SECOND EDITION

EFFECTIVE TRAINING

Systems, Strategies, and Practices

P. Nick Blanchard
Eastern Michigan University

James W. Thacker
University of Windsor

PEARSON

Prentice
Hall

Upper Saddle River, New Jersey 07458

Library of Congress Cataloging-in-Publication Data

Blanchard, P. Nick.
    Effective training : systems, strategies and practices / P. Nick Blanchard, James W.
Thacker.—2nd ed.
        p.   cm.
    Includes bibliographical references and index.
    ISBN 0-13-032739-5
    1. Employees—Training of.   2. Occupational training.   I. Thacker, James W.
II. Title.
    HF5549.5.T7B555   2003
    658.3′124—dc21

                                                                2003048296

Senior Editor: Jennifer Simon
Editor-in-Chief: Jeff Shelstad
Assistant Editor: Christine Genneken
Editorial Assistant: Kelly Wendrychowicz
Exec. Marketing Manager: Shannon Moore
Marketing Assistant: Patrick Danzuso
Managing Editor (Production): John Roberts
Production Editor: Kelly Warsak
Production Assistant: Joe DeProspero

Permissions Supervisor: Suzanne Grappi
Manufacturing Buyer: Michelle Klein
Cover Design: Bruce Kenselaar
Cover Illustration: Stock Illustration
Composition/Full-Service Project Management:
    BookMasters, Inc./Jennifer Welsch
Printer/Binder: Phoenix Color Corp.
Cover Printer: Phoenix Color Corp.

Credits and acknowledgments borrowed from other sources and reproduced, with permission, in this textbook appear on appropriate page within text.

Pearson Education LTD.
Pearson Education Singapore, Pte. Ltd
Pearson Education, Canada, Ltd
Pearson Education–Japan

Pearson Education Australia PTY, Limited
Pearson Education North Asia Ltd
Pearson Educación de Mexico, S.A. de C.V.
Pearson Education Malaysia, Pte. Ltd

10 9 8 7 6 5 4 3 2
ISBN 0-13-032739-5

To Claudia, whose understanding, love, and support continue to nurture and comfort, and to Mike and Brandon, sons who bring joy and delight to the old man.

N.B.

This book is dedicated to my longtime friend, wife, and companion Gabrielle, without whom I never would have written this book.

J.T.

Brief Contents

Contents

Preface

We created the idea for the first edition of this book while fishing on a beautiful lake in northern Manitoba. Both of us were teaching a human resource development course and were unsatisfied with the texts available at the time. Our main concern was that we really needed two texts for the course, one providing the theory and scholarship surrounding the learning-teaching experience and one providing the application and "how to" part of the experience. In this second edition we continue to focus on these dual objectives. We added an example of a training program for a small company called Fabrics Inc. and spread it across the appropriate chapters as an illustration of how the concepts can be applied. The case is developed step-by-step from needs analysis through design and evaluation. For example, in Chapter 4, the needs analysis process used in Fabrics Inc. is detailed so the student sees what is actually done. Then it is picked up again at the end of the design chapter and again the student is brought through the process to the end of design. This approach gives the student a real understanding of the things that need to be done and how they are actually done.

We continue to differ from other training books in that we place training activities in the context of organizational strategy. Whether you are a student or a practitioner, this book will be of both conceptual and practical value for developing training programs that meet strategic and tactical needs. At the same time, an overarching model of the training process will guide you step-by-step through the training procedures, from initial needs analysis through the evaluation of training's effectiveness. As human resource competencies become a significant competitive advantage, the pace and intensity of organizational training increases dramatically. Human resource development or "performance improvement" departments must demonstrate that their programs enhance competencies that are of strategic value. As a company's strategies change, the types of management competencies and styles need to change as well, and human resource development is responsible for this alignment. We address these and related issues because we believe that effective training practices are determined by the organizational context in which they occur.

Unique Characteristics of This Book

This book differs from others on the same topic in a number of ways. Those in italics are new to this edition. For example, we:

- Integrate training into the strategic planning process.
- Show the important relationship between organizational development practitioners and trainers.
- Provide an overarching model of the training process, with a more detailed model of each phase of the process, making it easy to see how each phase connects in reaching the training objectives.

- Provide an understanding of training and its implementation as it relates to the small business.
- Integrate learning and *design theories* into the development of training so the reader understands how theory helps design effective training.
- *Describe the step-by-step process of developing an actual training package as we move through each of the training process stages from needs analysis through the evaluation.*
- Provide numerous examples of actual training situations in companies to highlight aspects of the training process.
- Provide a step-by-step process for developing learning objectives with many examples of good and bad objectives.
- *Include appendixes in some chapters for advanced learning opportunities.*
- Use a contingency approach, identifying alternative approaches to the training process and the associated strengths and limitations, rather than a "one best way."
- *Incorporate a macro and micro theory of design into the design of training.*
- Provide a comprehensive case in Chapter 2 that is applicable throughout the text and is often referred to in the remaining chapters.

Other aspects of the text that we believe are important are:

- Learning objectives at the beginning of each chapter
- Case at the beginning of each chapter, sometimes split with its follow-up at the end of the chapter
- Questions, cases, and exercises at the end of each chapter
- An instructor's manual with sample syllabi, answers to questions at the end of the chapters, and a "test bank" of questions
- PowerPoint slides of all tables and figures

Learning objectives provide trainees with an understanding of what the training is trying to accomplish, and so they are an important part of the training process. Better learning is achieved if, at the beginning of training, people know where they should focus their attention. Therefore, at the beginning of each chapter we identify its learning objectives, stating what the reader should be capable of doing after completing the chapter. (The value of learning objectives and the characteristics of good objectives are discussed in depth in Chapter 5.)

Following the learning objectives is a case example to stimulate the reader to think about the issues that will be raised in the chapter. Throughout the chapter we refer back to the case to make specific points, asking the reader relevant questions about the case. Some of the cases are presented in totality at the beginning of the chapter; others are split into two parts, the first part stopping at a critical point, and the rest presented at the end of the chapter, so the reader can see how the issues were handled or what consequences resulted from the actions taken.

At the end of each chapter are discussion questions, cases, and exercises to enhance understanding. The instructor's manual provides more information about this material and offers additional ideas for teaching. It also includes sample course outlines and a test bank.

Another important difference in this book is the overarching model of the training process and its subprocesses. This model provides an understanding of the logical sequencing of training activities, from needs analysis to implementation and evaluation. The model demonstrates training as a system and how each of its processes are interconnected. Thus each phase of the training process (i.e., needs assessment, design, development, implementation, and evaluation) is covered in its own chapter. These chapters begin with a description of the types of input needed to complete that phase and the types of output produced. The bulk of each chapter provides a step-by-step description of how the input is transformed into the output. The output from one phase then becomes the input for the next.

For ease of reading we have not used the he/she convention when the context of the material requires a gender reference. Instead we alternate the use of gender throughout the text. We have received many compliments for this choice in the first edition and continue it here.

Most training books focus on large organizations that have access to many resources, ignoring the smaller companies with more limited resources. We address the training issues faced by smaller businesses in two ways. First, the contingency approach provides alternative activities and procedures, some of them compatible with limited resources. Throughout the book we address the applicability of various approaches to the smaller business. Second, many of the chapters include sections directed specifically at the small business. These sections provide possible alternatives and describe what some small businesses are actually doing in these areas. Unfortunately, the literature on small business training practices is relatively sparse. If you know of successful small business practices, we would love to hear about them and include them in subsequent editions.

We know that we failed to locate many of the excellent teaching techniques, exercises, and research applications that are available. Our goal is to improve this book continually so that it makes learning and teaching the joy that it can be. To that end we ask you to contact us with your thoughts, applications, exercises, and so on with the idea of sharing them. **You can reach us at Nick.Blanchard@emich.edu or jwt@uwindsor.ca.** Of course, any contributions will be acknowledged or cited as appropriate in future editions of this book.

Organization and Plan of the Book

We begin with an overview of training and a definition of key terms. The first chapter also discusses training's role in the organization, how training fits into the human resources (HR) function, and how the training function fits into the structure of large and small companies. Here we discuss training as a career. This chapter also presents the overarching training process model that is used to outline the organization of the book and provide an overview of the content of the remaining chapters. The chapter ends with a discussion of the key roles and competencies of human resources development (HRD) professionals.

Chapter 2 discusses strategic planning and the roles human resources and HRD play in this process. Here we show how input from the human resources function in general and the human resource development function in particular can influence strategic direction. We then proceed to discuss how these functions develop internal strategies and tactics to support the company's strategic plan. Throughout the text, we often refer back to this chapter to demonstrate how strategic issues drive human resource development decisions. We also provide an important link between organizational development (OD) practitioners and trainers, showing how the competencies of each of these disciplines complement and support the objectives of the other. In the remaining chapters we use an OD philosophy to address ways in which the training process and outcomes can be integrated into other organizational systems. This integration of the training process into a systems perspective provides the reader with an understanding of where training fits in the organization and how it operates.

The case example provides a discussion point for many of the topics in this and subsequent chapters, allowing the student to walk through a case from the beginning of the strategic plan to the development of training.

Chapter 3 provides the theoretical and conceptual framework for understanding the training process. It begins with a short discussion of the practical application of theory. A model of the factors that determine performance (motivation, knowledge, skills, abilities, and environment) is followed by a review of theories of motivation and learning. These theories are discussed in terms of their application to training. There follows a discussion of resistance to learning and applications of adult learning theory to overcoming this resistance. The chapter concludes with a discussion of individual trainee differences and offers training alternatives that can address such differences. The concepts and principles developed here are referred to throughout many of the following chapters, tying particular practices to the theoretical rationale for those practices.

Chapter 4 addresses the first phase of the training model presented in Chapter 1: needs analysis. An expanded graphic of this phase is presented and discussed at the outset so the reader will understand the organization of the chapter. The philosophy of needs analysis is discussed in terms of both its proactive use (as related to the strategic plan) and its reactive use (to deal with immediate concerns and changing conditions). The relationship between these two approaches is also explored. The steps involved in the needs analysis are discussed, along with the sources from which data can be gathered and to set training priorities. The chapter ends with a real example of a training process for Fabrics Inc., walking the student through the needs analysis as it is actually done for the company. An appendix provides issues related to the development of criterion measures for the more advanced students.

Chapter 5 begins with the second phase of the training model: training design. The outcomes of the needs assessment phase are shown as inputs to this phase. The chapter then identifies the activities conducted in the design phase of training. First is the development of the training/learning objectives. Here a formula for development of learning objectives is provided along with numerous examples of effective objectives. Next is the identification of organizational constraints on training and factors that will facilitate learning. The learning facilitation factors focus separately on the trainee and the training design. Next, factors that facilitate the transfer of learning back to the trainee's job are discussed. These factors are broken down into training design factors and organizational systems factors back on the job. We then discuss two theories of design (one micro and one macro) and demonstrate how they help in the design of a training program. We also integrate Social Learning Theory with the micro theory of design showing how they are related. At the end of the chapter, Fabrics Inc. is revisited and the process of design is examined step-by-step.

Chapter 6 provides the conceptual framework for determining which methods to use when developing a particular training program. It begins with a discussion of the importance of matching training methods to the desired training outcomes. The various training methods are then described, along with their strengths and limitations, using learning theory as a framework for this discussion. Included here are the relative costs; trainer versus trainee control over what is learned and how; effectiveness at developing knowledge, skills, or changing attitudes; and issues related to training group size and individual differences. The chapter concludes with a summary table of the various methods' effectiveness in meeting knowledge, skill, and attitude change objectives.

Chapter 7 discusses the same methods, but in terms of how actually to use them in developing and conducting a training program. The two parts to this chapter are development and implementation of training. For development we again provide a model to follow through the process examining the inputs (from the design phase) through to the outputs. Here actual forms that you might use, tables that provide step-by-step procedures for developing aspects of training, issues to consider in developing training using different methods, and so forth are provided. Then the model for implementation is provided, the outputs from the development becoming the inputs for the implementation. Here we follow the process of putting on the training and what needs to be done to assure success. Again the focus is on practical applications.

Chapter 8 begins with the model for evaluation and addresses the issues and activities involved in the evaluation phase of the overarching training model. While various evaluation issues are discussed in each phase of the training model, we provide the bulk of the information at this point in the book. Feedback from users of the first edition indicated that this placement allowed evaluation to be understood in the context of the overall training process. However, we stress the importance of incorporating appropriate evaluation activities into each of the other phases of the model. Chapter 8 provides guidance and actual examples of the various types of evaluation that can be used. At the end of the chapter we again revisit Fabrics Inc.

to provide the process that takes place at this stage of training. The appendix provides information related to the threats to validity, both internal and external, for more advanced study.

Chapter 9 contains two parts. First, the focus is on four special training topics: orientation, diversity, sexual harassment, and team training. In-depth discussion is provided, covering what organizations are doing in these areas and why it is important. Orientation training is used to provide an example of how to develop training, using the model provided in the previous chapters (needs analysis, design, development, implementation, and evaluation). A step-by-step process for developing this training is provided. Finally, a number of other special training topics are addressed in terms of their importance and what various organizations are doing in that area.

Chapter 10 begins with a general overview of a manager's job, then discusses the types of competencies needed by managers. This discussion includes the conceptual, technical, and interpersonal knowledge and skills, as well as personal traits or styles. In addition to the traditional listing of various types of management development programs that address these areas of competency, the capacity of our readers is enhanced through a model that allows the training professional to determine what competencies a manager in a particular organization needs. The model integrates the competitive strategy, organizational structure, and technology literature into a continuum that describes the organizational context in which managers must operate. This context then determines the relative value to the company that various managerial competencies and characteristics (such as style) are likely to provide. This chapter also discusses three important areas of managerial knowledge and competency: understanding of the organizational context, self-awareness and diagnostic skills, and adaptability. The special issues related to training top executives are also discussed. The chapter includes a discussion of the special needs of technical managers.

Acknowledgments

In a boat in northern Manitoba on a quiet sunny day, while we were catching our share of walleye, we conceived writing this book. Several years later, back on the same lake and catching fewer fish, we decided it was time to update and improve the first edition. From that time until now, many people helped make the second edition possible, and we are grateful to them. Of course, any errors or omissions are ultimately ours, and we bear responsibility for them.

The people at Prentice Hall were very helpful. Thanks to John Sisson, the managing editor who got the project off the ground; and our current editor, Jennifer Simon, whose advice and help were ultimately responsible for its final form. Thanks to Kelly Warsak, production editor at Prentice Hall, for her timely feedback and assistance in turning the product into its final form. Thanks also to those anonymous yet most important people whose diligence and skill in copy editing and production create the final images, text, and layout that make reading and learning a pleasure. Also a heartfelt thanks to Rebecca Faringer, who is able to detect the errors that everyone else misses.

We would like to acknowledge the contributions of both the academics and practitioners who shared their insights with us. Specifically, we would like to thank Mitchell Fields, University of Windsor; and Greg Huszczo and Rick Camp, both with Eastern Michigan University. Thanks go to Lee Sanborn of Ford Motor Company for providing information and access to portions of Ford's Production Systems training. Nina Adams helped us understand what virtual reality and multimedia mean in the world of computer training and we thank her. Thanks also to the folks at Simulearn who provided us with a unique experience in leadership training via computer simulation.

The reviewers of this book whose feedback helped us make improvements are Dr. Betty Hubschman, Barry University; David V. Day, Penn State University; and Dr. Robert C. Williges, Virginia Tech. Finally, for the number of times she had to retype chapters and renumber tables and figures, and did so with a smile, we wish to thank May Nhan. Her diligence and high spirits are always motivating for anyone who deals with her.

About the Authors

NICK BLANCHARD

Nick Blanchard completed his undergraduate studies in psychology at UCLA and his doctorate in industrial and organizational psychology at Wayne State University. He has served as head of the Management Department, Associate Dean, and is currently interim Dean and Professor of Management at Eastern Michigan University's College of Business. Among his accomplishments is the development, management, and continuous improvement of the on-site MBA program with corporate partner, Masco Corp. Nick's writings appear in both scholarly and applied publications. His earlier training text, *Toward a More Organizationally Effective Training Strategy and Practice*, was also published by Prentice Hall in 1986. He served as consultant and trainer to many organizations including Bethlehem Steel, Chrysler Corporation, Domtar Gypsum, Ford Motor Company, and various local and state government agencies.

JAMES THACKER

Jim Thacker received an undergraduate degree in psychology from the University of Winnipeg in Winnipeg, Manitoba, and his doctorate in industrial and organizational psychology from Wayne State University. He is currently a professor at the University of Windsor's Odette School of Business. His research has been published in both academic (*Journal of Applied Psychology, Personnel Psychology, Academy of Management Journal*) and practitioner (*Journal of Managerial Psychology, The Human Resource Consultation: An International Journal*) journals. He also coauthored the first Canadian edition of the text *Managing Human Resources* with Wayne Cascio, published in 1994. He has been a consultant and trainer in the private sector (Michigan Bell, Ford, Hiram Walker's, Navistar, H.J. Heinz) and public sector (Revenue Canada, CanAm Friendship Center). Prior to obtaining his doctorate, Jim worked for a gas utility as a tradesman and served as vice president of his local union (Oil, Chemical, and Atomic Workers) for a number of years. This firsthand experience as a tradesman and union official combined with his consulting and academic credentials provides Jim with a unique combination of perspectives and skills.

Overview of Training in Organizations

Learning Objectives

After reading this chapter, you should be able to:

- Define and differentiate among knowledge, skills, and attitudes
- Describe the similarities and differences among employee development, education, and training
- Describe the economic importance of training to business operations
- Describe various roles and expectations of training in large and small businesses
- Describe the components of a general open systems model and the corresponding components of the training processes model
- Describe the career options for trainers and the key roles and competencies associated with those options
- Describe the relationship between training, the human resources function, and line operations

---

Training a Key Factor in British Airways Turnaround

In the early 1980s, British Airways (BA) was in serious trouble. It lost £544 million (about $1.3 billion) in 1981–1982 and was continuing to lose money at the rate of about £200 a minute. The company faced laying off about 20,000 employees, closing down unprofitable routes, and disposing of substantial assets just to stay in business. In 1983 the board of

(continued)

(*continued*)

directors charged Colin Marshall with reestablishing the company as "the world's favorite airline," a title it once wore proudly. By 1987 Marshall and his executive team revitalized the company enough to merge with British Caledonian and be privatized. British Airways then showed a steady rise in performance and profitability, bringing it back to world-class status. Training was a significant part of Marshall's strategy for revitalization. However, he recognized that just training people was not enough. He knew that employees' new skills and abilities must be supported by the company's systems and procedures. Thus he insisted that the training be integrated with all the other "people" and business initiatives being developed.

The central focus of British Airways' strategy was a total dedication to the passenger. "Winning for Customers" was a core program in this strategy. It assessed managers' skills and identified areas for development. The carefully chosen title constantly reminded managers to focus their activities on what was best for the customer. Other human resource development (HRD) systems redesigned to support this strategy included the following:

- A program of performance feedback, used on a quarterly basis, to measure strengths and weaknesses of managers via a framework of "key" management practices
- A series of programs called "Managing Winners" developed to meet the training needs identified in "Winning for Customers"
- A number of customer-focused training initiatives to provide all employees with skills to deal with service failures and customer retention
- A new learning center, using state-of-the-art learning and training systems, open to employees at all levels

Training programs at BA are a part of an integrated system in which each program builds on the learning achieved in earlier programs. The following systems were put in place to ensure that training was linked to the customer service strategy:

- To ensure training consistency, a framework was developed specifying the skills to be developed in each training module.
- Professional capability performance standards (e.g., platform skills, content knowledge, and use of training methods) are set for trainers.
- Customer service training is compared to "best practices" both within British Airways and externally.
- Line managers are partnered with trainers to work out common language and concepts to ensure the practicality of training and its transfer to the job site.

These practices help to maximize return to the organization from the training investment. However, BA knew that training will not solve every customer service problem. The following seven-step process was used to identify the location and cause of the problem, then to develop the best solution.

1. Conduct customer satisfaction analyses to identify areas where customer service needs improvement.
2. Conduct "root cause" analysis to determine whether the problem stems from employees' abilities or from other factors such as motivation or work procedures.

(*continued*)

3. Develop the appropriate intervention strategy. If it is a training intervention, develop learning objectives. Analyze training alternatives to determine the most cost-effective approach.
4. Ensure collaboration on the training design between professional training staff and line personnel.
5. Set a tangible value for the training investment before training begins. Identify how much improvement in customer satisfaction is to be expected for training to be judged successful.
6. Determine whether this training is justified. If not, return to step 3.
7. Evaluate changes in customer satisfaction as a measure of the training's effectiveness.

In the mid-1990s British Airways recognized that it faced new and different challenges. Even though excellent customer service remained a competitive advantage, significant changes occurred in the air travel industry. For improvement to continue, British Airways needed to reinvent itself once again. With the input from a cross-section of employees, management redefined the mission, goals, and values to address: global economics, increasing competition, employee satisfaction, and continued improvements in customer satisfaction.

The restated mission, values and goals are as follows:

MISSION:
To be the undisputed leader in world travel.

VALUES:
Safe and secure, honest and responsible, innovative and team spirited, global and caring, a good neighbor.

GOALS:
Customers' choice—become the airline of first choice in key markets.
Strong profitability—meeting investors' expectations and securing the future.
Truly global—global network and outlook: recognized everywhere for superior value in world travel.
Inspired people—building on success and delighting people.

British Airways is one of the most profitable airlines in the world, reporting a £640 million profit for the year ending 1997. That same year they announced a £6 billion, three-year program to improve aircraft, products, facilities, and training for employees. Their success in the area of customer preference and satisfaction is, in part, evidenced by the numerous awards received from industry travel publications. British Airways' approach to human resources development dramatically improved its bottom line by establishing BA as a leader in customer service, creating a worldwide image as the preferred international airline.

This case is based on Fitz-Enz, J. 1997. *The 8 Practices of Exceptional Companies.* New York: AMACOM; and various news releases and information contained on the British Airways Web site, www.british-airways.com (accessed through December 2001).

Overview of Training

Training, in the British Airways case, enabled the company to adapt to changing conditions and be more effective in the marketplace. Experienced trainers know that effective training is structured as a continuous performance improvement process that is integrated with other systems and business strategies, as was true in the BA case. The key word here is *process*. The training process involves (1) identification of performance improvement opportunities and analysis of what caused the opportunity to exist, (2) identification of alternative solutions to the opportunity and selection of the most beneficial solution, (3) design and implementation of the solution, and (4) evaluation of results. A training program (one of many possible performance improvement solutions) would emerge from the training process.

Many people think that training of any sort will benefit the company. This assumption is just not true. When a training program is developed without using the training process, disaster usually follows. Such a program is likely to be unrelated to the needs of the company, the employees being trained, or both. When training is not designed to address a specific performance improvement opportunity, employees tend to discount its relevance and few changes will be seen in their performance. Likewise, companies quickly tire of training that cannot demonstrate its incremental value over its cost.

Training can provide employees with knowledge and skills to perform more effectively, preparing them to meet the inevitable changes that occur in their jobs. However, training is only an "opportunity" for learning. What is learned depends on many factors such as the design and implementation of training, the motivation and learning style of the trainees, and the learning climate of the organization. In the British Airways case, training is tied closely to the core business strategy of customer service. Training is a part of an integrated system in which performance is measured against criteria (best practices benchmarks) that are tied to strategic objectives. Employee performance at BA is systematically reviewed and feedback is provided on a regular basis. Performance problems are analyzed to determine the cause, and solutions are developed on the basis of this analysis. All the BA training programs were developed as an integrated and coherent whole with each program building on the learning from previous programs. Training is developed and implemented in partnership with line managers, so a clear link is created between what happens in training and what happens on the job. The training at BA is a good illustration of approaching training as a process and not just a program.

This text will take you through the complete training process as it is conducted under ideal conditions. Unfortunately, for most organizations ideal conditions do not exist. Often, insufficient money, time, or professional training staff are significant factors. Recognizing these limitations, we provide variations that, while not ideal, will do a reasonable job of accomplishing training objectives. Of course, these shortcuts exact a price, and we identify the major consequences of the shortcuts. We try to provide both "ideal" and more practical approaches to improving performance through training.

OPPORTUNITIES AND CHALLENGES IN THE NEW MILLENNIUM

As the new millennium unfolded never was the belief in training as a tool for organizational success stronger. In 2002, training budgets for North American companies with 100 or more employees totaled more than $60 billion despite the effects of September 11, 2001. At the same time economy, which began a decline in late 2000, continued to struggle. Although employee and development remains strong, pressure to demonstrate its contributions to the bottom increases. Until the mid to late 1990s managers relied primarily on faith that investing in training would produce improved financial results. Now evidence[1] shows that companies that invest more in training will show higher net sales per employee, gross profits per and ratio of market to book value.

Because of this evidence, companies continue to invest in training despite difficult economic times (unless they face severe financial problems). This trend creates many opportunities for training to expand its role and influence in the organization. However, as with most opportunities, some risk is also involved. Training departments face a broad array of challenges, a sampling of which are described next.

Changing Demographics

In the last half of the twentieth century major shifts occurred in North America, which will dramatically affect businesses in the next 10–20 years. Principal among these demographic shifts are the following:

- Aging of the population
- Lower birth rates
- Significant fluctuations in generational educational achievement
- Significant fluctuations in generational birth rates
- Increased diversity of ethnic and cultural makeup
- Differing values of newer generations of employees

These changes suggest that most companies now, or in the near future, face a severe shortage of skilled employees. Older workers retire, but fewer younger workers with the appropriate knowledge and skills are available to take their place. For example, the demand for educated, successful 35- to 45-year-olds is predicted to increase by about 25 percent over the next 15 years, when about 15 percent fewer people will occupy that age bracket.[2] Companies need to find ways to maintain the competency levels of existing employees and provide appropriate competencies to new employees. Training is one tool for this task.

Generation X and Y employees demand a more balanced lifestyle than their predecessors, and their leverage with employers has never been higher. Training must assist in the reshaping of organizations and jobs to meet these lifestyle demands. The advancement of technology allows many employees to work outside company walls, which requires new workflow systems and management processes that both old and new employees must learn to operate within. The increased diversity of the workforce will increase the demands on training to provide a workplace that is supportive of diversity while maintaining operational effectiveness. These challenges are just a few that result from the changing demographics companies must address, in part through their training function.

Knowledge Workers

The first decade of the twenty-first century will see the value of products and services determined more by the knowledge of the workforce and less by physical labor. This trend began with widespread use of personal computers in the mid-1980s and led to a "new economy." Many of the more dangerous and repetitive jobs of the past are now accomplished through remote-controlled systems and robotics. Because these jobs were primarily unionized, a significant drop in union membership occurred in the industrialized sector across North America. This drop in unionization resulted in conflicting strategies for union leadership. On the one hand, union leadership is demanding that employers provide training for the the rank and file to keep them up-to-date with modern operating methods. On the other hand, union leadership also understands that training can result in even further reductions in the number of unionized employees, reducing the size of the bargaining unit. Regardless, employers are both willing and determined to ensure that their employees are better trained because of economic pressures and consumer demands for higher-quality products and services. These demands require more effective and efficient job and workflow designs, staffed with employees who are committed to quality, show good judgment, are knowledgeable, and demonstrate multiple competencies. These changes create higher knowledge and competency requirements at every level in the organization. Training must address these needs because the supply of people holding these competencies is much smaller than the demand for those people.

Quality

As just mentioned, high-quality products and services are necessary just to stay in business in today's competitive markets, especially for businesses that provide products directly to other businesses. Typically they must demonstrate the quality of their products through quality systems developed by the purchasing company or by some globally accepted agency. For example, Ford, GM, and DaimlerChrysler impose their quality systems on suppliers. **ISO 9000** is an example of a quality system adopted by companies across the globe. It is a set of worldwide standards, ensuring consistency in product quality by all companies that become certified. These standards were developed by the International Organization for Standardization (ISO) in Geneva, Switzerland, in the late 1980s for the European Common Market. The standards, continually examined and updated, expanded into the United States, Canada, and more than 50 other countries. The basic process consists of five stages:[3]

1. Preaudit: Assessing how you are doing now
2. Process mapping: Documenting the way things are done
3. Change: Developing processes to improve the way things are done to reach a desired level of quality
4. Training: Training in the new processes
5. Postaudit: Assessing how well you are doing after the changes and continuing the improvement process

Training is itself a part of the standards, as indicated in point 4. A substantial amount of additional training is also required to meet the standards for certification. Training is required on a continuous basis even after certification is granted, because continuing audits ensure company compliance with the standards.

Obviously, the ISO process results in better-trained personnel. Companies involved in ISO also find improved efficiency and internal communication, cost reductions, and the ability to document quality control processes to their customers.[4] Glen Black, president of the Process Quality Association in Canada, compared ISO certified to noncertified companies. He found that the certified companies are six times less likely to experience bankruptcy, average 76 percent lower warranty costs in customer-discovered defects, and allow 36 percent less bureaucracy within their company structure.[5] A cost comes with achieving these benefits, however. Once the company makes the decision to seek certification, it must be prepared to engage in a substantial amount of training. For example, in the process of becoming certified, Carolina Fluids Components in the United States provided every one of their employees with 120 hours of training on all aspects of the business.[6] Assuming employees were paid a relatively low wage of $20 an hour, that is an investment of $2,400 per employee. Furthermore, training is only a part of the overall cost. Each business must determine whether the costs of ISO certification are justified by the benefits, but any company choosing to apply for certification must be prepared to engage in a substantial amount of training.

IMPORTANT CONCEPTS AND MEANINGS

The literature in training and development, like other professional disciplines, is continually evolving. As such, you will often find different meanings attached to the same terms. You will also find that different readings will use different terms for the same concept. Thus, it is important for us to be clear about the terms and concepts we are using. It is also useful for you, the reader, to have a good understanding of how terms are commonly used in the field and how they will be used throughout the text.

The basic terms and concepts used throughout the book are defined in the following sections. It is important to have a good understanding of them at the outset. Other terms will be defined as they first occur in the text.

Learning

Definitions for *learning* found in the literature vary according to the theoretical background of the authors. Unless otherwise indicated, the term **learning** in this text means a relatively permanent change in cognition (i.e., understanding and thinking) that results from experience and that directly influences behavior. This definition, of course, reflects our own theoretical assumptions. We will discuss this definition and others at length in Chapter 3.

KSAs

What is learned can be separated into different categories. Again, how these categories are defined differs according to the source. Traditionally, organizational psychologists used the categories "knowledge, skills, and abilities" (KSAs) to label the different types of learning outcomes. One drawback to this categorization is that the term abilities typically is not defined much differently from the definitions given to skills and knowledge. Abilities, for example, are defined as "general capacities related to performing a set of tasks that are developed over time as a result of heredity and experience."[7] Skills are defined as general capacities to perform a set of tasks developed as a result of training and experience.[8] The only difference seems to be whether heredity is involved. To our knowledge, the existing scientific evidence suggests that skills are influenced by heredity as well as by experience. Some authors make a distinction by categorizing skills as being psychomotor (behavioral) in nature, while abilities are categorized as cognitive. However, in that case, abilities do not differ from how knowledge is defined. The most commonly accepted definition of knowledge covers both the facts people learn and the strategies they learn for using those facts, all cognitive in nature. Although some would argue that abilities can still be distinguished from knowledge and skills, we believe the distinction to be of minimal value. On the other hand, attitudes are relatively easy to distinguish from knowledge or skills. In addition, it is scientifically well established that attitudes influence behavior and that they are learned.[9] Thus, to our way of thinking, attitudes must be part of any wholistic attempt to describe learning/training outcomes.

In this text the acronym **KSAs** refers to the learning outcomes, **knowledge, skills, and attitudes**. The three outcomes of learning are pictured in Figure 1-1. The way these three types of learning occur and the way they manifest themselves are interrelated, but quite different. We will be discussing these outcomes in depth throughout the text (notably in Chapters 3, 4, and 7).

Knowledge   The knowledge category of learning refers to these elements:[10]

- The information we acquire and place into memory (declarative)
- How information is organized for use into what we already know (procedural)
- Our understanding of how, when, and why information is used and is useful (strategic)

Declarative knowledge is a person's store of factual information about a subject matter. Facts are verifiable blocks of information such as the legal requirements for hiring, safety rules, and the like. Evidence of factual learning exists when the learner is able to recall or recognize specific blocks of information.

At a higher level is the person's understanding about how and when to apply the facts already learned, referred to as **procedural knowledge**. It assumes some degree of factual knowledge, because some information must be known about an object or activity before rules for its use can be developed. For example, one could not know when to apply the steps in an employment interviewing process (procedural knowledge) if she did not know what the steps were (declarative knowledge). Procedural knowledge allows trainees to understand the underlying

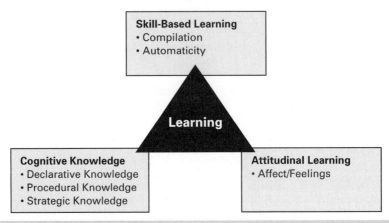

FIGURE 1-1 Classification of Learning Outcomes

rationale and relationships surrounding potential courses of action so they can apply their factual knowledge appropriately.

The highest level of knowledge is **strategic knowledge**. It is used for planning, monitoring, and revising goal-directed activity. It requires acquisition of the two lower levels of knowledge (facts and procedures). Strategic knowledge consists of the person's awareness of what he knows and the internal rules learned for accessing the relevant facts and procedures to be applied toward achieving some goal. When this type of knowledge is the focus of training or education, it is often called a "learning how to learn" program. For example, Bill is responsible for assuring that the hiring process for his company is both legal and is also effective at identifying the best candidate for the job. Bill must review and evaluate the various employment procedures to determine which, if applied correctly, would result in the selection of the best candidate *and* would fit within the law. He would use this strategic knowledge to access and evaluate previously acquired procedural and declarative knowledge to achieve the goal of a legal and effective hiring process.

Skills   We use Dunnette's definition of skill as the capacities needed to perform a set of tasks that are developed as a result of training and experience.[11] A person's skills are reflected by how well she is able to carry out specific actions such as operating a piece of equipment, communicating effectively, or implementing a business strategy. Skills are dependent on knowledge in the sense that the person must know "what" to do and "when" to do it. However, a gap separates knowing those things from actually being able to "do" them. A skill is a proficiency at doing something, beyond just knowing about it.

The two levels of skill acquisition are **compilation** (lower level) and **automaticity** (higher level). These two levels reflect differences in the degree to which a skill becomes routine or automatic. When a person is learning a particular skill or only recently learned it, she is in the compilation stage. Here a person needs to think about what she is doing while performing the skill. A person who masters the skill and uses it often reaches the automaticity stage. Here the person is able to perform the skill without really thinking about specific actions. In fact, thinking about it may actually slow the person's performance. Learning how to play tennis is a good example of the different stages of skill development. When you are first learning to play, you must constantly think about each aspect of hitting the ball, such as where to stand on the court, grip, and so on. Gradually, changes in how you grip the racket and your movement on the court become automatic, and thinking about them may actually reduce your effectiveness. One of the values of practicing as a learning technique is that through practice the behavior becomes more automatic.

Attitudes   Attitudes are employee beliefs and opinions that support or inhibit behavior.[12] In a training context, you will be concerned about employees' attitudes in relation to their learning of the training material and their job performance. The beliefs and opinions the person holds about objects or events (such as management, union, empowerment, and training) create positive or negative feelings about those objects and events. Thus, changing a person's beliefs or opinions can change the desirability of the object or event. For example, if an employee has positive feelings about a supervisor, those positive feelings are likely to become associated with the employee's job. If the employee learns from a coworker that the supervisor said negative things about her, job satisfaction is likely to be reduced, even though nothing about the job itself actually changed. What changed is the employee's belief about the supervisor's opinion of her.

Attitudes are important issues for training because they affect motivation. **Motivation** is reflected in the goals a person chooses to pursue and how hard they work toward achieving those goals. Goals and effort are influenced by how the person feels about things related to the goal (i.e., attitudes). Because a person's attitude influences his behavior, attitudes that motivate employees to perform or learn more effectively need to be addressed by training. For example, Lockheed Corporation began to be concerned about the security of their products and product development processes. They realized they needed either a significantly increased security force (which was financially costly) or to include security in the job descriptions of all employees. Lockheed chose the latter approach, using security awareness training and annual refresher training. The sessions were designed to change employees' attitudes about their jobs, so that everyone saw workplace security as part of their responsibility rather than only the responsibility of the security department. Five years after the start of the program, the number of reports of "suspicious incidents" increased by 700 percent.[13] Training in Action 1-1 on page 10 illustrates the importance of examining not only attitudes, but also knowledge and skills when designing training programs.

Competencies

A **competency** is a broad grouping of knowledge, skills, and attitudes that enable a person to be successful at a number of similar tasks. A carpenter, for example, has knowledge about different types of wood, different tools and their uses, and different types of finishes that can be applied to wood. This knowledge alone will not make that person a good carpenter. The carpenter may also possess a set of skills such as cutting, shaping, joining, and applying finish. These skills alone will not make a good carpenter. The carpenter may love working with wood, place a high value on quality, and find great satisfaction working on the details of planning a project. These factors alone will not make a good carpenter. It is the combination of these KSAs and others such as hand-eye coordination, visual acuity, patience, and judgment that allow the carpenter to become proficient. So, to be successful at carpentry or any other occupation a person must acquire multiple competencies. A trainer can identify the key KSAs that make a master performer successful at a given job, then group them into appropriate clusters. This provides a broad set of competencies required for the job. Then, linking these competencies to a set of behaviors that allow trainers to "know it when they see it," provides a valuable tool for hiring, training, and even determining pay rates for the job. We spend a great deal of time discussing KSAs because they are the foundation of competencies. Competencies are useful for understanding how the KSAs combine to influence job performance. The KSAs determine what types of training will improve competencies, leading to improved job performance.

Training, Development, and Education

The terms *training, development*, and *education* are used in different ways by various authors. Training is often described as focusing on the acquisition of KSAs needed to perform more effectively on one's current job. Development is used by many to refer to the acquisition of

---

TRAINING IN ACTION 1-1

TRAINING NEEDS IN THE STUDENT REGISTRATION OFFICE

The offices of the president and provost at a large university were receiving many complaints about the registration office being nonresponsive to student problems during registration for classes. The director of registration felt that, because of the high turnover in customer service representatives (CSRs), who handled student problems, most CSRs did not know the proper procedure. The director wanted to initiate training in registration procedures immediately and called in a consultant to assist in developing and conducting the training.

After listening to the director's description of what was wanted, the consultant said, "You're probably right. Of course, we could conduct a training needs analysis to clarify the exact nature of the performance problem." The director was concerned about the time required for a needs analysis and wanted to get training started right away. However, in agreeing that the needs analysis would determine specific problem areas, the director said, "Okay, do the analysis, but let's get started on training right away. I want them to know exactly what they are supposed to do."

The needs analysis revealed the steps and procedures that an effective CSR was required to complete in dealing with an unhappy customer. For example, one of the first steps was to identify and clarify the customer's problem. To do this step, the CSR was first to acknowledge the feelings the customer was displaying (e.g., anger or frustration) in a friendly and empathetic manner. Once these feelings had been acknowledged, the CSR was to determine the exact nature of the customer's problem through nonevaluative questioning (i.e., determining the facts without placing blame for outcomes).

Interviews with the CSRs established that they all knew the correct procedure and most could quote it word for word. However, observation of the CSRs at work showed marked differences in how the procedure was carried out. Further analysis of each CSR's skills in performing these tasks revealed that low skill levels and inappropriate attitudes were the primary causes of unsatisfactory performance. Even though nearly everyone "knew" what to do, some were not good at doing it. Others didn't believe it was important to follow every step. One CSR said, "Hey, if they get their problem solved, what do they care if I acknowledged their feelings?"

Certainly training was required in this case, but not the "knowledge" training the registration director thought was necessary. For those CSRs who lacked the behavioral skill to carry out the procedures, demonstrations and practice sessions with immediate feedback were provided. For those CSRs who had the skill but didn't understand the importance of all the procedures, training sessions were conducted in which the CSRs reevaluated their attitudes through various educational and experiential activities.

KSAs needed to perform in some future job. Some value may come from distinguishing between KSA acquisition for a current job and a future job, but we feel that the use of the terms *training* and *development* create confusion, because the creation of KSAs is largely the same regardless of when the KSAs are needed. One cannot develop KSAs without some form of training or educational experience. We use the terms *training* and *development* here to refer to distinct but related aspects of learning: Training is a set of activities, and development is the desired outcome of those activities. **Training** is the systematic process of providing an opportunity to learn KSAs for current or future jobs; **development** refers to the learning of KSAs. In other words, training provides the opportunity for learning, and development is the result of the learning. "Training departments" and "management training" are now called human resource development (HRD) departments and management development, respectively. The change in terminology reflects the change from a focus on the process (training) to a focus on the outcome (development).

Education is typically differentiated from training and development by the types of KSAs developed. Training is generally focused on job-specific KSAs, and education focuses on more general KSAs, related (but not specifically tailored) to a person's career or job. This distinction is satisfactory, but education should not be thought of as something that is done only outside the organization. For example, many organizations provide literacy training for their employees. This training is not tailored to the specific job requirements of these employees but is directed at developing general reading and writing skills.

The Role of Training in Organizations

Most moderate-sized to large organizations have a centralized training area, often called a human resource development (HRD) department. HRD is typically part of a human resources (HR) unit. Other HR units might include recruitment, selection, and compensation. The role of the HRD department is to improve the organization's effectiveness by providing employees with the KSAs that will enhance their current or future job performance. The focus is on the development of job-related KSAs. At the same time, effective training must address the personal needs of employees, helping them to learn, to grow, and to cope with the issues that are important to them. Focusing on KSAs that do not meet the needs of the organization is not productive. Likewise, unless the new KSAs are seen as relevant and important by the employees, they won't transfer back to the employee's job, wasting company resources. Truly effective training strategies and practices are those that meet the needs of the organization while simultaneously responding to the needs of individual employees.

Some examples that illustrate this point are depicted in Training in Action 1-2 (page 12) and 1-3 (page 13).

In these two examples, training was successful in developing new knowledge and skills, but it failed to take into account the needs of the organization or the employees. This failure prevented the knowledge and skills from becoming integrated into the day-to-day operations. In the first example, training met the needs of the supervisors but was rendered unusable by the organization's new policy. Because of past problems in the performance appraisal system, the organization felt a need to put in place a new system that included reviewing and documenting the formal appraisal. A more careful needs analysis would have identified this systems conflict, leading to more appropriate training or an intervention to prevent or modify the change in policy. In this case they might develop "periodic, informal appraisal interviews" so when it came time to do the formal interview, they would encounter few surprises and little "selling" would be required. Or they might intervene to change the new system so that the face-to-face interview could take place before the appraisal was finalized. This approach would allow for a more integrated approach to both the feedback and documentation aspects of the performance appraisal system. The British Airways case presented at the beginning of this chapter demonstrates the value of integrated personnel systems.

Training in Action 1-3 shows that training met the organization's need for developing problem-solving and team-building skills in employees. However, it failed to recognize the employee's concerns about fair workloads, recognition, and peer acceptance. As a result, the learning was not applied back on the job. A more thorough needs analysis would direct the training design to address the needs of both the organization and the employees. Chapter 3, on learning, motivation, and performance, discusses the many causes of performance problems and shows that training is a solution for only some.

TRAINING IN ACTION 1-2

SELLING PERFORMANCE APPRAISALS

The supervisors in a large electronics company badgered the training director for years to help them do a better job of conducting performance appraisal interviews. Most supervisors were using a "tell and sell" approach. They would tell the employee the problems they observed and try to sell the employee a corrective action plan. The supervisors and employees would constantly argue about the accuracy of the appraisal and the value of the corrective action plan.

Finally the training director put together an off-site workshop focusing on performance appraisal interviewing skills. The seminar emphasized a "problem-solving" approach, in which the supervisor and employee come to agreement on the "problem" and identify ways to solve it. The workshop cost the company a significant amount of money. Evaluations taken immediately after the workshop showed that the supervisors liked the approach and understood the steps and processes involved. They believed their problems with appraisal interviews were now

solved. Unfortunately, follow-up evaluations, taken a few months after the workshop, showed that none of the supervisors were using the problem-solving approach.

Further investigation revealed that a few weeks after the workshop, the HR department issued a policy modifying the performance appraisal procedure. The new policy required that the official evaluation documents, with the supervisor's signature, be forwarded to HR before any formal, face-to-face feedback sessions between supervisor and subordinate took place. Thus the supervisor's appraisal, without input from the subordinate, became official. Once HR received and filed the document, the supervisor was required to provide formal, face-to-face feedback to the subordinate. All supervisors used the "tell and sell" approach under the new policy because they had already submitted their official appraisals to HR. This required that they convince the subordinate that the appraisal was accurate.

TRAINING, BUDGETS, AND MANAGEMENT RESPONSIBILITIES

If you are like most business students you hope to be a manager or executive at some point in your career. Are competencies in training important to bring to that job? Managers are accountable for the performance of the entire area they manage. As a manager, the capabilities of your employees play a significant role in your ability to achieve the company's objectives. Thus managers need to participate in determining their subordinates' training needs and the type of training to meet those needs. After the training is completed, managers should play a role in judging training's effectiveness. As a manager, you also need to be involved in managing your own training and development. Clearly, training is a part of every manager's job, whether it is explicitly in the job description or implied from the objectives.

As organizations streamline operations and cut costs to become more competitive, many managers and supervisors will be asked to conduct some of the training themselves. This training can take the form of on-the-job coaching or more formal classroom sessions as topic area experts. This approach to training can happen in a business of any size but especially in smaller businesses where resources do not allow for full-time HRD professionals. Familiarity with effective training practices and strategies make a manager more valuable in any function or at any level in the organization.

Training is big business. U.S. organizations employing 100 or more employees budgeted a total of $54.2 billion for training and another $8.6 billion for training facilities and overhead in

---

TRAINING IN ACTION 1-3

TEAM BUILDING SIZZLES THEN FIZZLES

The director of a city utilities department felt that creating employee problem-solving teams would improve the quality of his operations and improve the efficiency of the department. All employees were provided the opportunity to participate in team building and problem-solving training. About 60 percent of the employees, including the director and his management group, signed up for the training. Three-hour training sessions took place once a week for 10 weeks. Employees, working on a common process within their department, were grouped into teams for three weeks of team-building training and seven weeks of problem-solving training.

At the beginning of the problem-solving training each team identified a problem in its area of operation and worked through this problem as it went through each step of the training. The team members were delighted to be learning new skills while working on a real problem. By the end of training, each group actually solved or made significant progress toward solving the problem it was working on. Evaluations taken at the conclusion of training indicated that trainees enjoyed the training and understood the steps, tools, and techniques of team building and problem solving. The director was pleased with the results and submitted a report to the city manager documenting the successes of the training.

Follow-up evaluation conducted six months later showed only one team still in operation. Other teams fell apart because workloads prevented their setting aside time for meetings, little recognition was given when problems were solved, nontrained employees resisted making changes in work processes, and/or teams were ridiculed by those who had not participated in training.

2002.[14] This figure was down slightly (about $2.5 billion) from 2001, due to the effects of the September 2001 terrorist attack, which substantially curtailed training-related travel. Smaller to midsized firms, employing 100 to 499 people, averaged about $185,000 per company for training; these companies make up about 79 percent of the Dun & Bradstreet database of U.S. organizations. Those employing between 500 and 999 people, about 10 percent of the database, planned to spend about $234,000 each. Of the $54.2 billion, $39.1 billion was spent for HRD staff salaries, and another $15.1 billion was allocated for outside services (seminars, conferences, materials, etc.).

What about other countries? Unfortunately, international surveys of training are not conducted on an annual basis. The American Society for Training and Development (ASTD) conducted a benchmarking study in 1999 that collected measures across companies from different nations. One study from these data reported training expenditures per employee for the United States, Japan, Europe, and Canada.[15] Firms in Canada averaged $530 per employee for training, while the United States averaged about $650. Europe was the highest at $960, while Japan was the lowest at $386. Obviously, these figures should be viewed with caution because companies participated voluntarily and represent a variety of sizes and industries. On the other hand, some evidence indicates that these figures might be representative. IBM Canada in the early 1990s, for example, with 12,000 employees, spent more than $36 million a year for training or about $3,000 per employee.[16] This amount compares to an average, for firms of the same size, of slightly under $4,000 for that time period in the United States. Thus, we can assume with some degree of confidence that Canadian employers spend about 20 percent less than U.S. employers on training their employees. A state of the industry report by ASTD comparing similar companies, showed that firms that train more employees and invest more per employee in training report higher financial and operational performance.[17]

One implication from this research is that the more effective companies see training as an important investment and are devoting substantial amounts of cash to training activities. Whether you are part of the training staff or a line manager, it makes sense to understand a part of the organization that commands this sort of financial attention. Although most training departments do not charge other parts of the organization for their services, 38 percent of the companies say they use a charge-back system, whereby departments must use part of their budget to pay for training services. This practice is most common in manufacturing, wholesale/retail trade, and public administration but is becoming increasingly common. Companies using this practice no longer view training as just a cost to the organization. Executives and managers in these companies expect a return on their training dollar investments. If training is not able to document the value of its products and services, it may find internal customers going to outside vendors for services. The HRD departments that can document favorable cost/benefit ratios will continue to get their fair share of budget dollars.

An example of this situation is Scepter Manufacturing of Ontario, Canada. Scepter is a plastic product supplier. In 1992 the company's training budget totaled $6,000 and covered about 150 employees. A change in company strategy necessitated training all employees in various new technical areas and cross-training in other jobs within their work area. Performance measures after the training and the implementation of new systems showed that scrap was reduced by 50 percent and defective parts were reduced from 5 percent to 0.1 percent. Was training worth it? "Yes," said the plant manager, who indicated that the training budget increased to $60,000.[18] Although it is somewhat time-consuming and complex to document how new KSAs result in increased operational profitability, the Scepter example shows it is both feasible and practical to do so. Chapter 8 provides the details for documenting and evaluating training results.

STRATEGY, TRAINING, AND ORGANIZATIONAL DEVELOPMENT

Today's competitive environment is more intense than ever before. Significant and rapid changes affect the business environment. One only has to think about the remarkable changes in technology, political boundaries and treaties, population demographics, and consumer preferences in the last decade to appreciate the turbulence of the business environment. Businesses will find themselves at a competitive advantage if they develop strategies that focus their internal strengths to meet their external opportunities and challenges. Most businesses continually evolve their competitive strategies. As strategies change, mechanisms are required to enable the organization's structure, systems, processes, and people to change with them. The alignment of all of these factors is accomplished through organizational development and training.

Organizational development (OD) is a set of processes (or interventions) designed to improve the ability of an organization to adapt to the demands of its environment, while meeting the needs of its employees.[19] OD interventions apply behavioral science concepts to facilitate the change of beliefs, values, attitudes, procedures, systems, and structure in an organization to match more closely requirements imposed by external forces (e.g., markets, competitors, technology, etc.). OD, then, is a set of planned activities that systematically change the way an organization operates so it better conforms to external conditions. For example, take the organization that determines it must develop teams to respond to an increased demand for innovation and customer focus. This company must do more than assign employees to teams. It must ensure that the corporate culture supports teams and that its systems do not punish those who try innovative approaches. These changes to the system and employee behavior are accomplished through OD and training.

Training is an obvious performance improvement method, accomplishing improvement through changing employee capabilities. To be effective, trainers must also be good OD practitioners. Because performance improvement is concerned with more than just delivering a set of KSAs, effective trainers are concerned with how employee KSAs will influence the effectiveness of the organization and the individual. Excellent trainers understand the organization's processes and systems and how these affect the employee's use of KSAs on the job. When something about the organization's operation restricts the employee's performance, the training practitioner must intervene to secure appropriate change. Had the trainer at the electronics company in Training in Action 1-2 intervened, the training could have been more effective and the organization more productive. The training director needed to be aware of the proposed policy changes for performance appraisals. With this information the director might modify the policy to reflect the problem-solving approach. Failing that, the training could be modified to provide supervisors with techniques for conducting the appraisals in ways consistent with the policy. If you were a consultant to the director of the utilities department in Training in Action 1-3, how could you have intervened to make the department's systems and processes more conducive to team problem solving?

Not all OD interventions are within the training practitioner's scope of responsibility, however, nor do all trainers actually apply OD techniques and principles. Rather, we want to point out the large amount of overlap between OD goals and activities and those of training. The effective trainer needs a basic understanding of organizational development. Helping organizations and employees change to become more effective is at the heart of the training enterprise. Therefore, organizational development concepts are used frequently throughout this book as we discuss the various training strategies and practices. Chapter 2 explores the relationships among business strategy, OD, and training.

Structure of Training Organizations

TRAINING AS PART OF THE HR FUNCTION

In most organizations, training is part of the human resource function. A typical HR function is depicted in Figure 1-2. Although HR departments differ to some degree across large organizations, most contain the components listed in the figure. The descriptions of the positions are necessarily broad, but they convey the differences in the types of activities performed.

To be effective, each of the functional areas within HR needs to integrate its goals, systems, and activities with those of the other areas. The training area, for example, must understand what the other HR areas are doing to ensure that everyone moves toward a common goal. When such coordination does not happen, issues such as those depicted in Training in Action 1-1, 1-2, and 1-3 will occur. HRD management that is closely involved with the other HR programs will understand what needs to be done to improve employee competencies that lead to accomplishment of the overall objective. Those HRD managers who do not will likely place those objectives in jeopardy, however well-intentioned they may be.

The relationship of training to other HR activities is fairly clear. The attitudes of employees toward their organization affect employee motivation and performance. HRD staff must understand this to determine training needs. Training itself can play a role in how positively or negatively employees view the organization. The employment activity controls the number of employees entering and leaving the organization and the competencies that come and go with new hires and terminations. The influx and outflow of employees change the capability mix within the organization. HRD must work in tandem with employment to ensure the proper mix is retained. New employees have special needs, such as orientation training, as do those leaving the organization (e.g., retirement seminars or outplacement workshops). HRD must gear up to meet those training needs and be aware of anticipated changes in the hiring or exiting trends of the company. HR planning and research are extremely important to the HRD area as organizational employment models and succession plans identify the future KSA needs of the organization. In addition, the

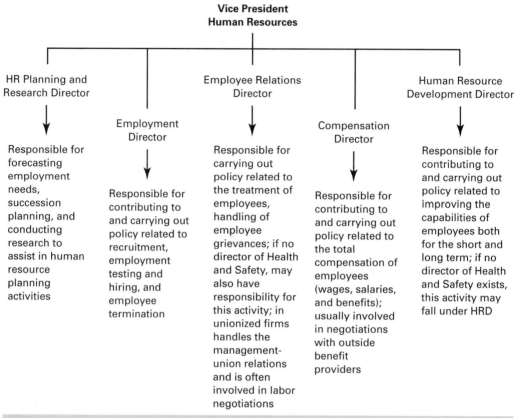

FIGURE 1-2 Human Resource Organization for a Large Company

research aspect of this HR function can assist the HRD area in understanding current organizational and employee needs. HRD, then, is one aspect of the organization's overall human resource strategy. The overall HR strategy is developed in conjunction with the organization's competitive strategy. For the HR strategy to be effective, each of the specialized activities within HR must understand its role in carrying out the strategy and must have its activities integrated with those of the other areas.

THE TRAINING ORGANIZATION

HRD departments vary considerably in how they are constructed. An example of how a training department in a large organization might be organized and the types of activities in which it might be engaged is provided next. This organization is reflected in the possible HRD career path depicted in Figure 1-3.

Within the HRD department, activities are often divided into management development and employee development. In a large company, each of these areas might be further divided into more specialized activities. For example, the employee development area might contain customer service training, employee orientation, health and safety training, and a separate training area for each of the organization's major operations. If the company is large, it might also have specialists working in evaluation and research, program design, materials development, and

Director HRD

Rotation through other HRD management positions

Manager, Training Support Services

Supervisor of Materials Development

Rotation through other specialist positions

Entry-level specialist position (e.g., training materials developer)

FIGURE 1-3 Possible Career Path in HRD

needs analysis. The customer service training coordinator, for example, could work with specialists in these areas to do the following:

- Determine the customer service training needs in the organization.
- Develop training programs to meet those needs.
- Develop materials to support the instructional methods to be used in the programs.
- Evaluate the effectiveness of the programs.

Entry-level positions in a large company's HRD department are usually at the specialist level. Thus a new hire with little experience but a good education in the training area could start out as a materials designer or a stand-up trainer, depending on her KSAs. In a large organization a career path might look like the one shown in Figure 1-3. The early rotation through the various specialist positions provides the novice trainer with solid, firsthand experience in all aspects of the training system. A person who has a solid grasp of the system (i.e., how it is "supposed" to work and how it "actually" works) will then be able to supervise one of the specialist areas. Supervisors must make sure not only that their particular area is running properly, but also that the area's activities are fully integrated with what other areas are doing. This requires a realistic understanding of the other areas' goals and how they operate. Some large companies also require that their HRD specialists spend time in a line position, to better understand the needs of line personnel. Thus at some point in the career ladder pictured in Figure 1-3 (probably between the supervisor and managerial positions), the training practitioner might supervise or work in a line operation for a period of 6 to 12 months, although this requirement is still fairly unusual.

In general, the smaller the organization, the more activities each individual is asked to perform. In a medium-sized company, the HRD activities of employee, management, and organizational development may all be carried out by a small group of people under the guidance of an HRD manager. Each individual is expected to perform all (or most) aspects of each of the activities. Smaller companies may not have an HRD or training department at all. Instead, a single individual may be responsible for all training activities. In even smaller businesses many of the HR responsibilities, including training, are decentralized out to the line managers. Human resources may consist of only one or two people who handle the core HR activities and act as consultants and facilitators for the line managers in carrying out HR responsibilities.

Another career path for a training and development professional is as a member of a training or consulting firm. Generally, entry-level positions require a minimum of several years of experience working in different areas of training. Most training or consulting firms are relatively small (1 to 15 people), and the staff must be capable of performing many activities, not just one specialty. In addition, the financial resources of these firms generally will not support a long and extensive training period. Employees are expected to be able to "hit the ground running," with only a minimum of orientation to the firm's philosophy, product, and service lines. Some large training or consulting firms do hire specialists in certain areas such as instructional design, materials development, and evaluation. However, these firms also prefer employees to have several years of experience as well as advanced degrees. Generally, they are able to recruit a sufficient number of applicants who meet the experience and education requirements, because their compensation package is typically much better than that of the smaller firms, although compensation levels vary considerably from firm to firm.

TRAINING IN LARGE AND SMALL BUSINESSES

Most business texts, especially those covering human resource management (HRM), focus on medium-sized to large businesses for a number of reasons, including the following:

- Research typically requires a larger sample size.
- Larger firms have the budgets to support research.
- Policies and procedures are more formalized, thus easier to track.
- The techniques described in HR texts usually require a formal HR function containing multiple areas of specialization, such as compensation, HRD, selection, and so on.

When small businesses are overlooked, a major component of the economic engine that runs North America is ignored.[20] Small to medium-sized business firms account for more than 60 percent of the private sector's contribution to the economy. Most of the workforce is employed at companies employing fewer than 100 people. Almost all businesses (98%) employ fewer than 100 employees, and 93 percent employ fewer than 20 people. No size criterion is universally accepted in the literature for categorizing a business as large or small. Some use fewer than 500 employees,[21] some 200 or fewer employees,[22] and others 100 or fewer.[23] We generally use the term **small business** here to refer to organizations with fewer than 100 employees, but we on occasion use examples with about 150 employees. Larger companies that employ fewer than 500 people are considered to be medium-sized.

The model of the training process that we present is applicable to both large and small businesses, but the ways in which it is implemented can differ dramatically with the size of the company. One difference is the number of employees that need to be trained. Because larger companies train greater numbers of employees, they must use a more systematic and controlled method of determining what training needs exist. In smaller companies the owner or president can have a close working knowledge of each employee and his or her training needs. Another difference is in developing training programs. The smaller business can easily determine what types of training are more or less important to the company's objectives and can design training accordingly. In larger companies, again, a more systematic and formal approach will be needed because the firm's strategies and objectives are more complex. In larger companies economies of scale can be obtained if common training needs across the workforce are identified, reducing the per-person cost of training. However, a more rigorous approach to identifying needs is required because more employees are involved.

Another difference between the large and small companies is that small companies can use less costly and formalized methods for evaluating training, because the results are more easily observed. Throughout the following chapters, where applicable, we identify strategies and practices that might be more appropriate for the smaller business. Where research results are applicable, we highlight their implications. When research is not available, we offer logic and applied examples.

Although many differences exist between smaller and larger firms in the way they deal with training, owners of small businesses have the same concerns as big businesses. Both identify as their number one concern the ability to obtain, develop, and retain a high-quality workforce. Both large and small businesses recognize that training is a critical component to increasing the quality of their workforce. So, even though training is just as important to the small business as to the medium or large business, the methods and practices they use are different. These differences suggest no "one best way" is available to determine training needs, design a training program, or evaluate the effectiveness of training. Nevertheless, a set of processes exists, which, if followed, lead to effective training regardless of organizational size.

A Training Process Model

OPEN SYSTEMS

Figure 1-4 shows a general systems model long used as a description of business organizations.[24] This model is called the **open systems model**. Open systems have a dynamic relationship with their environment.

As Figure 1-4 indicates, the system is open to influences from its environment and, in fact, depends on the environment for input. The system takes inputs from the environment and transforms them into outputs. Outputs enter the system's environment and may or may not influence future inputs into the system. A business is a type of open system, operating in the same manner as other open systems.

A system (such as a business) must be responsive to the needs and demands of its environment, because the environment provides the input needed for the system to replenish itself. For example, if a business is responsive to the needs of society by providing valued goods and services (output), it receives valued input from society in the form of financial and goodwill credits. These inputs are used by the business to continue operating. If the business does not provide sufficient value to its environment, it will fail because the environment will not provide the input necessary for the system to replenish itself. Although the business must meet the needs of its environment, it must also protect itself from aspects of the environment that are harmful to the system.

The dotted line in Figure 1-4 represents the barrier between the system and the environment. The spaces in the line indicate the barrier is semipermeable, allowing parts of the environment (input) and system (output) to cross over. The barrier represents the organization's policies, systems, and procedures that are designed to allow only certain components of the external environment to enter the system. For example, the company must hire employees (input), but it does not hire just anyone. It wants to hire only those who can make a positive contribution to the organization's goals (desirable input). Therefore, it sets up criteria for selecting employees from the labor pool, allowing only those with the proper qualifications to enter the organization. On the other hand, the company must comply with the laws set up by society or face sanctions (undesirable input), and some of those laws address the criteria that can be used in selecting employees (e.g.,

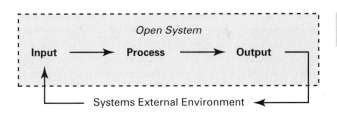

FIGURE 1-4 General Open Systems Model

equal employment opportunity and affirmative action). Thus input from one area of the environment (the law) influences the nature of barriers that allow input from another area of the larger system (the labor pool). The organization's policies, systems, and procedures allow it to examine and analyze the environment to determine which components of the environment to respond to and what response is most appropriate. These topics are covered in more depth in the next chapter, in the discussion of strategic planning and organizational development.

The British Airways case demonstrates that employee training can enable companies to adapt to changing conditions and be more effective in the marketplace. This increased effectiveness is made possible if training allows employees to learn how to improve performance and prepares them for changes in how their jobs are structured. However, training does not always result in these outcomes. Training is an "opportunity" for learning, but what is learned depends on many factors, including:

- How well the training matches the needs of the employees and the organization
- The quality with which training is designed and implemented
- The learning climate of the organization

At its worst, training can be an isolated program of activities unrelated to the goals of the business, the trainees' performance or the nature of their jobs. Think back to a time when someone was trying to teach you something that you did not think would be useful or relevant to you. Did you pay much attention? How much did you remember of what the person was trying to teach one week after the lesson? When a training program is designed without an understanding of the business reasons for the training and the ways in which the training will affect employee performance, employees tend to discount its relevance. Little learning or job improvement is likely to result. To avoid such training failures training professionals apply the following principles to maximize the effectiveness of training:

- Understand the needs of the organization and the trainees.
- Develop clear objectives for what the training should accomplish for both the organization and the trainees.
- Design and develop training to meet the objectives.
- Provide a supportive learning environment for the training.
- Design and conduct the training in a manner that motivates trainees to learn.
- Work with others in the organization to identify and remove barriers to using the new knowledge and skills on the job.
- Evaluate appropriately as feedback for improvement.

Our training process model is a systematic approach to ensuring that the principles listed are applied and training objectives are achieved. Training, at its best, uses the following model as a set of processes aimed at continuously improving employees and organizational systems, including the training itself. The key is a commitment to the training processes. In the British Airways case we saw that the training was tied closely to the core business strategy of customer service. Training was part of an integrated system in which performance was measured against criteria (best practices benchmarks) that were tied to strategic objectives. Employee performance was systematically reviewed and feedback was provided on a regular basis. Performance problems were analyzed to determine the cause, and solutions were developed on the basis of this analysis. Although many training programs were developed, they were integrated into a coherent whole with each program building on the learning from previous programs. Training at British Airways was developed and implemented in partnership with line managers, which created a clear link between what happened in training and what happened on the actual job. This continuity and integration illustrate training as a process and not just a set of programs. When training is structured as a set of processes, integrated with other systems and business strategies, as in the following model, the connections between training and day-to-day business practices are apparent.

TRAINING AS AN OPEN SYSTEM

Many open systems exist as part of another open system, and are called subsystems of the larger system. For example, a product assembly system is a subsystem of a manufacturing system, which itself is a subsystem of the company, which is a subsystem of the industry, and so on. In the open systems model, training can be seen as a subsystem within the larger system of HR, which is a subsystem of the company. Figure 1-5 illustrates some of the exchanges that take place between the training system and the larger organizational system. The organization's mission, strategies, resources, and the like all represent sources of input into the training subsystem. Of course, if the training department is part of a larger HR function, then these inputs would be filtered through that system. Organizational inputs are translated by the training subsystem into usable input such as organizational and employee needs, training budgets, staff, equipment, and so forth. The input is utilized to produce the output of the training system (improved KSAs, job performance, and so on). This illustration shows how interconnected the training activities are with what is happening in the organization as a whole. Unless training takes into account and meets the expectations of the business, the business will institute sanctions on the training system (e.g., reduced budgets, staff, and other resources) rather than providing it with more desirable inputs. Training in Action examples presented earlier demonstrate the consequences of a poor match between the training system and the organizational environment. The British Airways case provides an example of how a training system can be designed to ensure that training staff appropriately analyze and respond to the organizational environment. In the next chapter we take a closer look at the training environment.

TRAINING: A PROCESS

Implied in the open systems model is that training is a process, not just a program or a set of programs. To be sure, training does consist of programs. When a particular training need is identified, a training program may be developed to address that need. However, prior to this point the organization invested money in the training function, for which it expects a favorable return. At the end of the year the organization will determine how favorable the returns have been and determine what its next investment will be. Thus, viewing training as simply a program or set of programs, is too short-sighted. Effective training is about meeting organizational needs, not just conducting training programs. When training is viewed as a set of integrated processes in which

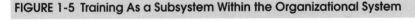

FIGURE 1-5 Training As a Subsystem Within the Organizational System

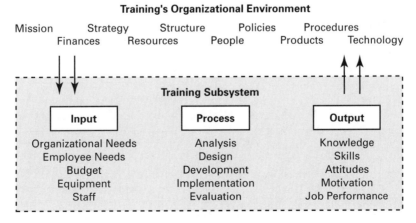

organizational and employee needs are analyzed and responded to in a rational, logical, and strategic manner, the organization will improve and is likely to invest in further training. Our model of training processes, depicted in Figure 1-6, reflects this approach.

Figure 1-6 is merely an overview of the process; a more detailed figure for each phase is provided at the beginning of each relevant chapter, where the input and output of each process is described in considerably more detail. For now we will briefly describe the phases and their inputs and outputs.

The training process begins with some type of triggering event. The **triggering event** is the recognition of an **organizational performance deficiency (OPD)**. When the **actual organizational performance (AOP)** is less than the **expected organizational performance (EOP)**, OPD exists. The discussion of analysis in Chapter 4 covers this topic in greater detail, including both when the OPD exists in the present and when it is anticipated for the future. In either case, when the firm recognizes an important OPD and believes training may be a solution, the training process is initiated.

Analysis Phase   An effective business is one that is able to scan its environment and determine the products and services it can provide to meet customer or market needs. Similarly, an effective training system begins with a determination of customer needs in the **needs analysis phase**. In this case the first customer is the organization. These needs show up as performance deficiencies. A performance deficiency would be indicated by things such as profitability short falls, low levels of customer satisfaction, or excessive scrap. These are deficiencies that reflect the current state of the company. A performance deficiency can also exist if the company is likely to perform poorly in the future unless changes are made. For example, when the ISO 9000 certification standards first came out, organizations wishing to do international business had an anticipated

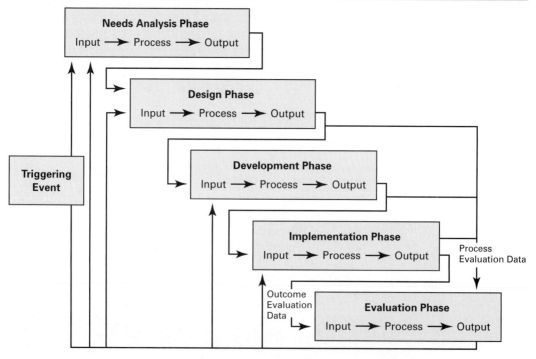

FIGURE 1-6 Training Processes Model

performance deficiency. They would lose business unless they were able to achieve certification by a certain date. On an individual level, when a manager is not able to perform some aspect of his current job at an acceptable level a performance deficiency would exist. When a manager has been targeted for promotion, any differences between her current capabilities and those she will need to perform well after the promotion would be anticipated performance deficiencies.

Once performance deficiencies are identified, the cause must then be determined. If the deficiency is caused by inadequate KSAs, then training becomes a way to satisfy the need. Because not all performance problems are due to KSA deficiencies, those problems for which training will be beneficial must be sifted from those for which training would not help. Performance deficiencies that are caused by motivation or equipment, for example, require a different solution. The performance deficiencies to be addressed by training are then prioritized.

This process of data gathering and causal analysis to determine which performance problems should be addressed by training is termed **training needs analysis (TNA)**. To conduct the TNA information needs to be collected from the organization as a whole, from the operational areas where problems exist, and from the people within the operational areas. The information collected is the input to the analysis phase. Output of the analysis phase consists of identification of training and nontraining needs and their priorities. Nontraining needs become inputs to other functional areas (for example, compensation and rewards, labor relations, organizational development, etc.). Training needs become the inputs to the design phase, where the training objectives are developed.

Design Phase   In addition to the training needs identified in the TNA, additional inputs to the **design phase** are developed from the organizational and operational analyses. These inputs include both the constraints placed on training and areas of expected support. Constraints and support occur in relation to things such as organizational plans, resources, and business cycles. Another set of inputs is derived from theory and research on learning; these inputs are used in the design of training programs to facilitate learning and the transfer of the learning back to the work site. Training objectives, that is, the outcomes a particular training program is to achieve, are developed as part of the design process, by examining training needs in relation to the identified organizational constraints and support. These objectives specify the employee and organizational outcomes that should be achieved as a result of training.

The second part of the design process is identifying the factors needed in the training program to facilitate the learning and its transfer back to the job, including identifying alternative methods of instruction. The factors needed to facilitate learning and transfer of learning as well as the alternative methods of instruction become inputs to the development phase of the training system. The training objectives become inputs to the evaluation phase. As you perhaps noticed, the evaluation process begins after identifying evaluation objectives and is conducted concurrently with the other phases of the training system. However, for convenience we discuss evaluation after discussing all the other phases of the training process.

Development Phase   Program development is the process of formulating an instructional strategy to meet a set of **training objectives**. The instructional strategy consists of the order, timing, and combination of elements to be used in the training program. Inputs into this phase are provided by the design phase and include the alternative instructional methods and the information relating to learning facilitation and transfer. All elements of a particular training program are determined during the **development phase**. The specific content, instructional methods, materials, equipment and media, manuals, and facilities are integrated into a training plan designed to achieve the training objectives. These outputs of the development phase serve as inputs to the implementation phase.

Implementation Phase   All the aspects of the training program come together during the **implementation phase**; however, it is a mistake to assume that everything will happen as planned. Therefore, it is useful to conduct a dry run of the training, similar to a dress rehearsal for a play, allowing the trainer to become familiar with the facility, equipment, and materials with no actual trainees present. A useful next step in the implementation process is a pilot training group, consisting of a small number of trainees representative of the larger population. Although the trainer is usually not at liberty to make major deviations from the training plan, many opportunities may be available to influence the effectiveness of the training. Trainee reactions to the training, how much they learn, and process evaluation data allow the trainer to identify areas of self-improvement. In addition, improvements to the training strategy can be identified from the pilot group evaluations. Once these refinements are made, the training is ready for full implementation.

The output of the implementation phase is the actual training that is conducted, the trainees' responses to training, their learning, their behavior back on the job, and its effect on key organizational outcomes. These outcomes combined with process evaluations are fed back to the appropriate constituencies within the training area and the rest of the organization, thus completing the evaluation phase.

Evaluation Phase   Although we discuss this phase of the model last, it actually begins during the development phase. Recall that evaluation objectives are an output of the design phase. These outputs become inputs to the **evaluation phase**. Another input is the organizational constraints. Time, money, and staff all affect how training is evaluated. The design of the training program (lecture, role plays, simulations) will dictate significant portions of the evaluation strategy. All of these inputs come together to determine the evaluation strategy and design. Carrying out the strategy and design results in two possible outputs: process results and content results. These outputs derive from the types of evaluation that are useful for training: process evaluation and outcome evaluation.

Process evaluation is a determination of how well a particular process achieved its objectives (i.e., outputs). Each phase of the training process model constitutes a process with inputs and outputs. For example, in the analysis phase a process evaluation would be concerned with the accuracy and completeness of the organizational, operational, and personal data collected. It would also determine whether the data were interpreted accurately, whether the cause of performance discrepancies was identified accurately, and whether the training objectives reflected all the key training needs that were feasible to address. Logical rather than statistical analysis is used for this type of evaluation. Collecting and analyzing process data can provide early warning of potential problems in the training program.

Outcome evaluation is conducted at the end of training to determine the effects of training on the trainee, the job, and the organization, using the training objectives as the standard. Outcome evaluation can also be used to improve training processes. Outcome evaluation data by themselves do not provide enough information for program improvement, but in combination with process evaluation data they serve as a powerful tool for improving programs. By examining outcome evaluation results from the first presentation of the course, you can determine whether all the training objectives were achieved. If they were, you can be fairly comfortable that the training processes are working as they should. However, if one or more objectives are not achieved, the training process evaluation data can then be used to identify problems in the process and corrective action can be taken.

Recall that British Airways developed standards for training outcomes, standards for consistency in the training approach, and standards for the trainer's professional capabilities. This evaluation of both process and outcomes allowed British Airways to improve not only their customer service, but also the effectiveness and efficiency of their training. Such an approach creates a continuous improvement process for training that is integrated with the continuous improvement of other organizational systems.

TRAINING AS CONTINUOUS IMPROVEMENT

Training is just one of several possible solutions to organizational and individual performance problems. Whether training is the right solution depends on the cause of the problem and the cost/benefit ratios of the other alternatives. Thus training processes are similar to problem-solving processes. Most problem-solving processes include the following steps:

- Identifying organizational problem areas (those in need of improvement)
- Determining the cause(s) of the problem
- Identifying, selecting, and implementing the best solutions
- Evaluating the effectiveness of the solution
- Implementing a feedback loop in which the evaluation results are used to determine the next course of action

Comparing this list with Figure 1-6 shows how our model of training processes serves as a problem-solving tool. The needs analysis phase identifies the problems and their cause(s). Training becomes a solution when the problem is caused by inadequate KSAs. Once training is identified as a solution, the design, development, and implementation phases result in a training program for the appropriate employees. The evaluation phase assesses both the training processes and the training outcomes.

This text will take you through the complete training process as it would be conducted under ideal conditions. Unfortunately, most organizations do not operate in ideal conditions. Insufficient financial resources, time, and training professionals represent just a few of the challenges faced by most companies. Recognizing these limitations, we provide variations to the ideal training practices and systems that, while not ideal, do a reasonable job of accomplishing your training objectives. Of course, these shortcuts exact a price, and we identify the major consequences associated with various alternatives. Thus we try to provide both "ideal" and more practical approaches to implementing the training processes. Nonetheless, even in less-than-ideal conditions, all of the training processes are critical to the success of your training. Although less-than-ideal methods may be used to carry out the training processes, elimination of one or more of the processes places the entire effort at grave risk.

SUMMARY

Training faces increasing demands to demonstrate results in terms of return on investment. With these demands come increased opportunities for the training function to influence the direction and operations of the company. Changing demographics, the steadily increasing competitiveness of the marketplace, high demand for and short supply of knowledge workers, and customer demands for high-quality products and services all challenge companies and their training departments.

Important concepts and terms in the field of training were defined and discussed including learning, the three types of knowledge, two levels of skill, and attitudes. The manner in which attitudes affect motivation which in turn affects behavior was explained. Though differing opinions exist in the field of training about what constitutes training versus development and education, training in this text will be considered to be the experiences provided to people that enable them to learn job-related KSAs. Education will be considered to be the experiences that enable people to learn more general KSAs that are related to, but not specifically tailored to a person's job. Development will be considered to be the learning that occurs as a result of training or education.

Evidence is accumulating that those companies that spend more on training are achieving better financial results. Improved operating methods (such as ISO 9000) and increasing employee competencies are also resulting in declining union membership. This trend places the leadership of unions in the dilemma of demanding increased training for their membership to ensure job security, while at the same time recognizing that higher-skilled employees allow the company to do more with fewer people.

Large firms may be able to engage in more elaborate types of training, but the processes that make for effective training are the same for both large and small to medium-sized enterprises. What differs are the methods used to complete the processes. Larger firms can rely on economies of scale to keep the cost of training per employee down. Small to medium-sized firms must also find economical ways of providing training. The way large firms organize their human resource activities into their operations differs from that of small to medium-sized enterprises. Larger firms maintain a more centralized HR department within which are many specialized functions. Small firms typically do not use a distinct HR department but spread the HR duties among the management of the firm. In larger organizations, HRD areas must understand and work collaboratively with other HR activities to achieve the organization's objectives. In smaller firms, it is not as much of an issue because HRD activities are carried out by line managers.

Many career options exist within the training field, ranging from outside consultant to internal specialist. A more traditional career path in training begins with an entry-level position as a specialist with a larger firm and moves to positions of greater responsibility until reaching a generalist position. The individual may then move into another area of HR or move to an external firm providing training services. However, this path is subject to many exceptions and many different entry points, depending on experience and qualifications. The skills and competencies of organizational development practitioners are important to training professionals as well. Likewise, the skills and competencies of trainers are important to OD professionals.

Effective training occurs as a set of phase(s) in which each phase acquires input, engages in a set of processes, and produces output needed for the next phases. The training process model provides a visual understanding of how the phases relate to each other. Although the model shows the phases occuring as sequential steps (needs analysis, design, development, implementation, evaluation), in fact these phases occur in a dynamic fashion with feedback from one phase leading to the next phase as well as recycling through some aspects of the previous phase.

KEY TERMS

- Actual organizational performance (AOP)
- Attitudes
- Automaticity
- Competency
- Compilation
- Declarative knowledge
- Design phase
- Development
- Development phase
- Education
- Evaluation phase

- Expected organizational performance (EOP)
- Implementation phase
- ISO 9000
- Knowledge
- KSAs
- Learning
- Motivation
- Needs analysis phase
- Open systems model
- Organizational development (OD)

- Organizational performance deficiency (OPD)
- Outcome evaluation
- Procedural knowledge
- Process evaluation
- Skills
- Small business
- Strategic knowledge
- Training
- Training needs analysis (TNA)
- Training objectives
- Triggering event

EXERCISES

1. Review the material in Training in Action 1-1. Assume you were hired to develop a training program for these CSRs. Write down the four most important knowledge, skills, or attitudes that you believe your training design must address and your reasoning for selecting these. If done as a group exercise, allow each member of the group to share the KSAs they identified

and their reasoning. Then, reach a group consensus as to the four most important KSAs and your rationale for including each KSA. Each group will then report to the rest of the class.

2. Describe your vision of where you will be in your career five years from now. How will training play a part in that career?
3. In small groups, discuss the training responsibilities of supervisors and managers who are not part of the HRD department. Prepare a list of what those responsibilities might be and a rationale for your choices.
4. Conduct an interview with a small business owner or manager. Get a good understanding of how they approach training in their company. What differences do you see in how this company approaches training and what was described in this chapter? What are the reasons for this difference?
5. Conduct a search of recent publications for an article that discusses a type of training that will be critical for one type of industry or segment of an industry. Select an article that identifies a specific company or set of companies that demonstrate this training need and summarize the article in one page or less.

QUESTIONS FOR REVIEW

1. Pick one of the following roles that most appeals to you: training manager, instructional designer, training instructor, training evaluator. What is the range of role competencies for that job (identify at least four different competencies)? Describe why that job is especially appealing to you.
2. Describe the relationship between the HR and the HRD functions in a large organization. How might a small organization handle the responsibilities of these two areas? What would a career path look like for someone starting out as a trainer in a consulting firm?
3. Define and provide an example (not used in the text) of the following:
   a. Each of the three types of knowledge
   b. Each of the two levels of skills
   c. An attitude
4. Consider the following problem-solving model. Based on the discussion in this chapter, describe how the training process model is or is not consistent with this model.

   PROBLEM-SOLVING PROCESS
   - Define and understand the problem.
   - Determine the cause of the problem.
   - Identify potential solutions to the problem.
   - Select the solution that provides the most benefits for the least cost.
   - Develop an action plan for putting the solution in place.
   - Implement the solution.
   - Evaluate and, if necessary, modify the solution.

Strategic Planning, Training, and OD

Learning Objectives

After reading this chapter, you should be able to:

- Describe the strategic planning process, its components, and their relationships
- Distinguish between an organization's external and internal strategies and describe the value of each
- Describe the benefits of using an HRD perspective in strategy development
- Describe the characteristics and major components of a learning organization
- Describe the differences, similarities, and relationships among competitive HR and HRD strategies
- Identify and describe external and internal factors influencing HRD strategy
- Identify possible HRD strategic alternatives and situations in which they might be appropriate
- Describe the field of organizational development and its relationship to training activities, including the value of cross-training between the two

---

Strategic Planning at Multistate Health Corporation

As you read this case think about the relationship among competitive strategy, the HR function, and HRD at Multistate Health Corporation (MHC). The case was written in 1994, and is real, but the corporation asked that its name not be used. The federal and insurance environment for health care changed substantially since that time; however, the

(*continued*)

(*continued*)

considerable change in governmental regulations and insurance procedures. At the time of their strategic planning, hospitals were reimbursed on the basis of a preset, standardized price for treatment rather than the "cost-plus" method used previously. The federal and state governments were putting increasing pressure on health care institutions to reduce costs. In addition, new medical technologies and procedures being developed were expensive to acquire and implement. MHC recently acquired subsidiary corporations to develop or acquire new procedures and technologies. The subsidiaries were to work in partnership with the regions to implement new procedures and technology.

MHC lost money every year since 1987. Currently it is experiencing an oversupply of bed space in most of the communities with MHC hospitals. Projections indicate that need for inpatient services will decline while the need for outpatient services will increase. Nontraditional health-related services are also projected to increase (e.g., services in which patients and their relatives are trained in self-care or care of relatives). In short, the market is becoming much more competitive while products and services are rapidly changing.

MHC just finished its corporate strategic planning process and planned to develop a two-pronged market strategy to deal with its changing business environment. One major area of focus is technology. The strategic planners departed from the previous strategy, opting to become a leader in the development of new health care technology and procedures. They felt the new developments would allow quicker recovery times, thus reducing the hospitals' costs. In addition, the technology could be marketed to other health care providers, generating more revenue. The drawback was that new technologies and procedures were expensive to develop and were often subject to long waiting periods before being approved by the insurers and government agencies.

The second prong of the strategy was to improve efficiencies in basic health care and outpatient services, which would allow them to continue to provide for the basic health care needs of the less fortunate. The substantial governmental fees, grants, and other revenues tied to this population would provide a profit only if efficiencies could be developed throughout the corporation.

IMPLEMENTATION ISSUES

Carrie Brown, hired 6 months earlier as corporate vice president of human resources, listened to several days of strategy discussion, without participating much. She now felt it was time to address the human resource implications of these strategies.

"While I agree that these are good strategies," Carrie said, "I don't know if we have the right people in the right places to carry them out. A few of our regional and divisional executives are already doing some of the things you're talking about, but most of them have grown up in the old system and don't know how to go about cost cutting in a way that doesn't diminish the quality of our service. Many of our divisions are in rural areas and haven't kept up with technology. We do have some middle- to upper-level managers who are up to date in cost cutting and technology implementation, but they are scattered throughout the organization."

Mitchell Fields, president and CEO of MHC, suggested, "Why don't we just move those people who have the capabilities to implement our strategies into positions where they have the power to make it happen?"

(*continued*)

strategic planning issues faced by MHC remain relevant today. The information pro
here reflects the organization in 1993 as it was completing its strategic planning pro

THE ORGANIZATION

Multistate Health Corporation (MHC) is a health care provider owned and opera
a religious order. MHC owns 30 hospitals and four subsidiary corporations, emplo
more than 10,000 people. Its headquarters is in Michigan with hospitals located in
states across the country. The overall organizational structure and the corporate F
structure are depicted in Exhibits 2-1 and 2-2.

COMPETITIVE STRATEGY

In line with their mission, which is rooted in the tenets of their religion, MHC fo
providing care to the indigent and less able members of the community. They we
reasonably successful until 1989 when the health care industry began to experie

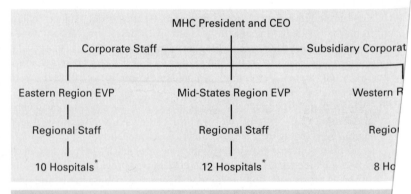

EXHIBIT 2-1

Each hospital has a CEO reporting to the regional executive vice president (EVP). H
referred to as divisions within MHC and have a CEO as well as a functional staff (inc
conducting divisional operations. Corporate HR is included as part of corporate staff,
Exhibit 2-2.

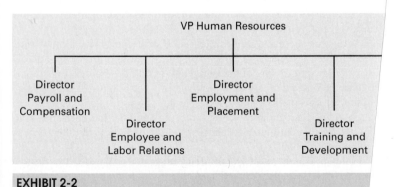

EXHIBIT 2-2

(*continued*)

"Unfortunately," Carrie said, "we have no accurate data about which of our people have the capabilities. It would be a mistake to move forward unless we're sure that we have the knowledge and skills on board to be successful. What I've discovered in the short time I've been here is that we have grown too large for our human resource information system. We're still doing most of the data collection on paper, and the forms used are different in each of the divisions, so we can't consolidate information across divisions, and even if we could it would take forever to do it by hand. We have different pay scales in different divisions, and you can't get a VP in Boston to take a CEO position in Iowa because he'd have to take a cut in pay. Basically, what I'm saying is that we don't have a coherent HR system in place to give us the information we need to put the right people in the right places.

"Another issue is that our current structure isn't conducive to setting up partnerships between the subsidiary corporations and the regions. The corporations developing the technology are seen as pretty distant from the regions and divisions. While the subsidiary corporations will bear the developmental or acquisition costs, they are going to want to pass those along to the regions and divisions. The divisions will then have to bear the costs of implementing the new technology and working out the bugs. Once all the kinks are worked out, the subsidiaries will be selling the technology to our competitors at lower prices (due to volume) than they charged the divisions. The corporation and subsidiaries are likely to profit from this arrangement, but the divisions are likely to show losses. As you know, our compensation of division executives is based on profitability. They are likely to resist cooperation with the subsidiaries. Our current systems don't let all of our businesses come out winners."

"I understand what you're saying," Mitchell said. "Our competitive strategy is for the big picture and the long term. If these HR issues are going to be a problem, we have to fix them right away. We are going to have to work out some way for both the subsidiaries and the divisions to come out winners in moving new medical technology forward. Assuming we are able to put our HR house in order. . . get the right systems and people in place. . . . Are there any other concerns about adopting our strategies?" Hearing no additional objections, he said, "Okay, then, let's get to work on putting an implementation plan together, and first on the list is our HR system."

(The MHC case is continued at the conclusion of the chapter. As you read the chapter, we identify concepts and principles that apply to this case.)

Overview

Most people understand the value of having a plan of action before starting a project. Though planning requires additional time at the beginning of a project, it can save considerable time by preventing mistakes and ensuring that important steps are not skipped. In fact, the cornerstone for most quality programs is a "plan-do-check" cycle to ensure that desired outcomes are identified and realized in the most effective manner. Whether for a large organization or a single department, planning is a key to organizational success.

Strategic planning is the development of relatively long-term objectives and plans for pursuing an organization's mission. The strategic plan provides direction to all units of an organization. For example, the HRD department must reference the strategic plan to determine priorities for developing employee KSAs. In addition to receiving direction from the strategic plan, functional areas can provide valuable input that shapes the development of strategies. Thus even though the HR and HRD function are both directed by organizational strategies, they should also help shape their content.

This chapter explores the relationship among HR, HRD, organizational development (OD), and strategic planning. In general we use the terms *HRD* and *training* synonymously. However, in this chapter, for the sake of clarity, the term *HRD* will refer to the functional area (department) that is responsible for managing training activities. *Training* will refer to the activities (i.e., training processes) being conducted by the HRD area.

Figure 2-1 illustrates the relationships between the organization's strategy and the activities of individual units in carrying out the strategy. The strategy provides direction to the individual units (departments) of the organization. The units develop or are given objectives that will help accomplish the strategy. To accomplish their objectives the units then develop their own strategies/tactics. Individuals within the unit are given (or develop) objectives that will help achieve the unit objectives through chosen tactics. Thus, when viewed from the HR unit, the strategy provides general direction that leads to the objectives for HR. These objectives require supporting tactics. The tactics lead individuals to achieve a set of objectives. In this way, plans providing direction for fulfilling the organization's mission are developed and coordinated throughout the organization. As you can see, the planning of strategy occurs throughout the organization, with each higher level of the organization providing direction to the lower levels. The process of developing strategic plans is similar whether the strategy is being developed for the entire organization or for some subunit. What differs is the type of information that is collected and analyzed in developing the strategy and the level of detail provided in directing actions.

In the MHC case, why did the HRD department need to be involved in shaping MHC's strategy? One reason is that the strategies depended heavily on the competencies of upper management and executive personnel. Without knowing the current capabilities of these individuals, the company does not know whether it has the capabilities to implement the strategy successfully. HRD can, and should be involved with strategic planning at three levels: organizational strategy, HR strategy (tactics), and HRD strategy (more tactics).

At the organizational level, HRD can contribute to the shaping of the organization's competitive strategy, though this role may not be obvious. In the MHC case the divisional staff's ability to carry out the strategy was seen as a problem. MHC decided to go ahead with their strategy, but would they be better served by adopting a strategy that matched more closely the KSAs of their staff? Perhaps MHC has enough time to identify the right people for the key positions and get them in place. If there aren't enough people with the desired competencies, what are the alternatives? Hire people from the outside? Train high-potential insiders? The answers to these

FIGURE 2-1 Linkages Among Strategy, Tactics, and Objectives

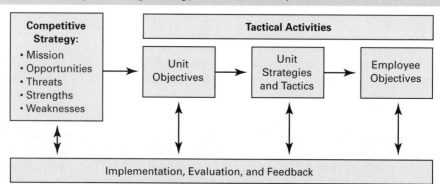

questions help to define the objectives and tactics used in pursuing the organization's competitive strategy.

The second strategic role for HRD is influencing the organization's HR strategy. The **HR strategy** is one level below the organization's competitive strategy and is the set of tactics HR will use to support the competitive strategy. In the MHC case the HR strategy appears to be one of promoting from within and "moving the right people into the right positions." It assumes that enough of the "right" people will be available to fill all the positions and that these people can be identified. To implement this strategy, the HR function needs to create a succession planning process and a corresponding executive development program for those identified as successors. Before committing to this strategy, Ms. Brown should consult with her HRD manager to determine the probable cost and time parameters of such a program. Of course, this and other HR programs will depend on a human resource information system (HRIS) that provides accurate and meaningful data necessary for HR planning.

The third strategic role for the HRD function is developing and implementing its own strategy. **HRD strategies** are the set of tactics used to support the achievement of the HR strategies, which are developed to support the organizational strategy. When viewed from an organizational level, HR and HRD strategies are tactics, containing considerably more detail about actions to be taken than is provided in the organizational strategy.

Assuming MHC continues its current strategic direction, what are the implications for HRD strategy? How does MHC determine the competencies of its executives? Assuming they conduct a needs analysis, how will they store and review the information? Clearly the development of the HRIS is an important first step. If they decide to develop their current executives, should these executive development programs be centralized at corporate HR or decentralized to the regions and divisions? Should they be developed in-house or farmed out to firms specializing in executive development? How does executive development fit into the culture of the organization? The answers to these kinds of questions provide the content of an HRD strategy.

Strategic planning and strategy implementation involve change. So HRD must understand the change process, which involves principles and concepts of organizational development (OD). OD uses the research base and set of techniques related to organizational improvement and managing change. As the organization's objectives and strategies change, the KSAs required of employees change as well. However, it is not enough simply to provide new KSAs. The organization's systems and procedures must change to support the use of the new KSAs if the desired change in performance is to occur. In the MHC case, what types of systems and procedures must change if the strategies are to be successful? The reward system? The way MHC is organized? The HRD process? The field of OD provides processes for identifying when systems and procedures need to change and how to manage the change. In the discussion of OD in this chapter we will focus on the strategic planning process and the ways HRD and OD can support each other. However, throughout the book we will also be addressing other OD issues as we discuss the training process.

Strategic Planning Process

If you scanned across the HRD departments of a wide variety of companies, you would observe many similarities. In fact, in the first chapter we indicated that the process of developing and providing training should be similar across organizations. However, as we pointed out in Chapter 1, many differences exist among organizations in how much training is provided, who gets trained in what areas, and who provides the training. Some companies' approaches to HRD help them achieve their objectives while the approach of others hinders the achievement of objectives. To understand why similar approaches to HRD might lead one company to be successful and the other unsuccessful, or why different approaches by two companies can each be successful, you must critically examine the relationship of HRD activities to the strategy of the company.

Different strategies and strategic planning processes have different HRD implications. The following discussion explains the strategy development process and the implications of differing competitive strategies as they relate to HRD. Some additional discussion of competitive strategy is provided in the management development chapter.

ORGANIZATIONAL MISSION

An organization's mission statement is a general statement that articulates why the organization exists and its commitments. The **mission** is the focal point for strategy development because it outlines what the strategy is designed to achieve. Here are examples of mission statements from two different types of organizations.

MISSION OF OZONE HOUSE (A SOCIAL SERVICE AGENCY)
Ozone House is a community-based, not-for-profit agency that seeks to help youth lead safe, healthy, and productive lives through intensive prevention and intervention strategies.[1]

MISSION OF FORD'S WINDSOR ENGINE PLANT, WINDSOR, ONTARIO, CANADA
Our mission is to continually improve our products and services to meet our customers' needs, allowing us to prosper as a business and provide a reasonable return for our stockholders.

These statements, though different, show many similarities. A good mission statement is a fairly general description of what the organization seeks to accomplish. It describes the products or services the organization provides, who it provides them to, and what it wishes to accomplish.

STRATEGY

The mission describes what the organization wants to accomplish; strategies define how the organization will go about doing so. The numerous definitions of **organizational strategy** all include the following elements:[2]

Strategies attempt to optimize the match between the organization's mission, what is occurring or is projected to occur in the external environment, and the organization's internal operations.

Strategies include

1. setting short- and long-term business objectives for the organization,
2. setting courses of action necessary to achieve those objectives, and
3. allocating the resources needed to carry out those actions.

Competitive Strategy
The literature dealing with strategy contains a great many categorizations and terms that refer to different types and levels of strategy. For simplicity we choose one, competitive strategy, to demonstrate the relationship between organizational strategy, HR, and HRD. What most companies call their **competitive strategy** concerns positioning themselves in the marketplace. This, their most important strategy, includes the set of interrelated internal and external choices made by the company to improve or retain its competitive position. Competitive strategy also provides the added benefit of a documented relationship to many aspects of managerial and organizational behavior.[3]

Three competitive positioning strategies illustrate a continuum of possible competitive strategies: market leader, market follower, and cost leader. We will briefly discuss all three, concentrating on the two ends of the continuum (market leader and cost leader). These two extremes clearly illustrate the implications for developing HR and HRD strategies that are consistent with the competitive strategy.

Market leader organizations, also labeled prospectors[4] and innovators,[5] find and exploit new product and market opportunities. Success depends on their capacity to survey a wide range of environmental conditions, trends, and events and move quickly into windows of opportunity. Market leaders typically use multiple types of technology capable of being used in many different ways.

The **market follower**, also labeled analyzer[6] and differentiator,[7] minimizes risk and maximizes profit opportunity by moving into a market after its viability is established by others. The success of the market follower depends on copying and improving upon products with an established market. Such organizations must be able to respond once markets are proven, but at the same time maintain operating efficiency in the market and product areas already established. These firms represent the middle portion of the competitive strategy continuum.

The **cost leader**,[8] also referred to as the defender,[9] represents the opposite end of the continuum from the market leader. Its main goal is to be the low-cost provider in the industry. Its success depends on its pricing competitiveness and having a product that is acceptable to the market (not necessarily the best). It achieves this success by producing a standardized product or service efficiently, by using economies of scale, low-cost labor, and perhaps by introducing innovative production methods.

Strategies reflect choices the organization makes about how to pursue its mission. An organization must choose from among a large number of often contradictory strategies. For example, one way to pursue a cost leader strategy (one prong of the MHC strategy), is to aggressively pursue competing bids from as many suppliers as possible, then accept the lowest bids from as many suppliers as needed to meet requirements. A different tactic is to develop long-term relationships with a few suppliers with capacity to meet your requirements, guaranteeing sole supplier status in return for meeting a specified price target. Both tactics can reduce the cost of supplied materials, but they result in different effects on the purchasing activities of the organization and on supplier relationships. Among the feasible alternatives, the company seeks to choose the one that will best achieve the mission. Which will be "best" depends on how the organization addresses its strategic contingencies.

STRATEGIC CONTINGENCIES

The success of a competitive strategy is contingent on the demands of the external environment and factors internal to the organization. Figure 2-2 represents the relationships among environment, strategy, structure, and technology.[10] As the figure indicates, strategy is the process of making internal adjustments to accommodate the demands of the external environment, while remaining true to the mission. Note, however, the arrow between strategy and environment shows influence in both directions, which reflects the fact that the choice of competitive strategy

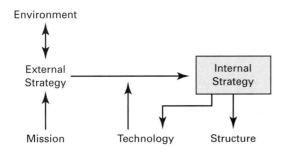

FIGURE 2-2 Mission, Strategy, Technology, Structure Relationship

may change the environment in which the firm operates. We discuss this topic further in the "External Environment" section.

Figure 2-2 also shows that the external (competitive) strategy requires an internal strategy to be developed and implemented. The **internal strategy** reflects how the organization must change in order to carry out the competitive strategy. The two key factors in the internal strategy are the organization's structure (e.g., division of labor, policies, procedures) and core technology (how the principle products or services are created). Because the core technology is so critical to implementing external strategy, it can influence the strategy that is adopted. Thus, when a competitive strategy is not consistent with the core technology, one of these factors must be changed. Again, this strategic choice is one the organization must make. External and internal strategies are aligned to maximize the match between environmental demands, the core technology, and the organization's structure. We now examine each of these strategic contingencies in more detail.

External Environment

An organization's **external environment** consists of elements outside the organization that influence the organization's ability to achieve its mission. Competitors, the economy, societal norms and values, laws and regulations, raw materials, suppliers, and technological innovation are examples. An environmental factor that is important to one organization may or may not be important to another, even if they are in the same industry. Because organizations differ (for example, their mission, internal resources, and operations), external factors will affect each organization differently. Each organization must examine its environment for threats and opportunities. The degree to which a factor needs to be addressed in the strategy depends on the size of the threat or opportunity. What kinds of environmental factors were important in the MHC case? Certainly governmental regulations, new technology, and MHC's competitors seem to be important areas to be addressed by their strategies.

The success of a competitive strategy can be significantly influenced by the uncertainty of the external environment. **Environmental uncertainty** is determined by two factors: complexity and stability. **Environmental complexity** refers to the number of factors in the environment and how interrelated they are. **Environmental stability** is the rate at which key factors in the environment change; the more rapid the change, the more unstable the environment. When the environment is more complex and unstable, it is more uncertain. When it is simpler and more stable, it is more certain. Table 2-1 depicts this relationship.

In more uncertain environments, the organization must be flexible and adaptable in order to respond effectively. A market leader strategy is consistent with this situation. More certain environments demand less need for flexibility, so a more rigid operating method can minimize costs and maximize profitability, a situation consistent with the cost leader strategy. Uncertain

TABLE 2-1 Factors Influencing Environmental Uncertainty

		Complexity	
		High	Low
Stability	High	Moderate Uncertainty	**Low Uncertainty**
	Low	**High Uncertainty**	Moderate Uncertainty

environments generally favor strategies using more decentralized decision making, whereas centralized decision making is usually more effective when the external environment is more certain. How would you characterize MHC's environment? Is it complex or simple, stable or unstable? Is MHC's strategy appropriate for its external environment?

The choice of competitive strategy puts the organization into a particular environment. In choosing a strategy an organization must analyze the environment for that strategy. For example, given two similar organizations, the one choosing the market leader strategy will by definition compete in a more uncertain environment. The cost leader, on the other hand, competes only in established and more stable markets. This environment may be more hostile, but it will experience a slower rate of change.[11] Thus, choice of strategy is often a choice of environment. At the same time, the state of an organization's external environment should influence strategy decisions. For example, in an industry such as telecommunications, the rapid changes in information technology and governmental regulations influenced many firms to shift their market position strategies more toward the market leader end of the continuum.[12] Although these generalizations are somewhat simplified, the concepts are generally supported by the literature and serve here as a heuristic for understanding the contingent nature of the relationship between strategy and environment.

Core Technology

Technology is how the work gets done in the organization. Each unit in the organization uses a technology to accomplish its tasks. **Core technology** refers to the main activities associated with producing the organization's principle products and services. A number of ways can be used to categorize technology.[13] Taking some liberties with these approaches, we use a simple continuum of "routine" to "nonroutine" technologies. At one end, the **routine technology** label is applied to tasks whose outcomes (1) are highly predictable, (2) demonstrate few problems, and (3) use well-structured and well-defined solutions when problems do occur. A high-volume assembly line, such as a garment factory or some automobile plants, are examples of routine technology. Such operations consist of highly specialized tasks and well-defined rules for coordinating activities. Decisions are usually top-down and highly formalized, leaving little discretion to the line employee. The routine technology is most often seen in the cost leader strategy. Even though the initial infrastructure required to put this technology in place can be expensive, its efficiency in high-volume production provides low production cost per unit.

A task using **nonroutine technology** is characterized by (1) results that are difficult to predict, (2) problems occurring often and unexpectedly, and (3) solutions to problems not being readily available and needing to be developed on a case-by-case basis. With this type of technology, management needs to provide lower-level managers and line employees with more decision-making authority to meet the challenges encountered. This responsibility, of course, means the firm needs employees with a higher level of KSAs. It is further complicated by the greater task interdependence characteristic of this technology, which increases the need for coordination and integration. Managers and workers need decision-making authority within their own areas, but their activities must also be coordinated with the activities of others. Thus, employees must be given clear goals and parameters for their work outcomes but be allowed to determine the best way to meet them. This type of technology is more typical of market leader strategies where the development and production of new products is key. The cost of the nonroutine technology may be high, but new products are able to command high prices in the marketplace. Leading-edge software and computer chip developers, such as Microsoft and Intel, are examples of such companies.

Structural Implications of Strategy

Organization structure refers to how a firm is organized (i.e., how labor is divided) and the policies and procedures used for coordinating its various activities. The structure is utilized to carry out the strategy and must be aligned to address both the strategic environmental factors and the core technology. An organization's structure involves many aspects, but we are interested primarily in three components: organizational design, decision-making autonomy, and division of labor.

Design   Organizations should be designed to ensure the effective operation of the core technology. **Organizational design** refers to the number and formality of rules, policies, and procedures created to direct employee behavior. An organization's design can be characterized as existing somewhere on a continuum ranging from mechanistic to organic.[14] A highly **mechanistic design** reflects an organization with highly defined tasks, rigid and detailed procedures, high reliance on authority, and vertical communication channels. The highly **organic design** reflects an organization that is flexible in its rules and procedures, has loosely defined tasks, is highly reliant on expertise, and places a high reliance on horizontal communication channels. Few organizations operate on the extremes of this continuum, but most lean more toward one end or the other.

The organic design places more emphasis on human resources and the mechanistic more on technical and financial resources. In the mechanistic design, employees' technical and interpersonal skills and behaviors are prescribed. In the organic design these skills and behaviors are permitted to evolve (within broad parameters) in order to supplement and complement the unit's technology. As you might suspect, the organic design is most appropriate for nonroutine technologies, whereas the mechanistic design is more appropriate for routine technologies.[15]

Decision Autonomy   The amount of authority given to employees in deciding how to complete a task and the degree to which they are able to influence goals and strategies for their work unit is called **decision autonomy**.[16] Individual or small group decision-making autonomy is a function of whether decisions are centralized or decentralized. Cost efficiencies are associated with more centralization, whereas flexibility/adaptability is associated with decentralization.[17] Thus centralized structures are more appropriate for cost leader strategies and decentralization for market leaders.

Division of Labor   The way in which the work is divided and organized is called **division of labor**. Of the many ways in which labor is divided, one is line (those working directly with the core technology) and staff (everyone else); another is management and labor. Some organizations divide themselves by products, others by customers or geography. Some divide the work into functional areas while others organize work around the processes in their core technology. Even though these divisions are important, we focus on how specialized the duties and responsibilities are within the organization. We place organizations on a continuum from narrowly defined (specialized) to generally defined duties and responsibilities. The more narrow the duties and responsibilities, the more centralized the decision making and the more mechanistic the organization will be. This results from the need to extensively coordinate the activities of employees whose scope of responsibility is fairly narrow. In organizations in which duties and responsibilities are more broadly defined, a more organic and decentralized structure is appropriate, allowing the employees to coordinate their activities less formally and providing more flexibility and adaptability for the organization. Again, you can see the close relationship between an organization's core technology and how labor is divided.

PROACTIVE AND REACTIVE STRATEGY

Formalized strategic planning is a proactive process used to decide how best to meet the demands of the environment in the near (e.g., next year or two) and long term (e.g., next 5 to 10 years). A **proactive strategy** requires a more formalized process typically involving sophisticated analytical and decision-making tools. It is proactive because it is a deliberate process for determining how the organization should respond to the anticipated business environment. Its purpose is to create a good fit between the organization and its future environment.

However, strategy can also develop in a more reactive fashion, evolving in reaction to short-term business conditions. In a **reactive strategy**, less formal analysis and planning occur and more attention is focused on the immediate future. Many suggest that both reactive and proactive strategies are necessary for an organization to be effective.[18] The formalized (proactive) process uses a best guess about what the future will bring; the day-to-day (reactive) operations confront what the future has actually brought. A strategic plan that positions the firm for long-term expectations but is modified by the firm's experience as it moves forward is preferable to either a rigidly held long-term plan, or to only reacting to short-term experience.

In the proactive strategy development, the organization typically identifies its strengths and weaknesses (internal focus) and compares them to the mission-related opportunities and threats (external focus) posed by the environment. The SWOT analysis (strengths, weaknesses, opportunities, and threats) is used to identify the organization's business objectives (e.g., market share, volume, profit) and its strategies (e.g., market penetration, product mix, pricing). The strategies are aimed at minimizing threats and weaknesses while taking advantage of the opportunities and strengths. Do you think that MHC engaged in SWOT analysis prior to developing their strategic direction? It seems as if they developed their strategy, then discovered the human resource weaknesses.

When the strategy is allowed to evolve in a more reactive form, the same processes take place but typically less formal analysis occurs and fewer people are involved in the decision making. Organizations that engage in both proactive and reactive strategy formulation typically use the reactive approach to continually fine-tune the strategic direction.

MATCHING INTERNAL TO EXTERNAL STRATEGY

Organizational strategy needs to be both externally and internally focused. As Figure 2-2 indicated, the external strategy is related to the environment. Technology and structure are the focus of the internal strategy. The role of strategy is to make the best possible match between the internal and external factors.

The competitive strategy is external. It is concerned with such factors as what product or service markets demand and what competitors are doing. It positions the organization to take advantage of opportunities and avoid threats. Internal strategies address issues such as organizational culture, design, division of labor, resource allocation, and innovation. Internal strategies aim to maximize the strengths and minimize the weaknesses of the organization. Together, the internal and external strategies are integrated to form the organization's strategic plan. The development of internal and external strategies is an interactive process with each being more or less dependent on the other. For example, a cost leader strategy would require strength in areas such as production efficiency (e.g., economy of scale), purchasing (e.g., supplier leverage), and labor cost (e.g., number of employees). If a firm is weak in these areas, adopting a cost leader strategy is difficult because the firm must transform its weaknesses into strengths. It is easier to adopt a strategy consistent with its existing strengths.

On the other hand, the environment may compel an organization to abandon its current strengths to pursue opportunities and avoid threats. Suppose a company developed moderate strength in areas supporting a cost leader strategy, but its many competitors are also strong in these areas (threats) and few or none are strong in market leader characteristics. If the analysis indicates strong opportunities for those developing new products, these factors may suggest that the firm develop a market leader strategy. Doing so would then require an internal strategy to develop the necessary strengths. The following example describes some potential internal strategies for a company that recently adopted a market leader strategy. The following changes to the internal processes and systems would act to support the external strategy:

- Increase the size and influence of product development and market research.
- Increase flexibility of production technology (i.e., the ability to shift from product to product quickly).

- Increase interaction between product development and market research (structure).
- Increase creativity within product development (structure).
- Align reward systems to support innovation (structure).
- Increase knowledge base of employees (technology and structure).

Training in Action 2-1 describes the experience of Hewlett-Packard Canada in strategy reformulation. As illustrated in this example, the external strategy must be supported by internal strategies that bring the structure and core technology into proper alignment. HR and HRD are typically key players in the development of these internal strategies.

HR AND HRD INFLUENCES ON COMPETITIVE STRATEGY

As noted in Chapter 1, the HR function is responsible for acquiring and maintaining the human resources needed by the organization. HR accomplishes these objectives through systems such as staffing, human resource planning, performance appraisal, compensation, health and safety, employee and union relations, and, of course, training. Each of these systems influences the organization. Integrated under the HR umbrella, they can enhance the organization's ability to mobilize the necessary human resources to carry out a competitive strategy. The organization's HR function is also a critical contributor to the analysis of organizational strengths and weaknesses. Analysis of information related to current employee capabilities is important in developing

---

TRAINING IN ACTION 2-1

BACK FROM THE BRINK

In the early 1980s Hewlett-Packard Canada was considered to be a slow-moving, inefficient company compared with its new competitors in the computer equipment business. Although it had state-of-the-art printers and other computer-related equipment, it was slow to get these products to the market and their prices were comparatively high. Business results were poor and projected to worsen. Furthermore, a recession was in full swing. A rethinking of the competitive strategy was necessary. Top management performed the normal strategic planning activities, but they also formed teams to target companies in need of computer equipment and to determine what HP Canada needed to do to win their business. After analyzing their environment and internal strengths and weaknesses, the HP strategic planning team adopted a strategy combining elements of both quality and cost leadership.

To address the internal weaknesses related to this strategy, HP Canada cut staff and streamlined operations. The sales force, for example, had been organized into separate groups specializing in one or a few products. Under the new structure the groups were merged into a sales force organized around customers but familiar with all products. HP Canada also relied on developing economies of scale in the production of its printers, pricing them competitively rather than taking large profit margins on their popular models. This strategy of getting a smaller unit profit from a larger volume of units combined with improvements in product quality vaulted Hewlett-Packard Canada back into a market leadership position. Profits increased in spite of a continued Canadian recession. By the late 1980s HP Canada positioned itself to be one of the toughest competitors in a competitive industry.

Source: Information derived in part from Yoder, S. 1991. A 1990 reorganization at Hewlett-Packard already is paying off. *The Wall Street Journal*, July 22, pp. AI, AID.

external strategies (e.g., market position) and the corresponding internal strategies (i.e., structure, technology).

Increased Importance of HR

Why should companies invest in developing a strategic HR management capability? The evidence indicates that firms that do so will significantly increase the market value of the firm.[19] Data collected from more than 2,400 firms show that firms with HR systems that achieve operational excellence and are aligned with the firm's strategic goals improve their market value by about 20 percent. This evidence suggests that investment in HR excellence and bringing business strategies and HR systems into alignment leads to competitive advantage.

In the early 1980s organizations began to recognize the importance of HR issues in making business decisions. Strategic HR management is now fairly commonplace, and the practice of using HR strategies to gain competitive advantage is increasingly evident, especially in successful organizations.[20] Fundamental changes occurring in the business environment over the last two decades make HR issues more central to long-term business success.[21] Table 2-2 lists many of these changes and their corresponding HR issues.

A common thread running through Table 2-2 is that to be competitive in an uncertain environment, organizations must respond more quickly, flexibly, and intelligently. A rapidly changing business environment requires constant adaptation and flexible use of resources. Employees must be more competent, and the organization must institute systems using that competence more effectively. This need creates an interesting dilemma. Just as organizations are requiring their employees to have higher levels of knowledge and skill, the supply of entry-level employees with these characteristics is shrinking. Evidence indicates that almost 30 percent of U.S. high school students fail to graduate and about 20 percent lack basic reading, writing, and arithmetic skills.[22] Another study noted that of those employees classified as requiring upgrading of basic skills, 67 percent had a high school diploma.[23] Even some business school graduates are found to lack some skills.[24] A report commissioned by the Association to Advance Collegiate Schools of Business (AACSB—International), the business school accrediting agency, states, "The corporate sector gives Business School graduates relatively low ratings in terms of their leadership and

---

TABLE 2-2   Conditions Increasing the Importance of HR Issues

High rate of change in market demand	Requires employees who can develop or adapt products and services quickly
High level of uncertainty in market demand	Requires employees who can forecast more accurately and react more flexibly
Rising costs combined with competitive pressures on profit margins	Requires employees with wider range of KSAs so fewer people can do more things well
High rate of technological change	Requires employees who are more technologically literate and current
More complex organizations (number and type of products, technologies, locations, customers, etc.)	Requires employees who can process and analyze complex information from a variety of sources
More diverse labor pool	Requires employees who can interact effectively in many cultural and ethnic contexts
Smaller labor pool	Requires more effective use of existing employees and better recruiting of new employees

interpersonal skills."[25] Using assessment center methodology, a study of approximately 350 students from four schools found minimal skill improvement from the start to the completion of their undergraduate course work.[26] The picture is no better in Canada, where 22 percent of the workforce is illiterate.[27] It is estimated that this lack of literacy skills costs U.S. industry about $60 billion a year,[28] and in Canada, about $4 billion per year.[29]

Even though both the public school systems and business schools continue to work hard to correct these problems, businesses are not waiting for the solutions. The general decline in the KSAs of the labor pool combined with a projected shrinking of the total labor pool spell problems for business. Thus, many firms are providing basic skills training to their employees as well as creating their own "universities." Organizations that place a high priority on employee competencies will also need to place a high priority on internal strategies for human resource development and staffing.

In addition to contributing to the development of the organization's competitive strategy, HR activities must support those strategies once they are adopted. Decisions about competitive strategy need to be reflected in HR strategy, and vice versa. For example, if the company's operations are labor intensive and a strong union consistently demands high wages and restrictive work rules, it would be foolish to adopt a cost leader strategy without addressing these issues first. Similarly, once the company makes the decision to adopt a cost leader strategy, HR must develop its own strategies for supporting cost leadership. Figure 2-3 reflects this relationship and some of the factors involved in developing an HR strategy. As this figure illustrates, HR strategy must be aligned with competitive strategy, and each influences the other. Let's assume a cost leader strategy requires a change in production technology (e.g., more automation); this change could be accomplished only if HR is capable of staffing the new technology. HR's input into the strategy formulation process might be the identification of what it would take to staff the proposed technology and the likelihood of being able to do so. Failure to address the HR side of the strategy could lead to the purchase and installation of a new technology that, among other things, is too costly to staff, creates labor conflict, produces conflicts in the existing culture, or requires lengthy training, thus delaying the implementation of the technology. Might any of these things happen at MHC?

HRD and Strategy Development

Throughout this text we emphasize that HRD is in the business of supporting the organization's strategies, goals, and objectives. In this supporting role, HRD contributes to the organization's competitive position in the following ways:

- Ensuring employees have the necessary competencies to meet strategic performance demands
- Identifying and assisting in the removal of barriers to desired performance
- Providing key information related to the development of competitive strategies

The last point, "providing key information," involves many issues. Obviously, HRD needs to provide an assessment of employee strengths and weaknesses relative to the competitive strategy. Unfortunately, many organizations don't think of HRD in this strategic sense. Product innovation or cost leadership strategies are often formulated with little consideration of employee capabilities, and it is only after implementation problems surface that HRD considerations may arise. These problems often result in costly delays in implementing the strategy, perhaps even dooming the strategy to failure. Assuming the competitive strategy requires increasing the competencies of employees, the various methods of approaching this task would need to be examined. From this evaluation, HRD could make an estimate of how long it will take before employees are ready to implement the strategy and the amount of resources required. This information is provided to the strategic planning group so it can determine the cost/benefit of the strategy.

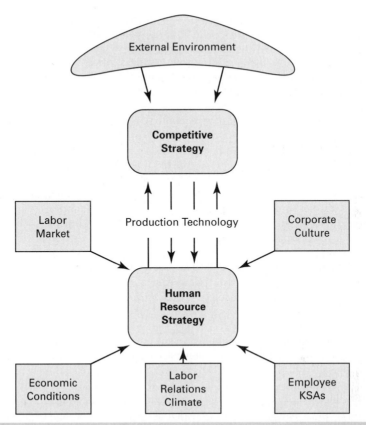

FIGURE 2-3 Relationship Between Competitive and Human Resource Strategies

Think back to the MHC case. What would have happened if Carrie Brown had not been invited to participate in the strategic planning session? Even with her input, will the plan be successful? It's clear that HR must deal with a number of issues before the competitive strategy can be put in place.

Staffing (new hires) is another way of improving the competency base of the organization. In the staffing approach, competencies would be imported through recruitment and hiring. Even here, however, HRD would need to be involved in orientation and any other "new employee training." Adding competencies through new hires implies current employees would be terminated or reassigned. The implication of this approach must be considered and factored into the strategy feasibility equation. If termination or reassignment becomes part of the internal strategy, training will likely be involved. For those reassigned, training in their new duties and responsibilities will be necessary. For those terminated, some form of outplacement training may be needed.

The Role of Competencies in Strategy Development

We are not suggesting that HR issues should be the only, or most important influence on the strategic direction taken by an organization. However, it should be part of the equation. The relative importance of strategic variables such as technology, financial assets, product, and human resources varies from one context to the next. Likewise, the importance of HRD issues to competitive strategy depends on how central employee expertise is to business success and the value of using current employees compared with acquiring new ones.

For firms that compete in markets where technical innovations are continuous and the rate of knowledge growth is high (e.g., electronic communications), employee expertise is a strategic asset. For firms in which change is slow or nonexistent or where markets are less knowledge-intense (e.g., food processing), HRD may have less strategic importance. However, any organization operating in a highly competitive market should consider giving employee competencies a high strategic value. Because new technology is always developing and continuous quality improvement has become standard in most industries, strategies for increasing employee competence can provide a competitive advantage. This connection is clearly illustrated in a 1999 special issue of *Human Resource Management*, a journal of the Society for Human Resource Management.[30] The special issue focused on strategic human resource management, and five case studies of how companies developed strategic human resource capabilities were presented. These case studies support what we said about the role of HR and HRD in the development and deployment of competitive strategy. Interestingly, all of the companies—Herman Miller, Lucent, Praxair, Quantum, and Sears—put into place employee competency models (particularly leadership) that were aligned with the strategies.

In formulating the firm's competitive strategy, the value of input from HR and HRD lies in the information they possess about the organization's ability to carry out different strategies. Organizations in market leadership positions, especially, must find ways to sustain their innovation advantage. Human resources are ultimately the only resource with the capability to adjust continually to changing market conditions. The development of human resource expertise provides a potentially inexhaustible supply of new ideas and creative approaches to the demands of the environment. Using employee knowledge as a major component of company growth and competitive advantage only recently began to be appreciated in strategy formulation.[31]

Once competitive strategies are formulated, HR and HRD adopt the more traditional role of supporting those strategies. Before we move to HRD's role in supporting organizational strategy, let's examine an internal strategy tied directly to both HR and HRD.

The Learning Organization: An Internal Strategy

The *learning organization* is a term used to describe an internal strategy for improving the competency base of the organization. The goal of a learning organization is to stimulate and capture individual learning in ways that allow the learning to be retained and spread across the organization.

Defining the Learning Organization   Many definitions explain the essence of the learning organization.[32] Here we attempt to combine the commonalities among them in our definition. The **learning organization** builds a sense of common understanding among individuals, enhancing their capacity to create the results they want to create through continually learning how to learn. Its systems support employees in creating, acquiring, and transferring knowledge to others. In a learning organization employees modify their behavior to reflect new knowledge. It is part of an overall competitive strategy in which knowledge is the competitive advantage. It requires large investments in time, energy, and people.

Even though it is an obvious fit with a market leader strategy, in which innovation separates winners from losers, it also has applications to every organization, including those that adopt cost leader strategies. Creating a learning organization is a challenging process. Its components are listed in Table 2-3. Organizational learning requires a focused support system and an infrastructure that can capture and deploy learning to those who seek it. Upper management must provide the appropriate climate and reinforcement, demonstrating commitment to the strategy even through the difficult initial stages of implementation.

TABLE 2-3 Components of a Learning Organization

Personal mastery	Involves the continual clarification and deepening of one's personal vision. It connects personal learning with organizational learning.
Mental models	Deeply ingrained assumptions and generalizations influence how we understand the world. Until these models are brought to the surface, little learning takes place that does not conform to these models.
Building a shared vision	Sets up a creative tension that pulls the visions of individuals into a common future that all desire, thus galvanizing a group toward goal accomplishment.
Team learning	Teams are the learning blocks of the organization. If the team does not learn, the organization does not learn.
Systems learning	This framework enables an understanding of the interrelationships rather than simply seeing the things that are related.
Systematic problem solving	The reliance is on the scientific method rather than guesses or hunches. Data, rather than assumptions, are used for decision making. People are skilled in the use of basic statistical techniques for analysis.
Experimentation	Distinguished from problem solving, its focus is on expanding knowledge rather than responding to current difficulties. Failure of experiments is accepted as a way of gaining knowledge.
Learning from experience	The lessons of experience are documented in a form that employees find accessible and understandable.
Learning from others	Knowledge is gained from what others do and how they do it, rather than from the results they achieved. Benchmarking and similar practices are encouraged.
Transference of knowledge	For the organization, rather than just individuals, to learn, knowledge must be documented and made transferable quickly and easily.

The primary responsibility of management, and the focus of management practices in a learning organization is to create and foster a climate that promotes learning. Management's task is not to control or be a corporate cheerleader or crisis handler; it is to encourage experimentation, open communication, promote constructive dialog, and facilitate the processing of experience.[33]

HRD's Role in the Learning Organization   HRD systems and employees are critical to the success of the learning organization strategy. They not only must know their field and craft well, but also must fully understand the organization and its strategic direction. They must be able to fashion learning experiences for employees that fit the culture, systems, and values of the organization. Learning organizations often require fewer employees because line managers are able to integrate many of the staff functions into their daily routine, especially with the HR function.

For example, the selection process is traditionally an HR activity, but in learning organizations this process might be handled by an autonomous work team that learned how to perform this activity. HR staff in such organizations learn how to improve HR processes so that fewer dull, routinized tasks are required, thus reducing staff and clerical support needs. On the other hand, the number of HRD personnel increases dramatically. The HRD professionals are doing less stand-up training but are creating more learning situations, opportunities, and systems.

James DeVito, vice president of Educational Research and Services for Johnson & Johnson, described their former role as learning stonemasons and their new role as learning architects.[34] As stonemasons, they were responsible for providing the content and the process of learning; as architects they are designing systems that allow individuals and groups to identify what they need to know and the best way of learning it. The learning organization radically changes the focus and core competencies required of HRD professionals. They now fulfill the responsibility of empowering employees to identify and meet their training needs.

Electronic information systems are critical to the success of this strategy. No organizational learning can occur without the capacity to store learning compactly and cheaply and to transmit it quickly and easily. Self-directed training delivery systems such as satellite broadcast systems, video discs, and networked learning libraries make it possible for people to learn what they need to know when they need to know it. This capability changes the paradigm for how the training function meets the training needs of the organization. Rather than directing the learning experiences of employees, training entails helping employees learn how to learn on their own and also developing the means for that learning to happen. Xerox, Samsung, and Corning implemented these systems with much success some time ago. Corning, for example, set a company-wide goal that 5 percent of each employee's annual workload would be spent in job-related training. A few years later, in 1991, *Business Week* recognized Corning as a prime example of an effective competitor.[35] Corning attributes its success to a commitment to employee and organizational learning.

At this point you might be wondering, "If this strategy is so difficult to implement and requires so much time, money, and commitment, why would a company decide to do it? Doesn't it face a fairly high risk of failure?" The answer is that the potential advantages are so large that companies are willing to take the risk. Let's assume the learning organization strategy is successful and allows a company to jump ahead of its competitors who are using a traditional training system. By the time this fact becomes apparent, the company already gained a substantial knowledge lead on the competition. Because of the difficulties in moving to a learning organization strategy, it will take the competitors some time to put this strategy into place. Meanwhile, the company is continuing to improve the competencies of its employees and increasing its competitive advantage. Because of its head start, competitors probably will require substantial time to catch up; perhaps some never will.

Although the learning organization strategy is still young, it shows great promise. It also presents traditional training organizations and training professionals with a significant threat. If the preceding scenario proves correct, the focus and technology of HRD and training professionals will shift dramatically. Those who fail to keep up will go the way of buggy whips and computer punch cards.

WHAT ABOUT SMALL BUSINESS?

We noted that strategic planning provides direction to the HRD department about the amount and types of training that are valuable to the organization. But is it necessary for small businesses to get involved in strategic planning in order to be successful? The answer is yes. Strategic planning is positively related to small business performance.[36] In spite of this benefit, many small business owners and managers do not engage in strategic planning.[37] Some of the reasons include the following:[38]

Not enough time	Too busy with day-to-day operations and concern about tomorrow are the excuses for not planning for next year.
Unfamiliarity	Lack of awareness of strategic planning or failure to see its value. See it as limiting flexibility.
Lack of skills	Do not have the skills nor time to learn them. Do not wish to spend money to bring in consultants.
Lack of trust	Want to keep key information to themselves. Do not wish to share this information with other employees or outsiders.

What can be done to encourage small businesses to become more involved in such planning? First, education about the advantages of such efforts would be useful. Even large organizations use the excuse that they are so busy fighting fires they cannot find time for planning. However, if they spent time planning, they might see fewer fires. Bringing small business owners and managers in touch with those who use strategic planning successfully in their small business is a good start for this education.

The skills issue can be addressed by using a less formal and rigorous process. Evidence indicates that small businesses that use a more informal strategic planning process can be more effective than those using more formal processes.[39] Additional evidence suggests that, at the very least, a formalized process produces no better results.[40] The emphasis on structured written plans in strategic planning may be dysfunctional for the small business. A less formal strategic planning process for the small business is provided in Table 2-4.

What about the issue of lack of trust? Research suggests that when faced with threats (SWOT analysis), small firms benefit by going outside the organization for help. Unlike large organizations, they are unlikely to have the necessary internal resources to address these threats.[41] Without a source that they trust, they will simply not obtain the necessary information or assistance. Small businesses need to seek out possible resources and establish appropriate relationships in "good times" so that they can be drawn on for help in "bad times."[42] The small business owner can evaluate the relationship during times when threats are not creating a crisis.

Will an increase in strategic planning result in a corresponding increase in the attention small businesses give to training? We believe it will focus attention on the "right" training. Training is often ignored as a strategic initiative because owners and managers do not have a clear model for making decisions about whether training activities will lead to a competitive advantage.[43] Involvement in strategic planning will provide such direction. As we discussed earlier, when the need for training emerges from the strategic planning process, it is clearly tied to the mission and objectives of the small business. For example, in companies that include ISO 9000 certification in their strategy, training is clearly value added because certification will not be granted without it.

One final point should be made about small businesses. Because they are small, communicating a strategic direction and implementing the plan should be considerably easier than with a large firm. The evidence indicates that, in implementing strategic plans, small companies needed to anticipate and prevent fewer problems than larger firms.[44] Some problems still do exist, however. For example, the small business that seeks to become a preferred supplier to a company doing business in Europe must receive ISO 9000 certification. Many small companies used the strategic planning process to determine whether becoming certified is worthwhile. The planning process allows them to see how certification fits their overall competitive strategy. Training in Action 2-2 shows how different companies used the strategic planning process to make the decision.

TABLE 2-4 Questions for the Strategic Planning Process in a Small Business

1. Why are we in business?
2. What are we trying to achieve?
3. Who is our competition and how can we beat them?
4. What sort of ground rules should we be following to get the job done right?
5. How should we organize ourselves to reach our goals and beat the competition?
6. How much detail do we need to provide so everyone knows what to do?
7. What are the few key things that will determine whether we make it? How should we keep track of them?

TRAINING IN ACTION 2-2

STORIES ALONG THE ROAD TO ISO

Rivait Machine Tools, which provides electrical discharge machining of steel, employs 14 people. The president, James Rivait, made an important strategic decision to diversify into the aerospace industry. To even be considered as a supplier in this industry, a company must be ISO 9000 certified. Eighteen months later and $100,000 poorer, Rivait achieved certification.

Early in 1993 Grace Specialty Polymers set out in a new strategic direction that required ISO 9000 certification. The strategic plan set a target of achieving certification for four separate locations by the end of 1994. To accomplish this goal, an executive steering committee consisting of the general manager and employees who reported directly to him was assembled. They were to provide the direction, commitment, and resources. Next an ISO implementation team was set up. This seven-member, cross-functional team was made up mostly of department managers. Although successful, the members of the team indicated it is not an easy process. Their assessment was that a company must be committed to getting it done. You can't have less than a full effort.

Reelcraft Industries embarked on an ISO certification program to improve processes. It took the company 2 years to achieve certification, and the paperwork it produced was awesome. The main difference is that Reelcraft now "builds quality in rather than inspecting errors out." Among the chief benefits are increased knowledge and skills and communication.

Cavalier Tool & Manufacturing examined the ISO process and determined that it did not make strategic sense for them at that time. Sometimes a customer faces a short-run emergency and needs a "down and dirty mold." "If we were ISO 9000 certified, we would not be allowed to take on that business. All your work must follow the ISO process, and so I would have to turn down this customer. I am not ready to do that," president Rick Jannisse said. Furthermore, he is not disposed toward the discipline required to be ISO certified. Examining the external environment, he realizes that he may be forced to become certified eventually, but not now. At least he is aware of the implications of the decision he is making.

Sources: Benson, R., and R. Sherman. 1995. A practical step-by-step approach. *Quality Progress*, October, pp. 75–78; Bible, R. 1996. Implementing ISO has made us better. *Industrial Distribution*, April, p. 128; Williamson, D. 1997. ISO rating: The sign of the times. *Windsor Star*, July 16, p. F1.

HRD's Role in Supporting Strategy

It is not enough for the organization to develop competitive strategies—these strategies must be followed with action, typically referred to as tactics. Figure 2-1 illustrated the links between an organization's competitive strategy and tactical activities. The strategies are implemented through a tactical action plan, which consists of the required actions and the unit(s) responsible for those actions. The process begins with assigning objectives to the different work units of the organization. The units must then develop strategies and implementation tactics to achieve the objectives. Eventually, they are translated into individual employee objectives. The objectives for the HRD unit, as for all functional areas, must be tied directly to organizational strategies. Of course, for HRD these will be filtered through the strategies the HR unit developed to achieve its objectives.

DEVELOPING AN HRD STRATEGY

Without a strategic plan, training is likely to be managed in a haphazard manner, its resources underutilized, and its full strategic value not realized. At the most basic level the training function must make strategic decisions about where it will focus its resources and energies. It also depends in part on the environment in which training operates, the resources available (financial, material, and personnel), and the core competencies contained within the training function. Analysis of these areas leads to strategic decisions about the technology that should be used to develop needed employee competencies. Because the bulk of HRD's environment is the organization, an organizational analysis will provide most of the data necessary for creating the training strategy. How to conduct this analysis and sources from which data can be obtained are detailed in Chapter 4.

The Training Environment

Just as the organization must align its competitive strategy with the demands of its environment, so too must the training function. The environment of the HRD function consists of the organization itself as well as some aspects of the organization's external environment. Key are the strategies adopted by the HR function. Figure 2-4 illustrates key factors in the selection of a training strategy. In any given organization the importance of these factors varies and additional factors may exist.

FIGURE 2-4 Environmental Factors Affecting the Selection of a Training Strategy

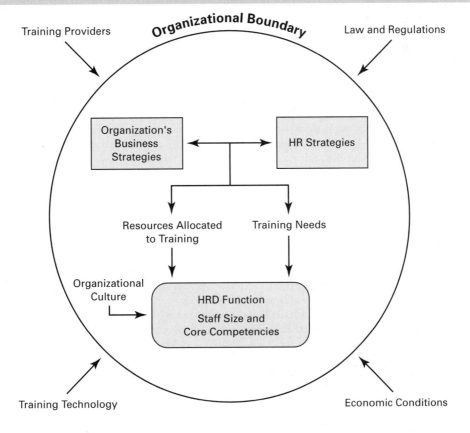

Factors External to the Organization   As Figure 2-4 indicates, some external factors are outside the organization, and others are outside the training function but internal to the organization. Factors outside the organization may exert their influence on the training function directly or through other parts of the organization.

External Training Providers.   Training providers such as private training and consulting firms, professional associations, and colleges and universities can be seen as either threats to or opportunities for the training function. They provide a threat as competitors providing similar products and services. In this sense their threat is to the size and perhaps even the existence of the training function. If their products and services are viewed as higher or equivalent in quality but less costly, the organization may decide to reduce or eliminate internal training. In addition, external providers can provide competitors with competencies. To the extent that employee competencies are a competitive advantage to the company, the training function needs to monitor the activities of external providers as benchmarks against which to judge their own performance.

External training providers can also be seen as opportunities. They can be used as resources for products and services that are not cost effective to develop internally or for which internal resources or capabilities are lacking. Some of the primary uses for external training providers are in new program development, specialized program development, needs analysis, and evaluation. These functions all require specialized competencies that may not be used on a continual basis. By going to outside providers, the company avoids the expense of narrowly focused full-time employees who are needed only on occasion. Additionally, development costs for new training programs are relatively high. However, an outside provider who specializes in the training program area will be able to spread development costs over many clients, lowering the cost to any one company.

Law and Regulations.   In formulating strategy, the training function needs to consider laws, regulations, and legal practices related to training because they affect important organizational outcomes and can have a profound impact on the demands placed on the training function. Some training is either legally mandated or strongly encouraged by the nature of the legal system. Mandated training focuses primarily on health and safety programs. Equal employment opportunity laws place restrictions on how training can be used, who has access to it, and who must be included in various types of training. Some types of training are encouraged because they reduce the employer's exposure to lawsuits. For example, nearly all medium-sized to large firms provide sexual harassment training, even though it is not required by law. Employers who provide such training to their employees reduce their liability exposure if an employee brings a sexual harassment suit against them.[45] More will be said about this in Chapter 9.

Training Technology.   Training technology refers to the tools, methods, and media through which learning opportunities are created and put into effect. For example, during the past decade we saw tremendous changes in the capabilities of interactive, multimedia, computer-based systems. In addition to hardware and software development, advances in learning theory, educational practices, and training facilities are all part of the technology of training. As these technologies change, training professionals must assess their implications for training strategy. A firm with a given set of training needs and limited resources to meet the needs must make a strategic decision about how the resources will be used. Investment in new training technology typically requires fairly large amounts of capital, reducing the firm's ability to meet some training needs in the short term. Failure to make the investment, however, will result in higher training costs and perhaps less effective training over the long run. If the technology is developing rapidly, an investment now may lead to quick obsolescence (as in computer hardware and software). However, it may also provide better and less costly training across a wide range of training needs. Early investment can lead to a competitive advantage, even if the technology must be replaced in a few years. This dilemma is faced by many training departments. For example, should a company invest in DVD technology, allowing it to integrate all aspects of training onto an easily portable disc, or stay with the more traditional videocassette technology? The start-up cost for the DVD system is about $100,000. A state-of-the-art video system costs about $1,000. Is the advanced technology worth the additional cost? The answer depends on how well it allows HRD to meet its strategic objectives. Thus the advances in training technology must be viewed with regard to the opportunities and threats they pose to HRD's mission and objectives.

    Economic Conditions.   Economic conditions are critical in the development of the organization's competitive strategy, and, therefore, on HRD's strategies. The economy also has other direct implications for the development of a training strategy. When the economy is robust, organizations tend to grow, and growth increases the demands on training (e.g., new employees need orientation and job training, employees need to change KSAs). Growth means larger training budgets and more difficulty attracting highly qualified staff (while full employment may be desirable for society, it means a tighter labor market for employers). It also means less time available for training, because everyone is working hard to take advantage of the "good" times. In times of economic downturn, the reverse is true.

    From a training perspective any phase of the economic cycle is subject to positives and negatives. Economic booms may be the best time to invest in new training technologies. It is difficult to schedule training then, but the budget is larger, and the immediate training needs will be for those trying to cope with the growth in customer demand, staffing, and the like. Economic downturns, on the other hand, typically place different demands on training. With reductions in the workforce, those remaining are asked to do more with less and to do it better. New systems and procedures may be implemented to improve efficiencies, all of which require training. Some organizations, rather than downsizing in times of economic recession, choose to use production downtime to upgrade employees' skills. The North American automobile manufacturers did this during the mid to late 1980s. Regardless of the organization's competitive strategy, HRD is well advised to take economic forecasts into consideration when developing its training strategies.

Factors Internal to the Organization   Competitive and HR strategies present important implications for the type of training strategy adopted. The competitive strategy determines the structure of the organization, policies and procedures, budgets, and so on. The HR strategy must align itself to these constraints while developing the structure of the HR function and its policies, procedures, and budgets. HRD's strategy must take these constraints into account. Figure 2-4 shows the resources allocated to training flowing from both HR and business strategies. These resources affect the feasibility of various training strategies. At the same time, HRD strategies must take into account the culture of the organization, in particular the training climate.

    Organizational and HR Strategy.   Because the market leader strategy depends on innovation, employee knowledge and skills are critically important. Highly skilled and knowledgeable people must be hired and developed. They need to work under a structure that allows them latitude in how they go about their work. Reward and feedback systems must focus on long-term rather than short-term performance. Some amount of failure must be expected as employees try out new ideas. The failure of an experiment can be positive if it brings the organization closer to realizing its objectives through the learning that occurs. If failure is punished, employees will be reluctant to attempt new things. Hewlett-Packard, Raytheon, and PepsiCo illustrate this philosophy by selecting highly trained and skilled employees, being committed to their long-term development, and developing systems that evaluate and reward employees for their contributions to the company's objectives.[46] HRD in this organization must adopt a strategy that builds on the already high level of competency brought into the organization. Would a learning organization strategy be appropriate here?

Cost leader organizations, in contrast, emphasize tight fiscal and management controls. Because their leadership position is dependent on their ability to produce high volumes at low cost, efficiencies and productivity are critical. Strategies for reducing costs include reducing the number of employees, reducing wages and salaries, using part-time and contract labor, and improving work methods. Conforming to standardized procedures is emphasized in these organizations, and training helps to ensure conformance. On-the-job training (OJT) techniques are used more frequently for line employees. It is only at the middle-management levels and above that more autonomous decision making occurs and that higher-level competencies are emphasized. In these organizations, training is more likely to be focused on management.

We identified just a few of the myriad of HR implications in any given strategy. The important point is that the organization's competitive strategy and the supporting HR strategies determine HRD's strategic direction.

Organizational Culture. An organization's culture is made up of the shared beliefs and basic assumptions its employees adopt as they adapt to the organization and its demands. The culture is reinforced and transmitted through formal statements, materials, policies, procedures (formal and informal), stories (real or invented) about key individuals and events, and the actions that prompt rewards and punishments. The culture of an organization determines what is valued. The training must fit within the culture of the organization, unless part of the organization's strategic plan is to change the culture. For example, companies sometimes decentralize training by using experts within each of the work units to provide training. This policy will not be successful if the culture devalues these experts. Likewise, training itself can be devalued by the culture because of a widely shared belief. Training directed at attitudes and attitude change would be applicable in this case. These cultural values must be taken into account when training strategy is developed.

THE TRAINING ENVIRONMENT AND AMOUNT OF CENTRALIZATION

Various factors in the HRD environment and their stability determine the degree of uncertainty faced by HRD in developing a training strategy. Remember, the level of environmental uncertainty is determined by two factors: rate of change and degree of complexity. Further, because each environmental factor influences not only the training function but also one another, more complex environments create more uncertainty: It is more difficult to predict how three things will interact than it is to predict how two things will interact.

The amount of environmental uncertainty has strong implications for centralization in the HRD organization. In predictable environments, where training needs and budgets are known quantities for the foreseeable future, the training systems should be more centralized and under more formalized controls so that the most efficient means of meeting the training needs can be realized. In uncertain environments, training systems should be more decentralized and flexible so as to adapt to changing conditions.

At extreme levels of centralization, all training is developed and provided by a central training function (e.g., corporate training). In an extremely decentralized training strategy, each of the separate units of an organization would acquire its own training. On-the-job training is an example of a decentralized training strategy, because each area's management is responsible for providing (or delegating) the development and implementation of OJT.

Different levels of centralization result in both advantages and disadvantages. More centralization offers greater assurance of common content and method, greater economies of scale for development costs, and higher competencies in those who develop and deliver training. On the other hand, decentralization increases the relevance of training to each specific area of the organization, creates more commitment to training, and ensures that training occurs where it is most needed.[47] Furthermore, because local managers are involved in the training, learning is more likely to be used on the job (transfer of training), and barriers preventing transfer are more easily addressed. Decentralization also results in managers' being more involved in the development of subordinates. Aspects of centralization are discussed in the strategies described next. As you read this section, think about how the strategies would apply to the MHC case.

SOME STRATEGIC TRAINING ALTERNATIVES

The strategic alternatives discussed here deal primarily with whether training is developed and implemented in-house or purchased from the outside, and the amount of centralization in making training decisions. The three strategic alternatives are each labeled in terms of the HRD function's role. In the primary provider strategy, HRD provides all training. The manager/ intermediary strategy uses the HRD function as a purchaser, manager, and monitor of training provided by outside sources. The mixed strategy is a combination of the two. These strategies represent only a few of the many HRD might consider; they serve merely to illustrate how training strategy varies according to the organization's competitive strategy and the environment in which HRD operates. These alternatives were selected because they are not unique to a particular strategic plan but rather can be applied to any company. Budget requirements and core staff competencies are discussed in general terms.

Primary Provider

In this strategy all, or nearly all, training is developed and provided in-house by the HRD department. Each phase of the training process is handled by specialists. The types of training needs that will be addressed, the development of programs to address those needs, and the evaluation of those programs are determined by a centralized HRD function. Because it is most effective in a stable environment where training needs do not change rapidly, it is most appropriate for cost leader companies. The principal advantages of this strategy are the control over the training content, consistency in delivery across the organization, and reduced training costs. It is more effective in larger organizations where a single training program can be applied to many groups of employees. Because the cost of development can be spread across a large number of employees, the cost per employee is reduced. Because a single program is developed to meet a particular training need, the content is consistent across the organization. Because the content and design of the program are developed by in-house specialists, it is tailored to the company's needs.

This strategy requires a fairly large centralized training staff. Core competencies for HRD departments using this strategy include all those necessary to identify training needs, design and develop training programs, conduct the programs, evaluate the programs, and manage the training processes and systems. Because of the resource requirements, it is usually adopted only by the largest companies.[48] It is not to say that all large companies adopt this strategy, only that they are more capable of adopting it. Many large companies successfully adopt a decentralized training strategy, whereas others successfully use centralized strategies.

A way to reduce centralization but maintain a low cost is to have training developed by the corporate HRD staff but conducted by other employees. This system places a higher reliance on train-the-trainer and self-learning methods (e.g., videos and computer-based training). In this approach, after the training programs are developed by the HRD area and then shipped out to the various business units, the training is completed by the trainee alone or facilitated by a business unit representative (e.g., supervisor or in-house technical expert). Those conducting the training will need to go through a train-the-trainer course to familiarize themselves with the content and methods. Even so, problems can develop in the effectiveness of training throughout the organization.

Suppose MHC identified "listening skills" as a problem area for hospital staff who must deal with patients and their families. In response, HRD developed a listening skills training program and also decided to decentralize the training and have it conducted by unit managers within the division. This type of training includes many experiential exercises and some behavior modeling. These managers would, therefore, need to demonstrate effective listening skills, be familiar with the exercises and skilled at facilitating them, and be skilled at providing constructive feedback. Because of differences in managers' training capabilities, different locations would receive different levels of training. For this reason, evaluation would become especially important. Often the strategic KSAs that training is intended to provide are subverted through modifications in the training content and design at the work unit level. One solution to this problem is to provide extensive training and develop reward systems that motivate the work unit trainer to be consistent in presenting the material and applying the methods built into the training. However, this level of monitoring can substantially reduce the cost advantage.

Manager/Intermediary

This strategy employs outside training venders for all or almost all training activities. The training function's role is to select and manage training suppliers. Suppliers may be training firms, consultants, professional seminars, college/university courses, and the like. A full commitment to this strategy would use outside vendors to conduct all aspects of the training process from the training needs analysis through evaluation.

For small businesses and organizations with a small or nonexistent training function, the manager or intermediary strategy is most typical. It is adopted primarily for budgetary reasons. These organizations employ a relatively small number of people and it is more economical to pay a vendor than to pay the salaries of a professional training staff.

This strategy is also appropriate for larger organizations whose training needs vary dramatically over short periods of time. Thus market leaders and those HRD departments that operate in uncertain environments will find many advantages in this strategy. It provides a flexible way of meeting changing and diverse training needs with professionally developed and administered programs. It also fits well with a decentralized HRD structure. A small central HRD staff is involved in the budgeting process, monitoring of training-related policies, and providing consultation and support to the various units. For example, compilation of lists of approved vendors, payment of vendors, and mandated training are decisions that might be made by the central HRD group. Then the different units of the organization (business units, divisions, geographical units, and the like) are free to select the vendors and programs best suited to their needs and within their training budget.

The core competencies required of the HRD function in this strategy revolve around the selection and management of training providers. Because a large number of firms and individuals offer training services, the manager must carefully screen potential providers. Obviously, cost is one factor to consider. Typically, the low-cost providers are those who recently entered the field. However, the fact that a provider is more expensive or experienced does not mean its quality is higher. Within your budgetary limits, the primary criteria should be the ability to provide the desired KSAs to your employees. Some key questions for making this determination are listed in Table 2-5. Of course, this list is not sufficient to evaluate the provider fully, but it provides a good start for making comparisons. These issues will be discussed more completely in Chapter 8.

Managing the training providers requires typical management competencies. The provider must be given clear direction—that is, the goals and expectations must be clearly spelled out. The various training providers and their programs need to be organized in a logical flow with minimal disruption to the activities of the company. The providers' activities need to be monitored to ensure they are acting to plan and goals are met. An open communication system must be established between the training function and the training providers so that both parties can access the needed information.

Under the manager/intermediary strategy, HRD staff costs are minimized because the actual training activities are contracted outside the organization. This strategy translates to substantial savings on employee salaries, benefits, and taxes. The cost per training session is usually higher,

TABLE 2-5 Questions to Assess Training Provider Capabilities
What is their background (education, experience, etc.)?
Have they ever provided these particular training programs or services before?
Have they conducted formal evaluations of their results? If so, what have been the results?
Can they give you the names of people in these companies who could speak knowledgeably about the trainer's products and services?
Can they give you names of those who were recipients of the service and those who brought the training provider into the organization and oversaw the training or the service?
Can they provide an outline of their approach or process? How do they go about developing a program, delivering training, or providing a training service?
If they are providing training previously developed, can they show you materials, such as handouts, exercises, and videos?
If these materials are not specific to your organization, how will they alter them to make them appropriate for your situation?

though, because the hourly or daily cost for training vendors is almost always higher than the comparable rate for in-house training staff (even including benefits and taxes). However, the training provider is paid only for the time actually spent providing the service. The contract ends once the training task is completed. With this strategy, no layoffs or staff relocations are required when the need for training slacks off. Also, because these outside firms have training programs on the shelf, the company pays less for program development. Although these costs are often built into the consultant's fee, they are typically lower because the training provider can spread them over many companies. Even when the training provider creates a customized program, much of the developmental work has already been done. Thus during times of rapid change and when training needs are more diverse the total costs for training can be substantially less when using external providers. Under more stable conditions, moderate-sized to larger organizations can meet a given set of ongoing training needs more consistently and at less cost via in-house training staff.

To reduce costs further, a train-the-trainer approach can be used with the manager/intermediary strategy. In this case, a training provider (rather than HRD staff) trains one or more employees to use the provider-developed program. For example, it may be too costly and disruptive for a small business (of, say, 15 employees) to send all its employees to a customer service seminar and workshop. Instead, the company might send the general manager to the workshop, then to a train-the-trainer session conducted by the workshop provider. Although the company would likely pay a fee for using the materials, when the general manager returns to the company, she can train the rest of the employees as time allows, and for little additional cost. The general manager can also modify the training, customizing it for the specific needs of the organization.

The Mixed Strategy

Most firms use some combination of the two preceding strategies, providing some training internally and contracting some to external providers. Decision making is centralized for some training activities and decentralized for others. Different philosophies suggest where centralization should take place and what training should be developed or conducted internally. One approach is to conduct ongoing training internally and contract to external providers all new training. New training is usually required when some aspect of the environment changes. This strategy allows the firm to be adaptable to changing aspects of the environment while focusing its internal efforts on ongoing training. If uncertainty surrounds the training that is required or how quickly the need will change, this strategy puts the company in a more flexible position to respond. In addition, less of the development costs of new training are borne by the company. A negative aspect, however, is that training developed by outside vendors can be less directly relevant to the employees and additional resources may need to be allocated to tailor the training to the organization. Also, if the training need becomes ongoing, plans should be developed to provide it internally, an action that will require agreement from the external provider. Another approach is to develop all new training internally and contract out ongoing training. This strategy reduces the size of the organization's training staff. Typically, trainers are individual consultants who are willing to work as contract employees for the firm. This strategy ensures the fit between the training and the training needs, but the organization must shoulder all the development costs. However, these costs may be offset by reduced staffing needs. A careful break-even analysis would determine whether reduced staffing would adequately compensate for increased development costs.

The more strategically important training is, and the more likely it is to be needed on an ongoing basis, the more likely it is to be developed and conducted internally. Specialized training such as that required for professional staff (e.g., accountants and engineers) is typically outsourced. This type of training is difficult to develop internally and expensive to maintain the needed expertise. For similar reasons, training related to obtaining certification or professional credentials is often obtained from external providers.

The mixed strategy may be appropriate for organizations with training needs that are extremely diverse from one sector of the organization to another. MASCO Corp., a home improvement and building products company with more than $3 billion in sales in 2000, is a good example. MASCO consists of an assortment of divisions producing different products and services. The corporation adopted elements of both the market leader and cost leader strategies. The training needs of the different divisions are unique for the most part. It would be expensive for MASCO to hire a centralized HRD staff to handle the training needs for all the divisions. It makes more sense for the HRD function to be decentralized to the divisions. On the other hand, MASCO is in the process of redefining its culture after a period of strong growth. As a part of this redefinition, the company is instituting an executive development program in which key executives and high-potential managers are given the opportunity to earn an MBA. This centralized program is provided by an outside vendor (Eastern Michigan University). Participants in the program fly in from all over the world to the MASCO training center for their courses. The company's HR executives and training staff work closely with EMU to ensure course materials meet MASCO's strategic KSA needs while reflecting the breadth and rigor of a traditional MBA program. Materials are often customized to reflect problems and issues MASCO is facing. It isn't the only training that the company centralized. As part of its strategy to realize synergies among its divisions, it instituted a training program in logistics, similar to the MBA program in that the content is customized by an outside vendor (Michigan State University) to meet MASCO's strategic needs. Again, employees from all divisions are invited to take part in the program. Thus, MASCO's mixed training strategy takes advantage of centralized programming for some of its strategic training while decentralizing the rest.

OD, Strategy, and Training

Organizational development (OD) is the field of study that deals with creating and implementing planned change in organizations. Obviously, strategic planning involves change—both in the way the organization interacts with its external environment and in how it manages its internal operations. Although many organizations fail to take advantage of OD in the development and implementation of strategic plans, we believe it has much to offer.

OD AND STRATEGY

Whether an organization's strategies are developed proactively, reactively, or both, they require support from the internal systems. Organizational change is an inherent part of the processes of developing and implementing strategy. Organizations must resolve three core issues in developing and implementing strategy:[49]

1. *Technical design issues.* These issues arise in relation to how the product or service will be determined, created, and delivered.
2. *Cultural/ideological issues.* These issues relate to the shared beliefs and values that employees need to hold for the strategy to be implemented effectively.
3. *Political issues.* These issues occur as a result of shifting power and resources within the organization as the strategy is pursued.

These three issues determine the organization's ability to achieve its objectives. In developing strategy, decisions such as what products to develop, how to manufacture them, and what marketing techniques to use will signal shifts in organizational values, power, and resources. These issues will need to be managed effectively to create support for, rather than resistance to, the strategic plan. The field of organizational development can offer a great deal in helping organizations manage change effectively.

Organizational development provides a research base and a set of techniques related to effective change. Careful understanding of the research and skillful use of the techniques allow change to occur in an objective, goal-directed manner that addresses both the needs of the organization and the employees affected by the change. OD uses an open systems, planned change process that is rooted in the behavioral sciences and aimed at enhancing organizational and employee effectiveness. A model of a generic planned change process is provided in Table 2-6.

The strategic planning process, if done properly, is an OD approach to change. The first step, establishing a compelling need for change, is what occurs in strategic planning during the environmental scanning phase. The need for change is made apparent when the strategic planners identify the threats and opportunities in the external environment and compare that information with what the organization is currently doing. When a gap exists between what the organization is doing and what the external environment requires (or will require), a need for change is established. Next the

---

TABLE 2-6 Steps in a Generic Planned Change Model

1. A compelling need for change is established.
2. Goals are developed and agreed to by the concerned parties.
3. The cause of the need for change is determined.
4. Alternative approaches for addressing the cause are identified and evaluated.
5. An approach to addressing the cause is selected.
6. The approach is carried out.
7. The results of the approach are evaluated.
8. The results are fed back to the organization.
    - If results are favorable, go to step 9.
    - If results are unfavorable, go back to step 4.
9. The change becomes internalized. The changes made become routine and the normal way the organization conducts its business.

company's business objectives are set (step 2 in the change model). The company's current strengths and weaknesses are analyzed to determine what internal changes are necessary (step 3). This information then provides the compelling need for internal change, and internal strategic objectives are developed for these areas. The rest of the steps in the OD model concern the development of **tactical activities** to achieve the strategic objectives.

Examples of OD Techniques

A wide variety of OD techniques are available. The few techniques briefly described here give you a flavor of the ways in which OD practitioners approach change. As you read through them, try to pick out the ways in which training would be useful to the technique or ways the technique could be useful to the training process. As we cover each phase of the training process in later chapters, we will refer back to these techniques and ways to overcome resistance to change.

Diagnostic and Planning Interventions (Macro)   These interventions attempt to help groups identify the current state of the organization, facilitate decisions about where the organization should be in the future, and develop plans for how to get there. They are highlighted because of their relevance to training needs analysis, design, and evaluation. Some of the most popular techniques in this area are survey feedback, organizational confrontation meetings, and force-field analysis.

Survey Feedback.   **Survey feedback** begins with the design and administration of instruments for capturing employee attitudes, perceptions, and beliefs about various aspects of their work life. This information is then analyzed and fed back to various constituencies in the organization. The process provides a snapshot of how employees view the organization. The value of this approach is that it provides objective data that can be used to implement change to address the problems and issues identified in the survey. This technique capitalizes on the participatory nature of OD because everyone is given the opportunity to provide input. Thus, the data are "owned" by everyone. After the data are analyzed, the results are fed back to those who participated in the process. Feeding back the data requires well-developed specialized skills. The results must be presented in a form that is understandable to the audience and in a manner that doesn't threaten them or make them defensive. At the same time it must convey the nature of the problem. One popular strategy for providing feedback is the "waterfall." In this method, the consultant first gives the results to the leadership group, which in turn presents the results to the people who report to them, and so on throughout the organization. What kind of training would be useful for those who will be presenting feedback to others? Obviously, they will need the appropriate presentation skills. Because feedback and subsequent planning sessions are done in group formats, skills in facilitating group discussions and problem solving will be desirable. Can you think of others?

Organizational Confrontation Meeting.   The **organizational confrontation meeting** is a technique designed to mobilize the resources of the organization in identifying problems and developing action targets and action plans. It is particularly useful when a gap exists in the understanding between leadership and the rest of the organization (such as when a new top manager is hired) or when the organization is in a state of stress. It was originally developed for upper management and professional staff but proved effective with many types of line and support groups.

To begin the process, representatives from each of the organization units (e.g., functions) are selected to participate as a member of a group. On a given date all the groups assemble and each is asked to identify problems it is facing. Because groups are made up of people from different parts of the organization, the problems are representative of what is going on across the total organization. The problems are compiled onto a master list that is shared with everyone. Each of the problem areas is discussed and categorized; participants are reformed into problem-solving groups. The new groups rank the problems and agree on action plans with timelines for solving the problems. These plans are reported to the entire group, discussed, and perhaps modified. Follow-up meetings are held periodically to report progress and plan future actions.

How does training relate to this intervention? Participants would likely need training. To be effective, participants require basic skills in listening, conflict management, win-win negotiations, group problem solving, providing feedback, and group dynamics.

Force-Field Analysis.   **Force-field analysis** is another technique OD practitioners use for helping groups understand a problem or situation and develop action plans. The underlying concept is that any situation can be explained by the sets of counterbalancing forces that hold it in place.[50] Force refers not only to physical forces but also to psychological forces that influence individual behavior. For example, if you wanted to understand why a work group is not following the new company procedures, you might examine the forces acting within and outside the group that influence the members' behavior. Tradition, reward systems, and group norms are forces that often exert strong pressure on group members, preventing them from trying new ways of doing things. Other forces that can influence group behavior are economic factors; individual KSAs; stereotypes of race, gender, and religion; and group conflict.

To understand a particular situation, you must first identify all the factors that exert influence on that situation. Then you must determine whether each factor is exerting force toward change (drivers) or against change (restraining). All the steps for using the force-field analysis are listed in Figure 2-5. The arrows show forces that are driving and restraining change. In this figure, the restraining forces are more numerous and larger than the driving forces, a combination that would create resistance to change in the people operating within the force field. The line of interaction, where these forces meet, symbolizes the current state: This line reflects the array of forces on either side which have created the current situation you are trying to change. Thus, for change to occur, actions must be developed to shift the force fields so that the forces for change are larger than the restraining forces.

FIGURE 2-5 Force-Field Analysis Model

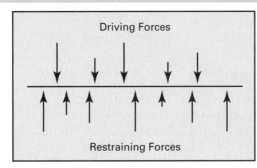

1. Identify the current state of the situation.
2. Envision the desired state.
3. Identify the forces restraining change.
4. Identify the forces that support or encourage change.
5. Assess the strength of the forces.
6. Develop strategies to:
   reduce the forces restraining change
   increase the forces for change (or capitalize on existing drivers).

This model helps groups and individuals understand the actions needed to overcome resistance to change. Research shows that change occurs more smoothly and quickly if the forces that are restraining change are reduced before or at the same time as driving forces are increased. Simply increasing the driving forces often results in escalated conflict. This conflict then becomes another force for resisting change as individuals become more defensive and positions harden.

Techno-Structural Interventions   These interventions address the structural configuration of the organization and its technological processes (how the work is done). Even though each of the following techniques addresses a different set of issues, they all use behavioral science and business operation models to assess the current state of the organization's technology and work systems. The objective of the analysis is to design systems and processes that are more effective in meeting the needs of the organization and its employees. Techniques in this area include job redesign, enrichment, rotation, and enlargement; collateral organizations; organizational restructuring; and responsibility charting. Programs such as total quality management, organizational reengineering, and the like are forms of techno-structural intervention. They are used to change how the work is done, the responsibilities assigned to individuals or groups, reporting relationships, and communication channels.

As you might expect, changes in these areas generate a great deal of conflict and resistance. To reduce this resistance, it is important to involve those who will be affected by the potential changes. Generally, a task force is formed with representatives from affected work areas, and the representatives are responsible for communicating from and to their respective areas. Rarely do more than a few individuals know all the critical information about the entire work process, so the first step is for individuals from various areas to educate one another about their operating processes. Once the group understands the entire process and its objectives, it attempts to redesign the process to better achieve the objectives. Often the changes in the sociotechnical system also require the redesign of other parts of the organization. The open systems perspective is used to connect any changes made to the operating system with other parts of the organization.

Once agreement is reached about the changes that are needed, an implementation plan is put in place identifying who will do what by when. This procedure is typically called responsibility charting. Generally, it is better to involve all those affected by a change in planning the change. However, in larger organizations, it is sometimes not possible. Whenever changes are made to the structure or work system, those who are affected, but were not part of the planning, will need to receive training to understand the changes. Additional training will be required for all those subject to redesigned work, changing the KSAs needed to function effectively.

LEVELS OF INTERNAL CHANGE AND RESISTANCE

Whenever internal change is planned, the plan should address three levels in the organization:

1. *The organization itself:* The way the organization is put together (what we call structure and design) must be examined to ensure that work is allocated appropriately and organizational systems are supportive of the change. This level of analysis identifies how labor is to be divided and what rules and procedures will govern operations.
2. *Groups and their interrelationships:* The way work is performed in the organizational units (i.e., the sociotechnical systems) and how the outputs of the various units are integrated is the focus of this level of analysis. The issues here concern the design of jobs within units of the organization and the interrelationships of the jobs to one another.
3. *Individuals within groups:* The changes in performance that will be required of employees must be identified and mechanisms—facilities, machines, equipment, and KSAs—put into place to enable the desired performance to occur.

Resistance to change is a common occurrence. Without sufficient motivation to change, resistance is natural. Change requires effort, new learning, and possible shifts of resources and outcomes. Often those satisfied with the status quo can create enough resistance to derail the change effort, even to the point that the business fails. A major factor in this resistance is the failure of the change process to address all three levels of change. For example, instituting a work-team system in the organization without addressing the performance-appraisal system will naturally cause resistance to the new approach. People ask, "Why should we work as a team if we're getting evaluated as individuals?"

Achieving successful change at one level, then, requires analysis and possibly interventions at all three levels. Consider the impact of a change in the organizational structure. Work would be allocated differently, so that some units might get work they hadn't done before while others might have certain jobs taken away. The affected units would need to change their work processes because they would have different amounts or types of work to do. These changes would require OD interventions at the group level. Here the OD practitioner is involved in the design or redesign of jobs and work systems and the associated interpersonal relationships. In addition, changes in how these work groups interact with others would be required, because they would now be producing something different. Employee resistance to new procedures would need to be addressed as jobs were being redesigned. At the individual level, employees would also need to acquire the knowledge and skills necessary to perform their redesigned jobs.

You might think that these three levels of change are intertwined only if the change occurs at the organizational level. However, they are integrated no matter where the initial change takes place, which is why it is important to take a systems perspective. Let's say you want employees to increase their skill at integrating quality control (QC) into their production work. Of course, training is an issue (the individual level). Is it the only issue for the change to be successful? Even if employee KSAs are developed, the job itself and the organizational systems must support using the KSAs. You will need to ensure that the design of the job supports the performance you want from your employees (techno-structural level). For example, the equipment and tools might need to be changed. If employees feel that QC is just a way for management to eliminate their jobs, they may resist this intervention. If so, simply providing new KSAs will not be enough. Work group norms (i.e., attitudes) will need to be changed to be consistent with QC objectives. At the organizational level, reward and appraisal systems would need to support the desired performance outcomes and work procedures. If the focus of the appraisal system does not assess the quality of the employee's work, but only the quantity produced, employees would not be likely to sacrifice quantity for quality. The appraisal system needs to reflect the importance of quality as well as quantity. The point is that the components of the organization (structure and design, jobs and employees) are interdependent, and changes in one need to be addressed as part of the overall change effort. The training needs analysis process (Chapter 4) provides a model for determining not only what training is needed, but also what other changes are necessary to support the training.

Another important point is that most change carries with it the need for changing employee attitudes. It is the central focus in overcoming resistance to change. It is most effectively accomplished through involving employees in the change process and through education and training. Involving employees develops commitment to the change for several reasons:

- They are intimately familiar with the current system and can make valuable contributions to the change effort, increasing its chances of success.
- They become knowledgeable about what will happen as a result of the change (reducing fear of the unknown).
- They are acting in a way that is supportive of the change by being part of the process, and their beliefs about the change become more positive.

Educating employees about the need for change also affects attitudes by allowing the employee to understand the consequences of not changing and the benefits that change can bring. Training allows employees to develop the knowledge and skills to be successful under the new conditions. Training in Action 2-3 provides an illustration of why change management must deal with all three levels.

TRAINING AND OD

Using OD's principles of change management helps ensure strategic plans are implemented effectively. Because training also focuses on change, the principles are applicable to training efforts as well. By including an analysis of organizational problems as an integral part of the training needs analysis, the organization ends up not only with training programs that address critical competencies but also an increased awareness of what problems need to be solved by other means. Trainers also use organizational information to design better programs so that potential application problems are included in the training rather than becoming surprises after training begins.

Despite the seemingly obvious advantages of collaboration between OD and training professionals, a gulf sometimes seems to separate the two. Consider the following examples:[51]

- An executive complains that his training and OD people cannot seem to work together.
- A training staff complains at length about a manager they consider unreasonable, attributing her faults to her background in OD.
- A training staff objects strongly when told that training needs analysis data could be used to identify performance problem solutions other than training.

Table 2-7 provides some insight as to why conflict such as in the preceding examples exists. OD practitioners are typically strategic, and executives are usually their clients. Trainers are typically tactical, and their clients are lower in the hierarchy (see Figure 2-1 for differences between strategy and tactics). It is the nature of the OD practice to challenge assumptions underlying organizational practices. Trainers typically take organizational procedures and practices as givens, trying to make people more effective within those practices. For example, suppose the needs analysis data show that the problems in a work unit are due to its manager acting inconsistently and arbitrarily. More OD professionals than training professionals would be willing to be guided by the data and confront the manager. Training professionals may be willing to say that no employee training needs were identified, but less likely to tell the manager that his or her behavior needs to change. OD professionals, however, are much more likely to get tagged with the "analysis paralysis" label than trainers, who are seen as "doers." Yet as Table 2-7 suggests, each would benefit by working closely with the other, because one's apparent weakness is the other's strength.

Why Trainers Need OD Competencies

Trainers can benefit from using OD if only because its planning procedures help to clarify what is needed in a given organizational situation. We believe that training programs will benefit from the application of many elements from the field of OD. OD's emphasis on participative approaches to problem solving suggests that training is better when trainees take an active role in the selection of their training opportunities and in the training itself. When involved in the planning stages, they are less likely to demonstrate resistance. This learner-focused orientation opens the communication channels and results in higher levels of motivation during the training program. A participative orientation also ties line managers directly to the training process by involving them in assessing their employees' needs, developing the training, and developing support systems for applying the training back on the job.

In the training needs analysis and training design chapters we emphasize an open systems approach. The needs analysis chapter focuses on understanding training needs in the context of

---

SELF-MANAGED WORK GROUPS AT AN AUTOMOTIVE PARTS PLANT

A southeast Michigan automotive parts manufacturing plant was divided into three manufacturing areas (Areas A, B, and C). The Area B manager, after some initial research, decided to install self-managed work groups (SMWG). An outside consultant was brought in to assist in the change. The following activities were carried out in the order presented:

1. A steering committee was formed consisting of the UAW plant bargaining committee chairperson, two other UAW representatives, the area manager, the plant industrial relations manager, two area superintendents, and the consultant. This group developed and managed the change process.

2. An analysis of Area B employees, supervisors, and productions systems was conducted to identify areas for piloting the SMWG concept. Three production processes were selected on the basis of employee and supervisor interest and on the ability of the production process to create natural groupings of employees. Although the way work was assigned in the team concept would change, the equipment would remain the same.

3. Training was provided as described here, with length indicated in parentheses.
   a. General orientation to self-managed work groups was provided to all employees in Area B. This orientation included an overview of the changes that would occur in the pilot groups, the process of determining how those changes would occur, the role of staff support functions (e.g., engineering, accounting, etc.), and a question-and-answer period. (2 hours)
   b. Supervisors and line employees in the SMWGs were provided with the following:

   - A more in-depth orientation, including the goals, roles, and expectations for the SMWGs and the salaried coordinator (formerly supervisor). In addition each SMWG developed a team mission and set team goals. (4 hours)
   - Basic team skills: interpersonal communication, interpersonal relations, conflict management, and problem solving. (16 hours)
   - Team building training for each group consisting of both instruction and trainer-facilitated application. After each component of training (e.g., development and assignment of roles) the team would apply that area to themselves. For example, after presentation of the team procedures material, the team would develop an "operating plan" for their work group describing how work would be assigned, how team meetings would be conducted, how coordination between shifts would occur, and so on. (20 hours)
   - Training in information management, group facilitation, meeting management, and stress management, to prepare supervisors for their new roles as salaried coordinators. Time was also provided for them to identify problems in carrying out their new roles and to develop potential solutions. (8 hours)
   c. Consultation for SMWGs and salaried coordinators was ongoing for a year after completion of the training.

This applied example demonstrates elements of effective change management at the group and individual level. However problems were encountered at the organizational level.

(continued)

TRAINING IN ACTION 2-3

(*continued*)

Group Level: All SMWGs were informed of why the change was desirable, understood what the change would mean to them personally, and what would be the benefits to Area B and the plant. Their representatives on the steering committee (UAW representatives for the line employees and management for the supervisors) ensured that their voices would be heard. Each work group helped to shape the way the change was implemented in their group by developing the team mission statement, goals, operating procedures, and so on.

Individual Level: Prior to implementation each individual could choose to remain in the work group or move to a different work group in the plant. Only a few individuals chose to leave their work groups. Extensive training provided each individual with the KSAs needed to be successful in the SMWG concept.

Organizational Level: This effort ran into problems in two areas. First, no changes were made in the performance appraisal system, so salaried coordinators were still evaluated on the criteria used for supervisors. Thus coordinators began reverting to their old supervisory behaviors, telling SMWGs what to do rather than helping the groups learn

what to do. Second, no changes were made in support systems such as engineering and accounting. Accounting would not furnish the SMWGs with cost and operating efficiency information in a form they could understand. Without this information the SMWGs were unable to determine whether they were meeting their goals. Equally troublesome was the relationship with engineering. Engineers were used to coming into an area and telling the employees what was wrong and how to fix it. The new system required them to work with the SMWG to determine both the problem and the solution. Engineers saw this process as a waste of their time, because they already knew what to do. As a consequence, engineers would frequently not show up at SMWG meetings or would dominate the meeting. Because engineering didn't report to the area manager, the manager had little control over how the engineers interacted with the SMWGs.

These problems could have been prevented if organizational systems had been addressed as a part of the steering committee's change management plan. The plant manager needed to be a part of the steering committee, because he was the only one with authority to make systemwide changes.

TABLE 2-7 Differences Between OD Practitioners and Trainers

Issue	OD Practitioner	Trainer
Role	Strategic	Tactical
Client	Top management	Middle- to lower-level management
Response to problems with organizational politics, structure, etc.	Challenge and confront	Work around or within the system
Organizational perception	Overly analytical	Gets things done

organizational systems. The design chapter emphasizes connections between the training program and other organizational systems. These connections help to ensure transfer of the training to the job. Furthermore, connecting the training to these other systems legitimizes it. Many trainers entered the field on the strength of their platform skills, but those skills are not sufficient to develop effective training or provide enriching experiences for the trainees. Many trainers told us of their frustrations when trainees were excited about what they learned but at the conclusion of training nothing changed.

OD can also help trainers enrich their own jobs. If they view themselves as part of an assembly line in which they are simply putting on one piece of the product, they will not see how their work relates to the final product. OD suggests that trainers need to understand why the training was developed, what the trainees are expected to do back on the job, and the obstacles they will face when trying to apply the training. When they understand the organizational context, having full knowledge of how what they do affects the desired outcomes, their job becomes more meaningful.

Why OD Professionals Need Training Competencies

While generally successful OD has experienced some glaring failures, many of which could have been avoided with a well-designed and well-implemented training program.[52] Earlier we identified the types of training required as a prerequisite or supplement to various OD techniques. OD interventions nearly always involve groups of employees in structured activities such as planning, problem solving, and intergroup conflict management. It is naive to assume that one can bring people together in new relationships to solve new problems, in a new situation with a new process, without prior training. These employees need to:

- Have a common knowledge and skill base in these areas.
- Understand group dynamics and be skilled in working in groups.
- Understand and be skilled at using a common problem-solving model.

If OD practitioners are not skilled in designing and implementing training programs, they must develop collaborative relationships with trainers who are. It provides an excellent opportunity for involving internal training resources in change efforts. It is especially helpful when an OD consultant (familiar with good training practice) is retained from outside the organization. When these two areas work together in a collaborative fashion, they will go a long way toward defusing any conflict between external consultants and the HR function.

If OD is to be a long-term effort, the change must be institutionalized into the way the company does business. In one study only about one-third of the OD efforts examined lasted more than 5 years.[53] This finding indicates that training is a critical component to institutionalizing the change. Three situations are identified as key times for training:

1. When the OD process is started, training is needed to provide education about the change process and to provide the necessary KSAs.
2. After the process has been in place for a while, some retraining or upgrading of KSAs is required to sustain the process.
3. As new employees enter the organization, they need an understanding of the process and the KSAs.

Although most organizations provide the initial training, few conduct follow-up training or modify their new employee training to include the new process and the related KSAs.

Integrating Training and OD

Trainers and OD professionals have legitimate differences in the nature of the change they are responsible for, but their interests are intimately connected. Each can provide valuable service to the other. Nonetheless, as we noted, they often are at odds with each other. One reason for the division between them is that companies typically organize around their different functional activities and OD and HRD departments are often separated.[54] This separation increases the differences in perspective, role, value of services, clients, and so on. An obvious solution, then, is to house them together in something like a performance improvement department within HR. This situation is a classic example of an organizational change effort that requires attention to critical change management issues. For example, such a department would need different measures of success than either currently uses. Success could be measured by its contribution to business results rather than the number of bodies passing through training courses or the number of teams built and facilitated by OD staff. This overarching goal would require trainers to identify system deficiencies that are likely to interfere with training and ODers to identify KSA deficiencies that are likely to interfere with system changes.

Companies such as Andersen Consulting-Education, AT&T Universal Card Service, and the U. S. Coast Guard made these changes and improved their business operations.[55] These companies found that integrating OD and training activities requires sponsorship from the top HR and other executives. One way toward full-scale integration of these activities is to develop pilot collaborations focusing on a particular business problem. This approach allows staff from each discipline to learn more about how the other operates and where the synergy exists. In addition, the HR executive needs to encourage people in both disciplines to learn as much as possible about the other. Another process that should lead to better integration of training and OD activities is having the staff in both areas work together to identify barriers to collaboration and identify ways to remove the barriers. This activity not only creates familiarity but also uses the OD principle of involving those affected by the change in the change process. By integrating the two activities, the organization also receives the potential benefit of cross-functional training, increasing the KSAs of both groups.

SUMMARY

An organization's strategy needs to be both internally and externally focused. Proper development of a strategy requires a SWOT analysis to determine its best fit in the market, given its own strengths and weaknesses. Competitive strategies from which an organization can choose include market leader, market follower, and cost leader. Each results in different implications for how HR goes about its business. The HR department needs to be involved in the strategic planning process, providing information about workforce readiness to meet alternative strategic directions. HR also provides input in relation to managing change arising from new strategic directions. From this and other information, a strategic direction is determined.

HR and HRD need to develop their own strategies to support the overall strategic plan. It is HRD's responsibility to focus on what changes in KSAs are required to meet the strategic objectives. HRD also needs to partner with other parts of the organization to identify any other roadblocks to achieving employee performance objectives and assist in removing them.

The choice of strategic direction will also help determine the way HRD is structured. Cost leader organizations operate in a stable environment and training can generally be centralized. Furthermore, training programs are not as likely to change, so the HRD department can develop much of its own training. Market leaders, on the other hand operate in an uncertain environment and the HRD department needs to be more decentralized. Training needs can change often and so the HRD department takes more of a "management of vendors" role.

Training is more than a program of providing KSAs to employees; it is an organizational change effort. As such the use of OD techniques are useful tool for trainers. Similarly, OD efforts often require training, so training skills are useful for OD technicians. To be more effective these two groups should consider working closely together and using each other's capabilities.

KEY TERMS

- Competitive strategy
- Core technology
- Cost leader
- Decision autonomy
- Division of labor
- Environmental complexity
- Environmental stability
- Environmental uncertainty
- External environment
- Force-field analysis
- HR strategy
- HRD strategies

- Internal strategy
- Learning organization
- Market follower
- Market leader
- Mechanistic design
- Mission
- Nonroutine technology
- Organic design
- Organization structure
- Organizational confrontation meeting
- Organizational design

- Organizational development (OD)
- Organizational strategy
- Proactive strategy
- Reactive strategy
- Resistance to change
- Routine technology
- Strategic planning
- Survey feedback
- Tactical activities

CASE ANALYSIS

The first part of this case was presented at the beginning of the chapter (pages 28–31). The following reflects HR's response to Mr. Field's directive.

HR FOLLOW-UP TO STRATEGIC PLANNING AT MHC

MCH determined that it needed to address the human resource implications of the new climate in health care and that some type of planning system was in order, so it hired an outside consulting firm. The consultants agreed that some type of system would likely be appropriate, but they were not ready to stipulate what that system would look like. They conducted some initial diagnostic interviews, lasting 1 to 2 hours, with all of the divisional CEOs, the regional EVPs, the corporate CEO, and the corporate vice presidents, including the VP of human resources and the VP of organizational development. The interview format is shown in Exhibit 2-3.

The following information was obtained from the interviews.

The current HR activities conducted at the corporate level follow:

1. To collect and store résumé-type information for all employees. This information includes demographic data, employment history, and performance evaluations.
2. To select divisional CEOs, regional EVPs, corporate officers, and staff professionals, and to assist at the regional and divisional levels in the selection of management-level employees, primarily through posting the position and through word-of-mouth about who is competent and available.
3. To sponsor occasional management development programs at the corporate level, although no system is in place to determine whether these are perceived as valuable or necessary. Most management development is done externally with tuition reimbursement, and some is done by individual divisions.

(*continued*)

    I. What is the purpose of this meeting?

    To enhance and develop the objectives of the human resource planning system (HRPS).

    II. What is HRPS?

    HRPS is a business planning system designed to provide quality data to enhance individual and organizational decision making in all aspects of human resource management.

    III. Why was I asked to participate in this meeting?

    Because you are a key decision maker, we want to ensure that HRPS fits the needs of your organization.

    IV. What specific information should I provide?

    We want your input regarding the following:

    1. Should administrative access to the data in HRPS be local, regional, or only at the corporate level?

    2. Who in your organization would use and benefit most from this system?

    3. What, if any, problems are there with current information used in human resource management decisions (i.e., recruiting, training, appraising, etc.)? For example, do you lack information as to which people are capable successors for certain jobs, and do you know what recruiting sources produce the best employees?

    4. What values of the corporation should be incorporated into HRPS? How might these values be incorporated?

    5. As you see it, ideally what job responsibilities will change in your organization as a result of HRPS?

EXHIBIT 2-3 Agenda and Clarification of Issues for HRPS

The interviewees expressed varying degrees of dissatisfaction with the following:

1. No system for comparing internal candidates for positions. Performance evaluation is decentralized.
2. No system for making known the criteria for positions. People do not respond to posted openings, because rejection is a block to future promotion. Recommendation from a higher-up is known to be necessary. A related complaint was that many CEOs will not recommend their best people, either because they rely on them or because the bright young people might eventually be competition.
3. No system for evaluating the KSA required of a CEO in one part of the corporation compared to that of another. For example, the CEO in Grand Rapids has different responsibilities compared to a CEO in Detroit, but no one at corporate knows what the differences are.
4. No corporate human resource philosophy/strategy guides the organization in its HR activities.

Individuals at the corporate, regional, and divisional level reported slightly different perceptions of the priority of needs for a human resource planning system (HRPS). See Exhibit 2-4. Although monitoring equal employment and affirmative action is in the company's mission statement, it was considered important by only one respondent. The various levels disagreed on what job classifications should be in the HRPS: Corporate and regional personnel preferred to include only executive-level personnel, and divisional personnel wanted to include data down to the first-level supervisor. As an interviewee stated, "The MHC value statement says that we respect the dignity of all

(*continued*)

Organizational Level	Improve Selection/ Search Process	Develop a Succession Plan	Forecast Critical Human Resource Skills	Develop Critical Human Resource Skills	Create and Utilize Career Development
Corporate	2	4	3	5	1
Regional	1	3	4	5	2
Divisional	1	5	4	3	2

EXHIBIT 2-4 Rank Order of Top HRPS Objectives by Organizational Level

individuals. To exclude people below the executive level tells them they are worth less." On the issue of control and administration of the HRPS, corporate and regional executives preferred corporate- or regional-level administration, while divisional executives had a strong preference for direct access. Some expressed concern that corporate administration would reduce divisional autonomy in human resource decision making. The degree of centralization had been a sore point for several years. The divisions previously operated individually as profit centers, but corporate headquarters was discussing the need for a more integrated approach.

After reviewing the consultants' report and meeting with the consultants, the executive committee (representing the three levels of management) arrived at consensus on the following HRPS objectives:

1. Improve the selection/search process for filling vacant positions.
2. Develop a succession plan.
3. Forecast critical skill/knowledge and ability needs.
4. Identify critical skill/knowledge and ability deficiencies.
5. Identify equal employment and affirmative action concerns.
6. Create a career development system that reflects the organizational mission.

The following HR philosophy was developed and was then approved by the board of directors of MHC:

As an employer committed to the value of human life and the dignity of each individual, we seek to foster justice, understanding, and a unity of purpose created by people and organizations working together to achieve a common goal. Therefore, we commit ourselves to the following beliefs:

1. People are our most important resource.
2. The human resource needs of the organization are best met through the development of employees to their maximum potential.
3. Justice in the workplace is embodied in honest, fair, and equitable employment and personnel practices with priority given to the correction of past social injustices. ■

CASE QUESTIONS

1. How would you characterize the fit between MHC's environment, competitive strategy, structure, and technology? Indicate any issues with this fit that might influence the success of the strategy.

(*continued*)

2. How could HRD influence the shaping of the competitive strategy?
3. In what ways might OD and training collaborate to maximize the effectiveness of the strategy? What forces are currently operating that drive or act to restrain the new strategy? Which of those need to change?
4. Given the strategy, how can HR be supportive with tactical actions? What type of structure should the corporate HR function adopt to match the competitive strategy?
5. Given the facts of the case, what would you suggest as an HRD strategy? Provide specific tactics that can be used by HRD to support the competitive strategy.
6. What sources of support and resistance are likely to exist in creating and implementing the new HRPS? What tactics could be used to reduce or eliminate the resistance?

EXERCISES

1. Conduct an environmental analysis of HRD's environment at the company you work for (if you're going to school and don't work, use the school's environment). What are the opportunities and threats to HRD in that environment? What demands does the environment make on the HRD department?
2. Form groups of three to five people, one of them having been provided with training by their employer within the last 2 years. Have this person explain the company's mission to the rest of the group. Then have the person describe the type of training he or she received. The group's task is to determine the linkage between the training and the mission.
3. Identify two organizations with different environments and core technologies. Describe what these differences are. Indicate how the HRD strategies of these companies might be similar or different. Provide a rationale for your conclusions based on concepts in the chapter.
4. Examine the mission at the institution you are attending. Examine the one for your area of study (if it has one). Do the two relate? On the basis of the mission and objectives, do a SWOT analysis through interviews with administration or using your own expertise. What major changes are indicated? How will they affect the way courses will be taught? What training might be necessary to meet these changes?

QUESTIONS FOR REVIEW

1. What factors might inhibit HRD managers from developing a strategic planning approach to training? How might these factors be overcome?
2. Think of possible strategic training alternatives other than those described in the text. Under what conditions would these be important in developing a training strategy?
3. Identify (through personal knowledge or research) an organization that utilizes HRD as a part of their competitive strategy. What role does HRD play in their strategy and how is HRD involved in the implementation of the strategy?

3

Learning Motivation and Performance

Learning Objectives

After reading this chapter, you should be able to:

- Identify the major factors determining human performance and their relevance to training
- Explain what motivates people and describe the factors influencing motivation
- Describe the cognitive and behavioral approaches to learning and their contradictory implications for instructional practices
- Describe different types of learning and how they relate to one another
- Identify a learning theory that integrates cognitive and behaviorist perspectives and describe how its processes and components relate to training
- Describe Gagné Briggs' nine events of instruction and their use
- Describe the causes of resistance to learning
- Explain the effect of group dynamics on learning and transfer of training
- Explain why different people need different training methods to learn the same things
- Identify the characteristics of training design that motivate learning and accommodate trainee differences

The Wilderness Training Lab

Claudia, a successful 33-year-old corporate marketing executive, found herself in the mountains of New Mexico preparing to climb a rope ladder attached to a tree. When she reached the top of the ladder, she would fall off backwards. It wouldn't be an accident. No, she wasn't suicidal or deranged. She was participating in an executive development program called Wilderness Training Lab.

At the corporate office in Michigan, she was known as an independent, smart, and tenacious businesswoman. She moved quickly up the corporate ladder from product research assistant to brand manager. Claudia had a reputation for micromanaging her subordinates and being a loner. When asked about these issues, Claudia replied, "When I was in college, I had a lot of group projects. At first I went along with group decisions and trusted others to do a good job, even though I felt anxious about putting my grade in the hands of someone else. It seemed to be a good way to get along in the group. Those projects received mediocre grades, and I'm only satisfied with being the best. Then I started to take over the leadership of every group I was in. I developed the plan, decided who would do what and what the timelines were, and always took on the most difficult and complex parts myself, all the time making sure the others were doing what they were assigned. From then on my group projects always got an "A." I carried those lessons with me into the workplace and I've had good success here too. Maybe it rubs some people the wrong way, but it works for me. The only trouble I'm having is keeping up with all my projects. Some of the other brand managers want to work with me on joint projects, but I don't have time. Besides, they probably just want me to do their work for them or steal my ideas. The VP of marketing will be retiring soon and only one of the seven brand managers will get that job. What's in it for me if I collaborate with them? Let each of us sink or swim on our own merits."

A few months ago, the VP of marketing, Sandy Cines, sat down with Claudia to discuss career plans. Sandy had always praised and encouraged Claudia's work, but this time he was a little reserved. He suggested, in rather strong terms, that she attend a Wilderness Executive Development Program. Claudia hesitated because of her workload and upcoming deadlines. Sandy said, "Well, I'll leave the decision up to you. The director of training and I have looked at your strengths and what you'll need for the next level as an executive. Technically you're very strong, but more important at the next level is building good interpersonal relationships. The training director recommended this program for you. But, as I said, I'll leave the decision up to you."

Claudia wondered what he thought was wrong with her interpersonal relationships. She had great relationships with customers, with outside vendors, and in her personal life. Relationships with her subordinates and peers needed to be different. She needed to be firmer and less flexible with them, didn't she? She didn't think she had bad relationships with her subordinates or peers. They never complained to her. However, Claudia decided it was pretty clear that Sandy wanted her to attend the Wilderness program.

In New Mexico she found a diverse group of men and women executives from all around the United States. Many confided that they had been sent by their organizations to "learn how to be more effective in groups." Most of them indicated they were interested and eager, but a little nervous about what was expected of them. They soon found out. They were divided into groups of 10 and taken out on the "course."

(continued)

(*continued*)

The first training exercise was climbing the "trust ladder." Doug, the program director, explained that the group members would have to rely on each other quite a bit during the coming week. To demonstrate that the group could be trusted, each person was to climb to the top of the ladder and fall backward into the group, who would catch the person in a proper manner. Doug showed them how. After everyone completed the exercise, they discussed risk taking, building and trusting one's support systems, being part of a support system, and communicating one's needs. Then came more challenging exercises: building and using rope bridges to cross a stream, white-water rafting, and—the most physically challenging of all—scaling a 13-foot wall. The front of the wall was sheer and smooth. On the other side was a platform on which two people could stand at about waist level with the top of the wall, and from which extended a ladder to the ground.

Everyone had to scale the wall and no one could stand on the platform until he or she had scaled the wall. The event was timed, and the groups were in competition with each other. The first thing a group had to do was develop a plan. Strong and tall people were needed to boost the others to a point where they could pull themselves over. Some stood on the platform and helped those who were not strong enough to pull themselves over. It was clear the first people over also had to be strong. Another problem was the last person over. Everyone except the last pair would have "spotters" in case of a fall and also the last person would have no one left to boost him or her to the top. Someone would have to act as a human rope, hanging down from the top so the last person could climb up him and over the wall. Therefore the last person would have to be light but strong enough to boost the second-to-last person up and to climb over the human rope. In order to determine the order, the group members needed to share with one another their strengths and weaknesses. Claudia wanted to be the last person so she could make sure everyone was doing what they were supposed to, and also because, as the last person over the wall, she would represent the group's successful completion of this exercise. Two of the strongest men in the group confessed to having injuries that would hamper them. Claudia realized that her tennis elbow would be a great liability. When it came to her turn to discuss her strengths and weaknesses, she was honest about her injury and indicated she would fit best somewhere in the middle where many people could help her.

When Claudia's turn to climb came, she called out to those on top what to expect— where she couldn't put much strain, and how she would indicate that someone was pulling too hard. Then she was being pushed up with spotters all around her, and the next thing she knew she was over the wall.

Later, when the members discussed the event, Claudia asked what impact her limitations caused in the group. Those who had been pullers replied "None." They said that because she told them about her problem ahead of time, they knew what to do.

While getting packed to go home, Claudia thought about how much she had learned about herself and her relationship to other people, especially at work. She recognized that she generally failed to trust others to do their part and so she was not being as effective as she could be. Her success came at a high price to herself because of the extra workload she imposed on herself. In addition, she wondered, "What was the price paid by my subordinates? How have my actions affected their attitudes and performance? Do I need to be so competitive with my peers? Is that behavior really in my or my company's best interests?" She knew she would have a lot to think about on the trip home.

A Few Words About Theory

Theories are speculative road maps for how things work. In fact, most of us develop our own theories to explain how the world around us works. The child yells, "I want an ice cream cone." He is told, "No, not until you ask properly." After a number of such incidents, the child begins to see that when he says please he is more successful than when he says "Gimme" or "I want." The child develops a theory of how to get things he wants; he must always say please. "Good" theories assemble a number of facts, show the relationship among those facts, and develop a logical rationale for what is likely to be true, given those facts. From theory, predictions or hypotheses can be generated and tested. If the tests show the predictions are correct, the theory is supported. If the new facts are inconsistent with the predictions, the theory is revised or discarded. Suppose the child in the previous situation takes his theory to the extreme. When he says "please", but is denied his request, he continues to badger the person saying "pleeeease, pleeease". If he soon finds this approach does not work, he may revise the theory. The new theory says "please" works more often than not, but if you have to say it over and over, it does not work. In fact it makes the person annoyed. This process of developing, testing, and reformulating theory is the basis of science. It is how new knowledge is created. A good theory is also practical:

- It explains facts as simply as possible.
- It predicts future events.
- It provides information on what can be done to prevent undesirable things from happening.

Theories are abstractions that allow us to make sense out of a large number of facts related to an issue. Effective training practices are developed from theories and theoretical constructs that describe how learning occurs, and what motivates people. This chapter addresses those models, concepts, and issues and thus is necessarily somewhat abstract. Unfortunately, some people may see little value in wading through the complex logic and rationale of theories. It is easier to just follow a set of instructions like a recipe. But, in training, as in business, a single recipe won't work. Recipes require standardized ingredients—businesses don't have them. Each organization is unique, with different missions, strategies, environments, technologies, and people. The interaction of these elements creates a different "chemistry" in each organization, making a "one best way for everyone" approach ineffective. Theories provide the guidelines, principles, and predictions that allow organizations to create the right recipe for their situation. Successful people in business pay attention to theory.

Firms in all industries from manufacturing to telecommunications, from energy production to health care (e.g., Ford, 3M, Microsoft, Motorola, Toshiba, Toyota, and Xerox) jumped ahead of the competition because they understood and applied theories. Some of these theories concern the product, others with how the product is made, and others with how the firm is managed. Rather than copying others, these companies understood the underlying theories related to what they were trying to do and applied them to their goals. As the quality guru W. E. Deming indicated, experience teaches nothing without theory.[1] He warns that unless you understand the theory behind someone's success, copying can lead to chaos.[2] Supporting this view is a survey of *Fortune* 1000 companies engaged in programs to improve quality (e.g., TQM, ISO 9000) and involve employees in decision making. The companies that applied the underlying models and theories correctly were getting the best results; those that simply put programs into place were getting the worst results.[3]

Let's consider pay systems as an example. Suppose you know of a company that pays its employees on the basis of how much they produce (i.e., a piece-rate system). The company is successful and the employees make a high wage. You decide to institute the piece-rate system in your company. Will it work? It might, but it might not. Its success will depend on your total reward system, what you are trying to accomplish, and what your employees value. For example, your employees may turn out a high volume of the product but at the cost of many problems with quality. They may produce more than you can sell. Piece-rate systems can create a "norm" in the work group that prohibits them from producing more than a specified amount (to avoid increases in the product/money ratio or to protect slower workers). In other words, the success of the piece-rate system is affected by the differences in the people and work environments.

Understanding motivational theory allows you to improve employee performance levels by applying the principles of motivation to your firm's unique circumstances. The same is true with training. Whether someone else's training program will work for you will depend on the needs of your company, your employees, and the training system you use. Copying without understanding is like taking someone else's prescription drugs. Even though they may have made someone else better, they could kill you.

What theories are important to the success of the training enterprise? If trainees don't learn, training has failed. Theories of learning are certainly important. If trainees learn but don't try to transfer the learning to the job, training has failed. Add theories of motivation to the list. If the trainees learn and try to transfer the learning to the job site, but obstacles in their work environment prevent them from making the transfer, training again has failed. It failed because the changes in the work environment that needed to support the desired behavior were not taken into consideration. Thus, in order to design and implement effective training programs, you need to understand how people learn, what motivates learning and performance, and how the learning and work environment affects motivation and performance. These topics are the focus of this chapter. The theories, models, and concepts discussed here serve as a foundation for the rest of the book. These theories and their implications for training will be referred to throughout the text, because they are related to each phase of the training process.

Understanding Motivation and Performance

Your job performance, your behavior in general, is a function of what you know, what you are able to do, and what you believe (KSAs). If you don't have the KSAs, you can't perform. However, additional factors are important in determining your performance. Figure 3-1 depicts a general **performance model**. This model indicates that a person's performance depends on the interaction of motivation, KSAs, and environment. Motivation arises from your needs and your beliefs about how best to satisfy those needs. Both motivation and KSAs are part of your memory and thinking systems (i.e., cognitive structure). **Environment** refers to the physical surroundings in which performance must occur, including barriers and aids to performance, as well as objects and events (cues) that you might see as indicating that your performance will be rewarded or punished.

Think back to the Wilderness Training case. Which of Claudia's KSAs allowed her to reach her current position? Her boss felt she lacked the interpersonal skills necessary for developing

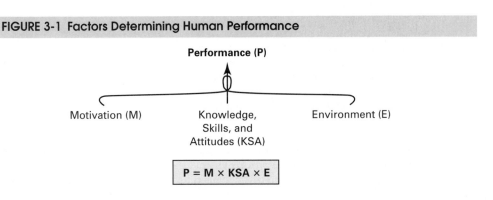

FIGURE 3-1 Factors Determining Human Performance

Performance (P)

Motivation (M)   Knowledge, Skills, and Attitudes (KSA)   Environment (E)

$$P = M \times KSA \times E$$

good relationships. Did she lack these skills or was she not motivated to use them? Apparently she had the skills, because she was able to develop good relationships with others with whom she was not working directly. The training director probably understood this fact, because he suggested the Wilderness Training rather than an interpersonal skill-building workshop. The Wilderness Training didn't teach people how to develop good interpersonal relationships as much as it broke down barriers that prevented those relationships from developing. The program worked on the motivation and attitudes of the trainees. What barriers in Claudia's work environment might keep her from developing these relationships? How about the upcoming retirement of the VP and that open position? What criteria could be used in evaluating managers, which would encourage them to develop positive relationships with peers and subordinates?

Each of the factors M, KSA, and E in Figure 3-1 can influence performance, but it is the combination of these factors that determines the person's performance. The likelihood of engaging in any activity, then, is limited by the weakest factor. For instance, no matter how knowledgeable or skilled you are, if you are not motivated to perform the activity—or worse, are motivated not to perform it—then you won't. If the environment does not support the activity or blocks it, then it doesn't matter how motivated or knowledgeable you are—you won't do it. For example, if necessary tools are not working or equipment is missing, you won't attempt the activity. Likewise, if the environment is sending signals that your performance will be punished, you won't perform. In Claudia's case, she seemed to want to stay at work and not attend the training. However, her boss gave strong indications that staying would be viewed negatively. Her environment changed, signaling that old ways of performing would not be rewarded and new ways would.

This model in Figure 3-1 is important for determining employee training needs. It helps us understand whether poor job performance is due to KSAs or other factors. It is also important in the design of training. When putting together the learning modules and training methods, the trainer must consider how they will affect the trainees' motivation to learn. Similarly, when selecting the training facility and materials, we must consider how they will interact with trainee motivation. When we ask trainees to use their new knowledge and skills back on the job, we must make sure the environment is supportive of this new way of performing. A deeper understanding of the three determinants of performance will increase your ability to design and implement effective training programs. First we look at motivation, presenting the most prominent theories and clarifying their relationship to the training enterprise.

MOTIVATION: WHY DO THEY ACT LIKE THAT?

Motivation is part of a person's cognitive structure and is not directly observable. Thus it is typically defined in terms of its effects on behavior, which are observable. Most of the scientific literature defines **motivation** as the direction, persistence, and amount of effort expended by an individual to achieve a specified outcome. In other words, the person's motivation is reflected by the following:

- What need(s) the person is trying to satisfy
- The types of activity the person does to satisfy the need
- How long the person keeps doing it
- How hard the person works at it

Consider Claudia, what need is it she is trying to satisfy? The growth need, the need to achieve and get ahead in the company. What types of activities does she get involved in? Well, she takes on extra projects, volunteers to work on task forces, works late, and so forth. How long has she been doing it? For about 2 years. And how hard does she work at it? Well, it seems pretty hard: 12 hour days and she often goes in on Saturday.

Motivation is goal directed and derives from both people's personal needs and the decision processes they use to satisfy those needs. Separate theories evolved to explain the relationship between needs and motivation and between decision processes and motivation. Needs theories attempt to describe the types of needs people have, their relative importance, and how they are related to each other. Process theories attempt to describe and explain how a person's needs are translated into actions to satisfy the needs.

Needs Theory

Our needs are the basis of our motivation, the reason for almost all of our activity. Understanding a person's needs helps you to understand his behavior. From earlier work by Maslow,[4] Clayton Alderfrer developed a **needs theory** of motivation called **ERG theory**.[5] ERG is an acronym representing the three basic needs of the theory: existence, relatedness, and growth. **Existence needs** correspond to Maslow's lower-order physiological and security needs. They are the immediate needs required to sustain life—needs for food, shelter, and the like—as well as the need for some security into the future for a safe and healthy life. **Relatedness needs** reflect people's need to be valued and accepted by others. Interpersonal relationships and group membership (work, family, friends, etc.) act to satisfy these needs. **Growth needs** include feelings of self-worth and competency and achieving one's potential. Recognition, accomplishment, challenging opportunities, and a feeling of fulfillment are outcomes that can satisfy these needs. Even though some disagreement exists in the scientific community about the relationships among these needs and their relative importance at any given point in life, few dispute the idea that these needs exist for everyone.

People work to satisfy their needs. So, understanding the types and strength of employee needs is important to the training process. It can help to identify some of the causes of poor performance and therefore determine training needs. Consider the employee who has strong relatedness needs but whose job is structured so that he must work alone most of the time. He may not be getting the required quality and quantity of work completed because he spends too much time socializing with others in the workplace. Additional technical KSAs will do little to improve his job performance. Some other type of training (perhaps time management) or some nontraining intervention (such as job redesign or counseling) would be more likely to result in performance improvement.

Understanding needs is also important in designing training programs and facilities. Trainers need to make sure that the environment and training methods—that is, how the training is conducted and where it takes place—meet the trainee's physical, relationship, and growth needs. We discuss these issues in depth in the chapters covering training design, development, and implementation. To get a sense of how training methods, materials, and environment influence trainee motivation, think back to the Wilderness Training case.

Although Claudia was motivated to attend the training because of her boss's pressure, was she motivated to learn when she first arrived or was she skeptical about the value of the training? What if she had been given a series of lectures on the importance of developing strong interpersonal relationships instead of the outdoor group experiences? Would she have been as motivated to absorb the lessons and apply them to her work? How strong do you think Claudia's relatedness needs were? Do you think training that focused on showing her how changing her behavior would result in increased acceptance by her peers would be effective? It seems apparent that Claudia did have high growth needs. The outdoor training presented her with a series of physical and psychological challenges, fitting in with her growth needs and motivating her to become an involved participant in the training.

The few empirical studies conducted on this topic tend to support Alderfer's notion that people can experience needs in all three areas simultaneously.[6] Which are more important depends on the relative satisfaction level in each area. Unsatisfied needs motivate us, and motivation decreases as needs in an area are satisfied. However, needs in these three basic areas tend to renew themselves, and needs in an area can expand. Though you may have a good job that provides you with food, shelter, and security, you can start to feel the need for better food, a larger and more comfortable home, a larger savings account or investment portfolio. Similarly, even though your relationships with family, friends, and coworkers may at first satisfy your relatedness needs, you may begin to feel that you would like the relationships to be better or closer, or that you want to develop additional relationships.

Sometimes our needs may conflict with one another, or one type of need may become more important than the others. Then we feel we must choose one over the other, which is what happened with Claudia. We cannot be sure how strong her relatedness needs are, but we do know that she saw them as conflicting with her ability to satisfy her growth needs at work. The wilderness training was designed to satisfy the trainees' needs for growth and relationships at the same time. Step by step, the training demonstrated how building strong interpersonal relationships could not only satisfy relationship needs, but also make greater accomplishment possible.

This example illustrates a central point about motivating trainees to learn. The best training incorporates opportunities to satisfy all three categories of needs. Existence needs are addressed, in part, through the training facility and accommodations. The trainees' physical comfort, level of hunger, and so on will make a difference in how much is learned. Demonstrating how the training will improve the trainee's competencies should also show how the learning can increase the trainee's security, another aspect of existence needs. Relatedness needs can be addressed through building a network of positive relationships among trainees and between trainees and the trainer. Growth needs can be addressed by using methods that provide challenging experiences that lead to the attainment of the target KSAs. By making sure your training program addresses all three categories of needs, you will go a long way toward motivating all trainees, because you offer something for everyone.

Need theory leads to implications for the training process even after completion of the training. Trainers need to make sure that trainees are able to see the links between their learning and the satisfaction of their needs. In Claudia's case, her boss provided some of that linkage by telling her how important relationship building is to her current and future job success (i.e., security needs). What could the trainers at the Wilderness Training Lab do to create these links? We discuss this issue more in the next section, because these links are the focus of the process theories.

Process Theories

Needs are only part of the motivation equation. The other part is the process of deciding how to go about satisfying those needs. **Process theories** of motivation describe how a person's needs translate into action. Although many types of process theories exist, we will focus on the two with the most direct implications for training: reinforcement theory and expectancy theory.

Reinforcement Theory   **Reinforcement theory** is relatively simple on the surface but can be difficult to apply. It does not provide all the answers for how needs are translated into action, but its major points are essential for understanding human behavior. The foundation for reinforcement theory comes from the work of E. L. Thorndike.[7] Thorndike's **law of effect** states that behavior followed by satisfying experiences tends to be repeated, and behavior followed by annoyance or dissatisfaction tends to be avoided. This principle was used by B. F. Skinner in developing the operant conditioning model and reinforcement theory.[8]

Reinforcement theory is closely related to the operant conditioning theory of learning. In fact, it is difficult to discuss this theory without discussing learning, because reinforcement theory and operant learning theory are part of the same theoretical package. The basic components of learning in **operant conditioning** are illustrated in Figure 3-2. A person is faced with an object or event in the environment (stimulus) and behaves in a certain way (response). That behavior results in an outcome (consequence) to the individual that is positive or negative. In the illustration the man has seen a book of great interest (environmental stimulus) on the way to work. He purchases the book and reads it (response) while continuing to walk to work. You can imagine the consequence. The environment provides stimuli that elicit behaviors and consequences that reinforce or punish them.

Stimulus ⟶ Response ⟶ Consequence   **FIGURE 3-2 Behaviorist Model of Learning**

In similar situations, the consequences of past behavior affect future behavior. How will the man in Figure 3-2 respond to books while walking in the near future? Operant learning theory says the man will learn to avoid reading and walking. A person's motivation (i.e., direction, magnitude, and persistence of behavior), then, is a function of her reinforcement history. Unfortunately, reinforcement theory provides no explanation of the processes involved in storing, retrieving, or using the lessons of past reinforcement. The model leaves us wondering how future behavior becomes influenced by previous reinforcement history. Nevertheless, the theory does convincingly predict the various effects on future behavior caused by the consequences of past behavior.

Skinner identified four types of consequences that can result from behavior:

1. Positive reinforcement
2. Negative reinforcement
3. Punishment
4. Extinction

When behavior results in either positive or negative reinforcement, the likelihood is increased that the behavior will occur in future similar circumstances. **Positive reinforcement** occurs when your behavior results in something desirable happening to you—either tangible (such as receiving money), or psychological (such as feeling pleasure), or some combination of the two. **Negative reinforcement** occurs when your behavior results in removing something you find annoying, frustrating, or unpleasant. This "good" outcome increases your likelihood of repeating the behavior. For example, if you have a headache, you take an aspirin and the headache goes away, the "aspirin-taking response" is negatively reinforced. Nothing is inherently desirable about taking the aspirin; its reinforcing power comes from its ability to remove the pain. Positive and negative reinforcement can be provided by the environment or by the person. For example, when a person is paid for work done, the positive reinforcement (pay) is provided by the environment. When a person feels a sense of pride and accomplishment after completing a task, the person is positively reinforcing himself.

Your behavior is punished when it results in something undesirable happening to you. **Punishment** decreases the likelihood of the response occurring in the future. Like reinforcement, punishment can be tangible or psychological or both and can come from the environment or be self-administered. In Figure 3-2 the environment provides the punishment. On the other hand, when we do things that violate our personal values and beliefs and therefore experience negative feelings, we are self-punishing that behavior. Punishment exists when you receive something unpleasant, or when you lose something desirable. The latter form of punishment is called **extinction**. For example, you may buy books by a certain author because of the positive feelings you experience as you read them. However, while reading the last two books by this author you did not experience those positive feelings. Therefore, you stop buying this author's books. When the person's behavior (like buying and reading the books) no longer produces the desired outcomes, the behavior is less likely to occur in the future. Figure 3-3 depicts the various types of behavioral consequences.

These definitions can be confusing or misunderstood, so let's look at a couple of examples. First think back to the Wilderness Training Lab case. What kind of reinforcement history did Claudia experience from working in groups? Her first group experiences in college resulted in the negative outcomes (for her) of mediocre grades. Because her cooperative behavior in groups was punished, she stopped it. When she changed her behavior to become more directive, monitoring and doing more of the important work, two consequences resulted: (1) she was positively reinforced by good grades; (2) she avoided the negative feelings of anxiety about having other group members not do their assignments well and the resulting mediocre grades. Her new group behavior was both positively and negatively reinforced over a number of years. It is no wonder then, that she continued to work in groups this way. Is it possible she avoided working in groups with her peers because she couldn't control those groups in the same way she could her subordinates? The training she received provided her with new group situations in which she was positively reinforced (e.g., recognition, accomplishment) for using a new set of group behaviors.

In another example, suppose Jon, a machinist, after working for a few hours, suddenly hears a loud, unpleasant screeching noise coming from the exhaust fans near his work area. He finds the electrical switch and turns the fans off, then later switches them on again, after which they work for the rest of the day. The same thing happens the next two days. The fourth day, after the fans have been running for a few hours, when he takes his break he shuts them off before the noise begins. When he returns from his break, he turns them on and they operate normally for the rest of the day. This behavior becomes a daily habit with Jon. What Jon does not know is that plant maintenance repaired the fan the evening before he began his "shutting it off at the break" behavior. Jon maintained his behavior because it was negatively reinforcing. By "giving the

	Desirable Consequences	Undesirable Consequences
Trainee Receives	Behavior Positively Reinforced	Behavior Punished
Trainee Loses	Behavior Punished (Extinction)	Behavior Negatively Reinforced

FIGURE 3-3 Types of Consequences That May Follow Behavior

fans a rest," he avoided the loud, unpleasant noise. Because this worked every time, it was self-reinforcing. It is how many workplace habits and "superstitious behaviors" develop.

Reinforcement Versus Punishment   Punishment can eliminate undesirable behavior in the workplace. However, several problems make it undesirable as a management or training tool.

- It does not motivate people to do things, only not to do things. It does not indicate what the desired behavior is, only what is not desired.
- If the undesired behavior is punished only sometimes, people will learn the situations in which they can get away with it. The saying, "While the cat's away the mice will play," neatly captures one problem with this technique: Punishment requires constant vigilance on the part of a supervisor and encourages employee efforts to "beat the system."
- If a person's undesired behavior is rewarding to him, the punishment must be severe enough to offset the behavior's reinforcing properties. Escalating negative outcomes to employees raises ethical, moral, and commonsense objections.
- Someone must do the punishing. This person becomes someone to be avoided. Supervisors avoided by subordinates experience leadership problems.

Positive and negative reinforcement are better tools for motivating and especially training employees. Negative reinforcement can cause the desired behavior to become self-reinforcing, like Jon's turning off the fans. When the person continually performs the desired behavior (avoiding the undesired behavior), negative outcomes are avoided. If the desired behavior is then also positively reinforced, the person not only avoids the negative outcome but receives a positive outcome. As with Claudia in the opening case, the result is a strong maintenance of the behavior.

With reinforcement, the person doing the reinforcing does not always need to be present for the desired behavior to occur. The employee actively seeks to make the reinforcing agent (e.g., supervisor or trainer) aware of her behavior. When punishment is used as the motivational or learning mechanism, the employee attempts to hide behavior so as to avoid the consequences. Obviously, a trainer or supervisor's job is much easier when employees are attempting to communicate what they are doing rather than hiding it.

Thus either positive or negative reinforcement is preferred over punishment as a strategy for motivating learning and behavior change. Used in combination, positive and negative reinforcement appear more effective than either used alone.[9] We discuss this technique later in the chapter when we review Gagné's learning types and "shaping" behavior. For those interested in finding out more about how to implement positive, humanistic, and effective work environments, we would encourage you to read Dick Grote's *Discipline Without Punishment*.[10]

Reinforcement theory suggests that any training must be concerned not only about the KSAs that are to be learned, but also about the consequences that are attached to the following:

- The learning process
- The old way of doing the job
- The new way of doing the job

These factors play a key role in determining how much is learned and how much is actually used back on the job.

As was mentioned, many unanswered questions arise when using reinforcement theory to describe the motivational process. Expectancy theory, however, provides some additional explanation and leads to many more implications for training.

Expectancy Theory   In 1964 Victor Vroom published a theory of work motivation called **expectancy theory**.[11] This theory describes the cognitive processes involved in deciding the best course of action for achieving one's goals (i.e., satisfying one's needs). A **cognitive process** is a mental activity such as information storage, retrieval, or use. Thinking and decision making are cognitive processes. In its most basic form, the theory proposes that a person's motivation can be explained by the relationship among three conceptually distinct elements:

1. The level of success expected by the individual (e.g., how well she will be able to do what she set out to do), which is termed Expectancy 1.
2. The individual's beliefs about what the outcomes will be if she is successful. The expected outcomes and their likelihood of occurrence make up Expectancy 2.
3. The individual's feelings about the various outcomes' positive or negative value. An outcome's subjective value is referred to as its **valence**.

In combination, these elements determine the individual's motivation (i.e., effort) to engage in a particular course of action. When situations allow different courses of action, as most do, the one with the highest motivation level is chosen. The motivation level for a particular course of action can be calculated mathematically with the following formula:

$$\text{Effort} = \text{Expectancy } 1_i \times \Sigma_{ij} (\text{Expectancy } 2_{ij} \times \text{Valence}_{ij})$$

Although this formula is useful for those conducting research on motivation, it is not particularly useful in the day-to-day activities of most people. It does, however, present some important implications for training and learning, which we discuss shortly.

To gain a better understanding of the expectancy theory framework, let's go back to Claudia at the point where she was trying to decide whether to attend the executive development seminar as suggested by her boss. Today is the last day she can register for the seminar, which starts in 2 weeks. She postponed the decision as long as possible and now must decide. She feels confident about her ability to complete this training successfully but she holds some doubts about whether it will teach her anything useful about running her marketing operation or working more effectively in a group. She knows that during the week she will be in training the marketing strategies for five important accounts will arrive on her desk and she will need to review and finalize them before forwarding them to top management. They are due on the Wednesday following training. In addition, her normal work will continue to pile up. Claudia faces the choice between incompatible performance goals and courses of action. Her cognitive processes, in expectancy theory terms, are illustrated in Figure 3-4.

Examining Claudia's situation in terms of expectancy theory, we see that her expectations of success (Expectancy 1) are high for both behaviors. The expectancy of 1.0 means she is 100 percent sure that she would successfully be able to complete either course of action. The Expectancy 2 links reflect the outcomes that Claudia anticipates if she successfully completes the seminar or stays at the office and completes her workload. If she turns down the training and stays on the job, she believes there is a 50 percent chance her boss will see her skills as inadequate. It would be higher, but she believes if she can do a superior job on these strategies, he won't think those relationship skills are so important. She believes it's 90 percent likely she will have feelings of pride and accomplishment for getting all her work completed on time. However, if she turns down the training, she believes there's only a 30 percent chance her boss will recommend her for promotion.

On the other hand, if she goes to the training, she believes the likelihood is 60 percent that her boss will evaluate her as having a more complete set of managerial skills. However, she will fall behind in her work, and it is a certainty (1.0) she will feel harried, overloaded, and depressed. Yet she sees the chances of being recommended for a promotion increasing to 60 percent if she goes to training. As the valences in Figure 3-4 shows, she values her boss's recommendation for promotion the most. She views having her boss evaluate her skills as being inadequate and the feelings associated with being behind in her work as the least desirable of the outcomes. Using the formula to calculate Claudia's motivation to turn down training and stay on the job, we come

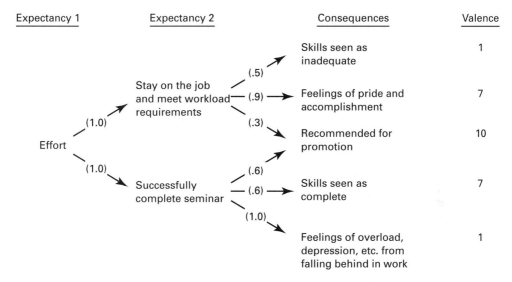

Valence values: a value of 5.5 would be neutral. Numbers below this reflect increasingly negative outcomes. Numbers above it reflect increasing desirability.

FIGURE 3-4 Illustration of Expectancy Theory

up with a force of 9.8. This result is arrived at by multiplying each Expectancy 2 by its respective outcome valence, summing the values, and then multiplying the total by the Expectancy 1 value.

Using the same procedure for the alternative goal, attending the seminar, we find a force of 11.2. Thus for Claudia the motivation to stay at work is less than the motivation to attend the seminar. Even though the actual values of expectancies and valences are interesting from a scientific perspective, from a practical standpoint it is the relationships among the elements of the model that are useful. This example illustrates the cognitive processes that link a person's goals, possible courses of action, and likely outcomes. These connections determine the person's motivation, and these connections are what is missing from the reinforcement theory. Of course, we simplified the situation considerably from what Claudia would actually face in the real work setting. Many other alternatives were available to her. She could delegate someone to cover most of the normal work coming across her desk (though she was not especially comfortable with delegating). She could arrange for the marketing strategies to be sent to her in New Mexico in order to work on them at night, after training, and on the weekend. Each of these alternatives would present its own expected outcomes and associated valences.

Faced with the situation Claudia faced, what would you do? It is unlikely that you would place the same value (valence) on the outcomes or give them the same likelihood of occurring. You might identify more or fewer outcomes. One of the things that makes this theory so useful is that it takes into account the fact that people view the world differently and are motivated by different things.

Few people would consciously go through the formal math or mapping of expectancy theory, but it is interesting to note that most training programs that teach decision making use a model similar to this one. More typically, we go through these processes unconsciously and in a less systematic fashion. We choose a particular way of behaving because of our expectations about the costs and benefits of that action. Relationships between our past behavior and its consequences are combined with current information to make inferences about the consequences of our future behavior. Some implications for training become rather obvious here.

To be willing to try, a person must believe he or she stands a reasonable chance of being successful. Expectancy 1 exerts the most influence on our behavior, because we don't waste our time trying to do things we believe we cannot do. Sometimes this belief is what makes people reluctant to go to training. So, trainers must demonstrate that success is likely for the participants. Second, and related to needs and reinforcement theory, trainers must make sure the right outcomes are attached to the successful completion of training. Trainees should be able to see clear connections between the content of training and important organizational and personal outcomes. Third, the training outcomes must be made as desirable as possible for the trainees rather than just the organization, the supervisor, or the trainer.

Self-Efficacy and Motivation

Feelings about one's own competency are reflected in the concept of **self-efficacy**, which is one of the better-researched constructs related to motivation. High self-efficacy is associated with a belief that one can and will perform successfully. Individuals with low self-efficacy are preoccupied with concerns about failure.[12] Research supports the belief that the higher the self-efficacy, the better the performance.[13] Not only is performance better, but in difficult situations those with high self-efficacy try harder, while those with low self-efficacy tend to reduce effort or give up.[14] In a training context, research shows that those with high self-efficacy beliefs are more motivated to learn, and are more likely to transfer that learning.[15]

Several factors combine to provide employees with an estimate of their ability to be successful:

- *Prior experience*: The person's past successes and failures and their consequences
- *Behavioral models*: Successes and failures of others observed attempting the behavior
- *Others' feedback*: The encouragement or discouragement provided by others
- *Physical and emotional state*: The physical or emotional limitations believed to affect ability to perform

Self-efficacy, therefore, plays a large role in the person's Expectancy 1 evaluation. The employee's feelings of self-efficacy are translated into behavior. If success is expected, the employee works harder, longer, and more creatively in anticipation of the positive consequences of a successful effort. If failure is expected, the employee acts to minimize the negative consequences of failure. For example, withdrawing from the activity (refusing to try) moves the person away from proven failure to simply "I didn't try." It also allows the person to say "At least I didn't put a lot of energy into it" or other forms of rationalization. The point is that the employee's self-efficacy sets up the person's behavior to fulfill the self-efficacy beliefs. In expectancy theory terms, if I don't believe I can successfully do something, then I won't exert the effort to do it, I'll do something else.

What can be done specifically to improve an individual's self-efficacy? The supervisor can provide the employee with confidence through persuasion. Convincing her that she is quite capable of succeeding in the training will help. Also seeing others who are similar to the employee succeed will improve the employee's self-efficacy.

Training can improve self-efficacy either directly or as a by-product.[16] If the employee experiences low self-efficacy regarding his or her abilities to perform the job, but evidence indicates he or she possesses the requisite KSAs, a program of improving self-concept and confidence is needed. When the low self-efficacy results from a true lack of required KSAs, attaining competency in these KSAs should increase the employee's self-efficacy, if the training allows the trainee to demonstrate mastery on a continuous basis. Trainers can also emphasize what the objectives are and the success of similar sets of trainees in the past.

Because self-efficacy is so powerful, it is useful to assess trainee self-efficacy before and during training, because self-efficacy beliefs seem to be a good predictor of both learning in the training environment and transfer of the behavior to the job.[17]

Understanding Learning

Learning has been probed and prodded by scientific inquiry since the late 1800s. The resulting theories led to practical application in both educational and industrial settings. The range of theoretical perspectives varied widely over the last century. Examining the rise and fall of the various theories, though intellectually fascinating, is beyond the scope of this chapter, and indeed of this book. Rather we examine the essential elements of learning theories and identify their relationship to training. Specific applications of the theories are provided in subsequent chapters.

WHAT IS LEARNING?

To understand the differences among learning theories, it helps to understand the difficulties of simply defining the concept of learning. Learning is not directly observable, but it is something that almost everyone says they experience. People can "feel" that they learned. Scientists assure us that it occurs physically, yet they are not sure how. It is clear from physiological evidence that learning is related to changes in the physical, neuronal structure of the brain and its related electrochemical functioning.[18] Unfortunately, much is still unknown about how or why these electrochemical changes take place. Learning, of course, is closely tied to memory: Whatever is learned must be retained if it is to be useful. Electrochemical changes created during learning apparently create a relatively permanent change in neural functioning that becomes what is commonly termed *memory*. Again, relatively few definitive answers exist about how or where learning is stored in the central nervous system.

Two Definitions of Learning

If we cannot actually observe learning occurring, then how do we know that learning occurred? We must use something influenced by learning that we can observe. That is, we must infer that learning occurred by looking at its observable effects. What things, influenced by learning, can we observe? The answer is that we are pretty much limited to observing the learner's behavior. For instance, in school you are often given tests to determine whether you learned. The behavior being observed is the way you answer the questions. In the workplace your supervisor might look for ways you perform your job differently after training. In science, concepts, events, and phenomena are given an operational definition, which means that the concept is defined in terms of how it is measured. Because learning is measured in terms of relatively permanent changes in behavior, this becomes the operational definition of learning for many theorists. Behaviorists in particular adopt this definition.

Cognitive theorists on the other hand, insist that even though learning can be inferred from behavior, it is separate from the behavior itself. By examining the ways in which people respond to information and the ways in which different types of behavior are grouped or separated, they developed theories of how information is learned. For cognitive theorists, learning represents a change in the content, organization, and storage of information (see the following section, "Example of Cognitive Theory"). The term used to refer to the mental processing of information is **cognition**. For cognitive theorists, learning is defined as a relatively permanent change in cognition occurring as a result of experience. These theorists discuss learning in terms of mental infrastructures or schema rather than in terms of behavior. Learning is seen as the building and reorganization of schema to make sense of new information. Bruner,[19] Gagné,[20] and Piaget[21] are among the cognitive theorists.

Implications of Behaviorist Versus Cognitive Approaches

At first the differences in the definition of learning may not seem to be important. It may seem to be a simple difference of whether learning is synonymous with behavior or with how information is processed, organized, and stored. However, these differences create widely different approaches to how education and training are conducted.

One obvious and important difference is where control of learning is believed to occur. The behaviorist approach suggests that learning is controlled by the environment. Certain external stimuli are present, the person responds to them, and certain consequences result. It is the model of learning implied in Figure 3-2 (page 79) and discussed earlier as part of reinforcement theory. In the behaviorist approach, the trainer controls learning by controlling the stimuli and consequences that the learner experiences. The learner depends on the trainer to elicit the correct associations between stimulus and response. Note that this model does not include the brain or any mental activity. B. F. Skinner's explanation of learning perhaps clarifies why he was sometimes referred to as a radical behaviorist. He defined learning as "a relatively permanent change in behavior in response to a particular stimulus or set of stimuli."[22] He proposed that "we learn to perceive in the sense that we learn to respond to things in particular ways, because of the contingencies of which they are a part." To paraphrase Skinner: We perceive things a certain way because of the consequences of perceiving them that way. Skinner viewed the brain in much the same way as he viewed the body, as just another organ in which certain neural activities are conditioned to occur, or not occur, in a given situation. The conditioning depends on the past history of consequences for those activities. Learning occurs when new consequences are experienced.

In contrast, the cognitive approach suggests that learning is controlled by the learner. Prospective learners come to training with their own set of goals and priorities. They possess a set of cognitive structures for understanding their environment and how it works. They even develop their own set of strategies about how to learn. The learners decide what is important to learn and go about learning by applying the strategies they developed and with which they feel comfortable. For cognitive theorists, the learner controls what is learned and how. The trainer and the learning environment facilitate that process to a greater or lesser degree. Adoption of one approach or the other leads to implications for how training is conducted and the atmosphere of the training environment. Table 3-1 lists some of the instructional implications of these two positions. For some learning situations, a behaviorist approach is better, and for others a cognitive approach works better.[23] We discuss this issue again later in the chapter.

TABLE 3-1 Some Training Implications of Cognitive and Behaviorist Learning Theory

Issue	*Cognitive Approach*	*Behaviorist Approach*
Learner's role	Active, self-directed, self-evaluating	Passive, dependent
Instructor's role	Facilitator, coordinator, and presenter	Director, monitor, evaluator
Training content	Problem or task oriented	Subject oriented
Learner motivation	More internally motivated	More externally motivated
Training climate	Relaxed, mutually trustful and respectful, collaborative	Formal, authority oriented, judgmental, competitive
Instructional goals	Collaboratively developed	Developed by instructor
Instructional activities	Interactive, group, project oriented, experiential	Directive, individual, subject oriented

Example of Cognitive Theory   The developmental psychologist Piaget identified two cognitive processes critical for learning: accommodation and assimilation. **Accommodation** is the process of changing our construction ("cognitive map") of the world to correspond with our experience in it. Piaget indicated that accommodation occurs through the creation of new categories, or schema, to accommodate experience that doesn't fit into existing categories. Assimilation is the incorporation of new experience into existing categories. In cognitive map terms, accommodation changes the map whereas **assimilation** fills in the detail. These two processes are most clearly evident in young children but exist in adults as well. Suppose Mike (age 8) is in the rear seat of the car with his younger brother Brandon (almost 2 and learning to talk) as Dad drives through some farmland. As they pass a pasture where horses are grazing, Mike points and says, "Look, Brandon, horses." Brandon responds hesitantly, "Horsies?" Mike excitedly replies, "Yes, that's right, horsies!" Dad glances back and says, "Good work, Brandon, you now know a new word!" Brandon is pleased and repeats the word several times to himself. As they continue driving, they pass another pasture with cows grazing. Brandon yells, "Look, Mike, horsies!" Mike or Dad is now faced with teaching Brandon the difference between horses and cows.

What is the learning process that took place? Brandon started out with no understanding of horse or cow. When presented with a new perceptual experience and a label, Brandon created a new cognitive category that might include the following parameters: "large, four-legged, brown, moving thing with a tail." So when Brandon saw the cows, they fit enough of the parameters that he attempted to assimilate this new experience into the category "horsies." If Mike and Dad do a good job of teaching Brandon the differences between horses and cows, he will learn to discriminate between these two and create a separate category for cows (accommodation). What he doesn't know yet is that later in life he will be taught to create new categories such as mammals and species and that both horses and cows are included in some categories but not in others.

The process of assimilation and accommodation reflects the way we organize our experience and the meanings we attach to the world as we encounter it. Our behavior will depend on how we accommodated or assimilated previous stimuli.

Integration of Cognitive and Behavioral Approaches

Both the cognitive and behaviorist approaches provide insight into the process of learning and furnish practical tools for increasing the effectiveness of training. We believe that the cognitive and behavioral approaches must be integrated to provide a full definition of learning. **Learning,** as we use the term throughout this text, is defined as a relatively permanent change in cognition, resulting from experience and directly influencing behavior. A fairly obvious implication of this definition is that changes in cognition and related behavior that result from things other than experience (e.g., effects of drugs, fatigue, and the like) would not be considered learning. The definition also implies that changes in cognition and behavior that are short-lived have not been learned. For example, memorizing a phone number long enough to walk from the telephone directory to the phone and dial the number would not fit into our definition. However, learning the mnemonic techniques that allow you to do that, would be learning, if they were retained over a relatively long period of time.

Learning, as defined here, is not dependent on behavior. Relatively permanent cognitive changes (new KSAs) can occur in the absence of observable behavior. However, only the learner would know whether the learning took place. For example, think of courses you took in which the material was presented in a lecture or audiovisual form. If it was effective, you changed your way of thinking about the topic or came to a deeper understanding of the material—even though you did nothing other than pay attention and think about what was presented. However, until you engage in some activity related to the topic, no one other than yourself would know that learning had taken place. This phenomenon could also happen with skills. Suppose you are a chef and you attend a seminar on preparing a dish. You observe the presenter enhancing the flavor of a dish using a technique of which you had no previous knowledge. You could go back to your kitchen, try the technique, and are successful on the first try. You acquired the "flavoring" skill through observation rather than behavior. However, you might not be sure you had acquired the skill until after you engaged in the behavior. Additionally, the more you use the technique, the more permanent (i.e., resistant to forgetting) it would become. Thus behavior is both an important measure of learning and a means of learning.

The debates between the cognitivists and behaviorists began some time ago, but the gap between the two positions is continually narrowing. One article pointed out that:

> To show that behavior is determined only by cognition, one would have to find a control group consisting of individuals who cannot think. Similarly, to provide empirical support for the argument that behavior is due to environmental consequences alone, one would have the impossible task of forming a control group for which there was no environment.[24]

Each of the two approaches produced valuable insights about learning. Learning theories that integrated the substantiated aspects of both approaches explain learning more completely than either singly. We discuss two such theories next.

Two Integrative Theories of Learning

The two learning theories presented here capture critical elements of both the behavioral and the cognitive approaches and weave them together in a coherent and compelling fashion. The first, Gagné's approach, is somewhat more behavioral. The second, Bandura's social learning model, includes more cognitive processes. Each, however, incorporates concepts and principles from both theoretical perspectives. We begin with Gagné, because he provides a systematic explanation of learning from the most elementary, associative form to higher-level problem solving.

GAGNÉ'S LEARNING TYPES

According to Robert Gagné, different types of learning can be categorized in terms of the events required for the learning to occur.[25] The eight types are presented in Table 3-2. All but type 1 (signal learning) and type 2 (stimulus-response learning) require competence at the preceding levels of learning. Type 1 is simply a different type of learning, and type 2 learning does not depend on it. The other types of learning exhibit a hierarchical dependency on the lower types. For example, type 4 (verbal association) requires competence at type 3 learning (shaping).

Both the behavioral and the cognitive approaches to learning are embodied in Gagné's learning hierarchy. It should be clear from reviewing the table that the behavioral approach provides greater explanation for simpler forms of learning and serves as the foundation for more complex forms of learning. As learning becomes more complex, an increasing reliance on cognitive constructs and processes emerges. Thus, which approach is "better" depends on the type of learning on which you are focused.

Type 1: Signal Learning

Signal learning is the association of a generalized response to some signal in the environment. It typically involves learning to emit a nonvoluntary response to some signal that in the past did not produce that response. For example, when an optometrist examines your eyes, she may put you in front of a machine that blows a puff of air into your eye. This puff of air causes you to blink your eye. If a red light came on just before the puff of air, you would probably learn to associate the puff of air with the red light and begin blinking when the red light comes on. At that point you learned to blink (generalized response) in response to the red light (signal).

TABLE 3-2 Summary of Gagné's Eight Learning Types

Learning Type	Description
1. Signal learning	Learning a general response to a specific signal. Pavlov's classical conditioning falls into this category.
2. Stimulus-response (S-R)	Learning a single response to a stimulus situation. Basic forms of operant conditioning fall into this category.
3. Shaping	Chaining together of two or more S-R associations. Originally termed *chaining* by Gagné, we have called it shaping to avoid confusion with other parts of the text.
4. Verbal association	A chain of two or more verbal associations. Basically the same as shaping, but the application to language makes it a special case because it involves internal links to language capabilities.
5. Multiple discrimination	Ability to make different but appropriate responses to stimuli that differ to greater or lesser degrees.
6. Concept learning	Typically called generalization learning. Reflected by the ability to make a common response to a class of stimuli demonstrating some common characteristic or relationship but otherwise differing to greater or lesser degrees.
7. Principle learning	Represented by a chain of two or more concepts characterized by the development of a formal logical relation between concepts similar to an "if A then B" formulation, where A and B are concepts.
8. Problem solving	Involves the retrieval of two or more previously learned principles and their combination to produce a novel (to the learner) capability reflecting a higher-order principle.

Behaviorist approaches to learning trace their roots in the early signal learning research. Pavlov's principles of the conditioned reflex (classical conditioning) are perhaps the most widely known.[26] Pavlov wasn't studying learning, he was examining the physiology of digestion. He was studying the amount of salivation produced by various substances placed on the tongues of dogs. As the story goes, Pavlov observed that the dogs began to salivate upon his entering the lab, thus playing havoc with his desire to determine the amount of saliva produced by various substances. He speculated that over time his entrance was followed so often with substances placed on the dogs' tongues, that the dogs learned to salivate on his entrance.

Table 3-3 shows how the classical conditioning, or signal learning, process works. Step 1 reflects the state of affairs before conditioning takes place. Certain factors in the environment (unconditioned stimuli) produce automatic responses in animals and people (unconditioned

TABLE 3-3 Classical Conditioning Process

Step 1. Unconditional stimulus (Meat powder)	$\longrightarrow$	**Unconditioned response** (Salivation)
Step 2. Conditional stimulus paired with unconditioned stimulus (Buzzer followed closely in time, over many trials, by meat powder)	$\longrightarrow$	**Unconditioned response** (Salivation)
Step 3. Conditional stimulus (Buzzer alone)	$\longrightarrow$	**Conditioned response** (Salivation)

responses). If we place an unconditioned stimulus such as meat powder on a dog's tongue, an unconditioned response would be the dog's salivation. That is, the dog need not be trained (conditioned) to salivate when meat powder is put on its tongue. However, this salivation response does not occur to every stimulus that might be in the dog's environment, such as a buzzer. If, however, you sounded that buzzer just before putting meat powder on the dog's tongue, over a number of trials the buzzer would become a conditioned stimulus. The dog is learning (being conditioned) to associate the buzzer with the meat powder. However, you are still putting meat powder on the dog's tongue, so the salivation is really a response to the meat powder and remains an unconditioned response. This situation is reflected in step 2 of Table 3-3. In step 3 you stop putting meat powder on the dog's tongue after sounding the buzzer. If the dog salivates at the buzzer, you created a conditioned response (salivation) to a conditioned stimulus (the buzzer). This response can be extinguished (removed) by continually sounding the buzzer without offering the meat powder. Over time, the conditioned response gradually disappears. Through conditioning, a response to one stimulus can be transferred to another, unrelated stimulus.

Signal learning occurs frequently in the workplace, though it typically receives little attention. The noon whistle blows at the factory and the digestive juices of the workers begin to flow. Sparks fly from the welding machine and your eyes blink, even though you are wearing goggles. Signal learning is the most rudimentary form of learning and is somewhat relevant for skill development. However, most skill development requires a more complicated sequencing of behavior than can be explained by the pairing of unconditioned and conditioned responses. Operant conditioning and reinforcement theory (learning types 2 to 5) provide a more compelling explanation for skill development.

Type 2: Stimulus-Response Learning

Stimulus-response learning, like classical conditioning, is elementary but forms the basis for more complex types of learning. Essentially, it is the association of a single response to a single stimulus. It differs from type 1 learning because the response in type 2 learning is considered voluntary. In signal learning the unconditioned response becomes conditioned to occur to a stimulus that does not innately produce it. In stimulus-response learning the association occurs as a result of the consequences of the response. This type of learning is also called operant conditioning[27] and instrumental learning.[28] Reinforcement theory is a part of the stimulus-response learning paradigm. It is difficult to observe this type of learning in adults, or even young children, because they have already developed millions of these types of associations and integrated them into more complex behavior patterns. The relevance of this type of learning to more advanced forms is the underlying nature of how these stimulus-response relationships are formed. This relationship was addressed earlier as part of the reinforcement theory discussion.

Stimulus-response learning is the foundation for all skill development. By itself it is generally too elementary to be of much value in organizational training programs. The principles of reinforcement and punishment are, however, quite relevant for the more complex types of learning that follow.

Type 3: Shaping and Chaining

Any complex behavior can be broken down into a set of simple behaviors, arranged in chronological order. **Shaping** refers to the process of learning to link the appropriate behaviors to one another (the behavioral set) and learning the reinforcing consequences that are linked to the behavioral set. It establishes the learning of complex behaviors through what is called "reinforcing successive approximations" to the desired end behavior. That is, the person learns the first part of the behavioral sequence and it is reinforced. When the first part is learned, the next part of the sequence is learned and reinforced. This process continues until the desired combination of simple behaviors (stimulus-response connections) are integrated into a coordinated set of behaviors. The end result is that the person learned to perform a more complex behavior.

When using shaping during training, a trainer would first break the complex behavior that must be learned into smaller, simpler behaviors that are well within the trainee's capabilities. The trainee is shown how to order the behaviors and asked to perform them in the proper order. The trainer reinforces the trainee each time his behavior moves closer to the standard than the previous attempt. After demonstrating that he learned a part of the sequence, he is no longer reinforced for that single behavior but only for learning more of the sequence. At the conclusion of training, only the complete set of behaviors that demonstrates learning of the complex behavior is reinforced. The following example illustrates the shaping process and resulting learning. Suppose a production supervisor is frustrated by a machinist who consistently turns out a high volume of product but whose work area is always littered with debris and oil. This mess not only is a potentially hazardous environment for the machinist, but causes a half-hour delay for the operator on the next shift, who must clean up the area before beginning work. The supervisor speaks to the machinist about this problem, and the next day the machinist stops work a half-hour early to clean up the area. The half-hour of lost production results in the machinist's turning out less product than required. When the supervisor discusses this situation with him, the machinist replies, "What do you want, high volume or a clean area?"

Here is a complex behavior pattern that the supervisor needs to change. The supervisor consistently gave praise for producing at a high volume. The machinist values the praise and perhaps even sees it as related to some future reinforcement (such as a raise or a promotion). The machinist learned to operate his machine continuously except for two 15-minute breaks and during lunch. While the machine is in operation, debris and oil accumulate on the work surface and floor. During a work shift the debris and oil are scattered and pushed around the work area. By observing the machinist's sequence of behaviors, the supervisor can identify changes that will produce both the high volume of production and the clean work area. The machinist's current pattern of behavior is shown in Figure 3-5 as Machinist's Initial Behavior. If the machinist were to spend a small amount of time keeping the work area clean throughout the shift, less debris and oil would be scattered and less overall time required to clean. The supervisor needs to modify the machinist's pattern of behavior to match the Machinist's Modified Behavior in Figure 3-5, where the number of times the machinist cleans the work area is increased.

The supervisor can discuss the behavior pattern with the machinist and get his agreement to try the new approach. Discussion and agreement will not be enough, however. The supervisor must, in the beginning, also be diligent in visiting the machinist's work area just prior to breaks, lunch, and quitting time to supply the necessary reinforcement for keeping the work area clean throughout the shift. He should continue doing so until the desired behavior pattern is established.

FIGURE 3-5 Machinist's Behavior Patterns Before and After Modification

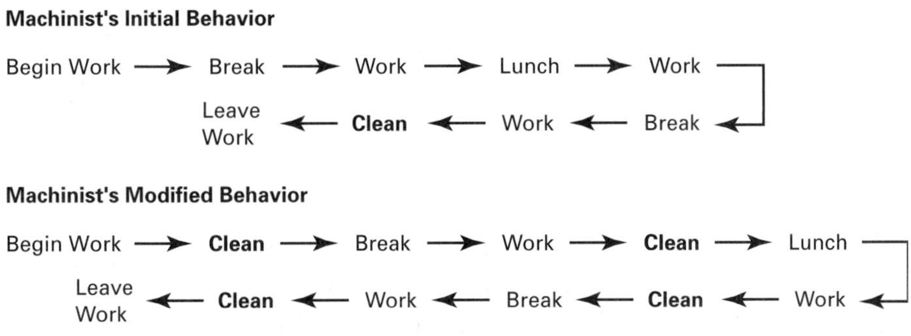

Machinist's Initial Behavior

Begin Work → Break → Work → Lunch → Work

Leave Work ← **Clean** ← Work ← Break

Machinist's Modified Behavior

Begin Work → **Clean** → Break → Work → **Clean** → Lunch

Leave Work ← **Clean** ← Work ← Break ← **Clean** ← Work

Because the machinist is learning a new, more complex behavior pattern, the supervisor must accept that at the start productivity will be high and cleanliness low at times and at other times the reverse will occur. Because the machinist already knows how to produce high volume, the supervisor should withhold praise for high productivity unless it is accompanied by a clean work area. In the beginning, the supervisor should praise even small improvements in the cleanliness of the work area as long as productivity remains at an acceptable level. For example, if some attempt at cleaning the area was made prior to the first break, the supervisor might say, "Well, the area is looking better. I see you're trying to keep it cleaner." However, praise should be withheld (but encouragement given to do better) if cleanliness showed no improvement just prior to the lunch break. At this point the supervisor might say, "I know it's hard to keep the area clean and concentrate on running the machine, but I'm sure you'll be able to do better after the lunch break."

The key to shaping is to reinforce movement in the direction of the desired behavioral pattern and to withhold reinforcement when behavior moves away from that pattern. Behaviorists call this technique reinforcing successive approximations. In our machinist example, any time the machinist is able to improve the cleanliness of the work area and maintain acceptable production levels, it would constitute an approximation to the ultimate desired behavior pattern of maintaining high productivity levels and a clean work area.

The second operant conditioning concept important to training is **chaining**. This process describes how the outcomes of behavior come to acquire their reinforcing or punishing properties. A fundamental assumption of chaining is that all outcomes acquire their positive or negative value through association with the feelings produced by their physical effects. Food is usually valued positively because it produces physical effects that are subjectively experienced as "good." Money is also a positively valued outcome, yet it has no direct physical effects. It acquires its positive value because of its association with things that do create those physical effects. The reinforcement value of money, then, is chained to the reinforcement value of the things that money can acquire. Although food is a **primary reinforcer** because it is directly linked to physiological effects, money is a **secondary reinforcer** because its value comes from its links to primary reinforcers.

Primary reinforcers are sometimes used in the training environment; such as refreshments provided at the start of the program and at other times throughout the program. The trainees begin to associate the reinforcing properties of the refreshments (a primary reinforcer) with the training. Training starts on a positive note because it is chained to the positive value of the refreshments. This association becomes so strong in some companies that trainees are upset if refreshments aren't provided.

Chaining affects training in other ways as well. Because of chaining, it is often difficult to know whether a particular outcome will be seen by the trainee as positive or negative. For example, public praise is often believed to be a positive reinforcer. Sometimes, however, public praise from the trainer can be punishing because of the norms of the work group. Peers may see a person receiving praise from the "boss" as being an "apple polisher" and may ridicule or make sarcastic remarks to the person. Rather than reinforcing the person's behavior through praise, the trainer unknowingly punished the behavior.

The trainer must understand as clearly as possible how trainees will perceive the outcomes with which the training is linked. This point relates to Expectancy 2 and valence concepts of expectancy theory. The work unit norms and the culture of the organization will strongly influence whether training is chained to positive or negative outcomes. Shaping and chaining can be useful for understanding employee work performance and for improving trainee motivation and attention in the design of training.

Type 4: Verbal Association Learning

Among the primary focal points of education and training is the acquisition of knowledge, concepts, principles, and problem-solving ability. However, underlying all these elements is the ability to make appropriate associations among various objects and actions that are symbolized by the learner's vocabulary. Nearly all training involves the communication of fact and meaning through language, written or spoken. Though the exact process remains largely a mystery, it is clear that objects, events, and actions are placed into memory along with corresponding verbal symbols. These verbal symbols are the language we use to communicate with each other.

The pairing of a verbal response to an object or event in the environment is the most elementary type of **verbal association learning**. Mechanically, the process is similar to that of operant conditioning. A fundamental difference is that the stimulus (object or event) becomes internalized as language. Thus the word *house* is associated with the various stored experiences the person has had with houses, and he differentiates this word from other words (e.g., tent). The labeling of objects and events is required before the person is able to form concepts by associating two or more language symbols. As with stimulus-response learning, the consequences of verbalizing the associations will enhance or discourage their use in the future. In this way, verbal sequences become memorized, either intentionally or unintentionally.

Obviously, one measure of learning is the degree to which the person is able to identify and use the language of the subject matter appropriately. For example, we cannot easily determine a manager's decision-making process by simply observing the decision or watching the manager as she makes the decision. The decision itself, whether right or wrong, does not indicate how or why it was chosen. However, the manager's ability to describe the factors and processes that led to the decision will indicate the level of both subject matter knowledge and decision-making skill. This information can be used to design training to meet the subject matter or decision-making skill needs of the trainee. If, however, the manager is not able to verbalize these factors and processes, training must begin at the verbal association level to provide the trainee with the vocabulary necessary to describe relevant subject matter factors and decision-making processes.

Often it is assumed that if the person cannot communicate effectively about a particular subject, she lacks the knowledge and skill to behave effectively in the area. However, the person may know the principle or concept but be unable to express it in language understood by the trainer or those in the job environment. What is missing is a common set of language symbols. Even though the person may be able to perform the task, if she is unable to communicate it effectively it indicates a lack of communication skills.

Of course, in training it is also important not to use unnecessarily complex phrases or words. We observed one company in which the line employees were given training designed for middle- and upper-level managers. The line employees complained that they had never heard of many of the terms used, and even when they understood the words, the sentences made no sense to them. You must start your training at the verbal association level of the trainees. This common language can then be used to develop understanding of the more complex language. When terms or phrases are complex but are integral to effectively communicating about a subject, by all means use them, but not until your audience understands them.

The following example illustrates verbal association as well as each of the remaining types of learning. Imagine you are conducting a management training seminar for first- and second-level managers. You are attempting to teach them to use the best management style for a given situation. You want to train them to identify important differences among situations and to apply the appropriate management behaviors in each situation. Ultimately, you would like them to be able to determine on their own how to interact with their employees in ways appropriate for the particular situation. Therefore, the managers must first understand the critical aspects of the situation and their behavior in those situations. This understanding begins with the appropriate verbal associations for the terms, concepts, and principles that will be used.

We will focus here on only two aspects of the situation: (1) the structure of the work itself, called task structure, and (2) the subordinate's need for independence. The trainees must understand the meaning of these terms if they are to learn how to identify the situation correctly. If the trainees are provided with a definition of the term *task structure*, they can use the verbal associations in the definition to form an abstract foundation for the term. A typical definition of task structure might be:

> The degree to which the process of production, the rules of the work unit, and other factors outside the direct control of the worker determine what, when, how, and where the work will be done.

If the trainee can reliably associate the preceding definition with the term *task structure*, it would be an example of complex, verbal, paired association learning. The difference between high and low task structure can be described by following the definition with a statement such as, "The more discretion the employee has in determining what, when, how, and where the work is done, the less structured the job is." Providing verbal examples is also useful in building an understanding of new terms. You might give the following example: "An assembly line job, for example, is typically more structured than a vice presidency." The trainer should use terms, examples, and concepts already known by the trainee as a base from which to work. In most cases the training objective is not merely to have trainees use, recall, or recognize appropriate words and phrases. Rather, they must usually demonstrate the ability to do something when it is appropriate to do it and not do it when it is inappropriate. The next two sections (discrimination and concept learning) deal with these types of learning.

Type 5: Multiple Discrimination Learning

Discrimination learning occurs when the person learns to identify the key aspects of a specific situation, which indicate that a particular response is appropriate. As was stated in the previous section, the relevant verbal associations must be acquired first.

Training people to distinguish among different parts of their surroundings must begin at simpler levels and advance to more complex. In simple multiple discrimination learning, only one aspect of the situation changes to signal that a different response is appropriate. Thus each aspect of the situation associated with different response patterns must be presented separately, so the linkage to behavior can be established for each one. In our example, we will deal with only the two situational factors and two types of managerial behavior. We want to teach trainees to discriminate among higher and lower levels of the situational factors and the managerial behaviors. We only use the extremes here, although in real training we would show the full range of situations and managerial responses. The two situational factors are "task structure" and "employee need for independence." The two types of managerial behavior are (1) initiating structure and (2) participative management. Initiating structure occurs when the manager provides direction to the employees regarding what, when, and how things are to be done. When using a participative management style, the manager seeks the involvement of employees in making decisions about what, when, and how things are done. Our goals are for the managers to learn the following:

- When task structure is high, the manager's initiating structure should be low.
- When task structure is low, the manager's initiating structure should be high.
- When the subordinate's need for independence is high, the manager should become more participative in setting goals.
- When the subordinate's need for independence is low, the manager should become more directive in setting goals.

This pattern is set out in Table 3-4.

As Table 3-4 suggests, the learner needs to discriminate not only between the situational factors of "task structure" and "subordinate need for independence" but also between the high and low levels. The same is true for the response categories "initiating structure" and "participa-

TABLE 3-4 Supervisor Behavior Patterns Recommended for Two Levels of Two Environmental Stimuli

| | Subordinate Need for Independence | |
Task Structure	*High*	*Low*
High	Low initiating structures	Low initiating structure
	High participation	Low participation
Low	High initiating structure	High initiating structure
	High participation	Low participation

tion." The supervisor must be able to identify when an initiating structure or participative management style is being used as well as the extent to which the style is being used.

For now, we are trying to teach the managers to discriminate between situations based on structure being high or low, or based on employee independence being high or low, so they can identify the appropriate managerial style. Training would focus on one factor at a time. A single type of situation would be used in which only the task structure or employee need for independence varies. We would try to use a job situation that everyone would be familiar with. If the trainees come from different areas of the organization, some of them may not be familiar with the job, so it must be explained. Only one job is used because if we vary both the job and the amount of task structure, the trainees may become confused about what they should be responding to. Once they learn to discriminate among the factors, we can move to the next level, concept learning. There we will use several jobs.

At first trainees are reinforced for recognizing aspects of the job that indicate something about its task structure. Once they can reliably recognize structural elements, they are asked to determine whether the information indicates that task structure is high or low. Reinforcement is no longer applied for just recognizing an element as related to task structure, but only for recognizing both the element and its impact on task structure. Can you see how the shaping concept is used even at higher levels of learning? Once the managers can correctly identify the level of task structure, they are ready to move on. Next we might ask them to indicate whether they would provide any initiating structure in the situation. We would follow the same procedure as before until they were consistently indicating the appropriate amount of task structure to use in the situation. The same procedures would be used for participation. The cycle would be repeated for situations involving employee need for independence. When all these are mastered, the trainees will be ready to learn to generalize their learning across multiple situations, which is known as concept learning.

Type 6: Concept Learning

Concept learning is defined as the ability to use a common abstract property to respond correctly to a variety of situations that differ widely in appearance. Whereas in discrimination learning the trainee learns to apply different responses to a single situation, here the trainees must generalize the same responses across many different situations. However, the supervisor trainees are not yet ready to apply the appropriate managerial behavior to both the task structure and employee need for independence. Again, we must teach one concept at a time. In the next type of learning, principle learning, these concepts can be combined into an integrated behavioral pattern. For now we are simply creating an understanding of each concept (task structure, employee need for independence) so that they can be recognized across different situations.

In the management training example, you want the trainees to generalize from the situations they encounter in the training environment to those they might find in the work environment. Suppose the trainees were managers and supervisors from production, sales, information systems, and accounting. You might use an assembly job to demonstrate a highly structured task because the technology, the programmed decision making, and the formal procedures best exemplify a highly structured work situation. Further, you might use a job in new-product engineering as a clear example of tasks with low structure, because this job demands a great deal of latitude in decision making, the tasks are usually new and nonroutine, and the duties are broadly defined. Although the trainees might do well discriminating high from low task structure in the training environment, this ability will not transfer back to their jobs unless they can generalize the concept of task structure to any job. When the trainees are able consistently to identify the level of task structure across a sequence of novel and distinct stimulus situations, the trainer can say that they learned the task structure concept.

Although trial-and-error learning can be used to establish a concept, it is usually not the best method. A systematic approach moving from simple to more difficult learning tasks is typically more efficient and leads to better retention. The trainer might begin with concrete examples that trainees can test to see whether their understanding corresponds with what is desired by the trainer. The best situations reference the trainees' experience. They can be real situations or hypothetical situations that are experienced vicariously (e.g., some case studies, simulations, or demonstrations). After mastering this experiential foundation, trainees must apply it to concrete situations that are different from their experience but contain the elements of the concept to be learned. In our example, these situations are not in the trainee's previous experience but they contain information about how structured a job is or how much independence employees desire. In the previous example, jobs in assembly and new product engineering were used to demonstrate the different levels of task structure, and trainees then generalized the concepts back to the areas that they were managing. When the trainee is consistently able to ignore elements unrelated to the concept and respond appropriately to elements of the concept across the novel situations, the concept is considered learned.

Concept learning applies to skills as well as to knowledge. In our example, we are interested in more than just the trainees' ability to know what initiating structure and participative management are, we want them to know how to do these things. Thus we use a similar approach, but this time linking behavioral rather than just verbal responses to situational cues. The trainee must learn to display the range of behaviors that constitute appropriate learning of the concept.

Observational and experiential training methods such as videos combined with role playing are useful here. Again we would apply reinforcement for successive approximations to shape the trainees' ability to behave in ways consistent with the concept (e.g., high and low initiating structure). When both the verbal and behavioral concepts have been mastered, the trainer is ready to move on to principle learning.

Type 7: Principle Learning

Principles are chains of concepts. Learning that occurs with types 3, 4, 5, and 6 reflects what we called declarative knowledge. **Principle learning** is required for development of procedural and strategic knowledge. The statement "Low initiating structure in a high task-structure work environment increases employee job satisfaction" represents three distinct concepts:

1. Initiating structure
2. Task structure
3. Job satisfaction

In order to learn this principle, the trainee must have already learned each of the three concepts. Again, memorizing the verbal chain in no way implies learning the principle, the discriminations, or the concepts. Learning the principle is demonstrated by its appropriate use in specific situations. Presenting the trainees with novel situations in which all the various factors and many irrelevant factors may be present, and determining whether they can apply the appropriate managerial behavior, will demonstrate whether they learned the principle.

In our continuing example, we need to present trainees with situations in which varying levels of both task structure and employee need for independence are present. If the training objective was based only on knowledge of the principle, we would ask them to indicate how they would respond to the situation. If skill development was also an objective, we would place them in these situations with instructions to demonstrate the appropriate managerial style. Role plays and some types of simulations are useful for this development. As always, starting with the concrete and progressing to the abstract while reinforcing successive approximations to the desired response pattern will strengthen the learning and reduce the likelihood of forgetting.

Type 8: Problem Solving

Problem solving integrates and applies more than one principle to produce a novel response or capability that results in a higher-order principle previously unknown to the learner. In our example, suppose you successfully fostered the learning of the principles matching participative management and initiating structure with the situational variables of task structure and employee need for independence. You might then present a videotape of an employee characterized as being low in self-esteem. Even though this employee tested well in the selection process, she hasn't been on the job long enough to know how well she's doing; nonetheless, she feels she is not performing well and is thinking of leaving the job for one not as demanding. None of the principles learned is directly applicable to this situation.

The ability to problem-solve would be evident in trainees who were able to generalize from the existing principles to develop a higher-order principle such as "managerial behavior that compensates for mismatches between employee characteristics and the work situation is effective." In this instance, providing support and reinforcement to the low self-esteem employee would compensate for the employee's low opinion of her work. Other managerial behaviors that provided similar support would also be appropriate.

By getting the trainees to share what they would do in the situation and why, the trainer can develop and reinforce the problem-solving capabilities of the trainees. The key in teaching trainees to problem-solve is to provide them with situations in which the existing principles do not directly apply but, if integrated, will provide a higher-order principle that will allow them to solve the problem.

When a problem is solved, something is also learned in the sense that the capabilities of the problem solver are enhanced in a relatively permanent way. The higher-order principle becomes a part of the trainee's knowledge. Of course, higher-order principles may be learned in the same fashion as regular principles. The difference is in the process of discovery, or the amount and nature of the guidance provided. In typical principle-learning situations, the trainer will cue and even model the higher-order principle in combination with appropriately reinforcing trainee responses that more or less demonstrate acquisition of the principle. The problem-solving type of learning occurs when the trainee is able to discover the new principle without (or with minimal) help. Research indicates that this latter type of learning produces a highly effective capability that is extremely resistant to being forgotten.[29] It is from the ability to solve problems that strategic knowledge is developed.

SOCIAL LEARNING THEORY

Albert Bandura and his associates developed a model of learning known variously as observational learning, vicarious learning, and most often, social learning theory.[30] One of its most important contributions to the science of learning was demonstrating that learning could occur without any overt behavior by the learner. That is, the learner didn't have to do anything except observe what was going on around her. No behavior pattern was produced and no reinforcement given.

The basic premise of **social learning theory** is that events and consequences in the learning situation are cognitively processed before they are learned or influence behavior. The processing of information leads to learning and changes in behavior. Certainly the consequences of behavior (reinforcement or punishment) influence the likelihood of that behavior in the future, but they do so as a result of how they are perceived, interpreted, and stored in memory. Thus, one can learn by observing the behavior of others and the consequences that result. This theory contradicts the strict behaviorists, who claim that learning can occur only as a result of one's own behavior and its consequences. The cognitive processes that are a part of social learning theory are motivation, attention, retention, and to some extent behavioral reproduction. Figure 3-6 illustrates the relationships among these cognitive processes.

Motivation

Although we discussed motivation at length earlier in this chapter, it is useful to see how it fits in with social learning theory. As the model indicates, motivation both influences and is influenced by the other processes. The learners' needs determine what things receive attention and are processed for retention. As is depicted in the model, social learning theory incorporates the operant conditioning concept of behavioral consequences affecting the likelihood of future behavior. However, whereas operant conditioning principles stipulate that the consequence can only be learned through learner behavior-consequence pairings, social learning theory suggests that behavioral consequences can be acquired through anticipatory learning. **Anticipatory learning** occurs when a person learns what consequences are associated with a behavior (or set of behaviors) without actually engaging in the behavior or receiving the consequences. By observing someone else's behavior, the observer can learn something about how to perform the behavior and also something about the consequences of the behavior. Thus this theory provides a model for learning through observation alone. For this reason, it is often referred to as a theory of observational or vicarious learning. The model of learning processes illustrated in Figure 3-6 is more than just observational learning, however. It combines cognitive and behaviorist concepts into a comprehensive set of integrated processes that are applicable to all types of learning, providing another set of tools for designing and implementing training. Additional motivational issues are discussed later in the "Motivation to Learn" section.

FIGURE 3-6 The Cognitive Processes Involved in Social Learning

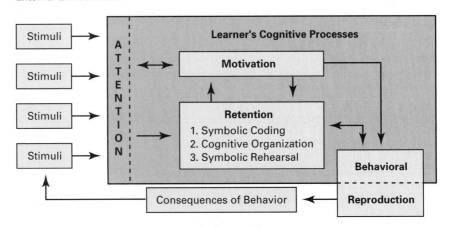

Attention

The learning process begins with the learner's **attention** becoming focused on particular objects and events in the environment (stimuli). Of the great multitude of objects and events in the typical environment, we notice many of them but pay attention to only some. The things we pay attention to are those that stand out for some reason (loud, bright, unusual, etc.) or those that we learn are important (e.g., lead to need satisfaction). This reaction is reflected in the fact that we are more likely to model the behavior of someone who is spotlighted in some way (highly publicized, unusually attractive, popular, etc.) than someone who isn't. Similarly, we are more likely to model someone who seems to receive a lot of reinforcement than someone who receives little.

The concept of attention is important in training. Making key learning points stand out so that the trainees will focus attention on them improves learning. Eliminating extraneous objects such as cell phones and beepers keeps trainees from becoming distracted during training. Making learning exercises fun and interesting keeps attention focused on the learning topic. However, exercises that are fun but don't relate to the learning objectives draw attention away from what you want trainees to learn, making the training less effective. These issues and others related to capturing trainee attention are addressed in the training design chapter.

Retention

Once attention is focused on an object or event, the incoming information is processed for possible **retention**. Some of the information will be retained, some will be lost. The more training is designed to facilitate the retention processes, the more learning will occur. The initial phase of retention is the translation of the information into symbols meaningful to the individual, called **symbolic coding**. It typically takes the form of reducing the external objects and events into internal images and verbal symbols. These symbols are then organized into the existing cognitive structure through associations with previously stored information. This process, **cognitive organization**, can be facilitated in training by asking the trainees to provide examples of how the new information relates to what they already know. This exercise serves two purposes. It allows the trainee to code more easily and store the information, and it allows the trainer to see whether the desired associations are being made. Other ways in which training can facilitate retention are discussed in the training design chapter.

To facilitate the retention process, the learner should "practice" the learned material through **symbolic rehearsal**, which involves visualizing or imagining how the knowledge or skill will be used. If the focus is on skill building, the trainee imagines using the skills in different situations. This exercise is usually fairly easy to do because the skill helps to define the situations. When the focus of learning is knowledge, it is sometimes more difficult to imagine how it can or will be used. For example, think back to when you were learning the multiplication tables. Most of us memorized these through constant repetition over many months, and that repetition provided us with the experience of using multiplication to solve problems. Each year as we advanced to the next grade, we were given more problems to solve that required multiplication. In contrast, storing information without any associations with personal use—in other words, just memorizing—typically results in only short-term retention. Students who have ever crammed for an exam are probably familiar with this phenomenon. Thus associating information with its uses enhances the storage and retrieval process. The symbolic rehearsal process can be thought of as mental practice. Observing others use the knowledge or skill provides additional opportunities for symbolic rehearsal, because as you watch them you can put yourself in their place. Symbolic rehearsal also increases the ability to generalize the learning to novel situations. The discussion on training design in Chapter 5 discusses other ways to enhance retention through symbolic rehearsal.

Behavioral Reproduction

Behavioral reproduction is repeated practice. The more a person practices using new information, the more it is learned and retained. The effectiveness of practice depends on how the practice is designed and reinforced, as we will discuss in detail in the training design chapter. Figure 3-6 shows the behavioral reproduction process as being a part of both the learner's cognitive processes and the external environment. This duality reflects the fact that behavior is initiated by the person's cognitive processes—the person must retrieve the appropriate behavior from storage and direct the body to perform the appropriate actions—and then the behavior itself actually occurs in and becomes part of the environment.

We already spent considerable time discussing the importance of behavioral consequences. One additional point is worth making, however. If consequences are to affect behavior, the individuals must be aware of these consequences. For example, assume a supervisor recommends an employee for a bonus but hasn't yet told the employee. Subjectively for the employee, it is not a consequence of behavior, even though objectively it is. Even when aware of a consequence, the person may misinterpret its value. The supervisor who is disappointed in an employee's performance and sarcastically says "Really nice job" may be misinterpreted by the employee as giving praise. Thus the person must be aware of and correctly interpret behavioral consequences if those consequences are going to have the desired effect. Effective training programs need to call attention to the desirable consequences of learning and of using the learning back on the job.

Relating Instruction to Learning

Learning theory describes how individuals learn. Much of what takes place during learning can be influenced by external events, which makes instruction possible. Gagné and his associates suggest effective instruction requires a "set of events" external to the learner, designed to facilitate the internal process of learning.[31] So, what things (external events) do we need to facilitate the trainees' learning of a particular objective? Put another way, can the sequencing of events in a training process increase the likelihood learning will occur?

The answer is yes. A particular order of presenting material will facilitate learning. Gagné and his associates provide a **micro theory of instructional design**, which is a guide for designing training. It is relevant for all three types of learning outcomes: cognitive knowledge, skill-based, and attitudinal. The theory provides nine steps (sets of events) to follow in developing training for a learning objective.[32] To be most effective this "set of events" should be arranged in a specific order as depicted in Table 3-5. Gagné and his associates do not indicate the nine steps are necessary for every learning objective, or that the sequencing must be exactly as indicated. They say:

> [T]hese events of instruction do not invariably occur in this exact order, though this is the most probable order . . . by no means are all of these events provided for every lesson. . . . Their role is to stimulate internal information processes . . . sometimes an event will be obvious to the learner and not needed . . . or provided by the learner themselves. . . . In using the checklist the designer asks, "Do these learners need support at this stage for learning this task."[33]

Let's go through each of the events using a learning objective related to teaching apprentice electricians.[34] The learning objective is to determine the amperage of an appliance, given the watts and voltage. The first event, "gaining attention," is obtained by showing a short video in which a family is in a kitchen, the lights are on, the radio is on, the toaster is on. One of the children plugs in the blender and when she turns it on everything shuts off, radio, lights and toaster, which gets everyone's attention. You then ask, "What happened here?" When the answer is given (a fuse was blown), you discuss why it happened and move to the second event: "inform the learner of the objective." The objective is to calculate the amperage of appliances in order to

TABLE 3-5 Gagné-Briggs Nine Events of Instruction

Instructional Event	*What It Does . . . Gets Trainee*
Gaining attention	To focus on trainer
Informing the trainee of goal (objective)	To begin to focus on the goal
Stimulating recall of prior knowledge (learning)	To retrieve prior learning to working memory
Presenting the material	To selectively perceive important parts of training
Providing learning guidance	To consider how the new material fits into her overall schema, and clarifies where it belongs for ease of retrieval
Eliciting the performance	To do it
Providing feedback	To perform effectively by reinforcing correct responses and assisting when incorrect
Assessing performance	To attempt a number of similar problems to determine whether she grasps the concept
Enhancing retention and transfer	To do more complex and varied examples of the concept and assess the success

Source: Gagné, R. M., L. Briggs, and W. Wager (1992). *Principles of Instructional Design.* Fort Worth: Harcourt Brace Jovanovich.

wire a room properly with the correct number and type of plugs, based on what will be used in that room. The next event is "stimulate recall of prerequisites." Here you would ask apprentices to recall the typical voltage in a house (it is 120 volts but for ease of calculation here we will round out to 100). You then ask, "Where is wattage for appliances found?" The answer is on a label on the back or side of the appliance. Then ask "What is the purpose of fuses?" The answer is to prevent circuit overload. Finally ask how their size is measured (amps).

"Presenting the stimulus" is done by providing the formula for determining amperage: Amps = Watts/Volts. Given the watts of the blender (1000 watts), you ask, "What is its amperage?" You may give a few more examples. Next, for the "provide learning guidance" event you ask them to go back to the example at the beginning of the discussion. Tell them the kitchen was all wired to one typical 15 amp fuse, and ask "Would the fuse have still blown if the toaster was not plugged in." They cannot give the correct answer because they need more information, so you discuss the need to have the wattage of everything in the kitchen to determine total amps. You then give it to them (100 watt light, 1000 watt toaster, 10 watt radio) and ask for the amps generated for each.

For the next event, "eliciting performance," you provide them with the wattage of a number of appliances (refrigerator 1000 watts, TV 300 watts, space heater 1400 watts, and so forth) and ask them to determine the amps each will require. To "provide feedback," you review the answers to the preceding questions and determine how well each apprentice understood the process. "Assessing performance" is done by providing the apprentices with a number of problems for which they need to calculate the amps of appliances. For the final event, "enhancing retention and transfer," you provide them with the following problem: You are going to wire a workshop. The appliances to be used in the workshop include a table saw, router, planer, drill press, sander, four lights, radio, electric heater, and so forth. You also give the wattage for each of the appliances. Then you ask them to indicate how many 15 amp circuits they would need to provide to be most efficient, and what they would put on the same circuit.

Using the theory helps you create a setting where learning is most likely. Another example is provided in Table 3-6.

TABLE 3-6 Example of a Lesson in Problem Solving

Objective: Given a drawing of a plot of land, the student generates a plan for a sprinkler system that will cover at least 90% of the land, using the least amount of materials (PVC pipe and sprinkler heads).

Event	Media	Prescription
1. Gaining attention	Live instruction and overhead projector	Show pictures of sprinkler coverage of a rectangular plot of ground. One highly successful (90%) coverage, one unsuccessful (70% coverage), and one using too many sprinkler heads. Show these rapidly, inviting attention to their differences.
2. Informing the learner of the objective	Same	The problem to be solved is to design the most efficient sprinkler system for a plot of ground—one that covers at least 90% and uses the smallest amounts of pipe and sprinkler heads.
3. Stimulating recall of requisites	Overhead projector	Have the learners recall applicable rules. Because the sprinkler heads they will use spray in circles and partial circles, rules to be recalled are (1) area of a circle, (2) area of quarter and half circles, (3) the area of rectangular areas, (4) the area of irregular shapes made by the intersection of circular arcs with straight sides.
4. Presenting the stimulus material	Same	Restate the problem in general terms, and then add specific details: (a) rectangular lot 50 by 100 ft; (2) radius of the sprinklers, 5 ft; (3) water source in the center of the lot.
5. Providing learning guidance	Same	The student will need to design tentative sprinkler layouts, draw them out, and calculate the relative efficiency of each. Guidance may be given by informing the learner of various options if it appears that rules are not being applied correctly. For example, "Could you get more efficient coverage in the corner by using a quarter-circle sprinkler head?" Or "It looks like you have a lot to overlap; are you allowing for a 10% non-coverage?" Ask the learner what rule he is following for placing the sprinkler.

TABLE 3-6 (continued)

6. Eliciting performance		
7. Providing feedback	Oral review by instructor	Confirm good moves, when in a suitable direction. If the learner doesn't see a possible solution, suggestions may be made. For example, "Why don't you draw four circles that barely touch, calculate the area, then draw a rectangle around the circles and calculate the area of coverage to see how much you have?"
8. Assessing performance	Instructor	Present a different problem using the same type of sprinkler, with different lot shape and size. Check the efficiency of the student's solution in terms of coverage and amount of materials used.
9. Enhancing retention and transfer	Worksheet	Present several different problems varying in shape of lot, position of the water source, and area a of sprinkler coverage. Assess the generalizability of student problem solving to these new situations.

Source: Gagné, R. M., L. Briggs, and W. Wager. (1992). *Principles of Instructional Design.* Fort Worth: Harcourt Brace Jovanovich.

Why Are They Resisting and What Can I Do About It?

Learning, like eating, is one of the most fundamental processes of survival, yet trainers and managers continually complain about trainees who do not pay attention, are disruptive, and generally demonstrate a resistance to the training they are receiving.

Often the older the trainees or the higher their education, the more resistance they show. If learning is a basic human process, why are so many complaints of this type made?

The first step to understanding **resistance to learning** is viewing learning as a performance outcome. Most learning is not something that happens automatically or unconsciously. It is an activity we decide to do or not do. From the performance model discussed earlier (see Figure 3-1 on page 75), we know that learning performance is determined by a person's motivation, KSAs, and learning environment.

MOTIVATION TO LEARN

Most trainees arrive at training with an elaborate and highly integrated **cognitive structure**. They already know a lot about themselves, their work, their company, and many other things.[35] The objective of training is to change some part of that cognitive structure so that the trainee's performance will be improved. Change creates anxiety, however, for the following reasons:

Fear of the unknown:	"Right now I know how things work, but I don't know how this training will affect things."
Fear of incompetence:	"I don't know whether I'll be able to learn this stuff."

Fear of losing rewards:	"What will happen to my pay, status, perks, among other things?"
Fear of lost influence:	"Will this training make me more or less valuable?"
Lost investments:	"I've spent a lot of time and energy learning to do it this way. Why change?"

These concerns deal with the trainees' needs, current competencies, and how training will change their current outcomes. These factors are addressed by expectancy theory, and the trainees' motivation to learn will depend on the answers to these questions. To the degree that the answers indicate that learning is worth the effort, the individual will be motivated to learn.

Even when trainees acknowledge the value of the training, they may believe the effort required to master the learning is just not worthwhile. The reluctance of many experienced managers to learn how to use computers is one example of this attitude. They are often bright and competent in other aspects of their jobs, but they continue to use their old ways of communicating and calculating, even though they see that the computer could increase their capabilities. Their already well-developed cognitive structures can make it seem too difficult to change all they already know and learn the new KSAs. The more difficult a task is, the greater the resistance is likely to be, usually in the form of withdrawal or avoidance. The benefits of doing a difficult task must be much higher than the costs to induce the person to do it. Why is learning more difficult for those with more extensive and developed cognitive structures?

In Piaget's terms, the accommodation process (developing new cognitive categories) is the most difficult, while assimilation (adding new things to existing categories) is relatively easy. Accommodation requires one to create new categories, which then need to be linked to other related categories. The more categories that exist and the more developed they are, the more difficult the learning. When assimilating, the learner simply adds new elements and rearranges associations among elements within a single category. When accommodating, not only must learners create a new category and place elements into that category, they must also associate this category with other categories. The elements within those categories must be modified to create the network of associations that appropriately incorporates the new information.

This type of situation occurs whenever a company changes the paradigms it uses for conducting its business. For example, think about what supervisors face when companies move from a traditional, centralized, hierarchical, autocratic decision-making process to a team-based, flexible, more consensus-based, employee-involvement system. From their experience and training in the traditional system, the supervisors developed a cognitive structure for how to get things done. They learned how to make all the decisions for their subordinates, and developed a system for communicating those decisions and ensuring that they are carried out effectively. These strategies were probably reinforced over many years. A new piece of equipment or a change in the work process brings new procedures that are learned and assimilated into the supervisor's decision-making structure relatively easily. Under the new, team-based, employee-involvement decision making, however, the whole process of making decisions must be relearned because the underlying organizational assumptions changed. For the supervisor, the focus is no longer on the quality of his decisions, but on the supervisor's ability to facilitate quality decisions by the team. Although some aspects of the supervisor's old decision-making process might still be useful, his cognitive structure must be changed to incorporate the new concepts, and the useful aspects of the old concepts must be reorganized and integrated with the new. For this reason, learning the new system will be more difficult for supervisors with a lot of experience than for a newly hired supervisor with little experience in the traditional system.

Resistance to learning also comes from defensiveness. The more experienced a person is, the more she has already learned, which means a more developed, integrated, and complex cognitive structure. A great deal of effort went into creating that cognitive structure. Training can, in a sense, be seen as an attack on a person's competence, especially if the training is mandatory. Trainees in this situation can also feel they are being told that the trainer knows more about how to run their area than they do. In these cases, they are likely to try to show the trainer, and the other trainees, that the training or the trainer is inadequate or irrelevant or that their current KSAs are better than what training has to offer.

This generalization is not to say that older, more experienced people cannot learn new things or discard old beliefs. They frequently do. As adults mature, they appear to go through periodic episodes of cognitive reorganization, in which concepts or principles of long standing are reevaluated.[36] During these cognitive reorganizations, knowledge that is of little functional value is discarded and new KSAs are discovered and integrated into their cognitive structure, especially in times of transition such as job or career changes. For adults, the key factor in discarding old learning and acquiring new is its practical usefulness. Training that seems abstract, theoretical, or otherwise unrelated to doing the job will likely be ignored or resisted. Training that can demonstrate its value and practical utility will find trainees eager to learn.

GROUP DYNAMICS

Another reason for trainees to resist learning new ways concerns **group dynamics** and its impact on motivation. The power and control of the group over its members was first noted in the Hawthorne studies of the 1920s and 1930s.[37] Even though members of the group were paid piece rate, the output from members of the group were always within a certain number of units. Examination of this study revealed that the group set a standard and rewarded those who remained within the standard, and punished those who did much more or much less. Thus the group norm of a certain number of units was generally followed.

The power of the group comes from rewards for members that follow group norms, or punishment for those who do not. These rewards or punishments can be as simple as talking to (reward) or shunning (punishment) a group member. (Punishment can also be severe such as slashing tires or physically threatening those who do not comply.) If you want to be a good group member, you must agree with and follow what the group decides is best. Consider the following scenario. Sarah arrives at the training center early, excited to be attending a workshop on how to communicate with customers more effectively. Fellow trainees are talking among themselves, making fun of the training. One of them says, "They are going to tell us how to do our job; I bet the trainer has never even done our job so how could he know." Another responds, "Yeah, these workshops are put together by those who never worked in a real job, but at least we can enjoy this as a day off work." Then one turns to Sarah and says, "Hey, I see you managed to con your boss into sending you here for a rest too—good work." To be part of the "in group" Sarah will have to agree, and as a result will probably not participate as much as she would like in the training. This behavior will affect the amount she learns.

Let's say that in spite of her (and everyone else's) lack of participation in the workshop Sarah did learn a few skills. Now she goes back to her workplace. There she hears coworkers comment, "Well did you enjoy your day off? Wasn't that training the stupidest stuff you have ever seen?" and "Can you imagine using that 'active listening' stuff on a real customer?" With such comments, what is the likelihood Sarah will want to try some of these new skills? Group dynamics is a powerful force that can drastically inhibit both learning and transfer of skills.[38]

Group dynamics can also be used to support high performance. The pajama factory experiments of the late 1940s compared employees in two groups where change was necessary in how the jobs were done.[39] In one group they were told about the changes, and in the other the members provided input into the changes. The no participation group showed a drop in productivity from the baseline, and the participation group showed an increase in productivity from the baseline. The most important factor in the difference was group norms that developed to either restrict output (no participation group), or increase it (participation group). More recent research indicates that trainees' perception of their work groups' support for training is a strong predictor of the likelihood the trainees will transfer what they learned to the job.[40] The control the work group exerts over the individual member is a double-edged sword. It is a good thing if the norms are developed in line with the organizational goals. One way of developing these norms is to allow input from the work group on decisions that will affect them. The movement toward more teams and teamwork in organizations provides such opportunities, but in order to assure the right norms are developed, these work groups need to be nurtured and made to feel valuable.[41]

Training That Motivates Adults to Learn

Learning occurs quite frequently in adults when it appears to offer practical application immediately or in the near future.[42] For example, a study showed IBM sales representatives averaged more than 1,100 hours a year in "new learning episodes." (A new learning episode was defined as a deliberate attempt to gain and retain some significant knowledge or skill for problem solving or personal change.) Professors, by contrast, averaged slightly more time (1,745 hours) on fewer episodes. Clearly, adults are not resistant to learning, but they are sometimes resistant to training offered by their companies. Why?

TRAINING RELEVANCE, VALUE, AND READINESS TO LEARN

Some of the most often mentioned reasons for adults engaging in new learning are problems on the job, job/occupational changes, home and personal responsibilities, and competency at some hobby or recreational activity. In the study mentioned previously, about two-thirds of the learning episodes were job related. The need to know and the readiness to learn are critical aspects in the success of adult learning programs.[43] The need to know refers to the value of the knowledge to the learner. Adults most often seek to learn when the learning is life-, task-, or problem-centered.[44] Readiness to learn refers to the amount of prerequisite knowledge (KSAs) the trainee possesses and the trainee's belief in his or her ability to learn the material. This aspect is consistent with the principles of self-efficacy and expectancy theory. People's motivation to learn a particular knowledge or skill set will be directly influenced by their belief that if they put forth the effort, they will be successful in their learning (Expectancy 1). Beyond this expectation, they must feel that the benefits of learning the KSAs outweigh the benefits of not learning them (Expectancy 2).

The challenge is to provide instruction in a context that overcomes the natural resistance of adult learners to changing their cognitive structures. Making the relevance and value of the learning clear, as it relates to the trainee's and organization's goals, addresses one source of resistance to learning. A second source can be addressed by ensuring that the trainee believes she can successfully master the training content. Over time, adults may develop feelings of low self-efficacy in certain areas and feelings of high self-efficacy in others. For those with a low self-efficacy for learning in general or for the specific content area of the training, the trainer needs to change the self-efficacy beliefs so trainees are more willing to attempt new learning. Doing so requires a careful match between the trainee's characteristics (KSA level, learning style preferences, etc.) and the design of the training. By demonstrating that learning in the subject area can be as easy as in areas in which trainees have high self-efficacy, trainers can overcome a significant type of resistance to learning.

ALLOWING TRAINEES CONTROL OVER THEIR LEARNING

As we pointed out, trainees walk into training with well-developed cognitive maps that reflect their experiences. Because these experiences differ from person to person, any given training group is likely to differ considerably in the KSAs they possess and in their learning strategies. Trainees often view these differences as hindrances to their learning and resist training with others who are dissimilar. However, these differences can be viewed as a learning resource if the trainees are willing to share their experiences and strategies and if the training environment supports such an exchange. In fact, adult learners prefer sharing their learning experience with others if the environment is supportive. Even though adults prefer to plan their own learning projects and to adopt a self-directed approach to learning, this preference doesn't imply a desire to learn in isolation. Rather, it reflects a desire to set their own pace, establish their own structure for learning, and employ flexibility in the learning methods. More often than not, adults seek learning assistance from others. In short, they do not mind learning from others, but they want to maintain some control over the learning experience. These characteristics suggest training that incorporates individualized components and also makes use of shared, relevant experiences will be most effective at overcoming resistance to learning.

Although it is true that many adults are able to learn new competencies even when they are not told the significance or usefulness of the training, they are much less likely to be able to apply these new competencies to their job. Research suggests that trainees receiving instruction on how to perform a set of skills show improved performance at the end of training, but fail to use the skills on their own or to generalize the skill usage to similar situations.[45] Training that provides instruction on the "how to" and includes the "why and when" results in improved performance, as well as continued use of the skill across appropriate situations.[46]

INVOLVING TRAINEES IN THE PROCESS

Training, then, should take into account the motivational and cognitive processes that influence the trainee's readiness and willingness to learn. Many writers emphasized the importance of participation, choice, personal experiences, critical reflection, and critical thinking as key characteristics of adult learning.[47] Involving the trainees in the learning process from needs assessment to design and evaluation addresses many of these issues.

Involvement is a key part of overcoming resistance to change. You may remember, from the discussion of OD principles in Chapter 2, that involving those who are affected by change in planning and implementing the change creates a sense of ownership. The result is increased commitment to the change, as well as better implementation. Supervisors, as well as trainees, should be involved in determining the training needs, because both are affected by the change. Supervisors have a clearer understanding of why new KSAs are necessary, how they fit in with the overall plans for the work unit, and the consequences of their employees learning or not learning the new KSAs. The trainees in turn see what KSAs they need to improve and understand why those KSAs will be of value. Involving trainees in needs analysis and other parts of the training process will be discussed in more depth in relevant chapters.

Individual Differences Related to Learning

Some interesting findings came from studies regarding the learning process for low ability and high ability individuals.[48] Goal setting as a motivational incentive does not always operate with the same magnitude for these two groups. When starting to learn a moderately difficult task, providing goals to those with low ability will inhibit, rather than enhance learning. Although the same is true for high ability individuals, it is not nearly as severe. High ability individuals, it seems, have the extra cognitive capacity to focus on goals as well as the new learning in the early learning stage. This difference disappears as the task is learned, and then goal setting enhances performance of both low and high ability individuals. Even though a difference separates the two groups, results from this research suggest that overall, it is wise not to introduce goal setting as a motivational device early in the training process.

Although we indicated that it is desirable to consider diversity among trainees as an opportunity, it is true only up to a point. For example, trainees who are substantially less knowledgeable than others can create significant problems. They may not be able to keep up with the material, or, if the material is presented at a slower pace, the more knowledgeable trainees are bored to tears. It's not only differences in KSAs that can create problems in a training group. A contingency approach to adult learning looks at the characteristics of trainees, such as those listed in Table 3-7, that suggest different approaches to training and development.[49]

The logic of using different approaches for trainees with different characteristics makes some sense, but research in most of these areas is sparse or nonexistent. Currently, research in the areas of resistance to change, absorption level, and topical interest provide some substantiation for providing different training designs to different populations. For example, those with low self-efficacy should have training that first addresses the self-efficacy issue; for those with a high sense of self-efficacy, this training would seem not only irrelevant, but probably demeaning. Of course, providing different training designs becomes more complex and more costly for the organization.

Differences in learning characteristics can have important consequences for training; however, providing separate training sessions may not always be the most practical or cost-effective way to achieve the organization's HRD goals. Thus training programs need to be designed to accommodate a sufficiently large group of trainees while at the same time considering individual differences. Training design issues are discussed in more detail in Chapter 5. However, training professionals should consider the following nine principles in developing training programs for their employees:[50]

1. Identify the types of individual learning strengths and problems and tailor the training around them.
2. Align learning objectives to organizational goals.
3. Clearly define program goals and objectives at the start.
4. Actively engage the trainee, thus maximizing attention, expectations, and memory.
5. Use a systematic, logically connected sequencing of learning activities so that trainees master lower levels of learning before moving to higher levels.
6. Use a variety of training methods.
7. Use realistic job- or life-relevant training material.
8. Allow trainees to work together and share experiences.
9. Provide constant feedback and reinforcement while encouraging self-assessment.

By applying these principles to training programs, the trainer can address the diversity of characteristics trainees bring to training within the context of a group learning environment.

TABLE 3-7 Dimensions for Trainee Assessment Prior to Training

1. Instrumentality	Desire for immediate applicability of the material to be learned
2. Skepticism	Need for logic, evidence, and examples
3. Resistance to change	Fear of unknown or personal consequences of change related to feelings about self-efficacy and locus of control orientation
4. Attention span	Amount of time before attentiveness is substantially diminished
5. Expectation level	Trainee's quality/quantity requirements of training
6. Dominant needs	Intrinsic and extrinsic motivators that drive the trainee
7. Absorption level	Pace at which trainee expects and can absorb new material
8. Topical interest	Trainee's personal (job-relevant) interest in the material

SUMMARY

An employee's performance is a function of their motivation, KSAs, and the environment. To understand motivation we turn to two types of theories of motivation: need and process. Need theories, such as ERG, explain what it is that motivates an individual. Process theories, such as expectancy theory, explain how individuals are motivated.

Two historical approaches to understanding learning are the behaviorist perspective (Skinner) and the cognitive perspective (Piaget). To fully understand learning we examine it from a more integrated approach through Gagné's learning types and Bandura's social learning theory. Both combine the behavioral and cognitive perspectives. The behavioral approach (reinforcement theory) focuses on the importance of the environment, and the cognitive approach (accommodation/assimilation) emphasizes the notion that learning can take place without any behavior being exhibited. Together they provide a more complete picture of the learning process than either can do alone. The process of learning provides the foundation for designing effective training. Gagné and colleagues provide this foundation with their theory of instructional design (nine events of instruction).

To motivate employees to learn you must first realize they already know a great deal, possess highly integrative cognitive structures, and have been successful to date. A number of reasons explain why they are hesitant to learn more material, such as fear of the unknown, of not being successful at learning the new material, and so forth. To motivate them you need to make the training relevant, of value, and be sure they are confident of being successful. Goal setting will increase motivation in the later parts of the training program, but will interfere with learning in the early stages. Finally, trainee involvement with each phase of the training process will facilitate trainee interest and motivation in the training.

One final concern in making training relevant is the issue of individual differences. In general we advise you to treat the diversity of individual characteristics in a training group as an opportunity. However, sometimes it will be best to develop separate training programs. Nine principles are offered for addressing individual differences in the design of training programs.

KEY TERMS

- Accommodation
- Anticipatory learning
- Assimilation
- Attention
- Behavioral reproduction
- Chaining
- Cognition
- Cognitive organization
- Cognitive process
- Cognitive structure
- Concept learning
- Discrimination learning
- Environment
- ERG theory
- Existence needs
- Expectancy theory
- Extinction
- Group dynamics
- Growth needs
- Law of effect
- Learning
- Micro theory of instructional design
- Motivation
- Needs theory
- Negative reinforcement
- Operant conditioning
- Performance model
- Positive reinforcement
- Primary reinforcer
- Principle learning
- Principles
- Problem solving
- Process theories
- Punishment
- Reinforcement theories
- Relatedness needs
- Resistance to learning
- Retention
- Secondary reinforcer
- Self-efficacy
- Shaping
- Signal learning
- Social learning theory
- Stimulus-response learning
- Symbolic coding
- Symbolic rehearsal
- Theories
- Valence
- Verbal association learning

CASE ANALYSIS

RICK'S NEW JOB

Rick recently received an MBA. At college he was known as smart, hardworking, and friendly. His good grades landed him an internship with Peterson Paper Products to head up their sales department. Near the end of the internship Val Peterson, the president and founder of the company, asked Rick to meet him after work to discuss the future.

PETERSON PAPER PRODUCTS

Peterson Paper Products, or PPP, was founded 17 years ago by Val Peterson. It purchases raw paper of varying grades and produces paper stock for business and personal stationery and greeting cards. Its annual sales topped $15 million, and it employs 80 to 90 people depending on demand. Sales gradually declined over the last 2 years after steady and sometimes spectacular growth during the previous 7 years. Competition increased markedly over the last 3 years, and profit margins dwindled. Although PPP is known for the high quality of its products, consumers are shifting from premium-priced, high-quality products to products with higher overall value. Through all of these changes PPP maintained a close-knit family culture. At least half of the employees have been with the company since the beginning or are friends or relatives of the Petersons or Mr. Ball, Val's partner.

Val Peterson, 53, holds the majority of stock in this privately held company that he founded. He began working summers in a paper company during high school. He supervised a shift at a paper plant while he went to college at night. After graduation he worked at increasingly higher management levels, occasionally switching employers for a promotion. Eighteen years ago he quit his vice presidency with a major paper product manufacturer to start his own company. Employees see him as charismatic, even tempered, and reasonable. He spends most of his time and energy on company business, putting in 12-hour days.

Rosie Peterson, 50, Val's wife, is the controller for the company and holds 5 percent of the company stock. Rosie never went to college, and her accounting methods are rather primitive (all paper and pencil). Nonetheless, she is always on top of the financial picture and puts in nearly as many hours as Val. She exerts a great deal of influence in the operations and the direction of PPP.

Walter Ball, 61, is both Mr. Peterson's friend and business partner. He owns 25 percent of the stock and has known Val since before the start of PPP. He is VP of operations, which means he oversees the computer information systems that run the paper production process and handles the technical side of the business. He is not current on the latest computer or manufacturing technology, but he loves the paper business. He says he will probably retire at 65, but most people say they'll believe it when they see it.

Diane Able, 41, is the customer service manager and is married to Steve Able, the chief engineer. Diane worked her way up in the company over the last 10 years. She is often asked to assist Mr. Peterson with projects because of her common sense, and he trusts her to keep information to herself.

Rick's Offer

When Rick met Mr. Peterson to "discuss the future," he was nervous. He knew Mr. Peterson liked his work so far, but didn't know if it was enough to extend his internship another 6 months. So far he

(continued)

(*continued*)

had worked only with Mr. Peterson on special projects and didn't know the rest of the management group well. He was flabbergasted when Mr. Peterson said, "I was thinking that you might like work here at PPP full time and help us out with our sales department."

The two of them discussed the problems in the sales area and talked about what could be done to boost sales. Rick agreed to start the next Monday. During this conversation, Rosie walked in and suggested they all go out to dinner. At dinner Rosie emphasized to Rick that PPP was a family operation, down to earth and informal. "You probably shouldn't try to change things too quickly," she warned. "People need time to get used to you. You have to remember, you're an outsider here and everyone else is an insider." Then Val moved the conversation back to what the future could be like at PPP.

Rick's Awakening

The first few days at work Rick spent in getting to know the plant and operations, meeting all the employees, and familiarizing himself with the problems in sales. He met with Val each morning and afternoon. He also met with the key managers, not only to introduce himself, but to convey his desire to work collaboratively with them in addressing the problems in sales. He was conscious not to flaunt his college education and to convey that he recognized he was a newcomer and had a lot to learn. In the middle of his second week, Val told him that his reception by the other employees was going very well. "Your enthusiasm and motivation seem to be contagious. Having you join us shows them that things need to change if we're going to reach our goals."

Rick noticed, however, that the managers always went out in groups, and he hadn't been invited along. He also wasn't included in the informal discussion groups that formed periodically during the day. In fact, the conversation usually stopped when he approached. Everyone was friendly, he thought; maybe it would just take a little more time.

By his third week Rick identified some of the problems in the sales department. Among the four salespeople, morale and productivity were moderate to low. He was unable to find any sales strategy, mission, or objectives. The records showed that Val was by far the leading salesperson. The others indicated that Mr. Peterson "always works with us very closely to make sure we do things right. If he senses there might be a problem, he steps in right away." After formulating a plan, Rick discussed it with Mr. Peterson. "First, I would like to institute weekly sales meetings so we keep everyone up-to-date. I also want to create a centralized sales database," he told him. Mr. Peterson smiled and agreed. Rick felt he was finally a manager. He did feel that he should have mentioned his idea for creating a sales department mission and strategy, but recalled Rosie's caution about not moving too fast.

Rick discussed with Mr. Ball the possibility of using the centralized computer system to run word processing and spreadsheet software on terminals. Mr. Ball was concerned that the data in the spreadsheets could be accessed by outsiders. Anyway, he didn't think the system could handle that task because its primary function was production. Puzzled, Rick asked if a PC could be allocated to him. Mr. Ball said that no one in the company had one.

"Well," Rick thought, "I'll just have to bring mine from home." The next Monday Rick walked through the office carrying his computer. Several of the other managers looked at him quizzically. Making light of it he said, "I'm not smart enough to keep everything in my head and I don't have enough time to write it all down on paper." As he was setting up the computer he got a call from Val. "Rick, that computer you brought in has caused a heck of a ruckus. Can you lie low with it until I get back late this afternoon?" Rick thought he sounded strained, but chalked it up to overwork. He agreed and left the computer on his desk, partly assembled. Five minutes later Rosie walked into his office.

"Do you think it's funny bringing that thing in here? What are you trying to prove—how backward we all are? How much better you are with your big initials behind your name? You're still an outsider here, buster, and don't forget it."

(continued)

Rick tried to explain how much more productive the sales department would be and that he had tried to use the company's computer system. However, Rosie wasn't listening. "Did you think about checking with me before bringing that in? With Val or even Walter? Don't you think we have a right to know what you're bringing in here?" Rick knew argument would do no good, so he apologized for not checking with everyone first. He said he had a meeting with Val for later to talk about it. Rosie said, "Good, talk to Val, but don't think he calls all the shots here."

At the meeting with Val, Val agreed that the computer would certainly help solve the problems in sales. "But, you have to be sensitive to the feelings of Rosie and the other managers. It would be best if you didn't use the computer for a while until things calm down."

The next day Walter walked into Rick's office. He told Rick he had moved far too fast with the computer. "That's not how it's done here, son. Maybe you're spending too much time listening to what Val says. He isn't really the one to talk to about these kinds of issues. Next time you just ask old Uncle Walter."

Without his computer, Rick spent the next few weeks building the database by hand and conducting sales meetings with his staff. He tried to set up meetings with Mr. Peterson, but Val was usually too busy. One day, Rick asked Diane Able about not being able to see Mr. Peterson and she said, "You know, you monopolized a lot of his time early on. Those of us who worked closely with him before you came were pushed aside so he could spend time with you. Now, it's your turn to wait."

"Are you the one who's been spending all the time with him?" Rick asked. "Well, it's been me and some of the other managers. We've really been taking a beating in sales so we need to figure out how to reduce our costs," Ms. Able answered. A few weeks later Rick was called in to Val's office. Val began, "Rick, you know we've been going through some bad times. We're reducing head count and I'm afraid you're one of the people we're going to let go. It has nothing to do with your work. You haven't really been here long enough to have either succeeded or failed. It's just that we had unrealistic expectations about how quickly things in sales would turn around. I feel terrible having to do this and I'll do everything I can to help you find another job."

After packing his things and loading up the car, Rick sat in his car and stared out the window. "Welcome to the real world," he thought to himself. ■

CASE QUESTIONS

1. Why do you think Rick was let go? How does reinforcement theory apply to this situation?
2. Explain Rosie's and Walter's reaction to Rick's computer in terms of resistance to change. How might Rick have used the concepts in this chapter to approach the computer situation so as to gain acceptance?
3. Explain Rick's inability to "fit in" using social learning theory. Where did the breakdowns occur?
4. If Val hired you to develop a management training program for the senior managers at PPP, how would you go about designing the program? Provide appropriate theoretical rationale to support your position.

EXERCISES

1. The following steps provide practice in implementing a social learning strategy.
   a. In consultation with a friend, coworker, or fellow student, identify a target behavior the person doesn't currently have but would like to have.
   b. Develop a social learning strategy for the person to acquire that behavior.
   c. Implement the strategy.
   d. In small groups or with the entire class describe what you tried to do and what happened.

2. In discussion groups of four to six people, identify the differences among you that impact the kind of training you would prefer. Use Table 3-7 on page 108 to start your discussion, but don't limit it to only those characteristics. What accounts for the differences and similarities among your group?

3. Observe an introductory course in computer programming. Then observe an introductory course in art or music. Which course uses a more behavioral and which a more cognitive approach to learning? If possible, interview the instructors to find out why they use the approach they do. Describe the match between the instructional approach and the subject matter.

4. Use the following to see how expectancy theory explains differences in student motivation.
   a. In a small group discuss the most important outcome you want to achieve in this class (it may or may not be a letter grade). Have each person indicate how valuable that outcome is to him or her using a scale from 1 = "not at all desirable" to 10 = "extremely desirable."
   b. After a person describes her most important outcome, ask that person to indicate how motivated she is to achieve this outcome compared with the other things she wants to do this term (use a scale of 1 = "not at all motivated" to 10 = "extremely motivated").
   c. Then ask the person to describe the things that must be done (performance level) in order to achieve that outcome.
   d. Next, ask the person to indicate the Expectancy 1 level (her belief that she will reach the performance level). Then ask the person to describe Expectancy 2 (the likelihood that successful performance will result in the outcome). Use probabilities (e.g., .1 = "very unlikely," .5 = "50% chance of happening," .9 = "very likely") to reflect expectancies.
   e. After everyone completes step d, examine the expectancy linkages to see how well they conform to the person's level of motivation. Discuss any discrepancies and why they exist.

5. This exercise is for those who are working together on a project. Without conversation among members of your group, write a list of the group's norms for performance on the project. When you are done, indicate whether you followed each of the norms and why. Once everyone has finished the tasks above collect all the responses and mix them up. Then hand them out. Allow each person to read the responses they received and compile the responses on a flip chart. Once all responses have been read discuss the implications of your group's perception of performance norms.

QUESTIONS FOR REVIEW

1. Explain the behavioral and cognitive approaches to learning. Which is most relevant to training? Explain your answer.
2. List an example for each of Gagné's learning types 3 through 8 and how each can be used in training. Use examples not used in the text.
3. You are a trainer who is explaining expectancy theory to a group of managers so they can better understand and deal with employee motivation problems. One of the managers says, "I don't have time for this theory stuff. I want real-world training that helps me in my job." How would you respond to the trainee? What is your rationale for your response?
4. List the nine events of instruction as outlined by Gagné-Briggs, and indicate how you would use them in a training situation.
5. Explain why different people need different training methods.
6. How does a work group exert control over the performance of a worker? Provide a rationale for why this "power" is a positive or negative thing.
7. How can training be designed to motivate learning and accommodate trainee differences?

CHAPTER 4

Needs Analysis

ANALYSIS PHASE

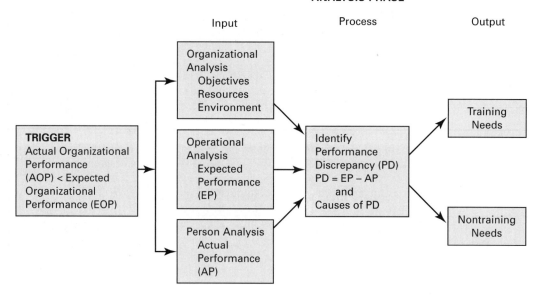

Input   Process   Output

TRIGGER
Actual Organizational Performance (AOP) < Expected Organizational Performance (EOP)

Organizational Analysis
  Objectives
  Resources
  Environment

Operational Analysis
  Expected Performance (EP)

Person Analysis
  Actual Performance (AP)

Identify Performance Discrepancy (PD)
PD = EP – AP
and
Causes of PD

Training Needs

Nontraining Needs

Learning Objectives

After reading this chapter, you should be able to:

- Describe the purpose of a needs analysis
- Describe what a competency is and why it is useful
- Explain the differences between proactive and reactive needs analysis and the situations favoring the use of one over the other
- List and describe the steps in conducting a needs analysis
- Describe the rationale for using performance appraisal information for a needs analysis and what type of performance appraisal method is appropriate
- Describe the relationship between needs analysis and the design and evaluation of training

114

Developing a Training Package at Westcan

Chris, a human resource manager at Westcan, was called into her boss's office one morning. Irven, the new VP of HR was telling her, "I just saw an old training film called *Meetings Bloody Meetings*, starring John Cleese. It deals with effective ways of running meetings. They showed it at the executive development seminar I'm attending." Irven, a competent and well-liked engineer, was promoted to vice president 3 months earlier. Although he had no HR expertise, he had been an effective production manager, and it was hoped that he would provide a measure of credibility to the HR department. In the past, HR had been seen as the department that forced its silly ideas on the rest of the company with little understanding of how to make those ideas work.

"With the number of team meetings we have company-wide, I think we need some training on how to conduct effective meetings," Irven said. "Everyone can use this training. It will be high profile and we can begin to gain the respect we need to be effective. What do you think?"

"Well," said Chris "I. . . ."

"Oh yes," Irven interjected, "I talked to a few managers this morning and they were enthusiastic about it. It's the first time I have ever seen managers enthusiastic about any type of training. Do we have such a training package available?"

"No, I don't believe so," Chris replied.

"Well," said Irven, "we need a one-day training session. It must be interesting, useful, and generalizable to all managers. Okay?" With that, Irven stood up, signaling that the meeting was over.

Chris went to work designing the training. She began by going to the local university and viewing the meetings film her boss had seen. Then she examined some books that dealt with meetings. She then decided she had a good idea of what made meetings effective, then called Larry, a friend at Satellite Systems, to see what he had. He faxed over a copy of a lecture he had given on the do's and don'ts of an effective meeting. It was nicely broken down into three parts: pre-meeting, meeting, and post-meeting. That information and a simulated meeting (to provide hands-on practice) could make up the one-day training program. Chris had never written a simulation and would need some help. She put in a call to one of her subordinates, Karen, a recent university graduate who had majored in HR. Karen would surely be able to help develop a simulation.

Why Conduct a Training Needs Analysis?

What is wrong with the situation at Westcan? It is a scene that repeats itself in some form every day. The boss wants some training, and the HR manager complies. After all, the boss must know what kind of training employees need, right? Maybe not. Recall from Chapter 1 that a training needs analysis (TNA) is a systematic method for determining what caused performance to be less than expected or required. The focus of training is performance improvement,[1] which becomes obvious if you turn back to the beginning of the chapter, and look at the analysis phase figure. Note the "trigger" for doing a needs analysis is a organizational performance discrepancy (actual or expected). Is there one at Westcan? There may be. In this situation a VP suggesting training could be considered the "trigger" to conduct a needs analysis. However, to answer the specific question about where a performance discrepancy exists, a needs analysis is required. Simply recognizing an enthusiasm for such training does not answer that question.

If a problem is evident with meetings, are all meetings ineffective or just some? Do all managers feel the same or just a few? Is the problem with knowing how to run an effective meeting or are other issues causing the meetings to be ineffective? How much do these managers already know about meetings, and how skillful are they at applying this knowledge? These and other questions need to be answered before Chris begins to design the training program for effective meetings. Yet, Chris assumes she knows what is required and begins to develop the training based on these assumptions without conducting a TNA to determine exactly what the deficiencies are. Think about this scenario as we examine the process of a TNA. Would you want to be in Chris's shoes? We refer back to this example throughout the chapter and at the end we give you the rest of the story.

A TNA is important because it helps to determine whether a deficiency can be corrected through training. In some cases the TNA determines that employees lack necessary KSAs to do the job, and training is required. In other cases employees have the KSAs to do the job, but roadblocks to effective performance are discovered that need to be removed. Training professionals make sure the right training is provided to the right people by conducting a needs analysis. As we indicated earlier, Chris at Westcan, is overlooking a critical part of the training process. She did not complete a TNA, instead relying on her boss telling her what type of training is needed. She jumped directly to the training design phase. By first conducting a TNA, she could accomplish several important things:

- Increase the chances that the time and money spent on training would be spent wisely.
- Determine the benchmark for evaluation of training.
- Increase the motivation of participants.
- Align her training activities with the strategic plan.

Why spend thousands of dollars, or more, on a training program no one needs. With increased concern about costs in organizations today, it is important that all departments, including human resources, justify expenses.

A TNA provides a benchmark (pre-measure) of the skills trainees possess prior to training. This benchmark can be compared to a measure of the skills acquired in training (post-measure). With pre- and post-measures, it is possible to demonstrate the cost savings or value added as a result of training.[2] Although some evaluation designs do not require them, pretests provide a logical benchmark for evaluation. The needs analysis can provide that pretest.

It is always better if trainees are motivated to learn when they come to training. A TNA ensures that training focuses on KSAs the trainees really need. Training that is perceived as relevant is more likely to create interest. Consider the employees who are sent for training but do not need it. Are they going to take the training seriously? Probably not. In fact, their lack of interest may be distracting to those who need the training or, worse, may cause the other trainees not to take the training seriously. The needs analysis also allows the trainer to explain at the start of training, how the training will be useful. A good TNA ensures that only those who need the training are included, and provides the data to show trainees why the training is needed.

As we discussed in Chapter 2, implementing a strategic plan requires careful analysis of the organization's human resource capabilities. A TNA is the process for determining the degree to which employees possess the necessary KSAs to carry out the strategies. The resulting training can then be designed to align with this strategic plan. The TNA also provides HRD with information as to the relevance of training to the strategic plan.

Conducting a TNA is not always necessary. For example, when an organization is trying to convey a new corporate message or instill a new culture (attitude change), it is advisable to educate all employees. Consider a company's concerns regarding sexual harassment. To be sure everyone is aware of how seriously top management considers breaches of their "sexual harassment" policy, company-wide education on this issue should take place. Sending everyone to a workshop on sexual harassment ensures that management's expectations regarding this issue are clear. It also demonstrates to the courts the employer's position, should an employee consider a sexual harassment lawsuit.

Another situation in which a TNA might not be necessary is when team-building skills are needed for new teams. Here the goal is to build the dynamics of the team so that the members work together cohesively and effectively, as well as to provide the relevant KSAs. Everyone on the team must be part of the training, even though he or she may already possess many team KSAs.

For most types of training, however, a needs analysis will increase the relevance and effectiveness of training. For example, team building for teams that have been working together for a while would benefit from a TNA. In this case the needs analysis focus is on the team, not the individuals. Only teams that demonstrate problems in effectiveness or cohesion (the trigger) would go through a TNA to determine what training (if any) was needed. Teams already functioning effectively would not need to attend, so the overall cost of training is reduced.

When to Conduct a Training Needs Analysis

As the needs analysis model at the beginning of the chapter indicates, a needs analysis is conducted when a triggering event occurs. A triggering event occurs when one or more key decision makers communicate that a performance problem exists and it needs to be corrected. Who the key decision makers are will vary from company to company and may include the head of HR or HRD. The performance problem may or may not actually exist, but the key decision maker believes it does. At this point the TNA is initiated. It may be formal and thorough or informal and cursory. In any case, the purpose of the TNA is to find out whether the performance problem actually exists, and if so, is it worth fixing and what is its cause.

The triggering event will determine which of two approaches to needs analysis will be taken. These two approaches are called proactive TNA and reactive TNA, and differ in where they are focused. A **proactive TNA** focuses on an anticipated performance problem in the future. A **reactive TNA** focuses on a perceived performance problem in the present. Let's look at an example of each.

First, in an example of the proactive approach, an organization decides as part of its strategic plan to implement statistical process control (SPC) to improve the quality of its widgets. So, sometime in the near future the expected performance (EP) for employees producing the widget will include the "use of SPC methods." Potential for a future discrepancy exists if the employees do not have these KSAs. This potential gap triggers a proactive TNA, to determine whether employees will be able to perform as expected when SPC is implemented. An assessment of these employees' actual performance (AP) reveals they have little ability to do the simplest of arithmetic. Because arithmetic skills are needed in the use of SPC methods, this discrepancy will need to be addressed before SPC can be implemented. So, a proactive TNA is conducted when the expectation is that a deficiency might occur based on changes planned in the organization.

The reactive TNA, on the other hand, is triggered by a current discrepancy. For example, the number of widgets produced per week is expected to be 5,000. The AP is 4,300, indicating a discrepancy that needs to be investigated. Both types of TNA follow the same procedures, and the slight differences in orientation will be discussed in more detail later.

The TNA is conducted because a performance discrepancy may occur for many reasons (see Figure 4-1), only one of which is a lack of KSAs. Consider the problem at the telecommunications company Ameritech. Installation and repair employees were asked to make sales pitches to customers about Ameritech services and equipment when on a service call, with the hope of increasing revenue. Examination of the company data on sales indicated few sales took place. The AOP was less than EOP, triggering a TNA. Note, in Figure 4-1, a number of possible causes of the PD are listed. If the cause is not a KSA deficiency, then some nontraining solution is required to alleviate the discrepancy. In the Ameritech situation, it was not a training issue.

FIGURE 4-1 Model of Process When Performance Discrepancy Is Identified

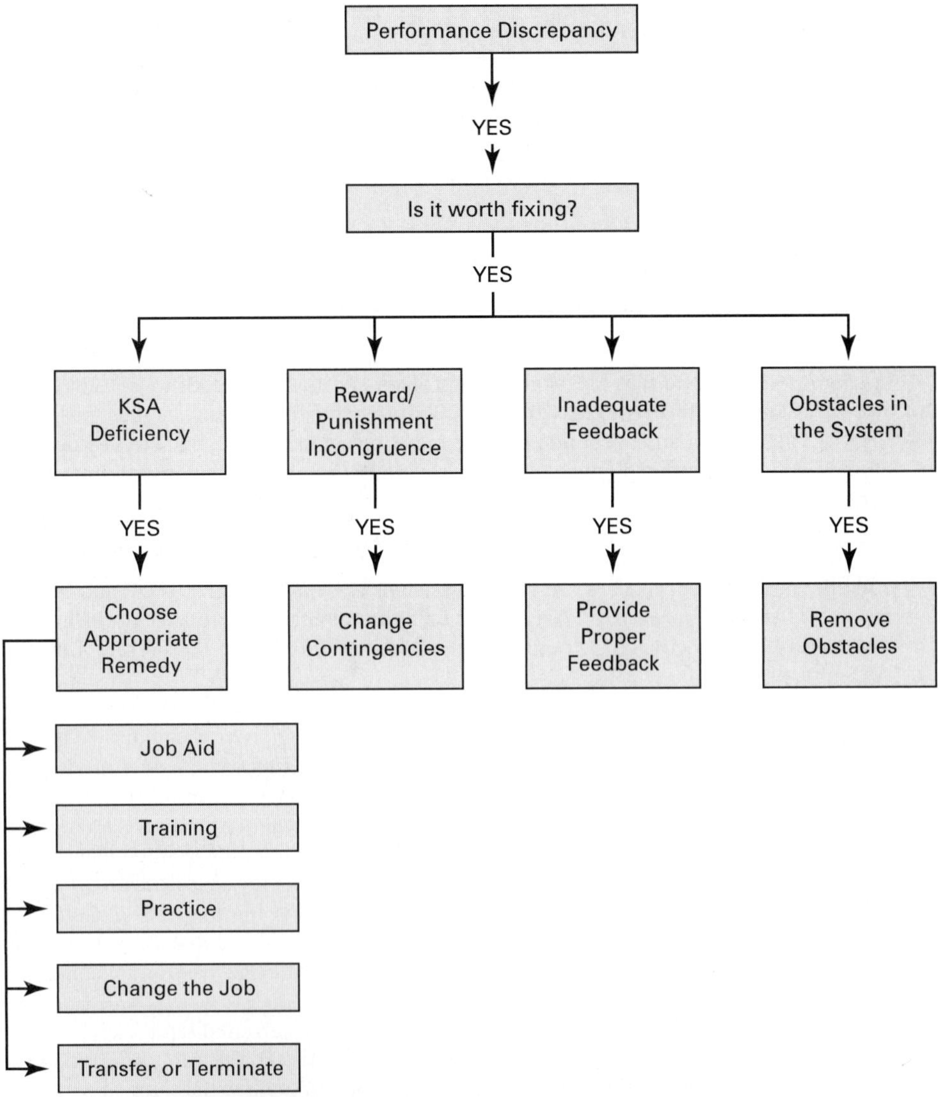

Source: Adapted from Michalak, D. F., and E. G. Yager. 1979. *Making the Training Process Work.*

Installation and repair employees' performance was based on the time it took to complete a call. A certain amount of time was allotted to each type of call. If you took longer than the time allotted for a number of calls your performance would be rated as below average. This time allotment was not changed when employees were asked to stick around and try to sell some products and services. So, most employees simply did not spend any time selling. Reward/punishment incongruities were causing the PD. We return to examine Figure 4-1 in more detail later, but now let's examine where we look for discrepancies.

Where to Look for Performance Discrepancies

Identifying performance discrepancies is not accomplished by looking in any single place. Archival data such as profitability, market share, grievance levels, productivity, and quality measures provide some appropriate indicators of how the organization is operating and where problems are arising. Table 4-1 provides a list of sources for gathering data related to potential discrepancies. The first one, "organizational goals and objectives," could identify discrepancies at the present time. Let's assume that quality is an important part of the strategic plan, and the objective for rejects (EP) is less than one per thousand. The actual performance (AP) is 12 per thousand. A definite discrepancy exists here; because AOP < EOP, a reactive TNA is implemented. Alternatively, we could determine from the strategic plan that a discrepancy will arise in the future. The new strategic plan indicates a substantial modernization of the plant. One of the objectives is to purchase new computerized machinery. Although no discrepancy is identifiable at the present time, one certainly might be when the new equipment arrives. This possibility means the HRD department will need to focus on assessing current employees' KSAs for operating the new machinery. If their KSAs are not sufficient, then a PD exists for the future. Because the potential for a future discrepancy prompts a TNA, it would be a proactive TNA.

The second on the list, "labor inventory," is also useful to determine discrepancies in the future and what types of training need to take place to prevent such a discrepancy from occurring. Knowing that a number of senior engineers are retiring over the next few years triggers the HRD department to start training those in line for promotion to obtain some of the necessary skills. Not being aware of the retirements could lead to a discrepancy because the company would lack enough senior engineers to manage the expected number of projects.

Data sources 3 through 8 provide information about areas where potential performance discrepancies might exist. Knowing the number of grievances are primarily coming from particular supervisors helps focus on those supervisors and their areas. Identification of high absenteeism in a particular area or an accident rate that is increasing provides the HRD department with early signs of problems. Quicker identification of problems leads to quicker solutions, regardless of whether they are training problems. This is one secret to an effective HRD department. Cindy Baerman, the Human Resource Development Officer of Miller Brewing company, began showing up to production meetings a few years back. She received funny looks, as the meetings were held to focus on production problems. Why would HRD want to be there? As Cindy pointed out, "What better place to learn of the kind of performance problems line managers are having?"[3] For her, constant monitoring of production problems was a critical role in the early identification of performance discrepancies, and a focus on continuous improvement. Being able to react quickly to maintain and improve performance is the first step in a continuous performance improvement framework, so important in today's environment.[4]

Now let's examine the analysis used for determining whether the PD requires a training or nontraining intervention. To make this determination, let's return to the analysis phase of the training model at the beginning of the chapter. It provides a framework for discussing the TNA process.

TABLE 4-1 Data Sources for Locating Performance Discrepancies

Data Source Recommended	Training Need Implications	Example
1. Organizational Goals and Objectives and Budget	Where training emphasis can and should be placed. These provide normative standards of both direction and expected impact, which can highlight deviations from objectives and performance problems.	To maintain a quality standard of no more than one reject per thousand. Goal is to become ISO-certified and $90,000 has been allocated to this effort.
2. Labor Inventory	Where training is needed to fill gaps caused by retirement, turnover, age, etc. This provides an important demographic database regarding possible scope of training needs.	Thirty percent of our truck drivers will retire over the next 4 years.
3. Organizational Climate Indexes	These "quality of working life" indicators at the organization level may help focus on problems that have training components.	
a. Labor-management data, strikes, lockouts, etc. b. Grievances c. Turnover d. Absenteeism e. Suggestions f. Productivity g. Accidents h. Short-term sickness i. Observation of employee behavior	All these items related to either work participation or productivity are useful both in discrepancy analysis and in helping management set a value on the behaviors it wishes improved through training once training has been established as a relevant solution.	Seventy percent of the grievances are related to the behaviors of six supervisors. High absenteeism for clerical staff. Accident rate for line workers increasing.
j. Attitude surveys	Good for locating discrepancies between organizational expectations and perceived results.	Line workers' attitude toward teamwork is poor.
	Valuable feedback; look especially for patterns and repeat complaints.	Perception that promotions in the office are on basis of favoritism.
k. Customer complaints		
4. Analysis of Efficiency Indexes	Cost accounting concepts may represent ratio between actual performance and desired or standard performance.	
a. Costs of labor		Labor costs increased by 8 percent in the last year.
b. Costs of materials c. Quality of product		Number of rejects increased by 30 percent since the new batch of line workers began work.
d. Equipment utilization e. Costs of distribution		

TABLE 4-1 (continued)

Data Source Recommended	*Training Need Implications*	*Example*
f. Waste		Waste steel increased by 14 percent since we began using part-time workers.
g. Downtime		The Hi Hoe (a digging machine) has been down for repairs four to six times a week since the new machine operator was hired.
h. Late deliveries		
i. Repairs		
5. Changes in System or Subsystem	New or changed equipment may present training problem.	The line was shut down about once per day since the new machinery was installed.
		Waste has doubled since purchasing the new cutting tool.
6. Management Requests or Management Interrogation	One of the most common techniques of identification of performance discrepancies.	The production manager indicates a drop in quality since the layoffs.
7. Exit Interviews	Often information not otherwise available can be obtained, especially in problem areas and supervisory training needs.	Almost all the production workers who quit indicated the pressure for production as the main reason.
8. MBO or Work Planning and Review Systems	Provides performance review, potential review, and long-term business objectives. Provides actual performance data on a recurring basis so that baseline measurements may be known and subsequent improvement or deterioration of performance can be identified and analyzed.	

Source: References for all of these methods can be found in Moore, M., and P. Dutton. 1978. Training needs analysis: Review critique. *Academy of Management Review* 3:532–45.

The Framework for Conducting a TNA

Recall from Figure 1-6 in Chapter 1, all five phases of the training model consist of an input, a process, and an output. The "input" for the analysis phase is made up of organizational analysis, operational analysis, and person analysis.[5] The "process" is where we determine the specific nature of the PD, and its cause or causes. The "output" provides us with either training or nontraining needs—and in some cases—both. Next, we provide a general description of the three inputs as an overview of the whole analysis prior to digging into the details of each.

Organizational analysis involves looking at the internal environment of the organization—influences that could affect employee performance—and determining its fit with organizational goals and objectives. It is this analysis that provides identification of PD at the organizational level. Imagine Company ABC that decides one of its goals is to become team oriented in its production operation. Examining the various policies of the organization reveals an incentive system that pays up to 15 percent of base pay for individual productivity above quota. This focus on individual productivity is not in line with the new goals of a "team approach, and could cause team members to be more concerned with their individual performance." It needs to be removed or changed to align with the goals of a team-based approach. The organizational analysis is also an examination of how the internal environment affects job performance. In the ABC example, if both Bill and Mary again do not come to the team meeting, does it mean they are not interested? Perhaps, but it is more likely they are working on beating their quotas so they will receive the bonus pay. Finally, the organizational analysis identifies constraints on training. Consider the small business owner who employs unskilled assembly-line workers, who are unable to read well. He wishes to move to a more team-oriented approach. The owner does not have the funds or time to develop a remedial reading course, which presents an organizational constraint and leads to the development of training that does not require reading.

Operational analysis examines specific jobs to determine the requirements (KSAs) necessary to get the job done (i.e., expected job performance). This process is generally called a **job analysis**, or task analysis, and requires an extensive analysis of a job to determine all the tasks necessary to perform the job at the expected level. After all tasks are identified, the next step is to determine the KSAs necessary to perform each of the tasks. Each task needs to be examined by asking the question "What knowledge skills and attitudes are necessary to be able to perform this task at the expected level?" The KSAs obtained from the analysis are the ones that an incumbent must have in order to perform at the expected level. A number of ways can be utilized to obtain this information, such as interviewing incumbents and their supervisors, observing the job, and so forth.

Finally, **person analysis** examines those who occupy the jobs to see whether they possess the required KSAs necessary to do the job. Here we measure the actual job performance of those on the job to see whether they are performing at an acceptable level. This task may seem easy enough; simply look at the supervisor's appraisal of the incumbents. As you will see later, however, many problems can arise with performance appraisals completed by supervisors, such as halo, leniency, and other effects. So, as a result, other methods are also used to obtain this type of information. Asking incumbents themselves, for example, or asking coworkers are two other methods. All methods have strengths and weaknesses that will be discussed in more detail later.

These "inputs" are conceptually distinct, but in practice much of the information is gathered at the same time and is closely interrelated. For example, information related to all three types of analysis can be collected from the job incumbents. Questions would include "Do any particular organizational policies or procedures that you must follow negatively affect your job performance?" (organization analysis); "Describe for me the tasks you perform when you first arrive at work" (operational analysis); "Do you believe you are lacking any skills that, if you had them, might enhance your ability to perform at a higher level?" (person analysis). Now let's examine each of these inputs to a TNA in more detail, and then look at some specific issues surrounding the two types, proactive and reactive.

ORGANIZATIONAL ANALYSIS

As noted earlier, organizational analysis can be "triggered" in response to a new strategic plan (proactive) or some identified performance discrepancy (reactive).

Regarding the former, think back to Chapter 2, and the strategic planning process. HRD is involved in this process to ensure that those determining the strategic plan have the necessary information to make the right decisions in terms of the direction the organization will take. When the strategic plan is finally decided upon, then HRD must respond to that plan. The organizational analysis in response to a strategic plan is a major undertaking. First, it involves examination of the strategic plan (mission and strategies), which describes where the organization wishes to be and how it will get there. Then, the analysis of the organizational environment provides information as to where the organization is currently. The discrepancy between these two—where an organization wishes to be (expected performance) and currently is (actual performance)—is a performance discrepancy. The organizational analysis determines where this discrepancy is located. We then focus our attention there and ask: Is the identified discrepancy worth fixing? If yes, then we know where to conduct our operational and person analysis. Consider the organization that makes the decision to increase customer satisfaction through better integration of production and sales. They will pursue this goal by adopting a team structure in these two areas. The "wishes to be" (expected performance) is having these employees operating within teams. An organizational analysis of where the organization is at the present time (actual performance) shows all management and office employees in production and sales are operating in teams, and doing so effectively. However, no teams are operating at the shop floor. The shop floor, therefore, becomes the area of focus.

When an organizational analysis is done in response to a particular performance discrepancy (reactive), it is usually of less magnitude than one done for strategic planning (proactive). Such an analysis could occur when a unit fails to meet its objectives. For example, production records might indicate production in Frank's crew dropped steadily over the past 2 months. It is now 15 percent below expected. Production in Frank's unit is the PD. Now you begin looking for the causes of the discrepancy.

To sum it up, an organization analysis focuses on the strategies of the organization, the resources in the organization, the allocation of these resources,[6] and the total internal environment.[7] The internal environment includes an examination of structures, policies and procedures, job-design work-flow processes, and other factors that facilitate or inhibit an employee's ability to meet job performance expectations. This assessment is necessary to help identify the cause of discrepancies and specifically to determine whether discrepancies are, in fact, training issues. According to Nancy Gordon, a TNA analyst at Ameritech, about 85 percent of all requests for training turned out to be related to issues that could not be addressed by training. They were, instead, incongruencies in the organizational environment that inhibited or prevented the appropriate work behaviors (see Training in Action 4-1). An organizational analysis, then, should be able to provide information about the following:

- The mission and strategies of an organization
- The resources and allocation of the resources, given the objectives
- The factors in the internal environment that may be causing the problem
- The impact of the preceding factors on developing, providing, and transferring the KSAs to the job if training is the chosen solution to the PD

Mission and Strategies

In the organizational analysis, an examination of the mission and strategies helps the analyst place the training in a particular context. Consider the Ford Engine Plant mission statement presented in Chapter 2, which stated "Our mission is to continually improve our products and services to meet our customers' needs, allowing us to prosper as a business and provide a reasonable return to our stockholders." A strategy that arose from that mission statement was to focus on the team approach for continuous improvement. One type of training to support this strategy is training in problem solving. Problem solving training requires openness and trust to be effective and is therefore in line with the team approach. If the workers in the plant are offered training in traditional negotiations skills, is this in line with the team approach? Perhaps not. Traditional negotiations training often teaches that it is useful not to reveal all your information, but instead hold back and attempt to get the best deal for yourself (or your department). To offer

---

INCONGRUITIES IN THE ORGANIZATIONAL ENVIRONMENT

A bank manager decided that in order to increase profits, he would send all his tellers to a training workshop about the products and services the bank offered. He wanted the front-line employees (tellers) to provide such information to customers who came into the bank. This practice would increase the amount of products and services sold.

The manager developed a method of tracking the number of products and services sold so he would have a measure of the success of the training. After a time he noticed no increase occurred in sales. Training did not result in an increase in sales. What went wrong?

Analysis revealed that when tellers returned from training, they also returned to the same appraisal system in place before the training. Performance assessment was based largely on the number of customers the teller was able to process. Why would a teller risk receiving a low performance rating in order to spend time telling customers about the products and services being offered by the bank?

Source: Adapted from Johnson, C. 1995. Making your training stick. *HR Magazine,* May, pp. 55–60.

---

such training would at best not reinforce an environment of openness and trust, and at worst actually counteract it.

The organizational mission and strategies also provide the priorities for training. Training resources are always finite, so decisions must be made as to where to spend the training budget. If, for example, "Quality is job one" at Ford, the analyst knows that development of KSAs relating to quality should receive priority. Thinking back to the Westcan case, can you identify how the company's priorities would be related to training needs?

Resources

Capital Resources   When the term *resources* is used, issues of finance, equipment, facilities, and the like usually come to mind. Recall in Chapter 2, during the **strategic planning** phase, decisions are made as to where money would be spent. If a large expenditure is made on new equipment for the machinists or toward becoming ISO 9000 certified, these strategic decisions will help determine the priorities for the HRD department. In the case of purchasing new equipment for the machinists, the priority is clear, we need to concentrate on the assessment of the machinist position. We need to assess the machinists' level of KSAs to determine whether they need training to operate the new machinery. This focus is based on the financial decisions made at the strategic level. Likewise, the strategic choice of becoming ISO 9000 certified indicates to the HRD department that it would need to provide support in that area. In both these cases, significant company resources will be directed toward these strategic initiatives. After all, if the employees are not able to operate the new equipment or engage in the tasks required for ISO certification, the money put toward those initiatives will be wasted.

The other main concern for HRD is based on its own budget. Decisions as to how to provide the required training is a function of the money HRD has to spend. Hiring external consultants versus internally developing training depends on a number of issues, not the least of which is the cost. In the Westcan case, Chris decided to develop the training herself. Hiring a consultant to provide the training might get better results, but Chris would have to weigh that against other training needs at Westcan, given her limited budget.

Human Resources   The two stages of examining the organization's human resource KSAs include the more general strategic needs assessment and the more specific assessment of the training needs. First, at the strategic level, HRD provides top management with the skill levels and potential of the current human resource contingent to support various strategies. This way top management knows the capabilities of their employees and can factor them into their strategic decision making. Heinz Canada's Leamington plant decided a number of years back that their strategic plan was to focus on the efficient production of ketchup. They wanted to purchase a state-of-the-art automated ketchup maker. The HRD department provided top management with information on the KSAs of the current workforce. This information indicated no one had the skills necessary, and in fact many had reading difficulties, so operating computer-controlled machinery might be a concern. Because the strategic planning group knew this information early in the strategic planning phase, they were able to make an informed decision about how to proceed. They considered the following choices:

- Abandon the idea of purchasing such equipment, and consider alternative strategic plans.
- Hire employees who had the skills to operate such machinery.
- Train current employees to operate the machinery.

Note the first choice is to abandon that particular strategic plan over one where existing skills of the employees are available. That choice was not followed, and Heinz choose to move forward with the plan, and to train employees (rather than hire new employees with the skills), which again was a strategic decision. Because they addressed the issue early, they gave themselves plenty of time to train employees to perform at the necessary skill level.

The strategic analysis provides a great deal of information about the capabilities of the workforce. This information assists in the decision as to what strategic plan will be followed. However, it is not enough. Once a decision on a strategic plan is approved, the focus moves to the area where priorities are identified from the strategic plan.

This second stage—the specific TNA level, identified from the HR strategy—focuses on those employees who are identified as facing performance discrepancies in areas important in the strategic plan. This focus would be the machinists in one of the earlier examples. What about in the Heinz example? Recall that none of the Heinz employees show the required KSAs to operate the machinery being proposed. So, although they are effective employees at the present time, a PD will develop when the new equipment arrives. The HRD department priority is to provide the employees with the requisite KSAs so when the ketchup machine arrives they will be prepared to operate it.

Organizational Environment

The other main objective of the organizational analysis is to examine the various structures (e.g., mechanistic or organic) and designs (e.g., pay systems and reward policies) operating in an organization to determine how congruent they are with the performance objectives of the unit in which the discrepancies were identified. Identifying these incongruencies early, and changing them, will help ensure that when training is complete, it will transfer to the job.

Consider two organizations:

Organization A decides to move toward a more team-oriented approach. The mission and objectives reflect this recent change in company policy. Among the present procedures is the use of a suggestion box, which provides rewards for individual suggestions for improving company performance.

Organization B's mission and objectives can be summed up as "quality is most important." One of the organization's policies is that performance appraisals for first-line management provide a measure of how well these managers meet productivity quotas, but they measure nothing related to quality.

In the first scenario, does the individual incentive system reinforce or hinder the team approach? If, after training and implementation of the team approach, no innovative ideas were forthcoming, would that mean the training was not effective? You cannot really tell. The skills may be learned but not transferred to the job. Consider the reward/punishment incongruence (see Figure 4-1) between rewarding for individual ideas (suggestion box) and instituting a team approach. Identifying this incongruence and removing it before instituting the team approach would facilitate transfer of the training. Training in Action 1-2 (page 12) and 1-3 (page 13) also show where organizational analysis could identify a reward/punishment incongruence that needed to be addressed in order to facilitate transfer of training.

In the second scenario, would you expect training in quality issues to be effective or is training even needed? The results may be attainable by simply redesigning the performance appraisal to emphasize quality. These examples illustrate the value of conducting an analysis of the organizational environment as it relates to performance deficiencies. Consider one other point. The analysis at the environment level should not be conducted until you have an idea what jobs are targeted either for their performance deficiencies or because of future changes. This targeting allows a certain degree of focus when you are conducting the analysis; you gather data that are relevant to those jobs only. Otherwise, you may gather an enormous amount of information on jobs that may be irrelevant and therefore a waste of valuable resources.

Where to Collect Data

Once a discrepancy is identified in a specific department or location, then the cause of the discrepancy needs to be determined. The assumption *is not* that training is required to alleviate the discrepancy. Don't forget what Nancy Gordon said: about 85 percent of training requests turn out to be solvable without training. To gather data, Table 4-2 identifies potential individuals you may wish to interview and points to raise with them. Note the similarity between the "What to ask" in Table 4-2 and Table 4-1.

OPERATIONAL ANALYSIS

When a performance discrepancy is identified, you conduct an operational analysis in conjunction with the organizational analysis in order to fully understand the nature of the discrepancy. The operational analysis determines exactly what is required of employees in order for them to be effective. Let's say you are investigating why production unit A is showing a steady increase in rejects. The actual performance of unit A is 15 rejects per thousand. Expected performance is one reject per thousand. You note that the increase in rejects corresponds with the hiring of nine new production workers. You might be tempted to say the problem is the new employees did not receive enough training. You might be right, but you really do not know for sure. The operational analysis helps you to:

- Determine what KSAs are required by employees in unit A in order to meet the expected performance.
- Determine the characteristics of the task environment (workflow, equipment functionability, ergonomic concerns, and so forth) that are required for performance to be able to meet expectations.

Note that at this point, operational and organizational analysis overlap because they both examine factors that can contribute to a deficit in performance. Table 4-3 provides a number of sources for obtaining such information. Techniques for obtaining task and KSA data are usually some type of job analysis, and sources are shown in Table 4-3. The most frequently used process includes questioning both the incumbents and supervisors of the incumbents. Let's now examine this process of analyzing a job, and the issues you need to consider.

TABLE 4-2 What Do You Ask and of Whom?

What to Ask	*Who to Ask*
Mission Goals and Objectives	
What are the goals and objectives of the organization?	Top management
How much money has been allocated to any new initiatives?	Relevant department managers, supervisors, and incumbents
Is there general understanding of these objectives?	
Social Influences	
What is the general feeling in the organization regarding meeting goals and objectives?	Top management
What is the social pressure in your department regarding these goals, objectives, and productivity?	Relevant department managers, supervisors, and incumbents
Reward Systems	
What are the rewards, and how are they distributed?	Top management
Are any incentives tied to the goals and objectives?	Relevant department managers, supervisors, and incumbents
What specifically do high performers get as rewards?	
Job Design	
How are the jobs organized?	Relevant supervisors and incumbents, perhaps relevant department managers
Where does their work/material/information come from and where do they send it when done?	
Does the design of the job in any way inhibit incumbents from being high performers?	
Job Performance	
How do employees know what level of performance is acceptable?	Relevant supervisors and incumbents
How do they find out if their level of performance is acceptable?	
Is a formal feedback process (e.g., performance appraisal) utilized?	
Are there resources for help if required?	
Methods and Practices	
What are the policies/procedures/rules in the organization? Which if any inhibit performance?	Relevant department managers, supervisors, and incumbents

TABLE 4-3 Data Sources for Operational Analysis

Sources for Obtaining Job Data	Training Need Implications	Practical Concerns
1. Job Descriptions	Outlines the job's typical duties and responsibilities but is not meant to be all-inclusive.	Need to determine who developed them. Sometimes written up quickly by supervisor or incumbent with little understanding of what is required.
2. Job Specifications	List specified tasks required for each job. More specific than job descriptions. Specifications may extend to judgments of knowledge and skills required of job incumbents.	May be product of the job description and suffer from the same problems.
3. Performance Standards	Objectives of the tasks of job and standards by which they are judged, and may include baseline data as well.	Useful if available and accurate, but often organizations do not have formal performance standards.
4. Perform the Job	Most effective way of determining specific tasks, but has serious limitations in higher-level jobs because performance requirements typically have longer gaps between performance and resulting outcomes.	Many concerns. Time required to do job fully, skills necessary, and safety concerns all make this method unlikely as an option. Easy, short-cycle-type jobs are a possibility.
5. Observe Job–Work Sampling		Useful again for short-cycle, primarily behavior-based jobs. Even there, however, must be aware that the impact of being observed can influence behavior.

6. Ask Questions About the Job
   a. Of the job holder
   b. Of the supervisor
		Most often used method and when done correctly can provide accurate data. To be useful should ask the both the job holder and his supervisor.

7. Review Literature Concerning Job
   a. In professional journals
   b. In practitioner journals
   c. From other industries
	Useful for determining specific issues related to the job and what is being done by others and what the results are.	Need to be sure information is relevant to your organization.

Analyzing the Job

The following steps are worth considering when you are about to analyze a job.

What Is the Job   The first step is to determine exactly what job is going to be analyzed. In today's environment, a common job title can mask real differences in the tasks that are done. An extreme example is at Honda Manufacturing, where everyone's job title is "associate," from the line worker to top management. Other organizations use the same job title for employees who do different tasks, because they work in different departments, geographical locations, and so on. Therefore, it is important to define clearly the parameters for the job to be analyzed. Welding discrepancies in the Honda shop, for example, would require an examination of the job of associate in the welding shop only. Once the job is defined, it should be clear how many employees work in the target job and where they are located.

Where to Collect Data   As Table 4-3 indicates, data can be gathered from a number of sources. Job descriptions and specifications may be good sources of data for understanding the job and its basic requirements. If this information was originally gathered through a job analysis you can be more confident of its value. Even if it was not gathered in such a manner, it provides a basic understanding of the job (through reading the job descriptions and so forth) and is useful before starting to ask questions of these employees.

Whom to Ask   When analyzing the job, you need to know what tasks are performed on the job. For this information you ask incumbents and supervisors. Incumbents are asked for two reasons:

1. They are the employees who do the job and know exactly what tasks are being performed.
2. Trainees will feel more ownership from any resulting training if they were included as part of the data collection.

Often the tasks required vary with an incumbent's experience. In this case, you need to choose a cross-section of incumbents based on tenure on the job.[8] A service person for a gas utility might start out relighting appliances (furnaces, water heaters and so forth). After some experience they are expected to troubleshoot domestic appliances, change thermocouples, fan controls, and so forth. After a few more years, they could be expected to work on commercial appliances in restaurants. After a number of years they would graduate to larger commercial furnaces and other high-yield gas appliances.

Data should also be gathered from the incumbents' supervisors for the following reasons:

- This information provides a different perspective and helps yield a well-rounded concept of exactly what is required.
- When discrepancies are noted between what the supervisor and the incumbents say, an investigation into the reason for the discrepancy can provide useful information.

Earlier we suggested that trainers need OD skills. In this instance, those skills would provide an effective way of resolving such differences between incumbents and supervisors regarding how the job should be performed. A more proactive approach is to avoid conflicting beliefs between subordinates and supervisors in the first place. You can do this by implementing the job expectation technique.[9] Using this technique, you would facilitate a meeting between subordinates and supervisors to discuss the job responsibilities of the subordinates. The goal here is to clarify job expectations. Although this process sounds simplistic, it requires trust and respect between supervisors and their subordinates. In reality, many job incumbents learn about their job through working with other incumbents and through trial and error.

Who Should Select Incumbents   The selection process should be done by the job analyst, not the supervisor or manager. If you let supervisors make the decision they may choose on the basis of who is available at the time, who they prefer to give the opportunity to, or any other reasons that quite likely would result in a biased sample. Perhaps more important, however, the incumbents may question the real purpose of the assessment and provide inaccurate data.

How Many to Ask Different jobs in any organization are filled with different numbers of incumbents. One incumbent makes the decision easy. When large numbers of incumbents are involved, the more individuals you obtain information from, the better picture you will be able to construct of the job. Furthermore, the more involved in this process incumbents are, the more committed to the training those incumbents are likely to be. At a minimum, talk to a representative sample of incumbents covering all aspects of the job. How you choose this sample is discussed under the next heading.

Exactly how many to ask is determined by your method of data gathering and the amount of time available. Let's say that each of five levels within the job consists of 20 incumbents, for a total of 100 incumbents. You have chosen to interview in small groups. You could have four interview sessions, each with five incumbents; one from each level. If time allowed, you might want to double the sessions to eight for increased participation and a more representative sample.

How to Select The best way to select the participants is through representative sampling of all those incumbents who are performing "adequately or better" on the job. The incumbents need to be placed into subgroups based on relevant characteristics, such as their level in the job (e.g., mechanic 1, mechanic 2). Once the categories are developed within the job, the job analyst should choose within these categories on the basis of other factors, such as years in the category, performance level, gender, and so on, in order to ensure that different views of the job are obtained. Note that we do not advocate random sampling. Random sampling is effective only when you have large numbers of incumbents who are similar, which is seldom the case in a particular job. One other consideration: If the organization operates in more than one location, particularly in different cities, you need to have input from different locations.

What to Ask About Several job analysis techniques are available for gathering information about a job. Two main categories are worker-oriented and task-oriented approaches.

Worker-Oriented Approach. The **worker-oriented approach** focuses on the KSAs that are required on the job, rather than the tasks or behaviors. Figure 4-2 provides an example of questions from a worker-oriented approach (position analysis questionnaire). A drawback of the worker-oriented approach is that task statements are not available to show how the KSAs are linked to the tasks. Such a link is useful in justifying the KSA requirements. This link was not shown at Canadian National Railroad a number of years back. For the job of carman, it was determined that you needed to have a certain amount of strength to do the job. When women applied they were told they simply were not strong enough to do the job. After discrimination charges were filed against the railroad, a judge asked management to indicate what tasks required such strength. Management was forced to improvise. No documentation was available to indicate any specific tasks that required a certain amount of strength. The railroad lost the case. You might think that for a TNA, such a link is not necessary. However, it is precisely this linkage that tells you what KSAs are responsible for the performance discrepancy you are investigating.

Task-Oriented Approach. The **task-oriented approach**, as the name implies, identifies the various work activities (tasks) required to perform the job. Only after the tasks are identified, do you systematically examine these tasks to determine the KSAs necessary to perform the tasks. This approach is different from the worker-oriented method, which focuses immediately on the KSAs used to do the job.

One example of the task-oriented approach is the **job-duty-task method**. The process is depicted in Figure 4-3. Note that the job is identified first, then each of the duties is written out. The writing out of the duties provides a stimulus to generate tasks and subtasks for each of these

Information Input

Note on Rating "Importance to This Job":

Each of the items in the questionnaire that uses the "Importance to This Job" scale is to be rated on how important the activity described in the item is to the completion of this job. Consider such factors as amount of time spent, the possible influence on overall job performance if the worker does not properly perform this activity, etc.

Code	Importance to This Job
N	Does not apply
1	Very minor
2	Low
3	Average
4	High
5	Extreme

1. _____ Far visual differentiation (seeing differences in the details of the objects, events, or features *beyond arm's reach;* for example, operating a vehicle, landscaping, sports officiating)

2. _____ Depth perception (judging the distance from the observer to objects, or the distances between objects as they are positioned in space; for example, operating a crane, operating a dentist's drill, handling and positioning objects)

3. _____ Color perception (differentiating or identifying objects, materials, or details thereof on the basis of color)

4. _____ Sound pattern recognition (recognizing different patterns or sequences of sounds; for example, those involved in Morse code, heartbeats, engines not functioning correctly)

5. _____ Sound differentiation (recognizing differences or changes in sounds in their loudness, pitch, and/or tone quality; for example, piano tuner, sound system repair)

FIGURE 4-2 Worker-Oriented Approach

FIGURE 4-3 Form for Recording Task Analysis Results Using the Job-Duty-Task Method of Job Analysis

Job Title: _____ Specific Duty: _____

Tasks	Subtasks	Knowledge and Skills Required
1. _____	1. _____	_____
	2. _____	_____
	3. _____	_____
2. _____	1. _____	_____
	2. _____	_____
	3. _____	_____
3. _____	1. _____	_____
	2. _____	_____

Source: Adapted from Mills, Pace, and Peterson. 1988. *Analysis in Human Resource Training and Organizational Development.* Reading, MA: Addison-Wesley.

duties. From the duties you get the relevant tasks, and from each of these tasks you might have some subtasks. Once all the tasks are identified you then go through them and identify the KSAs required to perform all the tasks, hence the justification for requiring these KSAs. (It is also possible to list all duties first, then tasks and subtasks for each duty, then go back and identify the KSAs for each of the tasks and subtasks. It is equally appropriate to go through each duty, determine the subtasks, then identify the required KSAs before moving to the next duty.)

Identifying the duties, tasks, and subtasks is done by examining (e.g., interview, observation) incumbents' behavior (what they do). Systematically examining each duty and inquiring about the tasks required yields the list of tasks necessary to do the job. Identifying the required KSAs is not as obvious, but still relatively easy to obtain by examining each task and asking the question, "What knowledge, skills, and attitudes are necessary to perform a particular task?" Once you are involved in the job analysis, it becomes apparent that incumbents and supervisors are able to determine the required KSAs. Based on the form from Figure 4-3, an example of an analysis of the job of a human resource professional is depicted in Figure 4-4.

FIGURE 4-4 Applying the Job-Duty-Task Method to the Job of Human Resource Professional

Job Title: <u>HRD Professional</u>   Specific Duty: <u>Task Analysis</u>

Tasks	Subtasks	Knowledge and Skills Required
1. List tasks	1. Observe behavior	List four characteristics of behavior Classify behavior
	2. Select verb	Have knowledge of action verbs Have grammatical skills
	3. Record behavior	State so understood by others Record neatly
2. List subtasks	1. Observe behavior	List all remaining acts Classify behavior
	2. Select verb	State correctly Have grammatical skill
	3. Record behavior	Record so it is neat and understood by others
3. List knowledge	1. State what must be known	Classify all information
	2. Determine complexity of skill	Determine whether skills represent a series of acts that must be learned in a sequence

Source: Adapted from Mills, Pace, and Peterson. 1988. *Analysis in Human Resource Training and Organizational Development.* Reading, MA: Addison-Wesley.

Another step in the process is to determine how critical each of the tasks is, and how important it is to be able to perform the task at the time of hire. By determining this aspect, you are able to identify those tasks that new employees will be expected to be able to perform at the time of hire, and those that will require training (those that new employees will not need at the time of hire). To obtain this information, ask those providing information to rate each of the tasks on a scale such as the one depicted in Table 4-4. This step not only documents the importance of the tasks, but also provides valuable evidence for which KSAs will be used in selecting employees, and which employees will be trained on. Finally, the KSAs necessary to

TABLE 4-4 Assessment Procedure Followed by a Large U.S. Computer Firm

1. *Define the job in question.* The analyst met with management to discuss the scope of the assessment. It was determined the assessment would include all salespeople in the company.
2. *Determine who to ask.* Because of possible differences between what was being done in offices in different states, incumbents who work in each state would need to provide input. Furthermore, because of the different types of equipment being sold by different salespeople, it would be necessary to have a representative number of incumbents from these subgroups.
3. *Determine what method to use.* Because a large number of incumbents were located in different geographical regions and sold different equipment, the questionnaire method was chosen. It would allow a large number of incumbents to provide input that could be easily analyzed.
4. *Develop a questionnaire.* For a questionnaire relevant to the job, the analyst obtained job descriptions from the various locations and for the different types of hardware being sold. He then met with incumbents (in small groups) as well as supervisors (in separate small groups) to obtain input on what tasks were done. After the tasks were identified, he asked them to indicate the KSAs they believed were necessary to do the tasks. The small-group interviews were scheduled so that out-of-state incumbents who were to be at the head office for other reasons were able to attend, thus providing input from the various states.
5. *Rate the importance of tasks and KSAs.* The questionnaire included all the tasks and KSAs identified. Two ratings were requested for each task and KSA. The first related to how important the task (KSA) was to successful job performance as follows:

How Important Is the Task
  1 Not Very Important Poor performance on this task will not affect the overall performance.
  2 Somewhat Important Poor performance on this task will moderately affect the overall performance.
  3 Important Poor performance on this task will affect the overall performance.
  4 Very Important Poor performance on this task will seriously affect the overall performance.

6. *Rate task importance for new hires.* The other rating was related to how important it was to be able to do the task successfully at the time of hire. The scale for that rating follows.

Importance at the Time of Hire
  1 A person requires no specific capability in this area when hired. Training will be provided for an individual to become proficient in this area.
  2 A person requires only a basic capability in this area when hired. Experience on the job or training is the primary method for becoming proficient in this area.
  3 A person requires considerable proficiency in this area when hired. Training is available only to provide "fine-tuning" once the person is on the job.
  4 A person requires complete proficiency in this area when hired. Training is not available to help an individual become proficient in this area after being placed on the job.

TABLE 4-4 (continued)

7. *Send out questionnaire.* The questionnaire was sent to all incumbents and their supervisors.
8. *Analyze data.* Returned data were analyzed to determine if any differences existed between states and between salespeople who sold different hardware.
9. *Display analysis.* Those tasks that came up with a mean rating of 2.5 and above were placed in the relevant quadrants as shown here.

		Importance at Time of Hire	
		Below 2.5	At or above 2.5
Task Importance	At or above 2.5	Training	Selection
	Below 2.5	Not Important	

perform each of the important tasks and subtasks are identified. These aspects too should be rated for importance to the job and importance at the time of hire.

What if the number of incumbents is large, and they are scattered across the country? Table 4-4 provides the process used to identify the tasks and KSAs for salespeople at a large computer firm in the United States with offices all across the country. Because of the breadth of the job—many different types of equipment (hardware) were sold—and the many different locations, the needs analysis was a major undertaking. The effort was worthwhile, however, because important information was obtained. For example, it was determined that irrespective of type of hardware sold (cash register or computer), similar tasks and identical KSAs were required. It was also determined that the job was the same in Los Angeles as it was in Detroit. Finally, from the importance scale, it was determined that a number of tasks and KSAs, although performed, were not critical to effective job performance. For example, "knowledge of computer operations," "knowledge of program language," and "ability to write simple computer programs" were beneficial but not necessary because it was possible to obtain such support in the field.

From these data the company was able to refocus its selection procedures to include the KSAs necessary at the time of hire, and to provide its training department with a clear picture of the training necessary after the salespeople were hired.

To understand the difference between the worker-oriented and task-oriented approaches, note the different results that would be obtained using each of these methods, depicted in Table 4-5.

TABLE 4-5 A Comparison of the Outcomes for Worker- and Task-Oriented Approaches to Job Analysis

Job	*Task-Oriented Approach*	*Worker-Oriented Approach*
Garage attendant	Checks tire pressure	Obtain information from visual displays
Machinist	Checks thickness of crankshaft	Use of a measuring device
Dentist	Drills out decay from teeth	Use of precision instruments
Forklift driver	Loads pallets of washers onto trucks	High level of eye-hand coordination

If No Incumbents Are Available   In today's environment of fast-changing technology, jobs are under constant change. In some cases new technology creates a job that requires skills distinctly different from the jobs it is replacing. For example, at a large food-processing plant, management ordered a state-of-the-art machine to make a particular product previously made with low-technology equipment. This new machine required new skills. The question was: How do you perform a job analysis for this job when no incumbents are available to ask? Dr. Mitchell Fields, a professor at the University of Windsor, was approached by Heinz of Canada to assist in determining the selection and training requirements for the new job. Table 4-6 describes the steps Dr. Fields took in determining these requirements.

What You Should Get from the Job Analysis (expected performance)

The job analysis should result in a list of all the important tasks and KSAs required to perform the job. Both sets of information are necessary. The task information is important for these reasons:

- Identifying the expected behavior that needs to be performed on the job and performance deficits
- Developing actual training programs
- Making subsequent evaluations of the training[10]

Knowing all the tasks that are necessary to be effective in a particular job provides justification for the KSAs employees are expected to have. Recall the railroad example earlier. A thoroughly developed list of the tasks linked to the necessary KSAs would show the true relationship between the problem of upper body strength and the job. In fact when the railroad finally did a proper job analysis, they found that upper body strength was not required.

Having a list of job related tasks will also help you develop training. By knowing the tasks to be performed you can develop training that closely resembles the real job. Consider the job of customer service representative. We determined one of the important tasks is to "deal with irate customers." We use these tasks to help us develop role plays that closely emulate the real job. Using real task behaviors in training makes the training more relevant and interesting to trainees, as well as assists in the transfer of training.

Finally, we can use the task information to develop tests that are reflective of not only the training, but more importantly what is required on the job. These can be used in the "person analysis" phase to identify those with training needs. The tests can also serve to evaluate the effectiveness of training. The task identification leads to the identification of the KSAs necessary to do the job. Let's now examine this process in detail.

Knowledge   All jobs require some type of knowledge. The job analysis should provide a list of tasks that, when examined, will point to the knowledge requirements necessary to be successful. For example, if one of the tasks identified is to edit manuscripts using Microsoft Word, then an inferred declarative knowledge requirement would be knowledge of the editing functions in MS Word software. Going back to our customer service job, we find that knowledge of "steps in a conflict resolution model" would be important.

An Alternative Approach.   Assessing the need for declarative knowledge is possible using the traditional job analysis just discussed. Some argue, however, that with the increased complexity of jobs, analysis of tasks alone is not sufficient; we need to determine the knowledge requirements at the procedural or strategic levels.[11] The concern is that if the job is reduced to individual tasks, the interrelatedness and complexity of the job is lost.

The operational analysis for higher levels of knowledge would be accomplished by examining the mental models of experts. Here an "expert" could be a high-performing incumbent or

TABLE 4-6 Job Analysis When No Incumbents Are Available

The food-processing company was unionized, and the union contract stipulated that new jobs go to existing employees. The company wanted to be sure those selected would have the KSAs to do the job. Most of the employees did not have much formal education, and their reading level was low, so it was important to determine the level of skill required to perform the job. It was decided to use a selection test, but employees whose reading level affected their ability to take a test were not to be disqualified unless reading was an important part of the job. Dr. Fields outlines how he conducted the job analysis.

1. Contacted the manufacturer of the new equipment and asked if that or similar equipment was being used elsewhere, so that data could be obtained from another company. In this case, the setup was customized for the company and no other application existed.

2. Obtained specifications and operating manuals for the new machinery. The manuals were incomplete and difficult to understand. In fact, they were more complex than they needed to be. As a result, initially it was thought that a high level of reading comprehension would be necessary.

3. Interviewed engineers responsible for designing the new machinery. Here I received important information as to its operation. However, the engineers tended to overestimate the level of aptitude required. They believed that operators would be making modifications to the programming software. Further discussions revealed that for the operator's job, reading requirements were minimal. The operating manuals were needed only for maintenance and repair.

4. Obtained blueprints and layouts of the physical equipment, as well as flowcharts of the operating software. This material indicated that the operators would be required to interface with a user-friendly, icon-driven software package (far less complicated than the complex programming tasks envisioned by the engineers).

5. Identified two main tasks. First, the operators would be required to keep track of the mechanical operations of a number of different (but integrated) assembly operations. It was determined, therefore, that mechanical aptitude was necessary. Second, the operators had to look at a VDT (video display terminal) display (two-dimensional) and make decisions about the assembly-line operation (three dimensions). Having skill in spatial relations, therefore, would also be important.

6. On the basis of the skills identified, I suggested two subtests of the Differential Aptitude Test for use in selection of employees: mechanical comprehension and spatial relations tests. All operators were selected from current employees. The major advantage to these two tests is that reading level (which was determined not to be important) is not a critical factor.

someone who performs the same job in another context (e.g., computer programmer). These types of analysis would be useful when more advanced training is required. Techniques such as multidimensional scaling and link-weighted methods can be used to identify such structures.[12] Space does not permit us to explore this area in detail, but those interested in this approach should consult more advanced texts.[13]

Skill   A list of all the skill requirements to perform the job successfully will result from the job analysis. Consider the customer service representative. One task for this job would be to "deal with an irate customer," which would require conflict resolution skills. The outcome from the job analysis will result in a number of such skills being identified. The complete list of required skills would provide the needs analyst with an understanding of all the job requirements.

Attitude

What are the attitudinal outcomes from the job analysis? The job analysis gives an understanding of the tasks that must be done. For each task required, knowledge and skills are inferred. The same is true for attitudes. Asking the question, "Can you think of any attitudes or feelings a person could have that might facilitate or inhibit an employee from doing any part of this job well?" should generate some ideas. Consider a job that requires working in teams to solve problems. A response to the preceding question might be, "A person should have a positive attitude toward the team approach" or "The person should have a positive attitude toward working with others." These responses provide the analyst with information on what needs to be addressed in training. Just such an issue was of concern in the new Ford assembly plant (see Training in Action 4-2). Here, incumbents were unavailable because the plant was not open yet. The needs analysis was conducted using their supervisors, who were brought on board early to prepare the plant for opening.

Competency Modeling

Rather than focus on identification of specific KSAs for a job, some organizations opt to develop "key competencies" for a job. A **competency** is a cluster of related knowledge skills and attitudes that differentiate "high" performers from average performers.[14] This definition is specific to

---

TRAINING IN ACTION 4-2

CHANGING ATTITUDES TOWARD THE TEAM APPROACH

The Ford plants moved toward a team approach to producing their product. In fact the team approach is part of the "Ford Production System." The Windsor Engine Plant was a new plant, which entered an agreement with the Canadian Auto Workers that employees from other plants would be given first choice of the new jobs.

Employees transferred from other plants for many reasons: cleaner plant, closer to home, old job being phased out. Few if any transferred because of the potential for working in a team environment. In fact, it is well known that the Canadian Auto Workers traditionally oppose such efforts. In the case of the Windsor Engine Plant, they made an exception.

In a determination of the skills needed, it became evident that many of the employees would be older, and the concern was that they would be set in their ways (generally against the team approach). The training program consisted of traditional skills training necessary for a team approach (communication skills, effective meeting skills, problem-solving skills), but another component was designed to influence attitudes toward the team approach.

This "other component" consisted of an orientation to the process of the team environment. Modules were designed to show the advantages of the team approach for the company and workers. An exercise called "Best Job/Worst Job" allowed trainees to see that their own description of what a "best job" would look like was the type of job a worker would have in a team environment. The training also provided a 6-hour session on individual growth and self-fulfillment. It was assumed that helping employees to focus on these issues would improve their attitudes toward the team approach.

Did the training significantly affect attitudes? No one knows for sure. After all the time and money spent on the training, no formal evaluation of the process was conducted. This omission should not be a surprise, as you will see in Chapter 8 on evaluation.

North America, as other countries such as the United Kingdom and Australia define competencies as simply "what someone needs to be doing to be competent at their job."[15]

Some disagreement arises as to whether deriving competencies is a process different from job analysis; with some experts indicating the process is the same, but the majority suggesting it is different.[16] The majority indicate the major difference is job analysis derives "tasks" or the "what" that is done on the job, leading to the determination of knowledge and skills. These experts do not include attitudes in job analysis data. A competency-based approach focuses on all the characteristics that underlie successful performance, not just the knowledge and skills derived from the tasks. Competency modeling places equal weight on attitudes, feelings and motivation. Given that job analysis in our model incorporates attitudes, we agree with both sets of experts. Although the data derived are somewhat different for competencies, the process for determining competencies is similar to the typical job analysis. Before discussing the "how to" regarding competencies, let's look at the makeup of one.

Consider the competency of "time management." For this competency, skills include delegation, prioritizing, and making "to do" lists. A knowledge and attitude component is also involved. Knowledge of the value of a manager's time (for example $120 per hour) would help managers see the value of determining what they do themselves and what they need to delegate. Attitudes reflecting "I have no one I can trust to do this" or "I can't say no" or "It is quicker if I do it myself" all get in the way of effective delegation, which in turn affects time management.

Why Competencies Although we agree that competencies are obtained in a similar manner, and much of the information gathered is similar to job analysis, some differences are evident. Competencies, when compared to KSAs, exhibit the following characteristics:[17]

- They are more general in nature.
- They show a longer-term fit.
- They include knowledge, skills, feelings, and motivation.
- They tie into corporate goals.

Competencies tend to be of a more general nature and therefore applicable to a number of jobs. In some cases the competencies are applicable to everyone at a particular level no matter what department (all supervisors), or even multiple levels of a job (all management). Northern Telecom, for example, developed a set of competencies relevant to all of their managers (see Training in Action 4-3). Note that for different levels of management, the competency remains the same, but the behaviors expected are different. In this way the focus is always on the same key competencies, but with different behavior, depending on the management level.

In today's environment jobs are always changing. Even lower-level jobs are under constant change, in many cases requiring more decision making and so forth. Because of this constant evolving, the specifics obtained in job analysis can become dated. The more general focus of competencies is advantageous to such ever-changing jobs.

Using competencies makes it easier to identify the affective (feeling orientation) aspects of work performance. For example, organizations increasingly focus on issues such as "meeting customer expectations." This area of the job, which requires dealing with people rather than producing goods, requires a broad view of good performance. Many argue that this broad view is easier to obtain using competency models.

Finally, in the process of developing the job competencies, a great deal of effort is made to understand the business context and competitive strategy. Then competencies are developed with a focus on these broader goals of the organization in conjunction with the specific job in question.[18]

Concerns About Competencies One advantage of job analysis is that, when done correctly, the method is scientific and defendable in court. More important, it reflects what is required to do the job, making selection, training, and performance appraisal relevant and valid. To date, no

---

TRAINING IN ACTION 4-3

LIST OF COMPETENCIES RELEVANT FOR ALL LEVELS OF MANAGERS AT NORTHERN TELECOM

Northern Telecom started with the development of a list of core values for the company.

Excellence: We have only one standard, excellent.

Teamwork: We share one vision and are a team.

Customers: We create superior value for our customers.

Commitment: We do what we say we do.

Innovation: We embrace change.

People: Our people are our strength.

From the "People" value, a performance appraisal and development process was instituted. In separate meetings with their supervisor, each employee is given the opportunity to work on development of objectives and development of themselves. The common competencies applicable to all managers are defined differently at each level.

One of these competencies and the relevant descriptions are listed here.

Competency	Demonstration of the Competency		
	First Level	Mid Level	Senior Level
Customer orientation	Develops customer consciousness in others. Communicates and resolves conflict. Ensures work (own and team) exceeds customer expectations.	Understands customer needs and translates to the goals of the organization. Fosters process improvement and change with linkages to customer groups. Instills and maintains customer focus of work unit.	Establishes a relationship at the strategic level. Gains trust of customers. Formulates strategies to meet identified and anticipated requirements. Is considered by customers to be an extension of their organization.

challenges to competency models have been raised, but they simply are not developed with the same rigor as a job analysis.[19] Also, as often occurs with new ideas, organizations develop competency models with little understanding of the process. Training in Action 4-4 is a good example of this situation. Competency models, however, will continue to be developed, particularly for training and development, for the following reasons:

- Training based on only task analysis can be dated quickly as work undergoes dynamic changes.
- The nature of work is changing and more hourly employees are being expected to do much more in the way of decision making and customer satisfaction, rather than simply producing a product.

DEVELOPMENT OF COMPETENCIES

Scott Parry is the chairman of Training House Inc., a consulting firm in New Jersey. He was discussing some issues with a client when the topic turned to competencies. The client indicated to Mr. Parry that she had just completed a 6-month survey of her company's managers to determine what essential competencies were needed in a world-class performance team. The competencies would be used as a guideline for recruitment and training in her company.

She indicated that so far, she had gathered 78 competencies, and asked Mr. Parry if he would mind looking at them. Perhaps, she said, he could think of some important ones that they had not thought of. Of course Mr. Parry, whose training firm deals with these issues all the time indicates that when done properly, somewhere between 10 and 14 competencies should result.

The problem is that most managers and many trainers do not understand what a competency is. When an exercise such as this one is set up to generate competencies, often what is obtained is a list of what managers believe is important to effective performance. The following list contains nine that were obtained from the client in question.

Initiative	Negotiation	Analytical
Self-esteem	Counseling	Intuitive
Decisiveness	Interviewing	Action-oriented

This looks like a list of what you would like in an ideal employee, and not what is required to be effective on the job, which is the problem. Too often the exercise is not done in a methodologically sound way to obtain the information you really want; and so you get wish lists of traits, characteristics, skills, and attitudes with little organization to them.

Source: Parry, S. 1998. Just what is a competency? *Training*, June, pp. 59–64.

- Corporate downsizing is forcing a move away from tightly defined jobs to a more flexible work design.
- Competencies help the HRD department focus its training.

This latter point is particularly important. Recall that with limited resources, decisions need to be made regarding what to offer in the way of training. A list of key strategic competencies for all managers makes the decision much easier. The competencies are not only related to each managerial level in the organization, but also tied to the strategic direction of the organization. This linkage provides a strong indication of the importance of these competencies and that all managers need to be proficient in them.

In summary, some concern that competencies are not developed with the rigor of job analysis may be raised, and the lack of specificity may not be able to stand court challenges when they occur. We argue that as with any tool, proper methodology will result in relevant and definable competencies. Organizations that determine they would like to use competencies should not abandon job analysis, but use this methodology to demonstrate the link between KSAs of the relevant jobs and the key competencies.

Procedure A number of methods have been used to develop competency models.[20] Some, as noted in Training in Action 4-4, are not as effective as others. In fact, Maxine Dalton of the Center for Creative Leadership indicated that about 70 percent of competency models are just a list of positive attributes obtained in a half-day meeting with senior management.[21] Generally, more methodologically sound procedures entail the following process:

- Meet with upper management to:
  - Determine strategies/goals specific challenges or specific focus.
  - Generate some tentative competencies.
- Identify specific jobs.
- Meet with high performers from those jobs, and their supervisors to:
  - Determine critical incidents that make "high performers" different from average performers.
  - Focus on the aspects that tie into the strategic direction of the company.
  - Formulate some tentative competencies.
- Determine the competencies that overlap with upper management competencies.
- Verify the preceding information with another group of high performers and their supervisors.
- Link this information to job analysis information obtained from the job to articulate specific KSAs that make up the competency.

Regarding the last point, competency models are more general and fit a number of jobs. Linking these competencies to the KSAs of the target job will assure that the competencies are not only valid, but also able to stand up in court. This linkage also provides you with the information you need to develop training. Without the KSAs that make up the competency, you will not be able to determine what training should look like.

The data gathered in the operational analysis are used to determine what expected (acceptable) performance is. From this information measures of expected performance (criteria) are developed. Development of these criteria are important, as they will be used not only to measure how employees are doing, but also as one measure of training success. Criterion development is complex, so Appendix 4.1 at the end of this chapter provides some in-depth understanding of the issues for the advanced student and others interested in developing good criteria. The appendix will also help you better understand the criterion issues discussed in Chapter 8 on evaluation.

PERSON ANALYSIS

Once the tasks (or competencies) and KSAs required to meet performance expectations are clear (operational analysis), the needs analyst determines who is not meeting these expectations. A person analysis is the methodology for identifying those incumbents who are not meeting the performance requirements. Recall from the training model the formula for a performance discrepancy is

$$\text{Expected performance} - \text{Actual performance} = \text{Performance discrepancy}$$

A **performance discrepancy** is most often thought of in the reactive sense, that is, as the difference between expected performance and actual performance. For example, assume the standard number of snowmobile trailers a "Builder Class 2" is expected to produce per day is 1.5. For the last 3 weeks three employees in this class are averaging 0.6 trailers per day. The discrepancy is 0.9 trailers per day.

In the proactive analysis the expected performance is what is needed in the future (and will likely require new KSAs), and actual performance is the current performance level (with present KSAs). Consider the trailer manufacturer in the preceding example. He decides to purchase equipment that will bend the trailer frame to the correct shape, eliminating a number of welds. The engineering studies indicate that this change in production process will increase the "Builder Class 2" output to 3 trailers per day. At the present KSA level "Builder Class 2" employees are expected to produce 1.5 trailers per day. Here the performance discrepancy for the person is the "future" required performance level (3 trailers per day) less their predicted performance level in the future given their current level of KSAs. This discrepancy will be 1.5 trailers per day. Will this require training on the new equipment? Only a TNA can determine the answer.

Where to Collect Data (Actual Performance)

Sources available to obtain person analysis information are shown in Table 4-7. Three of the more commonly used sources will be discussed in detail: performance appraisal, performance data, and proficiency tests (cognitive, work sample, assessment centers). Another source that will be discussed, one that is less commonly used, is the attitude survey.

Performance Appraisal   If the performance appraisal actually provided an accurate assessment of an employee's deficiencies, other assessment tools would hardly be necessary. Unfortunately, performance appraisals often suffer from a lack of reliability and validity for a number of reasons:

- Lack of supervisor training on how to use appraisals
- Lack of opportunity for the supervisor to see substantial amounts of a subordinate's performance
- Rater errors such as halo, leniency, and others effects
- Poorly developed appraisals and appraisal processes

If appraisal instruments are developed properly and the process of completing them followed conscientiously, performance appraisals can be a valuable source of employee training needs. The literature, however, suggests this is not often the case.

   Supervisor Ratings.   Performance appraisals are most often completed by supervisors.[22] For both political and interpersonal reasons these appraisals are often less than accurate assessments of the incumbents' KSAs.[23] This inaccuracy is less likely to occur where performance appraisal information is gathered specifically for general development of the employee, and where the climate in the organization fosters such development.[24]

   A number of things can be done to minimize problems with supervisor ratings, including the following:

- The appraisal system should be relevant to the job. Sometimes appraisals are too generic to be appropriate. Also they need to be acceptable to both supervisor and employee.[25]
- The supervisor must have access to relevant information to make accurate appraisals. As noted earlier, in some cases supervisors are not in contact with subordinates often enough on the job to be aware of their performance.[26]
- The supervisor must be motivated to provide accurate ratings. To help ensure accuracy the performance appraisal should be for the TNA only. Some organizations actually put an appraisal in place that is used only for developmental purposes. As Murphy and Cleveland note, "[I]t is likely that a supervisor experiences little conflict when information from a performance appraisal is being used for providing feedback to employees on their strengths and weaknesses and to recommend employees to training programs."[27]

Furthermore, it stands to reason that an incumbent is more likely to accept the appraisal ratings when she stands to benefit from the evaluation by receiving appropriate training.

   A method being used by some large companies to identify training needs is called work planning and review. The supervisor holds periodic meetings with subordinates to assess whether they met particular goals set earlier, what problems they are experiencing meeting these goals, and what, if any, training would be useful. Corning Glass, for example, identi-fies 14 dimensions of performance and lists three to six behaviors within each of these

TABLE 4-7 Data Sources for Person Analysis

Data Sources for Obtaining Data	*Training Need Implications*	*Remarks*
1. Performance Data	Include weaknesses and areas of improvement as well as strengths. Easy to analyze and quantify for purposes of determining subjects and kind of training needed. These data can be used to identify performance discrepancies.	Supervisor ratings are often done poorly, with no real incentive to do them well, and a lot of good reasons not to.
a. Productivity		
b. Absenteeism and tardiness		
c. Accidents		
d. Short-term sickness		
e. Grievances		
f. Waste		
g. Late deliveries		
h. Product quality		
i. Downtime		
j. Repairs		
k. Equipment utilization		
l. Customer complaints		
2. Observation–Work Sampling	More subjective technique but provides both employee behavior and results of the behavior.	This is done effectively in some situations such as customer service where employees know that the telephone calls they answer from customers can be monitored from time to time.
3. Interviews	Individual is only one who knows what he believes he needs to learn. Involvement in needs analysis can also motivate employees to make an effort to learn.	Need to be sure employee believes it is in her best interest to be honest, otherwise she may not be as forthcoming as you would like.
4. Questionnaires	Same approach as the interview. Easily tailored to specific characteristics of the organization. May produce bias through the necessity of prestructure categories.	Same concerns as the interview.
5. Tests		
a. Job knowledge	Can be tailor-made or standardized. Care must be taken so that they measure job-related qualities.	Care in the development of scoring keys is important and difficult to do if not trained in the process.
b. Skills		
c. Achievement		

TABLE 4-7 (continued)

Data Sources for Obtaining Data	Training Need Implications	Remarks
6. Attitude Surveys	On an individual basis, useful in determining morale, motivation, or satisfaction of each employee.	Important to use well-developed scales.
7. Checklists or Training Progress Charts	Up-to-date listing of each employee's skills. Indicates future training requirements for each job.	The following (7–9) rely on supervisor ratings, see (1).
8. Rating Scales	Care must be taken to ensure relevant, reliable, and objective employee ratings.	
9. Critical Incidents	Observed actions that are critical to the successful/unsuccessful performance of the job.	
10. Diaries	The individual employee records details of her job.	
11. Devised Situations	Certain knowledge, skills, and of attitudes are demonstrated in these techniques.	Useful but again care required in development of scoring criteria is important.
a. Role play		
b. Case study		
c. Conference leadership training sessions		
d. Business games		
e. In-baskets		
12. Diagnostic Rating	Checklists are factor analyzed to yield diagnostic ratings.	
13. Assessment Centers	Combination of several of the preceding techniques into an intensive assessment program.	Although expensive to develop and operate, these are good because they use multiple raters and multiple exercises to assess ratees. Also criteria for performance are well developed.
14. Coaching	Similar to interview—one-to-one.	Must choose coaches carefully and train to be most effective.
15. MBO or Work Planning	Provides actual performance data on a recurring basis related to organizational (and individually or group-negotiated) standards so that baseline measurements may be known and subsequent improvement or deterioration of performance may be identified and analyzed. This performance review and potential review are keyed to larger organizations' goals and objectives.	Good process when implemented properly, and review systems are supported by top management.

dimensions. These behavioral statements become the goals. Supervisors are asked to read each behavioral statement and provide written examples of how the subordinate did or did not behave in the described manner (see Table 4-8). If the subordinate is having problems meeting these objectives, the supervisor works with him to help him reach the objectives. One way of helping is to provide relevant training, when applicable. Even in the most progressive appraisal system, when supervisors rate subordinates, other concerns need to be taken into account. Various types of rater bias such as halo[28] and leniency[29] effects should be addressed through training. Another concern is that for some jobs, such as teaching and sales, supervisors do not often get to see the employee in action. Sometimes the supervisor is unfamiliar with the job details. Perhaps the best way to deal with these concerns is similar to the method suggested for dealing with gathering job analysis data: the more perspectives, the better the picture. For this reason it is useful to consider others as potential raters of an employee's performance.

To summarize, supervisors provide an important perspective in determining the needs of their subordinates. To be useful, however, supervisors need training in the use of appraisals, the appraisals need to be relevant to the job and acceptable to the supervisor and subordinate, and the appraisal should be used only for the assessment of the subordinates' needs.

Self-Ratings.   Self-ratings are a possibility for determining the needs of employees. Much of the research on self-ratings suggests that the individual tends to overrate her capabilities. However, evidence also indicates that the inflated ratings are a function of the rating instruments rather than the individual attempting to sound better.[30] Also, when self-raters understand the performance system, they are more likely to agree with supervisor ratings.[31] These findings suggest that self-ratings are accurate where subordinates are more involved in the development of the appraisal process.

McEnery and McEnery examined self-ratings and supervisory ratings gathered for a needs analysis related to training.[32] They noted that self-ratings were inflated, but were also more discriminating in identifying different needs than were supervisory ratings. Furthermore, the results suggested that supervisory assessment of "subordinate needs" more closely resembled the needs of the raters themselves. More recent research noted that self-ratings actually have lower measurement errors than supervisor ratings on some performance dimensions.[33] In short, self-ratings are an important part of any needs assessment.

The 360-Degree Performance Review.   Generally, the more sources used to gather information, the higher the reliability and validity of the results. This supports use of the 360-degree performance review, by which an individual rates himself on a number of dimensions and receives ratings on these dimensions by his supervisor, peers, subordinates, and sometimes even customers.[34] The resulting information is fed back to the individual. The broader view provided by this method takes pressure off the supervisor, especially when others in the loop agree more with the supervisor than with the individual. These data provide a springboard for dialogue between the supervisor and subordinate regarding the subordinate's needs.

TABLE 4-8 Work Planning and Review at Corning

Dimension	Behavioral Statement	Written Example
Applying quality principles	Sets high standards for self and others; puts a great deal of emphasis on error-free work.	Developed written requirements for all suppliers on the Stafford project and encouraged others to do the same.

The advantages of this process are that the various groups see the person under different conditions, maintain different relationships with the individual, and also have different expectations regarding performance. Some evidence indicates that ratees find feedback from peers and subordinates particularly useful in planning their developmental goals.[35] Furthermore, as already noted, the more sources of information, the better. The disadvantage to the 360-degree performance review is the amount of time it takes and its cost of implementation. If it is not properly integrated into the company's HR system, it can also lead to negative results.[36] So, for it to be effective, a supportive climate is necessary for development in general,[37] and as always, support from top management is helpful.

To summarize, those performance assessments designed to focus on development (e.g., WP&R) are more likely to provide accurate data than more generic or all-purpose appraisals. Also, to determine developmental needs, both supervisory ratings and self-ratings should be gathered. Both parties need to be involved in the assessment process. As McEnery and McEnery suggest, the supervisor provides a valuable perspective on the needs of the subordinate. The subordinate gains insight into his needs through discussion with the supervisor. This process will also improve communication between the supervisor and subordinate and serves to improve the accuracy of the assessment. If 360-degree feedback data are available for the meeting between the supervisor and subordinate, so much the better. These data will allow for an examination of the performance from a broader perspective. It is important, however, that if 360-degree feedback is being used, it must be incorporated into the organization properly. An example is found in Training in Action 4-5. Here, United Parcel Service uses 360-degree feedback and training as an ongoing process of performance improvement.

TRAINING IN ACTION 4-5

UNITED PARCEL SERVICE USES 360-DEGREE FEEDBACK AND TRAINING

At United Parcel Service (UPS) in Louisville, Kentucky, about 1,200 management employees participate in an automated 360-degree feedback process. Managers are measured on a number of critical skills such as "customer focus," "people skills," "business values," and so forth. But, before any of this evaluation happens, HR trainers hold mini training sessions to explain the purpose and process of 360-degree feedback to those involved. At these sessions, training is also provided on how to give and receive feedback.

After receiving training, peers, supervisors, and subordinates rate a manager once every 6 months on the critical skills. They do so by completing a questionnaire. The manager then sits down with her supervisor and discusses the feedback. The manager then sets objectives for improvement over the next 6 months. The manager can choose to attend programs that provide skills training and practice in the areas requiring improvement. Six months later the manager receives another round of feedback that indicates any improvement in the areas targeted. How is the process being received? Hope Zoeller Stith, trainer at UPS, indicates that information sessions that incorporate discussion about the purpose of the process, along with the feedback training, helped everyone see the benefits of the process. Employees reacted positively, Stith says.

Source: Wells, S. 1999. A new road: Traveling beyond 360-degree evaluation. *HR Magazine* 4:83–91.

Performance Data   Many different measures of performance are used, depending on the nature of the job. In some production jobs, the amount of scrap, the number of units produced, and quality (number of rejects) are all measures that could be used. For management performance, the number of projects completed on time as well as consistency in meeting objectives could be measures.

A different approach is to examine the causes of a performance discrepancy.[38] This approach looks at consensus and distinctiveness as they relate to the deficiency. **Consensus** refers to the degree to which the performance discrepancy is limited to a few (low consensus) or observed in many individuals (high consensus). **Distinctiveness** refers to the degree to which the discrepancy is specific to one area of the person's performance (high distinctiveness) or is present across a number of areas (low distinctiveness). These two issues need to be considered jointly. The four possible combinations are charted in Table 4-9. High consensus and high distinctiveness mean that the discrepancy occurs in a number of the incumbents and is specific to one dimension of performance. For example, the incumbent does not meet his quota of selling notebook computers, which is also true of 70 percent of the other incumbents (high consensus). The incumbent does meet the quota for selling full-size computers, monitors, and software, so it is only the notebook computers that seem to be a problem (high distinctiveness). This result would suggest that it is not a KSA deficiency, but rather a deficiency elsewhere (e.g., the product is not competitive or the commission is too low on the product).

Low consensus and low distinctiveness suggests that the discrepancy may be a KSA concern, because others in the department do not seem to have the same problem (low consensus), and the incumbent also has trouble on other facets of the job (low distinctiveness). However, keep in mind that other causes for the discrepancy may also be factors, such as a difficult sales territory. The distinctiveness/consensus categorization is meant only as a guide.

When consensus and distinctiveness are opposite (high/low or low/high), it is less clear whether the performance deficiency is a KSA issue or due to some other factor. In these cases, a closer examination of the incumbent and the situation would be necessary to determine the cause of the performance deficiency.

Proficiency Tests   Rather than rely on ratings of job performance, an alternative is to test the individual under controlled conditions. Two types of proficiency testing are cognitive and behavioral.

Cognitive tests measure levels of knowledge. Plumbers need to understand government regulations for installing water and drainage systems in a house, supervisors need to understand the procedures for assigning overtime, salespeople need to understand the procedures for accepting returned merchandise. Any job has a certain amount of knowledge attached to it, and a test to measure that knowledge can be developed. Tests of declarative knowledge can be paper-and-pencil. A concern of using such tests is that they will reflect the reading level when reading is not an important skill for the job. If you are concerned about the knowledge level of

TABLE 4-9 Likelihood of Deficiency Being a KSA Issue

		Distinctiveness	
		Low	High
Consensus	High	Unsure	Low
	Low	High	Unsure

incumbents and reading is not a required KSA, paper-and-pencil tests would not be appropriate, unless they were given orally (see Table 4-4 on page 133 for a description of such an example).

Paper-and-pencil tests offer a number of advantages, such as the following:

- Can be given to large numbers of individuals at once.
- Can be scored easily.
- Provide an effective method of determining areas where there is a lack of knowledge.

The disadvantages include the following:

- Time and effort are required to develop a comprehensive test that is both reliable and valid.
- If the test is other than true-false or multiple choice, developing effective scoring keys takes a great deal of time.

Recall from the operational analysis discussion (and Chapter 3) that higher levels of knowledge could be assessed through measures of mental models. Examples of a traditional test for declarative knowledge (Figure 8-10) and a test of higher levels of knowledge (Figure 8-4) can be found in Chapter 8.

Behavioral tests measure skills and are important means of determining an employee's needs related to skills required on the job. Such tests can incorporate *work samples*, which are simply work situations designed to reflect what actually happens in the workplace. Standardized rating methods are developed so everyone is presented with the same situation and measured according to preset criteria. For example, a welder may be required to measure and cut three pieces of channel iron, then weld them at right angles to make a U; a salesclerk may be required to respond to an irate customer who provides standardized antagonistic responses to the salesclerk's handling of a situation; a manager may be required to make a presentation to a boss on the advantages of going global. *Assessment centers* are an expansion of the work sample approach. They often involve a number of work samples and a number of assessors who evaluate the individuals in different situations. Although assessment centers are costly to develop and administer (they often require two to three days off-site), they provide a comprehensive analysis of needs, especially for managerial positions.

Surveys Attitudes are an important part of organizational effectiveness. If, for example, the team approach is an organizational objective, then attitudes toward this approach are important. Surveys of various attitudes are conducted routinely in some organizations. In such a situation, a scale related to the attitude toward teamwork could simply be included. If this practice does not exist, it might be useful to consider instituting one. At the very least, organizations could survey trainees before training to determine how they feel about teams and teamwork (if teamwork was a performance discrepancy).

Developing attitude scales requires a great deal of skill, and it is much better to use well-developed scales found in the literature. Texts such as *Assessing Organizational Change*[39] and *The Experience of Work*[40] contain a number of attitudinal measures. Another source that publishes such scales is the Institute for Social Research at the University of Michigan.[41]

GATHERING TNA DATA: FINAL THOUGHTS

For a conceptual understanding of the types of data required, it is useful to divide the TNA into three distinct factors: organization, operation, and person. Practically, however, when conducting such an analysis, you will find they are highly interrelated and often conducted at the same time. These factors are illustrated in the example (Fabrics Inc.) at the end of the chapter and also in Chapter 9 when a hypothetical orientation is developed. Looking at sources for each analysis (Tables 4-1, 4-3, and 4-7), you will see a great deal of overlap. If you were interviewing incumbents regarding operational analysis, for example, you would at the same time obtain information regarding roadblocks to getting the job done (organizational analysis). In the person analysis, when you examine performance data and compare consensus and distinctiveness, you can determine any structural reasons for the poor performance (organizational analysis).

Once the operational analysis data determine the KSAs for the job, the person analysis defines whether each of the relevant employees possesses these KSAs. For those who do not, the discrepancy between what is required and what the employee has serves as the impetus for developing the necessary training.

For the TNA to be effective, it is important that the development of employees is of high concern to both the individual and the organization. It is more likely to occur when an organization does the following:

- Puts procedures in place that allow for developmental appraisals to take place regularly and separate from appraisals used for other personnel decisions.
- Allows the individual to provide input into the process (self-appraisal).
- Places a high value on developing subordinates (by rewarding supervisors who spend time doing so).
- Provides opportunities for employees to receive the training and mentoring necessary for development.

However, having these procedures in place is not enough! Numerous stories recount supervisors who simply go through the motions of a performance appraisal and employee development, then get on with the "real work." Such attitudes are likely to undermine any system. Subordinates' perceptions of the process must be positive, and they must believe training will be useful in their development, particularly when self-assessment is being used in the TNA.[42]

Outcomes of TNA

From a TNA you will be able to determine what caused (or will cause) a performance discrepancy. Review Figure 4-1 on page 118. As Figure 4-1 shows, the first steps in a TNA are identifying performance discrepancies and deciding whether they are important enough to fix. If they are, you need to determine the cause of the discrepancy (through a TNA). Once you know the cause, you can determine what needs to be done to alleviate the discrepancy.

We are now at the outcomes portion of the TNA model (analysis phase) presented at the start of the chapter. The analysis process determines the discrepancy and then the causes of the discrepancy. The outputs are nontraining needs and training needs.

NONTRAINING NEEDS

Nontraining needs include those that show no KSA deficiency, and those characterized by a KSA deficiency, but where training is not the best solution. First, let's discuss those that show no KSA deficiency (see Figure 4-1).

Nontraining Needs (No KSA Deficiency)

Here, nontraining needs are those performance discrepancies caused by

- Reward/punishment incongruencies
- Inadequate or inappropriate feedback
- Obstacles in the system

No amount of KSA development will improve performance in situations where these problems exist. These causes of performance discrepancies should be uncovered in your organizational and operational analysis.

Reward/Punishment Incongruencies Is working at the expected level of performance punishing for some or all those working in a particular job? As Training in Action 4-6 indicates, the answer can be yes. The punishment/reward situation can be even less obvious. Suppose an employee who works much harder than the others notices he is treated exactly the same as those who just do the bare minimum. It may not be long before he stops making the extra effort. In such cases, training this employee is not going to help. Training may still be useful, but not training of the employee. Instead, the supervisor should be trained on how to motivate employees. What is needed here is for the supervisor to know how to provide rewards to the employees based on their performance. Systems also need to be in place to motivate the supervisor to reward employees appropriately.

Feedback Another nontraining need comes from employees not receiving appropriate feedback. Numerous examples tell of employees who believe they are good performers but their supervisors believe otherwise. Supervisors generally dislike providing negative feedback.[43] In fact, some suggest that it is the most disliked of all managerial activities.[44] Once again the problem is not a training issue for the subordinate, but it could be for the supervisor.

Obstacles in the System A third reason performance may be deficient is that conditions in the workplace obstruct the desired performance level. Receiving material too late, using worn-out machinery, and being constantly interrupted are but a few of the possibilities that could hinder performance. Once identified, these roadblocks need to be removed, a task that can be complex and in some cases may require high-level support. Suppose a supervisor has too many reports to file each week and this responsibility takes away from the time needed for helping subordinates. The reports are requested by middle management. The only way to reduce the amount of paperwork (if that is the answer) is to request that middle management reduce the number of reports they receive or find another way to generate the reports (see Training in Action 4-7). This task is not an easy one, but as you can see, providing the supervisor with KSAs (helping behaviors) to help the subordinate will not solve the problem.

Nontraining Needs (KSA Deficiency)

Now, let's examine the nontraining needs where a KSA deficiency is present. As Figure 4-1 indicates, even KSA deficiencies have a number of possible solutions, only one of which is training.[45]

TRAINING IN ACTION 4-6

PUNISHMENT FOR PERFORMANCE

At a Canadian gas utility, one of the tasks required of repairpersons was to change gas meters in residences. Each meter was taken in to be tested every 6 years. Most employees changed 15 per day. When the system became computerized, it allowed management to send a serviceperson to one or two streets in a particular area to change meters, instead of having calls all over the city. Management believed that because of the lower amount of time now necessary to drive between the homes, productivity would increase substan-tially. It did not. In fact, for the majority of employees it remained at 15.

What was the problem? A norm had been set by the servicepeople. Very few would change more than 15 meters, a standard that had been set by the majority. The punishment was that those who violated the standard suf-fered ridicule and shunning by the rest of the service staff. Because they all unloaded their meters at the same time and at the same loca-tion, those who were breaking the norm were easily spotted and "punished."

SELF-MANAGED BARRIER REMOVAL

A telephone company department manager was required to examine a number of computer-generated reports, provide input on them, and then send them to higher-level management each month. The manager never knew what was done with the reports, but they took a great deal of time away from other, more important work. After discussions with a consultant hired to do a needs assessment for other purposes, the manager decided to stop sending two of the reports. A few months later nothing had been said about the reports being late. The manager decided to stop sending a third report. Two days after the third report was due, the manager received a call asking where it was. It was sent promptly. Six months later, after still not hearing anything about the first two reports no longer being sent, the manager shared this information with other district-level managers, and they stopped sending the reports as well. The consultant left the organization a few months later and still no one had asked for the reports.

Certainly a more organizationally correct approach would be to ask higher management whether the reports were necessary. The concern by the manager was that the answer would be yes even though the reports were not used.

Job Aids   A *job aid* is one solution. This is a set of instructions, diagrams, and the like, available at the job site to provide guidance to the worker. It is useful if the task is complex, if it requires a number of steps, or if it is dangerous to forget a step. Airline pilots use job aids—a list of things they must do prior to takeoff—so they do not forget any of the steps required. General Motors Electromotive Division in Chicago provides workers with a job aid in the wiring of the locomotives. It is simply a diagram that shows where the wiring runs, which colors branch off, and where to connect them. Because of the number of wires in the harness, memorizing their locations would be difficult. Following the diagram makes a complex task manageable.

Practice   For tasks that are important, but performed infrequently, employees can forget or become less proficient at the skill. For example, police officers are required to practice on the firing range each month. Schools conduct fire drills as practice for an important task that may never occur. In these cases, providing the practice is meant to prevent a performance discrepancy. If a performance discrepancy in an infrequent task is discovered, periodic practice sessions should be considered to ensure that the discrepancy does not continue to occur, particularly if its occurrence can have serious consequences.

Changing the Job Itself   This approach may seem extreme, but it is sometimes worth considering. A number of years ago salespeople in automobile dealerships were responsible for the total job of selling a car. The most difficult part of selling is "closing the deal," which requires certain KSAs that are difficult to impart through training. As a result, many car salespeople did not last long in the business. This discrepancy led the dealers to change the job. They provided the salesperson with the skills to show the car, discuss various options, and negotiate to a certain extent. Then, when it came to closing the deal, the salesperson could send the customer to the sales manager. Thus the job was changed so that the salesperson no longer needed that skill.

Finally, if these options or training is not possible, the decision may have to be to transfer or terminate the individual.

TRAINING NEEDS

For those performance discrepancies that are due to the employees' lack of KSAs and for which training is a solution, you will need to list and describe the KSAs clearly and unambiguously. These KSAs are then used to develop training objectives, which will be discussed in detail in the next chapter.

Approaches to TNA

Now that we have examined the general approach of conducting a TNA, let's examine the two approaches (proactive and reactive) more specifically.

PROACTIVE TNA

The proactive TNA focuses on future human resource requirements. As Chapter 2 described, the HR function needs to be involved in the development of a strategic plan (SWOT analysis). From the resulting unit objectives, HR must develop unit strategies and tactics (see Figure 2-1 on page 32) to be sure the organization has employees with the required KSAs in each of the critical jobs based on future KSA requirements. Two approaches can be taken to develop needed KSAs:

1. Prepare employees for promotions/transfers to different jobs.
2. Prepare employees for changes in their current jobs.

An effective, proactive procedure used for promotions and transfers is succession planning. **Succession planning** is the identification and development of employees who are perceived to be of high potential. The first step in development of a succession plan is to identify key positions in the organization. These positions, if left vacant for any length of time, would negatively affect organizational functioning. In practice, these positions often are high-level management positions such as vice president of finance, plant manager and so forth, but they could be at any level (e.g., moldmaker if the position is key to the operation and difficult to fill). Once the positions are identified, employees with the potential to fill these key positions are identified. Information is then provided on employees' readiness to fill the position if it becomes vacant. This information becomes the TNA.

When preparing employees for changes in their current jobs, it is important that the TNA identify the changes that are expected based on strategic objectives. Once expected changes are determined, new KSAs required for that job can be identified. These future KSAs can be compared with the incumbent's current KSAs, and any resulting discrepancies can then be addressed through training. Consider Heinz. When they determined that they would be moving to a high-tech Ketchup machine, it was necessary to determine what KSAs would be necessary to operate it. Training in these KSAs then occurred before the new equipment was in place.

Organizational Analysis

The proactive approach starts with the strategic plan and objectives. The analyst tries to determine the best fit between the organization's current internal environment (structures, policies, procedures, etc.) and the future expectations. Questions regarding the formal structure might include the following:

- Are pay practices congruent with the new direction taken by the company? *Example*: Would a strict hourly pay structure fit if the plan was to treat each department as entrepreneurial?
- Is the emphasis of the new priorities congruent with the performance appraisal system? *Example*: If the priority is quality, does the performance appraisal have a dimension to measure this?

- Is the strategy congruent with the current practices? *Example*: The new strategy is to move to a more positive union-management relationship. Currently a policy does not allow any union business to be conducted on company time. Should this policy be revisited?
- Are enough employees available to accomplish the objective? *Example*: You plan to improve quality to meet ISO 9000 standards, but are constantly rushed because of a lack of personnel.

Informal procedures might be evaluated with the following questions:

- Are norms in place that would restrict output?
- Will workers believe that changes in performance are required?
- What formal procedures are short-circuited by informal procedures, and what are the implications (perhaps the formal procedure is inappropriate)?

These questions need to be asked at all levels in the organization, but specifically at the departmental level where more meaningful data will be found. Often those in higher levels of management take a different view of the impact of various policies on behavior.

Operational Analysis

Jobs are dynamic, always changing over time. Today, however, the changes in some jobs are much more dramatic than in the past. Employees need to be prepared for these changes. The job analyst must gather information not only on what tasks are done, but also on what tasks will be required in the future. This **strategic job analysis** is defined as identifying the KSAs required for effective performance in a job as it is expected to exist in the future.[46] Data gathering is identical to that in traditional job analysis, with the addition of a section called "gather information on the future." For this section you need to look at changes in areas of societal values, political/legal issues, economics/market/labor, technology, and others, and how those changes would affect the job in question. In this case, you need input from more than just incumbents and supervisors, including the following:[47]

- At least one person responsible for corporate strategy and closely tied to the job in question
- Someone who is aware of how the competition structures the job (technologically and from a human resource standpoint)
- An efficiency expert (internal technology/communication expert)
- Someone who worked his or her way up through the job in question
- A forward-thinking incumbent (one willing to suggest new ideas)

This list is not exhaustive and serves only as a guide. Once you gather these data, you can complete a revision of the tasks and KSAs based on these changes. The training function then uses this information coupled with person analysis to determine future training needs. The previous discussion about what to do if no job incumbents are available is helpful here. In reality no job incumbents exist if the job will change in substantial ways.

At first this task seems rather horrendous—and if the organization is doing it for the first time, it is. The first step is to identify the critical jobs. For example, if the primary function of the organization is writing software, the computer programmers' job will be more critical to the effectiveness of the organization than the file clerks' and should be examined first. Likewise, if the organization is making parts for the automotive industry, moldmaking might be a critical job.

Person Analysis

Assessment of the person (does she have the required KSAs?) is identical for the proactive or reactive TNA, and so the information presented earlier on person analysis is applicable.

Let's Do It

Let's go back to the Multistate Health Corporation (MHC) in Chapter 2. The strategic plan was outlined, and from it arose a number of potential objectives for HR, related to developing an HRPS. Let's examine these objectives as they affect a critical position, that of the CEO. No clear documentation exists of the required KSAs for the 30 CEOs of the hospitals; as a result no one knows the KSAs needed to be promoted to CEO. To deal with this and other positions in the organization, the MHC executive committee developed six objectives. The first step in addressing these objectives (as they affect the position of CEO) is to conduct an operational analysis of the CEO position. Recall how the job analysis was conducted for the large computer firm (Table 4-6 on page 136). You could use a similar process here and conduct interviews, given the small number of incumbents. You can interview all incumbents (four or five small group meetings), or hold one meeting with six CEOs: two from each region, one from the largest and one from the smallest hospital in that region.

At the meeting, ask the CEOs to list all the tasks and subtasks they perform, or prepare a partial list from previous conversations to use the time available most efficiently. Then, using a scale similar to the one in Table 4-6, ask each of them to rate each task on its importance for the job, and importance at the time of hire. Based on the ratings provided, determine which are important. Those tasks that are important for the job are the only ones that are considered. You need to examine these tasks to determine whether any differences distinguish between geographical locations or large versus small hospitals. If any are noted, they need to be resolved. If a large number of critical tasks are different, the jobs themselves could be different and may need different titles. It may also be that the task was not identified as important by some because it never was required. The task of "effective cost cutting" may not have been identified in some smaller hospitals because it was not used. It is still an important task for CEOs (assuming CEOs in larger hospitals indicated it as important), and would be included, although some CEOs may not have the KSAs to do it effectively, as noted in the case. Once you identify all the tasks, it is useful to classify them into broader duties, as outlined in Figure 4-3.

Next you need to identify the KSAs necessary to perform each task. These KSAs will be used to make either selection or training decisions, depending on where they were classified concerning "need at the time of hire." Publishing the ones required at the time of hire for the recruitment process makes the selection criteria clearer to all.

A team of subject matter experts on the position of CEO (see the discussion of strategic job analysis in the "Operational Analysis" of the preceding section), should be consulted to develop the strategic part of the job analysis (how the job might look in 5 years). This information, when compared with the information on current requirements, highlights what the future requirements would likely be.

Let's look at one duty. From the job analysis, one duty might be defined as the "development of subordinates." You might identify these tasks related to that duty:

- Initiates action to identify developmental needs
- Provides timely feedback to help subordinates improve
- Provides subordinates with the opportunities to develop
- Meets with subordinates to discuss performance and development
- Coaches subordinates in a manner that allows them to improve their skills

A number of other duties (and relevant tasks) would of course be identified. Finally the KSAs necessary to perform the tasks would be identified. From the preceding list of tasks, KSAs that would be relevant include:

- Knowledge of the performance review process
- Knowledge of basic coaching skills
- Skill at providing feedback in an effective manner

- Skill at interviewing
- Positive attitude toward the participative approach to problem solving
- Positive attitude toward helping others

Based on the assessment of the skills of the 30 CEOs at MHC, some or all of these KSAs may be lacking and training may be necessary. To determine which CEOs need which KSAs, the person analysis is conducted.

For the person analysis, let's just focus on the specific KSAs necessary to appraise performance. Here you want to know about CEOs' knowledge of the appraisal process, skill in providing effective reviews, and attitude toward these reviews. This information is obtained in part by asking CEOs directly (a subpart of your job analysis meeting). If managers have no confidence in a performance appraisal system, they will have no compunction about telling you that "it's not worth the time" or "it's never used anyway so why bother." If they do not believe they have the skill, they might also tell you that. Another place to obtain such information is from the CEOs' subordinates. You might get information from subordinates such as: "She really tries to do a good job but is constantly telling me what I need to do and never asks my opinion" or "He tells me I have a bad attitude. I'm not sure what he means but am in no mood to ask either." These types of comments suggest a lack of skills on the CEO's part, or it is possible the CEO has a negative attitude toward the process. Again, asking the CEO directly could determine which it is. You can also use the option of behavior testing to assess the skills. Put CEOs in a role-play situation where they must provide feedback to an employee, and score them on how well they do.

For the organizational analysis part of the TNA, some information has already been gathered from interviews conducted by the consultants. One of the objectives based on those findings was the inclusion of a succession plan. It provides the mechanism for supplying instant information on who should be considered for the next promotion, rather than relying on individual CEOs to make that determination. Of course, you need a standardized performance review system in place to make such determinations.

The job analysis provides relevant data for developing standard performance appraisals necessary in both promotion and developmental decisions. With such a system in place, each CEO would be responsible for completing performance reviews on his subordinates and providing developmental plans for them. This process would help to deal with the lack of interest by some CEOs in recommending their subordinates. Although not explicitly noted, one important measure of the CEOs' performance appraisal would need to be how well the CEOs prepare and develop their subordinates for promotion. This measure, as part of their performance review specifically, along with the use of a succession plan in general, will serve to encourage all CEOs to work toward developing their subordinates for promotion.

REACTIVE TNA

The reactive TNA begins with an existing discrepancy in job performance. In this sense, Figure 4-1 represents a more complete picture of the reactive process. A middle manager may notice that production is dropping, a supervisor may see that a particular employee's performance declined, or human resources may note an increase in grievances from a particular department. Once you identify a discrepancy, you need to determine whether it is worth fixing. Although this decision may be based on financial implications, it does not have to be. For example, the company notes that one department has lower ratings of supervisory consideration (as rated by subordinates) than the organization expected. The cost of this lower rating would be difficult to assess. It may take a long time (if ever) to notice any significant impact on the company's bottom line. If the company makes a strong commitment to developing a good employee-management relationship, it may decide to try to alleviate the problem.

In the reactive TNA, you still conduct the organizational analysis, operational analysis, and person analysis, but the distinction among them is even more blurred for the following reasons:

- The focus is primarily on the one department.
- Those who demonstrate the discrepancy (and their peers and subordinates) are the key persons to be interviewed about all three components.
- The discrepancy focuses the issue on a particular part of the job (e.g., interactions with subordinates as previously noted).

Organizational Analysis

Organizational analysis deals with the three issues identified to the right of the KSA deficiency in Figure 4-1. A complete analysis of all four aspects of Figure 4-1 is necessary regardless of whether the issue is a KSA problem. Even if a lack of KSAs is identified as a problem, other roadblocks may still be in place that will prevent performance even if the KSAs are learned.

Operational Analysis/Person Analysis

In the reactive approach, the performance discrepancy is already identified, because it triggered the analysis. This discrepancy determines where the focus of the TNA will be. From this initial discrepancy, an examination is needed to flush out the cause of the discrepancy, as described earlier.

Let's Do It

When a reactive performance discrepancy is identified, it is best to work from the discrepancy and deal only with those issues indicated from the analysis of the discrepancy. Instead of moving step by step through this analysis, let's look at Training in Action 4-8, an actual example of this process.

From the information provided in Training in Action 4-8, will training help? You cannot really determine the answer yet, although some factors identified suggest few external forces acting on the professors to change their teaching.

Let's suppose you did talk to the professors and they told you that they always teach this way and suggested that their job was not to entertain but to teach. Through some subtle questioning, you determine that they do not seem to understand some basic skills about making a lecture interesting and effective. They evaded questions about how an effective overhead should be set up, how questions can be used to obtain interest, and so on. Thus a KSA deficit is revealed. Would training alone be enough? It might, if the training were designed in a way that was interesting and it motivated the professors to go back to the classroom to try some different ideas. They would more likely try these new ways of teaching if organizational changes were made that encouraged them to improve. For example, when they reached an average on teacher evaluations of 3.5 on a 5-point scale, the professors could be offered a bonus (in the form of travel money or computer equipment if a cash bonus were not possible). Changes in the way pay increases are offered, with heavier emphasis on teaching, would also help. If these professors are not full professors with tenure, more emphasis on the importance of student evaluations in getting tenure or promotion would encourage professors to be more concerned with their teaching. Even personal interest by the dean could be effective. The dean might meet with the professor and indicate a concern with the performance; they could set goals for improvement and then meet on a regular basis to encourage the change. All these changes combined with a well-designed training program that would also motivate the professors should result in an improvement.

WHERE DO YOU START WHEN YOU HAVE A PERFORMANCE DISCREPANCY?

Students in a training and development class decided that for their class project they would like to determine why some professors are interesting and informative, whereas others are not. The needs analysis of this performance discrepancy (PD) would help to determine whether the issue is training or something else.

They examined the PD using operational analysis (expected performance) and person analysis (actual performance). As is noted in Table 4-3, one way of obtaining expected performance data is to observe the job. The group of students observed the job (lecturing) of professors for 2 years, and also using data from other students they interviewed, they developed a list of behaviors they believed made lectures interesting and informative.

For person analysis (actual performance), the students used observation and performance data (see Table 4-7). Using the observation method, the students identified six professors who were considered to show a performance discrepancy. These data were compared with other performance data (published student surveys) about the professors' teaching skills, which verified the observations. An attempt to verify this information further was made by asking the dean to provide student (customer) complaints about professors over the past 2 years. The dean declined to provide such information.

The organizational analysis was then conducted. Because of the nature of the discrepancy (only business school professors were studied), the organizational analysis focused primarily on the business school. Examining the university-wide mission and other documents was not necessary. From Figure 4-1, questions about the reward/punishment incongruence, inadequate feedback, and obstacles in the system were examined. This step was done through an interview (management interrogation as noted in Table 4-1) with the dean of the business school. Questions related to adequate feedback were (1) Are other performance ratings of professors used? (2) Do the professors receive feedback on their performance? The dean's answer was that the only measure of their teaching performance is student surveys and any unsolicited complaints from students. Regarding feedback, the professors receive the student evaluations along with a ranking of themselves and all other faculty members based on these data. Any student complaints would also be made available to the professor. The dean noted that the same professors tended to be rated low each year but again declined to provide specifics. A question related to reward/punishment incongruence was: What happens to those who are rated high and low? The answer was nothing; no extrinsic rewards or punishment were given for being a good or poor teacher. Finally, in response to a question about obstacles in the system, the dean emphasized the pressure for publications. "Publish or perish" were the words he used. Promotions, tenure, travel, and other rewards were all provided to those who published on a regular basis.

REACTIVE VERSUS PROACTIVE

From a systems perspective, it makes sense that a proactive approach would be better than a reactive approach. Obviously, anticipating needs is better than waiting until they cause problems. Companies that integrate the training function with strategic objectives are more readily able to respond to the rapidly changing technology and business conditions that are an everyday part of corporate life.[48] However, even when operating proactively, the organization will at times need to react to something happening in the environment; strategic plans are not meant to be cast in concrete. Using a combination of proactive and reactive strategies allows an organization to be most effective. It is, in fact, possible that a proactive approach is more important for market leader organizations than for cost leader organizations.[49] Market leaders need to be much more aware of their environment and anticipate how they will respond to that environment, otherwise they will not survive.[50] In reality, however, many organizations operate from a reactive perspective when it comes to training.

The Small Business

Some suggest the small business is not simply a miniature large organization, but a unique entity in itself.[51] This assessment may be true, but many of the procedures necessary to be effective are similar. In a small businesses, the procedures that management decides to implement are likely more important, because errors in judgment that create challenges for large companies (such as the building of the Edsel car by Ford) could destroy a small business. Therefore, the proactive approach to training would seem to be more important for the small business. Furthermore, in smaller organizations it is easier to integrate a proactive approach because fewer employees are involved.

Top management of a small business (president or owner) is usually responsible for any training.[52] This setup creates a problem, because this individual often does not understand how a proactive approach to training can be advantageous.[53] In fact, much of the dissatisfaction with training in the small business sector is a function of the reactive approach, which responds to a crisis with a "quick fix." The small business owner/manager needs to realize that sound training practices tied to the strategic plan will in the long run pay off, as Metro Tool and Die discovered (see Training in Action 4-9).

Other evidence indicates that more small manufacturing businesses are undertaking TNA. Many want to become ISO certified. David Alcock works for the Canadian Plastics Training Center (CPTC) in Toronto, which provides training to many of the small moldmaking companies in the region. He says that because of the investment required in becoming ISO certified, companies are requesting a TNA to obtain the maximum effect for their training dollars. He noted that in the last few years more than half of the company's customers (which are mostly small businesses) requested a TNA.

The time factor is always a concern for any business, but particularly for small business. So, for small business, the TNA often seems a waste of time. Techniques can speed the process of working through a TNA, but generally these techniques require a trained analyst to be effective.[54] Here are some tips for the small business HR person or manager to consider when faced with conducting a TNA:[55]

- Be clear on what you are going to do.
- Examine existing available data.
- Develop some ideas related to the issue and test them in your data gathering.
- Collapse the steps.
- Use technology.

The most important thing is to clarify what the issue is and map out what you plan to do before venturing out to do it. Look for records, minutes, and any other documentation related to the

---

TRAINING IN ACTION 4-9

TRAINING: WHERE IS THE RETURN?

Metro Tool and Die of Mississauga, Ontario, has 42 employees, most of whom have little education or training. Mr. Panteno, the owner, was interested in improving the quality and efficiency of his shop. He contacted Fabian Hogan, a consultant with the Ontario Skills Development Ministry. After an assessment, Mr. Hogan suggested that all employees receive education in basic literacy skills and training in blueprint reading and instrumentation die setup. Conducting this training would entail a considerable expense, but the consultant convinced Mr. Panteno that the invest-ment was, in the long term, a good one. At 3:30 every day training sessions were held on company premises and company time. Was this commitment to training worthwhile? Since completion of the training, rejects dropped from 7,500 per million to 325 per million. The company won the prestigious Xerox quality award in a worldwide competition. It recently provided one of its customers with a $9,600 cost savings. In the owner's own words, "Training has paid for itself. There is no tool and die company like us. We are a small company using big-company tactics."

Source: Adapted from MacKinnon, D. J. 1992. Training days at metro tool. *Toronto Star*, April 22, pp. C1–C2.

---

issue for guidance on what to look for and where to look. Determine who you need to talk to and what questions you will ask. (A reexamination of Tables 4-1 and 4-2 might be helpful here.) Sometimes it is difficult to help employees understand exactly what you are after. Consider Fred, the only salesperson in your organization who consistently gets letters of praise from customers and high repeat business. You call Fred in and ask him what he does that makes him so successful. His response is "I don't know, I just treat them well." You might provide a scenario that outlines a particular behavior, such as "When a customer comes in Bill greets them by name, asks about the family, asks them questions about themselves, then asks what he can do for them today...." And so forth. Once Fred hears the scenario he can correct, or amend it so the scenario fits what he does. You provided Fred with a template from which to provide information to you. Clearly one way to speed up the process is to collapse the steps. For example, meet with everyone at once and give them what you think your solution is to the problem. Now ask for candid responses to questions such as "Is this an adequate description of the problem?" "Is the proposed solution the best one?" "What would you do differently?" "What would prevent the successful implementation of this solution?" Of course you need to be assured that everyone at the meeting is willing to be open and honest. Finally, the use of e-mail, discussion boards, and so forth can help you gather information from a number of employees with minimum time spent actually meeting. A discussion board is where you can place your problem or issue, and ask for comments. You return to it from time to time to review comments and questions and pose new or follow-up questions. E-mail is also a way of soliciting input. Simply get a group on an e-mail list and conduct meetings using the technology.

Problems can arise with the shortcuts, however, leading to less-than-ideal solutions. Still, the shortcut is better than not doing a TNA. Remember, the ramifications of not doing a TNA is often wasted time and money on things unrelated to solving the problem. So, even for a small business it is important to do something, rather than nothing, even if it is less than ideal. An example of a quick-and-dirty approach to TNA is provided in Training in Action 4-10. Here the minimal time required might have resulted in substantial savings in terms of not having to find new workers and train them.

TRAINING IN ACTION 4-10

NEEDS ANALYSIS FOR A SMALL BUSINESS: HOW COMPLICATED DOES IT HAVE TO BE?

A business that manufactures trailers is only 8 years old. It has 52 employees, 36 of whom work on the shop floor under one job classification. The company recently installed a computer-based process for tracking the various costs associated with its manufacturing. The first thing management noticed was that 9 of the 36 workers took much more time building trailers than the rest. This was true for all trailers—custom, large, and small. Do these nine need training?

What Was Done

The owner asked the supervisor about these employees and the supervisor suggested that they were "not our best employees." He said he would watch them to see if they performed better. The supervisor monitored their work for about 2 weeks, during which time three of the nine quit and one simply stopped coming to work. The other five remained, but their work performance did not change. In fact, it seemed to deteriorate. Finally, the owner, in talking informally with one of the other employees, asked him what he thought the problem might be. "Too much pressure is being put on them lately," he said. "Before, when they were building a trailer, if they had a problem they would come to one of us to ask for help. Now that Mike [the supervisor] watches every move they make, they are afraid to come and ask."

It turned out that these employees had trouble reading the blueprints and seven or eight times a day needed to ask someone what to do next, which adversely affected their performance. When they were being monitored, they were afraid to admit they did not know how to read the blueprints, so four simply left and the performance of the other five got worse.

What Should Have Been Done

Recall that low distinctiveness (the nine build all trailers more slowly than others do) and low consensus (only nine have such a problem) suggest a training problem. With this knowledge, further needs assessment could be done by simply asking the nine what the problem is. It is important to frame the questions as helping: "I notice you are not able to build the trailers as fast as many of the other employees. What parts of the job are most difficult?" Even asking the other workers the cause of the problem would likely reveal the deficiency. Another possibility might be unobtrusive observation (rather than monitoring, which scared them). This action would uncover their constant requests for help reading the blueprints.

Notice that these actions do not constitute a full-blown needs analysis. They are, however, much better than doing nothing at all, which resulted in needlessly losing four employees.

ASSISTANCE FOR SMALL BUSINESSES

Small-business owners can access resources to aid them in training their employees. The different levels of government assist in various ways to help fund training. For example, most states have small business development centers (SBDC) that provide assistance in training. In California, customized training programs assist companies in becoming ISO 9000 certified and are available from the California State Department of Education at no cost. Instructors with factory experience conduct a TNA and develop training based on the analysis, making the training organization-specific. As a result, employees can see its advantages to their job. The major hurdle to these programs is convincing management of their value. Also the training must be integrated into the overall plan of the organization, or it is not successful.[56]

In Canada the Federal Business Development Bank (FBDB) assists small businesses in various ways, one of which is to provide training seminars on topics important to them. The main problem with these resources is that many small businesses do not take advantage of them. One of the authors was recently talking to Arnold Gavel, a small business owner from Winnipeg who was being sued for wrongful dismissal. The owner was amazed that the terminated employee was able to sue. When asked if he had ever attended the various types of seminars offered by the FBDB, the owner replied that he had seen advertisements for them but never thought they were of interest. Was one related to training managers how to discipline and discharge? Probably.

When the small business does not have the time or expertise, government-sponsored consultants can provide support. Furthermore, in most universities, graduate students in psychology or business would welcome the opportunity to become involved. These individuals often operate under the watchful eye of highly trained professors and are willing to do the work at a fraction of the cost a professional would charge, simply for the experience. In fact, if the situation provided research possibilities, the project might be done for free. For those who argue that small businesses simply cannot afford the time to do a comprehensive TNA, we argue the opposite; they cannot afford not to. It is better to do something rather than nothing, as noted in Training in Action 4-10 .

TNA and Design

We return now to the opening case, Westcan. Remember Chris was all set to begin developing an "effective meeting" training program. As you read the rest of the case, think about the things you learned about conducting a TNA. Note the TNA Westcan uses is much simpler and less formal than some we discussed. However, the value of doing the TNA is quite obvious.

The needs assessment shows that training was required at Westcan, but not the training Chris first imagined. Her problem was that she didn't have enough information to understand the types of needs the managers had. Without this information, she began to design what she thought would be a good "effective meeting" training session. What would have happened if she had gone ahead with her original plan? After conducting the TNA, she is now in a much better position to design an appropriate training program. The next step is to develop a clear set of training objectives that will drive both the design and evaluation of training. The importance of sound training objectives cannot be overstressed. Chapter 5 provides a step-by-step procedure for developing these objectives and meshing them with training design issues and constraints.

Developing a Training Package at Westcan (continued)

Chris told Karen about the conversation with Irven and what she had put together. Chris said, "What remains is to develop the simulation. Can you help?"

"Sure," said Karen, "but it's too bad you are so far along. I may have been able to help you in designing the training."

Chris indicated she had not put a great deal of time into designing the training and was open to any suggestions.

Karen suggested that Chris consider doing a needs analysis. "In a way, you completed a partial operational analysis by determining what is required in running an effective

(continued)

(*continued*)

meeting. What we don't know is where the managers are deficient; we call that a person analysis. One way to obtain that information is to ask the managers to describe how their meetings currently run and the areas they see as ineffective. Their answers should reflect the areas in which they are deficient. Also by asking the managers what training they want, we could ensure the training was relevant. Another method would be to sit in and observe how they run their meetings. It would allow us to identify deficiencies they might be unaware of," said Karen. Karen noted that in her brief time at Westcan, it seemed that pre-meeting information was well distributed and understood: agendas were given, notice of meetings always contained the relevant information, and so on.

"You might be right," said Chris. "I simply never thought of asking them." Together they developed a questionnaire asking questions related to effective meetings, such as "What would you like to see contained in a one-day effective meeting workshop?" "How well do the meetings with your staff stay on track?" They also got permission to sit in on a number of meetings.

The returned surveys and meeting observations indicated most managers understood the rules of effective meetings. All had at one time or another attended a lecture or read material on running an effective meeting. The problem was that they had never been able to turn the knowledge into action. They knew what to do, just not how to do it. They wanted practice with feedback from a professional. They also wanted the training to be for the intact teams they continually operated in, which required that management and nonmanagement from a team attend the same training and learn the behaviors required for effective meetings together. After going through the TNA with Karen and documenting all the information, Chris said to Karen. "Well, it looks like the training I was going to provide was way off the mark compared with what we now know they need. I owe you a dinner."

SUMMARY

Training is a reasonable solution when a performance deficit is caused by an employee's lack of KSAs. Most problems identified by managers as requiring training actually do not. Most such problems are a function of reward/punishment incongruities, inadequate feedback, or obstacles in the system. A TNA will reveal the reason for the problem.

When training is required, a TNA assures that it is focussed on the deficiencies in KSAs identified. The training will then be relevant for those attending, and hence more motivating for the trainees. The likelihood is higher that training will be successful when a TNA is conducted because:

- The appropriate KSAs required to do the job are identified (operational analysis).
- The KSAs of the employees in that job are determined (person analysis) so only those needing training are trained.
- Roadblocks to transfer of the training are identified (organizational analysis) and removed.

The organizational analysis is designed to assess the capital resources, human resource availability, and the environment in which the work is conducted. It is important to understand the amount and type of resources available and what type of environment the affected employees work in. Often employees are not performing at the expected level for reasons other than a lack of KSAs. The organizational analysis identifies these reasons so they can be rectified. Even where KSAs are the problem, other remedies can be considered before training, such as job aids, practice, and so forth.

The operational analysis provides information pertaining to what the KSA requirements are for the job in question. Observing the job, doing the job, and examining job descriptions and specifications are some of the ways of determining this information. The most often used, however, is to ask incumbents and supervisors what is required in a systematic way.

The person analysis provides information as to each employee's specific level of competence regarding the KSA requirements. A number of methods can be used to determine competence levels, such as examination of performance appraisals, testing, or simply asking employees where they encounter problems. Each of these approaches offers advantages, and the one you choose depends on factors such as time, availability, and so forth.

Two types of TNA are proactive and reactive. With proactive TNA, HR is active in the development of the strategic plan, providing information on the HR capabilities in the context of the proposed plan. Once the strategic plan is determined, it is the responsibility of the training department to prepare the employees (through training) identified as needing new or updated KSAs. Then, by the time the strategic plan is fully implemented, employees who required updating already received it. In this process, the "potential deficiency" is never realized because employees receive the training to prepare for the changes before they affect productivity.

The reactive TNA is far more common, and is in response to a specific deficiency noted in a department or job. Here, the TNA needs to be completed more quickly, because the deficiency is already hurting productivity. Given that strategic plans are seldom implemented without problems and changes, an effective organization uses both types of TNA, proactive and reactive.

THE TRAINING PROGRAM (FABRICS INC.)

This section is the beginning of a step-by-step process for developing a training program. Here we examine the TNA for the program and in subsequent chapters, we will continue the process through to the evaluation.

Fabrics Inc., once a small organization, recently experienced an incredible growth. What was, only 2 years ago, a business where the owner was also the supervisor of 40 employees, is now a firm of more than 200 employees. The fast growth proved good for some with the opportunity for advancement. The owner called a consultant to help him with a few problems that emerged with the fast growth. "I seem to have trouble keeping my moldmakers, and some other key employees," he said. "They are in demand, and although I am competitive regarding money, I think the new supervisors are not treating them well. Also, I received some complaints

from customers about the way supervisors talk to them. The supervisors were all promoted from within, without any formal training in supervising employees. They know their stuff regarding the work the employees are doing so they are able to help employees who are having problems, but they seem to get into arguments easily and I hear a lot of yelling going on in the plant. When we were smaller I looked after the supervisory responsibilities myself, and never found a reason to yell at the employees, so I think they need some training in effective ways to deal with employees. I only have nine supervisors—Could you give them some sort of training to be better?"

The consultant responded, "If you want to be sure that we deal with the problem, it would be useful to determine what issues are creating the problems, and from that, recommend a course of action."

(continued)

⟨ THE TRAINING PROGRAM (FABRICS INC.) ⟩

(*continued*)

"Actually, I talked to a few other vendors and they indicate they have some traditional basic supervisor training packages they could use and, therefore, they could start right away. I really want this fixed fast," the owner said.

"Well, I can understand that, but you do want to be sure that the training you get is relevant to the problems you experienced, otherwise it is a waste of money. How about I simply contract to do a training needs analysis, and give you a report of the findings. Then, based on this information, you can decide whether any of the other vendors or the training I can provide best fits your needs in terms of relevancy and cost. That way you are assured that any training you purchase will be relevant," said the consultant.

"How long would that take?" the owner asked.

"It requires that I talk to you in a bit more detail, and also to those involved, some of the supervisors and subordinates. If they are readily available I would be done this week with a report to you early next week," the consultant replied. The owner asked how much it would cost, and after another 15 minutes, agreed to the project and they returned to the office to write up the contract for a needs analysis.

The interview with the owner (who was also the manager of all the first-line supervisors) was scheduled first, and included an organizational and operational analysis. What follows is an edited version of the questions related to the organizational analysis.

Direction of the Organization

Q: What is the mission of the company? What are the goals employees should be working for?

A: Don't really have time for that kind of stuff. I have to keep the organization running.

Q: If no mission, how do employees understand what the focus of their job should be?

A: They understand that they need to do their job.

Q: What about goals or objectives?

A: Again, I do not have the time for that and I have never needed such stuff in the past.

Q: That may be true, but you are much larger now and do need to communicate these things in some fashion. How do employees know what to focus on: quality, quantity, customer service, keeping costs down?

A: All of those things are important, but I get your point. I never actually indicated anything about this to them. I simply took it for granted that they understood it.

Q: What type of management style do you want supervisors to have, and how do you promote that?

A: I just assumed that supervisors would supervise like I did. I always listened to them when they were workers. I believe in treating everyone with dignity and respect, and I expect others to do the same. I do not have any method to transmit that except to follow my style.

HR Systems

Q: What criteria are used to select, transfer, and promote individuals?

A: I hired a firm to do all the hiring for me when I was expanding. Told them I wanted qualified workers. As for the promotion to supervisor, I picked the best workers.

Q: Best how? What criteria were you using?

```
┌─────────────────────────────────────────────────┐
│        THE TRAINING PROGRAM (FABRICS INC.)        │
```

(*continued*)

A: Well, I picked those who were the hardest workers, the ones who always turned out the best work the fastest, and were always willing to work late to get the job done.

Q: Are there formal appraisal systems? If yes, what is the information used for promotion, bonuses, and so forth?

A: Don't have time for that. I believe that people generally know when they are doing a good job. If they are not, I will not keep them.

Job Design

Q: How are the supervisor jobs organized? Where do they get their information and where does it go?

A: Supervisors receive the orders for each day at the beginning of the day and then give it out to the relevant workers. They then keep track of it to see that it is done on time and out to the customer.

Reward Systems

Q: What incentives are in place to encourage employees to work toward the success of the organization?

A: Well I think I pay them well.

Q: Does everyone receive the same amount of pay?

A: At the present time yes, because they are all relatively new supervisors. I do plan to give them raises based on how well they are performing.

Q: But you indicated that you do not really have a method of informing them what you are measuring them on. How are they to know what is important?

A: Well, I will tell them. I guess I need to be considering that issue down the road.

Performance

Q: How do the supervisors know what their role in the company is?

A: Well I told them they needed to supervise the employees, and what that entailed.

Q: How do they find out how well they are doing in their job? Is there a formal feedback process?

A: I talk to them about how they are doing from time to time, but I get your point and will think about that.

Q: Are there opportunities for help if they are having problems?

A: Take this problem with the yelling and getting employees angry at them. I have talked to them about it and have offered to get them training.

Q: How do they feel about that?

A: Actually they thought it was great. As I said, none of these supervisors have had anything in the way of supervisory training.

Methods and Practices

Q: What are the policies, procedures, and rules in the organization? In your view how do they facilitate or inhibit performance?

A: I really do not think there is anything hindering their performance. I am always willing to help, but I also have work to do. That is why I hired supervisors, so I would not have to deal with that part of the business.

After gathering information on the organization, the consultant next gathered operational analysis data from the manager (owner). The consultant used the method provided in Figure 4-3. What follows is a portion of the completed form.

```
┌──────────────────────────────────────────────────────────────┐
│              THE TRAINING PROGRAM (FABRICS INC.)               │
└──────────────────────────────────────────────────────────────┘
```

(continued)

JOB TITLE: SUPERVISOR

SPECIFIC DUTY: BE SURE WORK IS COMPLETED AND SENT TO THE CUSTOMER ON TIME

TASKS	SUBTASKS	KSAs
Organize jobs in manner that assures completion on time	Examine jobs and assess time required	Knowledge of types of jobs we get
		Knowledge of times required for jobs to be completed
	Sort and give jobs to appropriate employees	Organization and prioritizing skills
		Knowledge of employees' capabilities
Monitor progress of work	Talk to employees about their progress on jobs	Knowledge of proper feedback
		Effective feedback skills
		Helping attitude
	Examine specific job products during production to assure quality	Knowledge of quality standards
		Quality assessment skills
Listen effectively	Provide feedback to employees about performance	Knowledge of effective listening skills
		Knowledge of conflict styles
		Conflict resolution skills
		Knowledge of proper feedback
		Effective feedback skills
		Positive attitude for treating employees with respect

And so forth . . .

Next, the consultant met with the supervisors, first as a single group of nine to do an operational analysis, then individually to discuss their individual performance. He chose to use a slightly different approach to the operational analysis because he expected they might have some problems working from the form used with the owner. The following excerpt comes from that interview.

To begin the meeting, the consultant said:

I am here to find out just what your job as supervisor entails. This step is the first in determining what training we can provide to make you more effective in your job. First we need to know what it is you do on the job. So I am going to let you provide me with a list of the things you do on the job—the tasks. Let me give you an

> ### THE TRAINING PROGRAM (FABRICS INC.)

(continued)

example of what I mean. For the job of a salesperson, I might be told a required task was to "sell printers." This description is too general to be useful, or you might say you must "introduce yourself to a new client," which is too specific. What we need is somewhere in between these two extremes, such as "make oral presentation to a small group of people." Are there any questions? OK, let's begin.

Q: Think of a typical Monday. What's the first thing you do when you arrive at work?

A: Check the answering machine.

Q: That is a little too specific. Why do you check the answering machine?

A: I need to return any important calls from suppliers or customers.

Q: What do these calls deal with?

A: Complaints usually, although some are checking on the status of their job.

Q: Anybody else do anything different from that?

A: No.

Q: Then what do you do next?

A: Examine the jobs that have come in and prioritize them based on their complexity and due date.

Q: The task, then, is organizing and prioritizing the new jobs you received. What next?

A: Meet with each subordinate and see how they are doing and distribute the new work.

Q: Tell me what "see how they are doing" means.

A: I make sure they are on schedule with their work. I check their progress on the jobs they are working on.

Q: OK, so check on progress of subordinates is the task. What next?

A: After all the work is distributed I check to see what orders are due to be completed and sent out today.

Q: OK, but I guess that assumes everyone is on schedule. What do you do if someone is behind in their job?

A: Depends how far behind. If it is serious, I may simply take the job away and give it to someone I think can do the job faster.

A: I don't do that. I find out what the problem is and help the person get back on track.

Q: So you spend some time training that person?

A: Well sort of. It is not formal training but I will see why the person is having problems and give some of my "tricks of the trade" to speed things up.

Q: Anybody deal with this issue differently?

A: I don't usually have the time to do any training. I will give it to someone who can do it, or in some cases just do the job myself. Sometimes that is faster. After all we have all this useless paperwork that we have to do.

Q: I want to come back to the paperwork, but first, you are saying that no standard exists for dealing with employees who are having problems with particular jobs?

A: Sure there is. The boss expects us to train them, but with the pressure for production, we often don't have time to do that.

A: Well, I agree with that. Even though I do stop and spend time helping, I often feel the pressure to rush and probably do not do a good job of it. I do try and tell them what they need to do to improve in the particular area.

[Although the format used in the session starts first thing in the morning and continues through a typical day, clues often emerge as to other tasks that are done. The mentioning of "tell them what they need to do to improve" causes the consultant to focus on that task and what other tasks are related to it, because the owner did indicate providing feedback was an important task.]

THE TRAINING PROGRAM (FABRICS INC.)

(continued)

Q: OK, let's look at the issue of telling them how to improve. We could think of that as giving feedback to employees. What other tasks require you to discuss things with subordinates?

A: We are supposed to deal with their concerns.

A: Yeah that's right, and also we are supposed to meet one-on-one with them and discuss their performance. Trouble is these new employees are know-it-alls and not willing to listen.

A: You're right about that. On more than one occasion many of us resort to yelling at these guys to get them to respond.

A: Boy is that ever true.

Q: What about the paperwork?

A: Well it is stupid. A clerk could do it, but we are expected to do it. If we do not, then billing and other problems come up, so we have to do it or else.

A: Yeah, it takes away from us being out here where we are needed.

And so forth . . .

Other questions that might be asked:

What is the next thing you would do in the afternoon?

The next?

What is the last thing you do in the day?

That pretty much describes a typical day (Monday in this case). Is there anything you would do at the beginning of the week (Monday) that is not done at other times?

How about at the end of the week? Is there anything you do then that is not done during the rest of the week?

Is there anything that you do only once or twice a week that we missed?

Now think about the beginning of the month. What do you do at the beginning of the month that is not done at other times?

How about the end of the month?

Is there anything that is done only a few times a month that we might have missed?

The beginning of the year?

The end of the year?

Are there any tasks that we may have missed because they occur only once in a while?

You will note that often it is necessary to redefine the task statements for the incumbent. This "art comes with practice." The following list contains of some of the tasks and relevant KSAs obtained from the TNA.

TASKS	KSAs
Deal with customer complaints	Knowledge of effective listening processes
	Knowledge of conflict resolution strategies
	Listening skills
	Conflict resolution skills
Organize and prioritize jobs	Knowledge of types of jobs received
	Knowledge of time required for various jobs
	Organization and planning skills

```
┌─────────────────────────────────────────────────────────┐
```

(*continued*)

Check on progress of subordinates work/
   Provide feedback on performance

Knowledge of proper feedback processes

Knowledge of effective listening processes

Listening skills

Communication skills

Positive attitude toward treating employees with respect

Deal with concerns of employees

Knowledge of effective listening processes

Knowledge of communication strategies

Listening skills

Communication skills

Positive attitude toward helping employees

Next, for the person analysis the individual meetings with supervisors were conducted, as well as one with the owner (supervisor of the supervisors). The questions came right from the job analysis and asked about the supervisors' knowledge of the areas identified, as well as the skills, and their attitudes toward issues identified as important in their job. The introduction to the interview was:

> From the interviews I have listed a number of knowledge, skills, and attitudes that are necessary to be an effective supervisor here at Fabrics Inc. I would like to ask you how proficient you believe you are in each of them. By the way, do not feel bad if you have no understanding of many of these concepts: many do not. Remember the information gathered will be used to determine how to help you be a better supervisor, so candid responses are encouraged. In terms of having knowledge of the following, indicate to me if you have no understanding, a very low level of understanding, some understanding, a fair amount of understanding, or complete understanding.

The results of the TNA identified a number of KSAs (training needs) that were deficient, as well as some nontraining needs.

Addressing Nontraining Needs

The following nontraining issues need to be addressed to help ensure supervisory training will be transferred to the job:

- Have owner (either with others or on his own) determine what the goals and objectives of the company are, and what aspects of performance should be focused on.

- Set up a formal appraisal system where in one session, the owner sits down with each supervisor to discuss performance and set objectives. In another session performance development is discussed.

- Use objectives set for the year and clarify how rewards (bonus, pay raises, and so forth) will be tied to the objectives.

- Set up similar sessions for supervisor and subordinates in terms of developmental performance review (at a minimum). Also consider incentives based on performance appraisals.

- Hire someone to relieve the supervisors of some of their paperwork so they can spend more time on the floor.

And so forth ...

> ┌───┐
> ## THE TRAINING PROGRAM (FABRICS INC.)

(continued)

Training Needs

A number of training needs were evident from the needs analysis beyond what was indicated by the owner. Specific to those issues, however, supervisors were particularly candid in indicating they had never been exposed to any type of feedback or communication skills. They had no knowledge or skills in these areas. Attitudes in this area were mixed. Some believed that the best way to provide feedback is to "call it like it is." "Some of these guys are simply not willing to listen, and you need to be tough," was a typical comment from these supervisors. Others believed that treating subordinates the way you would like to be treated goes a long way in gaining their support and willingness to listen.

A partial list of training needs includes lack of knowledge and skill in:

Effective listening

Communication

Conflict resolution

Effective feedback

Measuring employee performance

Motivating employees . . . and so forth

At this point we will leave "the training program" with the needs identified. The next step is the design phase. Near the end of the discussion on training design in Chapter 5 we will return to Fabrics Inc.

KEY TERMS

- Behavioral test
- Bias
- Bias in performance ratings
- Cognitive tests
- Competency
- Consensus
- Content validity
- Developmental discrepancy
- Distinctiveness
- Group characteristic bias
- Halo effect
- Job analysis
- Job-duty-task method
- Knowledge of predictor bias
- Operational analysis
- Opportunity bias
- Organizational analysis
- Performance discrepancy
- Person analysis
- Proactive TNA
- Reactive TNA
- Reliability
- Strategic job analysis
- Succession planning
- Task-oriented approach
- Validity
- Worker-oriented approach

CASE ANALYSES

CASE 1

Fred recently became a manager at a local hardware store that employs about six managers and 55 nonmanagement employees. With the coming of the larger chains such as Builders Square to the area, the owner is concerned about losing many of his customers because he cannot compete on the basis of price. The management team met and discussed its strategic response. It determined that the hardware store would focus on particular items of hardware and make personalized service the cornerstone of its effort. Fred's responsibility was to train all nonmanagement employees in good

(continued)

(continued)

customer relations skills; he was given a budget of $70,000. The owner gave Fred a number of brochures sent to the company over the past few months.

One of the brochures boasted, "Three-day workshop; $35,000. We will come in and train all your employees (maximum of 50 per session) so that any customer who comes to your store once will come again."

Another said, "One-day seminar on customer service skills. The best in the country. Only $8,000 (maximum participants 70)."

A third said, "Customer satisfaction guaranteed on our customer satisfaction training for sales clerks. Three-day workshop, $25,000. Maximum participants 25 to allow for individual help."

Fred liked the third one, because it provided personalized training. He called the company in to talk about its offering. The consultant said that by keeping the number small, he would be able to provide actual work simulations for each of the trainees to practice. He also indicated he would tailor the simulations to reflect the hardware store. Fred noted they would need two sessions and asked the consultant if he could take a few more per session to accommodate the 55 employees. The consultant agreed. The training went ahead, and the cost was under the budget by $20,000. ■

CASE QUESTIONS

1. Do you agree with Fred's choice? Why?
2. What else might Fred do before choosing a training package? Describe your approach in some detail.
3. If training went ahead as indicated, how successful do you think it would be? Explain your answer using concepts from this chapter.

CASE 2

You manage the HRD department of a large electronics manufacturing firm (LEM). Fourteen people report to you (see HRD organizational chart in Exhibit 4-1). LEM manufactures radios and pilot information systems for passenger aircraft manufacturers. It has about 250 salaried employees and about 1,400 hourly paid employees operating out of a single plant that is highly mechanized. Many of the operations are automated, with highly sophisticated robotics and sensing equipment. About half the hourly paid employees operate this type of equipment. They monitor the equipment's performance, make adjustments as necessary, and occasionally perform routine maintenance. Repairs and major maintenance are done by the maintenance department. The other half of

EXHIBIT 4-1 HRD Organization Chart

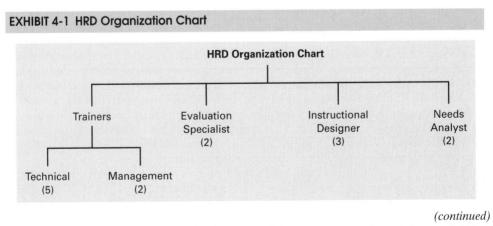

(continued)

(*continued*)

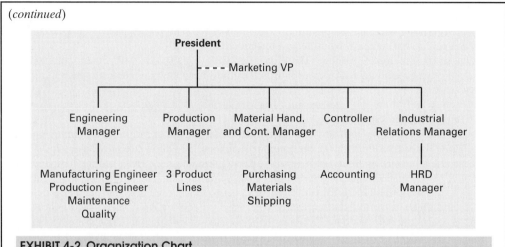

EXHIBIT 4-2 Organization Chart

the hourly paid workforce is engaged in manual operations such as wiring, assembling component boards, and assembling product housings. The salaried workforce is divided between engineers and management administrators. The structure of the organization is depicted in Exhibit 4-2.

The pace of change for both product and manufacturing technology is increasing dramatically, so much so that within 2 years a new process will be installed that will reduce the need for the hourly workforce by one-third. The reduction will come primarily from the manual operations and will reduce the need for salaried supervisors by a proportional amount. Currently, the union representing the hourly workers is resistant to "team" approaches. However, it has yet to be made aware of the new manufacturing process or the proposed workforce reduction. In spite of the union's formal posture, management instituted two experiments in work redesign in which small work groups determine work procedures, monitor their quality, and do their own interfacing with materials and shipping. These experiments contributed to improving the quality of these products, and the hourly employees feel quite attached to this way of doing business.

Competition is fierce in this industry, yet the marketing vice president and president recently secured two new contracts. One is to produce a new and highly secret passive restraint sensing system, which if successful will reduce passenger injuries in a crash by at least 50 percent. The second is a state-of-the-art radar interpretation system that will provide warning to pilots of air disturbance and air traffic and simplify existing radar interpretation. Putting these products on line will require dropping one of the old product lines (probably the radio) because of space limitations.

Management generally views the training organization as useful in acquiring financial resources to support professional development opportunities, obtaining certification/recertification in various disciplines, and providing several in-house seminars/workshops that were well received. The hourly paid workforce takes a different view of training. Their training focused on machine/equipment operation, safety, and literacy. Some seminars and workshops in teams and quality were not well received at all. In fact, the only program that was well received by the hourly paid workforce is the literacy program that HRD strongly pushed. After two years in existence, this program is well thought of by both rank-and-file and union leadership.

You, the HRD manager, and the industrial relations manager will meet with the president and vice presidents to discuss the strategic plan for LEM over the next 2 years. The industrial relations manager presented you with several questions to consider in preparation for the meeting. (See the following case questions.) ■

(*continued*)

CASE QUESTIONS

1. What performance discrepancies have you identified (separate into proactive and reactive)?
2. What KSAs will employees, both hourly and managerial need to meet expected performance in the short term (less than 1 year)? Provide your rationale.
3. What are the long-term KSA needs of LEM at both the hourly and managerial levels? Give your assumptions about the business's environment and technology.
4. What nontraining needs have you identified? Provide your rationale.
5. Based on the information provided here, what recommendations would you make regarding how the HR function should be used over the next 2 years?
6. Assuming your recommendations in question 5 are accepted, what is your strategic plan for training and development? Identify which needs identified in questions 2, 3, and 4 will be met by HRD and which by other HR systems.

EXERCISES

1. In a small group, analyze the job of "student." What are the duties and tasks required? From these tasks, list the KSAs that students need. Are any in your group deficient in any of these KSAs? Now identify and list the workshops offered to students to help them be successful. Are these relevant to the KSAs you identified? What additional programs would you recommend be offered?
2. Do the same job analysis for students in another field and compare it with yours. Are the KSAs the same for a student in science and arts? In law or engineering? What (if anything) is different?
3. Talk to someone you know who is currently working and see whether it would be possible to do a TNA on a particular job classification or on his or her job. Even interviewing only a few employees would provide enough information to give you an idea of how to conduct the TNA.

QUESTIONS FOR REVIEW

1. What is the purpose of a TNA? Is it always necessary?
2. What is the difference between proactive and reactive TNA? When is proactive better?
3. What are competencies, and why are they popular in training departments? How are competency models related to job analysis?
4. Describe how you would go about analyzing the future training needs of your university.
5. To obtain person analysis data, why not just use the performance appraisal completed by the supervisor? How can you obtain the best information possible if performance appraisal data must be used? How do self-ratings fit into this approach?

Appendix 4.1

One of the critical components in training is the development of appropriate tests (criterion) to accurately measure success in training. You need accurate measures for assessing KSAs during the TNA, for feedback during training, and to evaluate the training once completed. This section provides both a conceptual framework for understanding the criterion measures, and a practical guide as to how to develop sound criteria.

THE CRITERION

The operational analysis identifies the "type" of behavior expected in order for the job incumbent to be successful. This information is used in evaluating the training. The standards used in evaluations are called criterion measures. A criterion is defined as a standard by which a decision or judgment can be made.

Because you obtain this information from the TNA, it is important to understand the issues that relate to the developing of good criterion measures that are both reliable and valid. Let's first look at these two issues (reliability and validity) to help you understand the complexity of developing sound criteria for assessing the effectiveness of a training program.

Reliability

Reliability is a measure of the consistency of an outcome and is often measured using a correlation coefficient. It can be measured two ways: across similar measures (split half), and across time (test retest).

For the *split half method*, let's assume that 100 multiple-choice questions are used to test your knowledge on this course. To determine the reliability of the test, the instructor splits the test into two; even-numbered questions and the odd-numbered questions. He considers them as separate tests, even though the 100 questions were given at the same time. So, adding up the score of the odd-numbered and even-numbered questions provides two scores for each student. Correlating the two scores, he determines how reliable the test was. A high correlation would suggest that the test was highly reliable.

In the *test retest method*, the instructor gives you the test today (all 100 questions) and again in three days. He correlates student scores from the two time periods. Again, a high correlation between the two sets of scores would indicate a reliable test.

Highly reliable criterion measures are important. Consider a criterion for a machinist who completed training: He must produce a shaft exactly 4 centimeters thick. A test is constructed that requires the trainee to produce a shaft with the correct specifications. To pass the test, the trainee must produce a shaft whose measurement can be off by no more than 2/1,000ths of a centimeter. The evaluator measures the shaft with a micrometer (a measurement instrument able to detect differences in thousandths of centimeters). She finds it 1/1,000ths of a centimeter too large. If she measured it tomorrow, she would find the same results. If another instructor measured it using the same procedure, he would find the same results. This criterion is highly reliable. If a ruler is used instead of a micrometer, the results may still be reliable, but less reliable because the less-accurate ruler makes judgment errors in reading the scale more likely. Developing well-designed instrumentation, therefore, is important to obtaining a reliable measure, whether it be for a machinist or a measure of interpersonal skills.

Although developing a reliable instrument is important, of equal importance is the reliability in the use of the instrument. Both the instrument and the procedure used in applying it affect the reliability of the results. Consider the micrometer. Without training, the evaluator would not know how much to tighten the instrument around the shaft before obtaining the measurement. If one evaluator tightened it as much as he could and another tightened it just until she felt the first sign of resistance, the difference in results could be more than the 2/1,000ths of a centimeter tolerance allowed.

Relationship Between Reliability and Validity

Reliability is the consistency of a measure, and **validity** is the degree to which you are measuring what you want to measure. As an example, imagine that a rifle manufacturer has two new rifles and wishes to test for their ability to hit the bull's-eye. He places the first rifle in a vise-like mechanism to prevent deviation, which occurs if a person were doing the shooting. For the purpose of this discussion, we will change the terminology for validity slightly. We will say validity is "doing what you want it to do" rather than "measuring what you want to measure." Conceptually, these notions are the same. In the vise, the first rifle is aimed at a target 50 yards away, and five shots are fired. Each shot hits the target (see Figure 4-5A). Is the rifle (instrument) consistent (reliable)? As you can see, the five bullets struck the target but they are all over the place. The rifle is not reliable. Nor is it valid (doing what you want it to do: hit the bull's-eye). There is no point trying to make the rifle valid (doing what you want it to do) because it has no reliability; you need reliability before you can have validity. The next rifle is placed in the vise. This time the five shots are all in the upper left-hand corner of the target (Figure 4-5B). Is the rifle reliable? Yes, since it consistently hit in the same place for all five shots. Is it valid? No, it did not hit the bull's-eye. We now adjust the sight and fire; all five hit the bull's-eye (Figure 4-5C). Is this rifle reliable? Yes, the bullets were all in relatively the same place (consistent). Is it valid? Yes, all five hit the bull's-eye as well.

From this example it should be clear that you can have a reliable test that is not valid, but you cannot have a valid test that is not reliable. You need consistency of a measure before you even consider expecting all the bullets to hit the bull's-eye. Reliability, therefore, is a primary concern, but only because you need it to have validity.

Validity

Validity, as the degree to which you are measuring what you want to measure, is more difficult to assess than reliability. Consider the question, "Has training resulted in learning?" Learning is a physiological process that takes place in the brain. We are unable to assess this process directly, so we test individuals and, on the basis of their scores, we infer whether learning takes place. It is not a direct measure of the learning process but an inference based on behavior.

To better understand the issues here, let's examine the ultimate criterion.[1] The ultimate criterion is what we would like to be able to measure if it were possible to do so. It would include the exact indicators of success. However, we are never able to measure the ultimate criterion, because it is simply a theoretical construct. We must settle for what we are able to measure: the actual criterion.[2] Examining the relationship between the ultimate criterion and the actual criterion provides us with insight into the problems associated with criterion development. The actual criterion can be thought of in terms of its relevance, deficiency, and contamination in relation to the ultimate criterion (see Figure 4-6).

Criterion Relevancy   The criterion relevancy is the portion of the actual criterion that overlaps the ultimate criterion (see Figure 4-6). It would be the true validity of the actual criterion. However, given that we can never measure the ultimate criterion, an empirical measure of this validity (a correlation between the ultimate criterion and actual criterion) is not possible. This problem illustrates the need for logical and rational analysis in developing the actual

FIGURE 4-5 A Comparison of Reliability and Validity

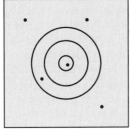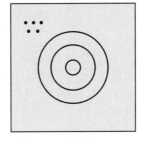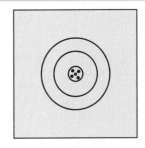

A   B   C

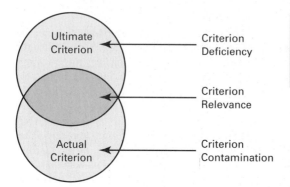

FIGURE 4-6 Diagram Illustrating the Criterion (Constructs) of Deficiency, Relevance, and Contamination

criterion to obtain an approximation of the ultimate criterion.

Let's look at an example in which training is designed to improve interpersonal relationships. Raters evaluate the learning by rating a trainee's behaviors in a scripted role play. The degree to which the raters are trained, to which the scales to be used in rating are well developed, and to which examples of acceptable and less acceptable behavior are clear to the raters are all factors that contribute to the validity (overlap of actual with ultimate) of the criterion. Because these will never match the ultimate criterion perfectly, deficiencies and contamination will always be factors. The more rigorous the development of criterion measures and processes, however, the more the actual criterion will approach the ultimate criterion.

Criterion Deficiency Criterion deficiency is the part of the ultimate criterion that we miss when we use the actual criterion, or the degree to which we are not measuring important aspects of performance. The factors that make up a trainee's ability to produce parts with a tolerance of a few thousandths of a centimeter are more complex than simply being able to do it under ideal testing conditions. Factors such as noise in the plant, the different types of parts that need to be machined, climate in the plant, and supervisor-subordinate relationships contribute to making a machinist successful. Our measure of success (producing one part in a training room) will obviously be deficient when compared with an ultimate measure of a successful machinist (the ultimate criterion).

Criterion Contamination Just as any measure will miss some important aspects of true success

(criterion deficiency), so will it contain some part that measures aspects not related to the true measure of success (criterion contamination). This part of the actual criterion does not overlap with the ultimate criterion.[3]

The two main categories of contamination are error and bias. **Error** is random variation in the scores on the criterion. It is, by definition, not correlated with anything. Error is, therefore, not as great a concern as bias. Although it lowers validity, it does not cause misrepresentation of the data, unless it is too large. Then, of course, it can result in the criterion becoming invalid. A high error content could be caused by poor training of the evaluator, poorly developed instruments, or other factors.

When the contamination is **bias** rather than error, it is correlated with other measures. It can result in spuriously high correlations between the criterion and these measures of success. Four sources of such bias are opportunity bias, group characteristic bias, bias in ratings, and knowledge of predictor.[4]

Opportunity bias occurs when certain individuals have some advantage that provides them with a higher level of performance, irrespective of their own skill level. For example, the criterion used to determine transfer of training is the number and quality of parts turned out by the machinist on the job. To determine whether training is effective in transferring learned skills to the job, you might correlate the scores on the training exam with performance 1 year later. In other words, the learning measured in the training evaluation is used as a predictor of future performance on the job. Analysis of these data indicates that those who scored highest on the test in training also produced the most and best quality (i.e., a high correlation was found between success in training and overall success after training). What is not known is that those who scored the highest in training received as a reward the newest and best machines to work on. The relationship between the two scores was contaminated by the fact that the better trainees received the better machines, and it could be that these machines provided the opportunity for success.

Group characteristic bias occurs when something about the group creates higher (or lower) performance, irrespective of an individual's capability. What if the trainees who did well were placed with supervisor A, who was progressive and participative in her approach, and those who did less well in training were placed with a more authoritarian supervisor who would "keep an eye on them"? Once again, those who did better in training may produce more and better-quality products as a function of the climate created by the supervisor. Those working for the authoritarian supervisor could in fact be restricting output in protest.

Another possible contaminant of the criterion is **bias in performance ratings**. The measure of transfer of training is often determined by the supervisor. The subjective ratings of supervisors are often used even in areas where objective data are available, because the objective data are often flawed—some workers have better territories (sales), better equipment (machinist), or a better environment (clean, well lit). In many cases the supervisor does not take these issues into account when rating subordinates. The **halo effect**, another type of rating bias, is a powerful force in rating subordinates. It occurs when a supervisor rates a subordinate on all dimensions of performance on the basis of knowledge of only one dimension. For example, Susan is well organized, so she is a great performer; Bill is excellent at running a meeting so he must be excellent at organizing, decision making, and interpersonal skills. To be effective in rating subordinates, supervisors need to rate each of the dimensions of the job separately and carefully so as not to allow one particular dimension to influence others.

The final possible contaminant is **knowledge of predictor bias**. The criterion for success in training could be thought of as a predictor of later performance on the job; successful training should contribute to successful performance. If, however, the supervisors were aware of the level of success in training, this information could influence their performance ratings.

DEVELOPMENT OF CRITERIA

It may seem that developing sound criteria is impossible. Not so. As we discussed previously, the operational analysis identifies the level of acceptable performance. From this analysis, criteria can be developed. Once criteria are established, the next step is to carefully develop instruments to measure the criteria. The instruments should leave as little as possible to the judgment of the rater.

Consider cognitive (declarative) knowledge. For the job of internal auditor, one of the tasks (expected behavior) is to know which reference books to use for each of the auditing issues. A part of the knowledge required then is to know what is in the various reference manuals. Training would require the trainee to learn what was contained in the various reference books. A criterion for success would be demonstrating this knowledge.

In developing a measure of the criterion, the goal is to have it as objective as possible. In this case, a multiple-choice test of the material would be an excellent method. The advantage of a well-designed multiple-choice test is that minimal judgment is necessary, so no matter who scores the test, the outcome will be the same (highly reliable). Given that well-designed multiple-choice tests can accurately measure any cognitive (declarative) knowledge,[5] we strongly suggest their use when possible.

Developing sound criteria for skills may be more difficult, and they may not be as reliable. However, instruments to measure skills, if carefully developed, could still meet reliability requirements. Some examples are presented in the discussion of evaluation in Chapter 8, under "Fabrics Inc."

With skill development, the trainee begins to learn more and more procedural, rather than declarative, knowledge. Procedural knowledge is more difficult to recall.[6] Furthermore, the appropriate criterion measure should be behavioral. The internal auditor may have as an expected behavior "Calm an irate department head." The expected behavior is to be able to calm down someone who becomes irate. The skill required to accomplish this behavior could be "active listening skills." A measure of the criterion would be how a trainee behaves in a role-play situation in which the role player becomes angry at something the auditor says.

In the case of measuring the criterion of "calming an irate department head," it is critical to develop clear rules and examples of what is and is not acceptable. Also it is important to train raters in the use of the rules and to provide examples. The more familiar the raters are with good, average, and poor responses, the more reliable the measure can be.

Validity in such instances is primarily what is called **content validity**. It is obtained when an expert examines the criteria on the basis of her knowledge of the TNA.[7] It is important, therefore, to conduct a good TNA, for everything that follows from it (both training content and evaluation instruments) is based on that analysis.

The time and effort spent developing a sound criterion are critical to the training process. Once developed, the criterion is used to determine several things:

- The expected level of performance (operational analysis)

- Whether the incumbent can reach it (person analysis)

- The training needs for those who cannot reach it (a training objective)

- A measure of training effectiveness for those taking the training (measure of success)

Training Design

DESIGN PHASE

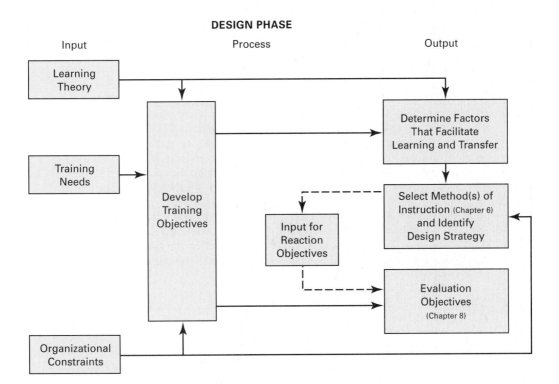

Learning Objectives

After reading this chapter, you should be able to:

- Describe the purpose of training objectives, the criteria for evaluating such objectives, and the advantages of developing these objectives
- Write a learning objective that meets the criteria for a good objective and accurately reflects needs analysis data

- Write a proposal for a training program
- Describe the motivational, KSA, and learning environment factors that act to facilitate trainee learning
- Use elaboration theory and the Gagné-Briggs theory of design to design a training session
- Describe the implications of motivation theories for training design
- Discuss the relationship between Gagné-Briggs theory of instruction and social learning theory
- Appropriately apply principles derived from learning theory to design a training session
- List and describe the factors that make it likely that learning gained during training will transfer back to the trainee's job

---

The Real World of Training . . . What Is Wrong Here?

CASE 1

At a large training establishment operated by the government, a course was offered in which trainees learned how to operate and repair a large, complex electronic system. The goal of the course was simple: develop trainees' ability to operate and maintain the electronic system. It was impossible to provide every trainee with his or her own system to practice on, but the instructor decided to increase the amount of trouble-shooting experience by providing classroom exercises on troubleshooting. The instructor posed various problems for the students to solve. For a specific problem such as a burned-out capacitor, he asked the students to identify the symptoms that would appear (e.g., the control board would not operate). After the training, the instructor was surprised to learn that many trainees were not doing well on the job. They seemed to be able to operate the equipment, but when it came to troubleshooting, they were not performing well.

CASE 2

The chief instructor of a 32-week military course examined the grades of the last four groups to complete the course. He noted an unusual trend. Students did poorly on the first exam, then did considerably better on the second and third exams. Then the students did poorly on the fourth but got better on the fifth and sixth. This trend continued throughout the 32 weeks, even for the brightest students. What was going on here?

The training model (design phase) at the start of the chapter provides an overview of the process we will follow in this chapter. We use information from the TNA along with organizational constraints and learning theories (inputs) to determine the training objectives (process part of the design phase). One of the outputs from the design phase, covered in this chapter, is an understanding of the factors that facilitate learning and the transfer of training. This understanding is obtained from learning theory (input). The other outputs that come from the design phase are:

- Identifying the most appropriate method of instruction, given the training objectives and our understanding of what facilitates learning and transfer (Chapter 6)
- Determining the evaluation objectives based on the training objectives (Chapter 8)

Chapter 6 provides the information on the various methods of instruction. Using social learning theory we indicate which methods are best for different objectives. At the end of the chapter, a table is provided to assist in making the decision as to the most appropriate method to use, based on objectives of the training. The evaluation objectives (the other output) are one of the inputs into development of the evaluation (Chapter 8).

Now, on to the design of training. As noted previously, the design phase provides a guide for what you need to do after determining the training needs of employees. Training needs, learning theories, and an understanding of the constraints that are placed on the HRD department are the inputs into the first step in the design phase—development of objectives. These objectives are then used to drive the design of training (content, methods, materials, etc.). Decisions about training design integrate what we know about "how people learn" (learning theory) with "what they need to learn." From there we develop the appropriate training. Of course, the plan must take into consideration any constraints (money, time, facilities, etc.) the organization may have. On the basis of all this information, a particular design is created and a training program is developed.

Suppose you completed a TNA and identified that supervisors need training in effective communication skills. You then need to make some decisions, such as the following:

- What method of training to use
- How much time to allot for the training
- How many trainees to train at the same time
- Whether training be on company time (overtime)
- Whether training be voluntary or mandatory
- On or off-site location for training

How we decide these issues is to some extent based on organizational constraints. If the HRD department does not have the resources to develop the program, or supervisors cannot be off the job for more than a half-day, these factors will help shape what the training will look like and how it will be offered. Let's look at these organizational constraint issues in more detail.

Organizational Constraints

In a perfect world, it would be possible to develop the perfect training program for every training need identified. For our supervisors who need the effective communication training we could develop a 2-week intensive training package using the most effective methods with lots of practice built in. Reality prevails, however, and many constraints around which training must be designed need to be considered. Many of these constraints influence the type of training you are able to offer. Table 5-1 provides a list of some of these constraints and various ways to approach training design. This list is not exhaustive and serves primarily as an example of the ways in which organizational constraints affect the methods and approaches used to meet the training needs. We discuss two major categories of constraints: organizational/environmental and trainee population. Each affects the issue of whether to train and the type of training you will be able to offer.

ORGANIZATIONAL/ENVIRONMENTAL CONSTRAINTS

Budgets are generally limited, so you must make choices about who gets trained and what type of training they receive. One way of making these decisions is to use the strategic direction of the organization to set priorities. The strategic planning process, when completed, provides a

TABLE 5-1 Constraints and Possible Ways of Dealing with Them

Constraint	*Suggestion for How to Handle*
Need high level of simulation[a] because: 　Law (fire drills)	
Task is critical to the job (police firing gun)	Incorporate a longer lead time to prepare simulations/ role plays.
Mistakes are costly (airline pilot)	Purchase simulators.
Trainees vary in amount of experience	Consider modularization.
Trainees have large differences in ability levels	Use programmed instruction[b]. Have high level of trainer-trainee interaction.
Mix of employees and new hires trained on a new procedure	Consider different training programs because of possible negative transfer for employees but not for new hires.
Long lag between end of training and use of skill on the job	Distribute practice through the lag. Provide refresher material or models for the employees to follow.
Short lead time	Use external consultant or packaged training.
Bias against a type of training (role play, etc.)	Develop proof of effectiveness into the training package. Use another method.
Few trainees available at any one time	Use programmed instruction.[b]
Small organization with limited funds	Hire consultant or purchase training. Join consortium.

[a]This constraint results if you are forced to provide a more costly training program involving simulators or costly practice sessions and so forth.
[b]This method of instruction is discussed in Chapters 6 and 7 and provides self-paced learning.

rationale for determining who gets how much of what kind of training. Recall the MHC case presented in Chapter 2 and discussed again in Chapter 4. Its HR philosophy is that people are the most important resource and that HR needs are best met through employee development. This philosophy provides a guideline for training choices. The case suggests training for management on how to use the new performance appraisal process should be done before money is spent on developing a succession plan. A common performance appraisal process is necessary before effective succession planning can be introduced. Once a succession plan is developed, the choice might be whether to spend money on training managers to use the succession plan or on developing their interviewing skill for the selection process. Once again, although both are necessary, the strategic plan would indicate that if only one can be done at this time, it should probably be developing the interviewing skills.

Even if the organization does not have a clear strategic plan in place, it is a good idea for the top managers in HR to develop their own mission and goals for the HR area. This is accomplished by meeting with executives to discuss priorities. Such meetings help define HR priorities and determine how to put resources in line with the direction of the company. A side benefit is that the process may stimulate top management to engage in strategic planning.

The technological sophistication of the organization affects which type of training you are able to offer. If, as in the MHC case, you are dealing with a number of locations and have little or no access to computer networks or videoconferencing you will be severely constrained in the type of training you can offer.

Decisions about training priorities must also follow the law. Certain training requirements are mandated by the Occupational Safety and Health Act in the United States and provincial health and safety regulations in Canada. A recent U.S. study indicates that 29 percent of organizations provide safety training on a weekly or monthly basis, and another 36 percent on a quarterly or yearly basis.[1] How much of this training is a function of the Occupational Health and Safety Act is unclear, but it is likely that the act plays an important part. For example, employers must tell employees what hazardous waste they are exposed to, educate them about the risks, and provide them with the KSAs to handle the waste in a safe manner. Training in this and other safety areas should have high priority.

In addition, Title VII regarding discrimination in employment and the Americans with Disabilities Act (ADA) in the United States and the Human Rights Commissions in Canada have in some instances ordered organizations to train employees on issues related to discrimination. The same survey mentioned earlier notes 18 percent of organizations provide sexual harassment training on a weekly or monthly basis and another 50 percent on a quarterly or yearly basis.[2] Much of this training may be out of fear that if they do not provide such training they may be open to legal problems in the future. These legal issues are discussed further in Chapter 9. So, a certain amount of training budgets must go toward such training, taking money away from other possible training. We are not suggesting that this type of training is in any way inappropriate or unnecessary, just that its effects on a fixed training budget may mean that other possible training activities are curtailed.

Budgeting for Training

The budgeting process is presented from the perspective of the HRD department that charges its customers (departments in the organization) for the services it provides. This budgeting process is, for the most part, similar to an outside consultant bidding on a project. Charging for services is occurring more frequently because HRD departments are required to justify their existence like other departments. In fact, in some cases, they are expected to market their training outside the organization as well as inside.[3] So, when providing estimates you need to understand you are competing for resources, and need to be as accurate as possible. Otherwise you could lose the training to an outside consultant, or have the training put off until some later time.

Initial estimates can be difficult to determine accurately and you may want to provide the client with some varied scenarios. Because the estimate is often expected before a needs assessment is done, several scenarios are helpful to decision makers. Before a TNA, you really do not have a clear idea of what training is required and how much. All you begin with is the triggering event, as explained in the TNA chapter. You could provide budget estimates for different training scenarios or deal with this issue the way it was done in the Fabrics Inc. example presented at the end of Chapter 4. Recall, the consultant offered to do a TNA, which would then provide a clearer idea of what was required. The consultant then offered to bid on the training, based on the TNA like anyone else. This bid would be more accurate because the issues were identified and amount of training required was clearer.

Once you have an idea of the length of training, you need to estimate the amount of time it will take to develop the training for delivery. The more accurate this estimate is, the more accurate your costing will be, and the more credibility you will have with clients. The amount of time to prepare can be estimated from the length of the training program. The ratio of preparation time to training days varies a great deal, however. It can range from 12:1, where much of the material is in some form of readiness, to 300:1, if it is computer-based training with little already prepared. In many cases when training is requested, the client wants an answer fairly quickly as to the approximate cost. To respond quickly, Brooke Broadbent, a training consultant, developed a method for estimating how long it will take to develop training. This guide is shown in Table 5-2. Depending on a number of factors, including your expertise in developing training you can roughly calculate the length of time it will take to develop the training. Imagine you are bidding

TABLE 5-2 Guide to Determining Time Required to Prepare Training

Variables	Level of Effort for Design		
	Low	*Medium*	*High*
Who			
1. The designer's knowledge and skills related to instructional design	Extensive knowledge and skills	Moderate knowledge and skills	Minimal knowledge and skills
2. The designer's knowledge of the training subject matter	Extensive knowledge	Some knowledge	No knowledge
3. The size and complexity of the target training group	Small, homogeneous	Medium, moderately complex	Large, complex
4. The designer's and the client's track records for sticking to plans	Always stick	Sometimes stick	Never stick
What			
5. The number of instruction modules	Few (5 modules)	Several (8 modules)	Many (12 modules)
6. The elements included in the training materials	Participant materials only	An instructor manual and a participant manual	An instructor manual, a participant manual, overheads, and job aids
7. The client's or organization's expectations regarding packaging	Minimal (produced in-house)	Modest (desktop publishing)	Extensive (professionally produced)
8. What is considered final product	Designer completes first draft, client rest	Designer completes up to the pilot	Designer completes all drafts, finalizes after pilot
How			
9. Data collection	A focus group made up of a few well-informed people	A focus group and a few interviews	Several focus groups and several interviews
10. The designer's interaction with the client	Deals directly with top decision maker	Deals with more than one level of decision makers	Deals with a complex labor-management committee
11. The client's level of involvement	Approves general direction and final draft	Reviews and approves key materials	Reviews and approves all materials
12. The program's degree of interactivity	Minimal	Moderate	Extensive
	Effort		
	Low	*Medium*	*High*
Totals	_____ × 1 = _____	_____ × 2 = _____	_____ × 3 = _____

Add the weighted totals from the high, medium, and low columns to get an estimate of the number of days it will take to develop 1 day of instructor-led training.

Source: Broadbent, B. 1998. The Training Formula. *Training & Development* 52:41–43.

on a 1-day workshop on effective communication. Examining Table 5-2, you check "low" for all but the last factor (degree of interactivity). For this item you rate "high" because of the extensive interaction within the training program. Based on the table, the training will require 14 days to prepare (11 + 0 + 3). From this information you could simply calculate an overall cost, but it might seem high to a client who does not know what is involved in the development of training. So, it is useful to have some sort of breakdown as depicted in Table 5-3. In such estimates it is a good idea to build in a contingency fund of about 10 percent, which will help cover unforeseen costs. This portion is indicated under miscellaneous. The "rate" should include both the trainer's fee as well as overhead costs. In the example depicted in Table 5-3 if the training is to be presented only once, the cost of the total training package would be $15,400 plus the cost of the 1-day training session. If it is to be offered 10 times, then the total cost of the development can be amortized over the 10 sessions, making its cost per session or employee much less.

So far we have only dealt with the developmental costs associated with training. For the total cost, you need to include direct costs associated with putting on the training (trainer compensation, travel, facilities, food and beverages, and so forth), indirect costs, overhead costs, and participant compensation. These costs are described in Table 5-4. Also for a more inclusive estimate of the total costs associated with putting on a training program, see Table 5-5.

Trainee Population

What if the TNA identifies two or more subgroups with the same training objectives but different levels of KSAs. A single training program to meet all their needs is difficult to develop. Let's go back to our supervisors who need the communication training. What if in the TNA we discovered that half of them previously received training in active listening, and were reasonably proficient in it. The effective communication model we plan to use in the training of supervisors involves five steps; the first step is active listening. The training, therefore, could be designed in a modular manner in order to provide only the relevant modules to each subgroup. In our supervisor example, the first module would be skill building in the active listening process, and only those not already proficient need attend. Then, all of the supervisors would receive the effective communication training, with the understanding that all were proficient in the active listening portion of the model.

Sometimes the needs analysis identifies a wide variability in the KSAs of the target population. In this case, the training design could provide individualized instruction, accomplished through computer-based or video instruction, although both take a long time to develop. Another alternative would be to allow for small classes and a high level of interaction between each trainee and the instructor.

TABLE 5-3 Proposal for Developing a 1-day Workshop on Effective Communication

Action	Time	Rate	Total
Prepare			
Interview relevant employees to determine issues and context to develop training	1 day	$1,000	$ 1,000
Develop objectives and plan for developing training, including identifying appropriate strategies (methods) to be used in instruction; also development of evaluation objectives	2.5 days	$1,000	$ 2,500
Develop training materials based on objectives	8 days	$1,000	$ 8,000
Develop visual aids and evaluation material	2.5 days	$1,000	$ 2,500
Miscellaneous			$ 1,400
TOTAL			$15,400

TABLE 5-4 Types of Costs in Training Programs

Development Costs

All costs related to the development of the program are included, plus the cost (or proportion) of any front-end TNA and of evaluation and results tracking. The cost of all program and materials design, any computer-based programming, and any piloting of the training are also included. These costs can be amortized over the life of the program (if it is planned for more than 1 year) to prevent overly high costs in the first year.

Direct Costs

These costs are directly attributable to the delivery of the training program. The criteria for inclusion in this category is that if training were cancelled the day before it was to begin, the cost would not be incurred. Thus travel, materials (that could be used in the future), facilities, food and beverage (unless a cancellation charge applies), equipment rental, and trainer compensation are included.

Indirect Costs

This category consists of any nondevelopment item that would be incurred even if training were cancelled the day before it was to start. It would include trainer compensation for preparation, materials purchase/duplication (if not usable in the future), marketing expenses, administrative and clerical support (compensation rate for time spent on project), and any materials already sent to trainees.

Overhead Costs

These costs reflect the program's share of the general operating costs of the training and development department (or the business, depending on the size and nature of the organization). For a large organization with its own training department, these costs would include the program's share of the purchase and maintenance of training equipment, clerical and administrative support, and training facilities, among other costs. For a small business that purchases the training externally, no overhead costs are likely to be involved. On the other hand, if a training and consulting firm develops a workshop for a client, the overhead would be considered to be the workshop's share of the normal operating expenses of the firm. Often this expense is calculated as a portion of revenue generated or as a fixed charge per day of training.

Participant Compensation

While participants are attending training, their salaries and benefits should be included as a cost of training. Another way to approach this expense calculation is to include only the cost of replacing those employees while they are in training. Thus for a management training program lasting 3 days, these managers may not be replaced; other managers may be asked to assist the work unit in routine matters, and the manager attending training is expected to handle everything else outside of training time. In these cases, no participant compensation cost was included because no organizational cost was incurred for replacing the trainee. An opportunity cost arises, however, because many things didn't get done that would be done if the manager were doing his regular job. Legitimate arguments can be made for and against including the participant compensation costs in these cases. Most organizations will have a policy on the matter.

Evaluation Costs

Costs are associated with evaluating the training to see whether it was successful. Here development of the assessment tools, time spent administrating them, and analyzing and preparing reports should all be included as well as material and travel costs if necessary.

TABLE 5-5 Training Costs for Grievance Reduction Training	
Developmental Costs	
1. 20 days of director's time at $50,000 per year	$ 4,000
2. 5 days of trainer's time at $30,000 per year	$ 600
3. Materials	$ 1,000
Direct Costs	
1. 5 days of trainer's time at $30,000 per year	$ 600
2. Training facility rental for 5 days at $150 per day	$ 750
3. Materials and equipment	$ 2,000
4. Coffee, juice, and muffins	$ 600
Indirect Costs	
1. 1 day of trainer preparation	$ 120
2. 3 days of administrative preparation at $20,000 per year	$ 120
Participant Compensation	
1. 30 supervisors attending 5-day workshop (average $35,000/yr.)	$21,000
Evaluation Costs	
1. 6 days of evaluator's time at $30,000 per year	$ 720
2. Materials	$ 800
Total Training Costs	**$32,310**

Note: Calculations for the personnel costs are based on a 250-day work year.

In some instances trainees hold negative feelings about a particular training technique. If this attitude is known during the design stage, a different technique can be considered. Alternatively, the design could build in attitude-change modules at the beginning. We found, for example, that many managers do not want to role play in training. We often hear arguments such as "This is silly" or "These never work." One way to handle this resistance is simply to call it something different. The term *play*, for some, suggests it is not serious learning. Sometimes when we present the technique, we suggest it is time for some "behavioral practice." This simple change in terms causes the exercise to be received more positively. The point here is that if, through the needs analysis, you discover a particular method of training is disliked because of past experience or word of mouth, you need to include in the training design a method of changing the perception or use another method when possible.

Refer back to the design phase of the training model and note that with these two inputs—TNA and organizational constraints—we develop the training objectives.

Developing Objectives

The term **training objectives** refers to all the objectives that are developed for the training program. The most important types of objectives are presented in Table 5-6. The term **trainee reaction objectives** refers to the objectives set for how trainees should feel about the training and their learning environment. The training's **learning objectives** describe the KSAs that trainees are expected to acquire throughout the training program, and the ways that learning will be demonstrated. **Transfer of training objectives** describe the changes in job behavior that are expected to occur as a result of transferring the KSAs gained in training to the trainee's job. **Organizational outcome objectives** describe the outcomes the organization can expect from the

TABLE 5-6 Types of Training Objectives

1. Trainee Reaction Objectives	Describes the desired trainee attitudinal and subjective evaluations of training
2. Learning Objectives	Describes the type of behavior that will demonstrate the learning, the conditions under which the behavior must occur, and the criteria that will signify that a sufficient level of learning occurred
3. Transfer of Training Objectives	Describes the job behaviors that will be affected by training, the conditions under which those behaviors must occur, and the criteria that will signify that a sufficient transfer of learning from training to the job occurred
4. Organizational Outcome Objectives	Describes the organizational outcomes that will be affected by the transfer of learning to the job and the criteria that will signify that organizational outcome objectives were achieved

changes in the trainees' job behavior due to the learning. Ideally, a training program would develop objectives in all four areas.

IDENTIFYING OBJECTIVES

The TNA is a critical part of determining what the objectives of training should be. To summarize briefly: The result of integrating the organization, job, and person analyses is the identification of performance deficiencies, their negative effect on organizational outcomes, and also identification of the cause of the deficiencies (i.e., motivation, KSAs, environment). With this information you then determine the following:

- Which performance deficiencies can and should be addressed by training
- Which KSAs need to be learned in order to change job behavior so that the performance deficiencies are reduced or eliminated

From the performance deficiencies we set the learning objectives, the transfer of training objectives, and the organizational outcome objectives. Trainee reaction objectives can be linked to the person analysis but may also include areas not addressed in the needs analysis. For example, consider that you determined in the person analysis that a group of line employees do not like training. Their bad memories of school color their view of training as an extension of that experience, and since school their only training was on the job. A reaction objective here might be "At the end of training, trainees will respond to questions about their experiences in the training environment with either a positive or very positive response." Based upon this objective you need to consider, in the design of training, methods to assure these trainees do not experience the training in the same way they experienced their schooling.

Although the content of the various types of objectives differ, the structure and process of developing good objective statements is the same. Objectives are statements about what is expected to be accomplished. A good objective has three components.[4]

1. **Desired outcome:** What should be expected to occur?
2. **Conditions:** Under what conditions is the outcome expected to occur?
3. **Standards:** What criteria signify that the outcome is acceptable?

It is difficult to write good objectives. You must be careful to ensure that the three components are specified in unambiguous terms and the full range of expectations is addressed.

WRITING A GOOD LEARNING OBJECTIVE

We focus attention on the writing of learning objectives for two main reasons:

1. Learning objectives are often more difficult to write.
2. Learning is the critical component of the whole process.

Learning can be observed only through its influence on behavior. Thus when you are writing learning objectives, you need to think not only about what will be learned, but also how the learning will be demonstrated. Learning is also the most critical objective. If the trainer isn't clear about what is to be learned, the appropriate learning is not likely to occur and the other objectives will not matter and will not be achieved. For example, it doesn't matter to the trainees' supervisor or the CEO if a terrific learning environment is created and trainees enjoy the training if the trainees don't learn what they need to learn. If they don't, then performance deficiencies won't be corrected and the organizational outcome objectives are not likely to be met. Thus, clearly articulated learning objectives are a critical first step in developing an effective training program.

Desired Outcome: Behavior

The desired behavior must be clearly and unambiguously worded. Anyone reading the objective should be able to understand what will be required by the learner to demonstrate she learned the KSA. A learning objective that states "to understand fully how to splice electrical wire" is ambiguous. It fails to specify what the trainee will be able to do. What behavior will indicate that the trainee "understands fully"? Recall what we said earlier—think not only about what will be learned, but how the learning will be demonstrated. A clearer learning objective would be "will be able to splice electrical wires of any gauge." This statement indicates what the learner should be able to do at the end of training. Consider another example: "The trainee will be able to differentiate (by sorting into two piles) between computer chips that are within specification and those that are outside of specification." Here it is clear what is expected, but not how the trainee is expected to differentiate between the computer chips.

Conditions

Explaining the conditions under which the behavior must occur further clarifies exactly what is required. In the preceding example, it is not clear how the trainee is to determine whether the computer chips are within specifications. Is it a visual examination, or is a tester used? Providing the conditions makes the objective even clearer: "Using an ohmmeter and chart, the trainee will be able to differentiate (by sorting into two piles) between computer chips that are within specification and those that are outside of specification."

A description of the conditions (assistance or barriers) under which the desired behavior will be performed should be provided. For example, the statement "Using an ohmmeter and chart" indicates the help that is provided. If the objective began with the phrase "Without the use of reference material," it is clear that the trainee must discriminate between the chips without using any aids.

Writing in conditions is necessary in some cases and not in others. In the following example, it is critical to know that the pie charts must be developed using a specific software package: "present the results of an accounting problem in pie chart form, using the Harvard Graphics software." Conditions should be included only if they help clarify what is required.

Standards

Standards are the criteria for success. Three potential standards are represented by accuracy, quality, and speed. For example, a learning objective might define accuracy as being "able to take a reading off an altimeter with an error of no more than 10 feet." A quality standard might be indicated by the statement, "is within engineering specifications 99.9 percent of the time." Or if speed is a critical concern, "will be completed in 15 minutes or less."

Here are a few examples of training objectives for a telephone repairperson in training. The Desired behavior is **bolded**, the conditions are *italicized* and the standards are <u>underlined</u>.

> *Using a drop wire, bushing and connector, but without the use of a manual,* **the trainee will splice a drop wire** <u>according to the standards set out in the manual</u>.
>
> *Using a standard climbing harness and spikes* **the trainee will climb a standard telephone pole** <u>within 5 minutes, following all safety procedures</u>.
>
> **The trainee will splice** <u>according to code</u>, **six sets of wires** <u>in ten minutes</u> *while at the top of a telephone pole wearing all standard safety gear.*

The Formula for Writing the Objective

The outcome specifies the type of behavior, the conditions state the where, when, and what tools will be used, and standards describe the criteria that will be used to judge the adequacy of the behavior. Remember that a learning objective should clearly state what must be accomplished by the end of training. Let's take the steps one at a time.

- Write out the "desired behavior." Here the verb needs to describe clearly what will be done: a "doing" verb, such as *count, place, install, list, solve, replace, sort, recite,* is used to indicate some action. Do not use the word *understand.* Always make sure the verb describes an action.
- Now add the conditions under which the behavior must be done. This description encompasses the use or nonuse of aids. So, "using an ohmmeter," "using reference material provided," "using a standard climbing harness and spikes," "while at the top of a telephone pole," "without the use of a manual," "without the use of a calculator," are all examples of conditions that would be expected in certain situations.
- Finally, it needs to be clear what standards for success will be used. How will the trainee know he successfully completed the training? What level of accuracy is required? Is quality or speed an important part of success? "According to code," "following all safety procedures," "within 5 minutes," "according to the manual within 15 minutes," "with no more than 3 errors," "obtaining a score of 80 percent," are all possible standards.

Now, to test whether you have written a sound training objective, ask someone to read it and explain exactly what she believes a trainee needs to do, under what conditions, and how the trainee will know if she is successful. If the person can articulate these factors, you succeeded in writing a good learning objective.

For some examples of typical learning objectives before and after using the formula, see Table 5-7.

The other three types of training objectives listed in Table 5-6—reaction, transfer of training, and organizational outcome objectives—require similar components. For example, a transfer of training objective might read as follows:

> After completing training, participants, at their regular job station and using an ohmmeter and chart, will be able to separate acceptable (within specifications) from unacceptable (outside specifications) computer chips with an accuracy of 99.99% while sorting a minimum of 10 chips per minute.

Attitudes

Sometimes attitudes as well as knowledge and skills are the focus of training. You might ask, "How do you write a learning objective for an attitude?" When the goal of training is attitude change, the focus of training activities is to provide the trainees with information that contradicts

TABLE 5-7 Learning Objectives Improved

Before	*After*
Upon completion of training the trainee:	*Upon completion of training the trainee:*
Will be able to apply theories of motivation to different situations.	After reading a scenario of an unmotivated student, and without the use of any outside material, identify orally to the class what you would do to motivate the student, and explain which theory you used and why. Trainee must identify at least three motivators and tie to correct theory. Must be correct on four of five scenarios.
Will be able to recognize and identify different personalities, and know how to motivate them.	Will be able to watch a fellow trainee role play a situation and correctly explain in writing what type of personality is being exhibited, and what to do to motivate him/her. Trainee must be 100 percent correct on the personality and identify at least two motivators.
Will understand what is necessary to have an effective team.	When asked, trainee must provide orally to the trainer five things that are necessary to have an effective team and be 100 percent correct.
Will have knowledge of three types of active listening, and be able to use the appropriate one in a particular situation.	Correctly identify in writing three types of active listening that were identified in training, when asked.
	In a role play, respond verbally to an angry comment using one of the appropriate active listening types, then explain to the class which was used and why.
Will be able to say no to boss and peers when asked to do extra work.	In a role play, respond correctly to the situation using one of the ways of saying "no" from the training manual, then explain to the class which you used and why with 100 percent accuracy.

inappropriate attitudes and supports more appropriate attitudes. Thus, training does not focus on changing attitudes specifically, but rather providing new knowledge. This new knowledge might consist of alternate views and information related to the attitudes. Learning objectives for attitude change, therefore, should focus on acquisition of the relevant information rather than the resulting attitude change.

Consider training that is attempting to improve attitudes toward teamwork in a group of trainees who all scored below the midpoint on a TNA teamwork awareness survey. In this case the learning objective might read as follows: At the end of training, trainees will demonstrate an increased awareness of the positive aspects of teamwork (new knowledge) as demonstrated by a 50 percent improvement on the team awareness survey.

Recall that the reason we want to affect an attitude is to influence behavior. In this example, we want trainees to have positive attitudes so that once they are back in the workplace they will participate fully in team meetings and provide input. The transfer of training objective in this case might be "After completing training, the participants will attend all team meetings (assuming participation is voluntary) and, using the skills taught, provide ideas and suggestions in those meetings." Another might be "After completing training, the participants' performance rating in team meetings (as completed by all team members) will average one point higher than before training."

Why Use Training Objectives

Developing good training objectives takes time, effort, and careful thought. Why bother if it is the actual training that will determine whether trainees acquire the KSAs, not the objectives? In fact, some HRD specialists seriously question the value of specific objectives.[5] Some concerns about the use of objectives include the following:

- Waste valuable time
- Inhibit flexibility
- Move focus from other areas
- Unrealistic for management training and other soft areas of training
- Not practical in today's workplace

Regarding the first concern, the argument is that resources are often scarce and the time taken to develop the objectives takes away from more important endeavors. On its face, this generalization may be true, but the objectives guide the development of training, and may even result in less time to develop the training because of the clear guidelines they provide. Go back and look at the objectives in Table 5-7. Note in the "After" column how much clearer the focus is regarding "what will be trained" when compared to the "Before" column.

In terms of inhibiting flexibility it is often felt that objectives inhibit the flexibility of the trainer to respond to trainee needs. The counterargument here is that a comprehensive TNA is designed to determine the trainee needs, and the objectives focus specifically on those needs. It does, perhaps, inhibit the flexibility of the trainer to go off on tangents that she might like to, but adhering to a focused direction is a positive thing.

Moving the focus from other areas is again the point of having objectives. The idea is to keep the focus on the topics identified in the TNA.

Some suggest that concrete objectives are not possible in management training or areas such as time management or interpersonal skills.[6] Again, we argue that whatever the training, you want to achieve certain outcomes; those outcomes need to be translated into objectives. With time management, for example you want trainees to gain some cognitive knowledge about strategies for time management. You want them to develop skills to use in the workplace. Trainees must know the skills before they will transfer into the workplace. So, articulating an objective that states, "At the end of training, trainee will demonstrate time management skills by completing an 'in-basket exercise' within 45 minutes, and be able to provide an appropriate time management rationale for each decision," makes perfect sense.

Finally, some say objectives have outlived their usefulness. They are too specific for today's complex jobs.[7] We need to find methods that are better at determining what is required for effective performance. Although this reasoning may be true at a more macro level, the purpose of objectives as a guide for training development is still valid. The complexities of the job will surface during a TNA, but it is still necessary in any job to have competence in specific KSAs to be an effective performer.

The majority of HRD specialists agree that training objectives are important from a number of stakeholder perspectives, such as the:

- Trainee
- Designer of training
- Trainer
- Evaluator of training

THE TRAINEE

Trainees benefit from training objectives for a number of reasons, including the following:

- They reduce anxiety related to the unknown.
- They focus attention.
- They increase the likelihood that the trainees will be successful in training.

High levels of anxiety can negatively affect learning.[8] Not knowing what to expect in a situation creates anxiety. Training objectives provide a clear understanding of what will be taking place over the training period, which reduces the anxiety felt from not knowing what to expect. The objectives also focus attention on relevant topics to be trained. Don't forget, attention is the first step in the learning process. Thus from a learning theory perspective, it is important to let the trainee know what the performance expectations are and to be able to refer to them throughout the training. Also, as was indicated in the chapter on learning, this information will assist the learner in both focusing attention and cognitively organizing the new information.

Finally, learning objectives increase relevant learning,[9] and the likelihood that trainees will be successful in training. This makes sense according to goal-setting research,[10] which indicates that when specific and challenging goals are set (such as would be set by the training objectives), the probability is higher that these goals will be achieved than when no goal is set or an instruction to "do the best you can" is given.[11]

THE TRAINING DESIGNER

The learning objectives guide the designer of the training or the purchaser of a training package. The training objectives directly translate the training needs into training outcomes. With clear objectives, you can check the training methods and content against the objectives to ensure that they are consistent. Furthermore, evidence shows that following behavioral objectives results in development of better lesson plans.[12]

Suppose the designer is told to "design training to provide salespeople with skills in customer service." Does the designer design a course in interpersonal skills so salespeople learn how to be friendly and upbeat? Does the designer design a course in product knowledge so the salesperson can provide information about the various products and their features to customers? Does the designer design a course in technical expertise so salespeople can assist customers in getting the product to work effectively? Consider the learning objective that reads "After completing training, participants will, using paraphrasing or decoding and feedback (desired outcome), respond to an angry customer (conditions), suggesting two alternate remedies judged by the customer to be appropriate for resolving the problem (standard)." This learning objective provides a clear, unambiguous goal for the designer. The designer can then design a course in active listening (paraphrasing and decoding and feedback), with the focus on dealing with angry customers. Without that guidance, the training may not be designed appropriately.

THE TRAINER

With clear learning objectives, the trainer can facilitate the learning process more effectively. Clear, specific objectives allow the trainer more readily to determine how well the trainees are progressing and make the appropriate adjustments. In addition, the trainer is able to highlight the relationship of particular segments of the training to the objectives. Some trainers may see objectives as infringing on their freedom to train the way they want to. It is probably for those trainers that objectives do the most good, keeping the trainer on the right track.

TRAINING EVALUATOR

Evaluating training is much easier when objectives are used, because these objectives define the behaviors expected at the end of training. With no clear indication of what training is supposed to accomplish, an evaluator has no way to assess whether the training was effective. It is analogous to the army sergeant who tells the private, "Dig a hole here." The private starts to dig and the sergeant walks away. After digging a few minutes, the private begins to worry because he knows he's in trouble. He doesn't know how deep the hole should be, how long, or wide, or anything else. When the private sees the platoon leader walk by, he asks him, "How am I doing on this hole, sir?" The platoon leader, of course, says, "How should I know?" When good objectives are developed, the evaluator simply needs to assess whether the stated outcomes and standards are met.

Facilitation of Learning: Focus on the Trainee

Recall from Figure 3-1 the factors influencing performance ($P = M \times KSA \times E$). Many issues exist within each of these factors that will make it easier or more difficult for the trainee to achieve the learning objectives.

KSAs (INDIVIDUAL DIFFERENCES)

The TNA supplies not only information on the need for training, but also on the trainees' readiness for such training. Let's take the example of employees recently hired or promoted. They were selected because of their KSAs, but they need some initial training to learn the specifics of this particular job at this company. Perfect selection techniques would ensure that those hired have the requisite KSAs to be successful in training, but few selection techniques are perfect. Even the best selection practices result in a certain number of individuals who are selected but subsequently are not successful. If these false positives—those predicted to be successful but are not—can somehow be identified in the TNA, the design of training might be able to address the issues that would prevent them from being successful.

For example, some who are identified as in need of training may not have the requisite KSAs to make use of the training methods and materials that would be effective for 90 percent of the other potential trainees. Providing a remedial training module for this group, prior to the regular training, may increase their likelihood of successfully completing training.

The selection process sets minimum criteria (based on a job analysis) that individuals must meet in order to be selected. Even here, however, if all met those criteria, some individual differences in abilities would be evident. Some will show higher levels of the KSA in question, and others may not possess the minimum skills (e.g., false positive). Needs assessment data that show large differences among the potential trainees indicate that the training design must be adjusted to address the differences, which relates back to Table 5-1, organizational constraints. If the variance in KSAs is large, you need to consider a design that allows those with lower levels of the KSAs to "catch up." Otherwise the training is demotivating by being too boring for some and too complex for others.

By not accounting for trainee differences, companies can be the losers. Bob Filipczak, staff editor for *Training* magazine reports on an insurance company that hired a number of older workers for its call center.[13] The company believed that an older voice could relate to older customers better. The older workers were sent through the company computer training program. Many of them quit before completing training and those who did stay were substandard performers. The company decided it was simply a bad idea to hire older workers as they were not capable of learning the new technology. After discussions with a consultant, the company decided to try again. This time the training would not be required to be completed in the same time frame. Trainers were able to work more closely with the older trainees. The result, performance on the job (after training), was on par with the younger employees.

Just how important is the individual difference issue? Consider the following:

- More than 200 ethnic backgrounds and cultures characterize the U.S. population, the largest being German, Irish, Mexican, African, and Italian.[14]
- More than half the U.S. workforce now consists of non-Caucasian and ethnic minorities, immigrants, and women.

- In 1996, 34 percent of U.S. immigrants came from Asia, and only 16 percent from Europe.[15]
- In the United States, about 26 million Americans were born in another country.[16]
- In the United States, white males will make up only 15 percent of the increase in the workforce over the next decade.[17]
- Canada has the highest per capita immigration in the world.
- In 1997, only 18 percent of immigrants to Canada came from Europe and 3 percent from the United States.[18]
- In Canada, aboriginal unemployment is about 30 percent; both provincial and federal legislation encourages employers to hire them into the workforce.
- New technology and government legislation in North America is making it easier for the disabled to enter the workforce.

These facts suggest a different workforce emerging in North America. With this increase in diversity will come an increase in individual differences in more than just KSAs. Different cultures and ethnicities mean different ways of viewing the workplace and its norms and values. Care in the needs assessment to understand the special requirements of some individuals will help tremendously in designing a successful training program.

Individual differences in background and traits may result in differences in how people learn.[19] Note in Figure 5-1, the training design A produces better results for those at all levels of the particular trait, suggesting that training design A is the method of choice. In Figure 5-2, however, design A provides positive results for those high in the trait, but not for those low in the trait. In contrast, training design B provides positive results for those low in the trait, but not those high in the trait. Here, those low in the trait should receive training design B, whereas those high in the trait should receive training design A.

The individual difference issue is complex, and interactions are not easily generalizable to different situations.[20] It usually makes more sense to think of additional rather than different training for employees who differ in KSAs. When clear differences do exist in learning style preferences, two options are available. All trainees can receive the same training, but it needs to be designed so that all trainees' learning style preferences are accommodated. In this situation, different methods of instruction would be incorporated into each learning topic. This method offers

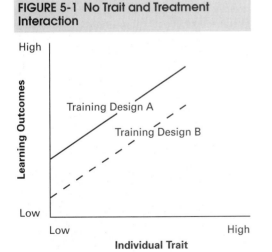

FIGURE 5-1 No Trait and Treatment Interaction

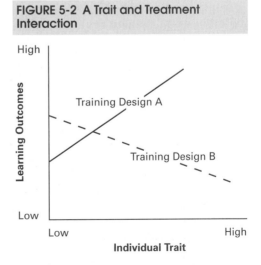

FIGURE 5-2 A Trait and Treatment Interaction

the advantage of covering the same learning point in different ways, facilitating the learning process for everyone. Disadvantages include increased time to complete training and higher costs to design than the time and costs involved in simply providing one mode of instruction. However, this expense must be weighed against the cost of putting people through training who are unable to learn the required KSAs.

An alternative is to create separate training programs designed around the learning style preferences of each group. Here the training is tailored to the preference of the training group, but multiple training programs need to be designed, developed, and implemented. Time for everyone to complete training is minimized, but cost of development remains high.

MOTIVATION OF TRAINEE

As the performance formula ($P = M \times KSA \times E$) indicates, if motivation is lacking, no learning is likely to occur. Thus training should be designed not only to provide KSAs, but also to motivate trainees to learn those KSAs and apply them to their jobs.

Expectations Toward Training

Those who come to a training program with positive expectations are more successful. Trainees who agree with such statements as:

- "Even if I fail, this training will be a valuable experience."
- "I will get more from this training than most people."
- "I have a better chance of passing this training than most others."
- "If I have trouble during training, I will try harder."

are more likely to meet the training objectives than those who do not.[21] The reason is that those with positive expectations are more motivated. Consider that if such expectations were determined during the needs assessment, an intervention could take place for those with unfavorable expectations. These interventions might include:

- Showing the trainee that he or she has the ability to complete training
- Clarifying the outcomes associated with completed training
- Showing that positive outcomes are more likely to occur if training is completed

Evidence indicates that doing these things increases motivation to learn.[22]

Suppose one of your supervisors has poor relations with her subordinates. Sending her to training to provide her with better interpersonal skills is fruitless unless she sees the value in such training. If in the TNA it is determined that she has low expectations and sees no value in the training, she could be asked to attend a pretraining workshop. You design the workshop to show the advantages of a positive relationship between supervisors and subordinates. The workshop also previews the training, showing that participants can learn the skills if they put forth the effort. Attending such a pretraining workshop, the supervisor would more likely be motivated to learn the skills.

Expectancy Theory Implications

Let's return to the intervention we suggested previously. We have trainees whom we believe have negative expectations regarding training. By intervening before training and providing the trainee with information that shows they can succeed in the training we are influencing Expectancy 1 (E1, the belief that effort will lead to desired performance). By clarifying the positive outcomes of training we assure the trainee is aware of all the positive outcomes of being successful in training. Finally, by showing that training increases the positive outcomes we influence Expectancy 2 (E2, the belief that desired performance will lead to desired outcomes). Increasing the expectancies (1 and 2) and also the number of positive outcomes, will have the net effect of increasing motivation to be successful in training.

No one consciously goes systematically through all the steps suggested in expectancy theory to make a decision, but unconsciously such a process does occur. Understanding the process, you might be able to influence someone's motivation by changing that person's expectancies or by identifying positive outcomes as previously noted. An example will illustrate the point. A TNA in the area Bill supervises found lower than expected productivity. It was also found that Bill's subordinates were afraid to talk to him about problems they experienced doing their work. An interview with Bill revealed that he believed that the best way to supervise was to be tough. "If they are afraid of what I might do to them if they screw up, they will work harder," he said. Bill seemed to like the idea that subordinates were afraid of him. Based on this information, Bill was encouraged to attend a training workshop. The workshop covers active listening, effective feedback, and other skills designed to teach supervisors how to interact better with subordinates, peers, and superiors. Will he be motivated to learn these skills? Let's look inside Bill's head, as represented in Training in Action 5-1.

To answer the question of whether Bill will be motivated to learn, we need to examine the factors in expectancy theory. What does Bill consider as possible outcomes of successful training, and what is the attractiveness (valence) of each of the outcomes? An examination of Training in Action 5-1 indicates he sees one outcome as a promotion, and it is a fairly attractive outcome (7 on a 10-point scale). Less stress is another outcome, but that is not especially attractive (4 on a 10-point scale). All together Bill identified six outcomes that might occur if he is successful at training. If he is unsuccessful, three outcomes are identified by Bill, and all three are attractive; the lowest being an 8 on a 10-point scale. Notice that Bill does not perceive that his training can have any impact on the productivity of his workgroup.

Now let's examine the likelihood that Bill believes that the outcomes he identified will actually occur (E2) if he is successful/unsuccessful in training. If successful in training (improves his interpersonal skills) the likelihood of him being promoted is low (0.2 or a 20% probability). The likelihood he will feel less stress is quite high at 0.8. All others are somewhere in between. If he is unsuccessful (does not learn the new skills), the probability that he will not have to change his behavior (he will behave in the same manner as before) is 1.0, or absolutely guaranteed. By not being successful in training, no one would expect him to change his behavior. Similarly, because he has not changed his behavior, employees will still be afraid of him (probability of 1.0), he will be the same old Bill, and he will not be ridiculed by his peers. As for Bill's belief about his ability to complete training successfully, he believes that if he really tries, it (E1) is 0.5. If he does not try he believes the likelihood of being unsuccessful is 1.0, or guaranteed to happen. So, let's determine whether he is likely to try in training through the following calculations.

FORMULA

$$E1[(E2_{outcome1} \times V_{outcome1}) + (E2_{outcome2} \times V_{outcome2}) + \ldots + (E2_{outcome6} \times V_{outcome6})]$$

where V is the valence, or attractiveness of the outcome.

WILL TRY IN TRAINING

$$0.5[(0.2 \times 7) + (0.6 \times 8) + (0.7 \times 6) + (0.8 \times 4) + (0.4 \times 7) + (0.6 \times 9)] = 10.9$$

WILL NOT TRY IN TRAINING

$$1.0[(1.0 \times 10) + (1.0 \times 8) + (1.0 \times 9)] = 27.0$$

Based on these calculations, it is clear that Bill will not try in the training. The motivation to not try is substantially higher than the motivation to try. So, what can be done to influence Bill to

---

TRAINING IN ACTION 5-1

What are the outcomes Bill sees and their attractiveness (valence) to him (on a scale of 1 to 10) if he is successful in training versus if he is unsuccessful?

Outcomes If Successful	Valence	Outcomes If Unsuccessful	Valence
Promotion	7	Does not have to change behavior	10
Better at job	8		
Less tension between Bill and subordinates	6	Employees still afraid of him	8
		Not ridiculed by coworkers for being a nice guy	9
Less feeling of stress	4		
Better relationship with union	7		
Fewer grievances	9		

How likely is it that if Bill is successful or unsuccessful, these outcomes will actually occur (Expectancy 2)? These expectancies are based on Bill's belief that they will occur and range from 0.0 (not at all likely to occur) to 1.0 (guaranteed to occur).

Outcomes If Successful	(Exp. 2)	Valence	Outcomes If Unsuccessful	(Exp. 2)	Valence
Promotion	0.2	7	Does not have to change behavior	1.0	10
Better at job	0.6	8			
Less tension between Bill and others	0.7	6	Employees still afraid of him	1.0	8
Less feeling of stress	0.8	4	Not ridiculed by co-workers for being a nice guy	1.0	9
Better relationship with union	0.4	7			
Fewer grievances	0.6	9			

Finally, how likely does Bill think it is that he could learn the new skills if he really tried (Expectancy 1)? This likelihood is also expressed as a probability (0 to 1.0).

In this case, Bill believes the skills will be difficult for him to learn, and he also believes that "leopards cannot change their spots." Therefore, Bill believes that if he really tries, there is only a 0.5 chance he will be successful. On the other hand, if he does not try, he definately (1.0) will not learn or change his behavior.

learn? A number of approaches can be taken. First, recall from Chapter 3 that expectancies are beliefs about the way things are. They can be influenced in a number of ways (e.g., past experience, communication from others). If Bill heard from other supervisors that the training was not difficult, he might change his belief about how difficult it would be to successfully complete the training (Expectancy 1). If Bill learned supervisors who were successful in training were promoted more often than others, this information would influence Bill's belief that if he completed training he would get promoted (Expectancy 2). If those who go to training generally receive higher pay raises and Bill is not aware of this fact, you can make him aware of the relationship between training and the raise (Expectancy 2). This relationship will add to Bill's calculations an additional positive outcome with a high probability of occurring.

It is also possible Bill did not consider some potentially positive outcomes such as "Improved productivity in his area," "Respect from upper management," "Better relationship with family and friends" (because he will be able to use the skills in his personal life as well), and "better able to persuade others of his point of view." Once made aware of these outcomes, depending on their attractiveness, the motivation to try may be altered to try rather than not. For example, "Respect of upper management" might be a given (E2 = 1.0) for all those who successfully complete the training. If this outcome is highly attractive to Bill, it would go a long way toward changing the decision to "try."

Other ways to influence Bill's motivation to learn focus on enhancing Expectancies 1 and 2 and clarifying the types of outcomes that will result from successful training. As Bill's supervisor, you could:[23]

- Discuss Bill's job performance and job-related goals and reach agreement that he needs to improve some set of KSAs in order to achieve those goals. Providing focus on goals presents specific outcomes the trainee may not have considered.
- Agree that this particular training program is the best alternative available for achieving the desired improvement (Expectancy 1).
- Agree that demonstrated improvement in the identified KSA area will result in desirable outcomes for him (Expectancy 2).

These steps should result in Bill's realizing the advantages of successful training and make his attitude more positive. In the design of training, therefore, it is important to include such pretraining interventions. An integral part of the design might be working with the supervisors to ensure that the suggested discussions take place.

In large organizations with well-organized human resource functions, the trainee-supervisor discussions might take place in the formal performance review. A portion of any thorough review is the developmental aspect. As noted in Chapter 4, this tool is useful for the supervisor to use with subordinates in determining training needs and increasing the motivation to learn.

Implications from Conditioning and Reinforcement (The Environment)

Classical Conditioning Recall from Chapter 3 that classical conditioning takes place without awareness. We salivate when we smell something we like cooking, because of prior learning. Emotional responses can be conditioned in a similar manner. A trainee who had bad experiences in school may feel anxious and even sick on entering a training room set up like a school classroom. Those trainees who experience high stress in their jobs become conditioned to feel stressed when they arrive at work. Eventually just seeing the building begins to create the stress because the two events are so often paired. Having someone in such an emotional state does not facilitate effective training, which might be a good reason to hold the training off-site for employees of this type. The point here is that some situations are associated with unpleasant emotional conditioned responses. Pleasant emotional responses are conditioned to other situations. When designing training, in most circumstances, you want to create situations that are pleasant. When the trainees are comfortable both physically and emotionally, they are better able to focus their attention on training. For these reasons, it is useful to know in advance as much about the trainee as possible.

Operant Conditioning   Recall from Chapter 3 that if a particular behavior is immediately followed by a reward, that behavior is likely to be repeated. Also, punishment that immediately follows a particular behavior will decrease the likelihood of that behavior continuing. Training should be designed with these principles in mind. To facilitate learning, trainees should be reinforced for their efforts to learn, regardless of their degree of success. As training progresses, rewards should be given for closer approximations to the derived behavior. Shaping as discussed in Chapter 3 is the model most frequently adopted by effective trainers. The following are important points to consider in the design of effective training:

- Know the things your trainees will see as rewarding and those that will be seen as punishing.
- Plan to reward at lower levels for effort and higher levels for success using successive approximations.
- Use both tangible and intangible rewards. Don't underestimate the power of trainees learning how to self-reward. Sometimes trainers will give coupons to trainees as a recognition and reward for participating in training exercises. These coupons are then redeemed at the end of the day for prizes (books related to training, other mementos related to the training).
- Don't forget that feedback is a reinforcer and key element in learning. Design feedback to show what the trainee did well and what needs improvement.

The following example illustrates these points.

Some trainees are reluctant to role play. However, role plays are one of the more effective methods for achieving behavior change. If role plays are incorporated into the training design, it is important to also design a procedure for ensuring that positive reinforcement rather than punishment follows. For example, the two trainers might first act out a simple role play to demonstrate how it is done. After it is over, the trainers each thank one another and point out some positive things that each did during the role play. They might then indicate that they would like someone volunteer to do another simple role play, and when the trainee is finished you and the other trainees applaud the efforts. Of course, this approach is successful only if the applause is seen as both real and reinforcing. You might then give the trainee feedback, highlighting the positive things done. Then you present the trainee with a "participation ticket" that can later be exchanged for a training memento.

Goal Setting

Goal-setting research consistently demonstrates that specific, challenging goals result in higher motivation levels than do no goals or the goal of "do the best you can."[24] Specific goals direct the individual's energy and attention toward meeting the goal. A number of conditions related to goal setting affect performance.[25]

- Individuals who are given a specific, hard, or challenging goal perform better than those given specific easy goals, "do the best you can" goals, or no goals.
- Goals appear to result in more predictable effects when they are given in specific terms rather than as vague intentions.
- The goal must be matched to the ability of the individual so that the person is likely to achieve it. Being able to achieve the goal is important for individuals' self-efficacy, for that is how individuals judge their ability to perform well on the tasks. For this reason, the analyst will need to design intermediate goals that reflect progress.

- Feedback concerning the degree to which the goal is being achieved is necessary for goal setting to have the desired effect.
- For goal setting to be effective, the individual needs to accept the goal that is set.

What is the application of this research to training? Well, what better way to capture the interest and attention of trainees than to provide them with individual goals? Learning objectives (discussed earlier) are a form of goal setting and could provide challenging, specific goals. These goals provide the measuring stick against which trainees can evaluate their progress and from which they derive self-satisfaction as they progress.

So far we examined issues related to getting and keeping trainees interested in the training. What remains is how to facilitate the learning process. In this regard, a number of important factors needs to be addressed when you are designing a training program. These issues will be presented under two headings: facilitation of learning and facilitation of transfer. Facilitation of transfer, of course, also helps facilitation of learning.

Facilitation of Learning: Focus on Training Design

To develop effective training programs, it is important to understand learning theory, or more specifically how individuals learn.[26] Among many learning theories, we choose to focus on social learning theory. This theory provides a broad understanding of the process of learning, yet is relatively easy to understand.

SOCIAL LEARNING THEORY

Let's examine the parts of social learning theory as they relate to training. Specific training events that correspond to the specific learning processes are illustrated in Table 5-8.

Attention/Expectancy

Social learning theory (see Figure 3-6 on page 98) indicates the trainee's motivation influences where attention is directed. Trainees attend to things in the environment that are most important to them. Thus the environment and process should be structured so that the most important things are the learning events and materials. Attention detractors need to be removed and creature comforts attended to.

Eliminating Distractions The room should be at a comfortable temperature, not too hot or too cold. People are generally comfortable at a temperature between 71 and 73 degrees Fahrenheit,

TABLE 5-8 Learning Processes and Corresponding Training Events

Attention/Expectancy	Learning environment, pretraining communications, statement of objectives and process, highlighting of key learning points
Retention	
Activation of memory	Stimulation of prior related learning
Symbolic coding and cognitive organization	Presentation of various encoding schemes and images, associations with previously learned material, order of presentation during training
Symbolic rehearsal and cues for retrieval	Case studies, hypothetical scenarios, aids for transfer of learning (identical elements and principles)
Behavioral Reproduction	Active and guided practice (role plays and simulations)
Reinforcement	Assessment and feedback (positive and/or negative)

with humidity level about 50 percent. The walls should be a neutral but pleasant color, free from distracting objects (e.g., posters, notices, and pictures unrelated to training). The room should be soundproof and have no view to the outside. If the room has windows, close the shades or curtains. Ideally, the learning facility will be away from the workplace so that trainees can concentrate on learning rather than be sidetracked by what might be going on at work. If the training must be conducted at the work site, establish a rule that no interruptions are allowed (from bosses, subordinates, or others who "just need a few minutes with . . ."). This rule also means no phones, beepers, or other communication devices while training is being conducted. Because communicating with the work area can be important, the training facility should have a system for incoming messages that can be delivered to trainees during breaks and after completion of training.

The seating should be such that trainees will not become uncomfortable over a 2-hour period, but not become so comfortable that they must fight off sleep. A comfortable, flexible, cloth-covered chair with armrests should be chosen. Trainees will also need a surface to place their training materials on and for writing.

Schedule training activities with the following rule in mind: "The brain can absorb only as much as the seat can endure." Thus breaks should be scheduled so that trainees do not have to sit for too long at one time. Provide refreshments if trainees are likely to be hungry at the start of or during training. A growling stomach is a significant force in taking the trainee's mind off the learning. Remember, food is a reinforcer, so you will be creating positive associations for your training while keeping trainees attentive. If lunch is provided, it should be light and not contain large amounts of carbohydrates, which tend to make people drowsy. Also avoid turkey, because it is sleep-inducing. Remember how you feel after a turkey dinner? Obviously, alcohol should be avoided.

Attracting Attention   The first steps in motivating the employees and setting their expectations are to notify them that they will be participating in the training, inform them of the nature of the training, and explain its job-related benefits. This communication should, at a minimum, indicate the training objectives and agenda. State the objectives again at the outset of training, and review them at strategic points throughout. Reiterating the objectives helps to keep the focus of training on the desired outcomes and attention on the important training activities. However, it is not enough for the trainer simply to state the objectives from time to time. The trainees must accept those objectives. To this end, you might ask trainees to describe how accomplishing the objectives will lead to resolving job-related problems. This exercise not only focuses trainees' attention on the training objectives, but builds commitment that will facilitate the transfer of new KSAs back to the job.

In addition to accepting the training objectives, trainees must also feel that the objectives are achievable. This principle comes directly from both expectancy theory and goal setting. Here's how achievable goals can be designed into the training. At the start of training, the overall objective may seem difficult if not impossible to achieve. You should point out that the overall objective is just the final step in a series of obtainable subobjectives. Research on goal setting suggests that following these procedures will result in higher levels of trainee learning.[27] Suppose the overall objective of a 1-day seminar was "To calm an irate customer without giving in to his request using the conflict resolution model." The thought of calming an irate customer using a method (conflict resolution model) that the trainees know nothing about could create a high level of anxiety. An intermediate objective that stated, "Respond to a single angry comment using active listening," does not seem as imposing and would provide a view of one of the steps toward reaching the overall objective.

Finally, the trainees' attention should be focused on the critical aspects of each step in the learning process. Techniques for highlighting the important points should be built into the learning activities so that the appropriate material is processed into permanently stored information.[28] The method of highlighting will vary according to the instructional method (e.g., case study, lecture). In the example of conflict resolution training discussed previously, suppose the training included a videotape of the correct steps. As the video progressed through the various stages of the conflict resolution model, these steps would flash on the bottom of the screen. This model begins with active listening, so as the video showed the person using active listening, "Active Listening" would be flashed on the bottom of the screen. This device would give the trainee an idea of how to perform each step and how the steps integrate into the total model.

Retention

An individual goes through four stages in the process of retaining something she is taught:

1. Activation of memory
2. Symbolic coding
3. Cognitive organization
4. Symbolic rehearsal and cues for retrieval

Activation of Memory   Information that is attended to is transformed into symbolically coded (typically as language) long-term memory. From there it is called up when the appropriate cues are present.[29] Before the symbolic encoding process can begin, relevant prior learning must be stimulated, so connections between the new information and the old can be established. This process can be facilitated by the trainer through stimulating the recall of the relevant prerequisite learning or prior supportive learning.

An illustration of this process is the management development example in Chapter 3 (under type 4—verbal association learning—of Gagné's learning types) in which we wanted managers to examine the structure of the subordinate's work and need for independence. Here we will focus on the subordinate's characteristics. Recall that different ways of treating employees are used, depending on their work environment. Assume the trainer wants the management trainees to learn the "relevant employee characteristics" for matching managerial behavior to the needs of the subordinate. The trainer can stimulate the recall of the prerequisite learning by asking the trainees to "try to remember the names of the relevant employee characteristics and what things differentiate them from irrelevant characteristics." Recalling supportive, prior learning can be stimulated by asking the trainees to draw on related experience. In this case the trainer might say, "Think back to employees you've dealt with in the past. How would you determine which of their characteristics would be relevant to the management style you adopt with them?" This activity would recall information supporting the new learning, providing a context for the new learning to occur.

Symbolic Coding and Cognitive Organization   Once the appropriate prior learning is recalled, the trainee is ready to encode the new information. The trainer can facilitate the encoding process through the technique of **guided discovery**. Typically the trainer makes statements and then asks a question. Let's assume the trainees just watched a video of a supervisor and a subordinate discussing the subordinate's work performance. Following the video the trainer might say, "Remember, certain employee characteristics are more closely related to how the employee approaches the work situation. In the video, how did the employee approach the work situation and what characteristics are most likely to influence this approach?" The statement is intended to stimulate relevant prior learning, and the question is designed to allow the trainee to discover the appropriate rule from the cues provided. The question shouldn't contain all the information needed for the answer but should suggest a strategy for discovering the answer. Engaging in guided discovery helps the trainee develop a coding scheme that relates the new learning to prior learning.

Encoding can also be enhanced through the use of images, in addition to being coded as verbal propositions. When **symbolic coding** incorporates both verbal propositions and images, retention of the information is improved, probably because image retention and language retention occur through different cognitive channels.[30] Thus, the addition of visual material in support of the oral and written language increases the trainees' ability to remember the information.

Cognitive organization is intimately tied to symbolic coding. The way information is organized during training and the prior learning that supports learning the new information shape the way the new information is organized into the cognitive structure. Likewise, the visual images used in training provide suggestions for how information fits together. When you develop the materials and the flow of a training program, you should make sure the new learning builds on relevant older learning. The flow of training should help the learner organize the new material by providing various organizational strategies.

Symbolic Rehearsal and Behavioral Reproduction Symbolic rehearsal and behavioral reproduction are types of practice. **Symbolic rehearsal** is practicing symbolically, as when the trainer asks the trainees to imagine a hypothetical situation and discuss how they would behave. At this point, the trainees aren't actually doing what they have learned to do—they're thinking, talking, or writing about it. Case studies provide one form of symbolic rehearsal. Trainees read about a situation and describe how they would handle the situation.

Behavioral reproduction is the transformation of the learning into actual behavior. Pilot training provides a clear example of the difference between these two types of practice. Pilots go through an extensive training process in learning how to fly a new aircraft. They read manuals, attend lectures, watch videos, and engage in computer-assisted, self-paced learning modules. Once a sufficient amount of learning occurs, the pilot trainees demonstrate their knowledge of procedures through discussions with the trainer and one another about what they would do in specific situations. They are given written or visual scenarios and asked how they would respond. All of these activities are symbolic rehearsal. When trainees demonstrate sufficient cognitive command of the aircraft's systems, procedures, and capabilities, they are put into flight simulators, which allow them to practice flying the aircraft. After they demonstrate competence flying the aircraft in simulation, they fly the actual aircraft under the supervision of an experienced pilot. The simulation and supervised flights are behavioral reproduction activities.

STRATEGIC KNOWLEDGE

In the past, training was designed to provide trainees only with the KSAs needed for their particular job. Many organizations found that more broadly based training leads to greater organizational effectiveness. In many cases, physical work is being replaced by knowledge work.[31] A study by Arthur Andersen found that in Canada's best-managed companies the use of management teams was a common approach.[32] This use of teams is on the increase all over North America. The Center for Study of Work Teams at the University of North Texas indicates about 80 percent of the *Fortune* 500 companies use teams with half or more of their employees.[33] To be effective in the team approach, employees need a broad understanding of how their jobs interact with other jobs. In these companies job-specific training is supported with information about the job's relationship to other parts of the organization. This type of training incorporates aspects of strategic knowledge development because it allows trainees to understand when and why to use their new KSAs.

Strategic knowledge development increases the breadth of what is learned by extending the training content to include learning when and why KSAs are appropriate and developing strategies for their use.[34] The strategies that are developed revolve around the planning, monitoring, and modifying of behavior. The trainee would not only learn how to perform the task but also how to behave strategically and adaptively. Table 5-9 compares a traditional skills training format with a format that includes training in strategic knowledge. You can see that the main difference is that the strategic knowledge training provides information as to when the skill is used and why it is important. Trainees are also provided with practice sessions in determining when to use the skill.

TABLE 5-9 Comparison of Traditional and Strategic Knowledge Training

Traditional Training	*Strategic Knowledge Training*
Step 1. **Declarative knowledge (what) is presented.** Workers are told that the materials are designed to teach them to read and interpret quality control charts used throughout their organization.	**Step 1.** **Declarative knowledge is presented the same way as in traditional training.**
	Step 2. **The context of the procedures (why and when) is added by instructing workers about the importance of the skill and the appropriate time for its use.** It is explained that if the assembly line workers could read and interpret quality control data, mistakes would be caught earlier and the product saved because traditionally quality control measures are taken after a specific number of items have been produced.
Step 2. **Procedural knowledge (how) is presented.** Workers are assisted in recalling specific math skills. Then stimulus materials and information required to master the task are presented. Examples of charts with various readings are provided and the workers are shown how to record charts during production, and interpret the data.	**Step 3.** **Procedural knowledge (how) would be presented the same way as in traditional training.**
Step 3. **Workers practice using the charts and interpreting the results.**	**Step 4.** **Workers practice using the charts and also practice determining when and why to use them.** Workers are provided opportunities for rehearsal and reinforcement of both conditional and procedural knowledge.
Step 4. **Workers are given feedback.**	**Step 5.** **Workers are given feedback (same as in traditional training).**

Source: Adapted from Schmitt, M. C., and T. J. Newby. 1986. Metacognition. *Journal of Instructional Development* 9:29–32.

Facilitation of Transfer: Focus on Training

Transfer of training refers to how much of what is learned in training transfers to the job. Training can result in the following transfer outcomes:[35]

- **Positive transfer:** A higher level of job performance
- **Zero transfer:** No change in job performance
- **Negative transfer:** A lower level of job performance

The goal is to have training result in positive transfer to the job.

Research into factors that influence transfer of training focused on three areas: conditions of practice, identical elements, and stimulus variability. The research also provides evidence that the nature of feedback, the strategies used for retention, and goal setting can influence how well the training is transferred back to the job.

CONDITIONS OF PRACTICE

Opportunities for trainees to practice can be designed in a number of ways. Each will facilitate the transfer of training more or less effectively depending on the nature of the KSAs to be learned.

Massed Versus Spaced Practice

Which is more effective—having trainees practice continuously for 4 hours, for 1 hour on 4 different days, or for a half-hour on 8 different days? Research demonstrated that material learned under the latter approach, **spaced practice**, is generally retained longer than material learned under the first approach, **massed practice**.[36] This finding is one of the most replicated in the psychological research,[37] and found additional support for simple motor tasks in a recent meta-analytic review of the research.[38] However, spaced practice requires a longer training cycle and management generally resists it. Training departments need to become more creative in developing their training to allow for spaced practice. Instead of the traditional 1-day workshop, eight 1-hour sessions at the beginning of the workday might be possible. Instead of a 5-day workshop, consider once a week for 5 weeks. This approach also gives trainees time to think about and even practice the knowledge or skill on their own.

Regarding more complex tasks, the recent meta-analytic review is inconclusive. The value of using spaced practice for complex tasks is not as critical.[39] Tasks that are difficult and complex seem to be performed better when massed practice is provided first, followed by briefer sessions with more frequent rest intervals.[40]

Whole Versus Part Learning

Which is better, **part learning** or **whole learning**? Whether trainees should learn parts of the task separately or learn the whole task all at once depends on whether the task can be logically divided into parts. In many cases it is just too difficult to design part task training.[41] Whole training devices are much easier because the design can be modeled after the real device (e.g., pilot training simulators). James Naylor suggests that even when the task can be divided into parts, the whole method is still preferred in the following circumstances:

- When the intelligence of the trainee is high
- When the training material is high in task organization but low in complexity
- When practice is spaced rather than massed[42]

Task organization relates to the degree to which the tasks are interrelated (highly dependent on each other). For example, in driving a car, the steering, braking, and acceleration are highly interdependent when you are turning a corner (high organization). Starting a standard-shift car, however, requires a number of tasks that are not as highly organized (pushing in the clutch, putting gear shift in neutral, placing foot on accelerator, turning key to start). **Task complexity** relates to the level of difficulty of performing each task.[43]

In the design of training, it is often not practical to attempt to subdivide the task into meaningful parts. If it is possible to subdivide them, you would still need to use the whole method if the task organization were high; if task organization were low, however, you would use the part method.

As an example of high task organization, imagine training a backhoe operator to dig a hole by first having her practice raising and lowering the boom, then practice moving the outer arm in and out, and finally moving the bucket. This sequence simply does not make sense. Ultimately the trainee has to learn how to open each of the valves concurrently and sequentially in the digging of a hole. An example of low task organization is the maintenance of the backhoe. Here, a number of tasks (check the teeth on the bucket, check the hydraulic oil, inspect boom for cracks) are not highly organized, so each could be taught separately.

A third option, **progressive part training**, can be used when tasks are not as clear in their organization. Consider the training of conflict resolution skills. Imagine that the model to be taught involves four steps (actively listen, indicate respect, be assertive, and provide information). These tasks are interdependent, but might also be taught separately. In this case a combination of the two types may make sense. First the trainees learn and practice active listening; then active listening and indicating respect; then active listening, indicating respect, and being assertive; and finally the whole model. In this way, the trainee learns each step but at the same time learns the integration of the adjoining step.

Whole, part, and a combination of the two (progressive part) learning are represented in the following diagram:

Training Type	Phases				
	Phase 1	Phase 2	Phase 3	Phase 4	Phase 5
Whole	A+B+C+D	A+B+C+D	A+B+C+D	A+B+C+D	A+B+C+D
Part	A	B	C	D	A+B+C+D
Progressive Part	A	A+B	A+B+C	A+B+C+D	A+B+C+D

As mentioned previously, even though these different ways of training a task are potentially viable, for complex tasks the use of "whole learning" is preferred for reasons explained later in the discussion of elaboration theory.

Overlearning

Overlearning is the process of providing trainees with continued practice far beyond the point at which they perform the task successfully.[44] This concept is similar to automaticity. The more a task is overlearned, the greater the retention.[45]

Overlearning is particularly valuable for tasks that are not used frequently or if the opportunity to practice them is limited. In a study of soldiers assembling and disassembling their weapons, one group (the overlearning group) received extra trials equal to the number of trials it took them to learn the task. Another group (refresher group), received the same extra number of trials as the overlearning group, but at a later date. The final group (the control group), received no extra trials. The overlearning and refresher groups both outperformed the control group, but the overlearning group also retained more than the refresher group.[46] Even when material/skills are overlearned, however, it is important to put mechanisms in place to reinforce the use and practice of the learned behaviors on a continuous basis, especially when it is a newly learned knowledge or skill.[47]

When trainees practice a skill beyond the ability to simply do the task, the responses become more automatic and eventually do not require thinking. For this reason, overlearning is most valuable for tasks performed in high-intensity or high-stress situations such as emergencies. For example, when in pilot training in the air force, one trainee recalls that numerous times during initial training the instructor would pull back the throttle of the aircraft and yell, "Emergency!" He did it frequently, and soon the trainee discovered that thinking was not even required—the emergency procedures became automatic. This reflexive nature is important in a situation where correct responses are critical.

In Chapter 1 we defined the concept of automaticity, a closely related concept to over-learning. It could be thought of as an outcome of overlearning, although it could also occur after a great deal of on-the-job practice. It is a shift to a point where performance of a task is fluid, requires little conscious effort, and, as the name implies, is "automatic."[48] Automaticity, through overlearning, should be designed into training when the task will be performed in high-stress situations or those that are encountered infrequently but must be performed correctly.

MAXIMIZE SIMILARITY

Maximizing similarity is also known as **identical elements**. The more the elements in the training design are identical to the actual work setting, the more likely it is that transfer will occur.[49] Two areas of similarity are possible: the tasks to be performed, and the environment in which they are to be performed. How do you increase similarity? A newscaster reading the news on television must use a teleprompter (the task) while someone is talking to him via an earphone (environment). After the basic skill is learned, to ensure transfer, the trainees practice the skill in an environment similar to their actual workplace environment. A machinist is exposed to the background noise of the factory floor and the interruptions common to the job. The secretary is exposed to the office noise as well as the interruptions that occur in the office.

VARY THE SITUATION

It is much easier to use the concept of identical elements for motor or technical skills, where most of the elements required for learning are in the job situation. When conceptual or administrative skills are required, as in management training, a great deal of variability often characterizes typical situations, and the use of identical elements simply is not effective. In such cases, the general principle approach is more useful.[50]

General Principles

For much of management training, it is impossible to provide specific training for what to do in every situation that might arise. It is necessary, therefore, to provide a framework or context for what is being taught, which is what strategic knowledge training attempts to do. Training through general principles will better equip trainees to handle novel situations.

You are teaching managers how to motivate employees and you tell them that praise is a good motivator. A manager goes back on the job and begins praising workers. Some workers are not motivated, and in a some cases, they even become less motivated. The manager is at a loss. If, however, the managers are taught some general principles about motivation, they would understand the responses they get and alter their own behavior. The principles related to expectancy theory suggest that certain reinforcers are attractive to some and not to others. Furthermore, it indicates that praise must be a function of performance to be motivating. The manager could think through these principles and identify what change was required in order to motivate those not responding to the praise. For some of these employees the attractive outcome may be for the manager to say nothing and stay away when they perform at an appropriate level.

OTHER CONSIDERATIONS TO FACILITATE TRANSFER

Knowledge of Results

Providing feedback (**knowledge of results**) to a trainee is important to learning and the transfer of training back to the job. Feedback performs three functions:[51]

1. It tells trainees whether their responses are correct, allowing for necessary adjustments in their behavior.
2. It makes the learning more interesting, encouraging trainees to continue.
3. It leads to specific goals for maintaining or improving performance.

When you provide such feedback, it is better to indicate that the level of performance can be controlled by the trainee. Sometimes inexperienced trainers will try to be supportive by suggesting that the task is difficult so any problems in mastering it are understandable.[52] This approach reinforces low self-efficacy. Feedback that indicates that a trainee can master the task improves a person's self-efficacy, and trainees with high self-efficacy tend to be more motivated and achieve more.[53]

Frequent opportunities to provide feedback should be part of the training design. Providing feedback takes a rather long time if the group is large, because the trainer needs to get to all trainees and monitor improvements. To help overcome this problem, other trainees can be used to provide feedback. For example, three-person groups can be used in interpersonal skills training. One of the three acts as an observer of the behavior and provides feedback to the person who is practicing.

Combination of Relapse Prevention and Goal Setting

A major reason training does not transfer to the job is, once back on the job, the trainee faces many of the same pressures that caused reduced effectiveness in the first place. Marx[54] instituted into his training, a system of **relapse prevention** modeled after a successful approach to assisting addicts to resist returning to their addictive behavior.[55] The strategy sensitizes trainees to the fact that relapse is likely, prepares them for it by having them identify high-risk situations that will result in relapse, and finally helps them develop coping strategies to prevent such a relapse.

Goal setting has also been shown to increase the likelihood of transfer.[56] With goal setting, the trainees are required to meet with fellow trainees to discuss the goals and how they will accomplish them. Furthermore, trainees are required to keep a record of their goal accomplishments, return these records to the trainer, and promise to meet at a later date to discuss these accomplishments publicly. This public commitment—through documentation of behavior, discussions with fellow trainees, and monitoring by trainers—further increases the likelihood of transfer.

Some evidence shows that relapse prevention without goal setting is not always successful.[57] So, Marx incorporated both the goal setting and public commitment into his relapse prevention training.[58] This revised relapse prevention training includes the seven steps presented in Table 5-10. Some of the relapse prevention strategies (step 4) used in the training are presented in Table 5-11. In preparation for this relapse prevention training, trainees complete a relapse prevention worksheet (Figure 5-3) to get them to begin thinking of the issues involved.

This combination of relapse prevention and goal setting is a powerful tool for encouraging transfer. The relapse part uses both cognitive and behavioral components to facilitate long-term maintenance of the newly learned behaviors.[59] Trainees leave the training expecting that relapse is a strong possibility but possessing a repertoire of coping responses to deal with it. The addition

TABLE 5-10 Seven Step Relapse Prevention Training

Step	*Purpose*
1. Choose a skill to retain	Helps manager to identify and quantify the skill chosen. Goal setting and monitoring of the skill require clear definitions of the skills often requiring help from the trainer. "Be nice to my employees" is not clear enough and needs to be revised to something more concrete such as "Provide praise to employees when they meet their quota."
2. Set goals	Once a skill is defined and quantified, then identify appropriate definitions of what a slip (warning that goal is in jeopardy) and relapse (more serious disengagement from goal) are. From this identification, goals are set as to what is desired. For example, the goal might be to praise at least five employees a minimum of once a day when they meet their quotas. Then define what a slip is: "Two consecutive days where five employees are not praised; and what a relapse is: "A week where targeted behavior is not met."
3. Commit to retain the skill	Need to think about the reasons for maintaining the skill. Trainees complete a matrix (item 3 in Figure 5-3), which helps them organize and prioritize reasons for maintaining the skill.
4. Learn coping (relapse prevention) strategies	These strategies help increase awareness of potential trouble spots, how to respond emotionally and behaviorally, where to get help, and so forth.
5. Identify likely circumstances for first relapse	Here the trainees are asked to think of a situation that would most likely cause them to slip back to old behavior, prepares them for when it really happens, and provides a nice transition to the next step, which is practice.
6. Practice coping (relapse prevention) strategies	With an understanding of what will cause a slip, trainees work in small groups practicing (using role plays and so forth) how to maintain the skill in such situations.
7. Learn to monitor target skill	Develop feedback mechanisms to help you monitor the frequency of using the specified skill. Use of whiteboard in office or notepad where you can check off each time you use the skill.

Source: Adapted from Marx, R. D. 1982. Relapse prevention for managerial training: A model for maintenance of behavior change. *Academy of Management Review* 7:433–41.

TABLE 5-11 Coping Strategies for Relapse Prevention

Step	*Purpose*
Understand the relapse process	Understanding that relapses are common and can be expected better prepares the trainee for such events. When a slip or relapse occurs, it is expected.
Recognize difference between training and the work setting	In training lots of positive feedback often comes from peers and the trainer. This support creates some overconfidence about how easy it will be to continue with the new skill when back on the job. However, you need to think about the likelihood that this attention and feedback will not happen back on the job, so realize the transfer will be more difficult.
Create an effective support network on the job	Identify and enlist others who can support you back on the job. Peers who also attended the same training, superiors who are supportive can be asked to provide you with needed feedback on how you are doing.
Identify high-risk situations	Determine times, situations where you are likely to slip back to old behavior. These cognitive "fire drills" help you to determine cues that signal a potential slip.
Reduce emotional reactions that interfere with learning	Understanding slips will happen and not reacting with feelings of failure or tendency to blame the poor training. These responses are self-defeating and being aware that they are likely to occur prepares you to take them in stride. Realize that it is a part of the learning process and does not reflect poorly on you or the training.
Diagnose specific support skills necessary to retain new skill	Determine what support skills are necessary to assist in the transfer of the trained skill. Consider the skill of allowing the team to make the decisions, rather than the supervisor. This pattern is difficult to change, and the skill of time management is an important collateral skill. If you are always running behind, the tendency to make the decisions yourself or push the team to hurry will interfere with the taught skill. You need to be aware of this behavior and if necessary get training in the collateral skills as well.
Identify organizational support for skill retention	Determine who in the organization will be support for the skill and actively seek them out for assistance in providing feedback. Ask supervisor to give feedback even if initially the supervisor is not that interested in doing so.

Source: Adapted from Marx, R. D. 1982. Relapse prevention for managerial training: A model for maintenance of behavior change. *Academy of Management Review* 7:433–41.

A Plan to Apply Skills Back on the Job

1. What is the skill/technique? (Be specific.) _____

_____

_____

2. What will using the skill/technique look like? (Be specific.) _____

_____

_____

3. What are the positive and negative consequences of using and not using this skill?

	Positive (+)	Negative (−)
Using Skill		
Not Using Skill		

4. What will a "slip" look like? _____

_____

_____

5. How will you feel if you slip back to old techniques? _____

_____

_____

6. Under what circumstances is a slip likely to occur? _____

_____

_____

7. What support is needed? _____

_____

_____

Source: R. Noe, J. Sears, and A. Fullemcamp. 1990. Relapse training: Does it influence trainee's post training behavior and cognitive strategies? *Journal of Business and Psychology* 4:317–28.

FIGURE 5-3 Relapse Prevention Worksheet

of the goal setting and public commitment further provides an incentive for transfer. Recent research indicates this method is particularly effective where the climate for the transfer is not supportive.[60]

Facilitation of Transfer: Focus on Organizational Intervention

In Chapter 4 we noted that once you identify a performance deficiency, you will need to assess how much of the deficiency results from inadequate KSAs, and how much from other factors. Remember what Nancy Gordon from Ameritech said: many of these deficiencies are a function of organizational forces and not a lack of KSAs. Just as these forces can interfere with effective performance, they can also interfere with new learning and inhibit transfer. To increase the likelihood of transfer, therefore, it is useful to harness as much help as possible back on the job.

SUPERVISOR SUPPORT

One of the key determining factors for the transfer of training is supervisory support.[61] Supervisors need to understand the behaviors being trained and provide support for trainees who use these new behaviors back on the job. In addition, research indicates that transfer is more likely when supervisors provide trainees with desired outcomes upon successful completion of training.[62] These actions on the part of supervisors will go a long way toward facilitating transfer.

Supervisors can affect their employees' learning and transfer of training in other ways as well. If employees who are motivated to improve (involved in their own development) receive support from their supervisors for such developmental activity, this support enhances their motivation.[63] Also, motivation to learn can be enhanced when employees understand realistic information regarding the benefits of their development activities.[64] Two other factors that affect motivation to learn are the employee's perception of training relevance, and reducing the negative side effects (like work that piles up) of attending training.[65] These two factors can also be controlled to a great extent by the supervisor.

PEER SUPPORT

Research indicates peer support can also have a positive impact on transfer of training.[66] If the trainee is the only one from a department who receives training, no peers back on the job may understand how to provide social support. In some climates this situation could result in pressure from more experienced peers to "forget all that stuff." With the right climate, however, peers can provide the proper support to use the training. What is the right climate? Learning must be considered an integral aspect of the organization's ongoing operation, becoming part of the employees' and managers' responsibilities. If everyone is involved in the learning process, it continues beyond the classroom. Most important, all employees must understand and support overall organizational objectives. By involving the entire workgroup in training, the resulting peer pressure will support company goals and objectives. With this type of climate, it is possible to use peer support in a more formalized manner. Peers could be considered potential coaches. Although it is the supervisor who is generally thought of as a coach to help recently trained employees transfer their skills to the workplace, this role can be accomplished by experienced peers.[67] The peers would receive training as coaches and be provided with specific checklists to evaluate trainees periodically on their performance. In addition, more experienced peers can serve as mentors, willing to answer questions and provide advice, guidance, and support to remedy the difficulties trainees may encounter in applying the new skills to the work situation.

We discuss strategies for dealing with different climates in a later section. For now, it is sufficient to note that it is the responsibility of the training department to inform upper management of the advantages of creating such a climate if the goal is to encourage transfer of training.

TRAINER SUPPORT

Conventional wisdom is that the trainer's job is done when training is over. More recent research, however, demonstrates the value of continued trainer involvement in the transfer of training. Trainees who commit to meet the trainer and other trainees at some later date to discuss transfer of training, use the training more effectively.[68] Thus, value derives from the continued involvement of the trainer who can be a useful resource in helping trainees work through any problems encountered in the workplace.

One idea in this regard is to have trainers monitor trainees at some point after training to assess how they are doing and provide feedback.[69] As a trainer you would sit in and observe the trainee in a situation where she is required to use the trained behavior. To be effective, the **sit-in:**

- Must be voluntary on the part of the trainee
- Must be confidential between the trainer and trainee
- Must be used only for developmental purposes, not administrative

During the sit-in the trainer must not interrupt the interaction between the trainee and others, but provide feedback only after the session is over. After all, "Who is better to be coaching the trainee on behaviors that were learned in training than the trainer?"[70]

Using the trainer in a follow-up to facilitate transfer of training might spread the trainers rather thin. However, it is important to consider the investment already made in training. If transfer does not occur, the investment is lost.

REWARD SYSTEMS

As noted earlier, valued outcomes contingent upon successful training enhances training transfer.[71] Operant conditioning is a powerful regulator of behavior. Employees are quite adept at determining which behaviors can get them in trouble, bring them rewards, or result in their being left alone. If trained behaviors are not reinforced, then the likelihood is small that such behaviors will be exhibited. Part of your responsibility as a trainer is to work with the supervisor and other parts of the organization to align reward systems to support the behaviors learned in training.

CLIMATE AND CULTURE

In a systems approach to training, as many forces as possible in the organization need to be focused on reinforcing the learned behaviors in order to ensure transfer. Although supervisors, peers, and reward systems all influence an organization's climate and culture, these factors need to be discussed in their own right.

Climate

Climate can influence the transfer of training.[72] Climate is generally conceptualized as the perception of salient characteristics of the organization.[73] Such salient characteristics as company policies, reward systems, and management behaviors are important in determining the organizational climate. Supervisor support, peer support, and so forth all are part of the total climate that will reinforce the use of the trained skills, but they alone do not make up an organization's climate. Other climate factors such as company policies and the attitudes reflected by upper management regarding training, if positive, will also support the transfer of training. Consider how trainees perceive training. If they believe adequate resources (time and money) went into the development of training, trainees are more motivated to attend and learn. The message here, is that the company cares enough about this training to devote valued resources. If these characteristics don't describe the climate, it may be better to not offer training at all.[74] Cultivating such a supportive climate toward training therefore is important and does facilitate transfer.[75]

Climate is related to and in many ways reflects the culture of an organization. When asked, "What is useful in promoting transfer of training?" HR specialists and supervisors responded that it is critical to have a culture that supports training.[76]

Culture

Culture is defined as a pattern of basic assumptions invented, discovered, or developed by a group within the organization. It can be considered a set of shared understandings about the organization.[77] One type of culture, a continuous learning culture—reflected by the shared understanding that learning is an important part of the job—shows a positive impact on the transfer of training.[78] A continuous learning culture is influenced by a variety of factors such as challenging jobs, social support (peer and supervisor), and developmental systems that allow employees the opportunity to learn continuously and receive appropriate training. Our discussion of the "learning organization" in Chapter 2 described how such a culture is formed.

Influencing Climate and Culture

Given the importance of climate, what can be done if the climate is nonsupportive or neutral regarding training? Changing climate and culture in an organization is a long and difficult process and must be done from the top. Issues related to the mismatch of the training goals and organizational climate and culture should surface in the organizational analysis part of the needs analysis. This information would then be provided to the top HR manager.

Evidence in North America indicates that the human resource department of organizations now carries more influence in organizational decision making than in the past[79] and employees in these departments are better trained in human resource issues.[80] With this increased influence and training, HR professionals are responsible for helping the company leadership to understand and resolve conflicts between organizational strategies and objectives and the existing climate and culture. Training in Action 5-2 provides an example of things that, incorporated into the training process to facilitate transfer, help to change the learning climate and culture.

TRAINING IN ACTION 5-2

HELPING TO ASSURE TRANSFER

Dr. Richaurd Camp is a consultant to a number of organizations in the United States and abroad. A few years back, an executive search firm hired him to train their employees on effective interviewing techniques. This task was a key part of their work. Dr. Camp, in a meeting with their management, discussed the importance of approaching the training as an organizational intervention, and the need to consider a number of organizational factors to assure the training transferred to the job. The client would be spending a great deal of money on the training and was willing to do what was necessary to assure transfer, which would be especially difficult because the international company is highly decentralized.

After a number of meetings with management, Dr. Camp designed a 3-day workshop to provide the interviewing skills requested. The first group to go through the training consisted of all the top managers, including the president. This training not only provided them with the necessary skills, but garnered their support for the process throughout the organization. He then began training all of the other employees from the top down. At the beginning of each training session, to indicate the importance of the training to the trainees, a video of the president of the company was shown. In the video the president indicated the importance of the training and how it would make them a more effective organization. Furthermore, in attendance at each training session was a senior manager who also verbalized support for the training. The manager was also able to provide real-life examples of when employees used old versus newly trained skills, and answer questions that arose about using the training back on the job. This reinforcement put the training in a real organizational context for the trainees.

In each local area, "stars" were identified (those using the process effectively) who were used as resource persons to facilitate transfer. After training, employees were also assigned coaches (recall everyone received the training, so experienced coaches were available). To reinforce the importance of using the skills on the job, Dr. Camp developed a "1-day refresher" training and went to the various offices to provide it. Part of the "refresher" training was to share concerns about the difficulties in implementing the process and to generate ideas on how to make transfer easier. At the end of this training Dr. Camp encouraged trainees to send him copies of the "outcome of an interview process" so he could provide them with feedback to again facilitate effective transfer to the job.

(continued)

TRAINING IN ACTION 5-2

(continued)

Dr. Camp then suggested the company develop a task force to examine how effective the transfer of training was and consider other steps that could be taken to assure that what trainees were learning was transferred to the job. A representative of the task force began meeting with employees (while they were at different training sessions) to explore ways of facilitating the transfer. One of the ideas to come from these meetings was that each trainee team up with another trainee who was at the training session. When they got back to their respective offices throughout the world, they would stay in contact, providing support,

feedback, and ideas for dealing with obstacles to using the trained skills.

How successful was the training? Management determined some bottom-line results that suggest the training helped them be more profitable. Does everyone use the skills as effectively as they could? No, but the organization continues to work on ideas to encourage the transfer. Recently the task force began discussing the possibility of videos and online information to introduce the skills and to reinforce the correct use of them.

Design Theory

With an understanding of the factors that facilitate learning and transfer, we now provide two **design theories** that incorporate much of this information. Various theories are related to the effective design of training. Some, such as component display theory,[81] are specific to only cognitive learning, and others focus only on attitude change.[82] For more information on these and many others you should consult *Instructional Design Theories and Models* by Charles Reigeluth.[83] For our purposes we will examine two design theories with a broader application: elaboration theory,[84] a macro theory of design, and the micro theory of Gagné and Briggs.[85]

Theories of training design are not theories in the traditional sense, because they do not predict cause-and-effect relationships. What they do is prescribe methods of presenting material (what is to be learned) in a way to enhance the likelihood that the material will be learned. So, instructional design theories offer guidelines as to what methods to use in what situations in order to design effective training.[86]

ELABORATION THEORY

Elaboration Theory (ET) is a macro theory of design. It is based on a holistic alternative to the part/whole sequencing that is usually followed in training. This holistic approach is more meaningful and motivational for learners,[87] because from the start they see and get to practice the complete task. It is relevant only for complex tasks (and is not applicable for the design of attitudinal training). To understand when to use elaboration theory, it is necessary to understand the issue of sequencing. **Sequencing** is the process of how to group and order the content of training. It is directed at facilitating the "cognitive organization" aspect of social learning theory.

If you are training employees in the use of a number of computer programs (word processing, spreadsheet, e-mail use), sequencing is not important, and it does not matter which you teach first. If the operating system is Windows and it is a part of the training, it would be necessary to present it first (because all other programs require its use). In this case, sequencing is important. Sequencing is only important when a strong relationship exists among the topics of the course. So, if your training included producing charts from the spreadsheet program and integrating them into a necessary word processing document, some sequencing will be necessary.

For the purposes of training different topics, two sequencing strategies are possible: topical and spiral (see Figure 5-4). Topical sequencing requires the complete learning of one topic before moving to the next task. Spiral sequencing requires learning the basics of the first task, then the basics from the second task and so on. After completing the basic understanding of all tasks, the learner moves to the second level of the first task to do the same thing. The advantages and disadvantages to each of these strategies are depicted in Table 5-12.

A training program is seldom all one or the other, but a combination of the two depending on the relationships among the tasks being taught. Consider a weeklong workshop for supervisor training on topics such as effective feedback, effective communication, providing performance reviews, running an effective meeting, problem solving, and so forth. In sequencing these topics, it makes sense to have feedback and effective communication before performance reviews, because they will provide help in doing an effective performance review. They can also be taught separately, using topical sequencing strategy. Consider another topic, problem solving. If you were teaching a six-step problem-solving process, you might combine the methods of sequencing. Learning to define a problem correctly and brainstorming might be taught topically before the problem-solving model is presented, because they are stand-alone topics. Then the six-step model could be taught using the spiral method. Because some tasks are learned independently, the learning process is facilitated. The complexity of the overall problem-solving process and interrelationship among the steps do suggest the use of the spiral approach.

Here is where elaboration theory comes in. Recall it is only applicable to complex tasks and is based on what Charles Reigeluth calls the **Simplifying Conditions Method (SCM)**. As he states:

> Regarding complex tasks, the SCM sequencing strategy enables learners to understand tasks holistically.... Holistic understanding of the task results in the formation of a stable cognitive schema to which more complex capabilities and understanding can be assimilated.[88]

FIGURE 5-4 Comparison of Topical and Spiral Sequencing

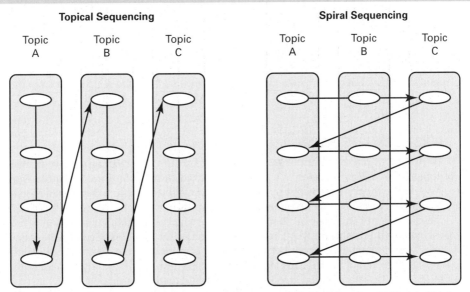

Source: Reigeluth, C. 1983. The elaboration theory. In *Instructional Design Theories and Models*, Vol. 2, edited by Charles Reigeluth. Hillsdale, NJ: Lawrence Erlbaum Associates.

TABLE 5-12 Comparison of Topical and Spiral Sequencing

	Advantages	*Disadvantages*
Topical	Concentrate on topic, no interference from other topics	Once learned, you move to the next topic and the first is forgotten
Spiral	Built-in synthesis and review. Interrelationships are more obvious and understood	Disruption of learner's thought process when moving to next topic

SCM is based on the notion that for all complex tasks, simple and more complex versions exist. Consider driving a car, which is considered a complex task. Driving on an empty lot is much less complex than on a freeway during rush hour.

The SCM is based on two parts, epitomizing and elaborating. **Epitomizing** is the process of identifying the simplest version of the task, which is still representative of the task as a whole. **Elaborating** is the process of identifying progressively more complex versions of the task. In the design of training the epitomizing version of the task is taught first, followed by increasingly more complex (elaborating) versions of the task until the desired level of complexity is reached. Consider the job of air traffic controller. The task is complex; they must assist a number of aircraft landings under various weather conditions. Training would take place in a simulator where the computer would simulate aircraft landing at the airport. First, we determine the epitome: the simplest version of the task possible while still representative of the complex task. It would be where only one aircraft is on the screen, no wind or other adverse weather conditions are present, and the pilot is responding perfectly to the trainee's instructions (when told to turn to heading 040 and descend at 100 feet per minute, the pilot response is exactly that). Once this epitome is mastered, a number of elaborations of the task must be mastered, each more complex, until the complexity required on the job is reached. In the air traffic trainee's situation, the first elaboration is to add a light crosswind, then perhaps errors in responses from the pilot; first regarding the heading, then both heading and descent. The final elaboration would be matched to the expectation of an air traffic controller in the field.

The major advantage of this approach to training is the more complete tasks are presented immediately, which should foster better understanding, and motivate trainees as they see the relationship between what they are learning and the job-related tasks immediately. Evidence indicates that ET is not only effective, but also appealing to trainees.[89] Students wanting to know more about the theory and see actual examples of its use are referred to work by Carson and Curtis and others.[90]

GAGNÉ-BRIGGS THEORY

To provide a micro theory of design we turn to the Gagné-Briggs theory of instructional design,[91] discussed in Chapter 3. It is applicable to cognitive, behavioral, and attitudinal learning. As a micro theory, it provides a set of procedures to follow for each instructional event to enhance learning. The theory identifies nine events of instruction (see Table 5-13). Note how these events of instruction are tied to social learning theory. Gaining attention is the same for each theory. Informing of the objectives further activates a process of getting the trainees' attention focused. Stimulating recall of prerequisite learning ties into activation of memory and so forth. Let's examine the nine events of instruction in more detail. As we do so, we will refer back to relevant sections of social learning theory for additional information.

TABLE 5-13 Gagné-Briggs Nine Events of Instruction

Instructional Event	*Relation to Social Learning Theory*
Gain attention	Attention
Informing the trainee of goal (objectives)	Attention
Stimulate recall of prior knowledge	Retention: Activation of memory
Present the material	Retention: Activation of memory/semantic coding/cognitive organization
Provide guidance for learning	Retention: Semantic coding/cognitive organization through guided discovery
	Retention: Symbolic rehearsal
Elicit performance (practice)	Behavioral reproduction
Provide informative feedback	Reinforcement
Assess performance	
Enhance retention and transfer	Reinforcement

Source: Gagné, R. M., L. Briggs, and W. Wager. 1992. *Principles of Instructional Design.* Fort Worth: Harcourt Brace Jovanovich.

Gaining Attention

You can gain attention in a number of ways (raise voice, clap hands, or a comment "Now watch me carefully"), but you are better off when you tie getting attention to the training at hand. If the training was in problem solving, for example, you could ask the question, "How do you go about solving a problem?" or "We have high absenteeism, what should we do about it?" These types of questions focus discussion on the types of problems trainees face and their typical problem-solving approaches. This initial focus leads nicely into the introduction of the problem-solving training objectives. Another way to gain attention is to have the CEO/president welcome the trainees and indicate how important the training is to the future of the company. This approach was effective for the training developed by Dr. Camp in Training in Action 5-2. High-level support for training is always important, and when you can get a key decision maker to take time to convey it, it is especially effective in getting trainees' attention.

Informing the Learner of the Goal (Objective)

We covered learning objectives and their importance in depth. Clearly this step is important in getting the trainee focused and aware of not only what needs to be learned, but also what will be required when training is complete. Also it is useful to tie the training back to the job and how it will help trainees be better performers. Having done a TNA this will be an easy task.

Stimulating Recall of Prior Relevant Knowledge (Learning)

This step is important in order to be sure that the trainee has accessed the information/knowledge necessary for the learning that is about to take place. At the moment of learning, all relevant prerequisite capabilities must be highly accessible to be part of the learning event.[92] Suppose you are about to conduct some "team problem solving" training. Previously you did some brainstorming training and problem definition training. You need to get trainees thinking about these topics so the previous learning will be accessible to the problem solving training. You can ask for an explanation of brainstorming from a trainee or focus a discussion on these two topics and show how they are related to the present learning task. Or simply review the two topics with a high level of participation from trainees.

Present Material to Be Learned

Material is presented in a logical and understandable format. This point seems obvious, but recall that what the trainer may think obvious may not fit in the trainees' schema. To ensure understanding, the method of instruction should include a number of questions designed to elicit responses from trainees regarding their level of understanding. Highlight important points with verbal emphasis (raise voice, slow down presentation for effect). Use easel sheets with bold print to highlight important learning points. Also, eliciting examples from trainees serves to ensure trainees understand the material. The training in team problem solving should list the steps on an easel board for all to see, with substeps provided under each of the main headings. Some simple examples of problems and the procedure to solve them could be on a video for effect. The video could be stopped at each step to highlight the step and the preparation for the next step. These examples reflect ways in which the organization and presentation of material assist the trainee in their symbolic coding and cognitive organization.

Provide Guidance for Learning

The key here is to guide the trainees to the appropriate answer/conclusion, not tell them the answer. Get trainees to examine the possibilities related to the topic, both right and wrong. When the solution is reached, the overall discussion will have helped trainees obtain an in-depth understanding of the topic. Provide them with a problem and ask for possible alternatives. For example in problem solving training, give trainees a problem such as "absenteeism is high" and ask them to "define the problem" (the first step in problem solving). This task gets trainees thinking and providing different perspectives. These different perspectives are shared by everyone and all can assess (depending on whether the response was correct) their own level of understanding. Providing numerous examples allows the trainees to see the generality of the material to many situations. Asking for their examples confirms that the material is being put in the correct context.

Elicit the Performance

Here trainees actually do it. For example, in the case of learning a problem-solving model, they now would work in teams to solve a real problem. The problem should be similar or even the same problem they have been discussing all along. It should also be the simplest type of problem they are likely to come across. Until now, working through the solution was piecemeal; now they as a team do it as a whole integrated process without interaction with other teams or the trainer. Once successful, provide a more complex problem to solve — even suggest they use one they previously encountered in their workplace.

Provide Feedback

Once the team completes a process, a feedback session as to how they did is essential. Feedback can be provided in numerous ways. Videotaping the session and going over it with the team (time consuming), sitting in on parts of each meeting and providing feedback, or having another team watch and provide feedback are all methods used to provide feedback. The type you use will, to some extent, be a function of the time available and the number of trainees. Of course designing a program in which training is spread over a number of weeks would allow for more individual feedback between training sessions, but the benefits must be weighed against the cost of trainer time. The important thing is that trainees know what they are doing right and wrong and are able to make corrections before training is complete.

Assess Performance

The Gagné-Briggs theory indicates you should assess learning after each of the topics is taught. So, after training on effective feedback skills and before moving to performance appraisal training, you need to assess the learning that took place regarding feedback skills. The assessment need not be formal, especially when a formal evaluation may be planned for the end of the training program. But some method of determining whether the trainees learned the material is necessary. Questioning (for cognitive knowledge) is one way to assess. Asking trainees for a behavioral response (for a skill) is also a form of assessment. This approach has two purposes: it confirms that learning that took place, and also provides for additional practice at recalling the knowledge, or performing the skill.

Enhancing Retention and Transfer

An important part of any training program is the transfer of the training to the job. Designing the program to facilitate retention and transfer is one of the more critical components of the training design. If cognitive knowledge is what the training is about, the opportunity for review (retrieval of the information) needs to be provided at spaced intervals after the training is complete. The same goes for skills. All of the support processes discussed earlier are relevant here. For an example of using the design theory to develop training, see Table 5-14.

The Small Business

Small businesses follow more sophisticated human resource policies today than in the 1980s.[93] In fact, a recent study suggests that many of their policies and practices are not much different from those of large businesses.[94] In another study, a comparison of small and large companies that implemented total quality management found that the small companies were equally involved in human resource activities such as training, and equally successful in producing quality products.[95] This finding suggests small businesses are beginning to realize the importance of sound human resource practices. The major difference between small and large business is the impact successful training can have on the organization as a whole.

Much of what was discussed earlier is relevant for any size organization. Ensuring that employees are highly motivated to learn and presenting interesting and relevant training is the same no matter the size of the company. Again, the major problem in many training programs is not the learning of the skills, but the transfer of these skills to the job. To our mind, given the requirements necessary for transfer of training, the small business enjoys a definite advantage. We see that climate and a continuous learning culture go a long way toward ensuring transfer of training. Although any organizational change is difficult, a small organization should be able to accomplish climate and culture change faster and more easily than a large one. Furthermore, in the small business, top management's commitment should be easier to obtain and to demonstrate. In many of the large company interventions conducted by the authors, top management provides written or verbal support for the intervention, but little else. Most of our dealings are with the human resource manager rather than the CEO or president. Although we stress the continued involvement of upper management, we often have little interaction with top management once the intervention has begun. Top management typically feels they must spend their time on more important things.

In the small firm, it is often the CEO or owner who makes decisions about the type of training and development that will be provided.[96] Access to these individuals is much easier and the ability to influence them is therefore greater. Because of their greater involvement, they often develop a clearer understanding of their role in making training successful. Training in Action 5-3 provides an example of this involvement.

Will the training in Training in Action 5-3 transfer? According to the research, it stands a good chance. The fact that the organization is small enough that all could attend the same training at the same time and experience the same things will help the transfer process. This situation simply could not occur in a larger company.

TABLE 5-14 Cognitive Portion of "Giving Effective Feedback" Using the Gagné-Briggs Nine Events of Instruction

A sample training design using the Gagné-Briggs model

Event	Feedback Training
Gain attention	Ask questions of trainees to initiate interest in topic of feedback: "Who has received constructive feedback that they actually appreciated?" If some have, ask them what it was about the feedback that made it better than other feedback they received. If no one has, ask what it was about previous feedback that made them not appreciate it. Have brief discussion about what is wrong with typical feedback we receive and what would make it better.
Inform of goal	Show objectives and discuss; tie to previous discussion.
Stimulate recall of prior knowledge	Ask "How do you behave when you are trying to help someone versus when you are disciplining them?" "How do you behave toward someone you are trying to help (helping is what feedback is all about)?" Get trainees to verbalize things they do such as "provide it in private," "do it as soon as possible," and so forth to put them in a helping frame of mind, with their rules for helping in their "working memory."
Present material	Share a list of what makes for effective feedback—be specific, not general; be descriptive, not evaluative; and so forth. Present it on easel sheet in bold. Provide examples for each item.
Provide guidance	Provide trainees with multiple examples (some good, some poor) and ask for input as to effectiveness. Give handout sheet with a number of feedback statements and ask trainees to rate their effectiveness. Get trainees in small groups to discuss their results and come up with a group consensus as to which are good and which are not so good. Have them provide a rationale. Now go through each and ask trainees to discuss in terms of their responses.
Elicit performance	Performance here is cognitive knowledge about what is effective and not effective feedback. Ask trainees to form groups of three. Have one of the three teach the others the rules of effective feedback with examples. Then switch so each trainee has the opportunity to show they know the information well enough to teach it to others, and provide their own unique examples.
Provide feedback	The other two trainees receiving training complete an evaluation form giving feedback to the one doing the training (in the groups of three). The trainer also goes around to each group and provides feedback.
Assess performance	Conduct a quiz that asks trainees to recall the rules for effective feedback. Go through a list of feedback examples (similar to the ones earlier) and indicate which are effective, as well as which are not effective and why they were not effective.
Enhance retention and transfer	Trainees will be back to learn the behavioral component of the training in a week. At this time review will take place to facilitate retention.

TRAINING IN ACTION 5-3

REAL SUPPORT

The Sandwich Community Health Center is a service-oriented organization with about 35 employees located in the community of Sandwich, Ontario. The executive director and assistant executive director of the organization wanted to integrate the two areas of the organization (clinical and health promotion) as well as develop a team approach to much of the community care they offer. After a discussion of the issue, a consultant conducted a TNA and provided training on communication skills and conflict resolution.

Everyone attended training, even the executive director. This involvement by top management sent an important message about the importance of the training. Top management also insisted that the training be evaluated. Knowing that an assessment will be made at some future date kept everyone focused on the need to change. Finally, although no formal culture assessment was made, the interviews conducted in the TNA clearly indicated a climate of continuous learning.

Outcomes of Design

As noted at the start of the chapter, it is necessary to understand the various factors that facilitate learning and transfer, in order to develop effective training programs. It is one of the three outputs of the design phase. Table 5-15 provides a summary of some of these factors and how they are related to the theories of design presented earlier.

Two other two outputs are the identification of evaluation objectives, which will be presented in Chapter 8, and the identification of alternative methods of instruction, which is presented in Chapter 6. In Chapter 6, the link between the learning objectives and training methods is presented; a table at the end of Chapter 6 summarizes this information.

TABLE 5-15 Learning and Transfer Factors As Related to Social Learning Theory and Gagné-Briggs Theory of Design

	Social Learning Theory	*Gagné-Briggs Nine Events of Instruction*	*Factors to Consider*
Pretraining	**Attention/Expectancy**		
	Influence expectations and attitudes of trainees		Identify those with low expectations/poor attitudes and send to pretraining workshop to improve.
			Provide information to influence expectancies and identify positive outcomes of training.
	Demonstrate the need for training and set goals		Do needs analysis so only relevant trainees attend training.

(continued)

TABLE 5-15 (continued)

	Social Learning Theory	Gagné-Briggs Nine Events of Instruction	Factors to Consider
			Have supervisors discuss performance of trainee and set mutual goals based on future training.
			Have learning objectives distributed ahead of time.
Training Beginning	**Attention/Expectancy** Create/reinforce positive attitude toward training	**Gain attention**	Allow time for suitable instructor and trainee introductions and develop a relaxed atmosphere.
		Inform trainee of goals	Allow for time to go through needs analysis, show learning objectives, and discuss usefulness on the job; draw examples from trainees.
	Eliminate distractions		Choose site where anxiety level will be low (see classical conditioning).
			Choose proper facilities.
During	**Retention** Make relevant		Continue to focus on training objectives.
		Stimulate recall of prior knowledge	Develop links between previous learning and the new learning (activation of memory).
		Present material	Use multiple media and make interesting.
			Ask questions and get involvement.
	Make interesting	**Provide guidance for learning**	Get trainees involved (symbolic rehearsal).
			Use relevant examples and offer many of them.
	Behavioral Reproduction/ Reinforcement Encourage learning	**Elicit performance**	Provide relevant practice process (including maximum similarity and/or different situations).

(continued)

TABLE 5-15 (continued)

	Social Learning Theory	Gagné-Briggs Nine Events of Instruction	Factors to Consider
		Provide feedback	Let trainees know how they are doing.
Ending	**Reinforcement** Be sure trainees see results of training	**Assess performance**	Provide time for examining objectives to see what was accomplished.
			Provide time to evaluate performance level accomplished and provide feedback.
	Sensitize trainees to difficulty in transfer of training	**Enhance retention and transfer**	Incorporate relapse-prevention strategy.
			Provide commitment of trainer to meet with trainees to facilitate transfer.
			Develop trainee goals for transfer of training.
Post-Training	**Reinforcement** Facilitate transfer		Obtain support from supervisor/peers/trainer to help trainee in transferring the training to the workplace.
			Ensure that reward systems are in line with newly trained behaviors.

The Real World of Training . . . What Is Wrong Here

Were you able to figure out what went wrong in the two cases at the beginning of the chapter? Both deal with the need to develop good behavioral objectives.

CASE 1

Recall the incidents discussed in Case 1 at the beginning of the chapter. Training in troubleshooting did not transfer well. What went wrong? Would more training help the employees become better troubleshooters? Let's reexamine the training that took place. The instructor provided a problem, and the trainees indicated the symptoms that would result from the problem. This "problem/symptom" sequence was the exact opposite of what they would be required to do on the job which involved seeing a symptom and then

(continued)

(*continued*)

determining the problem. Had proper learning objectives been developed before the design of the training, the instructor would have realized this mistake. For example, consider the learning objective, "Upon describing what is wrong with the system (a symptom), the trainee will immediately be able to describe all the possible problems that might cause these symptoms." Had this objective been developed before training, the type of training required would have been more obvious.

CASE 2

In Case 2, all the students followed a cycle of doing poorly on tests 1, 4, 7, 10, and 13, and much better on the other exams.

Further analysis revealed that the 32-week course was divided into five subsections, each of which had three tests. Also each subsection was taught by a different instructor. So on the very first test, the students did not know what to expect and did poorly. Once they understood what to expect on the tests, they improved on the remaining two tests. When a new instructor arrived, they prepared as usual only to find the type of test had changed; once again they did poorly. When they understood what the new instructor wanted, they did better. It was the "getting used to what the instructor wanted" that caused the cycle. Objectives were vague and students did not know what to expect. The chief instructor then developed learning objectives for all subsections, which provided guidance to both instructors and students as to what exams would be about. The problem disappeared.

Source: Mager, R. 1975. *Preparing Instructional Objectives*. Belmont, CA: Pitman Learning.

SUMMARY

In the design of training a number of factors need to be considered, the first being organizational constraints. How long you will be given to prepare and present training, how much of a priority it is and how much you can spend, will place constraints on the type of training you will offer. Once these questions are answered, you need to determine the type of trainees, their current level of KSAs, their motivation to learn, and how homogeneous they will be as a group in terms of these factors. Answers to these questions will provide you with a framework from which you will need to develop the objectives for training.

Training objectives provide clear unambiguous goals for the training. An effective objective contains three parts: (1) desired behaviors, or what the trainee is expected to be able to do; (2) conditions, or what help/environment trainees will face when performing the expected behavior; and (3) standards, or what will be required to be successful. Training objectives should be developed for reaction to training, learning, transfer the job, and organizational outcomes. These objectives provide guidance for designing and developing the training. They also provide the trainer with clear instructions on what to train and how to do it. Finally it informs the trainees what to expect.

In the design of training two aspects need to be considered: learning and transfer. To facilitate learning the design must address the motivation of the trainees and the environment training will take place in. Social learning theory and the Gagné-Briggs micro theory of design provide a framework for setting up each instructional event in a manner that is most effective. To facilitate transfer, consider issues such as type of practice, whole or part learning, overlearning, similarity to the job, and so forth. Also the use of a combination of goal setting and relapse prevention helps trainees transfer the KSAs to the job.

Just as important to transfer is the support of the supervisor and peers in the work group. Another method to assist transfer is to arrange "sit-ins" by the trainer. Finally, congruent reward systems and a supportive climate/culture need to be present to ensure transfer.

Elaboration theory, a macro design theory, is a useful guide for determining sequencing of events and just how to present them in a training context. This theory argues that one should focus on the whole rather than part learning, but to make the whole as simple as possible at the beginning and then make it more difficult in stages until it reaches the level of complexity in the workplace.

This chapter sets the stage for showing the link between the learning objectives and the methods used to provide training. By understanding what makes a good learning objective, and the groundwork in terms of what facilitates learning and transfer based on theory, you are now ready to examine the methods of training and the link between these methods and the learning objectives.

THE TRAINING PROGRAM (FABRICS INC.)

This continues the description of the Fabrics Inc., training program begun in Chapter 4. Recall that Fabrics Inc. grew quickly and experienced problems with its supervisors. In Chapter 4 we described how the consultant completed a needs analysis. From this TNA the consultant determined a number of areas where supervisors could use training. A partial list included a lack of KSAs the following areas:

Effective listening

Communication

Conflict resolution

Effective feedback

Measuring employee performance

Motivating employees

For the purpose of this exercise, we deal with only one: conflict resolution. The first step will be to develop the training objectives.

THE OBJECTIVES

Some of the learning objectives are as follows:

- The trainee will, <u>with no errors</u>, **present in writing the four types of active listen-**

ing, along with examples of each of the types, *with no reference material.*

- *When, in a role play, the trainee is presented with an angry comment,* **the trainee will respond** <u>immediately</u> **using one of the active listening types.** The trainee will **then explain orally the technique used and why,** *with no help from reference material.* <u>The trainee will be presented with five of these comments and be expected to correctly respond and explain a minimum of four.</u>

- The trainee will, <u>with 100 percent accuracy</u> **in writing provide each step of the conflict resolution model, along with a relevant example,** *with no help from any reference material.*

- *In a role play of an angry customer,* the trainee/employee **will show concern for the customer by listening and providing alternative solutions, using the steps in the conflict resolution model,** *with help from an easel sheet that has the steps listed on it.* <u>Trainee must use all the steps and two types of active listening in the role play.</u>

(continued)

> ### THE TRAINING PROGRAM (FABRICS INC.)

(*continued*)

- *After watching a role play of an angry person and an employee using the conflict resolution model,* **the trainee will,** *without reference to material, immediately* **provide feedback as to the effectiveness of the person using the conflict resolution model.** <u>Trainee must identify four of the six errors</u>.

Some examples of the other objectives are given here.

REACTION OBJECTIVE:
The trainees will upon completion of training **respond to a 15-item reaction questionnaire with** <u>minimum scores of 4 on a 5-point scale.</u>

TRANSFER OF TRAINING OBJECTIVE:
When an angry customer approaches the employee and begins speaking in an angry tone of voice, **the employee will** *immediately* **use the conflict resolution model behaviors to** <u>calm the customer down</u>.

ORGANIZATIONAL OBJECTIVE:
Three months after training <u>there will be a 75 percent drop in</u> **letters of complaint from customers**.

DESIGN ISSUES

Elaboration theory examines the design of training from a macro perspective. The conflict resolution process is a complex task that involves attending to cues at verbal, vocal, and visual levels, then responding in the appropriate manner using the four steps in the model. These steps are:

1. Active listening
2. Indicate respect
3. Be assertive
4. Provide information

Active listening is a complex task itself,[97] as is the total conflict resolution model. So, the first decision is what mix of "spiral/topical sequencing to use in training on the conflict resolution model. Active listening is a skill that can be used on its own, so we will use topical sequencing to train employees in active listening first. Then, we will use spiral sequencing to train the total conflict resolution model.

Teaching of the cognitive component of each of these skills will be completed before the skill training, but for brevity, we will discuss only the behavioral component. In teaching each of these skills, we will use the SCM proposed in elaboration theory. So, we first must determine the epitome, the simplest version of the task that still embodies the total task. For active listening, it will be to use the skill in an everyday situation, such as discussing which movie to see. The initiator (person in a role of disagreeing with the trainee) will simply disagree regarding a movie they both plan to see. This situation has no specific emotional component and should require minimal monitoring of the initiator by the trainee, because it will not result in meaningful argument. A similar epitome can be used for both active listening and the conflict resolution model, because the latter simply takes the discussion to a different level.

```
┌─ THE TRAINING PROGRAM (FABRICS INC.) ─┐
```

(*continued*)

The most complex task will require dealing with a great deal of anger on the part of the initiator of the discussion. Once the role plays at the two extremes are conceptualized, those in-between can be determined.

Now let's turn to the evaluation component as an output from the training design. To consider these outputs, we turn back to the learning objectives, which are:

- The trainee will, <u>with no errors</u>, **present in writing the four types of active listening, along with examples of each of the types**, *with no reference material.*

- The trainee will, <u>with 100 percent accuracy</u> **provide in writing each step of the conflict resolution model, along with a relevant example**, *with no help from any reference material.*

These, along with a number of similar objectives not shown, will require a paper-and-pencil test of declarative knowledge.

- *When, in a role play, the trainee is presented with an angry comment,* **the trainee will respond** *immediately* **using one of the active listening types.** The **trainee will then explain orally the technique used and why**, *with no help from reference material.* <u>The trainee will be presented with five of these comments and be expected to correctly respond and explain a minimum of four.</u>

- *In a role play where another trainee is playing an angry customer* the trainee **will calm the person using the steps in the conflict resolution model**, *with help from an easel sheet that has the steps*

listed on it. You may have identified "using the steps in the conflict model" as both a part of the behavior and as part of the standard. It is often the case that a statement of the behavior required will also provide information about the conditions and/or the standard. <u>The trainee must use each of the steps correctly.</u>

- *After watching a video of a sales clerk using the conflict resolution model to respond to an angry customer,* **the trainee will** *without reference to material* **evaluate the sales clerk referring to the steps in the conflict resolution model.** <u>The trainee must identify a minimum of four of the six errors.</u>

These objectives will require carefully developed standardized role plays. The role of the initiator will be scripted and standardized to provide each trainee with similar situations to respond to. In addition, a standardized scoring key, which will guide the scoring of a trainee in the behavioral tests, will be developed. These scoring keys provide examples of acceptable and unacceptable behavior of the trainee, and a rating scale for different responses. A scoring key will also be provided for the explanations (oral test) that follow the behavioral part of the test. The development process for these scoring keys will be provided in Chapter 8 in the discussion of evaluation.

We will return to Fabrics Inc., in Chapter 8 to provide the process for preparing to evaluate the training there. We will not be covering Fabrics Inc., in Chapter 7, where we discuss development and implementation of training.

KEY TERMS

- Behavioral reproduction
- Climate
- Conditions
- Culture
- Design theory
- Desired outcome
- Elaborating
- Elaboration theory
- Epitomizing
- Guided discovery
- Identical elements
- Knowledge of results
- Learning objectives
- Massed practice

- Negative transfer
- Organizational outcome objectives
- Overlearning
- Part learning
- Positive transfer
- Progressive part learning
- Relapse prevention
- Sequencing
- Simplifying Conditions Method (SCM)
- Sit-ins
- Spaced practice
- Standards

- Strategic knowledge development
- Symbolic encoding
- Symbolic rehearsal
- Task complexity
- Task organization
- Trainee reaction objectives
- Training objectives
- Transfer of training objectives
- Whole learning
- Zero transfer

CASE ANALYSES

1. Review the Multistate Health Corporation case from Chapter 2 and answer the following questions:
   a. In the implementation of the HRPS, what groups of employees are likely to need training? Think of this issue from a training design perspective as well as a training content perspective.
   b. For the type of training you envision for each group, what are the learning objectives? Write these objectives in complete form.
   c. For each group of employees that will need training, what are the organizational constraints you will need to address in the design of your training? What design features will you use to address these constraints? Be sure to address both the learning and transfer of training issues.
2. In the LEM case (2) in Chapter 4, suppose management decided to provide an outplacement workshop for management personnel who were being let go. A needs analysis indicated that what these individuals needed most was interviewing skills. How would you design a training program that would ensure trainees were interested and would get the most out of training (the focus is on the trainee)? ■

EXERCISES

1. You perhaps already noted that the learning objectives at the beginning of each chapter do not completely follow the three criteria we identified. They all describe the outcome in behavioral terms but do not identify the conditions or standards, which vary with the instructor. Assume you will be the instructor for this chapter and rewrite each of the learning objectives at the beginning of the chapter in complete form. Your trainees are corporate HRD employees and you are training them on the contents of this chapter. Additionally, write an objective for each of the other types of training objectives (trainee reaction, transfer of training, organizational outcome).

2. What is your grade point average since you started your education at this institution? Ho. hard do you work to maintain that average: 3 (very hard/hard), 2 (about average), 1 (enough to get by)? Now ask yourself why. Tie your answer into Expectancies 1 and 2 and the valence of outcomes. Break into groups that contain a mix of 1s, 2s, and 3s. Discuss what makes the person in your group a 3. Is it attractive outcomes (valence), confidence in ability (Expectancy 1), or belief that it will result in positive outcomes desired? From that information, is there any way you believe you could influence the 2s or 1s to be more motivated? What would you try to influence? Explain your approach in terms of Expectancies 1 and 2. How does this process relate to trainee populations in the workplace?

QUESTIONS FOR REVIEW

1. What are the four types of training objectives? Why is it necessary to formulate objectives for all four? Who benefits from learning objectives and why?
2. What can be done long before the trainee attends training to ensure that the trainee will be motivated to learn?
3. How does knowledge of classical and operant conditioning assist us in designing effective training?
4. How would you present training material in a manner that facilitates retention?
5. If a particular task was critical to saving life (police officer shooting a gun, pilot responding to an emergency), what factors would you build into the design of training to ensure that the behavior was both learned and transferred to the workplace?
6. To help ensure transfer of training, what would you do outside the training itself? Who would you involve and how? What about the organizational structure/environment?
7. Suppose you are designing a training program for a group of 40 employees. These employees come from a wide range of ethnic and cultural backgrounds and also have different educational and experience backgrounds relative to the content area of the training. What training design features would you use to address these constraints?
8. What is elaboration theory, and why is it useful in helping design training?
9. Discuss the Gagné-Briggs theory of design and its relationship to social learning theory.

CHAPTER

Training Methods

Learning Objectives

After reading this chapter, you should be able to:

- Describe the various formats, purposes, procedures, strengths, and limitations of the following training methods:
  - Lectures, discussions, and demonstrations
  - Computer-based training (CBT)
  - Games and simulations
  - On-the-job training (OJT)
- Describe the types of learning objectives for which each method is most suited
- Indicate the impact of the method on the learning process
- Identify the various audiovisual options and their strengths and weaknesses
- Evaluate multimedia tools as stand-alone training or enhancements to the various training methods

---

Sales Training at Motorola

More than a decade ago, Motorola developed a strategy for training its global sales force. A prominent feature of the strategy was that each year a master training plan for the sales force would be created. The company's strategic plans, business objectives, and operational tactics for each product would drive this plan. Once an initial plan was developed it was then reviewed and critiqued by senior management, the different divisions, the marketing function, and a training council. The input from these stakeholders would be synthesized into a master training plan agreed to by all the important stakeholders.

(continued)

(*continued*)

Designers of the sales training at Motorola first asked the question, "What outcomes do we want from salespeople as a result of the training?" Answers to this question become the training's specific learning objectives. Early on, it was decided that the training would be delivered to the sales force by video.

Once training content was designed, videos were produced by an outside company. The video training modules took from 3 to 6 months to produce. Videos contained live footage from production plants, customers' offices, and other locations, as well as studio footage, including professional actors in simulated sales situations.

Videos were used to train sales representatives in the following areas:

1. Product information

   - New products and system descriptions
   - Product applications
   - Competitive product analysis

2. Critical changes in policy and procedures

   - Changes in compensation plans
   - Sales contests

3. Market information

   - Market updates
   - Customer profiling
   - Location shots
   - Product usage in customer settings such as computer integrated manufacturing applications

4. Sales techniques

   - Review/reinforce/supplement skills developed during live courses
   - Model desired behavior in specific situations
   - Model undesirable behavior for critique/coaching

Videos and study guides were shipped to salespeople according to their need for the training. As many as 1,000 sales representatives might get a particular video training module. The sales representatives receiving a module would engage in self-study of supplementary materials that accompanied the video, watch the video, and follow directions in the video or supplementary materials. When salespeople felt they had mastered the material, they would complete an exam at the end of the study guide and call a toll-free number to transmit responses to the exam.

Salespeople who successfully completed a module received positive reinforcement through the annual "Make the Grade" recognition program. Results from the module exams were also factored into performance and merit reviews as well as promotional opportunities. Those who failed the exam were asked to go through the video and supplementary materials again before retaking the exam. If a salesperson failed an exam twice, the sales manager was notified.

Source: Adapted from Honeycutt, E., T. McCarty, and V. Howe. 1993. Sales technology applications: Self-paced video-enhanced training: A case study. *Journal of Personal Selling and Sales Management* 13(1):73–79.

Overview of the Chapter

The preceding case illustrates Motorola's use of many of the principles of effective training. The case also introduces issues yet to be discussed. Among these are the following:

- Given today's technology, is video still the best way to deliver the training?
- Given the content of the training, is video the most effective way to achieve training objectives?
- What role did cost of development, cost of delivery, and other constraints play in the selection of the video delivery system? Are those costs today different from the early 1990s?

This chapter provides a basic understanding of training methods, their components and variations, their strengths and limitations in terms of cost, suitable learning objectives, and other factors related to their effectiveness. At the end of this chapter we compare the ability of the various training methods to develop knowledge and skills and to influence attitudes. Once you select the methods for achieving your training objectives you will need to consider the merits of various delivery systems (e.g., computer-based, video, face-to-face, etc.) and other implementation issues. These considerations will be covered in Chapter 7.

Matching Methods with Outcomes

Every year, the selection of appropriate training methods to meet training objectives becomes more challenging. The growth of the training industry, the increased number of providers and the rapid advances in technology create an ever-growing number of methods and delivery systems. In this chapter and the next we provide a framework for sorting through the alternatives. However, no book will provide you with all possible alternatives, because by the time the book is written, new ones will have been developed. The material in this chapter and the next will, however, ground you in the basic methods and delivery systems allowing you to make good decisions in the future. Because instructional methods differ in their ability to influence knowledge, skills, and attitudes, you must be able to evaluate a method's strengths and weaknesses to make good decisions about its use. Before moving into that discussion, a brief review of the KSA definitions might be helpful. Refer to the definitions in Chapter 1 if you need more detail.

> Knowledge can be acquired at three distinct levels: declarative, procedural, and strategic. Declarative knowledge is the person's store of factual information, procedural knowledge is the person's understanding about how and when to apply the facts, and strategic knowledge is used for planning, monitoring, and revising goal-directed activity, including learning.
>
> Skills are a person's ability to carry out specific tasks such as operating a piece of equipment, communicating effectively, or implementing a business strategy. Skills combine knowledge of "what" to do "when" with the ability to do it. Two levels of skill acquisition are compilation (lower level) and automaticity (higher level), reflecting differences in the degree to which the skill becomes a routine or automatic behavior pattern.
>
> Attitudes are employee beliefs and opinions about objects and events and the positive or negative feelings associated with them. Attitudes affect motivation levels, which in turn influence behavior.

What might be the knowledge, skill, and attitude objectives in the Motorola case? Many training programs set learning objectives in more than one area, which will usually require you to combine several methods into an integrated whole, because no single method can do everything well. For example, among the methods used at Motorola are lecture, demonstrations, and simulations.

The various methods can be divided into cognitive and behavioral approaches, and trainers must understand the strengths and weaknesses of each. **Cognitive methods** provide verbal or written information, demonstrate relationships among concepts, or provide the rules for how to do something. These methods stimulate learning through their impact on cognitive processes and are associated most closely with changes in knowledge and attitudes. Though these types of methods can influence skill development, it is not their strength. Conversely, **behavioral methods** allow the trainee to practice behavior in a real or simulated fashion. They stimulate learning through behavior and are best used for skill development and attitude change. Thus either behavioral or cognitive learning methods can effectively be used to change attitudes, though they do so through different means. Cognitive methods are best for knowledge development, and behavioral methods are best for skills. What strengths do you think Motorola's video-based training offered for developing a sales representative's knowledge? How about skills and attitudes? What are the problems you see with using videotapes for developing sales skills? Do they provide an advantage over just reading about how to sell? Are they as helpful as a trainer who can answer questions and provide feedback? Let's look at the various training methods to see what they do well and not so well.

Lectures and Demonstrations

The lecture is one of the oldest forms of training, second only to demonstrations. In ancient times, before language developed, knowledge was transferred through demonstrations. Nearly all training programs contain some lecture component and a great many provide some type of demonstration. They possess similar characteristics, but are appropriate for different objectives. We will discuss the lecture first.

The lecture, printed or oral, is best used to create understanding of a topic or to influence attitudes through education about a topic. In its simplest form, the lecture is merely telling someone about something.[1] Do you think the Motorola videos contained any lecture components? Of course they did, because a video-taped lecture is still a lecture. When the trainer begins a training session by telling the trainees the objectives, the agenda, and the process that will be used in training, the trainer is using the lecture method. It is difficult to imagine training that doesn't use the lecture format to some extent.

Several variations in the lecture format allow it to be more or less formal or interactive.[2] The clearest difference is the role trainees are expected to play. The straight lecture does not include trainees interacting with the trainer. Adding discussion and a question-and-answer period invites the trainees to be more interactive in the learning process.

STRAIGHT LECTURE/LECTURETTE

The **straight lecture** is an extensive presentation of information, which the trainee attempts to absorb.[3] The lecture is typically thought of in terms of a person (the trainer) speaking to a group (the trainees) about a topic. However, the lecture may also take the form of printed text, such as this book. The only differences between a straight lecture and the same material in print are the lecturer's control of the speed at which material is presented, voice inflections and body language used to emphasize points, and of course the visual image of the lecturer. The lecturer can decide to vary from the training script, based on cues from the trainees, whereas straight text is limited to what is printed. Because of the many similarities, we view printed text as a form of straight lecture. Printed text should not to be confused with audiovisual aids to instruction, which will be covered later in this chapter.

A good lecture is well organized and begins with an introduction, which lays out the purpose of the lecture and the order in which topics will be covered. If it is an oral lecture the introduction should cover any rules about interrupting the lecture for questions and opportunity for clarification. The main body of the lecture, the topic content, follows the introduction. These parts of topic area should be logically sequenced so that trainees are prepared for each topic by the content of the preceding topics. The lecture should conclude with a summary of the main learning points or conclusions. Because lectures require long periods of trainee inactivity, a shorter version of a lecture, the **lecturette**, is often used. It has the same characteristics as the lecture but usually lasts fewer than 20 minutes if done orally. In print, the lecturette would be a shorter amount of printed text to read (e.g., this section on lecture and discussion compared to the whole chapter).

During a straight lecture or lecturette, the trainee does little except listen, observe, and perhaps take notes. Even when done well, it is not an especially effective technique for learning. However, it is useful when a large number of people must be given a specified set of information. The oral lecture should not contain too many learning points unless printed text accompanies the lecture. Trainees will forget information provided orally in direct proportion to the amount of information provided. Therefore, shorter lectures are usually better. However, longer lectures can be effective if the length is due to examples and clarifying explanation.

A major concern about the straight lecture method is the inability to identify and correct misunderstandings. When the only training objective is to acquire specific factual information, often better learning can be achieved at less cost by putting the information into text. Printed text and video can reach a larger number of people less expensively than a live lecturer can. Live lectures typically require paying for the trainer, facilities, travel, and other expenses each time they are presented. Using printed text or video allows the trainees to review the training material as often as needed for retention or after training to refresh the learning. In addition, because they can read or view the material at their leisure, lost productivity due to training is minimized. The only added value provided by the lecture is the credibility the lecturer can give to the material by his or her personal presence and the attention commanded through presentation skills.

DISCUSSION METHOD

The **discussion method** uses a lecturette to provide trainees with information that is supported, reinforced, and expanded on through interactions both among the trainees and between the trainees and the trainer. This added communication gives it much greater power than the lecture. Using logically sequenced lecturettes, each followed by discussion and questioning, can achieve higher-level knowledge objectives, such as principle learning and problem solving.

The discussion method provides a two-way flow of communication. Knowledge is communicated from trainer to trainees, and understanding is conveyed by trainees back to the trainer. Verbal and nonverbal feedback from trainees enables the trainer to determine whether the material is understood. If not, the trainer may need to spend more time on this area or present the information again in a different manner.

Questioning can be done by both the trainees and the trainer. When the trainees volunteer questions, they demonstrate their thinking about the content of the lecture. A trainer who asks questions stimulates thinking about the key areas that are important to know. Asking and responding to questions are trainer skills that will be discussed in the next chapter. For now the point is that questioning (by trainees or the trainer) and discussions are beneficial because they enhance understanding and keep trainees focused on the material. Furthermore, discussions allow the trainee to be actively engaged in the content of the lecture, an activity that improves recall and future use.

DEMONSTRATIONS

A **demonstration** is a visual display of how to do something or how something works. For example, later in this chapter we discuss on-the-job training, in which the trainer shows the trainee how to perform the tasks of the job. To be effective, a demonstration should, at a minimum, be accompanied by a lecture and preferably by a discussion. Whether demonstrating how to do something or how something works, the principles of an effective demonstration are the same.

To conduct an effective demonstration you should first prepare your lesson plan by breaking the task to be performed into smaller, easily learned parts. You would then sequentially organize the parts of the task and prepare an explanation for why that action is required. When performing the demonstration, you would complete each of the following steps for each part of the task:

- Tell the trainees what you will be doing so they understand what you will be showing them. It will also serve to focus their attention on the critical aspects of the task.
- Demonstrate the task, describing what you are doing while you are doing it.
- After you demonstrate each part of the task, explain why it should be performed in that way.

Demonstrations, like the lecture, can be differentiated by the level of involvement of the trainee. As with the lecture, the more the trainee is involved, the more learning will occur. The following steps increase the value of the demonstration.

After the trainer completes the demonstration:

- Ask the trainee to "talk through" the task before actually doing it.
- Give the trainee the opportunity to do the task and describe what he or she is doing and why.
- Provide feedback, both positive and negative.
- Let the learner practice.

STRENGTHS AND LIMITATIONS OF LECTURES AND DEMONSTRATION

In examining the strengths and limitations of the various methods, we focus on four major issues:

1. The cost in both financial and other resources required to achieve the training objective(s)
2. How much control the trainer has over the material that will be covered
3. The type(s) of learning objectives addressed
4. How the method activates different social learning theory processes

In the Motorola case, the company determined that it was more efficient to use video and print-based lectures, rather than classroom-style lectures and discussions. This approach probably was much less expensive than the cost of bringing all the salespeople to one central location, or sending trainers out to widely dispersed offices. However, to do it effectively, they needed to do extensive piloting of the video, to make sure that most of the questions that would arise in a classroom setting would be addressed by the video. Although Motorola chose to go the video route, many companies choose the classroom alternative, because of the relatively low cost of developing lectures and demonstrations.

The financial costs typically associated with developing and implementing lectures, discussions, and demonstrations include the following:

- Development costs related to creating the content and organization of the training
- Cost of ancillary materials to facilitate learning
- Compensation of trainer and trainee time spent in training
- Cost of the training facility for the program
- Travel, lodging, and food for the trainer and trainees

In terms of development and delivery, printed lectures are the most time-efficient. Oral lectures, followed by discussions and demonstrations require increasingly more time. Of course, the more questions, discussion, and participation allowed, the greater the amount of time required. If the training objective focuses on factual information and interaction is not important, printed text or a video lecture or demonstration will be more efficient and equally effective. The advantage of the live lecture is that it guarantees that everyone is exposed to the information. Printed or video lectures rely on trainees following instructions. For example, in the Motorola case, the employees were supposed to watch the video prior to taking the exam. However, they weren't supervised. Motorola used the exam to measure trainee knowledge of important aspects of the material whether or not they watched the video.

Control of Material and Process

Lectures, discussions, and demonstrations provide a high degree of trainer control over the training process and content. The material covered is predetermined by the trainer, as are the processes used to present the material. The trainees have little if any influence, other than whatever involvement was allowed in the TNA and program design process. However, as the training becomes more interactive, control shifts more to the trainee. Trainee questions or answers to questions shape the content of what is covered. The group dynamics help to shape the processes used by the trainer in presenting the information.

For example, in discussions, the order in which issues arise is determined partly by the lecture content, the types of questions raised, and the results of the discussion sessions. Discussions can move into tangential areas not specifically addressed in the lecture material but of interest to the trainees. Almost everyone at some point experiences the classroom discussion that wanders into interesting but irrelevant areas as a result of a well-placed question to the instructor about a favorite topic. Likewise, the trainee who attempts to replicate the demonstration may make errors in procedure, which can divert the trainer into explaining why that particular set of actions is inappropriate.

As the objectives for knowledge acquisition increase (i.e., Gagné's types), the amount of two-way interaction required for learning must also increase. For example, higher-level learning such as principle learning and problem solving require more discussion and questioning. An advantage of increasing trainee participation in the content is that it increases the amount that is learned. A disadvantage is that it decreases trainer control over what is learned and increases the time required for learning. Thus, if time or control of content is important, the amount and types of trainee questions and discussions need to be limited. Because discussion and questions can be limited or cut off, the trainer still maintains a greater control of content and process relative to other methods.

Learning Objectives (KSAs)

The lecture is most useful when trainees lack declarative knowledge or show attitudes that conflict with the training objectives. The printed or video lecture is more effective because they can be studied in more depth and retained to refresh learning over time. The discussion method is more effective than the straight lecture for learning higher-order knowledge such as concepts and principles and for attitude change. It is possible for the trainee to develop some degree of procedural knowledge via this method, though other methods that allow viewing and practicing of procedures (e.g., computer- and video-based training, and simulations) are generally more effective. Because discussions provide only information (not opportunities for behavioral reproduction), they should be used only for knowledge or attitudinal objectives.

If the training objective is skill improvement, the demonstration may be appropriate. However, training objectives often include both knowledge and skill development; that is, the knowledge is a prerequisite for the skill. For example, the training objective may be to improve managers' ability to conduct effective meetings. First the managers would need to know the components of effective meetings (facts) and when and how to use them (procedures). The lecture/discussion method may be appropriate for meeting the factual and some of the procedural objectives, but you should address the skill development objectives through methods that show trainees how to conduct meetings and allow practice in doing so. The demonstration is appropriate for complex tasks. For example, an expert might be used to train new assembly line workers in the programming of robots. In the Motorola case the videos provided demonstrations of how to operate new products.

The discussion method is more effective than the straight lecture at producing attitude changes. Because attitudes consist of a person's beliefs and feelings about an object or event, they can be modified by new learning. The lecture, and especially the discussion, can change employee attitudes by providing new insights, facts, and understanding as illustrated in Training in Action 6-1. The demonstration may also influence attitudes. For example, a new product demonstration is intended not only to show how the product works, but also to generate enthusiasm in the sales force about the product. Behavior modeling is a type of demonstration we discuss later, and it can be an effective way to change attitudes, because changes in a person's behavior are typically followed by changes in attitude. We discuss this further in the section on simulations and games.

TRAINING IN ACTION 6-1

CHANGING MANAGERIAL ATTITUDES ABOUT
PROBLEM-SOLVING TEAMS

An automobile parts manufacturer planned to implement employee problem-solving teams. A training needs analysis of middle- and first-level managers conducted prior to implementation showed that managers were resistant to these proposed changes in the work design that would give hourly employees more authority in making decisions. Of the many reasons for this resistance, two of the most common statements were "These decisions are ones we are supposed to be making" and "This change will reduce the need for managers. Some of us will lose our jobs."

Training provided to these managers was designed to give them the KSAs necessary to function in the new team-based system. A portion of the lecture/discussion was devoted to addressing concerns about reducing managerial positions. It was explained that the company did not intend to lay off or terminate any managers as a result of this change, but would reduce the size of the managerial workforce through attrition.

Another part of the discussion addressed the change in duties and responsibilities of first-line managers. It was explained that the supervisors would be given new duties and responsibilities, taking the place of those tasks transferred to the hourly problem-solving teams. These new responsibilities, facilitating team problem solving and decision making, serving as liaison between the team and other parts of the organization, acquiring resources for the team, doing long-range planning, and so forth were incorporated into a new performance appraisal for first-line managers. They would no longer be evaluated in the areas that would be handled by the problem solving teams.

During the discussion sessions following the lecture the managers expressed fears and concerns not previously addressed in the lecture portion. The trainer was able to address these issues either directly, by indicating other parts of the training program that dealt with those issues, or by indicating a willingness to bring someone in to address the issues at the next session.

These lecture, discussion, and questioning periods made it clear to trainees that no manager would be terminated just because some of their current responsibilities were being transferred to the teams. Although the managers were losing some responsibilities, they were gaining others. Their performance reviews would be based on the new responsibilities. This shift made it clear that they needed to develop the KSAs necessary to carry out the new responsibilities. A subsequent survey of these managers showed a significantly more positive attitude about the problem-solving team concept than before training.

Learning Processes

In describing the effects of the various methods on learning processes, we return to social learning theory. If you want to review these learning processes (attention, retention, and behavioral reproduction), they are found in Chapter 3 and specifically Figure 3-6 on page 98.

The lectures, discussions, and demonstrations are good at capturing trainee attention, at least in the short term. They show some strength in the area of retention, especially discussions and demonstrations. Even though only demonstrations are good at facilitating behavioral reproduction, lectures and discussion may develop attitudes that are supportive of the desired behavior.

Table 6-1 lists the basic components of the lecture/discussion. These components are discussed more fully in Chapter 7, but are presented here to show the impact each component has on the various learning processes. Table 6-2 lists the basic components of the demonstration and their impact on learning processes.

TABLE 6-1 Basic Lecture/Discussion Components and Effects on Learning

Lecture/Discussion Components	*Learning Process Affected*
1. Orientation	Attention
Presenting information so that trainees understand the direction the lecture is headed and the organization for getting there.	
2. Enthusiasm	Attention
Presenting information in a manner that conveys the topic's importance and inherent value.	
3. Variety	Attention
Using voice, gestures, various components listed in this table, and audio-visual aids. For printed lectures this component is minimized.	Retention: Symbolic coding
4. Logical organization	Retention: Cognitive organization
Presenting information in a logical order and providing logical transitions between topic areas.	
5. Providing explanation	Retention: Symbolic coding Cognitive organization
Describing facts, concepts, and principles in a clear and easily understood manner.	
6. Giving directions	Retention: Cognitive organization Symbolic rehearsal
Providing instructions in a manner that allows trainees to understand what they are to do and how to do it.	
7. Illustrating	Attention Retention: All areas
Providing clear, interesting, and relevant examples of how information can or has been applied (both correctly and incorrectly).	
8. Comparing and contrasting	Attention Retention:
Articulating the similarities and differences, advantages and disadvantages, and so on of relevant topic areas.	
9. Questioning and discussing	Attention Retention: All areas
Seeking information from the trainees regarding their comprehension, their content-related ideas, and stimulating the trainees' thought processes (e.g., Socratic questioning). This component is not possible in printed lectures.	
10. Summarizing	Retention: Cognitive organization
Highlighting important concepts covered in a manner that links the topics/ideas together.	

TABLE 6-2 Basic Demonstration Components and Their Effects on Learning

Demonstration Components	*Areas of Learning Affected*[*]
Present	
• Tell	Attention
• Demonstrate	Retention:
• Explain	Symbolic coding
	Cognitive organization
Try Out	
• Trainees talk through the task	Retention:
• Trainees do task while describing what they are doing and why	Symbolic rehearsal
	Behavioral reproduction
• Trainer provides positive/negative feedback	
• Trainees practice	

[*]From social learning theory as illustrated in Figure 3-6.
Source: Adapted from Gold, L. 1981. Job instruction: Four steps to success. *Training and Development Journal*, September, pp. 28–32.

Attention   Done properly, lectures and demonstrations attract and maintain the attention of trainees. In fact, of the three learning processes (attention, retention, and behavioral reproduction), attracting attention is what the lecture does best. Demonstrations, when combined with lecturettes are better than either alone at covering all the learning processes. Although it can be easy to gain the attention of the trainees at the start, one of the limitations, especially of longer lectures and demonstrations, is that trainees' attention can wander. Printed and video lectures offer the advantage that the trainee can put down the lecture when attention begins to wander and come back to it when in a more receptive mental state. For live lectures, a good lecturer will speak at about the rate of 125 words per minute, but the average person processes information at a rate equivalent to 400 to 500 words a minute. Thus a trainee's attention can fluctuate dramatically over the course of just a 1-hour lecture. Attention begins to decline after 15 to 20 minutes and begins to pick up again only near the end.[4] This phenomenon is a primary reason for the use of lecturettes. Likewise, demonstrations should be short enough to maintain trainee attention, while providing the necessary information about how to complete the task. Discussion, if properly managed by the trainer, acts to heighten attention and refocus thought processes.

Retention   Retention involves the processes of symbolic coding, cognitive organization, and symbolic rehearsal. The lecture's strongest link in the retention process is the first step of symbolic coding. A symbolic coding system is provided during the lecture when the trainer is describing, explaining, and illustrating the learning points. The words and images used are the trainer's way of symbolically coding the meaning of the material. Likewise, in the demonstration, the actions of the trainer are symbolically coded. The words and actions of the trainer are translated by the learners into their individual symbolic coding schemes. The challenge for the trainer is to present the material in a way that the trainer's and learner's symbolic codes hold the same meaning. The discussion/question method helps align the trainee's symbolic coding with the training objectives. Putting the lecture into print, or creating a video for a demonstration, facilitates the trainee's symbolic coding process by allowing the trainee more time to adjust her coding to that used by the text or video. This adjustment increases recall of the information at a later date (e.g., back on the job). Using visual aids, such as graphics in a text or image projections in a live lecture, will facilitate the trainee's coding process by providing additional cues. The more varied the stimuli used to present the same material, the more accurately the information is coded.

Organizing the coded information into already existing or new cognitive structures is what social learning theorists call cognitive organization. The organization of information determines the ease of recall and how appropriately it is used when it is recalled. When trainees become actively engaged in integrating concepts and principles into their cognitive structures, the cognitive organization process is facilitated. Thus, demonstrations allow more opportunity for cognitive organization than straight lecture. Discussion and questioning allows trainees to clarify their understanding of the lecture and organize it appropriately. Better cognitive organization occurs when the trainees are free to discuss various aspects of the new knowledge and its relationship to already existing knowledge and to question the trainer about actual or hypothetical situations where they might use the knowledge.

Demonstrations, by their very nature, stimulate symbolic rehearsal. By simply watching the trainer demonstrate the task, the learner is encouraged to think about doing it, especially if the learner knows he will be asked to do the task when the trainer is finished. Lectures present greater difficulty in this area. The lecturer can and should stimulate symbolic rehearsal by making suggestions about how the knowledge could be applied. However, these suggestions are not as powerful as the trainee imagining how it is applicable to her specific situation. Properly managed, a discussion/question session can facilitate this symbolic rehearsal. For example, as a trainer you might ask the trainees to think about ways in which the knowledge could be used in their work area and write their ideas down on a flip chart. You could then organize the trainees into small groups and encourage each individual to report his or her thoughts to the group. You might say to the group members, "As you listen to others describe how they could apply this knowledge, imagine you were applying it that way in your work area. When the person is finished, discuss the application idea and how it would apply in your area." This process would not only surface misunderstandings and possibly clarify them, but would assist in the cognitive organization of the information. The primary value, however, would be that each trainee was getting a chance to mentally practice (i.e., symbolic rehearsal) using the new knowledge in a variety of ways and situations.

Behavioral Reproduction   The lecture/discussion approach does not provide for practicing actual behaviors, so it is not appropriate for skill development objectives. Although it might be valuable for developing the knowledge base required to learn a skill, or developing attitudes that support using the skill, it is not useful in developing the skill itself. On the other hand, the demonstration builds practice, hence behavioral reproduction, into the training. As discussed in Chapter 5, it is important for the trainer to monitor the learner's performance, providing appropriate feedback to assure the correct behavior is learned.

Training Group Characteristics

The Trainees   For any type of lecture to be effective, trainees should be at about the same general level of intellectual ability and possess about the same level of related content knowledge. If the trainee group is widely divergent in either of these areas, it is difficult to aim the lecture at the appropriate level of understanding. If the lecture is in other respects an appropriate method, the best approach then is to train such groups separately.

The discussion method allows more diversity in a training group, because the discussion period provides an opportunity for more active learning. Trainees who learn better in a more active mode have the opportunity to do so. Trainees also have the opportunity to learn from their peers as they participate in the discussion and ask questions.

The training group can be fairly diverse for demonstrations. However, the trainer must be able to observe each trainee performing the task. As with discussion, the trainees in a demonstration are able to learn, not only from observing the trainer, but also by observing other trainees performing the task and attending to the instructor's feedback.

Size of Training Group   Video or printed lectures have no training group size limitations. Live lectures or lecturettes can be given to groups ranging from just a few to hundreds of trainees. The discussion method, however, places restrictions on the size of a class. In general, it should be small enough to allow all trainees ample opportunity to participate in discussions and questioning. The appropriate size will depend on the complexity of the material and the amount of time allocated. The more complicated the material, the more questions that will arise and the more discussion that will be needed; therefore, fewer trainees can be accommodated. Alternatively, more time could be allocated to accommodate more trainees. It is important to remember, however, that no amount of extra time will compensate for too many trainees. The dynamics of large groups make it difficult or impossible for all to participate in a meaningful way. When trainees cannot participate meaningfully, they will inevitably become less involved and withdraw their attention.

A live demonstration can also be done with a fairly large group, as long as everyone can clearly see the demonstration. However, many of the advantages of the demonstration are lost when the group is large. To capture all the advantages of a demonstration, it should be limited to small groups. The group can be larger if additional trainers are available to monitor trainee practice on the task and provide feedback. A good rule of thumb is to have no more than five trainees per trainer when the demonstration involves hands-on practice by the trainees.

Computer-Based Training

Increasing demands for more knowledgeable and skilled employees, coupled with the need to cut costs, put pressure on HRD departments to provide training to more and more employees, at lower costs. Many companies are implementing **computer-based training (CBT)** as an alternative to classroom-based training to accomplish these goals. Some of the reasons for this shift are demonstrated in the following beliefs many companies hold about CBT:[5]

- Reduces trainee learning time
- Reduces the cost of training
- Provides instructional consistency
- Affords privacy of learning (errors can be made without embarrassment)
- Allows the trainee to master learning
- Is a safe method for learning hazardous tasks
- Increases access to training

The growth of electronic technology and connectivity created alternative training delivery systems and methodologies. About 75 percent of organizations surveyed indicated they provided training to employees through the Internet or an Intranet (accessible only to those in the particular organization).[6] Because the Internet is not a method of training, but rather a technique of delivering training, we will not deal with it in this chapter. Rather, we will cover this and other types of delivery systems in Chapter 7.

Computer-based training is so varied in its forms and applications that it is difficult to describe in concise terms. We stay with convention and broadly define CBT as any training that occurs through the use of a computer.[7] It differs from other methods in the fact that face-to-face interaction with a human trainer is not required. Under this definition, CBT goes by many different names. Table 6-3 lists some of these with a brief description.

PROGRAMMED INSTRUCTION

CBT uses many of the methods described elsewhere in this chapter, but it is a distinctive method in its own right because of its ability to move the trainee into and out of modules based on the trainee's individual learning relative to the training objectives. **Programmed instruction (PI)**, the

TABLE 6-3 Names and Descriptions Used for Computer-Based Training Approaches	
PI	Programmed instruction (PI) is used in computer-based programs consisting of text, graphics, and perhaps multimedia enhancements that are stored in memory and connected to one another electronically. Material to be learned is grouped into chunks of closely related information. Typically, the trainees are presented with the information in the chunk and then tested on their retention of the information. If they have not retained the material, they are referred back to the original information. If they retained the information they are referred to the next chunk of information to be learned. PI may be computer-based but is also found in printed material and interactive videos.
CBT	Training provided in part or whole through the use of a computer. *Computer-based training* is the term most often used in private industry or the government for training employees using computer-assisted instruction.
CMI	Computer-managed instruction (CMI) uses a computer to manage the administrative functions of training, such as registration, record keeping, scoring, and grading.
ICAI	When the computer-based training system is able to provide some of the primary characteristics of a human tutor, it is often referred to as an intelligent computer-assisted instruction (ICAI) system. It is a more advanced form of PI. Expert systems are used to run the tutoring aspect of the training, monitor trainee knowledge within a programmed knowledge model, and provide adaptive tutoring based on trainee responses.
ITS	Intelligent tutoring systems (ITS) make use of artificial intelligence to provide tutoring that is more advanced than ICAI type tutoring. ITS "learns" through trainee responses the best methods of facilitating the trainee's learning.
Simulations	Computer simulations provide a representation of a situation and the tasks to be performed in the situation. The representation can range from identical (e.g., word processing training) to fairly abstract (e.g., conflict resolution). Trainees perform the tasks presented to them by the computer program and the computer program monitors their performance.
Virtual Reality	Virtual reality is an advanced form of computer simulation, placing the trainee in a simulated environment that is "virtually" the same as the physical environment. This simulation is accomplished by the trainee wearing special equipment such as head gear, gloves, and so on, which control what the trainee is able to see, feel, and otherwise sense. The trainee learns by interacting with objects in the electronic environment to achieve some goal.

foundation on which CBT has been built, is a method of self-paced learning managed by both the trainee and the learning system (e.g., computer program or text). Although PI can also be used without a computer, today its principal use is in CBT. Higher forms of CBT, such as intelligent tutoring, are much more than PI, but the principles of PI are the basis on which these other techniques operate. PI is the process of leading a trainee systematically through new information in a way that facilitates the most efficient learning. At its most basic level, PI provides the trainee with information, asks a question, and based on the response goes to the next bit of information, and so forth. Table 6-4 describes the PI principles while at the same time providing an example of the PI approach. By working sequentially through the questions, you can get a feel for how this method works and what principles of learning are used.

In its most sophisticated form PI consists of a set of branches that might be activated depending on the answer provided by the trainee to a question. If the trainee provides a correct answer, one branch moves the trainee forward to new information. If the answer is incorrect a different branch is activated, taking the trainee back to review relevant information in more detail. This

TABLE 6-4 Programmed Instruction for PI

Learning Stem	Questions	Instructions
1. Many people think it is impossible to learn without making a large number of errors. Because *trial-and-error learning* is time consuming and creates frustration in the learner, most people don't like this method. After making a large number of errors, people begin to *lose their desire* to learn. Many trainers feel that if learning is carefully *programmed* to occur in a specific manner, people can learn without making a large number of errors.	1.a Learning by making a number of errors until the right response is discovered is called: 1.b What is likely to happen to people's desire to learn when they must use the trial-and-error method? 1.c When the material to be learned is prepared so that the trainee makes few errors it is said to have been carefully:	Compare your answers to those below: 1.a Trial-and-error learning 1.b It decreases 1.c Programmed If your answers closely match those above go on to section 2. If not, reread section 1, paying close attention to the italicized concepts. Then answer the questions again.
2. Programmed instruction (PI) operates on the principle that if *learning is programmed to occur in small steps*, few errors will occur. Another principle of PI is that if trainees are *given immediate feedback* regarding the appropriateness of their response, they will learn more quickly and complete a greater amount of material.	2.a If the goal is to reduce the number of trainee errors before the material is learned, how should learning be programmed? 2.b To increase the amount learned and the speed of learning, when should feedback given?	Compare your answers to those below: 2.a In small steps 2.b Immediately If your answers closely match those above go on to section 3. If not, reread section 2, paying close attention to the italicized concepts. Then answer the questions again.
3. Trainee learning is enhanced if the trainee is active in the learning process. PI asks trainees to *respond to questions putting the trainee in an active learning mode.* Because trainees learn at different rates, *they will learn best if they can move through the material at their own pace.* PI allows people to learn at their own pace. Finally, *frequent review of material helps trainees retain* the material for longer periods of time.	3.a Programming questions into the material enhances learning because it places trainees into a(n) _____ mode of learning. 3.b At what pace should trainees move through the material to be learned? 3.c Frequent review of material results in:	Compare your answers to those below: 3.a Active 3.b Their own pace 3.c Longer retention of the material If your answers closely match those above go on to section 4. If not, reread section 3, paying close attention to the italicized concepts. Then answer the questions again.

(continued)

TABLE 6-4 (continued)

Learning Stem	*Questions*	*Instructions*
4. In summary, PI allows trainees to learn more material more quickly and retain it longer with less frustration by (1) programming small learning steps resulting in fewer response errors, (2) requiring frequent active responses by the trainees, (3) providing immediate feedback to trainee responses, (4) allowing trainees to move through the material at their own pace, and (5) frequently reviewing the material.	4.a What are five principles that PI uses to improve the ease, amount, speed, and retention of learning? 4.b PI increases the trainees' desire to learn by reducing the number of _____ the trainee is likely to make.	Compare your answers to those below: 4.a (1) Small learning ing steps (2) Frequent and active response by the trainee (3) Immediate feedback (4) Self-paced learning (5) Frequent review 4.b Response errors If your answers closely match those above you have successfully completed the section on PI. If not, review section 4, and then answer the questions again.

format allows trainees to move through the material as rapidly as they are capable. Trainees who show a better grasp of the material (based on their responses) move rapidly through the material. The branches taken by those for whom the material is more difficult are different and will depend on the types of errors they make.

CBT applies PI techniques within a computerized format to create the learning experience. However, PI can also come in book, tape, interactive video, or other formats. We will focus on the computerized application, but keep in mind that the principles are the same regardless of format. In the mid-1980s CBT was a fairly novel idea. Today it is a mainstream approach, with about 80 percent of leading edge companies using it to some degree.[8] However, it is not appropriate for all types of training needs or situations.

INTELLIGENT TUTORING SYSTEMS

Intelligent tutoring systems (ITS) is the next generation of programmed instruction. It uses artificial intelligence to assist in the tutoring or coaching of the trainee. ITS not only provides guidance and selects the appropriate level of instruction for the trainee, but also learns from its own process (what worked and did not work in the training of the trainee) and based on this information, improves methodology for teaching the trainee. Intelligent tutoring is typically a text-based system, though graphics and other types of audiovisual aids are often built into the system.

ITSs consist of five components: a domain expert, a student model, a training session manager, a scenario generator, and a user interface.[9] The domain expert, sometimes called the expert knowledge base, is the set of knowledge about what is correct (e.g., the best way to perform a task, the knowledge one needs to be effective, etc.). The trainee model component stores information about how the trainee is performing during training, and what they seem to know. As the trainee responds to items, the information is used to tutor or coach the trainee. The training session manager is the component that interprets the trainee's responses and responds either with more information, coaching (helping the trainee explore the topic), or tutoring (guiding the trainee toward the correct answer). This component also determines how and when to remediate the trainee and what type of strategy to use in the remediation. For example, the session manager may act simply as a reference source (providing sources for the student to look up needed information) or possibly a tutor or coach (suggesting an appropriate response) or the session manager might decide to provide a demonstration.[10] The training scenario generator is the component that determines the order and level of difficulty of the problems that are presented to the trainee. Finally, the user interface is the equipment that allows the trainee to interact with the ITS. It commonly includes a computer keyboard, mouse, or joystick. Because ITS is able to do the following, it sets itself apart from simple programmed instruction:[11]

- Generate instruction that matches the individual trainee's needs
- Communicate and respond to trainee questions
- Model the trainee's learning processes (assess current level of knowledge; identify misconceptions, learning problems, and needs)
- Determine what information should follow based on previous trainee responses
- Determine trainee's level of understanding of the topic
- Improve its strategies for teaching the trainee based on the trainee's responses

An examination of Figure 6-1 illustrates how trainee responses allow the system to interpret the response and provide the trainee with specific training to address the problem.[12] Note that the three students depicted in Figure 6-1 all got the wrong answer to the addition questions, but each made different errors. The intelligent tutor determines that student A never carries over, student B carries over but sometimes inappropriately, and student C has trouble with simple single-digit addition. The tutor will then provide a different type of instruction to each of the students based on the diagnosis of the errors. This process continues with the tutor constantly reevaluating and providing new instruction until the learning objectives are achieved.

INTERACTIVE MULTIMEDIA

Interactive multimedia training integrates the use of text, video, graphics, photos, animation, and sound to produce a complex training environment with which the trainee interacts. Although simulation training is covered later in this chapter, interactive multimedia training is a form of simulation. We cover it now because it is a form of CBT and because it is much more than simulation. Typically PI is applied to the multimedia learning chunks to facilitate learning. Interactive multimedia allows the trainee to be placed into a real-life job situation, solve a specific problem, and receive immediate feedback as to the effectiveness of the decision made.[13] Training can be

FIGURE 6-1 Student Modeling Example

Student A	22 + 39 51	46 + 39 75
Student B	22 + 39 161	46 + 39 185
Student C	22 + 39 62	46 + 39 83

as simple as providing some declarative or procedural knowledge, or as complex as teaching how to diagnosis heart disorders or improve communication skills. The development of CD-ROM and DVD technology allowed interactive multimedia to grow rapidly over the last few years. In the early 1990s few firms used the technology. About 40 percent of those surveyed for an industry report in 2001 indicated they often used it for training. Only 13 percent indicated never using the technology.[14]

Using this technology, Nugget Brand Distributors developed a certificate in food safety training, which it markets to restaurants.[15] Jackson Hewitt Tax Service, with its huge number of part-time workers (in the tax season), needed a way to bring employees up to speed regarding tax changes. CD-ROM technology allowed them to distribute the information more easily and cheaply than printed material. The training did not require a trainer to be available. It provided training just at the time when the new employee needed it.[16]

As an example of what this technology is able to do, consider a program developed to train physicians. This training, all computer based, allows a medical student to take a medical history of a (hypothetical) patient, conduct an examination, and run lab tests. As part of the examination the medical student may choose to examine the patient's chest. The student clicks the "examine chest" button and is then asked to choose a type of examination to conduct (visual inspection, palpitation, or auscultation). Imagine you are the student and you click on auscultate (listen to sounds made by the lungs). You would hear the chest sounds that would be made by the particular patient.[17] Based on your interpretation of the sounds, you would make a diagnosis and click the button that represented your diagnosis. You would then be informed of the accuracy of your diagnosis. If your diagnosis were incorrect you would be given an explanation and moved to supplementary materials designed to provide you with the knowledge you needed to make a correct diagnosis. Training in Action 6-2 describes a training program developed by Marriott International to develop their employees' interpersonal skills. This method of training has application for knowledge, skill, and attitude development.

VIRTUAL REALITY

Virtual reality training (VR) puts the trainee in an artificial three-dimensional environment that simulates events and situations that might be experienced on the job. The trainee interacts with these images to accomplish goals. The effect is to give the trainee the impression of physical involvement or "a presence" in an environment.[18] That is, the trainee psychologically experiences the environment as real. To experience a computerized VR one wears devices such as a headset, which provides visual and audio information; gloves, for tactile information; treadmills or other type motion platforms for creating the sense of movement. Some even have the ability to supply olfactory information. Like IM, it is a type of simulation, but for the same reasons we chose to place IM in the CBT section, we have chosen to cover VR as a part of CBT rather than in the simulation section. As this industry evolves, many suppliers call their IM simulations *virtual reality*. Clearly, these formats do not meet our definition of virtual reality. One needs to be aware that much of what is called VR is in reality IM.

VR provides trainees with an understanding of the consequences of their actions in the work environment by interpreting and responding to the trainees' actions. Sensory devices transmit how the trainee is responding in the virtual workplace to the computer, allowing the VR program to respond by changing the environment appropriately. For example, a Police Academy trainee who is sitting in a simulated driver's seat of a police car, can look down and see the speedometer and all the gauges on the dashboard. Looking to the right, the trainee sees an empty seat, and so forth. When the trainee turns the steering wheel the view out of a windshield provides a visual representation of the car turning a corner. VR has been used to train police officers how to safely stop a speeding car, without the danger of using real people and automobiles. To date, VR has been used for training complex and dangerous skills such as flying outside

---

TRAINING IN ACTION 6-2

MARRIOTT INTERNATIONAL USES MULTIMEDIA TRAINING FOR SOFT SKILLS

Marriott International, a widely recognized name in the lodging industry, is noted for their people-oriented, high-touch culture. So, when their strategic plan indicated a commitment to growing from 900 properties to 2,000 in only a few years, a concern regarding ability to train such large numbers was raised. Analysis indicated that in the next 5 years, Marriott would be hiring about a million employees, and all would need training.

A training transformation team was struck to study the problem and find a solution. The solution that made the most sense was a set of multimedia training packages that use CD-ROM technology and operate from a traditional PC computer. One of these, "Front Desk Quest," provides soft skills training. To begin the training, the trainee logs on with an ID and password. An on-screen person greets the trainee and walks her through the training and is always available for help (by pressing the Help button). The trainee is presented with a series of different training modules, the culmination of which is a simulation where the trainee plays an active role in combining skills and knowledge learned earlier. In the simulation, trainees are presented with a situation in which they are required to determine,

from a set of choices, what is the correct thing to say or do. They then click on what they believe to be the correct response, and the computer program responds by playing out the scenario to show the student what happens if they make a correct or incorrect decision. If the trainee was correct the trainee sees the customer on the screen saying something positive. If the choice was not correct, the video may show an angry customer responding. The trainee is able to make alternate responses and see the customer reaction.

Trainees are able to sign on to the training at any time and start up where they left off in the previous session. They are able to go over previous exercises as often as they want, and track their progress. Management can also sign on and note the progress of employees.

Do employees like the new training format? Yes, reactions are consistently positive. Even those with minimal skill in the use of a computer find it easy to use and are going full speed in only a few minutes. As Starr Shafer, a manager at Marriott says, "They immediately give better service with greater self-assurance. And they say "Wow, I felt so comfortable doing it.""

Sources: Stauffer, D. 1999. High-tech training a huge win in Marriott's high-touch culture. Available from www.traininguniversity.com; Jensen, E. (Personal communication, January 31, 2002).

---

the earth's atmosphere,[19] to more traditional skills, such as teaching someone to speak in front of large audiences.[20]

STRENGTHS AND LIMITATIONS OF CBT

Costs

Arguments are made both supporting and criticizing the cost effectiveness of CBT. Because of the wide variety of CBT methods and applications, it is best to look at the factors that determine CBT's cost effectiveness.

Developing any CBT program from scratch is a labor-intensive process requiring knowledge and skills in learning, programming, and computer systems, so intial costs tend to be substantial. The software development typically requires significant lag time between when the need is identified and completion of the CBT program. This lag time is a limitation, because many training needs require relatively immediate attention. On the other hand, for certain types of training, the benefits of the CBT approach can outweigh the costs and lag time. The costs of developing and implementing a CBT program are related to the following factors:

- Number of trainees taking the course per year
- The cost of wages per hour for trainees while they are taking the course
- The cost of wages per hour for course developer
- The amortized cost of hardware to support the CBT
- The amortized cost of software used in the CBT
- Hours needed to complete the CBT program
- Hours needed to develop CBT course content
- The stability of the course content

In general, the development cost of CBT is higher than that of other techniques. These costs are not usually justified for a small number of people, but in situations where the training is not likely to change and where a large number of people need training, it can be a relatively inexpensive alternative to instructor-led training.

In addition to the cost of developing the training this method requires hardware. Consider programmed instruction. If training required the purchase of 20 computers, the cost would be about $30,000. If the computers are also used for other purposes (such as workstations), the cost can be amortized across all uses. Then only the proportion allocated for the CBT program is assigned as a cost of the program. Nonetheless, because programmed instruction requires each trainee to interact individually with the program, dedicated computer stations must be available for training.

Intelligent tutoring systems also have high development, delivery, and maintenance costs.[21] However, shells are being developed to significantly reduce these costs. Shells are specialized tools for constructing ITSs. They consist of a shell engine and a knowledge base. The shell engine is the intelligent tutoring aspect of the program, and the knowledge base is the information that needs to be trained. The shell engine is still expensive to develop, but can be amortized across a number of applications. The knowledge base, which will be specific to one application (training a salesperson to sell the automobile) is quickly and easily changed to fit another application (training the HR manager to explain why a grievance cannot be allowed).[22]

Multimedia is also initially costly to develop, but putting it on CD-ROMs for distribution is inexpensive. When produced in quantity they cost less than $1 each, far cheaper than copying the information on paper.[23] Also, sending the CD-ROM (compared to a paper version) through the mail to trainees at remote locations is cheaper. If the topic to be trained is generic, such as safe use of hazardous waste, various generic training programs are available at a reasonable cost. Consider the health and safety training programs offered by Comprehensive Loss Management of Minneapolis. They offer a number of canned CD-ROM training programs in safety (see Table 6-5) for $695. One hour of CBT instruction reportedly requires an average of about 200 hours of development time.[24] This estimate is probably conservative for multimedia and virtual reality development. Thus, the cost savings in training delivery and implementation must be weighed against the formidable development costs.

At this time, multimedia training through the Internet is typically too costly at the level of sophistication reached via CD-ROM. Investing in high-speed connections and extra software for trainees makes this format expensive at the present time. Continued technological advances will likely reduce costs in the future.[25]

Virtual reality training has not really caught on as expected. With the exception of industries where life-or-death consequences characterize some tasks, few adopters bought in to the concept.[26] Some suggest it is because it is poorly understood and a perception that it is expensive to

TABLE 6-5 Some Health and Safety Training Using CD-ROM Technology

Accident Investigation

Prevents costly accidents from reoccurring by investigating to find causes and implement steps to prevent them.

Training time 30–60 minutes. Price $695

Basics of Ergonomics

Helps workers understand injuries caused by repetitive motion and what to do to prevent them.

Training time 30–45 minutes. Price $695

Blood-Borne Pathogens

Helps workers understand the cause of Hepatitis B and HIV, the virus that causes AIDS. This course uses 30 interactions to teach workers what blood-borne pathogens are and the precautions to take to prevent being infected.

Training time 20–40 minutes. Price $695

Confined Space Entry

This training teaches workers concepts essential for a safe work environment when in a confined space. Twenty-nine interactive activities assess the level of understanding of the key learning objectives and let trainees apply what they learned in a safe environment.

Training time 30–45 minutes. Price $695

WHMIS: Learning the System

This training covers the Canadian regulations related to workplace safety as it relates to hazardous material.

Training time 45–75 minutes. Price $695

Minimum Hardware Requirements

Stand-Alone Training Station

Pentium 100 mhz

8 MB RAM, 10MB hard disk per course

Windows 95 or better

Soundblaster-compatible soundcard

4X CD-ROM

Networked Training Station

486/25 computer

8 MB RAM, 10MB hard disk per course

Windows 95 or better

Soundblaster-compatible soundcard

Source: Information available at http://www.clmi-training.com/cdrom_program_descriptions.htm.

develop. A virtual reality unit can cost as little as $20,000. After adding the design of the training, which, for a simple task such as training someone to speak in front of a large audience, is $20,000, the total might make VR reasonable in terms of cost.[27] When compared to something like an equipment simulator, the cost may not be that much more. However, the time to build a virtual reality program may be too long (8 months or longer in some cases).

Although all CBT technologies generally involve expensive start-up costs, they offer a major advantage that significantly reduces the cost: less training time. A number of studies examining various types of CBT (programmed instruction and multimedia) indicate that CBT learning takes less time.[28] In a more recent study, Air Force trainees were being taught troubleshooting of the hydraulic subsystems of F-15 aircraft. Evaluation of two teaching methods, ITS and the more traditional CBT using programmed instruction, indicated ITS not only results in faster training time, but more is learned.[29]

Control of Material and Process

Perhaps the most important advantage of CBT is its control over the content of the material, method of presentation, and movement of the trainee through sequentially structured learning episodes based on previous trainee responses.[30] If it is also a CMI system, the learner's progress is automatically recorded. Each trainee can move quickly through material that is already familiar or easily grasped. As the learner finds the material less familiar or more difficult, the CBT provides more instruction, tutoring, and explanation. The pace of learning is controlled by the interaction between the software and the trainee.

Typically, no trainer is present to deal with adverse trainee reactions to the materials or format, or to address questions the trainee may have. Pilot testing of the CBT attempts to identify these issues and incorporate appropriate segments into the CBT to deal with them. For example, at periodic intervals the program may query the trainee about his or her reaction to the material. On the basis of the trainee's response, the presentation is altered. However, this feature adds considerably to the cost of the program and is a difficult, if not impossible, task.

The CBT software determines the content and process of the training. If the material is properly developed, this method ensures that each set of prerequisite KSAs is mastered before the learner moves on to the next level. It also ensures that each topic area is covered. These features can be advantageous or disadvantageous compared with instructor-based training. The advantages are that it ensures consistency of topic coverage and topic mastery across all trainees. Sometimes, however, it is necessary to diverge from prescribed topic areas to heighten trainee interest or improve understanding. A live trainer could identify when such divergence is necessary; a software program can only present what it is programmed to present.

The trainee control problems associated with this approach might decrease its desirability for some situations. Because CBT is often used as a stand-alone method, control over who is actually going through training is lacking.

A few years ago a professor of an introductory MBA accounting course decided to use a CBT program to teach the basic accounting principles. Each student was provided with his or her personal password to sign on to the system. Students could complete their lessons at their convenience, as long as they completed the 10 modules within a 3-week period. The modules were linked so that the students were required to complete module 1 before they could begin module 2, and so on. According to the records generated by the program, everyone completed all the modules by the end of the third week. At this point the professor began his lectures and discussions about contemporary accounting practices. It soon became clear that many of the students didn't understand the basic principles. Further investigation revealed that a number of students recruited others to use their password and complete their CBT modules. The professor abandoned the CBT approach the following year.

Would the same thing happen in an organization where certain training is mandated (e.g., safety, sexual harassment) and the trainees are not particularly motivated to complete it? Might it also occur if rewards were attached to completing the training but not to actually using the KSA on the job? For example, employees in "pay for knowledge" systems have been known to divide the training among the members of the group so that one or two people complete the training for all the other members. If concerns arise about who is completing the training, you will need to develop additional control mechanisms to ensure that the trainees are completing the CBT themselves.

Learning Objectives (KSAs)

CBT is best used as a method for enhancing trainees' declarative and, in particular, procedural knowledge base. It can also be useful in developing some types of strategic knowledge, teaching some types of skills, and influencing attitudes. CBT can enhance the trainee's declarative knowledge through repeated presentation of facts, using a variety of formats and presentation styles. It can do an excellent job of describing when and how to apply the knowledge to situations relevant to the training objectives. It can develop procedural knowledge by providing opportunities to apply this knowledge to various simulated situations. CBT can document the appropriateness of the trainee's application and provide additional practice modules to improve areas of weakness.

Skill development is also possible with CBT but is sometimes limited in its ability to duplicate the actual workplace environment and situations. CBT can create task simulations that are highly consistent with the actual job. For example, CBT software that trains employees in the use of word processing, spreadsheet, and other computer-based software can easily replicate situations they will face when back on the job. For the more complex skills that require the use of natural language (e.g., interpersonal or conflict resolution skills) or psychomotor development (driving a forklift), CBT is less able to replicate the actual job situation.

Consider the Marriott hotel chain. They recently decided to change their "soft skills" training from the classroom to the computer terminal (see Training in Action 6-2). Although Eric Jensen, a director at Marriott headquarters, was initially hesitant about the ability of multimedia to train soft skills, he changed his mind. He indicates a positive reaction from trainees, improvement in test scores, and a savings of about $100 for each person trained is realized, compared to traditional delivery methods.

These "soft skills" typically involve interaction between two or more people. Developing these skills requires trainees to engage in the interaction and receive immediate feedback about their performance. It is extremely difficult for computers to simulate these situations realistically; traditional CBT cannot accurately do it. Just trying to capture all the oral and nonverbal behavior that people are capable of in responding to a particular statement is a monumental task. As Eric Jensen noted regarding the training at Marriott, "There is no 'intelligent tutoring' in terms of the system 'knowing' what kind of tutoring an individual needs. The program simply branches in certain areas, but the branching is limited, too, because of the enormous cost in trying to take many different options into account."[31] So, although the interaction is far from perfect, it does provide one-on-one feedback, and learning does occur.

As to the psychomotor skills, the National Guard trains its members on how to troubleshoot and repair Bradley tanks. In many situations the tanks are not available, and having members train in a VR environment is less expensive and seems to be as effective.

What do all these examples mean? They mean that CBT can be a useful tool in developing skills that are easily simulated electronically. CBT can also help trainees learn about more complicated skills, such as interpersonal skills. However, it is not as good as other methods at helping the trainee actually develop those skills through practice and feedback. For instance, unless it is a highly sophisticated VR program, it won't be able to observe the person and provide feedback on such things as standing too close when talking to someone or not maintaining good eye contact.

Attitudes and motivation can be influenced through CBT by addressing how objects and events are connected as well as the consequences of particular courses of action. The material presented in the CBT can alter how the trainee perceives objects, events, and consequences. The opportunity to experience or interact personally with the objects and events, however, is limited by CBT's ability to simulate reality. As a result, the emotional or affective side of attitudes may not be activated. This reason may partially explain why many adult learners prefer CBT to be combined with some form of instructor-based training.[32]

Learning Process

Attention CBT is generally seen as more interesting and motivating than instructor-based training such as the lecture and discussion. Trainees cite reasons such as feeling less threatened by the machine and their control over the pace of instruction.[33] In addition, CBT can integrate audio and visual effects that draw the learner's attention to the material, as will be discussed in the audiovisual section. For these reasons, CBT is good at capturing and retaining trainee attention.

Retention Certainly the CBT method provides many cues that can be used in the symbolic coding process. Textual, auditory, and oral cues can be integrated to allow trainees to use those that fit best with their learning style for coding the content of the training.[34] Because CBT can use a wide range of audiovisuals (AVs), it can be effective in facilitating trainees' symbolic coding. The AV aspects of the CBT also assist cognitive organization. This methodology provides its own organization of the material that may or may not correspond to the trainees' cognitive structures. However, it does break each learning segment down into small steps, making it easier to integrate. Through the accumulation of these small steps and their repetition until mastery occurs, CBT is able to shape the cognitive organization of the trainee in the desired manner. The ease with which the trainee is able to do this will depend on how closely the organization of the CBT matches the cognitive organization of the trainee.

As a cornerstone of the CBT approach, symbolic rehearsal presents each learning segment until mastery occurs. The CBT first moves trainees through mastery of the facts and then provides application segments in which the trainees apply the facts to specific situations. Trainees must imagine themselves in the situation and apply their knowledge to that situation; they then respond and receive immediate feedback on the appropriateness of their response. For example, suppose trainees were learning to take photographs. The CBT would provide a simulated situation such as the inside of a room, artificial lighting, and objects that are closer or farther away and would provide a description of what should be photographed. The trainees would then indicate the camera settings for taking the picture. The CBT can even provide feedback that shows what would happen in a real situation. Using the photography example, the CBT program could show what kind of photograph would be produced. It allows each trainee to continue to practice while providing immediate feedback, until she masters the simulation. This type of symbolic rehearsal borders on behavioral reproduction and is valuable for retaining the material.

Behavioral Reproduction Unless the material to be learned involves direct interaction with computers or software, it is difficult to provide behavioral reproduction through CBT. The photography example is not true behavioral reproduction because the trainee isn't using a real camera or a real scene. CBT is good at teaching what should be done and providing symbolic rehearsal, but is limited in teaching how to do it. Behavioral reproduction that requires natural language interaction or psychomotor skill development (e.g., handling customer complaints or welding a pipe) is generally not possible with CBT. However, advances in virtual reality might make these possible in the future.

What CBT does well is model appropriate behavior and provide simulations in which the trainee can apply knowledge. These components will facilitate the development of skills but do not provide the opportunities to actually reproduce the desired behavior and receive feedback. For example, CBT can be used to learn a foreign language. The trainee can learn the meaning of words, their correct usage, and even how to replicate the appropriate pronunciation, but will not learn to use the language conversationally until actually interacting with someone in the language and receiving feedback.

Training Group Characteristics

Typically, only one trainee can use a computer station at a time. Thus the number of stations limits the number of trainees that can be trained at the same time. However, because the training is available virtually all the time, this factor is not much of a problem unless a great number of trainees must be trained in a short period. If the CBT is on a CD or floppy disk, then trainees can take it home or anywhere they have access to a computer.

CBT takes into account many differences in trainee readiness, which means relatively few trainee limitations for CBT. Trainees must be able to read and understand the text and AV components of the CBT. Some people are initially uncomfortable working with CBT as a stand-alone method.[35] In addition, while computers and software are relatively easy to operate, some individuals still are unfamiliar with and intimidated by them. Computer KSAs are prerequisites for trainees going through CBT, so if you are considering this method, be sure to assess the trainees' reading levels, computer literacy, and attitudes about CBT. You can address these issues with some type of pretraining orientation or preparation program.

Games and Simulations

Training games and simulations are designed to reproduce or simulate processes, events, and circumstances that occur in the trainee's job. Trainees can thus experience these events in a controlled setting where they can develop their skills or discover concepts that will improve their performance. Equipment simulators, business games, in-basket exercises, case studies, role plays, and behavior modeling are examples of this technique. We discuss each of these techniques separately and then describe the strengths and limitations of simulations in general.

EQUIPMENT SIMULATORS

As the name suggests, **equipment simulators** are mechanical devices that require trainees to use the same procedures, movements, or decision processes they would use with equipment back on the job. Simulators train airline pilots,[36] air traffic controllers,[37] military officers,[38] taxi drivers,[39] maintenance workers,[40] telephone operators,[41] ship navigators,[42] and product development engineers.[43]

It is important that the simulators be designed to replicate, as closely as possible, the physical aspects of the equipment and operating environment trainees will find at their job site. This resemblance is referred to as the **physical fidelity** of the simulation. In addition, psychological conditions under which the equipment is operated (time pressures, conflicting demands, etc.) must also be closely matched to what the trainees experience on the job. This similarity is called **psychological fidelity**. Training in Action 6-3 describes what can happen when the fidelity of the match between simulation and work setting is less than adequate. The events described in this example were reported by a new sales clerk trainee; although there may be some perceptual distortions, it was nevertheless his reality.

The literature on sociotechnical approaches to organizational development provides guidelines for the design/redesign of equipment.[44] HRD professionals engaged in the design of simulators and their pretesting should involve those who will be using the equipment and their supervisors. Their input helps reduce potential resistance to the equipment and, more important, increases the degree of fidelity between the simulation and the work setting. In Training in Action 6-3, if trainers brought in experienced sales clerks or their supervisors to pilot the simulation, they might have identified the fidelity problems, which could then be corrected.

BUSINESS GAMES

The University of Washington debuted its *Top Management Decision Game* some time ago as a way for business students to see the theories in their textbooks put into action.[45] Since then, businesses moved from board games to computer-based simulations, using interactive multimedia and virtual reality. **Business games** are simulations that attempt to represent the way an industry, company, or subunit of a company functions. Typically, they are based on a set of relationships, rules, and principles derived from theory or research. However, they can also reflect the actual operations of a particular department in a specific company. Trainees are provided with information describing a situation and are asked to make decisions about what to do. The system then provides feedback about the impact of their decisions, and they are asked to make another decision. This process continues until some predefined state of the organization exists or a specified number of trials are completed. For example, if the focus is on the financial

---

SALES SIMULATION

Twenty-five retail sales clerk trainees were learning how to operate the company's electronic sales register system. The trainees each stood in front of a sales register that was actually an older model sales register refitted to serve as a training device. On a screen facing each trainee, a video depicted a customer waiting to make a purchase. On the counter, in front of the trainee the items this customer wanted to purchase were automatically brought forward on a conveyer belt. The trainee entered specific key strokes to activate the register for a new sale, picked up each item and scanned it into the register. When all the items were entered, the trainee entered more key strokes to total the sale. When the sale was totaled, the conveyer brought forward either cash, a check, or a credit card, simulating the customer's payment choice. The trainee entered different key strokes denoting a check, credit, or cash sale. If cash was used, the cash drawer opened. The clerk was to deposit the customer's payment and remove the correct amount of change, if any. Credit cards were scanned and automatically debited for the total of the purchase. Payment by credit card or check also required the customer's identification to be documented. Once payment was received, any change and the receipt were to be given to the customer. It was simulated by placing it in a bin on the counter. The purchased items were then bagged and given to the customer (again placed in the bin).

This simulation might be fairly good. Unfortunately, when the trainees were placed at the real registers the next day, things were quite different from their training experiences. First, the registers they used were a newer model than those used in training, so some of the keys were in different places. Second, people were standing impatiently in line. Some wanted to purchase items and others needed help with merchandise or wanted to know the location of items in the store. The clerks couldn't concentrate only on working the register; they also had to interact with the customers. The scanner wouldn't read some customers' credit cards. Some customers argued about the price of items, insisting it was on sale for a lower price, though the scanner indicated a higher price. Some customers had their items totaled up and then decided they didn't want one of the items, or that they wanted additional items. Needless to say, the simulation training proved less than helpful, and many considered it to have lowered their capabilities. They felt they made many key stroke errors because of the training. If they were allowed to just learn on the job, they would not now be unlearning portions of the previous day's training.

---

state of a company, the game might end when the company reached a specified profitability level or when the company must declare bankruptcy.

Many business policy simulations examine the total organization but some focus on the functional responsibilities of particular positions within an organization (e.g., marketing director, human resource executive). These latter types are often called **functional simulations**. Because the differences between the two types of simulations are rather trivial except for the focus and scope of the game, we group them together. A wide variety of business games and simulations are available. A good source for exploring them or learning how to develop your own game is the Association for Business Simulations and Experiential Learning. Its publication *Developments in Business Simulation and Experiential Learning* describes new business games and simulations. The association also sponsors an annual conference in which new exercises, games, and simulations are demonstrated and discussed.

Business games involve an element of competition, either against other players or against the game itself. Some of the purposes for which business games have been developed and used are listed here:[46]

- Strengthen executive and upper management skills.
- Improve decision-making skills at all levels.
- Demonstrate principles and concepts.
- Integrate separate components of training into an integrated whole.
- Explore and solve complex problems in a safe, simulated setting.
- Develop leadership skills.
- Improve application of total quality principles and develop skill in using quality tools.

Games that simulate entire companies or industries provide a far better systems perspective than other training methods. They allow trainees to see how their decisions and actions influence not only their immediate target but also related areas. Training in Action 6-4 describes one such simulation. The choice of criteria depends on the nature of the game and the goals of the training. A few years ago, British Airways needed to determine how customers and competitors would react to a new pricing and distribution model. They used a simulation designed by Advanced Competitive Strategies in Portland, Oregon, to test the new strategy. Based on the results, the strategy was revised. Barbara McCloskey, manager of leisure strategy, described the simulation as "rigorous, confrontational, informative and downright addictive."[47]

TRAINING IN ACTION 6-4

THE PEOPLE'S EXPRESS SIMULATOR

People's Express (PE) is an airline company that made quite a splash in the business news for a while during the 1980s, but was eventually acquired by a competitor. As a start-up passenger airline, it managed to capture a significant market share in just a few years. It was one of the first airlines to offer deep-discount air travel, with friendly, but no-frills service.

A simulation based on PE can be played individually or by several people adopting different top management decision-making roles within the company. The game begins with the decisions to be made after the company's first year in business. The player(s) must decide how much money to invest in new aircraft, new employees, quality/services, and marketing. The game utilizes industry and economic statistics from the time periods involved to determine the effect of the players' decisions in these areas. The game is played for a speci-

fied number of years or until specified financial criteria are reached (positive or negative).

If only a single player is involved, the game can be used to demonstrate the integrated nature of decision making in this business. Too much money invested in new aircraft means not enough trained staff to work the aircraft, higher payroll and training costs, and lower service levels. Too much investment in marketing and demand may outstrip capacity, wasting a portion of the marketing investment, creating unnecessarily high costs and resulting in lower demand in the future (due to turning away customers and lower service). The player must find the right balance between investments in these four critical areas. When multiple players are involved, the learning can also focus on how to reach consensus decisions and the importance of sharing information and strategies across functional areas.

IN-BASKET TECHNIQUE

The **in-basket technique** provides trainees with a packet of written information and requests, such as memos, messages, and reports, that would typically be handled in a given position such as a sales manager, a staff administrator, or an engineer. This popular quasi-simulation focuses primarily on decision making and allows an opportunity for both assessing and developing decision-making KSAs. Generally, the trainees are given a role (usually a type of job) to play, a description of the role, and general information about the context. They are then given the packet of materials that make up the in-basket and asked to respond to the materials within a certain time period. After all the trainees complete the in-basket, a discussion with the trainer follows, in which the trainee describes the rationale for the decisions. The trainer provides feedback, reinforcing decisions made appropriately or encouraging the trainee to develop alternatives for those made inappropriately.

A variation on the technique is to run multiple, simultaneous in-baskets in which each trainee receives a different but interrelated set of information. The trainees must interact with one another to gather all the information necessary to make an appropriate decision. This activity allows development of communication, as well as decision-making skills. It also includes elements of role play and business games training.

In-baskets are best at developing procedural and strategic knowledge. This knowledge is translated into decisions, so decision-making skills are also enhanced. These skills are primarily cognitive rather than behavioral. Typically, the trainee's decisions are simply written down. A few in-basket exercises require the trainee to "call" someone and communicate the decision or request additional information, such as in multiple, simultaneous in-baskets. In these cases, interpersonal skills can also be developed.

CASE STUDIES

Case studies attempt to simulate decision-making situations that trainees might find on the job. The trainee is usually presented with a written (or videotaped) history, key elements, and the problems of a real or imaginary organization or subunit. The written case study can be from a few pages to 100 or more. A series of questions usually appears at the end of the case. The longer ones provide a great deal of information to be examined and assessed for its relevance to the decisions being made. Others require the trainee to conduct research to gather the appropriate information. The trainee must then make certain judgments and identify possible solutions to the problem.

Typically, trainees are given time to digest the information individually. If time permits, they are also allowed to collect additional relevant information and integrate it into their solution. Once individuals arrive at their solutions, they may meet in small groups to discuss the different diagnoses, alternatives, and solutions generated. Then the trainees meet with the trainer, who facilitates and directs further discussion.

Cases reflect the typical situation faced by most managers; incomplete information about many of the factors related to a decision. The trainer should convey that no single solution is right or wrong; but many solutions are possible.[48] The learning objective is to get trainees to apply known concepts and principles and discover new ones. Their solutions are not as important as their understanding of the advantages and disadvantages that go along with the solution. The trainer must guide the trainees in examining the possible alternatives and consequences without actually stating what they are.

A variation of case study is the **incident process**, in which trainees are given only a brief description of the problem[49] and must gather additional information from the trainer (and perhaps others) by asking specific questions. Because managers gather most of their information from questioning and interacting with others, this activity is felt to simulate a manager's work more closely. In all case study methods, the information sorting and gathering process can be as much a learning focus as the nature of the problem being worked on. In such instances the focus is on understanding the criteria that separate relevant from irrelevant information and learning where and how to gather relevant information.

The decision-making aspects of the case study are focused primarily on developing strategic knowledge. The information-gathering aspects are skill development, because trainees actually perform this activity. However, feedback about information-gathering skills is generally not as heavily emphasized as the trainees' ability to analyze and make decisions.

ROLE PLAY

The **role play** is an enactment (or simulation) of a scenario in which each participant is given a part to act out. Trainees are provided with a description of the context—usually a topic area, a general description of a situation, a description of their roles (e.g., their objectives, emotions, concerns), and the problem they each face. For example, the topic area could be managing conflict and the situation might revolve around scheduling vacation days with the two parties in conflict being the supervisor and subordinate. The problem could be that the subordinate wants to take vacation the first week in August and the supervisor knows a big project comes due on that date. Once the participants read their role descriptions, they act out their roles by interacting with one another.

The degree to which the scenario is structured depends on the goals of the training. **Structured role plays** provide trainees with more detail about the situation as well as more detailed descriptions of each character's attitudes, needs, opinions, and so on. Sometimes structured role plays even include a scripted dialogue. This type of role play is used primarily to develop interpersonal skills such as communication, conflict resolution, and group decision making.

Spontaneous role plays are loosely constructed interactions in which one of the participants plays himself while the other(s) play people with whom the first trainee interacted in the past (or will in the future). This type of role play focuses on attitudes and is typically used to develop insight into one's own behavior and its impact on others rather than to develop specific skills.

In a **single role play**, one group of trainees role plays for the rest, providing a visual demonstration of some learning point. Other trainees observe the role play, analyzing the interactions and identifying learning points. Although this format provides a single focus for trainees and feedback from a skilled observer (the trainer), it does have some disadvantages. Those chosen to act as the characters may experience acute embarrassment at being the center of attention. They also do not have the advantage of watching others perform the roles. In addition, they may not play the roles in a manner that clearly portrays the behaviors that are the focus of training. Having people other than trainees act out the role play eliminates these problems but adds some cost to the training.

A **multiple role play** is the same as a single role play except all trainees are in groups, with each group acting out the role play simultaneously. Following the role play, each group analyzes the interactions and identifies learning points among themselves. Each group may report to the others a summary of its analysis and learning. This format allows a rich discussion of the issues, because each group will play the roles somewhat differently. It also reduces the amount of time required to complete the process but may reduce the quality of feedback as well. Trainees are generally reluctant to provide negative feedback to peers. Even if they are willing, they may not have the experience or expertise to provide constructive feedback. Videotaping the role play is another option. The tape could be used by the trainee for self-evaluation, and the trainer could examine them between sessions and provide individual feedback.

The **role rotation** method begins as a single role play. After the characters interact for a period of time, the trainer will stop the role play and discuss what happened so far and what can be learned from it. Then different trainees are asked to exchange places with some or all of the characters. These trainees then pick up where the others left off. This format allows both a common focus for all trainees (except those in the role play) and demonstrates a variety of ways to approach the roles. It keeps trainees more active than the single role play and allows feedback from a skilled observer. However, it requires the progress of the role play to be frequently interrupted, creating additional artificiality. Again, trainees may be inhibited from publicly critiquing the behavior of their fellow trainees and may be embarrassed to play a role in front of everyone else.

BEHAVIOR MODELING

Behavior modeling uses the natural tendency for people to observe others to learn how to do something new. This technique is most frequently used in combination with some other technique. For example, the modeled behavior is typically videotaped and then watched by the trainees. We included it in the games/simulation section because once the trainees observe the model, typically they practice the behavior in some form of role play or other simulation. However, the behavioral modeling process itself is distinctly different from these methods. Among the various different descriptions of behavior modeling, only minor differences are noted.[50] The behavior modeling process can be summarized as follows:

1. Define the key skill deficiencies.
2. Provide a brief overview of relevant theory.
3. Specify key learning points/critical behaviors to watch for.
4. Use an expert to model the appropriate behaviors.
5. Encourage trainees to practice the appropriate behaviors in a structured role play.
6. Provide opportunities for the trainer and other trainees to give reinforcement for appropriate imitation of the model's behavior.
7. Ensure the trainee's supervisor reinforces appropriate demonstration of behavior on the job.

Behavior modeling differs from both role plays and simulations by first providing the trainee with an understanding of what the desired skill level looks like. This method is based on Bandura's social learning theory and is focused on developing behavioral skills. However, steps 2 and 3 reflect the cognitively oriented learning features of the technique and steps 5 to 7 the behaviorist/reinforcement theory features.

A training module composed of all seven steps is developed for each skill to be learned. An overview module should also be provided, as well as a separate workshop for those who supervise the trainees back on the job. An example of this type of training is a package called "Interaction Management," consisting of more than a dozen 2-hour modules and an introductory overview module. It also includes a 2-day workshop for the trainees' managers, focusing on the managers' reinforcement of appropriate behaviors back on the job. A portion of the workshop uses behavior modeling as well.

Behavior modeling is useful for almost any type of skill training. It can be used for training in interpersonal skills, sales training, interviewee and interviewer training, safety training, and many other areas.[51] One method of behavior modeling makes extensive use of video modeling and feedback. The trainee first observes the behavior being performed by a model and then attempts to reproduce the behavior (step 5) while being videotaped. Through split screen devices, the model and the trainee can be shown side-by-side, and the trainee can see exactly where his performance needs to be improved. In this approach, the trainee can see what should and should not be done.

STRENGTHS AND LIMITATIONS OF GAMES AND SIMULATIONS

Even though games and simulations come in a variety of formats, they share many common strengths and limitations. When a specific format differs from others in this regard, we discuss it separately, otherwise our discussion of strengths and limitations applies to all formats.

Costs

The development costs of games and simulations vary from format to format. In general, equipment simulators are the most expensive to develop, but cost will depend on the nature of the equipment that is simulated. For example, millions of dollars are spent on aircraft simulators used to train commercial and military flight officers. On the other hand, retail clerks and bank tellers can be trained on the actual equipment they will use on the job, which can be moved back and forth from training to the job site. If the development costs of your equipment simulators are quite high, you might immediately dismiss this approach. However, you should look at the cost in relation to feasible alternatives and their outcomes, which may show the simulator to be cost effective. One alternative to an equipment simulator is on-the-job training, although this approach might not work for some types of training. For example, pilot trainees taking test flights will not be exposed to all the possible situations they might encounter in flying thousands of hours a year, so the trainees would not learn from this method as much as they could from a simulator. Certainly the company wouldn't want to place the aircraft and crew in dangerous situations, yet pilots will need to know how to respond in such situations. In addition, the cost of "flying" a simulator is a small fraction of the cost of flying an actual aircraft, which entails fuel, ground personnel, fees, and other expenses. Thus the total costs of using the simulation can be lower than alternative methods, even when the cost is quite high.

At the low end of development costs are role plays. A wide range of role plays, already developed and published, include instructions and suggestions for their use (e.g., *Organizational Behavior Teaching Journal* and textbook publishers). Many of these publications are free. If you want to develop your own, tailored to your company's needs, you can do so at little cost. Business games and simulations are somewhat more complicated, thus usually more expensive than role plays. The development cost of games and simulations varies widely depending on complexity and equipment requirements. Multimedia or computer-based presentations will be more expensive (see earlier discussion of these methods). Like other simulations, they have the advantage of being reusable, so the cost can be amortized across the number of trainees. Behavior modeling costs can range from moderately low to high, depending on the format used. Using an expert to model the desired behavior live (e.g., welding two plates together) simply involves the cost of the model. Because the model is typically an employee of the company, the cost is just the lost production while the expert is modeling. Using professional actors as models, as you might for interpersonal skills training, will add to the cost but may be worth it in terms of improved quality. Use of live models is more expensive than using videotaped models because the cost is incurred each time the model is used. Videotaping the model allows the videotape to be used again but adds the cost of creating it. Professionally developed videos can be fairly expensive and will be discussed more fully in the audiovisual section of this chapter.

The degree of flexibility built into the simulation or game will determine its cost effectiveness. For example, a cockpit simulator that is programmable and otherwise able to reflect the characteristics of many different aircraft will be more cost effective than one that can simulate only one type of aircraft. The same is true of business games and other types of simulations. A game or business simulation that is programmed to create different economic situations and business conditions will have a wider audience base and a longer useful life than one that does not.

The cost of making mistakes while in training must be factored into the cost/benefit decision when you compare methods. One of the primary strengths of games and simulations is that they allow trainees to develop and practice skills in a safe setting. Mistakes in business decisions can be financially disastrous. Mistakes in equipment operation can cause damage to the equipment and physical harm to the operator and others. Mistakes in interpersonal behavior can also result in financial losses to the company through lost customers, resentful employees, misinterpreted instructions, and the like. These mistakes may result in psychological harm to the trainee in terms of lowered self-esteem and confidence, increased defensiveness, and other negative effects. Simulations and games allow trainees the opportunity to develop their skills in a situation where the costs of making a mistake are low or nonexistent.

Control of Content and Process

When games and simulations are used, the content of what is learned and the processes used in learning are influenced by both the trainer and the trainee. The game or simulation provides a set of information that focuses on a particular content area. The People's Express Simulator (Training in Action 6-4), for example, focuses on integrating business decisions across functional areas to improve company profitability and growth. Games and simulations also provide instructions and guidelines that strongly influence the learning processes. So, by selecting an existing game or simulation or developing a new one, the trainer exerts control over the learning content and process. Many games and simulations are structured so that situations occur in a predetermined order, providing the trainer with greater control over both content and process. This control is desirable if all trainees will be exposed to the same situations back on the job. Arrest procedures for police or machine maintenance and troubleshooting for equipment operators are examples. Other games and simulations allow the situation to change according to how trainees respond. Here the trainee can exercise greater influence on what is learned and how. These types of games and simulations are useful when trainees must learn how to deal with a wide range of situations and how to apply general principles. Business and financial planning, decision making, and military battle tactics are areas where these types are particularly useful.

Once the game or simulation is chosen, the trainer can exert control over learning processes by instructing trainees on how they should proceed through the game/simulation and providing additional learning activities. Unfortunately, trainers sometimes use games and simulations without developing structured preparatory and follow-up learning experiences. Often they do so with the rationale of allowing the trainees an opportunity to be more spontaneous and active in the learning process. However, without the proper preparation, orientation, and follow-up activities, trainees will learn less than they could and may miss important concepts entirely. Their perception might then be that the exercise was fun and entertaining but irrelevant.

The format providing the least built-in structure is the unstructured role play, in which only a general set of guidelines is given to the participants beforehand. How the trainees interact while playing out their roles is under their control. Although the trainer controls the choice of situation and roles, the trainees control how they are carried out. By asking the role players to focus on certain steps in the learning process, such as saying, "First try to identify the cause of the conflict, and then try to generate win-win alternatives," the trainer exerts more influence. In the case of role plays, reduced structure allows the trainees to imagine the situation as it might occur on the job. The potential danger is that it may be so unstructured they don't take their roles seriously or they are unable to imagine how it could possibly apply to their job.

Cases provide more structure, particularly in setting the situation (i.e., characteristics of the organization). However, the trainees' process of analyzing the case is largely internal or influenced by the interaction within the training group. Through the manner in which trainers facilitate discussion of the case, they are able to exert more or less control over what trainees learn and how.

Equipment simulators generally provide the most structure. They must replicate the physical and psychological characteristics of the equipment and the environment in which it is operated. The simulator itself controls the content and process of learning. To the extent that the simulation is programmable, the trainer can manipulate the content. The trainer can also influence the focus of learning somewhat through instructions. Trainees exercise some control over what is learned by the responses they make. For example, one pilot trainee might experiment with different thrust, flap, and rudder alignments while in the simulator whereas another may use only the alignments indicated as proper. The first pilot learns what happens under a variety of alignments, the second learns only what happens under the proper alignments.

Learning Objectives (KSAs)

Games and simulations provide opportunities to learn through concrete experiences that require both theory and application. Theory provides the general principles that guide action. Application provides the opportunity to test those principles and understand them at a behavioral level, not just as abstract intellectual knowledge. As the philosopher Confucius said, "I hear and I forget. I see and I remember. I do and I understand."

Some types of knowledge enhancement and attitude change are achievable through games and simulations, but usually supplemental methods are required. In general, games and simulations do not attempt to provide declarative knowledge—some initial level of declarative and procedural knowledge is assumed. Games and simulations provide a context in which this knowledge is applied. If the focus of training is specifically on declarative or procedural knowledge acquisition, games and simulations are not the most effective methods. If, however, you want the trainee to understand how the knowledge should be applied and to develop strategies for doing so, one or more of the game or simulation formats is a good choice. Take the example of a business game in which several teams of trainees compete for product market share. The game makes some assumptions about the knowledge trainees have about basic marketing strategies (e.g., product, pricing, promotions, and location). It allows them to apply their knowledge and see the consequences of that strategy. The intent is not to teach what the components of marketing strategy are, but rather how to apply them in an integrated fashion. In the course of the game, trainees may learn more about each of the components and learn new principles about the relationships among the components. This learning occurs as a result of, or in conjunction with, their ability to develop and implement an integrated marketing strategy. In the process they learn new strategies for problem solving, and enhance their strategic knowledge.

For these and numerous other reasons, games and simulations do a good job of developing skills. First, they simulate the important conditions and situations that occur on the job. Second, they allow the trainee to practice the skill. Finally, they provide feedback about the appropriateness of their actions. Each of the formats is most appropriate for particular types of skills.

- Equipment simulators obviously are best at teaching people how to work with equipment.
- Business games are best for developing business decision-making skills (both day-to-day and more strategic) and for exploring and solving complex problems.
- The in-basket technique is best suited to development of strategic knowledge used in making day-to-day decisions.
- Case studies are most appropriate for developing analytic skills, higher-level principles, and complex problem-solving strategies. Because trainees do not actually implement their decision/solution, its focus is more on the "what to do" (strategic knowledge) than on the "how to get it done" (skills).
- Role plays provide a good vehicle for developing interpersonal skills and personal insight, allowing trainees to practice interacting with others and receiving feedback.

Role playing is an especially effective technique for creating attitude change.[52] It allows trainees to act out behavior that reflects their attitudes and to experience others' reactions as well as their own feelings about the behavior. This experience and feedback allow the trainee to make appropriate attitudinal adjustments. The role reversal is even more powerful as it requires the trainee to take a position opposite of their attitude. It allows the trainee to better understand why others may hold differing attitudes. One such situation would be the supervisor with a negative attitude about union officials asked to play the role of union steward defending an employee who had been treated unfairly. As an old role-playing saying goes: "Seeing's believing, but feeling's the truth." Although trainees may see the logic of a principle through a lecture and see its application in a video or CBT, they are able to feel its personal value only when they use it themselves.

Learning Process

Attention   One of the strengths of games and simulations is their ability to gain the attention of the learner. A potential drawback is that it may focus attention away from the learning objectives. The active learning process used by these training methods is generally more compelling to trainees than sitting through a lecture or reading a text. In most games and many simulations, the aspect of competition against oneself or others increases attention and enthusiasm. Many also use clever gimmicks that capture trainees' interest, but these aspects can also distract trainees from the real objectives of the training. Sometimes trainees get so engrossed in the competition or "figuring out" the gimmick that they fail to learn the principles or develop the skills the game/simulation was intended to produce. It is important for trainers to build modules into the training that prepare trainees to use the game or simulation by identifying the desired learning outcomes. Modules might also be planned for breaks during the simulation to capture learning that occurred and to refocus trainees on the learning objectives. In general, a debriefing module should always be included so that trainees can reflect and elaborate on what they learned.

Another important factor affecting trainee attention is the credibility of the game or simulation. When it does not realistically represent the key characteristics of the trainees' job, trainees will not take it seriously and will give it less attention. Consider a role play or simulation designed to improve union-management problem solving. It asks trainees who are members of union-management committees to work on resolving certain issues. If these issues are, in reality, already contractually mandated in the company, both sides must pretend that part of the labor contract does not exist. When this happens, trainees are likely to consider the training irrelevant and not take it seriously.

Retention   Games and simulations are best at developing trainees' skills in applying or using knowledge. This approach assumes the factual and procedural knowledge needed to play the game or use the simulation was already learned. This information exists as symbolic codes in the trainees' cognitive structure. Games or simulations do not do a good job of teaching facts or procedures, but they are especially good at enhancing factual and procedural knowledge through the repeated recall and use of the information during the training. Thus they serve to refine and reinforce symbolic coding. Games and simulations focus primarily on the cognitive organization and symbolic rehearsal processes. Because the trainee must use many different areas of knowledge to complete the game or simulation, the trainee is able to see the connections and relationships between the different areas. Learning these new connections and relationships allows trainees to solve problems and develop strategies for achieving goals. Most games and simulations require trainees to engage in symbolic rehearsal by having them plan out their action steps and anticipate their consequences.

Behavioral Reproduction   Of course, the real strength of games and simulations is their focus on learning by doing. Creating realistic situations in which trainees can apply their knowledge to goal-directed actions and receive fairly immediate feedback is critical for skill development. For games and simulations behavioral reproduction is a significant part of the learning process. In order for the desired learning to occur, the training design must include feedback to the trainees about their actions. This requirement follows from the principles of reinforcement and shaping discussed in Chapter 3.

Training Group Characteristics

Equipment simulators are typically used by one person at a time, which provides an advantage in that differences in trainee readiness can, to some extent, be addressed. As with all games and simulations, however, trainees must possess the prerequisite knowledge and skill to make effective use of the method. Equipment simulators do limit the number of trainees who can be trained on the device. This limitation becomes a problem when a large number of trainees must be trained in a short period of time.

Business games and simulations, including behavior modeling, typically use small groups ranging in size from three to eight trainees. Differences in trainee characteristics can be both an advantage and disadvantage, depending on the goals of the training. Differences in content knowledge or experience can be an advantage if one of the goals of training is to increase the awareness of how different people approach the situation. In a business game or simulation, for example, constructing a group of trainees from different functional areas of the business allows each trainee to learn how decisions in their area affect other areas. Thus, all trainees learn a more integrative framework for decision making. On the other hand, such groups generate more conflict and require more time for discussion and decision making. Other differences in content knowledge can be more troublesome. When some trainees in the group are more knowledgeable of basic business concepts than others, they can become irritated at having to educate the rest of the group. They see others as getting a lot more out of the training than they are. In general, it is best to make sure that groups are formed so that everyone shares relatively the same level of basic knowledge. However, group formation will depend on the training objectives. Having more knowledgeable trainees educate those less knowledgeable may be your method of choice. The point is that the trainer must take care to identify how trainee group composition matches the training objectives.

On-the-Job Training

The most frequently used training method, especially in smaller businesses, is **on-the-job training (OJT)**. OJT uses more experienced and skilled employees, whether coworkers or supervisors, to train less-skilled and experienced employees. OJT takes many forms and can be supplemented with classroom training. Instruction by coworkers or supervisors at the job site often occurs on an informal basis and is characterized by the following:

- It has not been carefully thought out or prepared.
- It is done on an ad hoc basis with no predetermined content or process.
- No objectives or goals have been developed or referred to during training.
- The trainers are chosen on the basis of technical expertise, not training ability.
- Trainers have no formal training in how to train.

Formal OJT programs are quite different. They are typically conducted by employees identified as having superior (not necessarily the best) technical knowledge/skills and who can effectively use one-on-one instructional techniques. Because conducting one-on-one training is not a skill most people develop on their own, organizations with formal OJT programs provide "train the trainer" training for these employees.

Formal OJT programs should follow a carefully developed sequence of learning events. Learning is usually achieved through the following steps:

- The trainee observes a more experienced and skilled employee (the trainer) performing job-related tasks.
- The procedures and techniques used are discussed before, during, and after the trainer has demonstrated how the job tasks are performed.
- When the trainer determines that the trainee is ready, the trainee begins performing the job tasks.
- The trainer provides continuing guidance and feedback.
- The trainee is gradually given more and more of the job to perform until he can adequately perform the entire job on his own.

The generalized instructional process just described is formalized in more detail as the job instruction technique.

JOB INSTRUCTION TECHNIQUE (JIT)

Job Instruction technique (JIT) uses a behavioral strategy with a focus on skill development, but some factual and procedural knowledge objectives are usually involved as well. JIT[53] was developed during World War II and continues to be a standard in evaluating OJT programs. JIT consists of four steps—prepare, present, try out, and follow-up—as shown in Table 6-6.

Prepare

Preparation and follow-up are the two areas that are most often ignored in OJT programs. Preparation should include a written breakdown of the job. The person responsible for the OJT may believe that, because of a familiarity with the job, written documentation is unnecessary. To ignore this step, however, is to miss seeing the job through the eyes of the trainee. A trainer who knows the job well is likely to be able to do a number of things without thinking, and these may be overlooked in training. A systematic analysis and documentation of the job tasks will ensure that all the points are covered in the training.

The next step is to prepare an instructional plan. First, the trainer must determine what the trainee already knows. The person analysis portion of a needs assessment provides this information. The trainer will need to review any data available from a completed TNA. If no TNA is available, checking personnel records and interviewing the trainee are ways of determining what the trainee knows and what training should focus on.

Finally, putting the trainee at ease is just as important in OJT as it is in the classroom. You must take care to create a comfortable learning atmosphere. One way to create such an environ-

TABLE 6-6 JIT Instruction/Learning Sequence

Basics of Instruction	*Areas of Learning Affected*[*]
Prepare	Attention and motivation
• Break down the job.	
• Prepare an instruction plan.	
• Put the learner at ease.	
Present	Retention:
• Tell.	Symbolic coding
• Show.	Cognitive organization
• Demonstrate.	
• Explain.	
Try Out	Retention:
• Have the learner "talk through" the job.	Symbolic rehearsal
• Have the learner instruct the supervisor on how the job is done.	Behavioral reproduction
• Let the learner do the job.	
• Provide feedback, both positive and negative.	
• Let the learner practice.	
Follow-Up	Behavioral reproduction
• Check progress frequently at first.	
• Tell the learner whom to go to for help.	
• Gradually taper off progress checks.	

[*]From Social Learning Theory: Figure 3-6

Source: Gold, L. 1981. Job instruction: Four steps to success. *Training and Development Journal,* September, pp. 28–32.

ment is to provide the trainee with an orientation to the OJT/JIT learning process. This orientation may or may not be provided by the JIT trainer. In this orientation you should help trainees understand their role and the role of the trainer in the process. The importance of trainee listening and questioning should be emphasized. Familiarizing trainees with the steps in the JIT process will reduce their anxiety because they will know what to expect.

Present

The four activities of this stage are tell, show, demonstrate, and explain.[54] First, tell and show. As the trainer you would provide an overview of the job while showing the trainee the different aspects of the job. You are not actually doing the job, but pointing out where buttons are pushed, where materials are located, where to stand, and so on. When finished, you demonstrate how to do the job and explain why it is done in that manner. If the job involves many components or is complex, you should cover only one segment at a time, in the same order in which segments occur when the job is performed. During the demonstration you would indicate why the procedure is performed in that particular way, emphasizing key learning points and important safety instructions.

Try Out

Before actually trying the behaviors, the trainee describes, to the trainer, how to do the job. This step provides a safe transition from watching and listening to doing (symbolic rehearsal). The trainee then attempts to perform the job and the trainer is able to provide instant feedback. The trainer should consider that any errors that take place are probably a function of the training, not the trainee. With this notion in mind, the focus will be on improving the method of instruction rather than on the inability of the trainee to comprehend. In any case it is useful to allow the trainee to learn from mistakes, provided they are not too costly. Allowing the trainee to see the consequences of using an incorrect procedure, such as having to scrap the product, reinforces the use of the correct procedures. Such an occurrence becomes a form of negative reinforcement, because using the correct procedures avoids the scrap. The trainer can help by questioning the trainee about her actions while the trainee is performing the job and by guiding the trainee in identifying the correct procedures.

Follow-Up

There is an inappropriate tendency for informal OJT programs to consider training completed after the previous step. The trainer must check the trainees' work often enough to prevent incorrect or bad work habits from developing. It is important that trainees feel comfortable asking for help during these initial solo efforts. The trainer should take every opportunity to reinforce trainees in areas where they are performing well. As trainees demonstrate proficiency in the job, progress checks can taper off until eventually they are eliminated.

APPRENTICESHIP TRAINING

Apprenticeship training, another form of OJT, is one of the oldest forms of training. Its roots date back to the Middle Ages, when skilled crafts and trades people passed on their knowledge to others as a way of preserving the guilds (similar to unions) they belonged to. Many similarities characterize today's North American apprenticeship programs. Apprenticeship programs are partnerships between labor unions, employers, schools, and the government. Most apprenticeships are in skilled trade and professional unions, such as boiler engineers, electrical workers, pipe fitters, and carpenters. In general, an apprenticeship program requires about 2 years of on-the-job experience and 180 hours of classroom instruction, though requirements vary from program to program.[55] Journeymen provide the training on the job, and adult education centers and community colleges typically provide the classroom training. An apprentice must be able to demonstrate mastery of all required skills and knowledge before being allowed to graduate to journeyman status. These programs are regulated by governmental agencies, which also set standards and provide services.

COACHING

Coaching is the process of providing one-on-one guidance and instruction to improve knowledge, skills, and work performance. Usually, coaching is directed at employees with performance deficiencies, but it can also be used as a motivational tool for those performing adequately. Although coworkers can be coaches, especially in team-based organizations, more typically it is the supervisor who acts as coach. One analysis suggests that in the past supervisors spent, on the average, only about 10 percent of their time coaching subordinates. In today's organizations they typically spend more than 50 percent of their time in such activities.[56] Although many different models describe how the coaching process works, the format generally follows an outline. The following outline looks at the process from the coach's perspective:

1. Understand the trainee's job, the KSAs and resources required to meet performance expectations, and the trainee's current level of performance.
2. Meet with the trainee and mutually agree on the performance objectives to be achieved.
3. Mutually arrive at a plan and schedule for achieving the performance objectives.
4. At the work site, show the trainee how to achieve the objectives, observe the trainee perform, and then provide feedback, This process is similar to JIT.
5. Repeat step 4 until performance improves.

As can be seen, coaching is similar to JIT, involving one-on-one instruction in how to perform a task. A key factor in the learning process is the interpersonal relationship between the coach and the trainee.

Even though coaching is clearly a skill-focused method, it can also be used for knowledge development (e.g., facts and procedures), although other methods are better for transmitting knowledge. Like the OJT trainer, the coach must be skilled both in how to do the task(s) and in how to train others to do them. HRD professionals typically do not perform the role of coach (unless they are coaching other HRD professionals). Rather, they train supervisors in the coaching process and develop the supervisors' interpersonal skills to make them more effective.

Mentoring is considered to be a form of coaching in which an ongoing relationship is developed between a senior and junior employee. The purpose of mentoring is to provide the more junior employee with guidance and a clear understanding of how the organization goes about its business. Whereas coaching focuses on the technical aspects of the job, mentoring focuses more on improving the employee's fit within the organization. Thus coaching emphasizes skill development, and mentoring emphasizes attitude development. Generally, mentoring is conducted only for management-level employees, though in some cases it is applied at lower levels. In the past mentoring was primarily an informal activity, but it is becoming formalized in many organizations. The concerns about untrained OJT trainers discussed earlier apply to mentoring as well.

TRAINING THE TRAINER FOR OJT

For OJT programs to be effective, the trainers must be motivated to serve in the training role, be skilled as trainers, and possess the interpersonal skills necessary to interact effectively with those they train.[57] The components for training the trainer should include the following:

- The company's formal OJT process (e.g., JIT), the policies and support provided by the organization
- Interpersonal skills and feedback techniques
- Principles of adult learning

Trainers' normal job responsibilities should be reduced while they are training others. Some reduction in productivity must be anticipated and built into job expectations. As with any other job assignment, performance as a trainer should be evaluated periodically with feedback and appropriate reinforcement.

STRENGTHS AND LIMITATIONS OF OJT

OJT is clearly a useful method for skill enhancement. Trainees learn their KSAs in the actual job situation, thus transfer of training occurs naturally. An additional benefit is that the OJT process will provide new employees with a rapid orientation to how the company operates. It also has the potential of developing more positive relationships among older and new employees and between supervisors and their subordinates.

A major concern in OJT is the competency of the trainer. The trainer must possess the technical competence, the training competence, and the motivation to train. Without all these characteristics, training is not likely to be successful. In addition, the organization must provide the trainer with enough time away from her regular job to do the training. This accommodation not only leads to better training, but demonstrates the organization's commitment to its OJT program.

Cost

OJT offers some clear cost advantages if it is done effectively. Trainees and trainers are both at the job site performing job activities. Though neither the trainee nor the trainer will be producing at full capacity, they are at least producing something. With other techniques, neither the trainer nor the trainee is engaged in producing the organization's products or services while training is going on. Also OJT does not require the purchase of expensive training materials such as simulators, games, or computer-based training modules. All the materials are part of the normal work equipment.

OJT also speeds up the learning process. No delay separates training from its application to the work situation. In addition, some evidence indicates that one-on-one training produces faster learning that is more resistant to forgetting.[58] The more efficient the training, the less costly it is.

One cost concern in implementing OJT is the cost of training the trainers. Unlike other methods, for a start-up OJT system most if not all of the trainers will need training. In addition, while other methods have one trainer for many trainees, this method uses one-on-one training. The drop in productivity due to having the more skilled employees conducting training must be added into the cost. In addition, companies should expect some increased waste, breakage, and downtime due to inexperienced trainees operating the equipment.

Control of Content and Process

The content and process of learning in OJT is controlled primarily by the trainer during the "prepare" and "present" stages of training. As training progresses to the "try out" and "follow-up" stages, the trainee and trainer jointly control the content and process, because it is the trainee's actions that determine what the next learning module will be. The training moves as quickly or as slowly as necessary for the trainee to master the learning. Thus, if the trainee is in the "talk through" portion of trying it out and misses some steps, the trainer might again demonstrate how the job is done. If the trainee is able to "talk through" the steps correctly, the trainer might be ready to move to the "instruct the trainee" portion. However, if the trainee said, "You know, I was just guessing on some of those steps," the trainer might repeat the "talk through" portion until the trainee felt confident of knowing all the steps.

Learning Objectives (KSAs)

The primary focus of OJT is skill development, but because we discussed this aspect previously, we will not deal with it here except to say that OJT is a good method of developing skills. OJT can also enhance the knowledge base of trainees and influence their attitudes. Through discussions with the trainer and through questioning and restating of techniques, the trainee can learn factual and elementary procedural information. However, classroom techniques and individual reading assignments are more efficient and do a better job of developing this type of knowledge. Advanced procedural knowledge and strategic knowledge are better developed through experiential learning such as OJT. This occurs through a combination of observation and discussion as well as through physical interaction with the equipment, materials, and other accoutrements of the job.

The attitudes new employees hold about their job and their company come from observing and interacting with others. OJT provides a great opportunity to get employees off on the right foot by clarifying the norms, expectations, and culture of the work unit. Of course, accomplishing this task will depend on the ability of the OJT trainer to convey these appropriately to the trainee.

On a final note, if knowledge acquisition is required to perform the job, OJT techniques should be supplemented with other techniques that are more suited to knowledge acquisition. Apprenticeship training is a good example. For skilled trades, it is important to develop the skills of the trade; however, certain knowledge is a prerequisite for that skill development. For that reason, a significant amount of classroom training is also required as a part of the training. Computer-based training, role playing, reading texts, manuals, and other techniques can all be combined successfully with OJT.

Learning Process

Trainees are likely to be relatively more attentive and more motivated during OJT, because it is easier to see a direct relationship between the training and job performance. Verbal and visual stimuli direct attention to key learning points. Periods of active practice require the trainee to attend to what they are doing and what is being said, thus increasing the learning potential.

The visual, auditory, and tactile cues in OJT assist in the symbolic coding process, providing many relationships among objects and actions in the work environment. Through observation, practice, and discussion, the trainee cognitively organizes these relationships into easily recalled patterns of behavior.

By asking the trainee to describe the steps in the operation (before letting the trainee perform the operation), the trainer is facilitating the symbolic rehearsal process. The trainee must imagine himself going through the operations as he describes the procedures.

Behavioral reproduction, of course, is a strong point of this method. The trainee practices small portions of the operation until they are mastered and then moves on to larger portions until command over the tasks that make up the job reach the level needed to perform the job alone.

Audiovisual Enhancements to Training

Audiovisuals (AVs) can be useful enhancements for meeting all three types of training objectives (K, S, and A) and are easily applied to any of the other methods discussed. **Audiovisual aids** consist of any physical, mechanical, or electronic media used to provide or assist instruction. Typically they are used as a supplement to other methods of training, rather than as a stand-alone means of instruction, though some are effective training devices by themselves.

The range of AV alternatives is quite large, from simple chalkboard or whiteboard text and images to interactive multimedia presentations. They can be grouped under the headings of static or dynamic media. **Static media** are presentations of fixed text or images such as printed matter, overhead transparencies, pictures/slides, and computer-generated projections. An AV is considered static if the material presented is stationary. **Dynamic media** create sequentially moving stimuli; that is, the information is presented in a continuously moving progression from beginning to end. Audiotapes and videotapes, computer-generated presentations, and moving film are examples.

STATIC MEDIA

Static media are generally not suitable for training as a stand-alone method. Rather they are used to augment and enhance other methods, in particular the lecture method, but they are adaptable to other training techniques as well.

Newsprint, Charts, and Posters

Newsprint, charts, and posters display information through words or images. They range from handmade, with felt markers and newsprint, to professionally prepared, glossy prints. An advantage of these presentations is they can be posted on walls or other vertical surfaces so the information is visible to trainees while other training methods are in use (e.g., lecture, role plays, video). For example, these media are frequently used to post an outline of the day's training and to display procedural steps related to the training material. They allow trainees to place the material that is presented at any time into the context of the total program. Figure 6-2 shows a poster that could be used during conflict resolution training. It might be left up during the entire training so that trainees are constantly reminded of the six steps the training focuses on. Posters and charts the trainer knows will be used during training should be prepared before training and checked for accuracy. The credibility of the training and the trainer will suffer if errors exist.

Projected Text and Images

In the past, the two methods of projecting text or images for simultaneous viewing by an audience were photographic slides and overhead transparencies. Today digital camera projectors and computer-generated projections are also used. Photographic slides are simply photographs of training-related text, graphics, or actual equipment. They require the subject matter to be prepared and photographed, the film to be developed, and the slides to be mounted and ordered in

FIGURE 6-2 Example of a Conflict Resolution Training Poster

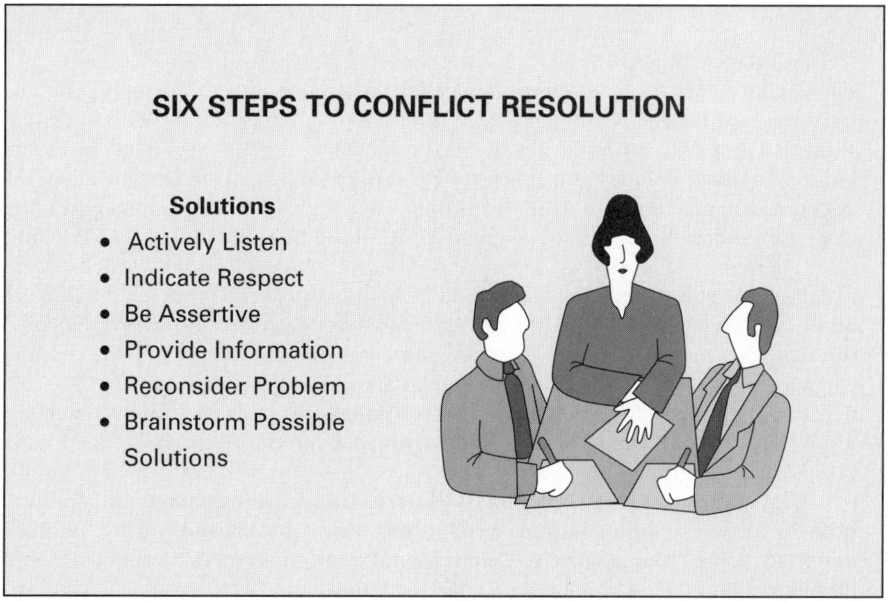

the correct sequence. This technology is used less and less frequently, but still offers some applications, particularly in scientific or medical training situations.

Creating overhead transparencies requires text and images to be transferred to the transparency material (generally clear acetate). It can be done by hand with transparency markers, but the result is not usually professional looking and can damage the credibility of the training. Computer-generated text and images as well as those copied from printed matter can be pasted together to create attention-getting and informative overheads. Although overheads can be created through a variety of mechanical devices, usually a computer system and image scanner are required.

Computer-generated projections are more sophisticated than overhead transparencies. Many popular office software packages contain "presentation" software components that allow you to create projections, discussion notes, and other training aids you can integrate into the presentation. Microsoft and Corel are two companies that produce such programs. Once the projections are created and placed in proper order, they can be downloaded onto a floppy disk or stored on the hard drive. During the training itself, the trainer will require a computer (typically a laptop or notebook) and a high-intensity digital projector. The computer communicates the image to be projected to the projector, which projects an enlarged image onto a screen. Most projectors will also project video images from a VCR, CD, or DVD player. The presenter can control the display of the projections with a mouse, clicking to move from one projection to the next, or time the presentation so that the image automatically advances to the next projection after a specified period of time.

Each of these methods fulfills the same purpose: to focus trainees' attention on specific content. In addition to displaying information, projections can aid the trainer in moving systematically through the components of the training. This feature is especially useful in training methods where the interaction between trainer and trainees may cause the trainer to stray from the training outline; the trainer can simply look to the projection being displayed to get back on track.

DYNAMIC AUDIOVISUAL METHODS

Dynamic AVs include audio-only tapes, moving film, videos, and computer-generated presentations. Dynamic visuals can also serve as aids to enhance other methods of training. However, unlike static visuals, these methods can be and frequently are used as the sole method of training.

Audio-Only Tapes

The audiotape has the same characteristics as the straight lecture. The only differences are that the audiotape is exactly the same each time it is used and provides no accompanying visual stimulus. Even while advances in video and computer-generated presentations reduce the popularity of audio-only tapes as training tools, they are an advantage in some situations. They are effective where the content of the training is primarily auditory recognition or auditory response. Almost 50 percent of companies with more than 50 employees use audiocassettes in their training.[59] One obvious instance is when the material to be learned requires specific responses to auditory cues. Telephone and radio operators of all types (e.g., 911 emergency operators, taxi dispatchers, and customer service line operators) can receive beneficial training through audiotape playback that closely simulates the work environment. Learning a foreign language is also a fairly common use of audiotapes.

Audiotapes are also useful when other forms of training are not available. For example, given the amount of time sales representatives spend in their cars, audiotape training can be a productive use of that time.

Thus advantages of this approach over the lecture are its portability and ability to be reused both for training additional people and for easy review and clarification by trainees. Also if it is important that all trainees receive exactly the same information, an audiotape will be better than a lecture.

Moving Film and Videos

Videos and motion picture film are good ways of both showing and telling trainees how to do something. They can present conceptual or factual information by integrating narration with visual illustrations, graphics, and animated depictions. These media are relatively portable and generally can be made available to trainees at their convenience. It is clear these media offer many advantages. No wonder 96 percent of companies with 50 or more employees used videotapes for training, making them second only to classroom instruction.[60]

Videos in particular are used as a stand-alone training technique. A video, like a lecture, is a one-way communication system, but with the disadvantage of no discussion/question session. A number of firms use video to enhance training in ways similar to those described in Training in Action 6-5. However, the use of interactive video technology is becoming more widespread, allowing more and more two-way interaction similar to that described in Training in Action 6-2. This type of training can be a complete training package, not just an audiovisual aid. However, short interactive video can be used to supplement other training methods.

The advent of widespread video recording and playback capability effectively eliminated the use of film. Many of the most frequently viewed training films have been transferred to the video format. The ease of use, both in developing the product and presenting it during the training, makes video superior to film in almost every instance. However, if a film that can be of value in training already exists, by all means use it (if you can find a projector).

Computer-Generated Dynamic Presentations

With the ability to project computer screen images onto a large screen and the increasing ability to digitize sound and image electronically, the computer is rapidly becoming a critical training tool. Multimedia software allows computers to store, modify, and reconfigure sound and image

---

TRAINING IN ACTION 6-5

USING VIDEO IN CATALOG SALES TRAINING

Here are two examples of how videos are being used to train employees working in the catalog department of two different types of organizations.

The Boston Museum of Fine Arts mails out catalogs of museum reproductions on a seasonal basis. They use seasonal and temporary labor to help keep costs low, but this practice requires constant training of new personnel. To meet this need they commissioned Creative Video Design to produce a training video for their telephone order takers. The video demonstrates how to greet the customer, how the phone system works, how to log on to the computer, enter the order, and so on. Another video was developed for the warehouse personnel demonstrating how to read and interpret inventory and shipping slips.

Talbots is a women's fashion merchandiser with hundreds of stores and a large catalog sales department. To make sure their catalog employees understand Talbots' total operations and particularly the way the catalog department works, they developed a series of videos. One provides a video tour of the catalog and store distribution center to new employees. Another video traces how a piece of clothing listed in their catalog makes its journey from the customer's order to delivery at the customer's home. A full understanding of the operations helps catalog salespeople give better service and advice to their customers.

Source: Adapted from *Catalog Age*, January 1994, p. 59.

as well as text to create nearly any combination of audio and visual presentation. Developing a computer-generated dynamic presentation (CGDP) does require considerably more hardware and software knowledge than do the presentation software packages discussed earlier. The development process is similar to that of producing a video but also includes converting all the components into digital media. As with video productions, it is advisable to use professionals to ensure the quality of the presentation.

STRENGTHS AND LIMITATIONS OF AUDIOVISUALS

Static AVs are one-way communication techniques and should rarely if ever be used as stand-alone training tools. The only exception is printed material such as books or pamphlets, which can be used alone if the material is simple and straightforward. This use typically occurs as self-study materials and not as part of a formalized training program. Because static media cannot demonstrate how to use the material, answer questions, or allow for interaction between the trainee and trainer, their value is greatest as a supplement to other methods. Because they are generally not appropriate as a stand-alone training method, we will compare static visuals with each other and with dynamic audiovisual methods.

Cost

Static AVs   An advantage of static audiovisuals is their lower development costs, which range from low (overhead transparencies, flip charts, and computer-generated projections) to moderate (photographic slides and professionally prepared posters). Implementation costs, on the other hand, range from low (flip charts and overhead transparencies) to high (computer-generated projections). The high implementation cost is entirely due to the cost of equipment. Overhead projectors are relatively inexpensive (several hundred dollars), slide projectors are slightly more, and computer image projection requires a relatively sophisticated system, which can range from $3,500 to $10,000. Of course, all this equipment is amortized across the training sessions in which it is used, so even the most expensive projection devices may be only a minor factor in the total cost of training.

Static visuals are reusable, so a trainee who didn't understand it the first time can look at it again and again. It isn't necessary, however, for the trainee to use the original materials. For a minimal cost, overhead transparencies and computer-generated projections can be copied to paper and given as handouts (slides are more expensive to convert). Providing these handouts will help to address any moderate to small differences in learning readiness among trainees.

Computer-generated overhead transparencies and projections provide a unique advantage because they are stored electronically. Any given display can be modified relatively easily by adding or removing text and images, reducing the cost of program modifications or adaptations. Slides, on the other hand, would need to be completely redone. For example, assume you produce 30 photographic slides for training human resource clerks in the proper procedure for processing a worker's compensation claim. It is not likely these slides would be much use in training supervisors about how to handle a workplace accident, even though worker's compensation claims are closely related. If computer-generated overheads or projections had been used, the original projections could be easily modified to delete irrelevant material and include the new material. Likewise, if 6 months later the government rewrites the worker's compensation laws, you will probably need to replace most of the slides for the HR clerks rather than modifying the existing slides. Technological advances in computer imaging and projection make slides less and less viable as static visual aids.

Dynamic AVs   Using a professional video production company is expensive. A completed video can cost from $700 to $1,200 per minute[61] or more, but it is often worth the cost because of the professional appearance of the video. Even developing in-house videos is fairly expensive, given the cost of labor, equipment, and so on. Developing an original CGDP can require even higher up-front costs than producing a video, because each component of the multimedia package must be developed, then digitized and integrated into a coherent, logically flowing package. The cost of development is lowered if the training components can be developed digitally in the first place.

Although the up-front cost is high, the per-person cost of producing a video can be low if the trainee population is large enough. Videos, film, and CGDP are portable and reusable. Videos and computer-generated dynamic presentations are easily and cheaply duplicated. Therefore, different trainees in different places can see them at any time, and they can be seen many times by the same trainee. This capability is valuable for refresher courses or for trainees who learn at a slower pace. Because of their reusability, the development cost can be spread over a large number of trainees, reducing the per-trainee costs.

When they are used for stand-alone training, the biggest advantage of videos and CGDPs is that trainees can view or study at their convenience. This capability can have a significant cost and time savings with regard to the trainees' and trainers' travel. For example, ADC Communications estimated it would cost about $150,000 to bring the company's 60 salespeople to the Minneapolis headquarters for a week of sales training.[62] By using stand-alone video training, this cost was eliminated. Because most employees can use VCRs and televisions in their homes, the company is not required to buy much equipment. The company should, however, provide on-site equipment for those employees who do not own the equipment or whose home environment is not conducive to learning. CGDP does not offer this equipment cost advantage, because the necessary hardware and software cannot be assumed to be widely owned by employees.

Finally, if employees view the tape at home or during free time at work, the productivity savings are substantial. If trainees must travel more than 200 miles to reach a centralized training location, they lose not only their productivity for the time at training, but also 1 or 2 days of travel time.

One way to cut the cost of video training is to rent or buy a video from commercial producers. A large number of commercially available training videos cover a wide variety of topics. Also videos and films produced primarily for entertainment can be used effectively in training. For example, we used segments of the classic film *Twelve Angry Men* (a film about a jury's deliberations during a criminal trial) to illustrate the problems and benefits of consensus decision making. Small portions of the movie *Falling Down* can illustrate various risk factors and warning signs for workplace violence. Television broadcasts can be used in a similar fashion. For example, textbook publishers now provide, as accompaniments to their textbooks, videocassettes containing segments of news programs and TV specials that relate to the content of the text.

Equipment costs vary across the media used. Film requires a projector and screen for presentation, and a video requires a VCR and television. Videos can also be projected onto large screens with a video projector. The technology is rapidly improving, and state-of-the-art projectors (costing about $4,000) can display large-screen images. This capability overcomes one of the disadvantages of the TV video, which is that only a small group of trainees can easily see it at the same time.

Control of Material and Process

Static AVs   Generally computer-generated projections are more easily controlled by the trainer than are other static visuals. The sequence of projections can be structured so material is displayed only when the presenter begins to discuss it. Text can be programmed to fade into and out of the projection with a click of the mouse. The mouse can also be used to point to or highlight particular parts of the projection. Finally, worry about slides or overheads getting out of order, being upside down, and the like is eliminated. Because the whole visual presentation is contained on a single floppy disk, it is more easily transportable than slides or overheads.

Although computer-generated projection offers many advantages, it also comes with a major disadvantage: It suffers all the potential problems of computer technology. Hard drives crash at inopportune times, floppy disks aren't readable by the operating system, viruses abound, and software and disk formatting compatibility issues must be solved. To avoid most of these problems, you can carry your own portable computer to the training site, but make sure a compatible backup is available. Of course, carrying a laptop reduces the convenience of having to carry only a single floppy disk.

Dynamic AVs The disadvantage of acquiring a commercially made video is that the information may not be specific to your company or your training content but rather must appeal to the largest audience. When you use such videos, you will likely need to augment them with additional training relevant to your trainees. You control the content and process of learning through selecting the video and creating the supplemental materials.

The portability of dynamic audiovisuals means that trainees can take them off the shelf and use them when convenient. To this extent, the trainee controls the learning process. However, watching a training video or multimedia presentation at home allows for many distractions. The process with which training occurs is completely in the hands of the trainee, who can stop the presentation at any point and do something else. Thus the desired level of learning may not be attained.

When video and CGDP are used as stand-alone techniques, the content and presentation format are controlled, but not the manner in which the trainee goes through the material. Particularly with video, trainees may fast-forward over parts they do not understand or are bored with. Thus evaluating learning is particularly important when this training technique is used.

Learning Objectives (KSAs)

Appropriately prepared and displayed audiovisuals will enhance almost any training and are especially effective for techniques in which the trainee is less active, such as lecture/discussion and some types of CBT. However, the nature of the learning objective will determine which type of audiovisual is most appropriate.

Knowledge Both static and dynamic AVs facilitate the trainee's knowledge development through their ability to activate or enhance learning processes. They focus trainee attention and provide visual stimuli that aid symbolic coding and cognitive organization. They are also useful for highlighting cues that will stimulate appropriate recall. AVs are most effective at enhancing declarative knowledge but can also be useful in developing procedural knowledge. Dynamic audiovisuals are more suited than static AVs for developing procedural knowledge, because they are able to model the steps required to perform the task and display a variety of situations in which the task is appropriate.

Skills Static presentation of information is not especially useful for skill building. It does not lend itself to facilitating development or the practice of skills. Dynamic presentations, however, can be useful in skill development and practice. For example, foreign language audiotapes use this approach. Dynamic audiovisuals can also make it easier to simulate the work environment. In police departments, for example, a film or video is used to place the trainee in the position of searching a building for an armed and dangerous suspect. The trainee must make decisions about what to do in a variety of situations such as the sudden appearance of objects and people, or entering a room with a closed door, and so on.

Another audiovisual technique increasingly being used is videotaping the trainee's performance during practice and using the video as feedback for skill improvement. Even though dynamic AVs can provide good models and instructions for skill development, they usually are not capable of providing feedback, so they should not be used as stand-alone methods. Interactive videos and CGDP provide the exceptions to this rule.

Attitudes Static and dynamic AVs, used in conjunction with other techniques, can facilitate attitude change by visually clarifying the relationships among objects and events that are the basis of trainee opinions and evaluations. For example, the Domtar plant in southern California used static visuals to display the consequences of not following correct safety procedures. This manufacturer of construction products used graphic displays of eye injuries in a safety training program to develop positive attitudes about wearing safety goggles. It also used pictures of employees working on various equipment with some wearing and some not wearing safety goggles; trainees were asked to identify the potential hazards to the individual in each picture. The process allowed the trainees to make the proper links between wearing the goggles and protecting themselves from injury. It is interesting to note that this plant won many safety awards from both the company and the state. The ability to provide visual documentation of the relationship between objects and events is a powerful source of learning and attitude change. Beliefs such as "wearing goggles is uncomfortable and unnecessary" are often reinforced by cognitive distortions and rationalization. Statements such as "If you're careful, you don't need goggles" and "I'm too experienced to get an eye injury" are examples of the kind of rationalizations heard at the Domtar plant before training. The trainer's words alone may not be sufficient to change attitudes. Visual displays allow the trainees to see that their distortions and rationalizations are inaccurate, making a change in attitudes easier to accomplish. Dynamic AVs can produce even more powerful images, because the connection between objects, actions, and consequences can be made even more explicit.

Learning Process

Attention   The phrase "a picture is worth a thousand words" reflects the importance of visual representation in the learning process. Static visuals provide the trainee with a visually based message, even if the image is simply enlarged text. Visual stimuli focus the trainee's attention when they represent a change in the environment. No matter how professional, a trainer's voice and image become familiar to the trainees after a period of time. When familiarity occurs, it becomes easier for the trainee's attention to wander. The periodic presentation of new visual stimuli activates the attention process. If the visuals are consistently similar in format (e.g., all text, black print, same font size) they too will lose their ability to attract attention. Combining graphic images, charts, and text and varying color to highlight key learning points will add zest to the training and maintain trainee attention. With dynamic audiovisuals the dynamic nature of the presentation itself attracts attention, because it is constantly changing.

The trainer should be careful that all AVs are integrated with the content of the training. When they show little relationship to the content, they become distracting and can actually reduce learning. This distraction can also occur if the trainer fails to manage the presentation of the visuals properly, such as incorrectly placing transparencies on the projector, standing in front of the screen, or otherwise interfering with the normal viewing of the visual. Trainees often begin to attend to the trainer's management of the presentation rather than to the content of the presentation, thus reducing learning.

Retention   Because different trainees learn more or less effectively through different media, the use of AVs provides additional modalities for learning. When several media are used to convey the same message, the message is more easily coded for storage and contributes more reference points. In general, visual communications are absorbed more quickly and retained for a longer time than auditory messages. Visual images are also more readily coded symbolically and recalled in their original form.[63]

The symbolic coding process is enhanced when pictures or graphic images provide visual cues that supplement or complement auditory or written cues. Combining cues from different senses results in more accurate symbolic coding and thus better retention.[64] Showing a variety of images, all pertaining to the same issue, presents trainees with a wider base of common cues to use in storing the information. Audiovisuals also are extremely good for demonstrating events and effects not usually observable or noticed. For example, enlarged images of tiny or microscopic objects are useful in many training settings. In the safety training example discussed earlier, trainees were able to see the effects of not wearing goggles. Eye injuries are often not easily observable, but the visual projections used in the training allowed the trainees to see what actually happened to the eye and what damage tiny bits of material can do. By making objects and effects visible, symbolic encoding becomes much easier.

Cognitive organization can be facilitated by graphic images that demonstrate how the training relates to familiar concepts. Pictorially representing these relationships makes integrating the new with the old easier than using verbal descriptions alone. Integration is likely to be easier and faster if the trainer is able to represent visually both the old cognitive organization and the new, showing the changes required. To the degree that the trainees' cognitive structures are different from each other, creating visual representations of them all is difficult. However, it can be accomplished by asking trainees to develop pictorial representations of their cognitive organization on flip charts. They can then use these representations to compare with the new organization being presented. For example, suppose jobs in a work group were redesigned because of a change in how the product is produced. During training, trainees could map out how the old job was performed. Then, after presenting the new work procedures, you could compare the old with the new and identify the areas where the new KSAs provided by the training will be needed.

Using AVs in training provides a common reference for all trainees. When you ask the trainees to "picture this" or "imagine you are . . . ," each trainee may hold a different image, but when you provide the image, they all receive the same sensory cues. When the trainees later recall the image, the frame of reference will be similar for all. Though a differential loss of information and detail is likely to occur across trainees, the basis of the recalled information is the initial image you provided.

AVs can be somewhat useful in aiding symbolic rehearsal. They provide visual cues that trainees can use to practice hypothetical applications of the training material. This process works in much the same manner as behavioral reproduction, described next. The difference is that in symbolic rehearsal the trainees are only imagining themselves applying the new learning. The AVs can help to create the context in which the symbolic rehearsal takes place as well as providing cues to assist in the symbolic rehearsal (as in guided discovery).

Behavioral Reproduction   AVs can be used to enhance the learning of a new behavior. By illustrating what to do, AVs can provide a model of how to perform. This modeling is usually accomplished best with dynamic AVs. Static or dynamic AVs can also be used to provide the appropriate cues for when to perform. For example, sometimes cue cards are given to trainees when they are practicing new behaviors. These aids need to be present and visible when the new behavior is first being practiced. In the training facility, supplying these cues shouldn't pose a problem. However, to allow opportunities for reproduction outside the training environment, the visual images must be easily portable. Many training programs provide pocket- or wallet-sized cards (static visual aid) to help trainees in practicing the new material back on the job. As we mentioned earlier, videos and CGDPs are portable but require equipment that may not be compatible with the trainee's workstation (particularly line employees). What AVs are not able to do is observe the trainee's performance and provide appropriate feedback. Thus, while AVs can enhance behavioral reproduction, they are limited as stand-alone tools for this type of learning.

The big advantage of CGDPs is that each component of the training can provide the audio-visual format best for meeting the objectives of that component. Some of these multimedia packages are now interactive, allowing the trainee to respond to questions and even pose questions, and thereby in some ways eliminating the one-way communication limitation of standard videos and static AVs. With interactivity comes two-way communication, though the limitations discussed earlier about the quality and type of interaction should be kept in mind.

Limitations for Learning   The principal limitation of static visuals is that they are typically not stand-alone learning tools. They are best used as enhancements to other methods. Because they are static, they cannot capture the full range of material that is dynamic. Even though it is possible to capture the essence of some types of dynamic material, such as the "steps in conflict resolution" or "tips for providing constructive feedback," dynamic audiovisual media will generally do this task more easily and with higher quality. Except for the most sophisticated dynamic AVs (i.e., interactive CGDP), they are unable to adapt to differing characteristics of the trainees or the situation. It is a "one-size-fits-all" technique. If trainees do not have the KSAs to learn from the AV, they won't learn no matter how many times they reuse it.

Trainee Characteristics

Obviously the trainees must be able to understand the AVs. This point may sound fairly trivial, but it is often overlooked. For example, the poster in Figure 6-2 assumes the trainees can read. If the trainees are managers, it is a pretty safe assumption. However, if they are line employees in an assembly plant, problems may arise. Not only must trainees be able to read, they must understand the terms. Even all managers may not know what the trainer means by "actively listen," "assertive," or "reconsider the problem." Displaying this poster without defining all the terms might create confusion for the trainees. The issue of understandability applies to all AVs, static and dynamic.

When wide differences in trainee readiness levels are present, AVs aimed at the highest level of KSAs may not be understandable to those at the lower level. If they are aimed at the lowest level, they will seem unnecessary and boring to those at higher levels. If a dynamic AV is being used as a stand-alone program, it is probably best to provide separate training AVs customized to the readiness levels of each group.

SUMMARY

We discussed in some depth the ability of the various training methods to address different KSA learning objectives. However, it is useful to summarize what each method does well. A summary is provided in Table 6-7. Please note that this table represents a general guide; more specific information is provided in the relevant sections of this chapter and Chapter 7. We rated the potential of the methods to achieve the various types of training objectives. Whether a method will reach its potential depends on how well the training is designed and implemented. Learning objectives are a critical factor in designing a training program, but other factors such as cost, control of training content, and learning processes also need to be taken into account. As the table notes, most of the methods are at least mildly effective in more than one area, and a particular learning objective can be met by more than one method. You may need to make trade-offs between effectiveness at meeting the learning objective and the cost of the method or the time required to develop it into a usable training program. These issues are discussed in the next chapter.

TABLE 6-7 Training Method Effectiveness at Meeting KSA Objectives

GOAL OF TRAINING

	Knowledge			Skills		
Training Methods	*Declarative*	*Procedural*	*Strategic*	*Technical*	*Interpersonal*	*Attitudes*
Lecture						
Straight[a]	3	2	1	1	1	3
Discussion	4	3	2	1	1	4
Demonstration	1	4	2	4	4	3
Computer-Based						
Text only	5	4	3	2	2	3
Simulation type	5	5	5	5	3	3
Simulations/Games						
Equipment	1	3	2	5	1	2
Case studies	3	2	4	2	2	3
Business games	2	3	5	2	2[b]	2
In-basket	1	3	4	1	2[c]	2
Role play	1	2	2	2	4	5[d]
Behavior modeling	1	3	3	4	5	3
OJT						
JIT	3	5	4	4	2	5
Apprentice	5	5	4	5	2	5
Coaching	3	5	4	4	4	5

Scale: 1 = Not effective
    2 = Mildly effective
    3 = Moderately effective
    4 = Effective
    5 = Very effective
[a]This rating is for lectures delivered orally; printed lectures would be one point higher in each knowledge category.
[b]If the business game is designed for interpersonal skills, this rating would be a 4.
[c]If multiple in-baskets were used, this rating would be 3.
[d]This rating applies specifically to role reversal.

KEY TERMS

- Apprenticeship training
- Audiovisual aids
- Behavior modeling
- Behavioral methods
- Business games
- Case studies
- Coaching
- Cognitive methods
- Computer-based training (CBT)
- Demonstration
- Discussion method
- Dynamic media

- Equipment simulators
- Functional simulation
- In-basket technique
- Incident process
- Intelligent tutoring systems (ITS)
- Interactive multimedia training
- Job instruction technique (JIT)
- Lecturette
- Mentoring
- Multiple role play

- On-the-job training (OJT)
- Physical fidelity
- Programmed instruction (PI)
- Psychological fidelity
- Role play
- Role rotation
- Single role play
- Spontaneous role plays
- Static media
- Straight lecture
- Structured role plays
- Virtual reality (VR) training

CASE ANALYSIS

TRAINING FOR CUSTOMER SERVICE SPECIALISTS

As a part of the president's initiative to remove "barriers to learning" at regional Midwestern University, an analysis of student services operations was conducted. That analysis revealed that the barriers deemed most important by students were those that would delay or prevent them from registering for classes. These barriers fell into three areas:

1. Resolving issues relating to fines accrued over the previous terms (e.g., library, parking, late fees)
2. Accurately completing forms and meeting processing deadlines for financial aid in time to enroll in classes
3. Acquiring appropriate advising so that they enrolled in the right classes (avoiding the problems associated with drops and adds)

As a result of this analysis, the university decided to create a new position called customer service specialist (CSS). The job description is presented here.

Classification Specification
Supersedes: New Classification
Title: Customer Service Specialist Grade: PT08

General Summary

Supervise, support, monitor, and assist with the continuous improvement of the work unit's customer service functions and related operational activities. Ensure quality customer service both in person and over the telephone. These activities require a working knowledge of the work unit's program policies, procedures, and regulations as well as an understanding of other departments and systems that interface with the work unit's activities.

Essential Duties

Personally provide and ensure that customer support staff provide positive customer service practices throughout the work unit, including greeting departmental customers in person or over the telephone, identifying their needs, obtaining necessary and appropriate information, and processing customer requests in a manner that will best meet the needs of the customer.

Monitor and ensure that customers perceive that customer service support staff treat them with courtesy, respect, tact, and a sincere desire to meet their needs.

Provide mediation and resolution to customer complaints and requests within delegated authority limits and consistent with departmental policies.

Communicate to customers the departmental policies and procedures related to their needs, and provide customers with appropriate forms and instructions.

Design and implement systems to ensure that forms turned in by customers are the appropriate forms for their service request and that they are complete and, where possible, accurate.

Work with the appropriate departmental administrator to identify the training needs of designated support staff in the work unit who provide direct customer service. Where appropriate, provide on-the-job training and coaching. Work with the designated department administrator to identify appropriate training experiences for customer service support staff.

Recruit, interview, and make recommendations in the hiring of customer support staff.

(continued)

(continued)

Identify processes and procedures in the department that are causing problems for groups of customers (not individuals) and work with department management toward their improvement. Where authorized, implement improvements in systems, processes, and procedures that will increase the customer satisfaction capability of the department.

Develop and maintain a network of contacts with other university departments that commonly interface with the work unit.

Interact with other university departments to resolve a customer's problem or meet the customer's needs.

Interpret and reconcile account records related to area of assignment.

Receive, read, and interpret correspondence and determine proper handling.

Perform other related duties as assigned.

Supervision Received

Supervision is received from designated departmental administrator.

Supervision Exercised

Supervision may be exercised, as determined by the appropriate departmental administrator, over customer service representatives, clerical support staff, and student support staff in the work unit who provide direct customer service.

Qualifications

Ability to read, write, interpret instructions, perform basic arithmetic, and communicate orally and in writing at a level typically acquired through the completion of an associate's degree is necessary.

Personal computing skills sufficient to utilize word processing and spreadsheet applications, and to perform file management and data input/retrieval functions are necessary. Knowledge of specific software applications and university information systems utilized in the work unit assigned is desirable.

Supervisory skills needed to provide direction to subordinates, monitor and manage subordinate performance, plan, organize, and coordinate the customer service activities are required, and supervisory experience is desirable.

Preference is given to those who master basic customer service and problem-solving skills as listed:

- The ability to communicate accurately and pleasantly with customers (across a wide diversity of cultural backgrounds) is necessary in order to identify customer needs and solve customer problems.
- The ability to communicate moderately to highly complex policies, procedures, and regulations and to ensure understanding of these while working under pressure (e.g., handling several requests at the same time) is required.
- Effective problem-solving abilities are required to (1) identify and prioritize customer service problems, (2) conduct a root cause analysis to determine the cause(s) of a problem, (3) develop a range of alternatives that will remove the cause(s) of a problem, (4) identify the alternatives that are most effective, and (5) develop an implementation plan for carrying out the alternative selected.
- Effective conflict management skills are required (e.g., defuse emotionally charged situations, clearly identify issues, clearly communicate procedures for resolving the issue, working with the customer to develop a resolution acceptable to the customer and the work unit).

(*continued*)

- Knowledge and understanding of university, state, and federal policies, systems, procedures, and regulations as they pertain to the work unit's ability to meet customer needs
and to areas of the university that interface with the work unit in meeting those needs.

Those hired without the preceding competencies will undergo training prior to assuming
job responsibilities. During the training period these individuals will be considered temporary
employees. Upon successful completion of the training, the classification will be changed to
permanent. Failure to complete training successfully will result in termination of employment
or reassignment to another position, at the discretion of the university.

Working Conditions

Work is performed in a typical office environment.

After the position was posted and advertised, 25 applicants were selected. Unfortunately, only
7 applicants were assessed as demonstrating the desired level of problem-solving and customer service knowledge and skills. ▪

CASE QUESTIONS

You are assigned the challenge of designing the training program for the temporary CSS employees
who must complete training before they become permanent CSS employees.

1. What are the training objectives for the CSS training program? Indicate how these objectives
   are tied to the KSA requirements. Assume that all trainees have associates degrees, but need
   KSAs in all other areas listed in the qualifications section.
2. Based on the training objectives, provide a training agenda and indicate the time allocated and
   order of modules in your program.
3. For each module, describe what the module is supposed to accomplish and the training methods you will use to accomplish it. Provide your rationale.
4. How will you evaluate whether each person in your training program mastered the knowledge
   and skill levels needed to perform as a CSS? Describe the types of questions you would ask of
   those supervising the CSS employees graduating from your program.

EXERCISES

1. Your instructor will assign you (or your group) one of the methods from the chapter.
   Contact the HRD department of a local business. Indicate that you are learning about training and would like to know whether they use the method in their training programs. If so,
   ask if you can schedule a time to observe the method being used. If they do not use the
   method or if you are unable to observe it, try another company until you are successful.
   While observing the method, take careful notes about how it is used. On a date specified by
   your instructor the class members will report their observations.
2. In small groups develop a role play. First determine the objective of the role play. It should
   be a limited objective that can be achieved in 15 to 20 minutes. Then develop all aspects of a
   role play that will achieve your objective.
3. Take 10 minutes to think about your best classroom-based learning experience and list the things
   that made it such a good experience. When the 10 minutes are up, use 10 additional minutes to
   think of your worst classroom-based learning experience and list the factors that made it such a
   bad experience. At the end of this time, the instructor will ask you to share your experiences.
4. Use the Internet to identify the types of games and business simulations that are available.
   From your research select four that list different learning content objectives. Prepare a one-
   to two-paragraph description for each.

QUESTIONS FOR REVIEW

1. Supervisors often resist taking on the role of coach. What can organizations do to encourage supervisors to be effective coaches?
2. Go through the different instructional methods and sort them into those you think would be most useful in training someone on the technical aspects of the job and those that would be most useful in the more social aspects of the job. Provide the rationale for your decisions.
3. Why are classroom-based training programs (lecture/discussion, role play, games, etc.) used so much more than individualized approaches to training? Do you think this choice is appropriate?

CHAPTER 7

Development and Implementation of Training

DEVELOPMENT PHASE

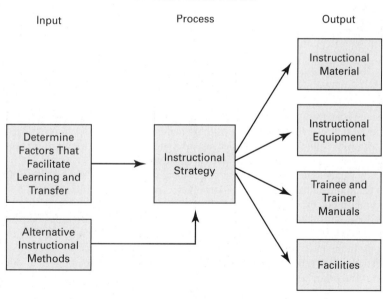

Input | Process | Output

Determine Factors That Facilitate Learning and Transfer

Alternative Instructional Methods

Instructional Strategy

Instructional Material

Instructional Equipment

Trainee and Trainer Manuals

Facilities

Learning Objectives

After reading this chapter, you should be able to:

■ Describe how to develop and implement the following methods of training in a manner that facilitates adult learning and meets training objectives:

- Lecture/discussion
- Computer-based
- Games and simulations
- Role plays and behavioral modeling
- On-the-job training

■ Choose appropriate AV for a given training objective and method

■ Choose the most effective seating arrangement based on the nature of the training

■ Examine a room and determine whether it meets training requirements

■ Describe the key trainer activities that lead to effective training

---

Jack Goes to Training

Jack, a 43-year-old machinist, worked for Scanton Industries for 23 years. It seemed that the need to learn something new was constant, and Jack was getting nervous about his job. The nervousness grew last week when he saw a new batch of equipment arrive. It looked something like the machinery he uses now, but it was hooked up to computers. Bill, his foreman, said, "It looks like you'll be going back to school for a couple of days, Jack. You're going to have to learn how to program your work into the computer." Jack smiled but felt sick to his stomach. He was always good with his hands, but he had never done well in school.

All Jack thought about all weekend was the training he would be going to. He fell asleep Sunday night thinking about it. He was awakened by the phone at 7:00 the next morning. It was Bill telling him training had been switched from the local training center downtown to the local school because of a sudden strike at the training center. The school was the only place available on short notice.

As Jack walked up the steps of the local school, he felt sick to his stomach again. He entered the hall and then the classroom. Everything was similar to what he remembered about school, except now each desk held a computer. Even the smell was the same, and it brought back memories. Some were good (the guys getting together between classes) but most were bad (being yelled at, taking tests, and doing poorly). As he sat in the wooden chair in the back where he used to sit, he looked out the window and began to daydream, just as in high school.

The other 20 trainees were quietly sitting around. All of them seemed as nervous as he. Suddenly someone burst through the door. "Hi, my name is Jason Reston. I'm your instructor for this course. You're here to learn some basic computer skills and how to program the various machinery that you will be using at work. I realize you come from different companies and will operate different machines, but the process for all of them is similar. First I am going to show you how to get signed on and into the program you will

(continued)

(continued)

be running. . . ." Jack was back from his daydream. Well, here we go, he thought.

At lunch Jack and Murray, who sat next to him in class, went to a local deli. "Are you keeping up?" Jack asked.

"Are you kidding? Are we going to be tested on this stuff?" asked Murray.

"I have no idea. If we are, I'm dead," said Jack.

The afternoon went slowly. The trainer simply gave an instruction and the trainees entered the information into the computer, then he gave another and they entered that. "How are we supposed to remember all this?" Murray whispered. The second day was worse. On a couple of occasions Jack was jolted out of his daydream while staring out the window. "Jack," yelled Jason, "Are you with us?" It was 3:00 on the second afternoon when Jason announced that they would be tested to see what they had learned. Jack looked at the test questions. Was he that stupid? He did not even understand many of the questions. Would he lose his job if he failed this test? He could almost hear his boss yelling at him, "You are fired, get out, get out!"

This case is an example of how not to conduct training. The anxiety Jack feels about going to training is exacerbated by the training room and the training itself. As we go through the chapter, think about what you would do to make the training more conducive to adult learning.

Instructional Methods

As Table 6-7 showed, most training methods discussed in Chapter 6 are at least mildly effective in more than one area. Chapter 6 provided information on each method to help you decide which is best suited to meet various goals of training. Now, we discuss the procedure for implementing the training.

LECTURE/DISCUSSION

When the TNA reveals a deficiency due at least partially to a lack of knowledge or to attitudes that are in conflict with the desired behavior, a lecture is an appropriate component of the training (see Table 6-7). A **lecture** is designed to transmit information, and it is most appropriate when addressing knowledge or attitudinal objectives.

If you are there simply to provide some basic information (such as the new benefits package), printed material is likely to be the most effective method. When training requires that trainees understand and integrate material before moving forward, you need two-way communication, not the style used by Jason Reston in the preceding case. Two-way communication is accomplished through the discussion method, which includes questioning.

Questioning

Questioning is a powerful tool that can help trainees discover for themselves the answers to questions asked. Questions also help the trainer determine whether trainees understand the information correctly and help create a common understanding. Trainers should be familiar with a number of types of questions.

Closed-Ended Versus Open-Ended Questions The **closed-ended question** asks for a specific answer. "What are the five strategies for dealing with conflict?" "What is the next step in the procedure?" This type of question is useful when you wish to assess learning or review previous material.

The **open-ended question** requires no specific response. In this case, no answer is a wrong answer—you are seeking an opinion. "What do you think about this method of problem solving?" "How would you approach this issue?" "What did you learn from that exercise?" These types of questions are useful for obtaining trainee involvement, generating discussion, and demonstrating the trainer is willing to listen to trainees' point of view.

Both types are useful. Closed-ended questions are useful when you wish to regain control of the discussion or to assess understanding of specific points. Use open-ended questions when you wish to relax the trainees or explore their beliefs and opinions about issues. Jason Reston could have used some open-ended questions to reduce the anxiety in his trainees.

Overhead Versus Direct Question   An **overhead question** is a question, either open- or closed-ended, directed at the whole group rather than one person in particular. They are nonthreatening because they do not require any particular person to respond. This type of question is useful when trainees are highly involved and readily respond. If no one responds, undesirable levels of tension can mount. However, increased tension is not always negative. Some trainers become anxious themselves if their overhead question isn't answered within 10–15 seconds. To relieve their tension, they answer the question themselves. Effective trainers understand that unanswered questions create tension in the trainees, which helps to focus trainee attention on the material being presented. This topic is discussed further in the "Encouraging trainees to respond" section. When only a few trainees are answering the questions, and it is the same ones over and over, it is wise to revert to the direct question.

The **direct question** is asked of a particular trainee. It is used to draw out nonparticipators and obtain differing points of view. As any trainer knows, a few trainees will often willingly answer any and all questions. If the same few trainees prevail over and over, many other trainees will tire of hearing from them and will withdraw. Keeping everyone involved in a discussion is an important skill required of an effective trainer. Most trainees begin responding to questions once they see that answering a question is a safe and rewarding experience.

Relay Versus Reverse Question   The trainer, when asked a question, re-asks the question of the group. This type of question is called a **relay question**. The trainer is asked, "How would this concept work in a unionized shop?" The trainer would respond, "An interesting issue. Does anyone have any ideas?" Relay questions allow the trainer to hear the trainees' views and then reinforce appropriate responses. It can lead to interesting discussions about the issue, which probably would not otherwise come up.

The **reverse question** is similar, except you state the question back to the person who asked it. Responding to the same question you might say, "Interesting question Bill. Your area is unionized; how do you think it would work there?" Use this approach when you, as the trainer, believe the questioner really wants to provide a personal point of view, but is hesitant. You can also use this technique if you want to get a feeling for how deeply the trainee wants to delve into the question. Be careful in redirecting a question back to the questioner, however. If you overuse it, you could inhibit trainees from asking a question for fear of having to answer it themselves.

Encouraging Trainees to Respond

Asking questions is only half the equation. You need to get trainees to respond. Here are some tips on how to encourage responses:[1]

- Do not rush to fill the silence. Trainers tend to show less tolerance for silence than do trainees. Sometimes waiting them out will work. Remember, the trainees are just learning the material, and it may take them a bit to mentally process through the material to arrive at an answer with which they feel comfortable.

- Ask them to write out an answer. Say, "Pick up your pens and write down a few reasons why workers are not motivated." Then allow them time for this task. Trainees are much more willing to read what they write than answer off the top of their heads.[2] This method also allows the trainer to ask specific trainees to respond as the pressure of the "unknown" question is alleviated. A variation is to ask trainees to share their responses with one or two other trainees and come up with a common answer. This technique further diffuses the accountability.
- Use the **guided discovery** method when faced with no response to a question. As the trainer you would not answer the question, but ask a new question that addresses much more basic material the trainees should already understand. When the correct answer is given, move to a slightly more complex question. Each question is designed to bring the trainees closer to "discovering" the answer to the question themselves. It encourages trainees to respond because the questions are easy at the beginning and the answer to the last helps to answer the next.

To facilitate the involvement of trainees, set the tone early. At the beginning of training, trainees may experience a certain amount of tension and reluctance to get involved. The ice-breaker is an excellent method of encouraging participation. It also helps trainees get to know each other and thereby feel more comfortable.

Ice-Breaker An **ice-breaker** is a game or exercise that prompts trainees to get involved in meeting and talking with others. It is designed to be fun but at the same time generate energy that will transfer to the rest of the training. Would this exercise be a useful way for Jason Reston to start his training? We believe so. The major reason given for not using an ice-breaker is that it takes up too much time; but this assumption is a mistake.[3] Consider the story of the tortoise and the hare. Without the ice-breaker, training starts off fast, but because of the lack of "getting to know others" and making discussion a legitimate part of training, it soon slows down and loses the race.[4] The choice of ice-breaker depends on the size of the group. One approach if the class is not too large, is to break trainees into triads. If possible, set up these groups ahead of time so group members do not know each other. Each trainee interviews one member of the triad, with the third as an observer. The questions should be simple but should help to get to know the person. For example, ask for the following information:

- Their name (for obvious reasons)
- Organization they are from and title (learn about the type of work they do)
- How long in present job (learn about their experience)
- What they like best about their job (learn about work person)
- What their hobbies are (learn about home person)

Once the interviews are complete, each trainee in turn introduces the interviewed person to the total group. This activity gets everyone talking to the total group, provides information on trainees, and releases a great deal of tension. If one of the objectives of training is to increase listening and communication skills, this ice-breaker pays double dividends.

Listening
In order to be effective, the trainer must demonstrate good listening skills. Good listening is difficult, for several reasons.

- We are able to process information much faster than someone speaks, which gives us opportunities to do or think of other things.
- We often believe we know what the person is going to say, so we interrupt to respond.
- We believe that speaking, not listening, is where the power and control are.

Listening therefore requires practice. Active listening, originally developed for clinical counseling, involves three steps:

1. Listen carefully to what is said.
2. Summarize in your mind what was said.
3. Feed the summary back to the individual.

Following this process helps keep you focused, but more important, it confirms to the speaker (and all other trainees) what's been said, leaving little room for misunderstandings. Training in Action 7-1 provides an example of active listening.

Other Techniques for Maintaining Interest

Effective questioning and listening will assist greatly in obtaining and maintaining trainees' interest, but trainers can do other things.

Move Around While Talking This technique does not mean you pace methodically back and forth, but rather you move out from behind the podium. If you must use a podium, move away from it from time to time. If you can, stay away from it altogether. Moving around while lecturing shows that you are comfortable with the material. If you approach trainees from time to time, talking specifically to them, you set a friendly atmosphere. The movement also requires trainees to follow you with their eyes, preventing the "glazed stare" that can occur if the trainer is stationary.

Use Nonverbal Communication Everyone is always sending out **nonverbal cues**, so it is important that these cues are the correct ones. Keep eye contact on a trainee who is asking a question; do not turn your back and walk away while the trainee is talking. Nod your head when a trainee answers a question, and hold eye contact. Also, maintain eye contact with the trainee group as a whole, while you are talking to them. Avoid talking to the overhead projector, the image on the screen, or your notes. Don't fold your arms, which can suggest that the discussion is over or that you are displeased. If writing on the board or flip chart, turn your head to the trainees while talking.

The key to nonverbal behavior is to convey enthusiasm about the information you are discussing. If the enthusiasm is real rather than feigned, this will show in your nonverbal expressions. Think of the last time you passionately argued a point of view. Were your arms out in front of you and your palms up? Perhaps you were moving your hands up and down in short gestures. It is unlikely your arms were folded across your chest.

TRAINING IN ACTION 7-1

ACTIVE LISTENING

Dialogue between trainer and trainee at the training workshop on decision making:

TRAINEE: This is training in decision making but I am in sales. What I want to know is how will this training help me?

TRAINER: You want to know how this training will help you improve your sales?

TRAINEE: No, not necessarily in sales . . . Just help me do my job better.

TRAINER: So you would like to know what the benefits of this training are and how these benefits will help you do your job.

TRAINEE: Yes, that's right.

What if you are not enthusiastic about the material you must present? This lack of energy can happen after presenting the same material a number of times. What do you do? First, you must realize how important enthusiasm is to effective training. Recall training sessions in which you were the trainee. It is easy to distinguish the good from the not-so-good trainer. The good one was enthusiastic. So, psych yourself up. Tell yourself you must generate enthusiasm. Give yourself reasons to be enthusiastic about the material. Remember, the trainees are not as familiar with the material as you. So, starting off enthusiastically will be infectious, for both the trainees and you.

Get Rid of Dysfluencies   Dysfluencies are those "and uh," "like," "um" space fillers injected into speech. Everyone uses them occasionally, but some use them far too often. This tendency is usually more prominent when a trainer is nervous or unsure. It becomes immediately noticeable, and trainees tend to focus on these utterances rather than the material. Videotaping your lectures, or simply asking others to inform you when you use them, can help you get rid of them.

Provide Variety   Recall from Chapter 6 that trainees' attention begins to decline after 15 to 20 minutes of lecture.[5] So, be sure to provide breaks, activities, and the like, to keep trainees interested in what you are saying. Keeping a watchful eye on the trainees can signal time for a break. Even a 5-minute stretch can help. Exercises or games (not to be confused with business games) are also valuable for gaining and maintaining interest (but make sure they are relevant).

Use of Exercises/Games   Introducing exercises or games that are fun and interesting is an excellent method for gaining attention and creating motivation. They are especially useful if they provide an entree to, or an example of, the training objective. These tools need to be used with a clear and definite purpose. We emphasize this point because of the experience of a colleague at a training workshop a few years ago (see Training in Action 7-2).

A number of models incorporate exercises into the learning process.[6] One such model is exhibited in Figure 7-1. This modification of an earlier model from Pfeiffer and Jones[7] allows trainees to experience first-hand a process related to the current training, then hear some information about the topic to compare what they did with what they learned. Then, they process the new information, generalize it to their situation, and attempt to apply it in a more relevant situation. Let's examine this process more closely.

Step 1: The Experience.   The learning experience begins with some sort of activity that ties into the training topic. In this way, all trainees share a common experience from which to begin. This first experience should not be too closely related to the actual work setting.

For example, when training managers to be better interviewers, one of the objectives is to teach them how to develop appropriate interview questions. The first thing you will probably realize is that most managers already believe they are good interviewers. So, how do you convince them training is necessary? To emphasize the importance of sound question development, the exercise (experience) is for them to help a committee select the new leader of a scout troop. Trainees take 10 minutes to develop their own interview questions. Then they meet in small groups and develop an overall list of questions, and the rationale for each. This list is posted on newsprint and discussed.

Step 2: The Lecturette.   After the experience, the trainer provides information (e.g., concepts and principles) related to the topic at hand. This can be in the form of lecture, video, and so on. In our example, a lecture would describe how to develop interview questions related to job requirements. Here you show how important it is to examine the job to determine what is needed rather than simply making up questions that sound good.

Step 3: Processing the Information and Experience.   After the experience and being provided with information regarding the same topic, trainees now work in small groups to discuss the experience, using the information they just received. In our example you might ask

---

TRAINING IN ACTION 7-2

USING GAMES IN TRAINING

A few years ago, Helen went to Amelia Island for a seminar that was heralded as an advanced seminar in process consultation. She even called the instructor to be sure that it would be advanced, not "an introduction to."

At the seminar Helen soon realized that although the other 11 attendees possessed a great deal of experience as trainers, they were not at an advanced stage of process consultation. It was also evident that the trainees were from a number of prominent companies across the United States. About halfway through the 5-day seminar they were put in two groups to learn about the different ways of intervening in a team's process. After receiving the information, the two groups were told to go off separately and develop a game for training the other group.

Each of the participants in Helen's group told of a game that was used in previous training and how much everyone liked it. Helen suggested developing a role play whereby they could demonstrate the various components of process intervention. One of the other trainees said, "No one likes role plays." "That's right," agreed another, and the group moved on to the more enjoyable games they were discussing. When they finally decided they would play the spider web game, Helen asked how they would tie the training into the game. Unanimously, they said that it was not necessary.

"The professor did not say we needed to do that" was the reply. "The game is to get the group interested in training. We'll move to the training after the game is finished" was another reply. Helen insisted that they somehow tie the game to the process consultation training they had been given, and reluctantly two of the group worked with her to accomplish this connection.

Back in the training room, the other group went first, getting Helen's group to play a game. After the game was completed, the professor asked, "But how does this activity tie into the training?" They all looked puzzled, and everyone in Helen's group looked at her rather sheepishly. When it was their turn, Helen's group did tie the training to the game but the professor commented, "It looks like you first decided on what game you wanted to play, then tried to fit the training into the game; it should be the other way around. First think what are you trying to accomplish, then find a game to meet that requirement."

The point to this story is that exercises and games that do not tie into the training objective are a waste of valuable training time. Although games are fun, their main value lies in their ability to reinforce the learning while providing a break in the routine.

---

the groups to analyze the questions they developed and answer the question, "What criteria did we use to develop these questions?" Another question might be, "How are these questions related to the job of scout leader?" Then each of the small groups could report to the total group what they discovered about how they developed interview questions.

Step 4: Generalizability. At this point it is important that the trainees see how the learning is relevant to situations outside the training. According to Pfeiffer and Jones, the key question here is "So what?"[8] You want the trainees to consider how this new information fits with the things they do back on the job. From the analysis and learning that took place, trainees should infer that scout leader interview questions can be developed in a better way and be able to generalize this to other similar situations. In our example, the trainees should decide the use of

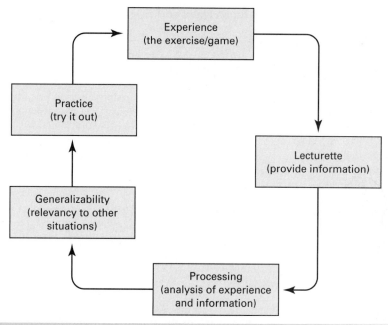

FIGURE 7-1 Experiential Learning Model

job-related information for developing interview questions is appropriate for all jobs. This point would be an opportunity to provide another lecturette on how to examine a job to determine the relevant questions to ask.

   Step 5: Practice.   The trainees receive another task similar in nature so they are able to practice the newly found skill. Note that in this step, the task should be more closely related to the actual job. In our example, the trainees could be asked to develop interview questions for selecting someone for their job.

Specific Behaviors to Avoid

The preceding ideas will help enormously in developing a lecture and training experience that provides the appropriate atmosphere for adult learning. For specific things to avoid when in front of the trainees, and suggestions on how to avoid them, see Table 7-1.

DEMONSTRATION

The demonstration is most useful when your training objectives are to increase procedural knowledge, technical skills, or interpersonal skills. It is often done in conjunction with a lecture, which explains what is being demonstrated and why it is done that way.

If the Choice Is to Use It   Developing a demonstration requires breaking it down into manageable parts or sequences. Just how long one sequence is depends on the total length of the whole demonstration and its complexity. Write out the sequence in a step-by-step manner so as to ensure nothing is missed. Be sure the explanation that coincides with the demonstration is clear. Once all the sequences and steps in the sequence are developed, ask someone to watch the demonstration and provide feedback.

TABLE 7-1 Typical Lecture Presentation Errors and Ways to Avoid Them

Errors	*Ways to Avoid*
Talking with back to trainees while writing on board or flip chart	Don't talk and write at the same time. Prepare flip charts ahead of time when possible. If considerable board work is required, use overhead transparencies.
Using highly technical words, unfamiliar jargon, or complex sentences	If technical words or jargon must be used, provide definitions. Simplify the language and sentences so meaning is clear. Pilot test at least part of the lecture with an audience similar to the trainees.
Providing examples or asides without much relevance to the trainees	The lecturer need not provide all the examples. Ask trainees to provide some of the examples or illustrations. In preparing the lecture, go to the supervisors of the trainees to get examples that are relevant.
Reading rather than lecturing	Prepare an outline of points to be covered rather than a word-for-word script. Be familiar with each point on the outline so that you are able to talk about it without reference to notes.
Speaking in a monotone	Listen to TV and radio commentators, paying close attention to when and in what way they change their tone and the pitch of their voice. Practice fluctuating the tone and pitch of your voice on tape and in everyday conversation. Use pauses in your lecture so you can think about how you want to say something.
Making distracting gestures	Videotape a lecture you are giving and observe your gestures. If they are distracting or irritating to you, the trainees probably feel the same way. Some gestures are useful and keep trainee attention. Don't stand stiff as a board either. The gestures you use are habits and can be practiced out or in.
Leaving projector on with no image or an irrelevant image	Get in the habit of glancing at the projected image as you are talking about the material it displays. When you are at the end of the material, you will see that it is time to turn the projector off, or change the image.
Losing your place in the lecture	Not being able to find your place happens most frequently because your notes are too detailed. Another technique is to check off topics completed.

The temptation is to not spend much time on this process as it seems so easy and obvious. However, you need to remember that the procedure (or whatever you are demonstrating) may be easy for someone familiar with it but for a novice it is usually not.

As the instructor you may conduct the demonstration alone. Trainees can follow along by visualizing each of the steps before they are performed to see whether they follow the correct sequencing. The best scenario, of course, is where each trainee has the materials needed to perform the operations being demonstrated. Each trainee is then able to copy the demonstration process immediately after watching. As trainees are performing the demonstration, the trainer moves around the room giving feedback. Even having teams of four to five trainees sharing the demonstration materials provides opportunities for them to watch others and do it at least once themselves. While one trainee is performing the demonstration, fellow trainees first visualize the steps in the sequence and then give feedback. This approach also presents opportunities for questions, instructor clarification, and group discussion, all of which contribute to a common understanding of what should be done when and why.

COMPUTER-BASED TRAINING

Computer-based training (CBT) a decade ago simply meant programmed instruction. Now CBT ranges from simple PI to virtual reality training, which is highly complex. All CBT training is costly and requires significant lead time to develop. One way to handle this expense is to amortize it over the length of the training. Rick Corry came up with a much more innovative idea. He worked for Owens Corning and was attending a seminar on multimedia training (a type of CBT) put on by a consulting firm. After listening to a presentation he got the idea of sharing the costs of multimedia training. The outcome of his idea is a company called LearnShare (see Training in Action 7-3). Its charter members can access more than 500,000 online development courses.[9] A company can join LearnShare and receive the benefits of membership at a cost of $50,000 for 2 years.[10] Advantages to membership include not only the cost savings due to the ability to buy in volume, but also the ability of member companies to share their "best practices" with each other.[11] LearnShare is successful, and the concept is a great idea for small companies to consider in the pursuit of all types of training, but particularly the expensive CBT.

Most types of CBT differ in what they are designed and used for, therefore we discuss them separately. Then we examine a few of the types of delivery systems used in training today, such as CD-ROMs and the Internet. First, let's look at the types of CBT.

Programmed Instruction and Intelligent Tutoring Systems

Programmed instruction (PI) is most effective for declarative knowledge. If declarative knowledge is the goal of training and there are a large number of trainees, the value of looking at PI is obvious. Once developed, PI can be transferred to whatever media is appropriate for the training (printed, floppy disks, CD-ROM, DVD, or Web site). Trainees then are able to complete the training at their own pace, on their own time (if desirable), and from different locations around the world. PI can automate the repetitive components of training just as machines do in manufacturing.[12] You are able to use PI to train the required knowledge base, and use the classroom and on-the-job for the hands-on practice. PI can also be used to teach procedural knowledge and some skills (computer). Recall from Chapter 6, PI can be a stand-alone type of training or it can be integrated into a multi-method training program.

Intelligent tutoring systems (ITS) are the next generation of PI, with all the advantages of PI and more. Intelligent tutoring systems not only provide the proper level of instruction but also learn from trainee mistakes. By analyzing the types of mistakes trainees make the system is able to alter training strategies for dealing with each trainee.

If the Choice Is to Use It   Development of PI is a long and arduous process, and in many cases not worth the cost and effort required. ITS is even more expensive to develop and requires specific expertise likely not found in your organization. With electronic training technology changing so fast, however, it is difficult to make recommendations that will hold even a short time into the future. ITS is definitely is worth considering, given the enormous advantages over simple PI. Numerous vendors offer relevant PI and ITS training available for purchase. Whether to buy off the shelf or to develop your own will depend on your cost/benefit analysis.

Interactive Multimedia and Virtual Reality

Both interactive media (IM) and virtual reality (VR) are multimedia training and simulations, but we separate them because VR is a much more sophisticated version of multimedia that uses hardware (helmet, gloves, etc.) to place you perceptually and psychologically into an environment. IM places you psychologically into the environment, but perceptually you are

---

THE HIGH COST OF MULTIMEDIA TRAINING

The software developer was extolling the virtues of multimedia training. "It will alter the learning landscape for the next millennium," he said to 200 training executives at a Boston conference. Rick Corry, newly appointed training executive from Owens Corning, listened with mild annoyance. He was recently told by one of these people that they would develop a nice CD-ROM training program for Corning for $150,000. The software developer went on to say that Corry's division would not be able to share it with other business units in Owen Corning. In fact, the corporation would not even own the copyright on the program for 2 years, during which the developer could sell it to anyone else it chose to.

When the speaker asked if there were any questions, Corry looked at all the others in the audience, and said, "I'm just wondering, why don't we get together and share what we have and fund what we need? After all, most companies have similar training needs in a number of areas: basic sales skills, time management, leadership skills, interpersonal skills." The room went silent. The speaker did not say a word. As the session ended, Corry was surrounded by training executives and collected 27 business cards from people who wanted to explore the idea. From that encounter came a consortium of nine large noncompeting manufacturing companies; it is called LearnShare. One of its goals is to develop partnerships with vendors of multimedia training, "but in a manner that is as good for us as it is for them," said Corry. With the consortium's combined revenues of more than $100 billion and 2.2 million employees, they are likely to carry some real clout with vendors.

One of LearnShare's first objectives was to determine similarities in the training needs across the different companies. LearnShare conducted a survey in all nine companies of the training material that was not related to processes or products. The result: 74 percent of the training was addressing the same needs. In other words, diversity training is diversity training no matter where it is taught.

The companies are already sharing non-multimedia training information and programs. Furthermore, they are sharing training space. Motorola, for example, allows managers at Owens Corning who are stationed in the Pacific Rim to sit in on some training Motorola is conducting in its facility there.

Source: Adapted from Blumfield, M. 1997. Learning to share. *Training* 34:38–42.

---

outside of the situation, looking in on it, if you will. Many of the producers of multimedia training use a much more liberal definition of virtual reality that includes most of what we define as interactive multimedia. What seems to be creating the confusion is the difference between IM based on traditional PI versus IM based on some form of artificial intelligence. IM using artificial intelligence is much more realistic in its ability to portray situations and its interaction with the trainee. So when reading about VR in trade journals you need to be aware of these distinctions. For some good reasons that are discussed later few actual VR training systems exist.

Interactive Multimedia Training systems that use interactive multimedia are capable of providing training related to almost any training objective. Most typically these systems take the form of computer-based simulations. The use of video and sound enables the training system to interact with the trainee. It can even be put into 3D for increased realism. Because of the number of new organizations specializing in IM development, the range of training possibilities has increased dramatically and reduced the cost. Organizations such as Volvo Heavy Truck, Michelin, IBM, Motorola, and Duracell make use of IM training. Applications from how to start up and shut down a production line, to "verbal interaction skills" or how to properly interact with an upset customer are available.[13]

One application, Virtual Leader, developed by SimuLearn Inc., utilizes artificial intelligence (fuzzy logic) to dynamically render graphics and dialogue to give the user a simulated real-life environment for learning and practicing persuasive leadership skills. In this example of high-end IM, the system is able to simulate realistic situations, interpret trainee responses within the logic of their leadership model, and show the trainee how his interactions influence simulated employees to behave. The simulation's intent is to teach people to monitor and appropriately balance power, tension, and ideas to align the work of others with the business goals (financial performance, customer satisfaction and employee morale). The authors received training in the use of the simulation and found it to be challenging and engaging. As with any off-the-shelf training product, the trainer will need to carefully evaluate its fit with the firm's training objectives.

If the Choice Is to Use It   Whether you decide to develop an IM program in-house or purchase it from a vendor, you should consider three factors: self-pacing, interactivity, and sophistication of the multimedia.[14] **Self-pacing** allows trainees to choose topics they wish to study, the difficulty level, and rate of instruction. **Level of interactivity** refers to the program's ability to allow trainees to respond to questions. The **sophistication of the multimedia** in this context refers to the relationship between the audio and video portions of the program. A good IM program should rate high on all three factors. Table 7-2 provides a checklist for ensuring that it does.

Should you decide to do it yourself, a number of texts are available to assist in the development of multimedia systems. If you decide to design the system yourself, you need to follow the procedures you would follow in any training design and development process. This approach sounds logical, but in discussions with Nina Adams, president of Adams I Solutions, a firm that designs IM training, it is often not the case. She told us,

> If I had one message to give people considering the use of IM training it is this: Understand the goals of the program you're going to develop before you do anything else. I recently worked on a project where the client was converting a live presentation to multimedia. The major problem was pulling out of the client what they wanted to accomplish . . . what they wanted people who went through the training program to think, do, or feel. It's amazing how many people develop a program without knowing what they're trying to accomplish. How do you know the program is "successful" if you don't know what you're trying to do?

Designing and developing IM training is always an option, but a number of companies such as SimuLearn are in the business. The more sophisticated and complex the material, the more likely you will need to contract with an outside provider. Often these materials can be tailored to fit the objectives of the company. In addition, many training programs can be generalized across organizations as indicated in our earlier discussion of LearnShare. LearnShare examined the training needs of its charter members and determined 74 percent of it was generic, and could be shared. Sharing in the purchase or development of IM greatly reduces training costs to any one company.

You should consider supplementing IM with other methods. This allows each method to provide unique learning opportunities while reinforcing the learning from other methods, thus improving the transfer of the training to the job. Instructor-guided discussion will generally be helpful as a supplement to IM. One thing that is evident after going through the SimuLearn leadership training is the energy it creates for discussing the experience and its connection to leadership development. Some of our conversation focused on the balance of realism and

TABLE 7-2 Points to Consider in Development of an Interactive Multimedia Program

Factor	High If	Low If
Self-pacing	• The pace of the program is entirely controlled by the learner. • Trainees can select menu options to determine the order of modules. • Trainees can skip lessons or segments at will and can exit the program from any screen. • Additional practice and more in-depth material are available upon request.	• The only way to control the pace of the presentation is by using the Enter key. • It is not menu-driven (i.e., the trainee can't select a particular lesson segment or skip segments). • Trainees can exit the program only at certain points.
Interactivity	• Trainees' responses follow instructional segments. • The program tests skills and judgments, not just facts. • The orderly sequence of topics is apparent to the learner.	• The program has long, uninterrupted lesson segments that offer no chance for the trainee to ask or answer questions. • The program tests recall instead of skills. • Segments do not build on one another. • The learner's answers are tagged right or wrong with no further explanation.
Multimedia	• The voices are distinct and natural. • A voice provides program instructions so that the trainee doesn't have to read them. • Sound and visuals reinforce one another. • Visuals use color and motion to reinforce the audio message and illustrate the idea presented.	• The sound or visuals are of poor quality. • There is no direct connection between the audio and visual material (the sound is limited to irrelevant music, for example). • The sound is restricted to a voice saying, "You are correct" or "Try again." • The visuals don't reinforce instructional points.

Source: Anonymous. 1993. Put SPIMM in your CBT. *Training*, February, pp. 12, 14.

artificiality, some on the relation of the leadership model to other models in the literature and some on our rationale for our personal scores. All of these topics, guided appropriately by an instructor, provide valuable insight for the trainees regarding theirs and others' responses and the different outcomes experienced. Other advantages to guided discussion include the following:[15]

- Enthusiasm of a facilitator for the training content encourages learning.
- It provides accountability in the classroom that is missing in e-learning.
- Instructor-led sessions are structured, away from work, and focus on learning.
- Questions and comments of trainees raise important issues and make it comfortable to talk.

- Many prefer to learn in a social situation.
- Learning occurs casually and indirectly when trainees interact.

These advantages do not mean that no learning occurs without these interactions, just that they facilitate additional learning. Another approach is to supplement the video learning with manuals and other material as Duracell did (see Training in Action 7-4). This approach too seems to result in a positive effect.

Virtual Reality   Virtual reality training is the next best thing to being there. It allows training on dangerous situations (police car chases, hostage situations) or other situations (flying, operating heavy equipment), where using the real thing is expensive. VR is accomplished through the trainee being surrounded by material and equipment that create the perception of reality. Often it takes the form of wearing electronic headgear and outer body garments that, through connectivity with a computer, allow the trainee to perceptually, psychologically, and to some extent physically experience a simulation as if it were actually happening. A simulator (to be discussed later) is a different type of virtual reality requiring no electronic headgear.

If the Choice Is to Use It   The cost to develop the software and purchase the hardware varies substantially based on complexity of training. A problem called "simulator sickness" is a more serious concern. This vertigo and general motion sickness comes with prolonged immersion in the computer environment. People show different tolerances in terms of how long they can last in such an environment, which, in addition to the cost and long lead time, makes VR training a risk not many companies are willing to take. For the most part, VR remains in the entertainment industry.[16] If you are going to use it, a number of organizations are available to help you, but expect a long lead time and possible problems with trainees when using it. Then, you need to test for any bugs in the program and check to see that the final product does what the storyboard suggests.[17]

TRAINING IN ACTION 7-4

DURACELL'S INTEGRATED APPROACH TO TRAINING IN CHINA

The battery manufacturing plant was to open in China to serve the growing Asian market demand for their product. They wanted to create a highly visual training process that would rely on graphics, animation, digitized photos, video, and Chinese text. The key component was the multimedia presentation, but it was supplemented with manuals trainees could take with them to use as a reference, printed job aids to assist with recalling more complex processes, and of course "hands-on" practice. It was felt that these backup methods were necessary to aid the trainee in retention and transfer.

The training was comprehensive and included health and safety, operations, quality, and fault finding. The goal was to create a standardized training process that would promote a safe work environment and facilitate the workforce in becoming as productive as possible, as fast as possible. How successful was this training? If motivation to learn is important in training, and we know it is, certainly that was high. From the moment the programs were installed, a crowd immediately formed around the workstations. Employees were anxious to be next to get their personalized training session.

Source: Marquardt, M. 1999. *Technology-Based Learning: Maximizing Human Performance and Corporate Success.* Boca Raton, FL: CRC Press.

Delivery Systems

Methods of delivering CBT are varied. Often when discussing CBT and computer delivery systems, the two are used interchangeably. The most common methods of delivery are:

- Local computers and local area networks (LAN)
- CD-ROM, DVD, local, and distance learning
- Internet and intranet

Local computer systems are housed at a specific location with the CBT loaded onto the hard drive of each computer. If the company uses a local area network (LAN), then it becomes possible to log into training on any company computer, even your own workstation. It allows access to training at any time with minimal inconvenience and minimum loss of time.

The CD-ROM or DVD saves companies hundreds of thousands of dollars in travel and lodging. It is often used to expand centralized training across multiple locations without the cost of sending trainees to a centralized location, or sending trainers all over the country. CD-ROMs and DVDs are small, easy to package and mail to all subsidiaries, allowing trainees to take the training with them wherever they go.

The Internet and intranets are also rapidly becoming a method for transmitting standardized training to satellite plants from a central location. Although many companies do not possess the bandwidth to use the Internet as a feed for training, they are able to download the training through the Internet/intranet, and use it at their location. Another advantage to this delivery approach is that the time trainees spend on the training and any evaluation of trainee learning can be recorded in a central location. It is also cheaper than creating large numbers of CD-ROM or DVD disks and mailing them to trainees.

This ability to provide training to multiple locations, coupled with the general busy lives most of us lead, brings a renewed interest in what is called distance learning. In the past, distance learning courses were called correspondence courses. With the advent of computers, distance learning takes on a new meaning, with options available that significantly improve the teaching process. Distance learning differs from other CBT in that it is instructor-led training. Typically this kind of training consists of a set of learning modules with associated lectures, videos, and trainee assignments to complete (reading, exercises, etc.). In addition discussions are held online through some type of caucus or chat room. Assignments and discussions are monitored by the trainer who can provide individual feedback. Good distance learning systems provide readily available technical support for both the instructor and the trainee. The firm must make the technical systems (hardware and infrastructure) available to trainees to take advantage of distance learning. Additionally, many of the commercially available distance learning systems will only work on certain Web browsers. The old adage "let the buyer beware" still applies, because of great differences in the quality of distance learning systems available.

As one final note, each type of CBT can stand alone, and in some cases this capability is sufficient. However, when possible, you should consider integrating your CBT with other methods. For example, training supervisors in active listening skills through an interactive video would provide the trainee with some level of skill. By coupling the video with some instructor-led, active listening role plays with real people, followed by trainee-instructor discussions of the experience, will lead to a much richer learning. Even declarative knowledge learned through PI could be supplemented with an instructor-led discussion on possible applications of the new knowledge. Remember, all the advantages discussed earlier related to guided discussion apply to any training conducted by an instructor. Combining CBT with these other methods, therefore, can only enhance the learning experience.

What About Small Business?

We already indicated options available to small business in terms of getting together to obtain a common set of training practices. Many Web-based training packages are also available. Like the distance learning mentioned earlier, these packages can vary from simple power point presentations online, to animated graphics, interactive exercises, and simulation.[18]

GAMES AND SIMULATIONS

We discussed some aspects of games and simulation in the preceding CBT section. However, not all games and simulations are computer-based and other aspects to implementing a game or simulation apply across electronic and nonelectronic media. Games and simulations offer many alternatives for trainees to learn through experience. As indicated in Table 6-7, games and simulations are best used for developing skills and attitudes. When you choose a training method to address a KSA, you need to think about the constraints of that format. Sometimes two methods are similar in what they are able to train (e.g., case study and business game), but time constraints permit only one to be used. The following will help you select the method that best fits your training objectives and organizational constraints.

Equipment Simulators

If technical skills in the operation or maintenance of equipment are the focus of training, one of the best instructional methods is the **simulator**. As noted earlier, simulators have long been used in the training of pilots, air traffic controllers, and other positions where errors on the job could be quite serious. These simulators are expensive to develop, but because errors on the job could be deadly, the expense is necessary.

The simulator can occupy the bulk of the training time. Tasks are attempted on the simulator, feedback is provided, then more simulator time is taken. Learning by doing is the major focus. At the same time, the instructor can be available to provide continuous and instant feedback.

If the Choice Is to Use It   Simulators can be used for most psychomotor skills training, but care must be taken in the development of a simulator. A temptation may be to use out-of-date machinery to reduce costs. Why use a brand-new piece of machinery for training when it could be on the shop floor and have a direct impact on productivity? This issue was part of the problem in Training in Action 6-3 (Sales Simulation). What must be taken into account is the reduction in transfer of training that is created by reducing the degree to which the simulation reflects reality. After all, if the skills do not transfer well, productivity is lost and training time and costs are wasted.

In addition to the equipment, the simulation must include all the features of the real situation (fidelity). Imagine a pilot learning how to fly a simulator that did not have a wind factor built in. Suppose in landing a real plane the pilot lines up with the runway and heads straight in, as taught, when suddenly a 30 mile-per-hour crosswind appears. This type of thing happened in Training in Action 6-2 when customers suddenly appeared with different requests and events that were simply not part of training.

The simulation should first require the skills to be displayed without complications from other factors, such as wind in the case of the pilot and customers in the case of the clerks. Once the trainee acquires the basic skills, however, the outside factors need to be introduced in the training. Increasing levels of complication are added to the simulation until the trainee reaches the desired level of proficiency.

BUSINESS GAMES, IN-BASKET, AND CASE STUDIES

As Table 6-7 indicates, if training objectives include developing cognitive skills, the case study, business game, and in-basket are all appropriate methods. However, these are not meant to be stand-alone techniques but are used in conjunction with other methods. Because each method differs in a number of ways, we discuss the requirements for each separately.

Business Games

Business games are used frequently to develop management skills.[19] Many of them are computer based. Generally the trainer works from the master program, and trainees work from their own disk with information related to their business and its environment. Trainees make decisions about what they wish to do and enter this information on a disk, which is given to the trainer. Data from all trainees are entered into the trainer's computer, and the computer generates feedback, which is then provided to the trainees. Computer-based business games typically begin with 50 to 100 pages of information that trainees need to read and become familiar with prior to engaging in the game itself.

Two types of games are intercompany and intracompany. The intercompany games require trainees to compete in a marketplace. The more complex games require decisions on where to build factories, what product to advertise, the level of quality of the product, how many salespeople to hire, how to pay them, and so on. Trainees are assigned to teams who compete against one another in the simulation game. As a result, the decisions made by each team affect the environment they all share.

Intracompany business games require teams or individuals to represent different functional areas in a single company. The process is similar to that of the intercompany, but without the competition. In fact, cooperation is usually required for success in the game. In the general method of instruction, trainees read the complete manual, then meet in teams to discuss a strategy and make the decisions. The team decisions are transferred to the trainer (game administrator) or computer. In organizations using computer networks, the trainee can input the data into the network for direct trainer access. Results are tabulated and fed back to the teams. Teams examine the feedback and any new information in light of the previous decisions and make another decision. This process continues over a number of decisions. Dr. Tony Faria, an expert in the field suggested that a minimum of 12 decisions need to be made in order for trainees to benefit from the exercise. The first four decisions provide trainees with a general understanding of the game and how the various factors interact; the second four provide a framework for competing; and in the final four, strategic decisions are made with enough knowledge to be meaningful.[20] After the final decisions are in and results tabulated, trainees meet to discuss the results, as well as the logic and criteria they used in making their decisions.

A relatively long period of time is usually required to complete all the decisions and conduct meaningful discussion afterwards. Training over a number of days or weeks is typical. Thus, this method would be difficult to use in a 1-day workshop. As indicated earlier, it is not a stand-alone method. Typically, the training program would alternate methods (such as readings, lecture, discussion) with trials on the simulation, continuing in this way to the end of the game, at which point a general discussion would take place. You will need to take steps to create sufficient trainee interest in the game to do the appropriate preparation between sessions to be able to make informed decisions. Typically, this issue is only critical at the beginning of the game. Dr. Faria found that trainees often become quite involved in games, spending a great deal of time determining their strategies.

If the Choice Is to Use It   If you decide to use a business game, you can likely find a relevant one. Available games cover a wide range of topics, such as marketing, accounting, finance, and general management. Make sure to match the game to your learning objectives. Prior to beginning the game and at its conclusion you should point out to the trainees what the learning objectives are and how the game relates to the objectives. These briefings will help keep trainees focused on the key learning points.

A business game requires a great deal of time to effectively incorporate into training. First you need to provide the knowledge base required to operate in the simulation. Then trainees need time to familiarize themselves with how the game works and the information about the situation the game is simulating. Then the game begins. Discussion sessions can take place at particular times during the playing of the game, but the main session would take place at the end. At this point you must take the time to be sure everyone is fully debriefed on game progress and encourage discussion about what was learned. It is useful for teams or individuals to present to the rest of the trainees the decisions they made and the results from those decisions. In these discussions a great deal of learning can take place.

In-Basket

If learning objectives focus around prioritizing, organizing and planning, and decision making, the in-basket can be an appropriate training tool. The **in-basket** is composed of a number of memos, phone messages, and other written requests typically found in an office "in-basket." The trainee must read and respond to them, in writing, in a limited amount of time (1 to 3 hours). The exercise requires a trainee to make decisions about a number of issues and to organize and plan his schedule for when he begins his new job (see Training in Action 7-5).

The in-basket process follows a standard format. Once the trainees complete the in-basket, the trainer conducts a general discussion about the way particular decisions were made and the criteria that were used. For example, the trainer may ask trainees what strategies they used to prioritize the information, asking questions such as, "What criteria did you use to determine which person to contact first when you finally arrived on the job?" "How did you determine in what order to address all the issues?" Then discussion can become more specific and address how trainees responded to actual items: "What did you do about the complaint that was 3 weeks old?"

The advantages and disadvantages of different approaches are highlighted in this discussion. During or immediately following the discussion you provide instructions covering alternative approaches to making the various types of decisions. Conclude with a discussion of the lessons learned and how these can be applied on the job.

It can take as much as half a day to complete the in-basket and the discussion that follows. Although it is a relatively short amount of time, other ways can be employed to reduce it further. Trainees can complete it prior to the start of training or as an evening assignment. In these cases, the time constraints around how much time the trainee can use to complete the in-basket are removed. If you are able to create the in-basket electronically, then the time limits can be retained. If the in-basket is completed outside of the training room, you should examine trainees' in-basket decisions before the training session. This review will allow you to develop meaningful questions and discussion topics for the group. Training time is then used to the best advantage. If time permits, you can provide feedback on the in-basket decisions to each trainee before the training session to help focus the trainees' attention on the areas of most importance to their individual development.

If the Choice Is to Use It   In-baskets are not as readily available commercially as simulations. One reason is that they are relatively easy to develop. You simply examine current jobholders' in-baskets for the material. Take papers from the in-basket, including filler material that requires no action (flyers, memos copied to the person, etc.) and follow the scenario from Training in Action 7-5. Use the trainee's current position as the position in the scenario. To provide the stress of real-life management, the amount of information that needs attention should be more than can be expected to be completed in the allotted time. To determine appropriate actions that should be taken, choose high performers from the job in question, and ask them what they would do. The attraction of the in-basket is that it is developed from real information from the trainees' organization.

TRAINING IN ACTION 7-5

TYPICAL INSTRUCTIONS FOR AN IN-BASKET EXERCISE

Salesperson In-Basket Instructions

Your name is Lee. You have been with Bennett Corporation for 1 1/2 years as a salesperson in the business machines marketing force on the East Coast. A position opened up in the Midwest region a few weeks ago when the salesperson, John Quitt, left the company and his customers without notice. The other salespeople in your new office tried to cover the calls coming in from the accounts you are to be assuming. Obviously, they were not able to handle all the calls, so you must do some catching up. Your transfer to fill this opening is still a week away, but the company flies you out to the midwestern office to go through your predecessor's overflowing in-basket. It is Sunday evening, April 13, and no one else is in the office. In 75 minutes you must leave to catch a plane to the Eastern Region Training Center, and you will not be able to be contacted for the week you are there.

Read through the items and decide on a course of action. It is imperative that you respond immediately because you will not be back for a week. All responses must be in writing so you can leave them for the other office personnel. Responses may include let-ter writing, memos to others or yourself, scheduling meetings, making phone calls (outline what is to be discussed), and so on. You may write your responses on the same memo you received, or the memo pad provided for you. Writing paper is also provided if you wish to write a letter. Be sure to attach any memos or letters to the appropriate item. It is your first trip to the Midwest, and you have not yet met any of your new coworkers.

An organizational chart and calendar are provided for your reference. Remember, you can spend 75 minutes to go through the in-basket.

Remember, every action you take or plan to take must be in writing. If you can't write it down, the assessor will have no way of assessing your performance.

It is advisable to read through the entire in-basket before taking any action.

Time Table

5 minutes	Read instructions.
75 minutes	Read and respond to in-basket items.

Please do not proceed until told to do so

Case Study

The general method of instruction for the **case study** is to ask each trainee to read the case and develop answers to the questions provided. Depending on the number of trainees, small groups can be formed to meet and discuss the case. Incorporating the different perspectives of each trainee, the group again answers these same questions. Then, all trainees meet with the trainer and discuss the case, focusing initially on the posed questions. Answers to these questions lead to different areas of the case. The trainer can refer to a previously prepared list of questions to ask depending on where the discussion goes.

The trainer facilitates the group discussion, keeping the communication climate open while ensuring that the focus remains on important learning points. The trainer acts as a catalyst by calling on trainees for opinions and encouraging others to confront aspects of a position they do not support. An important role for the trainer is to deflect requests from trainees to give the trainer's "solution" to the case.

Suppose problem analysis is the skill being trained. Here it is important that the trainer allow the case to go in the direction the trainees wish to take it, as long as they are pursuing a problem and analyzing it. The trainer must guide the trainees in examining the possible alternatives and consequences of each of their solutions. In this guided discovery approach, the trainer's solution is irrelevant to that process; in fact, it hinders it.

When using a case, sufficient time is made available for individuals to read and analyze the case alone, in small groups (optional), and then as a total group. It can all be done in 1 day, but, especially if the case is long, little time might be left to do anything else. If several training days are to be used, especially if the training is off-site and trainees are staying at a hotel, structured assignments can be built into the evenings. This option reduces the downtime of the training day. Of course, with a 1-day training period, you can always provide the case and ask that trainees read it and answer questions ahead of time. However, this technique is advisable only when you can be sure everyone will in fact read it ahead of time. Trainees are more likely to read the case if they realize they will be required to meet in small groups to discuss it.

If the Choice Is to Use It   If the decision is to use a case, a wide variety are available from various sources. Harvard cases are perhaps the best-known, although in Canada, the University of Western Ontario makes many available. These cases are often based on real organizations' experiences. The advantage of "real" cases is that you can enrich the case with up-to-date information from the organization, as well as "what the outcome of the case really was" and how it affected the company. If the decision is to use an already written case, it is important to make your selection carefully. The case must reflect the objectives of the training. For example, if the training is in advanced marketing mix analysis, the trainer must be sure the case is complex enough to allow such learning to take place.

Writing a case requires a special skill, and if you can locate one that fulfills the objective, it is probably preferable to use it. However, advantages are inherent in writing the case yourself. First, you can write it with the learning objectives in mind and, therefore, make it truly relevant. Second, it provides a real opportunity to assist with transfer of training by writing about the trainees' own organization.[21] The issues will be relevant to the training objectives and to the trainees personally. If you do decide to write a case, guides such as the *Handbook of Creative Learning* can assist you.[22]

ROLE PLAY AND BEHAVIOR MODELING

If the goal is to train in interpersonal skills, the two favored methods are the role play and behavior modeling. Both these methods require interaction between trainees. When assigning trainees to work together, do not pair up trainees who work together on the job for two reasons: first, the trainees might have a difficult time being serious, and second, roles could create animosity if problems already exist between the two trainees.

Role Play

The role play usually starts with one or two pages of background and description of what the trainees are to do. **Role plays** are reasonably easy to develop, and real problems and issues that exist in the organization can be used. They can be strategically placed throughout training to provide not only the skills practice but also a change of pace.

Feedback is an important component in the role play. As we noted in Chapter 6, the trade-offs necessary depend on the method of feedback. Sometimes the trainer asks one set of trainees to do the role play and provides feedback to them, with the help of the other trainees. This method places a great deal of stress on the trainees doing the role play, because all eyes are on them. Another concern with this process is that the role play is designed to provide learning by doing. In the single-group scenario, not everyone is "doing" (although we also do learn vicariously). An alternative is to have trainees rotate through the role play. The problem of stress still persists, however, and a great deal more time is required. A more expensive strategy, in which skilled observers at each role play watch and provide feedback, allows everyone to participate in the role play and receive professional feedback.

A method to consider is setting the trainees up in groups of three: the person creating the situation (initiator), the person who will respond using the skills, and the observer (who will provide feedback). Provide three sets of role plays that are different but contain the same learning points. Also provide sheets of "learning points to look for" regarding the three role plays. Now each of the trainees is given the opportunity to be in each position. The advantage is that this approach reduces the amount of time required to complete the process. The disadvantage is in the quality of feedback. Trainees are generally reluctant to provide negative feedback to peers, and even if they are willing, they are not experts, so feedback may not be accurate. Nevertheless, if it is set up with clear instructions and an understanding of the requirements, it can be an excellent learning tool. Each trainee is able to practice the skills, see how the skills work on them (as the initiator), and watch and provide feedback (as the observer). It may be useful to have the instructor and two volunteers run through exactly what is required (using a different role play) before starting. Another option is to videotape the role play. Then, the tape can be used by the trainee to self-evaluate; it can be used by peers in small groups to evaluate each other; or the trainer could examine the tapes between sessions and provide individual feedback.

If the Choice Is to Use It   Role plays are available in many textbooks and from other sources, but they are also reasonably easy to write. The advantage of writing a role play is that you can tailor it to the trainee population. Many trainees complain that the role play is too artificial. One solution might be to have trainees write their own. In the first session (several sessions are necessary to do this exercise) trainees would participate in some predetermined role plays. Using these role plays as a model, they write one based on their own experience.

Consider the following situation. Arnold is learning conflict resolution skills. Training to date provided him with the opportunity to role play a few different situations in which he used the conflict skills being taught. To make the role plays more meaningful, the trainer asks trainees to write their own role play for the next training session. She specifies that the role play should be a situation the trainee previously experienced, a conflict situation that the trainee did not handle very well.

Generally a role play includes two roles: the initiator (the person who starts the interaction) and the responder (the person who responds, using the relevant skills). Arnold thinks about past situations in which he experienced a conflict with others. Then, using the previous role plays as a model he writes about a disagreement with Chris, his office manager, concerning their computer software. He writes up the background that led to the conflict and what Chris had said to him. This role play will be the writeup for the initiator when he goes back to training. He will give it to a fellow trainee to role play and he will respond. He does not need to write up the responder's role because he was the responder and knows what the situation was. Hopefully the exercise will give Arnold an opportunity to respond in a more productive manner using the skills he is learning.

It is important not to make the role plays too complex or confusing. Generally, three problems are common with the written role play:[23]

1. Problems to be dealt with in the role play are not generally handled at the trainees' level in the organization. Thus the level of generalizability to the job is reduced.
2. Roles are often incomplete or misleading, creating confusion.
3. The script creates too many conflicts that cannot be resolved in the time allowed for the role play.

Some concerns may arise about the trainees' involvement in the role play. For some trainees the role play can be considered "fun" but not real, which lessens the generalizability to the job. Others find it stressful to act out a role with others watching. Table 7-3 provides tips on how to develop and present a role play.

Depending on the method used in providing feedback, the time frame for completing a set of role plays could be from 1 hour to 1 day. Preparing for the role play (along with a demonstra-

TABLE 7-3 Tips for Developing and Presenting Role Plays

Developing

- Carefully create your characters to prove your point. Provide two characters who are going to clash in exactly the way you want. For example, use one player to force another either to use the skills taught or to illustrate what happens when those skills aren't used. Don't write a script (unless you are teaching rote responses), but provide detailed background on characters' habits, attitudes, goals, personalities, and mood, as well as on the business restrictions that motivate or restrain them.

- Use role playing to illustrate one key problem. Don't try for more than one topic or you will diffuse the impact and distract the learners with too much information.

Presenting

- Take the time to introduce the situation. Give trainees enough background to understand what's at stake. Then assign the roles.

- Both the role plays and the discussions can get off the topic. To prevent digression, make sure participants understand your instructions. For example, tell them, "The customer service representative must (1) use the customer's name three times; (2) organize, clarify, and confirm the nature of the customer's problem; (3) empathize with the customer; and (4) offer to do something for the customer." If you plan to use observers to provide feedback, have each of them use an observation sheet to look for key behaviors and to respond to key aspects of the performance.

- If the role play gets off the topic, stop the performance and ask, "What are the problems here? Why isn't the conversation moving in the right direction?" Be assertive to ensure that they stay in character and on the topic.

- After the performance, always discuss what happened. It is when learning takes place. Ask questions of each player, and have the group advise the players. Encourage discussion. Challenge them with alternatives: "What would have happened if . . .?"

Source: Adapted from Mitchell, G. 1993. *The Trainer's Handbook.* New York: AMACOM.

tion) could take 20 to 30 minutes. With a large number of trainees, and each trainee role-playing in front of the rest, it could take the complete day. If the trainees are divided into groups of three, each trainee could do a role play, then return to the larger group and discuss the feedback with everyone in about 2 hours. If the role plays were videotaped, feedback could also be provided by the trainer at a later time. This system would be especially effective in a multiple-day training session off-site, where individual feedback sessions could be scheduled after dinner.

Behavior Modeling

The two differences between behavior modeling and role play are that in **behavior modeling**, (1) technical skills as well as interpersonal skills can be trained, and (2) the trainee views a demonstration of how to perform before being asked to perform.

Specific learning points should be identified, so the trainee recognizes what must be done. Developing a video that depicts the learning points is critical to this method. Although you could use a live model, the video is better for two reasons. First, it will be an accurate, standardized depiction of the required behavior. You can redo it until it is exactly the way you want it. Using a live model leaves room for variations or inappropriate behaviors. Second, you can insert into the video script learning points and the steps being followed. These descriptions allow the trainee to see the behavior and the specific point being highlighted at the same time.

In ideal behavior modeling, trainees watch the video of the model, perform the behavior, watch a videotape of their own performance (if videotaped), and finally receive feedback on their behavior. This method takes a great deal more time than the role play. If videotaping is used, the number of concurrent sessions that can take place is limited by the number of video cameras and VCRs available. Also a sufficient number of trainers must be available to provide feedback.

For maximum effectiveness, everyone must receive the practice and feedback, which, no matter how it is done, will require a great deal more time than the role play. You need to consider this factor in scheduling the training.

If the Choice Is to Use It   A difficulty in using behavior modeling is buying or developing the video of the modeled behavior. A number of videos are available, but it is important to preview them before purchase, because the quality varies considerably.[24] You may encounter the problem of matching the video to your learning objectives. Developing your own video is also a possibility, but cost, your ability to make a professional product, and the time needed may rule out that option. Table 7-4 provides a number of suggestions if the decision is to use behavior modeling.

TABLE 7-4 Things to Consider for Implementing Behavior Modeling

- Carefully select the trainer/program administrator who will set up and conduct the sessions. He or she must be skilled and experienced with this technique.
- Carefully consider whether this technique will meet your needs within your constraints of time and money. Unless you can identify specific skill deficiencies, present a positive model of the appropriate behavior, provide the time for each trainee to practice the behavior under the watchful eye of the trainer, and arrange for reinforcement from the manager of each trainee back on the job, you probably shouldn't select this technique.
- Identify real skill deficiencies in advance of training and involve the potential trainees and their bosses in this process. This activity will gain the key people's attention and their ownership of the objectives of the training sessions.
- Break the skills into small behaviors. Build a module around each small behavior and progress one step at a time, starting with a simple behavioral element, in order to gain confidence.
- Do not emphasize more than seven learning points during any one training module.
- Models used to demonstrate the correct way of behaving/handling a certain situation should have sufficient status to be credible yet easy for the trainees to identify with.
- Using a videotape of a model performing the correct behavior ensures that all groups of trainees will see a positive example and may reduce costs because it is reusable. However, this advantage may be negated, because it is difficult to find a model and a situation likely to be highly relevant and identifiable across diverse groups of trainees.
- Before trainees actually practice the desired behavior, ask them to verbalize the behavioral cues demonstrated by the model and then to visualize their pending performance. Verbalization may help improve generalization and use of the behaviors in new situations.
- A supportive climate that encourages experimentation must be established for the practice sessions. Emphasis on positive reinforcement rather than criticism increases self-confidence and learning.
- After each session, some behavior modeling experts provide a wallet-sized card that outlines the key learning points and critical steps. This reminder acts as a security blanket for the trainees to reassure them that they will know the crucial features as they attempt to apply the training back on their jobs.
- Conduct a review session after the completion of several modules in order to reinforce the learning points and to demonstrate the progress attained by the trainees.
- Manage the consequences of attempting the newly trained behaviors in the actual job situation. Work with the managers of the trainees to ensure that they set attainable goals for their subordinates, remove obstacles that may prevent trainees from attempting the new behaviors, and provide incentives for such attempts.

Source: Camp R., P. Blanchard, and G. Huszczo. 1986. *Toward a More Organizationally Effective Training Strategy and Practice.* Upper Saddle River, NJ: Prentice Hall.

ON-THE-JOB TRAINING

On-the-job training (OJT) is a preferred method for many organizations, especially small business. It is an appropriate approach in large companies as well when only a few trainees need training at one time. Many organizations do not follow a structured approach, however.[25] A structured approach such as job instruction training increases the effectiveness of training.

Job Instruction Training

Job instruction training (JIT) is one of the more effective structured approaches to delivery of OJT. Of the four steps in JIT—prepare, present, try out, and follow-up (see Table 6-6 on page 266)—the first and last steps are most often ignored by companies.

If the Choice Is to Use It Because you are not aware of what needs to be done you might ignore the preparation step. Table 7-5 provides an example of the preparation step for the job of press feeder. If it looks similar to the operational analysis in the chapter on needs assessment, it is. If an operational analysis was previously completed, the majority of the work outlined in Table 7-5 is already done.

The follow-up step may be ignored because it is not considered important. This step, however, is critical to ensure that the trained skills continue as they were taught. During the try-out step the trainee may demonstrate her capabilities in doing the job, but as with anything freshly learned, short-cuts, poor work habits, and incorrect procedures can creep into performance. By periodically dropping by to follow up, you can catch such performance discrepancies and correct them before they became habitual. Following up becomes less important as the trainee's performance becomes consistently acceptable.

Structured OJT is effective when done properly and supported by the organization. The seven steps provided in Table 7-6 help ensure successful OJT.

Apprenticeship

Apprentices spend a required amount of time in a classroom as well as in the workplace. The length of classroom training and on-the-job training varies from job to job. An apprentice cook, for example, requires 1 year of OJT and a week of classroom training, whereas a moldmaker requires 4 years of OJT with three 8-week classroom sessions.[26]

If the Choice Is to Use It Although formal apprenticeship programs are strictly controlled by the Department of Labor, nothing would stop an organization from setting up its own informal apprenticeship programs. The journeyman rank you provide your employees upon successful completion will not be transferable to other organizations, but you can take advantage of the process nonetheless.

Try to find and examine a comparable job with an apprenticeship program, and use it as a model. The classroom training is usually at a local community college, school of technology, or similar institution. Apprentices are usually off the job for their classroom training, but in designing your own you might be able to arrange night school classes, classes on the weekend, or some combination of the two. Correspondence school training is sometimes substituted for the classroom training.

Before venturing out to develop your own apprenticeship program, check with local government agencies regarding the programs available. Given that government is usually willing to help pay for the classroom training part of the apprenticeship program, it may be advantageous to make your program official.

Action Learning

Action learning isn't a method of training, but rather a strategy for implementing other methods. It provides a team of trainees with real problems to solve. It is "hands-on" learning through

TABLE 7-5 Job Breakdown Sheet for OJT

Dept: Metal Decorating   Prepared by J. Smith
Job: Feeder Pressman   Date: June 8

Main Steps	Key Points	Tools/Equipment Material	Safety Factors
Part I (Start of shift)			
1. Check level of fountain solution and refill if necessary.	Ask pressman which solution to use. Scratch mark shows minimum and maximum capacities.	All solutions kept in metal containers in storeroom	Do not spill on walkway.
2. Check level of varnish in wet varnish machine and refill if necessary.	Check card for type of material being used and determine amount of thinner necessary to obtain proper viscosity.	Same as #1	Very volatile and flammable.
3. Wash sponges, bucket, and gum containers.	Use same thinner as in #2.	Same as #1	Do not wash in enclosed area because of fumes.
Part II (Start a new bundle in press)			
1. Request lift driver to bring over new bundle.	Do not wait until bundle on press is almost finished.		
2. Check new bundle to be sure it is the correct one and is in good condition.	Pull the job ticket and check order number; examine top sheets and sides and corners of bundle.	Leather-palmed gloves	Always wear gloves when handling sheets to prevent cuts.
Part III (Whenever press is stopped)			
1. Lower elevator with bundle on it and cover with master sheet.	Lower only until top of bundle is at a convenient height.	Leather-palmed gloves	Wear gloves.
2. Unless otherwise instructed by pressman, wet plate on front unit.	Be sure entire plate is wet; dry spots can oxidize and damage plate.	Sponges and clear water	Be sure press is clear before wetting plate.

Source: Adapted from Gold, L. 1981. Job instruction: Four steps to success. *Training and Development Journal,* September, pp. 28–32.

which solutions to difficult problems are often found, and at the same time the trainees develop important KSAs. Action learning involves six components:[27]

1. Identification of an important organizational problem
2. A diverse group of executives or managers chosen to tackle the problem
3. Team use of a structured problem-solving approach
4. Team is authority to implement the solution
5. A commitment to learning from the process (which is as important as solving the problem)
6. A facilitator who helps the team focus on solving the problem and learning the skills needed to be effective

TABLE 7-6 Steps to Follow for Better OJT

1. Establish policy.

   Prepare a written description that puts the organization "on the record" as supporting structured OJT and makes a commitment to it. Make sure that the purpose of structured OJT is spelled out and is related to the company's other HRD efforts.

2. Establish accountability.

   Make clear who is primarily responsible for OJT. Write it into their job descriptions. Then ensure that part of their performance evaluation is based on how well they carry out this responsibility.

3. Review precedents.

   Make a few calls to find out what other organizations in your industry are doing about structured OJT. Do they provide training on the subject? If so, to whom? For how long? What is the course content? What cost savings can be traced to it? Use this information in efforts to design your program. It will also be useful in case your attempts to improve structured OJT in your organization come under attack. Nothing quiets critics faster than pointing out that "our competitors—or excellent firms in the industry—are doing it!"

4. Design and routinely conduct training on the principles of structured OJT.

   Supervisors and experienced workers are the most likely ones to conduct structured OJT in the workplace. In most organizations, they do not know how to do it. Teach them how and then sit back and take credit for the fantastic results!

5. Provide specialized support for line managers who use structured OJT.

   In most organizations, certain jobs are common entry points for employees. Design "off-the-shelf" lesson plans, job aids (checklists, procedures manuals, and training manuals), individualized learning contracts, and individualized training progress report forms for those jobs. They will save time and effort while improving the quality of structured OJT. Making that kind of support available enhances OJT by providing users with the tools to do it—and makes the HRD department a real partner with line management in improving structured OJT.

6. Avoid turf battles.

   Begin efforts to improve OJT on a small scale, in work units where supervisors or managers are supportive. Use your successes there as a springboard to other units and to additional resources.

7. Consider literacy skills.

   Do not assume that employees—or, for that matter, supervisors—are highly literate. Indeed, take advantage of efforts to improve OJT to assess performance problems that can be traced to literacy issues.

Source: Adapted from Rothwell, W., and H. Kazanas. 1990. Planned OJT is productive OJT. *Training and Development Journal,* October, pp. 53–56.

Many learning activities are embedded in this approach. Individuals must learn to use a common, structured problem-solving approach. They must develop a coordinated action plan. They must learn about the culture of the company and how change is accomplished. All these learning points and more take place with the guidance of a facilitator. The facilitator both facilitates the process and provides training in areas in which the team shows deficiencies. The facilitator suggests readings, provides lecturettes and discussions, and may use other methods to instill the KSAs required for the team to be successful. Many, if not most, **learning points** are achieved by the trainees as they are actually working on a project. However, the learning only becomes shared across the group as the facilitator leads the discussion. Without the facilitator little learning would occur. The managers would simply focus on the problem, ignoring the process, and do what worked in the past.

If the Choice Is to Use It The use of this tool for training must be approached from an analysis of the identified training needs. Putting together a group to solve a problem without this focus is nothing more than creating a task force. Thus, if executives need to develop in areas such as communication, team, and problem-solving skills or need a better understanding of the company culture or how to implement change, this method is a useful way to provide experiential learning opportunities. However, you must first carefully identify the primary KSAs you wish to derive from the experience. You will then need to make sure the individual team members come with the prerequisite KSAs needed for developing the higher-level KSAs. The cost of the training includes the cost of the facilitator, the trainees' time away from regular duties, and the cost of problem analysis, solution identification, and implementation. These costs must be weighed against the value of the solution produced and the increase in KSAs of the team members.

Coaching

The main difference between coaching and traditional OJT is that in **coaching** the supervisor continues to analyze the subordinate's performance, plan mutually acceptable action, create a supportive climate, and motivate the subordinate to improve.[28] Effective coaching requires a relationship between the coach (supervisor, peer) and player (employee) that motivates the employee to seek help from the coach in order to be a better performer.[29] Therefore, the role of the supervisor must change from controlling to collaborating.

Just as a needs assessment should be undertaken before it is decided that training is required, the supervisor should examine some basic issues before assuming that coaching is needed. Figure 7-2 outlines the basic questions the supervisor should ask. Note the similarity to Figure 4-1 (page 118) in the discussion of needs analysis.

In most cases, the coach is the supervisor or peer responsible for improving specific performance deficiencies. However, a significant increase occurred in the use of consultants as coaches for upper-level managers in recent years.[30] We discuss this trend in greater detail in Chapter 10.

If the Choice Is to Use It   Once it is decided that coaching is necessary, the five steps laid out in Chapter 6 should be followed. Skills required to be an effective coach are similar to those for an

FIGURE 7-2 Assessment of Need for Coaching

Question		Response
Do any obstacles in the system prevent effective performance?	⟶ Yes ⟶	Remove obstacles or revise expectations.
Do negative consequences follow good performance?	⟶ Yes ⟶	Change the consequences.
Do positive consequences follow poor performance?	⟶ Yes ⟶	Change the consequences.
Is the employee aware that improvement is expected?	⟶ No ⟶	Provide proper feedback.
Does the employee know how to improve?	⟶ No ⟶	Train or coach.
Could the employee improve performance if he wanted to?	⟶ Yes ⟶	Coach.

effective trainer. Good questioning techniques, active listening skills, and good feedback skills are all essential when coaching.

Mentoring

Mentoring is a form of coaching except it is usually not done by an employee's supervisor, and it is not as continuous as coaching. In the mentoring process a senior-level manager provides guidance to a junior-level manager (usually more than one organizational level separates them). In the past, mentoring was mostly informal, but more recently some organizations formalized the process.[31]

A number of features characterize successful mentoring programs, all of which should be considered if the decision is to use mentoring. These features include the following:[32]

- Top management support
- Integration into the career development process
- Voluntary involvement
- Assignment of mentees to mentors
- Relatively short phases to the program
- An established orientation
- Monitoring of the process

As in any organizational intervention, top management must truly support it. Allowing mentoring activities to take place on company time is one way of sending the signal that they are important. Providing rewards to successful mentors is also a way of indicating it is an appreciated behavior.

Also, mentoring needs to be integrated into the overall career development process. It must be seen as an extension of the mentees' development process. Internal access to training is needed, along with development programs and materials to supplement mentor/mentee activities. The mentor program needs to be voluntary. Forcing managers to take part in mentoring activities will do more harm than good. A reluctant mentor cannot provide the interest and motivation needed to assist someone in the organization.

It is helpful to assign mentors to mentees. Most formal mentor programs require a nominating procedure. Mentees are nominated by their supervisor and matched by the director of training to a mentor. It is a good idea to allow for switching, particularly if a match does not seem to be working.

Keeping each phase of the program short will help prevent potential mentors from being reluctant to take on mentoring responsibilities. Six-month cycles are enough time for a mentor to help a mentee in a significant manner while not being tied indefinitely to an assigned mentee. Mentors who find the process successful will sign up for another stint.

Provide an orientation for mentors and mentees. This is a formal process by which they can meet and hear about what worked in the past, and the role expectations for both in the mentoring relationship. The mentors should be allowed to do their mentoring in a manner congruent with their style, not be forced to follow a strict format. The orientation can provide some successful past mentors, who could describe how they took on the role. Presenting a few different approaches will reinforce that it is not necessary to follow a specific process.

Finally, it is important to monitor the mentoring process. This monitoring is critical to its success. At specific check points, both parties can be surveyed about the progress of the mentee. This survey could take the form of a meeting to discuss what has happened, a request for mini-reports on progress, or simply phone calls to ask how the process is working. Use this information to highlight successful mentoring relationships in company newsletters and other communications. This publicity will keep individuals motivated and keep the program visible. Plotting the career paths of mentees is another method of showing the success of the program.

Trainers for OJT

Apprenticeships use journeymen to train apprentices; coaching uses supervisors to improve subordinates' job skills and knowledge. OJT in general uses coworkers and supervisors as trainers. None of these people started out to be a trainer and likely none has formal training in how to be an effective trainer. Thus, any company that uses OJT should carefully consider the cost benefit of providing train-the-trainer training. In Chapter 6, we discussed the types of training OJT trainees should receive. Other issues related to OJT trainers are discussed here.

Selecting OJT Trainers   The best trainer isn't necessarily the person who can do the job the best. The best trainer is the one who has a good command of the job and who can interact effectively with others. Obviously, the trainer must understand and be able to perform the job well, but unless that person can also communicate knowledge to others in a supportive manner, little learning will take place. If those selected to be OJT trainers don't have these skills, training the trainer is indicated.

Motivating the OJT Trainer   Not only do trainees need to be motivated to learn, trainers need to be motivated to train. Trainers should also recognize the necessity of closely observing the trainee to ensure adequate skill development and to prevent the trainee from causing damage to equipment and property or injury to self or others. For it to happen, OJT trainers must be rewarded for spending the time training as well as for doing their job, which can be done in a number of ways. The important thing to remember is that someone who is training another employee should not be expected to perform at the same level of productivity as someone who is not. Some rewards must be provided for giving effective training. Think back to the proper process of OJT. It requires the trainer to methodically go through the steps of particular tasks and then observe as the trainee does the same. This process requires time, which will take away from the productivity possible if the trainer was doing his own job.

One way to motivate the OJT trainer would be to institute a different (higher) classification for someone who was capable of training other employees. This designation would provide prestige (and perhaps more money) for the position. At the same time the measure of performance for the trainer could be how well the trainee performs at the end of the formal OJT. Here, the motivation would be to turn out good trainees. If it is not done, and trainers are expected to perform their regular job at a similar level as nontrainers, then the result might well be what happened at a food service and vending company. They used experienced vending machine service route drivers to train new route drivers. The company attributed a history of high turnover among trainee drivers to the nature of the job, the low starting wage, and the hours required. The arrival of a new human resources manager led to a reexamination of this problem. Discussions with current trainees and trainees who had voluntarily terminated their employment in the recent past revealed that some of the trainers would do all the easy work (restocking the machines) and make the trainees do the "dirty" work (performing maintenance on the machines). Others wouldn't let the trainees do any of the work because it "slowed them down." Because the drivers were paid on the basis of the number of machines they serviced, rather than on an hourly rate, they were essentially doing the training for free.

What About Small Business?

OJT is the training method of choice for the small business. Many small businesses use peer training because they lack a budget for any formal training. The value of following the procedures outlined in JIT, whether the supervisor or a peer is to be the trainer, cannot be overemphasized. An up-front investment of time to train the OJT instructor and prepare the proper plan will ensure an optimal return on investment. Research suggests that structured OJT such as that described in JIT can get workers up to speed on their jobs in half the time regular training takes.[33]

Another important consideration is choosing the instructor. You need to choose an employee with a solid work ethic who correctly models the appropriate behaviors you want emulated. Remember, trainees will probably go to these trainers for help and other general information. These trainers will likely become de facto mentors to the trainee. Although these issues are important for any size organization, the impact on a small company will be greater, so these issues are more crucial. Of course apprenticeships are also excellent ways for small businesses to obtain a skilled workforce.

Audiovisual Enhancements

Identifying the appropriate type of media for each part of training is important to the development of the training program. If audio or audiovisual tapes need to be developed, a longer time frame or a larger budget (if they will be produced by a professional) will be necessary. Table 7-7 shows advantages and disadvantages of the various audiovisual methods.

TABLE 7-7 Advantages and Disadvantages of Audiovisual Aids

	Audiovisual Aid	*Advantages*	*Disadvantages*
S T A T I C	Charts/Posters	Ability to develop lists with trainees enhances group interaction; can post and refer to during training; use in lighted room	Difficult to view from a distance; bulky to transport
	Overheads	Able to overlay systems, flowcharts, etc.; easy to use; can see from a distance; use in lighted room	Can be distracting; projector can block view
	Computer-Generated Overheads	Able to develop flashy visual aids; use of color and control of points (one presented at a time); easily modified; easily controlled	Flashy presentation could distract from training; rely heavily on technology
D Y N A M I C	Audiotapes	Can learn at any time (even traveling to work); reusable	Single sensory input; no interaction
	Film and Video	Can demonstrate appropriate behavior; good for receiving personal feedback; can present and integrate conceptual information; some commercially available are reasonably priced and appropriate	High material cost; very high development cost; need to dim lights; store-bought not specific to company
	Computer-Generated Dynamic Presentation	Can be very flashy presentations; use of color and sound provide different stimuli for obtaining interest	Same as computer-generated overheads

STATIC MEDIA

Whether you are using a poster, newsprint, chart, or overhead, you need to be aware of certain rules when you are developing these static media. The biggest mistake made in using this medium is cramming too much information on the one poster, sheet, or overhead.

Newsprint, Charts, and Posters

Newsprint is probably the most often used aid in adult training. You can list learning objectives on it and post it on the wall for everyone to see throughout the training. During the training session you can generate lists related to the topic being trained, which is an excellent method for encouraging participation. These trainee-generated lists can be displayed on the walls of the training room to refer to as necessary.

Trainers can also prepare lists ahead of time. Depending on how they are prepared, these lists could be considered posters or charts. Guidelines for creating newsprint information (as well as posters) are similar to those for overhead preparation (see Table 7-8). Print in large (3-inch) letters using a wide-tipped marker. Keep the number of points to six or seven, and keep them brief.

Overheads

Most word processors are able to develop large print suitable for overheads, and photocopy machines or printers can transfer the image to a transparency. The advantages of the **overhead** are that it is used in a fully lighted room, and it is possible to build (overlay) a model or other visual aid. As an example, consider training on how to put together a piece of machinery. The first transparency would be the base. Each piece to be added could be on a separate transparency and you would "build" a model of the machine with successive overlays as you spoke. If the training was on how to complete forms, you would place a copy of the form on the overhead and write on the transparency to show the proper procedures. Similarly, you can place blank transparencies on the overhead and write on them as the discussion creates relevant points.

When you make transparencies ahead of time, it is useful to frame them with cardboard to keep them from sticking to each other or sliding off the table. Also number them so they will not be out of order when you are training. Table 7-8 provides some guidelines for developing transparencies.

Slides

Slides can provide a clearer look at things. Close-up enlargements of parts can present details not otherwise seen. The slides can be synchronized with an audiotape so the presentation is fully automated.

TABLE 7-8 Guidelines for Producing Transparencies

For each transparency:
- Present one idea or concept.
- Print in large letters (1/4- to 1/2-inch type, larger if by hand).
- Limit to 6 or 7 lines with 6 to 8 words per line.
- Use color for impact.

Computer-Generated Projection

Computer-generated projections are similar to overhead transparencies, but they can be presented in a more sophisticated manner using various software packages. They offer the advantage of combining art, photographs, and other graphic images with text. They also make your presentation more professional and give it pizzaz.

Resources Needed

The resources required differ according to the visual media used. Charts and posters simply require vertical surfaces to which they can be attached and a method of attachment (masking tape is an old favorite of trainers). However, resources for producing these visual aids can range from simple paper and markers to the cost of a graphic designer and professional printer.

Creating overhead projections may require several types of equipment. However, the simplest way is to create the material on a computer and then print directly to the transparency. A color ink-jet printer allows you to create professional-looking overhead transparencies. Special color transparency film is required for the ink-jet printer unless you have a color laser printer or a color copier that processes transparency film. Using overhead transparencies requires an overhead projector.

Creating computer-generated projections requires a computer of sufficient capability to handle the presentation software. For the computer-generated projections you need a computer and an integrated LCD/projector machine.

Projection media require a projection surface, usually a screen, but occasionally an off-white wall, free of objects, can be used. The projection area must be capable of being darkened so the images are clearly visible.

Planning the Use of Static Visuals

For effective static visuals, the room setup must allow easy viewing by all trainees. Seating should be arranged to allow a clear path for the projector's beam, and the projector should not block the trainees' view of the screen. Line of sight should also be clear for newsprint information. Here are some additional considerations:

1. Rehearse the presentation using the static visuals on the equipment in the room where training will occur. Doing so will reveal all the things you had forgotten about as well as the things you didn't know (e.g., the circuit breaker for the outlet won't handle the computer projection unit and the video equipment at the same time).
2. Bring extra equipment accessories. Extra projector bulbs, cables, extension cords, and easels should be at the training facility before training begins. Remember, Murphy's Law applies to trainers too. In fact, trainers face the following addendum: The more important the event, the more likely things will go wrong. Extra precautions are always wise.
3. Arrive at the training site early and check that all equipment is in working order. Make sure visuals are ready to operate when training starts (correct order, right side up, computer-generated projections ready, etc.).
4. If you are using computer-generated projections, bring along a set of traditional overheads (transparencies) for emergencies.

Protocol

When you use static visual aids, keep these points in mind:

- When using an overhead, place the pointer on the overhead rather than pointing at screen; doing this allows you to keep your focus on the trainees.
- Turn off the projector when it's not in use.
- Keep the line of sight to visual aids clear by placing the aid in a strategic location.
- Do not talk to the visual aid, but face the trainees. Turn to the visual aid to identify a point, then turn back to the trainees.

- When a visual aid is no longer being discussed, remove it.
- When you write on newsprint, try as much as possible to continue to face the trainees; do not stand in front of the easel or face it.

Trainee's Manual

Although not generally considered a static visual, the trainee's manual is an important guide to the training. To keep the trainees' interest and their complete involvement in discussions, you will find it useful to provide notes on all the information that you will be presenting. The trainees then will be able to pay more attention to what you and others are saying and doing, rather than being concerned about taking notes. The manual often includes all lecture materials, learning points, and supplemental readings. It also includes any exercises and some blank sheets for jotting down notes and lists in small group meetings.

The best holder for the manuals is a three-ring binder so the trainee can add information as training continues. It is sometimes better to keep certain information from the trainees until it is time to use it. Exercises are an example of material that should be held back. You do not want trainees being distracted from the current topic by trying to figure out various problems ahead of time.

Instructor's Manual

The instructor's manual provides all the information from the trainees' manual, as well as information on what the trainer needs to do and how to do it. It is a visual aid for the trainer. The format is to have the lecture notes on the right-hand side of the page, and the instructions for the trainer on the left-hand side. Instructions range from when to generate lists on newsprint, to what some of the expected information on the list might be and how to respond. For an example page from an instructor's manual see Table 7-9 on the following pages.

DYNAMIC MEDIA

Audiotapes

The **audiotape** is generally considered a stand-alone type of training. Like the straight lecture, it provides information. If you use the audiotape as a presentation, then the same rules that apply to presenting a good lecture apply to the audiotape.

Audiotapes can also be used for taping the actual sounds, or recreating the sounds required for training. For example, if you were training mechanics to understand the different sounds a transmission makes when it is healthy versus damaged, you tape the sounds from actual problem transmissions. Once developed, the audiotape could be used to teach trainees to recognize the different sounds an automobile transmission makes and what they mean. The same audio could also be used for testing trainees.

Moving Film and Videos

We tend to recall "stories" much better than general information. Well-told stories tend to get our attention and are more easily encoded into memory.[34] In developing a video, you face two issues: developing the story to catch the attention of the trainees, and the process of putting the story on video.

Construction of a story line requires five elements:[35]

1. A person (main character), has
2. a problem or conflict. The person
3. experiences an intervention/insight that
4. changes the main character, and
5. creates a new order. If you follow these rules in setting up your story, you will be successful.

Table 7-10 describes the points to consider in developing the story.

TABLE 7-9 Sample Instructor's Manual

Instructor's Notes	Time Schedule	Points to Be Covered	Reference

INSTRUCTOR'S NOTES
Moving forward: A role play

Purposes

1. Develop an understanding of how management (if you are union) or union (if you are management) felt about QWL involvement. (Role reversal)

2. Provide some insight into what the next step should be if one wishes to pursue a QWL effort.

3. Demonstrate concerns about moving forward in a QWL effort and the importance of addressing these concerns.

Instructor preparation

- This role play is designed for small groups of 8 people each (4 union and 4 management). Because the total number of participants in a given orientation will vary, you will probably have some unequal groups.

- Your objective should be to divide the groups so the total number in each group will be roughly the same.

Introduce role play and give instructions

Role play: Instructor preparation

- While the role plays are under way, the two instructors should be circulating among the various groups to give assistance as needed or to observe dynamics.

- Be sure to keep watch on the time and to give a notice when there are 5 minutes left to go.

- When time is up, ask for volunteers to tell:
  - How far they got
  - What decisions they made
  - How they felt (Role reversal)
  - What they learned

MOVING FORWARD: A ROLE PLAY

Hand out 10 cards, color coded for union and management.

Up until now, we have been concerned with discussing what QWL is, some advantages regarding getting involved and so on. But where do you go from here? If you decide to get involved in QWL, what's the next step?

With this next exercise, we hope to help you find the answer to some of those questions and at the same time have some fun. We are going to do this by letting each group answer the question: "Where do we go from here?"

We are also going to give everyone in the group a role to play. How many here have role-played before? . . . WAIT FOR SHOW OF HANDS.

I am sure each of you can vouch for how realistic and interesting role plays can be once you get going.

Each group will be made up of 4 union representatives and 4 management representatives. We would ask that you take a role opposite to the position you hold in the organization. In other words, if you are a union person, take a management role, and if you are a management person, take a union role.

(continued)

TABLE 7-9 (continued)			
Instructor's Notes	*Time Schedule*	*Points to Be Covered*	*Reference*
POST ROLE PLAY DISCUSSION.		**Role Play**	
Who would like to tell us how far they got in the project?		We have just handed out cards with these names written on them.	
How many completed all the points on the chart?		POINT TO PREPARED EASEL	
What did you come up with?		ROLE PLAY	**Prepared Easel**
Anybody come up with something different that they would like to share?		Management (Green) Union (Blue)	
So what do you think the purpose of the exercise was?		Lynn Pat Jan Jamie Tony Lee Kelly Fran	
What did you learn by participating in the role play?		So if you are a management employee, choose a card with names written in blue; if union, choose green names. This will give you one of the opposite roles.	
• If in Role reversal someone comments about seeing the other point of view, pick up on that. Emphasize that it's important to understand perception. How people see things is affected by their position, and it's important to try to understand where the other person is coming from.		If your table does not have an equal number of union and management individuals, then choosing an opposite role will not be possible, so just take a role similar to your position in the organization (management or union). Take the appropriate card and place it in front of you now.	
• If someone says they didn't get very far or it's really a complicated issue, pick up on this and emphasize that it takes a long time to get QWL going and we can't expect them to accomplish too much in this short of a time. Many meetings of longer duration are spent to get a QWL project going.		Any questions so far?	
		Before we begin, there are a few points I would like to cover about the role play.	
		(TURN TO NEXT EASEL PAGE)	
Also regarding complexity, suggest that it is a difficult thing to implement and one must be patient and realize that it is not an easy exercise. Implementation of a QWL project does take a lot of hard work—which can be at times frustrating (as you no doubt noted on this exercise).		ROLE PLAY	
		DO'S • BE YOURSELF • IMPROVISE OR MAKE UP FACTS THAT ARE NOT COVERED IN THE ROLE	**Prepared Easel**

TABLE 7-9 (continued)

Instructor's Notes	Time Schedule	Points to Be Covered	Reference
		DON'TS • DO NOT GO BACK AND READ ROLE ONCE YOU BEGIN	
		• DO NOT ASSUME SOME OTHER PERSONALITY	
		First (point to easel), be yourself. Most people are very good at acting if they make up their own lines. So act like you would in any situation.	
		Second (point to easel), improvise as necessary. If a question is brought up that is not covered in the roles, make up an appropriate answer consistent with your role. Use your own experiences and beliefs to help you in this.	

The second issue is the development of the video. Developing a training video is not just a matter of getting a video camera and a blank videocassette. In the first step, called storyboarding, you write exactly what will happen in the story, paying particular attention to the points outlined in Table 7-10. Once the story is developed, you are in the preproduction stage, and you need to acquire the resources necessary to produce the video. This process includes preparing the props and set, casting the parts, arranging for costuming, identifying necessary equipment and crew, and so on.

Scheduling for the shooting requires you to consider issues such as the rehearsals, the order in which scenes need to be recorded, and finally the actual days and times for recording. When the scenes are recorded, the various segments are then edited and integrated into the final product. All of these tasks require a solid understanding of the process. If you don't have a substantial background and experience in video production, the final product is likely to have an unprofessional appearance.

Computer-Generated Presentations

If you decide to develop computer-generated AVs, you can certainly enhance the credibility of training, especially if a great deal of lecture is required. The basic components your system will require are a portable computer (if you need to go off-site, for example) and software to run the system.

A number of programs are available that can do the job. Once you put all the information on the disk, you need to conduct a trial run to become comfortable operating it during training.

TABLE 7-10 Points to Consider in Creating a Story for a Video

Have one main character
- Must be realistic (not perfect)
- Have a problem, but otherwise successful

The problem
- Character has a major problem
- Can be personal internal struggle, or an actual problem with another employee
- Must build tension with this problem, character should come close to disaster (e.g., threaten to terminate employment)

Intervention/insight
- Character gains insight from
  mentor: Obi Wan Kenobi in *Star Wars*
  dream: Ghosts in *A Christmas Carol*

Too much story/too little story
- The general consensus is that if the story introduces too much extraneous material and too many actors, the points get lost.
- The other extreme is not enough story so trainees do not really understand why things are happening. Solid storyboarding will assist in preventing these problems.

Use of humor
- Humor can actually assist recall. For this reason, if you use humor, make sure the humor comes from the learning points. This way when trainees recall the joke they recall the learning point.

Learn from others
- Examine video developed by professional

Source: Adapted from Sneed, L. 1992. Making your video tell a story. *Training*, September, pp. 59–63.

Planning the Use of Dynamic Media

How close to the AV equipment should trainees sit in order to adequately view the material? A rule of thumb (whether static or dynamic visuals are used) is 1 foot of trainee distance from the screen for every inch of screen size. Thus, for a 32-inch TV screen the maximum distance trainees should be from the screen is about 32 feet. As for the sound, unless the room is wired and the TV adaptable to external speakers, volume can also become a problem. Adequate volume for those who are 7 feet from the TV will be too low for those who are 32 feet away, and making the sound adequate for those who are furthest away can make it too loud for those in the front. One solution is to create a semicircle around the TV, although this arrangement limits the number of people who can be comfortably seated. Learning to operate the equipment is also more difficult than with the other methods. Little skill is required to operate an overhead or slide projector. Significantly more skill is required to operate the computer or the image projection equipment and to load the software and get it ready to run properly. Finally, most projection equipment built prior to 1995 required dimming the lights so low that the atmosphere was more conducive to sleeping than learning. However, new technology solved that problem.

As with anything mechanical, it is important to try the system before training begins. Arrive early to check out all the equipment. Be sure remote controls for lights, video, and so on are operating and you understand how they work. Put the equipment through a trial run. Have a backup for any video or disk that will be used. Video machines do eat tapes, and disks do crash. Most training facilities have more than one VCR and computer, which are critical if an important part of training requires their use. Find out where the extra VCR is kept, and carry a portable computer as a spare, or arrange for backup overheads. Breakdowns do happen.

Protocol

When you are using dynamic visual aids keep these points in mind:

- Turn off the TV/computer or other visual aids when you are not using them.
- Keep the line of sight to visual aids unblocked. If the group is large, use two TVs placed in strategic locations connected to the single VCR.
- When you are talking about or discussing an issue (even for a short time) between film clips, turn the lighting up. Do not attempt to discuss issues in a darkened room.

Facilities

An important part of any training program is the environment. The best training is of little value if it is conducted in the midst of distractions, uncomfortable seating, difficulty in seeing audiovisual presentations, or similar problems. Attention to these issues, therefore, is critical. This issue was briefly discussed in Chapter 5 in the section on eliminating distractions.

THE TRAINING ROOM

Whether you design your own training facility or simply go off-site to train, you need to consider many factors in making your training room a learner-friendly environment. The following describes the type of training room that is ideal for most types of training.

It is best if the room is windowless. Windows can distract the trainees, as was evident in the case at the start of the chapter. Jack was easily distracted from the training for many reasons, but the window gave him a way to avoid the training. If the room does contain windows, be sure they are fitted with shades or curtains you can close. Light coming through the windows can create glare as well as be distracting. The walls should be blank—not decorated with pictures or brightly painted—and a nice neutral color, such as beige. Lighting should be adjustable so it can be dimmed for overheads, video presentations, and the like and be made brighter for the lecture, discussions, and exercises. The room should be close to square in shape. Rectangular rooms limit the type of seating arrangements possible. A rule of thumb is to avoid a training room whose length exceeds its width by more than 50 percent.[36] The room should be carpeted and have a sound-absorbing ceiling.

If the training is off-site, you want assurance that the walls are reasonably soundproof, especially if dividers separate the room. If it is your own facility, ensure that soundproofing is built into the room. Nearby breakout rooms for small group work would also be desirable and should be soundproofed.

The room should be equipped with its own temperature control, with quiet heating/cooling fans. This point may sound trivial—after all, who would build a training room with noisy fans? The problem is that contractors are good at building buildings but do not specialize in any particular type. When the new University of Windsor Business School was being built, a team of faculty members provided input into the design of the classrooms. This input helped tremendously in the development of user-friendly classrooms, but the team didn't think about fan noise. The result: one of the few complaints about the new building is fan noise. When the fans are on, it becomes difficult to hear students asking or answering questions.

Under the heading "nice to have," consider the following. Have tracks built onto the walls with a slot into which newsprint can be pushed, allowing for the hanging of charts and posters anywhere in the room. Whiteboards built into the walls at strategic locations will allow easy access to large writing surfaces. Built-in consoles that control lighting, audiovisuals, and computers provide easy access to the operation of these training aids. Be sure to have a remote control so trainers can operate the lights and AVs from wherever they are standing.

If AVs are built into the facility, make sure they are situated so that all trainees are able to view and hear them. Also make sure that they are not built into places where the equipment itself blocks sight lines.

Furniture

Choose tables and chairs rather than student desk-chairs. Tables should be movable so they can be set up in any configuration. An ideal table size is 5 feet long and 2½ feet wide. This size allows two people to sit comfortably on one side. Many configurations are possible by arranging the tables. Putting two tables together makes a 5-foot square where eight people can hold a group discussion.

Obtain padded chairs that are cloth covered (not vinyl), have castors, and are able to swivel. Trainees will be required to sit for extended periods of time, and comfort is important. In addition to providing overall comfort, the swivel and castors allow for ease of movement when trainees must form small groups or turn and work with another trainee. Armrests are also preferred. Being able to lean back and rest your arms creates a relaxing environment, conducive to learning.

Furniture Setup

The seating arrangements depend on the type of training being conducted. The typical configurations are classroom, U-shape, conference, and circle. The arrangement determines the degree of formality and where the attention is focused. It also affects the level of two-way communication.[37] To appreciate this point, consider the two extremes, circle and classroom (A and B in Figure 7-3). The classroom style (B) places the focus on the trainer and limits two-way communication between trainees, because the trainees are all facing one direction. If no tables are used, more trainees can be accommodated. This arrangement is called theater style. When a trainee sees such a setup, her role is clearly defined in her mind: she is there to listen. Now consider the circle. Here the focus is evenly distributed; no single person is being looked at. A trainee sees this style and his role is also defined: he will be a part of the discussion. Furthermore, this lack of focus makes it easier for trainees to debate and discuss issues among themselves.

To provide employees with information on the company's position regarding sexual harassment, for example, the classroom configuration is appropriate. Here the goal is to provide information, and the focus should be on the trainer. Most two-way communication is question-and-answer exchanges between trainer and trainee. Suppose the goal is to train managers to deal with sexual harassment. A circle is chosen, because the goal is to generate discussion about managers' experiences and discuss ways of handling them. In the circle, trainees face one another and the trainer is "one of the members" of the circle, with equal focus on all. Another obvious difference between these two configurations is that with the classroom, a larger number of trainees can be accommodated.

Various modifications of these two extremes can also be used. The semicircle (Figure 7-3C) encourages trainee discussion, allowing trainees to be face-to-face when the trainer is not talking. In this situation the trainer stands when presenting information and sits with the trainees to encourage discussion.

Perhaps the configuration used most often is the U-shape (Figure 7-3D). It is similar to the semicircle but allows for a larger group of trainees. The U-shape provides the main focus on the instructor, a fair amount of face-to-face with others for discussion, and the ability to have a reasonably large group (30 to 35 trainees), although with a larger group the U itself can become too large. The trainer must be careful not to move too deeply into the U and cut off those at the end. Also if flip charts are used, two sets may be needed to make reading them easy for all participants, particularly if the number exceeds 30. Placing the charts at the open end of the U and

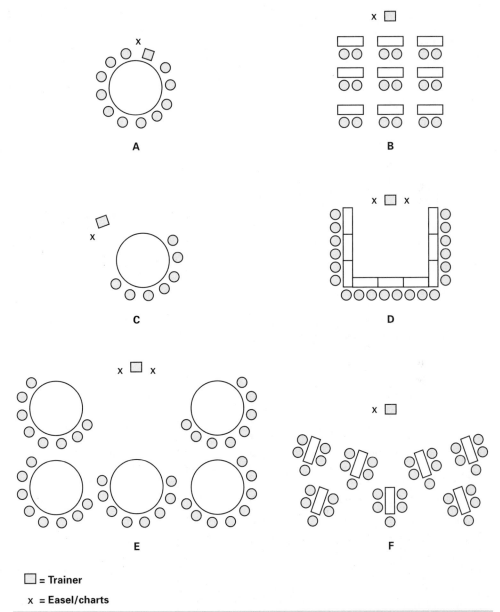

$\square$ = Trainer

x = Easel/charts

FIGURE 7-3 Different Seating Arrangements for Training

slightly inside (see Figure 7-3D) ensures you are not blocking the view and all participants can easily see the material.

In a slightly different version trainees sit at round tables in a semicircle (Figure 7-3E). This arrangement facilitates easy switching from lecturette to small group exercises or discussions. Figure 7-3F is similar but with rectangular tables. The other advantage of these configurations is that they set up small groups whose members can interact, making the training less threatening at the beginning.

OFF-SITE TRAINING FACILITIES

Although a certain pride can come from having your own training facilities, they can be expensive. Off-site training offers several advantages.

First, being off-site provides more assurance that trainees will not be interrupted. It is simply too easy to contact the trainee if she is on the same floor or even in the next building.

Another advantage is the change of pace it offers. Going to a hotel or conference center is not the same as going to work. Many trainees will associate staying in a hotel with vacation (unless they are traveling salespersons). This change of pace is even more important if a great deal of stress is associated with the job. Recall the discussion of classical conditioning. Regular pairing of work with stress will result in a feeling of stress upon arrival at the workplace. Off-site training in this situation might be more suited to the learning process. However, choose the off-site facility with care. Remember Jack and his training at the old school?

Going off-site also allows the trainer to choose a facility compatible with the needs of the particular training event. If breakout rooms, a classroom, U-shaped setup, or all three are required, you can choose the location that best fits the requirements.

The Trainer

Effective trainers need to have the KSAs related to both the subject matter content and the role of trainer. In addition, a trainer must establish credibility with the trainees. These KSAs will help but not be sufficient to establish the necessary credibility. We will discuss the KSAs first and then turn to establishing credibility.

TRAINER KSAs

It is useful to examine the KSAs of an effective trainer, presented in Table 7-11. Note that many of the requirements are similar to those suggested for an effective lecturer, which is important because almost all training includes a lecture component.

TABLE 7-11 Knowledge, Skills, and Attitudes Required of an Effective Trainer

Knowledge
Subject matter
Organization
Adult learning process
Instructional methods

Skills
Interpersonal communication skills
Verbal skills (ability to explain clearly)
  • Active listening
  • Questioning
  • Providing feedback
Platform skills (ability to speak with inflection, gesture appropriately, and maintain eye contact)
Organization skills (ability to present information in logical order and stay on point)

Attitudes
Commitment to the organization
Commitment to helping others
High level of self-efficacy

Just how much knowledge of the subject matter does the trainer need? The level of knowledge depends on the complexity of the subject matter. Highly technical subject matter requires a high level of such knowledge. Is the high level of knowledge more important than being a skilled trainer? Perhaps that question is not the correct focus, because both subject matter knowledge and trainer skills are important. We know that trainer skills are critical to effective training, so the better question is, "Which is more advisable, to train the trainer in the technical skills or to train the expert in training skills?" The answer, especially if the subject matter is highly technical or complex, is the latter. In the short term, it may be necessary to pair a technical expert with a training specialist, until the technical expert acquires sufficient training skill.

The trainer should possess a reasonable knowledge of the organization and trainees. Such knowledge increases the credibility of the trainer and helps her answer questions that come up regarding integrating the training back into the workplace.

Although most of the knowledge and many of the skills required of a trainer are trainable, it would be best to be able to begin with individuals who already possessed the attitudes identified in Table 7-11, because attitudes are more difficult to change.

TRAINER CREDIBILITY

The credibility of the trainer will have a significant impact on the effectiveness of training, so it is important to create a positive first impression and maintain it throughout the training.

First Impression

Typically, the favorable (or unfavorable) impression a job candidate makes in a "selection" interview is made in the first few minutes. The same could be said of the impression the trainer makes on trainees. Because this issue is so critical to effective training, the first few minutes need to be managed well. In the case at the beginning of the chapter, what kind of first impression do you think Jason Reston made? Did he establish any credibility with the trainees? Did he demonstrate a concern for their needs? Did he seem approachable?

What should a trainer wear? The answer is: You must know your audience. If you are unsure, ask. In many situations a business suit is a safe bet. If you are training accountants who all come to work in conservative business attire, you need to do the same. This same attire, however, could distance you from some other groups. If you are training line workers from a manufacturing plant, you may wish to dress more casually and not wear the uniform of management. Remember, you want the trainees to perceive you as someone able to help them in their job. To gain this credibility, you need to dress appropriately. Appropriate dress for training line workers might be casual dress—tasteful casual, but casual nevertheless.

What is equally important is that the clothes fit well, shoes are shined, and accessories match what you are wearing. This "first impression" will help establish your credibility.

Experience

The credibility of the trainer is also determined by credentials: where the trainer comes from and previous training done. For example, one successful trainer told about an early training assignment, at the age of 23, as part of a corporate training staff. The course was called "Nonfinancial Motivation Techniques." The trainees were first-line supervisors with an average of 6 years' experience in their positions and more than 10 years with the company. Ten minutes into the first training component (the lecture), one of the older trainees raised his hand and said, "Sonny, have you ever supervised a group of unskilled laborers?" The answer, of course, was no, but he qualified it with the fact that he had supervised white-collar employees. Several knowing smirks around the room made it clear that the trainer's credibility had been destroyed. Throughout the rest of the program, trainees were inattentive, lethargic, and occasionally rude. This trainer learned early on that trainer credibility is a key factor in the effectiveness of the lecture technique.

How could the trainer handle such a situation more effectively? One approach would be to set the context of the training at the beginning. He might say something like the following: "I will be presenting a number of nonfinancial techniques that you might be able to use to motivate your employees. These techniques worked for other supervisors in a variety of situations. First, I will explain the technique and then we will discuss how it might work for you or how it might be adapted to work for you. You know your work units better than anyone else, so I'm counting on everyone to help identify ways these techniques can be applied."

A trainer does not need to have the same work experience as the trainees to be effective. However, a trainer needs to be seen as having something worthwhile to offer. Here the trainer is offering some new ideas and expertise in facilitating the discussion of these ideas, but—and this point is important—the trainer does not dismiss or diminish the expertise of the audience. In effect, the trainer says, "Let's merge our separate areas of expertise to arrive at something we both want—more motivated employees."

Acknowledging the differences in experience at the beginning of training is also important. It allows the trainees to see that the trainer is aware of the differences and is taking them into account. For example, in the previous situation the trainer might say, "My experience has been supervising white-collar employees. How do you think the motivations of these employees differ from those you supervise?" After some differences are noted, the trainer might then ask, "At one time, most of you were unskilled workers. What were the things that motivated you when you were an unskilled worker?" This question would allow the supervisors to see that while individuals may differ in the things that motivate them, general categories of motivators apply for all individuals. The questioning process allows the trainees to test their assumptions and learn through self-discovery.

Integrated Instructional Strategy

The information presented in this text comes together in the instructional strategy used for a training program. The strategy is compiled in a written document, often called a program development plan. This plan details the methods, materials, equipment, facilities, and trainers for the training program. A variety of systems guide the documentation of the plan (program management timing charts, technical reports, etc.). Our purpose is to indicate what should be included in the documentation, rather than the form it should take. Important issues to address in your strategy are discussed next.

CONTENT: LEARNING POINTS

A **learning point** is an important piece of information that a trainee must acquire in order to accomplish the learning objective. Each objective provides specific information as to what needs to be learned. Consider this learning objective: "Solder 20 feet of 1/2-inch copper pipe, using elbows and unions, in 20 minutes or less with no leaks." In order to ensure no leaks, the trainee must pay specific attention to the cleaning of the copper pipe, the proper heating of the pipe, and correct application of the solder. These factors would be learning points, which the trainer would need to be sure the trainee mastered.

METHOD OF INSTRUCTION

We discussed a variety of training methods from which to choose, each offering strengths and weaknesses. Many of them, such as role play, behavior modeling, and case study, are not meant to be stand-alone methods, but rather to facilitate learning by providing alternative mechanisms for providing practice.

Although the method's effectiveness in meeting the learning objective should be the major criteria for selection, other considerations are costs, time needed to develop, and time allotted in the training session. If cost, for example, inhibits your ability to use the best method, you need to choose a different method that meets the budget but still provides the practice needed. Literacy of the workforce is another issue to consider. Methods such as programmed instruction and computer-based instruction rely on trainees' ability to read and understand. If they are not skilled in this area, alternative approaches are necessary, particularly if reading is not an important skill for the job.

FACILITIES, MATERIAL AND EQUIPMENT, AND TRAINERS

Facilities

If you are training in your own facility, be sure it is available and reserve it. If you are going off-site, you can be selective as to the design of the room. If breakout rooms are necessary or different seating arrangements (lecture, small-group discussion) are required, be sure the site can accommodate these circumstances. If dividers separate it from other rooms, inquire about the events scheduled next to you. Attending a training session when a motivational speaker or sales rally is happening next door can be distracting. If nothing is scheduled, get assurance that the booking office will be sensitive to your concerns if they book the rooms next to yours. Check the soundproofing of the panels that separate the rooms. Avoid booking rooms that lead directly to the kitchen unless you know they are soundproofed.

Materials and Equipment

Document all the material you will need such as text, overheads, and the like, and time frames for their completion. If you are developing material, allow sufficient time to prepare it properly. At off-site locations order the equipment and anything else being provided by others far enough in advance. If you can afford it and time is available, important charts, posters, and easel sheets can be professionally printed.

Trainer

How do you choose the trainer? One of the most commonly cited reasons for training not being effective is its lack of relevance to the trainee's situation. Comments such as "The training is great but it will not work in our plant," "You do not understand the problems we have," "My boss is the one who should be here, because the boss makes the decisions" indicate the concern trainees perceive as to the transferability of the training to their job.

One way to handle these concerns is to use middle managers as trainers.[38] Their involvement alleviates most of the preceding concerns, but some problems may arise. If the middle manager is the supervisor of some trainees, his presence could dampen these trainees' enthusiasm for training.

Larger organizations can overcome this issue by not involving managers in training people who report directly to them. Smaller organizations need to assure such trainees that they will be treated the same as others. As long as trainees do not perceive any different treatment, the word would get out that this system was okay. Another concern is the potential that the middle manager may spend too much time dealing with organizational issues rather than on the training topics. Solid training objectives would help to prevent this conflict.

Another way to develop a successful training program is likely not used enough because of the cost: using a seasoned trainer (e.g., outside or internal consultant) and a manager to team-teach the training program. The two could work from each other's strengths. An advantage of this approach is that the manager receives good on-the-job training on how to be an effective trainer.

THE STRATEGY

With the preceding information, the strategy can now be articulated. For each objective, a number of things are identified: facilities and configuration, learning points, methodology for training, and equipment and material required. Table 7-12 provides a useful outline to serve as a guide for completing the instructional strategy. It will help you systematically examine what is required and what sequence (in the case of more than one objective) makes the most sense. As each learning objective is considered (along with its learning points), the most effective configuration of methods, material and equipment, facilities, and trainers is determined. In Table 7-12 the lecture method provides the cognitive information; the simulation the actual practice. If the training is to teach supervisors how to deal effectively with conflict, the methodology might be lecture or discussion to provide information, depending on the sophistication of the group, and role play or behavior modeling to provide practice. Once you establish the methods to be used and the sequencing of the training, it is necessary to determine time frames for each of these activities. In most cases time is limited, and the inexperienced training developer tends to overload the material to be covered. Always allow for a reasonable amount of time for discussion and interaction, which is where most of the learning occurs.

TABLE 7-12 Components of Instructional Strategy

PROGRAM DEVELOPMENT PLAN

Name of Program: Pipe Fitting I

Target Population: Apprentices who successfully passed the gas fitters exam

Overall Training Objective: Trainees will be able to examine a work project and with appropriate tools; measure, cut, thread, and install the piping according to standards outlined in the gas code.

Learning Objective	*Learning Points*	*Method*	*Material and AV*
1. Using a tape measure, determine the length of and number of pipes necessary to connect the furnace to the gas meter in a manner that meets the gas code	1. Take into account the extra length necessary because of threading 2. Take into account that length is reduced by different fittings, e.g., street elbow, union, elbow, etc. 3. How to construct appropriate drop for furnace	Lecture and simulation	Training manual Overhead projector Assortment of 1-inch and ¾-inch fittings, elbows, street elbows, and unions Mock meter and furnace setup Tape measure, note pads
2. Use threading machine to cut and thread length of pipe required	1. Length of thread required 2. Importance of cutting and reaming, measuring, and use of threading machine oil	Lecture and simulation	Trainee manual VCR and TV Threading tape Threading machine Steel pipe Oil Tape measure

Facility and configuration:

Trainer:

Measures to assist transfer:

Method of evaluation:

Now, based on the type of training, you need to decide on the training facility and the seating configuration. Clearly documenting this information reduces the likelihood of mistakes. A problem may develop if the training required a great deal of face-to-face interaction among the trainees but the training facilities were too small to accommodate those interactions.

Mechanisms you plan to use to ensure transfer need to be documented, so it is clear what will occur once training is completed. Generally, you expect transfer of training to occur, but often little is done to ensure that it does. When no one person is responsible, the feeling of responsibility is diffused and transfer is soon forgotten.

Similarly, it is important to indicate the methods that will be used in evaluating the training, along with time frames. Once again, clearly outlining this information helps to ensure evaluation happens.

After the program development plan is carefully constructed and agreed on, the next step is to obtain or develop the instructional material, instructional media, and equipment as discussed earlier in the chapter. By methodically completing the program development plan and using it as a guide, you should be able to identify and develop everything required for training. The development phase of our training model depicts this process.

THE ALTERNATIVE TO DEVELOPMENT

For a number of reasons, an organization may choose not to develop its own course. A small business may not have the resources; large companies may not have many individuals to train or simply too many other projects in the works. In such situations, alternatives are available. You can either hire a consultant to use one of their prepackaged programs, or look to outside seminars for the training. One option is to hire a consultant to do all the work. It is an expensive alternative, but would result in a program tailored to your needs much as if you did it all yourself.

The Consultant

If the training you need is not specific to your organization, but more generic (e.g., conflict management, interviewing skills, or computer skills), you can find a consultant with a training package that can be adapted to fit your needs. The other extreme is to use the consultant's prepackaged program without any alterations, which will reduce the overall cost.

The advantage to prepackaged programs is that they are ready to go. The disadvantage is that they are not specific to your company. This trade-off may be more acceptable for a session on conflict resolution than a session on team development. In fact, many prepackaged programs can be used to supplement a company's own program. They can be less costly than hiring a consultant, but some are still expensive. Some consulting firms offer prepackaged programs and also provide training for your trainers. This option adds to the cost, but the training is usually quite good. If a great deal of training will be taking place in your organization, this option may be worth the extra expense if it is amortized over a number of sessions.

In deciding whether to use a consultant, consider questions such as the following:

- How many employees are to be trained, and will they need constant retraining?
- Can advantage be realized from involving a neutral third party (e.g., union-management cooperative ventures)?
- Is there a rush to get the training done?
- Do you have the expertise in-house?

If the decision is to use a consultant, make sure you consider the following:

- Ask for references, ask who they have trained, and be sure to follow up on this information (consultants vary in their expertise).
- Determine how much the consultant knows about your industry.
- See what the training objectives look like in some of their training packages.

- Find out how the consultant evaluates success in training.
- Make sure you know who will be doing the work. Often you meet the salesperson, not the trainer.

Outside Seminars

The outside seminar is training offered from time to time at local hotels, conference centers, and universities. These seminars are the least expensive and best alternative if you need to train only a few employees. For a sufficient number of attendees, these seminars may be brought to your site. On-site seminars can be tailored to your organization for a moderate extra cost. They can also include an evaluation component.

When choosing a seminar, consider the following factors:

- What are your training objectives? Skills require practice, and seminars often are too large to include practice sessions.
- Is any form of evaluation used? (Seldom is evaluation done.)
- How focused is the content based on your training objectives?
- You should also send someone to preview the seminar and report back on its potential value.

If you decide to purchase training, assess how it fits into the overall training strategy. Many companies are implementing team training because it is "the thing to do." Spending money on team training simply because others are doing it will only waste money. Training should be seen as a mechanism to support the organization's mission and goals. Other mechanisms must also be in place to support the training if it is to transfer effectively.

Alternatives for the Small Business

Jack Zenger, president of the Times Mirror Training Group in California, notes significantly more interest in training by small business lately. This interest is mirrored in Britain, where evidence indicates that training provides positive benefits for small business. Organizations with fewer than 100 employees reported 25 percent increase in training with about 60 percent reporting financial benefits from the training.[39] To achieve these benefits the small business may find it advantageous to hire a consultant or purchase prepackaged training. If so, it is important that they follow the same suggestions mentioned previously when choosing a consultant or packaged training.

Small businesses should also examine the feasibility of developing a consortium of small businesses that could all use the same training. LearnShare, mentioned earlier, discovered that 74 percent of their training is not specific to a particular organization's process or products.[40] The same is likely true for small companies. Why not take advantage of this commonality and work together to identify training needs and share in the cost of developing or purchasing relevant training? It is what LearnShare does. LearnShare recently developed an online training program called the leader survival kit.[41] Total cost of the program was $285,000, but by sharing the cost between companies it was only about $22,000 each. If this shared development expense can be done for e-learning, it can also be done for any type of training development, thus becoming affordable for smaller businesses. Also, given the number of small businesses around, the expense could be shared among more, making the cost of development even less.

E-learning is now an option for small business. Numerous businesses are providing a template for developing online learning. This way the small business gets affordable training they tailor to their needs. Quelsys, an e-learning firm in Norwalk Connecticut, allows trainers from other companies to use their authoring tools to build their training program. No cost is charged until employees begin to take the course, then the cost is on a per-employee basis.[42] Some companies are even more adventuresome and develop an online learning university (see Training in Action 7-6).

WHAT A SMALL COMPANY CAN DO

Walker and Associates, a telecommunications equipment distributor has just under 300 employees. A new president came on board who strongly believed in training and development of employees. He formed a partnership with GeoLearning Inc., a Web-based learning provider to create the Walker Institute of Training and Development, an online corporate university.

To facilitate using the Internet for training he then offered employees an interest-free loan to purchase a computer for home. At the same time he purchased a number of laptops for employees to check out for home or when they travel. Some employees were still a bit reluctant to use the net for fear of misusing it.

To help encourage e-learning Frank Russell, president of GeoLearning, provided much needed advice to Walker's president. "Start small, with a pilot program of a few employees, and get feedback from the naysayers," was his advice. This approach helped to launch the program. To further encourage its use, supervisors made its use one of the goals of employees in their performance review. They also integrated e-learning and its use into their orientation.

Note that these practices, starting with a pilot program, integrating the use of the Web training into an employee's first experience in the organization (orientation), and building it into performance appraisal, are all practices for any effective training, Web-based or not.

Source: Adapted from Tyler, K. 2001. E-Learning: Not just for e-normous companies anymore. *HR Magazine* 46: 82–88.

Small businesses often belong to industry-specific associations. These associations can provide a venue for discussing this idea to determine level of interest. The associations themselves could develop a consortium for their constituents. Even if a consortium is too complex a project to consider, what about purchasing a few prepackaged training programs? If a small business located three other companies with similar training interests, they save 75 percent of the cost.

Western Learning Systems of California is a variation on the consortium idea. It develops courses for larger companies but retains the copyright. It then markets these courses to small companies at a more affordable rate. They offer a 1-year membership for $5,000 that entitles a company to 75 classes at the rate of $195 per class.[43]

Another inexpensive way to train in some areas is to require that trainees read a particular book, then participate in a discussion group on the topic. The group is led by the person most knowledgeable about the subject. A company preparing for ISO certification asked a group of employees to read a book written by one of the quality gurus, Philip Crosby. They read a chapter, then met to discuss it. The manager prepared questions in advance to keep the discussion going.[44] Earlier we indicated how important trainee involvement is for adult learning. These discussion groups are the epitome of involvement. The informal training in this company became more formal after this initial orientation.

Although this method does not follow all the criteria we suggest for an effective training program, it might more than compensate by motivating its participants. No single best way to train has been established, especially when you consider the variations in cost benefit for different training alternatives. Training in Action 7-7 provides examples of various methods being used by small businesses.

| TRAINING IN ACTION 7-7 |

TRAINING IN A SMALL BUSINESS: DIFFERENT APPROACHES

Brenda Schissler, president of Staffmasters, a small temporary service provider in Lousiville, has 10 permanent employees. Each of them specializes in a topic (e.g., safety) and goes to outside seminars to gain relevant knowledge. Upon return, each is responsible for teaching the others about the particular issue.

Kevin O'Brian is the quality assurance person responsible for ISO standards at Rivait Machine Tools Inc., a 14-person operation in Windsor, Ontario. One basic type of work is done at Rivait Machine, so instead of providing training in the procedures required, they developed a "job aid," which is a checklist of tasks. The employee goes through the list, checking off each task as completed, then moving to the next task. This means training, except at the basic level, is not necessary.

You do not have to be big to win prestigious awards, but you do need training.

Custom Research Inc., is a market research company based in Minneapolis. Each of its 105 employees received a minimum of 130 hours of training in 1995. In 1996 it became the first professional service company and the smallest company ever to win the Malcolm Baldrige National Quality Award.

Steve Braccini, president of Profastener, a small business in California with about 150 employees, suggests that it is a good idea to send two rather than only one employee to a specific type of training. A single trainee might return with a skewed view of what took place. By sending two who then discuss the training with each other, you ensure a common understanding. Braccini believes this system results in a better overall product. Braccini makes one other important point: He always sends these employees to attend a "train the trainer" course before going on any training.

Sources: Exerpted from O'Brien, K. 1997. Personal communication. Rivait Machine and Tool, Oldcastle, Ontario, July 24; Zemke, R. 1997. The little company that could. *Training*, January, pp. 59–64; Filipczak, B. 1996. Training on the cheap. *Training*, May, pp. 28–34.

Finally, resources are available for small businesses to use in expanding their training capabilities. The U.S. Chamber of Commerce has a federation of programs and services division. Canada's equivalent is the Federal Business Development Bank. At these places, small business can obtain help in fulfilling training needs. The federation of programs, for example, states as its objective "to provide low-cost training to small businesses." The vice president, Roger Jask, did a needs analysis of the type of training required to keep small businesses alive, and from this analysis he developed a number of self-study courses that can be purchased for about $20 each. Exercises are included, and at the end of each chapter is a test that the trainee completes and sends to Jask to be scored. Also, at the end of the text a test is given in a similar manner. Passing the course earns the trainee a certificate indicating successful completion.[45]

Implementation

At this point you are ready to implement your instructional strategy. This phase of the training model is depicted on page 335. Note the outputs from the development phase are brought together and become the inputs for the implementation stage. Next, the "process" phase contains two steps that are important to take before your training is ready for general use.[46] They are first, a dry run, then a pilot program. The former is a "first test" of new material; here the

Implementation Phase

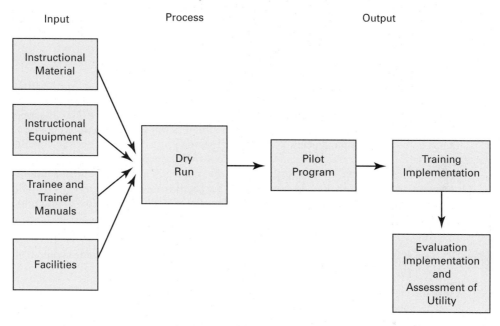

training package may not be presented in its entirety. The latter is the first full-blown presentation of the training using finished materials.

DRY RUN

The **dry run** is not designed to actually train the participants; it is to determine the value and clarity of the various pieces of the training program in a controlled setting. To assess its value, you need to get as many key perspectives as possible to view the training. The trainer should be someone involved in the training design and development. For an effective dry run, use some potential trainees, but choose them carefully, according to their diverse backgrounds, their general supportiveness of the value of training, and their willingness to provide feedback. More seasoned employees will be able to help evaluate the transferability of the training back to the job. You should also include some content experts who can provide feedback on the validity of the material and its usage. Some members of the training design and development team should also participate in the dry run. They can provide feedback as to how well the various pieces of the design fit together.

The dry run may not require that all the training modules in the program be tested. If you previously used a specific exercise, case, or role play with similar participants, the dry run for this exercise may simply involve the participants' reading the exercise and providing feedback as to its relevance. Working through the exercise and a full discussion may not be necessary. Other exercises, particularly newly developed ones, probably require the participants to go through the full process.

It is important to ask participants a list of questions after each exercise or module you test. For example, after participants complete a role play, you ask whether the situation is realistic for this organization. If it is not, future trainees may dismiss the training as being irrelevant. Other questions you may wish to ask are: Is the information and direction for the exercise clear enough for trainees to do the exercise? Was the time allocation too long or too short?

After the dry run is completed examine the feedback carefully and revise the training where applicable. Then it is time for the pilot program.

PILOT PROGRAM

The **pilot program** is different from the dry run in that trainees are there to be trained. It will be a full-fledged training program. The dry run refines the training to eliminate any major glitches. In the pilot, trainees are again chosen carefully. You want people who are generally supportive of training, and who are not likely to be disruptive. Trainees will spread the word about training to others in the organization quickly. You want that word to be as positive as possible, so that when new trainees come into the program they bring positive expectations. The pilot program will provide you with additional input to further refine the training (if necessary) and disruptions are not conducive to this process. You do, however, want a good cross-section of those who will be in the later training sessions to allow you to evaluate how the training comes across to different groups.

The main goals of the pilot program are:

- Provide the trainees with the relevant training.
- Assess further the timing and relevance of modules and various training components.
- Determine the appropriateness, clarity, and flow of material.

From the pilot program you obtain valuable responses and viewpoints, which are inserted in the trainer's manual. These inputs will help guide new trainers in what to expect. Another goal of the pilot is to provide an opportunity for future instructors to attend the training and experience what takes place firsthand. Finally, the pilot program will provide valuable feedback to designers regarding effectiveness of the training.

After the pilot, any further revisions are implemented. One final note: Although this pilot program will help to improve the program, examination and appropriate revisions should not stop here. Training evaluation goes on continuously. Transfer of the training to the job to positively affect organizational results is the primary objective of training. Thus training will continue to be modified until desirable outcomes can be reliably achieved.

TIPS FOR TRAINERS

A number of good tips for lecturing were featured earlier in the chapter. The following tips relate to other trainer actions that help deliver an effective training session.

Preparation

As a trainer you need to arrive early enough to be sure everything is in order. Check seating arrangements and make sure materials arrived. Before trainees begin arriving ensure all equipment is working and make sure you know how to operate it. Don't assume you can, turn it on and find out. Check the overhead projector to see that a spare bulb is stored inside. If not, find a spare (if you don't, you are tempting the fates). If you will be using a video, is the remote working, and do you understand it? Try it to be sure. Is enough newsprint available on the flip chart? Enough markers? As the trainer, you need to be sure everything is ready to go before the trainees arrive, otherwise you can lose your credibility before you get started.

The Beginning of Training

When trainees begin to arrive, greet them individually. Small talk with individual trainees before the session helps make them comfortable and, in turn, will facilitate discussion once the training begins.

Starting on time is important. Recall "reinforcement theory" discussed in Chapter 3. If those who arrive late discover training has not begun, the belief is reinforced that showing up on time is not necessary. A late start also punishes those who do arrive on time. For the rule of starting on time to be effective, however, you need to obtain commitment from the trainees.

Starting on time is important, but few trainers we know start exactly on time the first day. Most allow for some tardiness the first day when trainees may not know exactly where the training room is or simply did not give themselves enough time to get to the location. A good practice is to start training with an ice-breaker—an exercise that allows for those who arrive a little late to fit right in with little disruption.

Trainees may come with different expectations about what the training will be about, and they come for various reasons. After an ice-breaker, it is useful to ask trainees what they expect to get from the training. You simply ask each person or ask small groups to develop lists to present to the larger group. These expectations are written on newsprint for future reference. You can indicate to the trainees which of the points mentioned are a part of the training. For any points that are not part of the training design, you may offer to try and fit them in if they are appropriate. If not, explain why they are not appropriate for this training session. You should also promise to go back to the list periodically to be sure all things that you promised to cover were in fact covered.

Following or concurrent with this introductory step, go through the agenda to indicate what will be happening over the duration of the training. You explain how breaks will be distributed and how messages to them are handled. One way to determine these things is to ask for a short discussion regarding the rules that will be set down for the training period. In this way, the trainees abide by these rules because they helped develop them. If you want to expedite the process, you can prepare a set of suggested rules, and explain why they are useful. Then ask the trainees for any suggestions to modify, add, or delete from the list. At this point the rule of starting on time can be discussed and decided upon. Involving the trainees in setting the rule builds their commitment to the rule.

Setting the Tone

Dress   As suggested earlier, be sure to dress appropriately. If appropriately means business attire, you can loosen up after the training gets under way. Trainees need to feel comfortable, and if many show up wearing suits, you can signal a more relaxed nature by removing your jacket or loosening your tie if you are wearing one. You might say, "I think I need to loosen up a bit; please feel free to do the same." For training spread over several days, you might at some point on the first day ask the trainees to decide on an appropriate dress code.

The Podium   One of the authors was hired to assist a consultant in training automobile workers in a new plant. The consultant hired a number of local people because of the size of the project. Concurrent training sessions allowed us the opportunities to observe each other. One trainer was in the habit of sitting behind a table while talking to the trainees, another stood behind a podium, and the rest stood and moved around a lot, going back to their notes only occasionally. Which procedure is best? Again, it depends. Standing behind the podium or sitting at a desk is acceptable for one-way communication, but it is not the most effective style for training adults where two-way communication is important. In these cases, any barriers (desk, podium) present nonverbal impediments to the communication process. Additionally, seeing someone sitting behind a desk and teaching them might remind some trainees of unpleasant school experiences. Being out in front of a desk or podium and moving around helps make the trainer look more accessible and open to input. In any event, the two-way communication is much more important in the lecture/discussion method, whereas for the straight lecture a podium is perfectly acceptable. A skilled trainer will use the podium to signal to trainees when interruptions and comments are appropriate and when they are not.

Listening and Questioning

What separates the good from the average or poor trainer are their listening and questioning skills. This statement is not to demean presentation skills, but rather to stress the importance of listening and questioning. The techniques discussed earlier cannot be emphasized too strongly. If you are using the lecture/discussion method, use the experience and information provided by the trainees. Control the urge to tell them continually of your experiences. Remember that trainees relate to one another and their experiences more often than to yours. In the beginning you may want to share your relevant experiences to establish credibility and to show that sharing of experiences is desirable and useful. As training moves on you will want to encourage trainees to begin sharing their experiences that are related to the training.

Providing Instructions

It is important to provide clear instructions with each exercise you plan to use. Many role-play exercises are wasted because trainees don't understand exactly what is expected. Oral instructions certainly need to be provided, but a handout containing identical information is also useful for trainees to refer to. Even then, it is helpful to provide an example of what you expect. Once the exercise has begun, it's too late. It is discouraging to both the trainer and trainees if the trainees are confused and embarrassed because they misunderstood what they were supposed to be doing.

Dealing with Different Trainees

A successful trainer needs to understand how to deal with the various types of trainees he might encounter. Some need to be encouraged to become more involved in discussion, while others are far too involved.

Quiet Trainee   We already discussed methods for encouraging quiet trainees to become more involved (small group discussions, writing their answers first), and these approaches are usually successful. What if they do not work? If you organize a number of small groups for discussion sessions, one way to encourage the quiet trainee is to ask each group to rotate the person who is responsible for reporting back to the larger group. The quiet trainee will then take a turn reporting to the larger group, increasing his participation. However, too much pressure to become involved is not a good idea. If a quiet person is speaking up during the small-group sessions, he is providing input. Do not attempt to get these trainees to participate at an equal level to others if they are not so inclined. Doing so can create too much tension in the environment. If you tried all we proposed, with little change in the quiet trainee's behavior, don't push any further. Further attempts will only create barriers to the trainee's learning.

Talkative Trainee   The talkative trainee is usually far more of a problem than the quiet one. No matter what question you ask, this trainee wants to answer. Usually the answer involves a long story, and soon other trainees are rolling their eyes and tuning out. The trainer loses the trainees' attention, and valuable training time is wasted on irrelevant stories. You need to tone down that trainee's input, but not embarrass anyone. One approach is to ask others for their opinion. Say something like, "We have been making Lex do all the work here so far—how about someone else responding?" Or use the direct questioning technique to get the focus away from the talkative trainee. You can also speak to the talkative trainee in private, suggesting that you appreciate her comments but are concerned that others are not participating as much as they should. In this context, asking the talkative trainee to hold back on participation usually works.

Angry Trainee   Some trainees who come to training simply do not want to be there. They set out to ruin the session for everyone. You need to deal with such trainees early on before they disrupt the class. One of the authors was training line workers in team concepts and, although the union executive and most union members were supportive of the training, some were violently opposed. In the first session one of these trainees said, "I really do not want to be here; this training is management propaganda designed to weaken the union." The author's response was, "I have heard that said before; how do others feel about the training?" At that point a number of others indicated support for the training and, although the angry trainee did not participate much in the rest of the training, he did not disrupt it either.

If in such a situation, you found most trainees felt the same way, you would be wise to spend some time discussing the issue, because such an attitude will certainly affect training. The important point is to focus on how training can benefit them. One way to accomplish this task is to ask trainees to identify ways they would be able to use the training.

The Comedian   These trainees are a gift and a curse. They are a gift because when their jokes work, and if they are not put forth too often, they will do wonders to set a positive tone. Laughter is good medicine, and a comedian is able to provide it. The potential curse is in the nature and frequency of the jokes. Some jokes are clearly inappropriate. In other cases it is difficult to know what is offensive. However, you do not want even a small number of trainees to feel that a particular joke was offensive. Also if the comedians do get a lot of laughs, they are likely to continue to joke around. This behavior can disrupt the timing of the sessions and put the trainer behind.

What to do? If the joking gets out of hand or some jokes are inappropriate, you can talk with the comedian at a break. Indicate a concern that some of the humor is offensive to some of the other trainees or is distracting from the focus of training. In taking this approach, you need to indicate appreciation of the comedian's intention to contribute to the training, but reach an agreement about how often the jokes can be offered and what type of jokes are acceptable. This conversation should be enough to curb such behavior. Sometimes the comedian's jokes are directed at the trainer. In these cases the trainer must have a tough skin and be willing to laugh without taking it personally. This reaction will defuse any tension that may have been created, reduce the amount of distraction, and show the trainer isn't "too full of herself." It is only when the jokes become distracting or offensive that action needs to be taken.

Jack Goes to Training. . . (Continued from beginning of chapter)

"Get up. Get up, you're going to be late for the training!"

"Huh," grunted Jack. "What time is it?"

"It's 7:30 and you have to go downtown to the training center today, remember?" said his wife.

Wow, what a dream, thought Jack as he walked up the steps of the training center, feeling a little nervous. The training room was not at all like a schoolroom. No windows, no blackboards. As he entered the room, he was approached by a nicely dressed man who said, "Hi, my name is Doug. Welcome to the training center. Have you ever been here before?" The name tag indicated Doug was the trainer. He seems like a nice guy, thought Jack.

"There's some coffee and doughnuts over there—help yourself," said Doug. This might even be enjoyable, thought Jack, although he still felt a little apprehensive.

With introductions out of the way and the objectives and agenda explained, Doug summed up by saying, "So at the end of the two days you will be expected to take a set of specifications and program them into the machine. Are there any questions?"

"So there are no tests?" asked Jack.

"Well," responded Doug, "that is the test."

(continued)

(*continued*)

Jack was a bit confused, "But that is what we do at work—I don't see it as a test. A test is where I have to write down an answer to some question you pose about all this stuff."

"There are no paper-and-pencil tests, just behavioral tests," said Doug.

Suddenly it was lunchtime. Jack thought, "It was true, time does go fast when you are having fun. This sure isn't like school." All 23 trainees went to another room where lunch was served.

"I can't believe it. This is nothing like I expected," said Ron. Ron was the fellow whom Jack had to interview and introduce to the group in what was called an ice-breaker. That ice-breaker sure did a lot to get me relaxed and actually interested in the training, thought Jack.

Ron continued, "I always did poorly in school and was petrified about coming here." Jack responded, "Me too."

Ron said, "I like the idea of his periodically giving us mini tests. Gives us an idea of how we are doing and provides us with extra help if we are falling behind."

"Tests . . . oh yeah, I find it hard to consider them tests. They're hands-on, exactly what we will do on the job," said Jack.

Later Jack thought, "Wow, it's already over."

"Nice job, Jack. You are now certified on this piece of equipment," said Doug.

"Hey, Ron," said Jack, "do you believe how much fun learning can be?"

Ron agreed, "Doug was great. He kept getting our input and tying our experiences to the new stuff we had to learn. I never thought I would say this, but I would like to get more training like this."

"You bet," said Jack. "I still can't believe how great this was—especially after the dream I had."

SUMMARY

First we discussed the development of training. Most training uses some form of lecture or lecturette component. Much more is involved in an effective lecture than simply providing information. The effective lecture requires attention to a number of issues such as effective use of questions and proper listening skills. Details the instructor can attend to while lecturing, to keep trainees' attention, include walking around, eye contact, and general enthusiasm for the topic. Using games can not only provide interest, but also reinforce learning points.

Computer-based training is one of the fastest growing areas of training. CBT now comes in the way of intelligent tutoring systems that actually learn how to teach the trainee better as training progresses. Interactive multimedia training is able to train in all types of skills, including the soft skills like active listening and conflict resolution. Even with all the advances in CBT, it is still useful to combine it with other methods to capitalize on the advantages of more than one method.

Business games, in-basket, and case study methods are useful for developing cognitive skills. These methods in particular, however, are not designed to stand alone. Instructor-led discussions with trainees, when combined with other methods, create better learning.

Role plays and behavior modeling are two methods for effectively training in behavioral skills. Role plays in particular are easy to develop and implement. Behavior modeling is more complex to develop, because of the need for an effective model of the behavior. This training method is usually accomplished through a video, which can take a great deal of time to prepare and tends to be costly.

On-the-job training is the most used method of training. It takes many forms, such as apprenticeships, coaching, and the like. Many times, however, little thought or planning goes into it. To be effective it must go through the same rigor of development as any training program. Furthermore, care in the selection of the trainer is necessary if you really want the training to not only impart the appropriate skills, but also the proper attitude.

The use of static and dynamic media provide an important aspect of an effective training program. The more ways information is presented, the more likely it is remembered. Certain guidelines apply in using various media, and perhaps the mistake most often noted is related to the static media. It is the attempt to put too much information onto an overhead, flip chart, or power point presentation. With dynamic media, it is important to become familiar with the equipment before the training session. Nothing affects a trainer's credibility more negatively than delaying the start of training while trying to get some piece of equipment to work.

The type of training facility you choose is also important. Arrangement of the seating, and closeness of the trainer to the trainees should be a function of the objectives of the training, not the design of the room. Also noise levels from adjoining rooms or from outside needs to be determined before choosing a training room. The proper training facility then allows you to arrange the seating in a manner that best reflects what type of training will be taking place.

The trainer must be equipped with the proper skills to be effective. Credibility is also essential. Credibility can be obtained through first impressions and experience. You can exercise more control over first impressions and should strive to fit the expectations of the trainees. Dressing in a manner similar to those who are being trained is a good idea. No matter how you are dressed, however, you need to look professional with shoes shined, clothes fitting well, and so forth. Experience is more difficult to attain, and in some cases it may be wise to consider someone, more experienced and respected, who actually works with the trainees. Training them to be a trainer may make more sense than trying to provide a seasoned trainer with the experience required to be effective.

Before implementation of a large training program, it is useful to have a dry run in which you test the material to see how effective it is. This dry run is not an actual training session, but a process of going through the material and determining whether it is doing what you expect it to. The next step is a pilot program in which the first trainees go through the training, but you choose supportive trainees, so they can spread the word about the training program in a positive manner. Also you want constructive feedback from them to put the finishing touches on the program before it is formally launched.

Finally trainers need to be aware of behaviors that will enhance their effectiveness. Each session is likely to include a few trainees in a session who are difficult to deal with, and trainers need to know how to deal with them.

KEY TERMS

- Apprentices
- Audiotape
- Behavior modeling
- Business games
- Case study
- Closed-ended question
- Coaching
- Computer-based training

- Direct question
- Dry run
- Dysfluencies
- Guided discovery
- Ice-breaker
- In-basket
- Job instruction training (JIT)
- Learning point

- Lecture
- Level of interactivity
- Mentoring
- Newsprint
- Nonverbal cues
- On-the-job training (OJT)
- Open-ended question
- Overhead question

- Overheads
- Pilot program
- Questioning
- Relay question

- Reverse question
- Role play
- Self-pacing
- Simulator

- Sophistication of the multimedia

CASE ANALYSIS

Jim worked as a laborer for a gas utility in Winnipeg, Manitoba. When the opportunity came to apply for a backhoe/front-end-loader operator job, he was excited. Three people applied. To select the one who would get the job, the company asked each of them to actually go out and work on the backhoe for a day. Jim felt his chance for the job disappear, because he had never even driven a tractor let alone used a backhoe. When he went out, he did not know how to start the tractor. One of the other backhoe operators who was getting his machine had to show him. He managed through the day, and to his surprise, did better than the others. He was given the job.

On his first day at the new job, one of the other backhoe operators showed him where to check the hydraulic fluid and said, "These old Masseys are foolproof. You will be okay." Jim taught himself how to dig a hole by trial and error. He initially believed that the best way was to fill the bucket as much as possible before lifting it out of the hole and emptying it. He would wiggle the bucket back and forth until it was submerged and then curl it. When it came out of the hole, the earth would be falling off the sides. This job was not so difficult after all, he thought.

He cut through his first water line about 2 weeks after starting his new job. Going into a deep, muddy hole did not make the crew happy. After Jim cut through his third water line, the crew chief pulled him aside and said, "You are taking too much earth out with each bucket so you don't feel the bucket hitting the water line; ease up a bit." Water lines were usually 6 to 8 feet down, so Jim would dig until about 5 feet and then try to be more careful. It was then he pulled up some telephone lines that were only about 3 feet deep.

Realizing more was involved in operating a backhoe than he first thought, he sought out Bill Granger, who was known to have broken a water line only twice in his 15 years. It was said he was so good he could dig underneath the gas lines—a claim that Jim doubted. Bill said you need to be able to feel any restriction. The way to do that was to have more than one of your levers open at the same time. Operating the bucket lever and the boom lever at the same time reduces the power and causes the machine to stop rather than cut through a line of any type. Jim began to use this method but still broke water lines. The difference now was that he knew immediately that he broke a line. He could feel the extra pull, whereas in the past he found out either by seeing water gushing up or by hearing the crew chief swearing at him. He was getting better. Jim never did become as good as Bill Granger. In fact 2 years later he applied for another job as gas repairperson and was promoted, but the training as a gas repairperson was not much better. ■

CASE QUESTIONS

1. What are the potential costs to this lack of training? Why do you think the company operated in this manner?
2. What type of training would you recommend: OJT, classroom, or a combination? Describe what the training might entail.
3. What type of training environment would you provide?
4. Who would you get to do the training and why?
5. Would you consider purchasing a training program for backhoe operators? Provide your rationale.

EXERCISES

1. Check the room where your class meets. Does it meet the requirements of a good training room? What additions would make it more amenable to effective training?
2. Assume you are in training on conflict resolution. Think of a situation in which you got in an argument with someone, and write up the role of the person with whom you were in conflict. Follow the instructions in the chapter. Do not forget you need to write the role of the other person, not you, because you will play yourself. Show the role to a classmate and ask him or her to play it. As you play your part, try to behave differently than you did in the original confrontation. Although you do not have any training in the area of conflict resolution, simply try to remain calm and not turn the situation into a confrontation. Now debrief. How did it go? Was the role play useful in helping you practice being calm? Ask the classmate whether the role you wrote could be better in terms of providing information as to how the classmate is to act.
3. In a small group, each person takes a turn giving a 3-minute impromptu speech (on anything). Have someone designated as the bell ringer. Each time you use a dysfluency (uh, and uh, um, etc.), the bell ringer will hit a glass with a spoon (or make some other sound). Keep score for each person. Now over the next few weeks ask friends to tell you when you use these dysfluencies, and try to reduce them. Then get together with your group and redo the exercise. Do you note any improvement?
4. In small groups choose someone who worked in a particular job. Interview the person to determine the job requirements, and develop a procedure for providing OJT for the job.

QUESTIONS FOR REVIEW

1. You are asked to deliver a 2-day workshop for managers on effective feedback skills. It is focused primarily on performance reviews. Approximately 100 managers need to be trained. Describe what the content of the training would entail, methods you would use (e.g., lecture, case study, role play), and the instructional media and equipment you would want. Why? Also what type of room setup you would want? Why? Indicate how many sessions you would need for this number of managers. Why?
2. Describe the various types of questioning and when they are used.
3. What is the difference between role play and behavior modeling? When would you use one versus the other?
4. Describe the proper method for preparing and conducting OJT.

CHAPTER 8

Evaluation of Training

EVALUATION PHASE

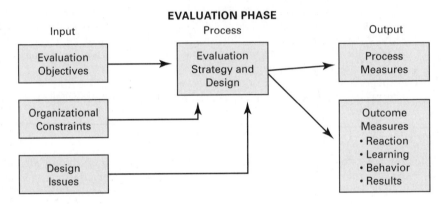

Learning Objectives

After reading this chapter, you should be able to:

■ Describe the pros and cons of evaluation and indicate which way to go on the issue

■ Describe the costs and benefits of evaluating training

■ Explain what process evaluation is, and why it is important

■ Describe the interrelationships among the various levels of outcome evaluation

■ Describe the various designs that are possible for evaluation, their advantages and disadvantages

---

Training Designed to Change Behavior and Attitudes

The city of Palm Desert, California, decided to provide training to improve employees' attitudes toward their work and to provide them with skills to be more effective on the job. The 2-day seminar involved a number of teaching methods including a lecture, films,

(continued)

(*continued*)

role plays, and group interaction. The topics covered were conflict control, listening, communicating, telephone etiquette, body language, delegation, taking orders, and others. Throughout the 2 days, the value of team work, creativity, and rational decision making was stressed and integrated into the training.

Before the training was instituted, all 55 nonmanagement employees completed a paper-and-pencil questionnaire to measure both their attitudes toward the job and their perception of their job behaviors. Supervisors also completed the job behavior questionnaire, a type of assessment, for each of their employees. All 55 employees were told they would be receiving the same 2-day seminar. The first set of employees (34 of them) was chosen at random.

The 21 employees who did not take the training immediately became a comparison group for evaluating the training. While the first group of employees were sent to the training, the others were pulled off the job, ostensibly to receive training, but simply took part in exercises not related to any training. Thus both groups were treated similarly in every way except for training. Both groups completed attitude surveys immediately after the trained group finished training. Six months later both groups completed self-report surveys to measure changes in their job behavior. Their supervisors were asked to complete a similar behavior measure at the 6-month mark as well.

The data provided some revealing information. For the trained group, no changes in attitude or behavior were indicated either by the self-report or by supervisor-reported surveys. This result was also true (but expected) for the group not trained.

Source: Adapted from Miller, S. 1990. Effects of municipal training on employee attitudes and behavior. *Public Personnel Management* 19:429–40.

Was training a failure in the Palm Desert case? Would the training manager be pleased with these results? Was the evaluation process flawed? These types of issues will be addressed in this chapter. We refer back to the case from time to time to answer these and other questions.

Rationale for Evaluation

Imagine a business that decided it wouldn't look at its profitability, return on investment, or productivity. You are a supervisor with this company, but you never look at how well or poorly your subordinates are performing their jobs. This is what training is like when no evaluation is conducted. Good management practice dictates that organizational activities be routinely examined to ensure that they are occurring as planned and are producing the anticipated results. Otherwise people, processes, and products or services that stray "off track" are provided with no means of getting back on.

Nonetheless, many rationalizations for not evaluating training continue to exist. A late 1980s survey of 45 *Fortune* 500 companies indicated that all of them asked trainees how much they liked the training, but only 30 percent assessed how much was learned, and just 15 percent examined whether behavior on the job changed.[1] Other evidence from that time suggested only 1 company in 100 used an effective system for measuring the impact and value of its training.[2]

This attitude is changing. In 1994, a survey of training in the United States found that for companies with 100 or more employees, 66 percent said they assessed learning, 62 percent assessed behavioral change, and 47 percent assessed the impact of training on organizational outcomes.[3] In 1996 another study indicated 70 percent assessed learning, 63 percent assessed behavior, and 25 percent organizational results.[4] Both studies show an increase in evaluation efforts since the late 1980s. A major reason given for this change is an increase in accountability for everyone. Top management is demanding evidence that training departments are contributing positively to the bottom line.[5] Dave Palm, training director of LensCrafters, knows first-hand about this trend. A frantic regional manager called Dave and told him that executives were looking to improve the bottom line and couldn't find enough evidence that training programs were providing a quantifiable return on the company's investment. Yes, they knew trainees were satisfied with training, but were they getting the bang for the buck? The conversation ended with the regional manager saying, "So, Dave, what are you going to do about it?" Dave had his wake-up call.[6]

On issues related to human resources, some studies suggest that Canada lags behind the United States.[7] A study by McIntyre in 1994 supports this finding in the area of training evaluation.[8] The study indicated that only 30 percent evaluate learning, 16 percent evaluate behavioral change, and 5 percent evaluate the impact of training on organizational outcomes. More recent data, however, indicate an improvement in Canada as well.[9] Regarding nonmanagement training, 31 percent of Canadian organizations evaluated learning, 47 percent evaluated behavioral change, and 36 percent evaluated organizational results. So, for both countries, this type of evaluation is becoming more commonplace. Nevertheless, for a number of reasons many still resist evaluation of training.

Resistance to Training Evaluation

Training managers can come up with a surprising number of reasons for not evaluating training, such as:

- Nothing to evaluate
- No one really cares about it
- Evaluation is a threat to my job

NOTHING TO EVALUATE

For some companies, training is a luxury that is provided as a reward for good performance, or simply something mandated so everyone must take their turn.[10] The argument here is that training isn't expected to accomplish anything, so there is nothing to evaluate.

The Counterargument   Even in cases where training is a reward or mandated, it is designed with some goal or objectives in mind. Some type of KSA change is expected from the trainees, even if it is just that they feel more positive about their job or the company. Once this goal or objective is identified, the objectives of training can be measured. Evaluation is simply measuring the degree to which objectives are achieved.

NO ONE REALLY CARES ABOUT EVALUATING TRAINING

The most common rationale for not conducting training evaluations is that "formal evaluation procedures are too expensive and time-consuming and no one really cares anyway." This explanation usually means that no one specifically asked for, demanded, or otherwise indicated a need for assessment of training outcomes.

The Counterargument   If an evaluation is not specifically required, it doesn't mean that training isn't evaluated. Important organizational decisions (e.g., budget, staffing, performance evaluations) are made with or without formal data on the effectiveness of training or its contribution toward organizational objectives. If no formal evaluations of training have taken place, decisions will be based upon the decision makers' impressions of training. Even in good economic times, the competition for organizational budget allocations is strong. Departments that can document their contributions to the organization and the return that can be expected on the investment of new budget dollars are more likely to be granted their budget requests. The question, then, is not whether training should be evaluated, but rather who will do it, how it will be done, and what data will be used.

EVALUATION IS A THREAT TO MY JOB

Considering that in the United States and Canada tens of billions of dollars are spent every year for training, why wouldn't companies evaluate this training? Fear of the result is one reason. Football coach Woody Hays, back in the 1950s once said he never liked to throw the forward pass because three things could happen and two of them are bad. The same could be said for evaluation. If time and money are spent on training and an evaluation determines that no learning occurred—or worse, job performance declined—tough questions will be asked. Although most managers are not likely to admit this concern publicly, it is perhaps the real problem. When we use the term *evaluation*, we too often think of a single final outcome at a particular point that represents success or failure—like a report card. This type of evaluation is called summative or outcome evaluation. When the focus is on this type of evaluation, managers are naturally concerned about how documenting the failure of their programs will affect their careers. Consider Training in Action 8-1. It provides an example of an evaluation designed to provide feedback so improvement (through training and practice) can take place. But when the focus shifted from "helping to improve" (**formative evaluation**) to measurement of success or failure (**summative evaluation**), the desire to participate in the process disappeared, and the airline threatened to discontinue it.

The Counterargument   Can you blame the airline (Training in Action 8-1) for wanting to opt out of the program? No, it is difficult to imagine anyone wanting to participate in a program where the information can be used against you. This type of summative evaluation is a legitimate reason for not wanting to evaluate. The main purpose of evaluation should not be an after-the-fact measure of accountability (summative evaluation), but a feedback mechanism to guide efforts toward success.[11] While trying to convince a client that the company's training should be evaluated, one trainer decided not to use the term *evaluation*. Instead he chose the term *data tracking*. He emphasized tracking attitudes and behaviors over time and supplying feedback to the training designers and presenters based on the findings. This feedback could then be used to modify training and organizational systems and processes to facilitate the training's success. The term *data tracking* did not imply the same connotation of finality as *evaluation*. Hence managers saw it as a tool for improving the likelihood of a successful intervention rather than as a pass/fail grade.

Was the evaluation in the Palm Desert case seen as summative or as a continuous improvement process? It is difficult to say without actually talking to those involved. However, if it was used for continuous improvement, assessment of the learning at the end of training could be helpful in determining the reason transfer did not take place. Based on this information the city could design additional interventions to achieve desired outcomes.

So We Must Evaluate

The arguments for ignoring evaluation of training make some sense, on the surface. However, they are easily countered when more carefully analyzed. Perhaps the biggest reason for abandoning the resistance to evaluation, however, is its benefit, especially today when more and more organizations are demanding accountability at all levels. Managers are increasingly demanding of training what they demand of other departments: provide evidence of the value to the organization.[12]

TRAINING IN ACTION 8-1

EVALUATION: WHAT IT IS USED FOR MATTERS

For 30 years, British Airways maintained a system in all its aircraft that monitors everything an aircraft and its pilot does. This information is examined continuously in order to determine any faulty aircraft mechanisms, and to constantly assess the skill level of the pilots. When a pilot is flagged as having done "steep climbs" or "hard" or "fast landings" for example, they are targeted for training to alleviate the skill deficiency. The training is used, therefore, as a developmental tool to continuously improve the performance of pilots. The evaluation is not used in a summative manner, as a measure of performance upon which disciplinary measures might be taken. The result for British Airways, one of the largest airlines in the world, is one of the best safety records in the world.

In the past, one of the major ways of determining problems in the airline industry in North America was to wait until an accident occurred and then examine the black box to see what problems occurred. The findings might indicate pilot error, or some prob-

lem with the aircraft. This information was then sent to all the major airlines for their information. This form of summative evaluation met with disastrous results. Recently, six major American airlines began a program similar to British Airways' approach. After all, it makes sense to track incidents and make necessary changes (in aircraft design or pilot skill level) as soon as it is noticed. In this way major incidents are more likely avoided. They are in fact using the evaluation information gathered as a feedback mechanism to ensure continuous improvement of performance, not as a summative evaluation of "failure."

This seemingly effective way of assuring high performance is about to come to an end in the United States, however. The Federal Aviation Administration (FAA) wants access to this information for possible use as a measure of summative evaluation of pilots. The airlines fear that the information given to the FAA could be used to punish airlines and pilots for certain types of behavior. As a result they are considering dropping the program.

Source: Orr, B. 2001. Toward safer skies. Available at CBSnews.com/now/story/0,1597,277042-412,00.shtml.

Other factors influencing the need to evaluate training are the quality movement, focus on continuous improvement, and organizational cost cutting.[13]

The image of the training function, especially by many line managers, is sometimes poor. By using the same process as line managers to demonstrate accountability, you can improve the image of training. Furthermore, the technology for evaluating and placing dollar amounts on the value of training has improved in the last several years. The caveat here is that we do not advocate a comprehensive evaluation of all training, because the value of the information must be worth the cost. Sometimes the cost of evaluation is simply too high.

Types of Evaluation Data Collected

Let's go back to the evaluation phase figure at the beginning of the chapter. Recall from Chapter 5 that one of the outputs from the design phase is evaluation objectives. These evaluation objectives are inputs (along with organizational constraints and design issues) to the evaluation phase of the training model. Remember that at the time of obtaining the design output you should begin developing evaluation processes and outcome measures concurrently with the development of training. The types of outputs from the evaluation phase are process and outcome evaluation. **Process** evaluation examines how the training was designed, developed, and carried out. **Outcome** evaluation determines how well training accomplished its objectives.

PROCESS DATA

One of the authors has a cottage near a lake, and he often sees people trying unsuccessfully to start their outboard motors. In going to their assistance, he never starts by suggesting they "pull plugs" to check for ignition or "disconnect the float" to see whether gas is reaching the carburetor. Instead, he asks if the gas line is connected firmly, if the ball is pumped up, if the gear shift is in neutral (many will not start in gear), and if the throttle is at the correct position, all of which are process issues. He evaluates the "process" of starting the engine to see whether it was followed correctly. If he assumed it was followed and tried to diagnose the "problem with the engine," he might never find it.

It is the same with training. If learning objectives were not achieved, it is pointless to tear the training design apart in trying to fix it. It might simply be a process issue: the training was not set up or presented the way it was intended. By examining the entire training process model you will see all the places that the training process might go wrong. In examining the training process, we suggest segmenting the analysis into two areas: process before training and process during training.

Process: Before Training

A number of steps are required in analyzing the processes used to develop training. Table 8-1 identifies a number of questions to ask during the analysis of the training process. First you can assess the effectiveness of the needs analysis from the documentation or report that was prepared. This report should indicate the various sources from which the data were gathered and the KSA deficiency that was documented.

Next you can assess the training objectives. Are they in line with what was found to be deficient? Were objectives developed at all levels: organizational, transfer, learning, and reaction? Are they written clearly and effectively to convey what must be done to demonstrate achievement of the objectives? It is important that you examine the proposed evaluation tools to be sure they are relevant. Based on the needs assessment and resulting objectives, a number of tools can be identified for assessing the various levels of effectiveness. We discuss the development of these tools later in this chapter. Then evaluate the design of the training. For example, if trainees' motivation to attend and learn is low, what procedures are included in the design to deal with this issue?

Finally, when you examine the actual design of the training package, you should assess the areas discussed in Chapter 5, especially those summarized in Tables 5-1, 5-10, and 5.14. By evaluating these issues before training begins, you can uncover any errors or omissions and correct them. If, however, you do not do so until after training occurred, the analysis will still help you diagnose why training outcomes were or were not achieved.

Would such an evaluation prove useful in the Palm Desert case? Yes. In that situation, as it stands, we recognize that training was not successful, but we do not know why. The process leading to the design of training may provide the answer. Another place the answer might be found is in the training implementation.

Process: During Training

One of the problems with collecting only outcome data is that, when the objectives are not achieved, it is never clear why. Did the training that occurred reflect what was proposed, designed, and contained in the training manual? If so, it is the design that must be changed. Or did the trainer or others in the organization make some ad hoc modifications? If this information were available in the Palm Desert case, analysis might provide information as to why the training was not successful.

TABLE 8-1 Potential Questions to Be Addressed in a Process Analysis (before training)

Were needs diagnosed correctly?
- What data sources were used?
- Was a knowledge/skill deficiency identified?
- Were trainees assessed to determine their prerequisite KSAs?

Were needs translated into training objectives?
- Were all objectives identified?
- Were the objectives written in a clear, appropriate manner?

Was an evaluation system designed to measure accomplishment of objectives?

Was the training program designed to meet all the training objectives?
- Was previous learning that might either support or inhibit learning in training identified?
- Were individual differences assessed and taken into consideration in training design?
- Was trainee motivation to learn assessed?
- What steps were taken to address trainee motivation to learn?
- Were processes built into the training to facilitate recall and transfer?
- What steps are included in the training to call attention to key learning events?
- What steps are included in the training to aid trainees in symbolic coding and cognitive organization?
- What opportunities are included in the training to provide symbolic and behavioral practice?
- What actions are included in the training to ensure transfer of learning to the job?

Are the training techniques to be used appropriate for each of the learning objectives of the training?

Source: Adapted from Camp, R. P., P. N. Blanchard, and G. E. Huszczo. 1986. Towards a more organizationally effective training strategy and practice. Upper Saddle River, NJ: Prentice Hall.

Imagine, for example, that the Palm Desert training required the use of behavior modeling to provide practice in the skills being taught. The evaluation of outcomes shows that learning of the new behaviors did not occur. If no process data were gathered, the conclusion could be that the behavior modeling approach was not effective. What if examination of the process, however, revealed that trainees were threatened by the behavior modeling technique and the trainer allowed them to spend time discussing behavior modeling, which left less time for doing the modeling. As a result, it is quite plausible that it is not the design of the training that is a problem, but the implementation of the training as it was designed. Without the process evaluation, this information would remain unknown, and the inference might be that behavior modeling was not effective.

Examples of implementation issues to examine are depicted in Table 8-2. Here it is up to the evaluator to determine whether all the techniques that were designed into the program actually took place. It is not good enough to determine simply that the amount of time allotted was spent on the topic or skill development. You must also determine whether trainees actually were involved in the learning activities as prescribed by the design. As in the previous behavior modeling example, the time allotted might be used for something other than behavior modeling.

Putting It All Together

"Actual" training is compared with the "expected" (as designed) training to provide an assessment of the effectiveness of the training implementation. You can obtain much of the necessary information for "expected" training from records and reports developed in the process of setting up the training program. A manual would provide an excellent source of information about what

---

TABLE 8-2 Potential Questions to Be Addressed in a Process Analysis (During Training)

- Were the trainer, training techniques, and training/learning objectives well matched?
- Were lecture portions of the training effective?
  Was involvement encouraged/solicited?
  Were questions used effectively?
- Did the trainer appropriately conduct the various training methodologies (case, role play, etc.)?
  Were they explained well?
  Did the trainer use the allotted time for activities?
  Was enough time allotted?
  Did trainees follow instructions?
  Was there effective debriefing following exercises?
- Did the trainer follow the training design and lesson plans?
  Was enough time given for each of the requirements?
  Was time allowed for questions?

Source: Adapted from Camp, R. P., P. N. Blanchard, and G. E. Huszczo. 1986. Towards a more organizationally effective training strategy and practice. Upper Saddle River, NJ: Prentice Hall.

---

should be covered in the training. To determine what actually was covered, someone can monitor the training. Another method is to ask trainees to complete evaluations of each module, asking them to evaluate process issues. Videotaping, instructors' notes, and surveys or interviews with trainees can also be used. Keep in mind that when you are gathering any data, the more methods you use to gather information, the better.

When to Use It

Who is interested in the process data? As you can see in Table 8-3, this information is used primarily by the training department to determine whether it is doing what it is supposed to be doing. The customers of training (defined as anyone with a vested interest in the training department's work) usually aren't interested in this type of information—they are more concerned with training outcomes.

Providing some process data, particularly data related to "during training," is important, even if it is only the trainer's documentation and trainee reactions. These data can be used by the trainer and others to assess what seems to work and what doesn't. Sometimes you will want more detailed process data, such as when training will be used many times, or the training outcomes have a significant impact on the bottom line. If, on the other hand, you are setting up a half-day seminar on the new computer software, collecting process information may not be worth the cost.

Once training and trainers are evaluated a number of times, the value of additional evaluations decreases. If you are conducting training done numerous times before, such as training new hires to work on a piece of equipment and the trainer is one of your most experienced, then process analysis is probably not necessary. If the trainer was fairly new or had not previously conducted this particular session, you might want to gather process data through direct observation by a senior trainer.

OUTCOME DATA

To be most effective we believe evaluations should be formative and focused on providing information to improve training, not summative or designed only to determine whether training is successful. Some disagree with this approach and suggest that formative evaluation ends when

TABLE 8-3 Who Is Interested in the Process Data

Training Department

Trainer	Yes, it helps determine what works well and what does not
Other trainers	Yes, to the extent that process is generalizable
Training manager	Only if training is not successful, or if a problem is present with a particular trainer

Customers

Trainees	No
Trainees' supervisor	No
Upper management	No

Source: Adapted from Camp, R. P., P. N. Blanchard, and G. E. Huszczo. 1986. Towards a more organizationally effective training strategy and practice. Upper Saddle River, NJ: Prentice Hall.

the training program is launched.[14] We suggest, however, that the focus always be on formative evaluation for these reasons:

- It removes the connotation of pass/fail, making evaluation more likely.
- It facilitates continuous improvement, a desirable goal even when training is deemed successful.[15]

This is not to say that summative or outcome evaluation is not important. Outcomes are the means by which you know how well the process is working. To determine how well training met or is meeting its goals, you need to examine the various outcomes. The four outcomes that are probably the best-known are reaction, learning, behavior, and organizational results.[16] These outcomes are ordered: reaction outcomes come first and will influence how much can be learned; next, learning outcomes influence how much behavior can change back on the job; then behavior on the job influences how much organizational impact the training can have. This description is a simplified version of what actually happens, and critics argue that no empirical evidence indicates that this relationship between these outcomes exists.[17] We discuss this argument in more detail later.

Reaction outcomes are measures of the trainee's perceptions, emotions, and subjective evaluations of the training experience. They represent the first level of evaluation and are important because favorable reactions create motivation to learn. Learning may also occur even if you find the training boring, or may not occur even if you find it interesting.[18] However, if training is boring it will be difficult for you to attend to what is being taught. Then you may not learn as much as you would if you found the training interesting and exciting. High reaction scores from trainees, therefore, assure the designers that attention was obtained and maintained, which is the first part of learning—getting their attention.

Learning outcomes are measured by how well the learning objectives and the overall training objective was achieved. The type of measurement used will depend on the measurement technology available to the evaluator and the type of learning being evaluated. Note the critical relationship between the needs analysis and evaluation. If the training process progressed according to the model presented in this text, you already identified how to measure learning during the training needs analysis (TNA). At that time you measured the employee's KSAs to determine whether they were adequate for job performance. The evaluation of learning should use the same measurement techniques as in the TNA. Thus the needs analysis is actually the "pretest." A similar measure at the end of training would show the "gain" in learning.

Job behavior outcomes are similarly measured in a manner consistent with the TNA. Remember, during the training needs analysis you identified performance deficiencies and traced them to areas in which employees were behaving in a manner that was creating the deficiency. The methods used for measuring job behavior in the TNA should be used in measuring job behavior after the completion of training. Once again, the link between needs analysis and evaluation is evident. The degree to which job behavior improves places a cap on how much training can improve organizational results.

Organizational results occupy the highest level in the hierarchy and reflect the performance deficiency identified in the TNA. It is the organizational result that often triggers reactive (as opposed to proactive) training. Here are some examples:

- High levels of scrap are being produced.
- Employees are quitting in record numbers.
- Sales figures dropped over the last two quarters.
- Grievances are on the increase.
- Number of rejects from quality control are rising.

Once again, if one of these organizational results triggered the training, it can be used as the baseline for assessing improvement after training. This process of integrating the TNA and evaluation also shows potential as a means of streamlining both processes and thereby making it more cost effective.[19]

Putting It All Together

If you evaluate each level in the hierarchy you are able to better understand the full effects of training.[20] Let's examine one of the items in the preceding list—a high grievance rate—as it relates to the training process and the four levels of evaluation.

The needs analysis determines that the high grievance rate is a function of supervisors not managing conflict well. Their knowledge is adequate but their skills are deficient. From the needs analysis, data are obtained for later comparison with skill levels after training has been completed. Tools for evaluation are developed at this time if they are not already available from the needs analysis. Training is provided, and then participants fill out a reaction questionnaire. This tool measures the degree to which trainees feel positive about the time and effort they invested in the program and each of its components. Assume the responses are favorable. However, even though the trainees feel good about the training and believe they learned valuable things, the trainer recognizes that the intended learning may not have occurred. Thus a test of conflict management skill is administered and the results are compared with pretraining data. If the results show that the trainees acquired the conflict management skills and can use them appropriately, the learning objectives were achieved. Will these skills then transfer to the job so the employees are using them in conflict situations? If we show that employees are using the skills, then the learning was transferred to the job. The next step is to see whether the grievance rate is declining. If it is, then you could, with some level of confidence, suggest that training is the cause of the decline. If you determined that learning did not take place after training, it would not make sense to examine behavior or results, because learning is a prerequisite. Now let's examine each of these four levels of evaluation more closely.

Reaction Questionnaire

What It Is   The data collected at this level are used to determine what the trainees thought about the training. Reaction questionnaires are often criticized, not because of their lack of value, but because they are often the only type of evaluation undertaken.[21]

The two types of reaction questionnaire are affective and utility.[22] An **affective questionnaire** measures our general feeling about training ("I found this training enjoyable"), whereas the **utility questionnaire** reflects our beliefs about the value of training ("This training was of practical value"). We focus here on the latter type, because we believe that specific utility statements on reaction questionnaires are more valuable for making changes.

Training reaction questionnaires do not assess learning, but rather the trainees' attitudes about and perceptions of the training. A number of categories should be considered in developing a reaction questionnaire, including the relevance of training; training content, materials, and exercises; trainer(s) behavior; and the facilities.

Training Relevance. Asking trainees about the relevance (utility) of the training they experienced provides the organization with a measure of the perceived value of the training. If most participants do not see any value in it, they will experience difficulty remaining interested (much less consider applying it back on the job). Furthermore, this perceived lack of value can contaminate the program's image. Those who do not see its value will talk with others who have not yet attended training, and will perhaps suggest it is a waste of time. Self-fulfilling prophecy proposes that if you come to training believing it will be a waste of time, it will be. Even if the training is of great importance to the organization, participants who do not believe it is are not likely to work to achieve its objectives.

Once trainee attitudes are known, steps can be taken to change the beliefs, either through a socialization process or a change in the training itself. Think about the Palm Desert case. What do you think the trainee reactions to the training were? Might this source of information help to explain why no change in behavior occurred?

Training Materials and Exercises. Any written materials, videos, exercises, and any other tools of instruction should be assessed along with an overall evaluation of the training experience. On the basis of responses from participants, you can introduce modifications to the training to make it more relevant to participants. Another reason for making suggested modifications is that it follows the OD principle of involving trainees in the process.

The value of a reaction questionnaire can be seen in Training in Action 8-2. Here the data provided information on how to develop an orientation to empowerment. Examining the reaction questionnaire responses proved valuable for determining that the Christie Handley videotape was seen by trainees as useful. It also indicated that almost three-quarters of participants perceived the role plays as useful. Open-ended responses at the end of the questionnaire asked trainees to indicate "which of the modules was most effective in helping you understand empowerment at Ameritech." Once again the Christie Handley videotape was listed by 20 percent of respondents and the role play by 16 percent. Although these percentages might seem low, they are not. Generally, open-ended questions are not responded to with great frequency. In this case, only about 40 percent responded. Furthermore, the next highest agreement for a module was only 2 percent. Taken in this context, the percentages are worth considering in developing the orientation. Using this information, rather than trying to guess what participants would find useful, the working committee and consultant were able to configure the orientation to increase positive perceptions.

Reactions to the Trainer. Reaction questionnaires are also useful in determining how the trainer's actions were evaluated by the trainees. Care should be taken to develop statements that specifically address the trainer's actions. General statements tend to reflect trainees' feelings about how friendly or entertaining the trainer was (halo error) rather than how well the training was carried out. Simply presenting an affective statement, such as "The trainer was entertaining," would likely elicit a halo response. For this reason, it is useful to identify specific aspects of trainer behavior you wish to be rated.

By asking about a number of factors important to effective instruction, you cause the trainee to consider how effective the instructor was in these areas. When the final question is asked, "Overall how effective was the instructor," the trainee can draw on responses to a number of factors related to effective instruction. This consideration will result in a more accurate response as to the overall effectiveness of the instructor. In other words less halo error will be involved. Note that the questionnaire in Figure 8-1 asks the trainee to consider several aspects of the trainer's teaching behavior before asking a more general question regarding effectiveness.

DEVELOPING AN ORIENTATION

An orientation for the introduction of an empowerment intervention was developed by a working committee at Ameritech. The orientation was to help employees understand the concept of empowerment, and why Ameritech and the Communication Workers of America developed a joint operating agreement that included the concept.

A great deal of work went into creating the orientation. Two videos and a role play were produced in addition to other materials and methods. One video showed some trial sites where rank-and-file members were interviewed about the process. The other video showed top management and union leaders discussing the empowerment process and answering questions from a panel of workers. After the training program was complete, the working committee reviewed the content, design, and materials.

The working committee questioned the value of using both videos. Members were also concerned that the role play in the orientation would not work because many of the rank-and-file "were not managers" and would not like role plays.

At that point the consultant suggested that a reaction questionnaire be drawn up to assess what participants in a few pilot orientation sessions saw as relevant. The orientation could then be adjusted according to the findings.

The reaction questionnaire asked, "How useful was the [component being assessed] in helping you understand the empowerment concept?" A sample question and the resulting data obtained are shown below. The percentage below the question represents the distribution of the 187 respondents. Note that the percentages do not add up to 100, because some participants chose not to respond.

How useful was the Christie Handley videotape in helping you understand the empowerment process at Ameritech?

1	2	3	4	5	6
Of little use	Of some use	Useful but too much time was spent on it	Useful, helped me understand the concepts	Very useful but not enough time was spent on it	Very useful, helped me a great deal to understand the concepts
4%	10%	8%	56%	7%	14%

Facilities and Procedures. The reaction questionnaire can also contain items related to the facilities and procedures to determine whether any element impeded the training process. Noise, temperature, seating arrangements, and even the freshness of the doughnuts are potential areas that can cause discontent. One way to approach these issues is to use open-ended questions, such as the following:

- Please describe any aspects of the facility that enhanced the training or created problems for you during training (identify the problem and the aspect of the facility).
- Please indicate how you felt about the following:
  - Refreshments provided
  - Ability to hear the trainer and other trainees clearly
  - Number and length of breaks

Please circle the number that reflects the degree to which you agree or disagree with the following statements.

1 = Strongly disagree
2 = Disagree
3 = Neither agree nor disagree
4 = Agree
5 = Strongly agree

1. The trainer did a good job of stating the objectives at the beginning of training.	1	2	3	4	5
2. The trainer made good use of visual aids (easel, white board) when making the presentations.	1	2	3	4	5
3. The trainer was good at keeping everyone interested in the topics.	1	2	3	4	5
4. The trainer encouraged questions and participation from trainees.	1	2	3	4	5
5. The trainer made sure everyone understood the concepts before moving on to the next topic.	1	2	3	4	5
6. The trainer summarized important concepts before moving to the next module.	1	2	3	4	5

7. Overall, how would you rate this trainer? (check one)

_____ 1. Poor—I would not recommend this trainer to others.

_____ 2. Adequate—I would recommend this trainer only if no others were available.

_____ 3. Average

_____ 4. Good—I would recommend this trainer above most others.

_____ 5. Excellent—This trainer is among the best I've ever worked with.

FIGURE 8-1 Reaction Questionnaire for the Trainer

Facility questions are most appropriate if the results can be used to configure training facilities in the future. The more things working in the trainer's favor, the more effective training is likely to be.

The data from a reaction questionnaire provide important information that can be used to make the training more relevant, the trainers more sensitive to their strengths and shortcomings, and the facilities more conducive to a positive training atmosphere. The feedback the questionnaire provides is more immediate than with the other levels of evaluation, and therefore modifications to training can be made much sooner.

Timing of Reaction Assessment   The timing and type of questions asked on a reaction questionnaire should be based on the information you need for evaluating and improving the training, the trainer(s), the processes, or the facility. Most reaction questionnaires are given to participants at the conclusion of training. The advantage is that the training is still fresh and the audience is captive. However, a problem with giving them at this time is that trainees may be tired after a full day of training and just want to leave. Filling out a questionnaire at this time may result in incomplete and less-than-valid data. In addition, the type of information you can get at this time is limited. The trainees may not know whether the training is useful on the job until they go back to the job and try it.

An alternative is to send out a reaction questionnaire at some point (1 or 2 months) after training. This delay gives the trainee time to see how training works in the actual job setting. However, the trainee may forget the specifics of the training, trainer behaviors, and aspects of the facilities. Another problem is that the response rate may be considerably less because respondents are no longer a captive part of the training environment.

Another approach is to provide reaction questionnaires after segments of a training program (e.g., after each day on a multiday training session). In such situations, it may be possible to modify training that's in progress on the basis of trainees' responses. Of course, this system is more costly and requires a quicker turnaround time for analysis and feedback of the data.

Regardless of how often reaction evaluation takes place, the trainer should specify at the beginning that trainees will be asked to evaluate the training and state when this evaluation will occur. It not only helps to clarify trainee expectations about what will happen during training, but also acknowledges the organization's concern for how the trainees feel about the training. It is important also that the data gathered be used. Trainees and the rest of the organization will quickly find out if you are simply gathering data only to give the impression that you care about their reactions.

Figure 8-2 provides a list of steps to consider when developing a reaction questionnaire.

Caution in Using Reaction Measures A caution is in order regarding reaction questionnaires, particularly those provided some time after training with the express idea of determining the amount of training that transferred to the job. Research suggests that responses sent out some time after training tend to indicate transfer occurred when other measures suggest it did not.[23] Thus reaction measures should not be the only evaluation method used for transfer of training objectives.

It is important to understand that reaction questionnaires are not valid measures of how much is learned.[24] They do, however, provide the trainees with the opportunity to indicate how they felt about the learning. How interesting the training is will affect their level of attention and motivation. What the trainees perceive the trainer to be doing well and not so well is also useful feedback to the trainer. You can use this information to make decisions about modifications in the training program.

Learning

Learning objectives are developed from the TNA. The difference between the individual's KSAs and the KSAs required for acceptable job performance define the learning that must occur. The person analysis serves as the pre-training measure of the person's KSAs. These results can be

---

FIGURE 8-2 Steps to Consider in Developing a Reaction Questionnaire

1. Determine what you want to find out (consider training objectives).
2. Develop a written set of questions to obtain the information.
3. Develop a scale to quantify respondents' data.
4. Make forms anonymous so participants will feel free to respond honestly.
5. Ask for information that might be useful in determining differences in reactions by subgroups taking the training (e.g., young vs. old; minority vs. nonminority). This could be valuable in determining effectiveness of training by different cultures, for example, which may be lost in an overall assessment. *Note:* Care must be taken when asking for this information. If you ask too many questions about race, gender, age, tenure, and so on, participants will begin to feel that they can be identified without their name on the questionnaire.
6. Allow space for "Additional Comments" in order to allow participants the opportunity to mention things you did not consider.
7. Decide the best time to give the questionnaire to get the information you want.
   a. If right after training, ask someone other than the instructor to administer and pick up the information.
   b. If some time later, develop a mechanism for obtaining a high response rate (e.g., encourage the supervisor to allow trainees to complete the questionnaire on company time).

compared to a posttraining measure to determine whether learning occurred and whether those changes can be attributed to training. The various ways of making such attributions will be discussed later in the chapter. As we noted, training can focus on three types of learning outcomes: knowledge, skills, and attitudes.

Knowledge Outcomes   Although most evaluations focus primarily on declarative knowledge, it is important to remember that training can also focus on two higher-level **knowledge outcomes**: procedural and strategic.

Declarative Knowledge.   If the goal of the training was to impart some sort of factual knowledge—such as "rules covering search and seizure" or "understanding the type of question that cannot be asked in an interview"— a test can be developed to determine whether trainees acquired this **declarative knowledge**. Paper-and-pencil tests are often used, one of which is the multiple-choice test. Multiple-choice tests offer many advantages. They are easy to administer and score and, when skillfully developed, accurately measure most declarative knowledge.[25] Some trainees may indicate they are not good at taking multiple-choice tests. However, evidence suggests that such tests consistently correlate highly with other forms of testing. A big advantage to multiple-choice tests is their reliability. Also, because of the number of questions you can ask, you can cover a broader range of the content than with other methods.

The major difficulty with this type of test is in the construction of the items. A complete discussion on how to write good multiple-choice questions is beyond the scope of this text, but some general rules to consider in constructing questions are found in Figure 8-3. More comprehensive information can be found in a book published by the American Society for Training and Development.[26] It may be wise to contact a local university and discuss the project with someone with the appropriate background. Even small companies with limited budgets should be able to obtain such help from a supervised graduate student eager to get some real-world experience.

Procedural Knowledge.   The second level of knowledge outcomes is **procedural knowledge**. Here the learner begins to develop meaningful ways of organizing information into mental models. Mental models are also known as cognitive maps, knowledge structures, and task schema. As noted in Chapter 4, experts develop more complex mental models for the way they organize their knowledge than do new learners.[27] As a result, the expert is able to access the solution strategy more quickly.

Assessing the organization of procedural knowledge can be accomplished through a number of techniques.[28] The key to these testing methods is that they identify the way the trainee organizes concepts. One method uses paired comparisons to determine how the trainee sees the

---

FIGURE 8-3 Procedures for Developing a Multiple-Choice Test

1. Examine objectives to gain a clear understanding of the content area you wish to test.
2. Write the questions in a clear manner. Shorter is better.
3. Try to choose alternatives to the correct response from typical errors made during training. Make alternatives realistic.
4. Do not consistently make the correct response longer than incorrect responses.
5. Four alternatives are usually enough. More take longer to read, and it is difficult enough to write three reasonable alternatives.
6. Pretest items by giving the test to those expected to know the material. Ask them for feedback on clarity. Note any questions that many of them get wrong.
7. Give revised items to a group of fully trained (experienced) employees and a group of not trained (inexperienced) employees. The former should score well and the latter should do poorly.

relationship between topics. For an example, trainees in a "train the trainer" course would be asked to indicate the relationships among a number of training concepts such as instructional design, criterion development, needs assessment, organizational analysis, and so on. Then these relationships would be compared with the relationships identified by an expert. Another method (see Figure 8-4) uses a configuration of concepts that are linked. Some of the links are blank, and the trainee must place the appropriate concepts in the blanks next to the ones it best fits with. Strategies for measuring these structures are too comprehensive to be discussed here, but a number of publications that deal with this topic are available.[29]

Strategic Knowledge.   The category of **strategic knowledge** deals with the ability to develop and apply cognitive strategies used in problem solving. It assesses the trainee's level of

FIGURE 8-4 Test of Knowledge Organization for Civil Engineers

The following list of concepts is related to road construction. Use them to fill in the appropriate blank boxes in the map. Try to fill in the boxes so that related terms or concepts are clustered together. Concepts can be related because they occur at the same time, one is necessary for the other, or one leads to the other.
Each of the listed concepts is used only once. Note that some of the concepts are already mapped for you.

Concepts:

Asphalt placement	Prime/tack coat	Striper
Compaction/rolling	Rollers	Striping
Cut/fill	Signage	Survey
Dump truck	Site access	Traffic
Hot materials		

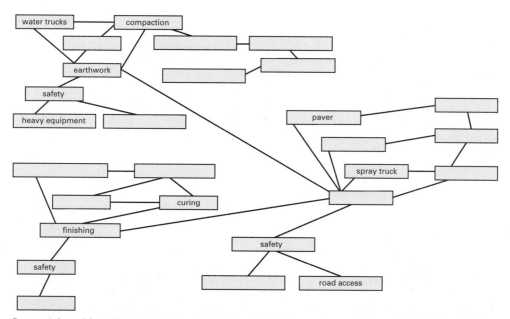

Source: Adapted from Hart, P., K. Kraiger, and T. Lamb. 1996. Summative evaluation of civil engineering 350: Civil engineering 448 and curriculum tests. Interim Technical Report for June to August 30.

understanding about the decisions or choices a trainee must make. Probed protocol analysis is one assessment method.[30] First, subject matter experts define a problem and the steps necessary to solve it. Trainees are then asked to explain step-by-step what they would do to solve the problem. Questions such as "Why would you do that?" "What would it mean if it did not help?" "What other test could you do?" help determine the trainees' strategies. Once again, for more detailed information a number of excellent publications are available.[31] One final note about cognitive (and other) tests. A common belief holds that a specific time limit needs to be given for a test. It is important to understand that speed tests provide different information than power tests.[32] Speed tests should be given only if speed in retrieving and using information is an important job characteristic. If, however, the critical component is accuracy of retrieval and use, time limits should not be used. In general, in power tests some sort of time limit can be provided. Without one, some trainees will remain for twice the time of others to check and recheck their answers. A good approach is to indicate a general time limit (e.g., about 1 hour). When the time is up, ask, "How much time do you need to finish?" This question is usually enough incentive for those who are simply reluctant to hand the test in.

Skill-Based Outcomes   Determining whether a skill or set of behaviors was learned is not the same as measuring whether they are used on the job. Obviously, if they are used on the job, they were learned. However, they may be learned but not used on the job. Knowing that the skill was learned is important, particularly if it does not transfer to the job. You then know that it is a transfer of training issue, not a learning issue.

Two levels of skill acquisition are compilation (lower level) and automaticity (higher level). Most training focuses on providing the skill training at the lower level, hence evaluations tend to be at the compilation level.

Compilation.   If the training being evaluated was in swimming, it is obvious you would not give a paper-and-pencil test to determine the learning that occurred. Similarly, if you are training supervisors in interpersonal skills, a paper-and-pencil test could provide information regarding what the trainee understands about interpersonal skills, but it will not identify the trainee's actual interpersonal skills.

Developing behavioral tests and standards for scoring such tests can be difficult. A number of situations need to be created in which the trainee is required to demonstrate the target skill(s). The difficulty lies in developing scoring standards. Consider a study that examined the training of machinists.[33] It was noted that passing the training was more a function of the trainer who was running the course than of the trainees. Different trainers used different standards for passing.

To address this problem, a standardized method was needed to provide points based on criteria outlined in the training objectives. These criteria were based on tolerance requirements and finished specifications. These criteria, once developed, gave the trainers clear standards from which to evaluate, thereby eliminating trainer differences. For certain skills (e.g., machining skills) a final product can be assessed by comparing what was produced to what was required. For other skills, such as those required for conflict resolution, assessment could be done through a structured scenario in which a person acts in an angry and aggressive manner and the trainee responds using the skills taught. Using multiple raters or standardized forms are possibilities for scoring these types of tests. What is important in developing such tests is achieving interrater agreement. This consistency is accomplished through standardized methods of rating that are clear to the trainer or whoever is required to conduct the testing.

Automaticity.   Skill-based training is generally evaluated at the compilation level. However, in some cases the skill must be so well learned that it can be done quickly and without much thought. For this level of skill, the evaluation would need to be much more stringent about what constitutes successful performance. One method for determining whether the trainee reached automaticity would be a speed test that required performance to be completed within a certain time. Emergency procedures for pilots would be an example.

Attitudes   As noted earlier, attitudes are an important outcome of training. At the conclusion of training, it is useful to assess any changes in attitudes that were learning objectives. Numerous attitude scales are available through journals (*Personnel Psychology, Journal of Applied Psychology, Academy of Management Journal, Academy of Management Review, Academy of Management Executive*) and books (*Assessing Organizational Change, The Experience of Work, Buros Book of Mental Measurements*). Developing attitude scales requires care, and you should use existing scales when possible rather than attempting to develop one. However, you may need to reword items in the survey to reflect your unique needs.

Assessing true attitude change is difficult. The primary assessment tool is a pre/post-measure of responses on an attitude scale. A scale measuring "attitude toward empowerment" is depicted in Figure 8-5. A comparison of responses before and after training that indicate an increase in positive attitude toward empowerment would suggest successful training. However, some doubts arise about such self-report measures, particularly if the trainees are identified. For example, the new employee might see the wisdom in hiding a dislike of team-based work after a concentrated orientation espousing the value of teams. Going to great lengths to assure respondents of their anonymity encourages honesty in trainee self-reports.

Timing of Assessment of Learning   Depending on how long the training is, it might be desirable to assess learning periodically throughout training to determine how trainees are progressing. Periodic assessment would allow training to be modified if learning is not progressing as expected.

Assessment should also take place at the conclusion of training. If learning is not evaluated until sometime later, it is impossible to know how much was learned and then forgotten.

FIGURE 8-5 Example of an Attitudinal Measure

Attitudes Toward Empowerment
Please indicate the degree to which you agree or disagree with the following statements.

1 = Strongly disagree
2 = Disagree
3 = Neither agree nor disagree
4 = Agree
5 = Strongly agree

1. Empowering employees is just another way to get more work done with fewer people. [reverse scored]	1	2	3	4	5
2. Empowering of employees allows everyone to contribute their ideas to the betterment of the company.	1	2	3	4	5
3. The empowerment program improved my relationship with my supervisor.	1	2	3	4	5
4. Empowerment brought more meaning to my life at this company.	1	2	3	4	5
5. Empowerment interventions should be introduced in other plants in this company.	1	2	3	4	5
6. The empowerment process provided a positive influence in labor-management relations.	1	2	3	4	5

In the Palm Desert case, the measures they took 6 months after training created a dilemma. Was the behavior ever learned, learned but forgotten, or was it learned but not transferred to the job?

Job Behavior Data

Once it is determined that learning took place, the next step is to determine whether the training transferred to the job. Assessment at this step is certainly more complex and is often ignored because of the difficulties of measurement.

A number of methods can be used to assess job behavior. These methods were covered in depth in the discussion of TNA in Chapter 4 and, in fact, the instrument used when conducting the needs assessment should serve well as the posttest evaluation tool. The primary sources of data are interviews, questionnaires, direct observation, and archival records of performance. Questionnaires are often preferred, for several reasons:

- Opinions can be obtained about specific behaviors from a large number of employees.
- The information can be tabulated to yield a numerical response.
- Respondents are anonymous, so it is more likely that they will be honest.
- A relatively short amount of time is required to gather the data.

Because this method of evaluation is so common, it is important to understand how to develop effective questionnaires. Figure 8-6 provides some guidelines.

Performance appraisals can also be used to document job and performance changes. As was noted in Chapter 4, one useful technique is the 360-degree performance review. If this type of appraisal is done on a regular basis, employees who go through training can be assessed by examining changes in their 360-degree feedback. Table 8-4 provides a portion of the results for an individual at a large U.S. corporation. Note the discrepancy in some of the dimensions. After training, if the behavior transfers to the job, the perceptions for certain dimensions should improve as rated by others.

Scripted Situations Some recent research indicates that scripted situations may provide a better format for evaluating transfer of training than the more traditional behavioral questionnaires.[34] Scripted situations help the rater to recall actual situations and the behaviors related to them rather than attempting to recall specific behaviors without the context provided. The rater is provided with a number of responses that might be elicited from the script and is asked to choose the one that describes the ratee's behavior. Research suggests that this method is useful in decreasing rating errors and improving validity.[35] An example of this method is depicted in Figure 8-7.

Finally, the trainer who includes coaching as a later part of training can observe on-the-job performance of the trainee. As was discussed in Chapter 5, these sit-ins facilitate transfer[36] and also help the trainer determine the effectiveness of the training in facilitating the transfer of training to the job.

Attitudes If attitudinal change was a goal of training, you should attempt to assess the success of transfer and duration of the attitudinal change once the trainee is back on the job. Assessing such attitudinal change can be accomplished through attitude surveys as discussed earlier. The same instruments used in the needs analysis and learning assessment can be used. If respondents' anonymity is ensured in such surveys, true attitudes are more likely to be reflected in the responses.

A study of steward training provides an example of the assessment of an attitude back on the job.[37] Training was designed to make union stewards more accessible to the rank and file by teaching them listening skills and how to interact more with the rank-and-file. Results indicated

1. Write simply and clearly, and make the meaning obvious.
   Bad: To what extent do supervisors provide information regarding the quality of performance of people at your level?
   Good: How often does your boss give you feedback on your job?
2. Ask one question at a time.
   Bad: Both the organization's goals and my role within the organization are clear.
   Good: The organization's goals are clear.
              My role within the organization is clear.
3. Provide discrete response options.
   Bad: During the past 3 months how often did you receive feedback on your work?

1	2	3	4	5
Rarely		Occasionally		Frequently

   Good: During the past 3 months how often did you receive feedback on your work?

1	2	3	4	5
Not once	1–3 times	About once a week	More than once a week	Once a day or more

4. Limit the number of response options.
   Bad: What percentage of the time are you sure of what your compensation will be?

1	2	3	4	5	6	7	8	9	10
0–10%	11–20%	21–30%	31–40%	41–50%	51–60%	61–70%	71–80%	81–90%	91–100%

   Good: What percentage of the time are you sure of what your compensation will be?

1	2	3	4	5
0–20%	21–40%	41–60%	61–80%	81–100%

5. Match the response mode to the question.
   Bad: To what extent are you satisfied with your job?

1	2	3	4	5
Strongly disagree	Disagree		Agree	Strongly agree

   Good: To what extent are you satisfied with your job?

1	2	3	4	5
Not at all	A little bit		Quite a lot	Very much

FIGURE 8-6 Guidelines for Writing Effective Questionnaires

TABLE 8-4 Example of 360-Degree Feedback Results

Skills Being Assessed	Very Low	Low	Average	High	Very High
Listening skills		S	P, B	E	
Managing conflict			S	P, B	E
Organizing			S, P	B, E	
Written communication			S, P	B	E

S = Subordinates
P = Peers
B = Supervisor
E = Employee being assessed

The following is a scenario regarding a school superintendent. To rate your superintendent, read the scenario and place an X next to the behavior you believe your superintendent would follow.

The administrator receives a letter from a parent objecting to the content of the science section on reproduction. The parent strongly objects to his daughter being exposed to such materials and demands something be done. The administrator would most likely: (check one)

____ Ask the teacher to provide handouts, materials, and curriculum content for review.

____ Check the science curriculum for the board-approved approach to reproduction, and compare board guidelines to course content.

____ Ask the head of the science department for his or her opinion about the teacher's lesson plan.

____ Check to see whether the parent made similar complaints in the past.

FIGURE 8-7 Scripted Situation Item for Evaluation of a School Superintendent

that when controlling for factors such as tenure as a union official and age, stewards who received the training behaved in a more participative manner (as reported by the rank-and-file) and were more loyal (an attitude) to the union (self-report on a measure of union commitment). For the union, the attitude "loyalty" was as important as the behavior. Loyalty will translate into many important behaviors that might not be directly measurable, such as supporting the union's political candidates and attending union functions.[38]

Timing of Job Behavior Assessment How long you wait before assessing transfer of training depends on the training objectives. If the goal was to learn how to complete certain forms, simply auditing the work on the job (pre- and posttraining) would determine whether transfer took place. This transfer assessment could be evaluated rather soon after training. When learning requires more complex behavior such as problem solving or conflict resolution skills, it might take longer for the trainee to become comfortable enough with the new behavior to exhibit it on a regular basis, and longer for others to notice that the behavior changed.

To understand this point, consider a more concrete change. Jack loses 20 pounds. First, the weight loss is gradual and often goes unnoticed. Even after Jack lost the weight, for some time people will say, "Gee, haven't you lost weight?" or "What is it that's different about you?" If this uncertainty about specific changes happens with a concrete visual stimuli, imagine what happens when the stimuli is less concrete and not consistent. Some types of behavioral change may take a long time to be noticed.

The training objectives should identify the point in time at which coworkers should notice the change in behavior. Specifically asking them to assess whether certain behaviors changed makes it more likely they will notice the change. In our example, if you were asked, "Did Jack lose weight?" and he had lost 20 pounds, you would more than likely notice it then, even if you did not notice it before.

Organizational Results

The objectives of training, whether proactive or reactive, are developed to solve an organizational problem—perhaps an expected increase in demand for new customer services (proactive) or too many grievances (reactive). The fact that a problem was identified (too many grievances) indicates a measurement of the "organizational result." This measurement would be used to determine any change after training was completed. Thus if it was initially determined that too many defective parts were being produced (low quality), the measurement used (number of defective parts per 100 produced) would be used again after training to assess whether training was successful. This assessment is your organizational result.

It is important to assess this final level, because it is the reason for doing the training in the first place. In one sense, it is easier to measure than job behavior. Did the grievances go down? Did quality go up? Did customer satisfaction go up? Did attitudes in the annual survey get more positive? Did subordinates' satisfaction with supervision improve? Such questions are relatively easily answered. The difficult question is "Are the results due to training?" Perhaps the grievance rate dropped because of a successful completion of negotiations and not the training given to supervisors in how to implement the contract. Or if attitudes toward supervision improved but everyone recently received a large bonus, the improvement might be spill-off from the bonus and not the training. These examples explain why it is so important to gather information on all levels of the evaluation.

The links between organizational results, job behavior, and trainee KSAs should be clearly articulated in the TNA. In this way a model is created that specifies that if certain KSAs are developed and the employees use them on the job, certain organizational results will occur. The occurrence of these things validates the model and provides some confidence that training caused these results. Thus the difficult task of specifying how training should affect the results of the organization is already delineated before evaluation begins. Because TNAs are not always as thorough as they should be, it often falls on the evaluator to clarify the relationship among training, learning, job behavior, and organizational outcomes. For this reason, it is probably best to focus on organizational results as close to the trainee's work unit as possible. Results such as increased work unit productivity and quality and decreased costs are more appropriate than increased organizational profitability, market share, and the like. Quantifying organizational results is not as onerous as it might seem at first glance.

Timing of Assessment of Organizational Results   Consistent tracking of the organizational performance deficiencies (e.g., high scrap, number of grievances, poor quality) should take place at intervals throughout the training and beyond. At some point after the behavior is transferred to the job, you should expect improvement. Consistently tracking the performance deficiencies in the organization allows a determination of when or if it occurs.

Relationship Among Levels of Outcomes

As suggested earlier, the research has not generally supported a relationship among these four levels of evaluation. For example, some studies show reaction and learning outcomes to be strongly related to each other.[39] Others indicate little correlation between results of reaction questionnaires and measures of learning of material.[40] As noted earlier a good response to the reaction questionnaire may simply mean you obtained the trainees' attention. This factor is only one of many in the learning process. The findings also indicate that the more removed from the actual training the outcome is, the smaller the relationship between higher- and lower-level outcomes. Figure 8-8 illustrates the hierarchical nature of the outcomes and the factors that can influence these outcomes.

The research showing no relationship between the levels make sense if one remembers that organizational outcomes generally are the result of multiple causes.[41] For example, productivity is affected not only by the KSAs of the employees, but also by the technology they work with, supplier reliability, interdependencies among work groups, and many other factors. Thus, while improvements can occur in one area, declines can occur in another. When learning takes place but does not transfer to the job, the issues to be concerned with are not learning, but transfer. What structural constraints are being placed on trainees so they do not behave appropriately? Beverly Geber, special projects editor for *Training* magazine describes a situation in which training in communication skills at Hutchinson Technologies, a computer component manufacturer, was not transferring to the job for some of the employees.[42] An examination of the issue

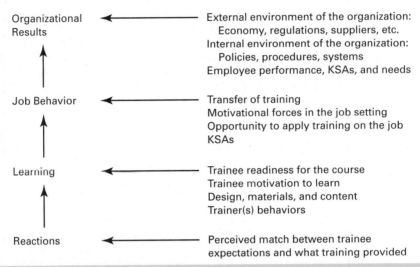

Organizational Results ←——————— External environment of the organization:
      Economy, regulations, suppliers, etc.
    Internal environment of the organization:
      Policies, procedures, systems
    Employee performance, KSAs, and needs

Job Behavior ←——————— Transfer of training
Motivational forces in the job setting
Opportunity to apply training on the job
KSAs

Learning ←——————— Trainee readiness for the course
Trainee motivation to learn
Design, materials, and content
Trainer(s) behaviors

Reactions ←——————— Perceived match between trainee
expectations and what training provided

FIGURE 8-8 Types of Outcomes and Examples of Factors Affecting Those Outcomes

(through focus groups of workers) disclosed that some employees were required to work in cramped space with poor lighting. These conditions made them irritable and unhappy. Did this situation affect their ability to communicate to their customers in a pleasant and upbeat manner? "You bet," said their human resource representative.

Evaluating the Costs of Training

Looking at the outcomes of training is only half the battle in evaluating its effectiveness. The other half is determining whether the results were worth the cost. If grievances do go down, and if the new behaviors are exhibited and the skills learned, then training might be considered the cause of the reduction, although cause-and-effect relationships are never a sure thing. The examination of all four levels of evaluation provide evidence of cause and effect, and appropriate designs enhance the level of confidence in cause and effect, but not to an absolute certainty. Many managers today still might ask, "So what? Was the training cost worth it?" In other words, did the benefits related to the reduction in grievances outweigh the training costs incurred? Training in Action 8-3 shows how one training director approached this question.

The "Is the training worth it?" question can be answered two ways:[43]

- Cost/benefit evaluation
- Cost-effectiveness evaluation

Cost/Benefit Evaluation   A **cost/benefit evaluation** of training compares the monetary cost of training to the nonmonetary benefits. It is difficult to place a value on these benefits, which include attitudes and working relationships. So, the labor peace brought about by the reduction in grievances is difficult to assess but rates high in value in comparison to the cost of training. The conflict resolution skills learned by supervisors provide the nonmonetary benefit of better relationships between supervisors and union officials. Although cost/benefit analysis is important and of value, it is also possible to assess the reduction in grievances (for example) in a way that directly answers the cost-effectiveness question.

EVALUATING TRAINING AT WALGREEN CO.

The Walgreen Co. in Deerfield, Illinois, provides pharmacy technicians to help pharmacists behind the counter in drugstores. Pharmacy technicians are support people who interact with customers and take refill information over the phone from doctors. They are also expected to determine whether generic drugs could be substituted for brand names and, if so, to ask customers if they would like the generic drug.

The pharmacists who hired the technicians were responsible for all the training, until Ann Marie Laures, corporate manager for Walgreen's training department, decided that a course for these technicians might be useful. Her department designed and implemented a training package that involved 20 hours of classroom training and 20 hours of closely supervised on-the-job training. Because technicians at Walgreen's 2,000 drugstores needed to be trained, this training would be costly, so Ann decided to determine how effective the training was.

She devised a questionnaire that asked questions such as: How speedily did the technician enter the data into the computer? How often did the technician interrupt the pharmacist with a question? How often did the technician offer generic drugs when applicable? She then sent these questionnaires to pharmacists who employed some technicians who received the training and others trained in the traditional way.

In almost all cases she found that the formally trained were more efficient and wasted less time than the traditional on-the-job trained technicians. The behavior of formally trained technicians was better in all respects. She went further, however, and assessed the organizational results as well. She discovered that sales in pharmacies with formally trained technicians exceeded those where technicians were trained in the traditional manner by $9,500 annually. The cost of training was $273 per employee, which suggests the formal training was a good decision.

Source: Adapted from Geber, B. 1995. Does your training make a difference? *Training*, March, pp. 27–34.

Cost-Effectiveness Evaluation   A **cost-effectiveness evaluation** compares the monetary costs of training to the financial benefits accrued from training. Two approaches can be used to assess cost effectiveness:

1. Calculation of the actual *cost savings*, based on the change in "results."
2. *Utility analysis*, which examines the value of overall improvement in performance of the trained employees.

The difference between the two is that the cost savings analysis only looks at the financial value of improvement in the problem that training was intended to correct (e.g., reduction in labor grievances). Utility analysis looks at all the ways in which the trainee's improved job performance will financially benefit the organization (e.g., reduced grievances, improved relations with labor force, less turnover, and so on).

Cost Savings Analysis (Results Focus).   The common types of costs associated with training programs were presented in Chapter 5, Table 5-4. These costs are compared to the savings that can be attributed to training. Let's look at our example from Chapter 5, Table 5-5.

Recall the cost of training was $32,310. Now let's determine the savings when training is completed. To perform this **cost savings analysis** we must first determine the cost of the current situation (see Table 8-5). The company averaged 90 grievances per year. Seventy percent of these (63) go to the third step before settlement. The average time required by management (including HR managers, operational supervisors, etc.) to deal with a grievance that goes to the third step is 10 hours. The management wages ($50 per hour on average) add $500 to the cost of each grievance ($50 × 10). In addition, union representatives spend an average of 7.5 hours at $25 per hour ($187.50) for those grievances, wages that are considered paid time as stipulated in the collective agreement. The total cost of wages to the company per grievance is $687.50. Thus, as noted in Table 8-5, the total cost for those 63 grievances that go to the third step is $43,312.50. Now, the savings as a result of training are indicated in Table 8-5.

In the first year, the number of grievances dropped by 50 percent, and only eight of those went to the third step. The drop in grievances suggests training was worth the cost. The drop should be coupled with a more positive relationship with the union and rank and file, a benefit some would say is value enough. But, let's calculate the actual cost savings. Sixty-three grievances cost $43,312.50 prior to the training, and the eight grievances after training cost $5,500. Thus training reduced the cost of grievances by $37,812.50. Subtracting the $32,310 training costs from this amount leaves a savings to the organization of $5,502.50 in just the first year. You will note that this conservative estimate does not include the cost of materials, facilities, and other overhead in the cost of grievances.

The data show a $37,812.50 return on a $32,310 investment. Dividing the return by the investment produces a return-on-investment ratio of 1.17. If the ratio is exactly 1.0, the training broke even. If it is below that, it cost more than it brings back to the company. In this case we calculate a 17 percent return on investment for the first year. Most companies would be delighted if all their investments achieved this level of return. In addition, the nonmonetary benefits described earlier are also realized. Presenting this type of data to the corporate decision makers at budget preparation time is certainly more compelling than stating, "Thirty supervisors were given a 5-day grievance reduction workshop."

TABLE 8-5 Cost Savings for Grievance Reduction Training

	Pretraining	*Posttraining*
Management Time (for those going to third step) 10 hours per grievance	10 hrs. × 63 grievances = 630 hrs.	10 hrs. × 8 grievances = 80 hrs.
Union Reps Time (paid by management) 7.5 hrs per grievance	7.5 × 63 grievances = 472 hrs.	7.5 × 8 grievances = 60 hrs.
Total Cost		
Management time	630 hrs. × $50 per hr. = $31,500	80 hrs. × $50 per hr. = $4,000
Union reps time	472 hrs. × $25 per hr. = $11,812.50	60 hrs. × $25 per hr. = $1,500
Total	$43,312.50	$5,500.00
Reduction in cost of grievances going to the third step		$43,312.50 − $5,500.00 = $37,812.50
Cost of training _____		−32,310.00
Cost saving for the first year		$ 5,502.50

Many training departments are beginning to see the importance of placing a monetary value on their training for a number of reasons:[44]

- HRD budgets are more easily justified and even expanded when HR can demonstrate it is contributing to the profit.
- HRD specialists are more successful in containing costs.
- Showing dollar value for training improves the image of the training department.

Remember Dave Palm from LensCrafters. He was told to demonstrate to top management what they were getting in the way of "bang for the buck." Well he did, and the result was that his training budget was doubled.[45] Training in Action 8-4 is a similar example. It is the story of Alberta Bell, where demonstrating the value of the training not only restored the original training, but also prompted management to consider increasing it.

Because of the time and effort required to calculate the value of training, many small business managers simply do not do it. However, assessing the value of training is not an exact science and can be done more easily by means of estimates. Table 8-6 provides a simplified approach for small business.[46] When estimates are necessary in completing this form, it is useful to obtain them from those who will receive the report (usually top management). If you use their estimates, it is more likely that your final report will have credibility. Of course, larger organizations can also use this method.

Utility Analysis.   In the previous example, training supervisors in grievance handling reduced the total number of grievances by 50 percent and the number going to the third step from 63 to 8. We calculated only the cost savings of the change in third-step grievances. **Utility analysis** permits us to estimate the overall value to the organization of the supervisors' changes in behavior. In other words, if those trained, on average, are better performers, and better performers are worth more in dollar terms, utility analysis allows us to estimate that increased worth. A general approach to utility is presented next:[47]

$$\Delta U = (N)(T)(D_T)(SD_Y) - C$$

where

ΔU = dollar value of improved performance

N = number of trainees

T = time the benefits will last

D_T = difference in performance between trained and untrained groups (in standard deviation units)

SD_Y = dollar value of untrained group's performance (in standard deviation units)

C = total cost of training the trained group

Some of the variables in the equation can be directly measured whereas others must be estimated. For example, N, C, and D_T can be objectively determined. On the other hand, determining how long the benefits will last is really an estimate, which will be more or less accurate depending on the estimator's experience with training, the types of employees involved, and so on. Calculating the dollar value of the untrained group's performance falls somewhere between. It is relatively easy, for example, to determine the compensation costs. However, it is often more difficult to translate their actual performance into dollar amounts. Recall our third-step grievance example. Even though we know what a third-step grievance costs in management labor compensation, we don't know the impact of those third-step grievances on the productivity of the work unit or the quality of the product/service. Thus, what is included in determining the

---

┌───┐

TRAINING IN ACTION 8-4

REDUCTION IN TRAINING TIME:
THE VALUE OF DEMONSTRATING VALUE

Telephone company Alberta Bell of Edmonton, Alberta, was looking for ways to reduce the cost of its operations. Downsizing and cost cutting were necessary to meet the new competitive environment. One of the decisions was to reduce the entry-level training program for their customer service representatives. The 2-week program was cut to 1 week. This move would save a great deal of money by reducing the cost of training and getting service representatives out "earning their keep" earlier.

Rudy, the manager of training at Alberta Bell, wanted to assess the value of this decision. By gathering information from data already available, he calculated the average time necessary to complete a service call for those who attended the 2-week training and compared it with the average for those attending the 1-week program. Those from the 2-week program completed a call on average in 11.4 minutes. Those in the one-week program took 14.5 minutes. This difference alone represented $50,000 in lost productivity for the first 6 weeks of work. He further analyzed the differences in increased errors, increased collectables, and service order errors. This difference was calculated at more than $50,000. The total loss exceeded $100,000.

He presented this information to upper management. Management quickly restored the 2-week training program and is considering making it longer.

Source: Adapted from Fitz-Enz, J. 1994. Yes you can weigh training's value. *Training*, July, pp. 54–58.

└───┘

dollar value of performance becomes a subjective decision. The final result will be an estimate of the value of the increased performance in dollars. Using the same example, an analysis of the possible utility is presented in Table 8-7.

Utility analysis is complex and beyond the scope of this text; what has been presented here is just a taste of the complexity. More complex models account for even more factors that may affect the true financial value of training outcomes.[48] Our purpose here is to demonstrate the difficulties of getting a true picture of the financial benefits associated with training outcomes. However, these complexities exist for any area of the business when you try to determine the effects of change. By becoming more quantitative in the assessment and description of training outcomes, training managers can put themselves on an equal footing with the other managers in the organization.

One important note regarding the use of utility methods for gaining support of the training program you wish to promote: Some recent research indicated that utility is not an effective method for garnering support for human resource policies. In fact, the research concluded that using utility analysis to bolster your claim as to the value of a project actually decreased managerial support for the project.[49] Until it is clear why this tendency is the case, it may not be wise to use this particular type of analysis to sell a project. It may still be useful for showing the benefits after the fact.

When to Use It

So, do we do a comprehensive evaluation at all four levels as well as a cost/benefit analysis for all training programs? No. To determine what evaluation should take place ask the question, "Who is interested in these data?" The different levels of outcome evaluation are designed for different

TABLE 8-6 Training Investment Analysis Work Sheet

Objective: _____

_____

Audience: _____

_____

Returns measured over: _____ One year: _____
Other: _____

_____

Part 1: Calculating the Revenue Produced by Training
Option A — Itemized Analysis

Increased sales:	_____	Additional sales per employee
	× _____	Revenues (or margin) per sale
	× _____	Number of employees
	= _____	Revenue Produced by Training
Higher productivity:	_____	Percent increase in productivity
	× _____	Cost per employee (salary plus benefits plus overhead)
	× _____	Number of employees
	= _____	Revenue Produced by Training
Reduced errors:	_____	Average cost per error
	× _____	Number of errors avoided per employee
	× _____	Number of employees
	= _____	Revenue Produced by Training
Client retention:	_____	Average revenue per client
	× _____	Number of clients retained
	= _____	Revenue Produced by Training
Employee retention:	_____	Average cost of a new employee (training plus lost productivity)
	× _____	Number of employees retained
	= _____	Revenue Produced by Training
Other:	_____	

Total Revenue Produced by Training:
$_____

Option B — Summary Analysis

_____ − _____ = _____

Revenue	Revenue	Revenue
After	Without	Produced
Training	Training	by Training

Part 2: Calculating the Return

_____ − _____ = _____

Revenue	Cost of	Total Return
Produced	Training	on Training
by Training		Investment

Source: Adapted from Hassett, J. 1992. Simplifying ROI. *Training*, September, pp. 53–57.

TABLE 8-7 Calculation of the Utility of the Grievance Training

Formula: $\Delta U = (N)(T)(D_T)(SD_Y) - C$

$N = 30$

$T = 1$ year (an overly conservative estimate)

$$D_T = .2 \ D_T = \frac{X_t - X_u}{SD(ryy)}$$

X_t = average job performance of the trained supervisors
X_u = average job performance of the untrained supervisors
SD = standard deviation of job performance for the untrained supervisors
$r\ yy$ = reliability of job performance measure

D_T is a measure of the improvement (in standard deviation units) in performance that trained supervisors will exhibit. Although obtaining the data is time-consuming (you need the performance appraisal data for supervisors, trained and untrained), the calculations can be done easily on today's computers.

$$SD_Y = \$14,000 = .40 \times \$35,000$$

The equation assumes average salary of $35,000. The .40 comes from the 40% rule, which is a calculation based on 40% of the average salary of trainees. This rule comes from the Schmidt and Hunter research. This and other methods to calculate SD_Y can be found in Cascio (1991). According to the preceding information, the utility of the training based on this formula is

$$(30)(1)(.2)(14,000) - 32,020 = \$51,980$$

Sources: Cascio, W. 1991. *Applied Psychology in Personnel Management*, 4th ed. Upper Saddle River, NJ: Prentice Hall; Schmidt, F., and J. Hunter. 1983. Individual differences in productivity: An empirical test of estimates derived from studies of selection procedure utility. *Journal of Applied Psychology* 68:407–14.

constituencies or customers. Note in Table 8-8 that the trainer is interested in the first three levels, because they reflect most directly on the training. Other trainers may be interested in these data as well if the results show some relation to their training programs. Training managers are interested in all the information. Both reaction and learning data can be used to evaluate the trainer and also promote the program to others (when positive). When it is not positive, the training

TABLE 8-8 Who Is Interested in the Outcome Data

	Outcome Data			
	Reaction	*Learning*	*Behavior*	*Results*
Training Department				
Trainer	yes	yes	yes	no
Other Trainers	perhaps	perhaps	perhaps	no
Training Manager	yes	yes	yes	yes
Customers				
Trainees	yes	yes	yes	perhaps
Trainees' Supervisor	not really	only if no transfer	yes	yes
Upper Management	no	no	perhaps	yes

Source: Adapted from Camp, R. P., P. N. Blanchard, and G. E. Huszczo. 1986. Toward a more organizationally effective training strategy and practice. Upper Saddle River, NJ: Prentice Hall.

manager should be aware of this fact, because it gives the trainer the information to intervene and turn the program around. The training manager's interest in transfer of training is to evaluate the trainer's ability to promote the transfer. Care must be taken in using this information, because many other factors may be present and operating to prevent transfer. Also, if transfer is favorable, the information is valuable in promoting the training program. These generalizations are also true for the organizational results. If the training manager is able to demonstrate positive results affecting the financial health of the company, the training department is bound to be seen as a worthy part of the organization.

Trainees are interested in knowing whether others felt the same as they did in training. They are also interested in feedback on what they accomplished (learning) as well as how useful it is to all trainees back on the job (behavior). A trainee's supervisor is interested in behavior and results, the main reason for sending subordinates to training in the first place. Upper management is interested in the results, although in some cases, where results may not be forthcoming, behavior may be the focus.

Does the interest in different levels of evaluation by different customers mean you need to gather information at all levels every time? Not at all. First, a considerable amount of work is required to evaluate every program offered. As with process data, it makes sense to gather the outcome data in some situations and not in others.

Again, the obvious question to ask in this regard is "What customer (if any) is interested in the information?" Although one of the major arguments for gathering the outcome data is to demonstrate the worth of the training department, some organizations go beyond that idea. In an examination of "companies with the best training evaluation practices," it was noted that none of these companies (IBM, Motorola, Arthur Andersen, etc.) were evaluating training primarily to justify it or maintain a training budget.[50] They evaluated (particularly at the behavior and results levels) when requested to do so by the customer (top management or the particular department). This selectivity is a function of the cost in developing such evaluations because these type of evaluations:[51]

- Need to be customized for each situation
- Are costly and time consuming
- Require cooperation of the customer

So, Arthur Andersen, for example, collects "results" only about 10 percent of the time. Motorola, on the other hand, evaluates only at the behavioral level, not the results level. Executives at Motorola are willing to assume that if the employee is exhibiting the appropriate behavior, the effect on the bottom line will be positive.[52] Training in Action 8-5 shows how various companies are dealing with evaluation, particularly behavior and results.

Certainly all levels of data gathering are important at different times, and the training professional must be able to conduct an evaluation at every level. So when and what should you evaluate? The answer is that it depends on the organization and the attitudes and beliefs of upper management. If they perceive the training department as an effective tool of the organization and require only behavior-level evaluation, that is the evaluation you do. However, this level may still require vigilance at the learning and reaction levels to ensure positive results. Darryl Jinkerson, director of evaluation services at Arthur Andersen, looks at the size and impact of the training before deciding how to evaluate it. Only those that are high profile, or where the customer requests it, will be evaluated at the results level.[53] What if training is a one-time event and no desire is indicated to assess individual competence (e.g., a workshop on managing your career)? Such a situation provides simply no reason to evaluate.[54]

TRAINING IN ACTION 8-5

EVALUATION: WHAT COMPANIES ARE DOING

Arthur Andersen and Co. uses reaction measures for all its training. Learning is assessed about half the time, behavior less than one-third of the time, and results only 10 percent of the time. The "results" are evaluated only for high-profile training or where the customer requests evaluation. In one of the executive training programs for presentation skills, videotaped presentations were used to evaluate both learning and behavior. Executives were videotaped giving a presentation. This exercise served as the needs analysis to identify candidates for training. It also served as the pretest for evaluation. After the training, they were videotaped again to determine whether learning took place. Six months later the executives were once again videotaped while making a presentation to a client. To measure improvement, the evaluators identified a number of the elements of a good presentation. Making good eye contact, not using nonwords (uh, um), and even the type or frequency of hand movements were quantified as a means of measurement (Geber, 1995).

Motorola developed a 360-degree performance appraisal process that they used as their behavior measure of leadership skills. The appraisal form is sent to the supervisors, their subordinates, and their bosses four times a year for 2 years, asking them to rate how frequently the supervisors display certain behaviors related to the leadership training (Geber, 1995).

Texas Instruments noted that once trainees left training, it was difficult to obtain transfer of training information from them. Because of the time and expense of gathering this information, it was generally ignored. Then an automated e-mail system was developed through which trainees, after being back on the job for 90 days, were contacted and asked to complete a survey related to transfer. This system increased the use of evaluations, reduced the time necessary to gather information, and provided a standardized process. Texas Instruments noted an improvement in the quantity and quality of participant feedback. It would seem easy enough to include an e-mail call to the trainees' supervisors for the same purpose (Overmyer-Day and Benson, 1996).

FPL Nuclear uses testing to assess learning. First, however, the test serves as the needs analysis to determine who needs the training. Second, it is used as a posttest to be compared to the pretest in assessing learning. Finally the test is administered a few months after training to assess the degree of retention. If trainees do not do well on the retention test, they are provided with refresher training (Dixon, 1996).

Sources: Dixon, N. 1996. New routes to evaluation. *Training and Development*, May, pp. 82–85; Geber, B. 1995. Does your training make a difference? *Training*, March, pp. 27–34; Overmyer-Day, D., and G. Benson. 1996. Training success stories. *Training and Development*, June, pp. 24–29.

Let's now return to Fabrics Inc. to see how their evaluation was developed.

⬡ **THE TRAINING PROGRAM (FABRICS INC.)** ⬡

We are now ready to examine the evaluation phase of the Fabrics Inc. training. We presented the training, and it is time to do the evaluation. In the design phase of the training process, one of the outcomes was evaluation objectives. Although we developed and implemented the training, it is critical to remember that the development of the tools for evaluation need to be done concurrently with development of the training, not after it.

Examination of the output of the evaluation phase of training indicated two types of evaluation: process and outcome. The process evaluation will consist of the trainer, during training, documenting the content phases and times taken in each of the training modules. These results will then be compared with the actual expectations regarding training content and times allotted.

For the outcome evaluation, four types are identified. The reaction questionnaire for trainers will model the one presented in Figure 8-1. For the training itself, the reaction questionnaire is shown in Figure 8-9.

Rate the following questions using the following scale anchors:

1 = Strongly disagree
2 = Disagree
3 = Neither agree nor disagree
4 = Agree
5 = Strongly agree

Active Listening Skills:

The training met the stated objectives.	1	2	3	4	5
The information provided was enough so I understood the concepts being taught.	1	2	3	4	5
The practice sessions provided were sufficient to give me an idea of how to perform the skill.	1	2	3	4	5
The feedback provided was useful in helping me understand how to improve.	1	2	3	4	5
The training session kept my interest throughout.	1	2	3	4	5

The pace of this part of the training session was

1. Way too fast
2. A bit fast
3. Just right
4. A bit slow
5. Way too slow

What did you like best about this part of the training?

What would you change?

Comments:

Note: A similar scale would be used for each of the other components of training that were taught.

FIGURE 8-9 Reaction to Training

(*continued*)

(continued)

For learning we need to revisit the learning objectives to determine what is required. We need a paper-and-pencil test for measuring the declarative knowledge (objectives 1 and 2), behavioral tests to measure active listening and conflict resolution skills (objectives 3 and 4), and an oral test to measure the procedural knowledge (objective 5). More specifically, the first two learning objectives

The trainee will, <u>with no errors</u>, **present in writing the four types of active listening, along with examples of each of the types,** *with no reference material.*

The trainee will, <u>with 100% accuracy</u>, **provide in writing each step of the conflict resolution model, along with a relevant example,** *with no help from any reference material.*

(and the others related to the training but not developed here) are accommodated using the paper-and-pencil test in Figure 8-10.

The next objective below is related to skill development for which we developed standardized role plays and guidelines to evaluate.

When, in a role play, the trainee is presented with an angry comment, **the trainee will respond** <u>immediately</u> **using one of the active listening types.** *The trainee will* **then explain orally the technique used and why,** *with no help from reference material.* <u>The trainee will be presented with five of these situations and be expected to correctly respond and explain a minimum of four techniques.</u>

These are depicted in Figure 8-11.

EVALUATION OF LEARNING

No specific time limit is set for this test, but most should be able to finish in about 1 hour. Answers to the questions should be written in the booklet provided.

Please read each question carefully. Some of the questions contain more than one part.

1. List four types of active listening and provide an example for each.
2. List the steps in the conflict resolution model. After each step, provide a relevant example of a phrase that could be used that would represent that step.
3. And so forth . . . .

FIGURE 8-10 Paper-and-Pencil Test for Evaluation of Learning

FIGURE 8-11 Training Evaluation Documents for Active Listening

SCENARIOS FOR EVALUATING LEARNING OF ACTIVE LISTENING SKILLS
Initiator's Role

Role Scenarios to Test Trainees (The initiator to be played by the same actor for all trainees)
Test Scenario 1
You were just asked by your supervisor (the trainee) to serve on the same committee again. You are angry that they always ask you. You start. Say angrily:

"OH NO, YOU DON'T. I'VE BEEN ON THAT COMMITTEE 3 YEARS IN A ROW AND IT TAKES UP TOO MUCH TIME."

(*continued*)

Test Scenario 2

Your supervisor just talked to you about following procedures. Why you—no one—follows procedures.

You start. Say angrily:

"WHY ARE YOU PICKING ON ME ALL THE TIME? I'M NOT THE ONLY ONE WHO DOESN'T FOLLOW THESE STUPID PROCEDURES."

You were just asked by your supervisor for a second time today whether you will be attending the weekly meeting.

You say angrily:

"I ALREADY TOLD YOU, I CAN'T ATTEND THE WEEKLY MEETING BECAUSE I HAVE TO COMPLETE THE STAFF REPORTS FOR TOMORROW."

And so forth (for a total of 5).

SCENARIOS FOR EVALUATING LEARNING OF ACTIVE LISTENING SKILLS

Trainee's Instructions

This test will require you to respond to five different short scenarios in which you are a supervisor, and you say something to a subordinate that elicits an angry response. You will be expected to respond using the skills of active listening. The description of each of the scenarios provides what you initially said to the subordinate. When you are ready for each of the scenarios to begin, nod your head to the initiator. At that time the initiator will say something. You need to respond to the comment, and when complete, explain to the evaluator the rationale for your response.

Scenario 1

You asked a subordinate to continue working on a particular committee for another year. Listen, then respond using active listening. Nod your head when ready ...

Scenario 2

You just talked to a subordinate regarding the importance of following procedures. Listen, then respond using active listening. Nod your head when ready ...

Scenario 3

Today is the day of your weekly meeting. You asked your subordinate if he/she would be attending the meeting, they said no. It is now time for the meeting and you call once more to check to see whether he/she can make the meeting. Listen, then respond using active listening. Nod your head when ready ...

SCENARIOS FOR EVALUATING LEARNING OF ACTIVE LISTENING SKILLS

Evaluator's Scoring Guide

General guide for scoring trainee.

Trainee fails the scenario if his/her response is focused on the issue instead of reflecting back what the initiator says. For example a poor (fail) response to the first scenario would be something where trainee responds to the concern by dealing with the issue "**But you are my best person for the job**" or "**You have to do it, I have no one else**" or "**Look, I am asking you as a favor to me.**"

FIGURE 8-11 (continued)

(*continued*)

Passing responses reflect back what the person is saying such as in the first scenario saying, **"So, you're saying that being on the committee interferes with you doing your job"** or **"You feel you have done your share regarding committee work."**

It is also important that the response does not sound like a mimic of what the person said. Although at this time we do not expect perfection regarding responses, the responses must at a minimum sound sincere. Refer to the tape recordings provided to understand the difference between what we consider mimicking and acceptable.

For each of the five scenarios there is an example of a poor (fail) response and an acceptable response. For the explanation expected after the trainee responds, we expect the trainee to be able to identify the type of active listening response used (paraphrasing, decode and feedback, summarizing) and why it was chosen. Answers as to why it was chosen are simply to be sure they understand the different methods and almost any answer is acceptable.

Scenario 1

The supervisor (trainee being tested) asked the subordinate to continue working on a particular committee for another year, and the subordinate responds. Listen to response and grade according to guidelines.

Unacceptable response: **"I am willing to talk about reducing the work you have to do if you will be on it."**

Acceptable response: **"YOU DON'T WANT TO BE ON THAT COMMITTEE AGAIN BECAUSE IT INTERFERES WITH YOUR WORK AND YOU FEEL YOU HAVE DONE YOUR SHARE."**

Scenario 2

The supervisor (trainee being tested) just talked to a subordinate regarding the importance of following procedures, and the subordinate responds. Listen to response and grade according to guidelines.

Unacceptable response: **"You are not the only one I have talked to about this."**

Acceptable response: **"YOU BELIEVE THAT YOU'RE THE ONLY ONE THAT I AM SINGLING OUT FOR NOT FOLLOWING PROCEDURES."**

Scenario 3

The supervisor (trainee being tested) called first thing in the morning and asked the subordinate if he/she would be attending the weekly meeting and the subordinate said no, he/she was busy. The supervisor just called again at meeting time to check to see whether he/she could make the meeting, and the subordinate responds. Listen and grade.

Unacceptable response: **"The meeting will only be an hour."**

Acceptable response: **"YOU'RE NOT ABLE TO ATTEND THE MEETING BECAUSE YOU ARE COMPLETING STAFF REPORTS THAT ARE DUE TOMORROW."**

And so forth . . .

FIGURE 8-11 (continued)

For the objective below the standardized role plays and evaluation are depicted in Figure 8-12.

In a role play of an angry customer/ employee the trainee **will calm the person, using the steps in the conflict resolution model,** with help from an easel sheet that lists the steps.

⟨ **THE TRAINING PROGRAM (FABRICS INC.)** ⟩

(continued)

SCENARIOS FOR EVALUATING LEARNING OF CONFLICT RESOLUTION

Initiator's Role

Role Scenario to Test Trainees (The initiator to be played by the same actor for all trainees)

Instructions for the Role Play

—Read the role a couple of times and get in the mood suggested.

—Be sure you understand the issues so you can present them without referring to the role.

—Once into the role, allow your own feelings to take over; if what the supervisor is saying makes you less angry then act that way, and vice versa.

—Do not refer back to the role after the role play begins, simply act the way you normally would do in such circumstances.

   —**Begin role play by presenting the points at the end of the role play with anger**.

   —**On at least one occasion after trainee begins to present his/her point of view, interrupt him/her to elicit assertive response. If he/she allows the interruption, interrupt again until he/she becomes assertive and asks you not to interrupt (maximum of four interruptions)**.

The Role

Your name is Pat. You are the longest-working machinist in the plant, with 25 years service. You taught many of those who are presently there, including most of those who were made supervisor recently. The company has been busy for the last number of years, and you have been called upon many times to provide the extra boost to get some projects out. You worked hard all your life and are starting to feel it in your bones. The work is getting harder and harder to complete, especially with the older lathes. With only 3 years to retirement, you are wishing you could afford to retire now. You are really wore out, that is, until you heard the news that the company just purchased one of those new computer-operated lathes. You feel confident that once you get to use the new machine you will be rejuvenated. In fact the thought of getting to work on one of these new machines gives you goosebumps. You have not felt this excited in years. Actually the thought of going back to school to learn about it is the most exciting thing, as it is making you feel young again. You are sorry you missed today's meeting at which they were going to talk about the new equipment, but your car would not start.

"Hey, did you hear the news?" your friend Bill called out.

"I don't think so, what is it?" you replied.

"They just announced that Fred is going for training on the new computer-operated lathe. I guess he will be the one operating it."

"Are you sure?" you ask.

"Yep, it was announced at the circle meeting this morning. He was selected to operate it and will be going for a 2-week training course next week."

You are furious. Fred was only just hired and is just a kid. You deserve first crack at the new machine, given your loyal service. Well that is it. Your supervisor (the young guy you taught how to run a lathe before he got promoted) never did get along with you, and now this. Well you are not going to take it. You walk into the supervisor's office and in a loud voice start off by saying

"What do you think you are doing? How can you give the new lathe to Fred, after all the years I have been here? This is not fair and I am not going to sit still for it."

FIGURE 8-12 Training Evaluation Documents for Conflict Resolution

⟨ **THE TRAINING PROGRAM (FABRICS INC.)** ⟩

(*continued*)

Be sure to continue the anger and bring up all the points mentioned in the role play. Go over them again and again until the trainee calms you down.

SCENARIOS FOR EVALUATING LEARNING OF CONFLICT RESOLUTION

Trainee's Role

Instructions for the Role Play

—Read the role a couple of times and be sure you understand the issues so you can present them without referring to the role.

—Do not refer back to the role after the role play begins, but you can jot down a few points for reference.

—Use the conflict resolution model to deal with the issue.

—When you wish to begin, nod at the initiator.

The Role

You are the supervisor of a manufacturing firm and have about 10 subordinates. They are all lathe operators, and you were also one until you recently got promoted. Your subordinates are all good people, and with the exception of Pat, who has been here 25 years and is a few years away from retirement, all are fairly young and have at most 10 years' service. Pat is a great machinist, knowing more than everyone put together. He taught you the job when you just started and although you never really hit it off with him, you do respect his ability.

You are pretty excited these last few days because the company just purchased a new computer-operated lathe. It is your understanding you will be getting a new lathe each year until all are replaced. You are moving into the new age. Choosing only one of your machinists to go to training and be the first one on the new machine was a difficult decision. All were likely candidates, with the exception of Pat, who was too old to learn the new machine, computer stuff and all. Furthermore, why train Pat on a new machine when he will only be here a short time. It makes more sense to train those who will be able to use the new skills for the longest time. Anyway, Pat really knows how to operate the older machine better than anyone, so why move him? Finally you came up with the perfect solution. The new guy, Fred, has not been trained on any machine yet, so training him on the new lathe would mean no one else needed training for the time being. Putting anyone else on the new machine would mean training Fred on the old machine, then when they are phased out, retraining him on the computer-operated lathe. So you announced it today at your circle meeting. Everyone was pretty quiet, but they will get over it. Too bad Pat wasn't there. Wonder if he is sick?

SCENARIOS FOR EVALUATING LEARNING OF CONFLICT RESOLUTION

Evaluator's Scoring Guide

General guide for scoring trainee.

Trainee fails the scenario if his/her initial response is focused on the issue instead of reflecting back what the initiator says. For example a poor (fail) response would be if the first comment to Pat was **"I did not think you wanted it"** or **"It is probably too complicated for you"** or "We **value your contribution**" or "You're the best we've got on the old machine, and we need you there."

Key to successfully passing this exercise is to:

—Actively listen to Pat (using the active listening skills)

—Questioning to obtain as much information as possible before dealing with the issue

FIGURE 8-12 (continued)

```
THE TRAINING PROGRAM (FABRICS INC.)
```

(*continued*)

   To be successful, it is expected that the trainee will use active listening and questions at least four to six times (preferably more) before moving to trainee's point of view. Key is to note how much the initiator calmed down.

—Being sure trainee indicates respect (must have at least one phrase such as **"I can appreciate why you feel you should have the opportunity to receive the training. It makes sense that you believe after such long and loyal service you should receive some reward".**)

—Be assertive, not aggressive, if necessary to present points

   When interrupted the trainee must use the proper assertive response to inhibit interruptions. Trainee is given four opportunities to be assertive as role requires interruptions until assertive response given (up to four). Note how that interruption is handled; trainee needs to be assertive (for example, **"I have carefully listened to everything you have had to say, I think it only fair that now you give me a chance to respond, okay**?"

—Provide supervisor's points as "point of view" not correct point of view

   The role play will begin with the initiator being angry. Response can be a summary of these points, paraphrase of one of them, decode and feedback regarding emotion expressed, but not anything dealing with the specific issue.

Evaluator Report Form

Put a mark next to each of the responses in terms of their type. Try to jot down the words used in some of the cases to enable you to provide specific feedback.

ACTIVE LISTENING
   Nonverbal Behavior
   Say More Responses
   Paraphrase
   Decode and Feedback
   Summarize

INDICATE RESPECT
   Use of active listening
   Questioning
   Show acceptance of other's point of view

BE ASSERTIVE
   Needs to be phrased in terms of YOUR POINT OF VIEW
      My perception is . . .
      It seems to me that . . .
      It is my belief that . . . and so forth.

PROVIDE INFORMATION
Use collaboration (problem solving) or compromise (negotiate). *Note*: Although this response is a part of the conflict resolution model, it is not part of the learning objectives for this training, hence it is not evaluated in this training program.

FIGURE 8-12 (continued)

   You will note that for the evaluator, a standardized scoring key, examples of acceptable and unacceptable behavior of the trainee, and a check list for different responses are provided.

   (The last objective is not provided here.)

Evaluation Design Issues

A number of texts provide excellent information on appropriate designs for conducting evaluations.[55] Unfortunately, many of their recommended designs are impractical in most organizational settings. Finding the time or resources to create a control group is difficult at best. Getting approval to do pretests on control groups takes away from productivity time and is difficult to justify.

Scientifically valid research designs are difficult to implement, so organizations often use evaluation designs that are generally not acceptable to the scientific community.[56] You can still have some confidence in your results with less rigorous designs. As you will note, some research designs are less than perfect, but you can find ways of improving them. The two designs most often used, and most criticized by scientists, are the posttest only and the pretest/posttest methods.[57]

BASIC DESIGNS

Posttest Only

The posttest-only method occurs when training is provided (represented by $\times$) and then a posttest is given (represented by T_2). The design is represented as $\times T_2$.

Some problems with the posttest-only design mean that in certain instances (discussed shortly) it is not a recommended choice. At other times, however, the method is completely acceptable.[58] The two possible goals of evaluation are:

1. To determine whether change took place
2. To determine whether a level of competence was reached

If the goal of the training is the latter, a posttest-only design should suffice. If, for example, legal requirements state that everyone in the company who handles hazardous waste be trained to understand what to do in an emergency, then presumably any training developed need only provide a test at the end to confirm that all trainees reached the required level of knowledge. As more companies are required to be ISO 9000 (or equivalent) certified, it will be increasingly important to prove that employees possess the required skills. As a result, certification will become the goal of employee training, and in that case the posttest only will suffice.

We mentioned frequently the value in doing needs analysis. If you conducted a needs analysis, you already collected pretest data, and so the posttest-only design becomes moot. Giving the posttest automatically applies a pretest/posttest design. Furthermore, in the absence of a TNA, archival data may serve as the pretest. Performance appraisals, measures of quality, and the like might allow for some pre/post comparison. Although such historical data may not be ideal, it could provide some information as to the effectiveness of training. Alternatively, you could identify an equivalent group and provide its members with the same posttest, thereby turning the design into a posttest only with control group. Suddenly you create a much more meaningful design.

The posttest-only design as it stands is problematic for assessing change. A number of other competing causes could be responsible for the change. (More information on competing causes can be found in Appendix 8.1 in the discussion of internal and external validity issues.) Nevertheless, we would agree with other professionals that any evaluation is better than none.[59] Gathering any pretraining information that might suggest that the level of KSAs prior to training was lower than in the posttest would help to bolster the conclusion that training was effective.

Pretest/Posttest

The other method used frequently by organizations is the pretest/posttest design. Here a pretest is given (T_1), training is provided ($\times$), and then a post test if given (T_2). This design is expressed therefore as $T_1 \times T_2$.

This design demonstrates that change occurred. Although you can demonstrate that KSAs changed, you are not able to say that training is responsible for those changes. For example, you may have been training a group of machine operators to operate new drill-press machines. Pretesting the trainees revealed that none knew how to operate the machine. After a 3-day training session, a posttest showed that, on average, the trainees were able to operate the machine correctly 85 percent of the time. A big success? Not if the supervisor of the work group says that the ones without training can operate the machines correctly 95 percent of the time by just reading the manuals and practicing on their own. A variety of reasons might explain why those who did not go to training are performing better on the job. Perhaps they already knew how to operate the machine. Perhaps a manufacturer's representative came and provided on-the-floor training to them. Or it could be that your training somehow slowed down the learning process. Therefore the suggestion might be that a control group is necessary.

In many instances using a control group is simply not an option. Does it mean you should not bother to do anything? Absolutely not. In fact, it is better to do something than nothing. We tend to focus on the negative aspects of the preexperimental designs rather than examine ways of using them most effectively when other options do not exist.[60] The pre/post-no-control group at least establishes that changes did take place. Were any extraneous factors present that might cause the learning? Acting like a detective and exploring the possibilities can serve to answer this question. Suppose Sue learned a great deal about operating in a Windows environment according to the pre/posttest. Did she do extra reading at home? Did she practice on her own irrespective of training expectations? Did she get some help from someone at the office or elsewhere? Simply asking her might indicate that none of those factors occurred, suggesting it was in fact the training.

Internal Referencing Strategy

Another way of dealing with the lack of a control group is **internal referencing strategy (IRS)**.[61] With this method, you include relevant and nonrelevant test questions in the pre- and posttest. Here's how it works.

Both pretests and posttests contain questions that deal with the training content as well as questions that deal with related content not in the training. In the pretest, trainees will do poorly on both sets of questions. On the posttest, if training is effective, improvement should show only for the trained items. The nonrelevant items serve as a control. In their research on the IRS, Haccoun and Hamtiaux noted that the results obtained from the IRS design were identical to those obtained when a control group was used.[62] This method deals with many of the concerns that arise when a control group is used, as well as other concerns. (See Appendix 8.1 for additional discussion.)

One final note. The IRS design can be used to determine improvement in KSAs, but research indicates it tends to show that training is not effective when in fact it is.[63] In other words, the training must provide a substantial improvement from pretest to posttest in order for it to be detected by this design.

MORE COMPLEX DESIGNS

Two factors need to be considered when developing a sound evaluation design:

1. Control groups
2. Random assignment

The **control group** is a group of similar employees who do not receive the training. It is used to determine whether changes that take place in trainees also take place for those who do not receive training. If change only occurs in trainees, it is probably due to training. If it occurs in both trained and untrained groups, it is probably due to some other factor.

Random assignment is the assignment of employees to either the control group or the training group by chance, to ensure that the groups are equivalent. It is more applicable to experimental laboratories than to applied settings such as in training, for two reasons. First, given the small number of employees placed in one group or the other, the theory of randomness is not likely to hold true. When we split a group of 60 employees into two groups of 30, it is quite likely that real differences will be present within the two groups. Random assignment works well when multiple groups of 30 are used, or when the total number of subjects is quite large (e.g., 500).

Second, it is unlikely that the organization can afford the luxury of randomly assigning employees to each group. The work still needs to be done, and managers would want some control over who will be in training at a specific time. For this reason, matching employees as best you can so the two groups contain a representative sampling makes more sense. The following discussion covers a number of designs that use control groups. We believe that assigning trainees through representative sampling is a more effective way of obtaining equivalent groups.

Posttest Only with Control Group

Posttesting only with a control group is represented by the following:

Trainee Group (representative sampling) $\times T_2$
Control Group (representative sampling) $\quad T_2$

If for some reason a pretest was not conducted or if you did not provide a pretest to a control group at the beginning of training, you can compare the trainees with a control group using a posttest-only design. Differences in test scores noted between the groups (trainees doing better) will provide evidence of the success of the training. The tendency is to downplay the effectiveness of this design because no pretest assessed equivalence of the groups before training. If the training and control groups were large enough to result in effective random assignment, you will be more confident of the findings. True randomness, however, is not ensured in a single set of trained and control employees. In this situation, **representative sampling**, matching employees on specific variables such as tenure, age, educational background, and other features will be more likely to provide equivalent groups, although one way to be more confident of equivalence is use of a pretest.

Pretest/Posttest with Control Group

The expression for pretest/posttest with a control group is:

Trainee Group (representative sampling) $T_1 \times T_2$
Control Group (representative sampling) $T_1 \quad T_2$

This design is one of the more favorable for eliminating most concerns about confidence in the results. The issue here is how equivalent the two groups are, given they were divided through representative sampling. A pretest can determine their level of equivalence. Equivalent pretests in both groups provide you with one more piece of evidence that the groups are equal, and posttest differences (if the trained group obtains higher scores) will suggest that training was successful.

Time Series Design

The time series design is represented by:

Trainee Group $T_1 \, T_2 \, T_3 \, T_4 \times T_5 \, T_6 \, T_7 \, T_8$

This design uses a series of measurements before and after training. In this way, the likelihood of any other factors causing the improvement are much smaller. Also, when everyone attends training at the same time (a one-shot training program), this design can be used whether the number is large or small. It can still be argued that because no control group is used, alternate reasons may explain the improvement. Recall, however, that in applied settings, the goal is to be as sure as you can about the results, given organizational constraints. If enough measures are taken pre- and posttraining to deal with fluctuations in performance, changes after training are certainly suggestive of learning.

Instances in which the training will be provided to everyone at the same time allow little room for elaborate designs, and the time series design becomes especially useful. If you gather data over a number of periods before and after training (and if they indicate training was successful), you can be more certain about the impact of training than if you simply conducted a pretest/posttest on the group. Remember, in an applied setting you will never be absolutely sure of the impact of training, but taking care to use the best possible design (considering constraints) is still better than doing nothing at all.

To make this design more powerful, consider adding a control group, expressed by:

Trainee Group $T_1 T_2 T_3 T_4 \times T_5 T_6 T_7 T_8$
Control Group $T_1 T_2 T_3 T_4 \quad T_5 T_6 T_7 T_8$

In this way, you are able to deal with the some of the concerns related to not having a control group.

Multiple Baseline Design

Multiple baseline design is represented by:

Trainee Group A	T_1	T_2	T_3	$\times$	T_4	T_5	T_6	T_7	T_8	T_9	$T_{10}\cdots$
Trainee Group B	T_1	T_2	T_3	T_4	T_5	$\times$	T_6	T_7	T_8	T_9	$T_{10}\cdots$
Trainee Group C	T_1	T_2	T_3	T_4	T_5	T_6	T_7	$\times$	T_8	T_9	$T_{10}\cdots$
Trainee Group D	T_1	T_2	T_3	T_4	T_5	T_6	T_7	T_8	T_9	$\times$	$T_{10}\cdots$

In this design, multiple measures are taken much as in time series, but each group receives the training at a different point in time. Each untrained group serves as a control for the trained groups. This approach deals with many of the concerns when no control group is used. Here the ability to say that changes measured by the test are due to the training is strong. If each group improves after its training, it is difficult to argue that something else caused the change.

WHAT DESIGN TO USE

Determining the true impact of training requires an investigation into the validity of evaluation results. A number of methods are available, and the more complex the design, the more valid the results. Other considerations need to be taken into account when you are deciding on an evaluation design. Innovation can provide good substitutes when the best is not possible. Consider the multiple baseline design. It is a powerful design and certainly is a possibility if a number of employees need to receive the training over time.

However, what if multiple measures were not possible? The following design would address many of the same concerns, and although it is not as elaborate, it certainly deals with many of the concerns regarding outside influences causing the change. If pretest scores are all comparable, and posttest scores indicate an improvement, these results are a strong argument for showing training was responsible.

Trainee Group A	T_1	$\times$	T_2		
Trainee Group B		T_1	$\times$	T_2	
Trainee Group C			T_1	$\times$	T_2
Trainee Group D				T_1	$\times$	T_2

We already mentioned that most organizations do not evaluate all training at all levels. Furthermore, even when evaluating training, many organizations do not use pretest/posttest or control groups in a manner that would eliminate concerns about the validity of the results. Dr. Dixon of George Washington University indicated that of the companies she investigated in her article "New Routes to Evaluation," only one, Arthur Andersen, used designs that would deal with many of the validity issues. Other companies, including IBM and Johnson Controls, follow such procedures only when asked by particular departments or higher-level management, or when they can defray some of the high cost of developing reliable and valid tests by marketing the final product to other organizations.[64] The demand for certification in some skills (primarily because of ISO and others' requirements) created a need for these types of tests.

When you are evaluating training, if using control groups or pretesting is not possible, remember other investigative methods can be used for assessing the likelihood that factors other than training account for any change in KSAs.

WHAT ABOUT SMALL BUSINESS?

For the small business owner, sending employees to training that is not effective could significantly affect the company's financial health. Consider the owner who is constantly terminating employees because they are unable (or unwilling) to do the job properly. They all receive training and most, but not all, turn out to be ineffective. Why? If training is not evaluated, you don't know whether employees are lost because the training is not effective or because of some other factor that is blocking effective performance

The small business owner might think it is not necessary to evaluate training because whether it was effective will be obvious by changes observed on the job after training. Actually this assessment is probably true; in a small business you would soon know if recently trained employees are performing at the expected level. However, if training is a significant cost to the owner, evaluating learning before and after training can still be of value. After all, the trainees may be learning on the job, and the training may not be adding anything to their KSAs.

Much of the training in a small business is **on-the-job training**. In such cases evaluation is often simply an assessment of the trainee's ability to learn. Examining the training process is not considered. As we discussed in the previous chapter, on-the-job training requires trainer skills just as does any other training. Simply placing a new employee with an experienced employee and expecting the experienced one to train is not wise. It can be worthwhile to evaluate the process of training that goes on, as well as the outcomes, especially if the position is at a lower level where, because of turnover or promotion, a rather high number of employees receive training.

Because a small business may have one or two employees who need training, using a training design to determine training success may be difficult.

Single-Case Designs

Single-case designs are often used to evaluate the training provided to professional counselors; it can also be used by managers to evaluate training when the number of employees is small.[65]

The single-case design uses data from one individual and makes inferences based on that information. To increase confidence in the results the multiple baseline approach could be used. Suppose two supervisors need to be trained in active listening skills. Because the business is small, both cannot attend training at the same time. Using a predetermined checklist developed for evaluating the training, you count the number of active listening phrases each of them uses in conversations with you. Take several measures over 3 or 4 weeks. Then one supervisor is sent to training. Continue monitoring the active listening after the person returns. Did the number increase for the trained supervisor and not the other supervisor? Now the second supervisor is given training, after which you continue monitoring the conversations. If both employees improved after training, you can infer that the training was effective. Although this approach is suggested for the small business, it is also useful in any sized organization with few trainees.

The movement to quality standards such as ISO 9000 creates a need for certification in a number of areas. Although the standards do not suggest how to evaluate training, they do specify that the organization must maintain training records and periodically evaluate training. The following excerpt comes from the QS 9000 requirements manual.

Training records can be diplomas, certificates, licenses, experience, resumes. . . . The standard does not suggest any specific method for evaluating training effectiveness. A popular method is annual review of training. . . . Results of the review are recorded and are used as feedback for revising and updating the training program. Another method is periodic assessment of individual employees.[66]

Certification can become both the documentation and evaluation of training, something that might explain why becoming certified is so popular (see Training in Action 8-6).

David Alcock of Canadian Plastics Training Center in the Toronto area says that even though few of the center's clients request an evaluation of training, such requests are on the increase. Most of the center's clients are small injection-molding businesses. The need for certification seems to be the driving force behind the necessity to evaluate. Canadian Plastics Training conducts standardized injection-molding training on its own site and provides a skill-based evaluation. A trainee who passes the skill-based test becomes certified as an injection molder. In many cases, employees are sent by their company for this training, but some employees pay their own way to improve themselves.

One reason these small companies do not evaluate is the cost. For in-house training done by Canadian Plastics Training, a late 1997 cost of evaluation for 20 employees to be trained to a higher-level classification was $25,000. Many small companies simply do not have those resources. Another issue noted by Alcock is what the evaluation would be used for. For example, suppose a unionized shop wants to upgrade the skills of the workforce. Sending them to training would carry with it the union's blessing. Evaluating the learning, on the other hand, might be met with a great deal of resistance. The union leadership and rank and file might be concerned about the company knowing how well the employees did on a test. Would the results be used to get rid of some employees? If not, what is the purpose of the evaluation? Convincing the union that evaluation is a way of assessing the effectiveness of training might be difficult to do, depending on the relationship between union and management. Training in Action 8-7 shows what one small company is doing.

Much of the preceding discussion relates to the evaluation of learning. What about organizational results in this case? After publication of the article on Scepter Manufacturing,[67] Villers was asked how he knew the drop in scrap and defective parts (results) was a function of training. His reply: "We are a small company, and it is the only thing that we changed." He makes an important point related to the examination of results in small businesses. When small business does training, evidence of the impact can be much clearer and faster. Also it should be easier to rule out alternative explanations for the change, without the need for the more complex designs.

Palm Desert

The Palm Desert case at the beginning of the chapter provides an example of an effort to evaluate using a control group and pre/post design. Even here, however, problems developed in the way evaluation was managed. One issue is that learning was not assessed. Only behavior change was assessed 6 months after training. We know the training did not transfer, but we don't know why. If it did not transfer because it was never learned in the first place, what was the reason? Was it perhaps that simply too much material was expected to be learned in a 1-day seminar? Examining the process of developing the training might reveal this problem, and the training could be revised before being implemented. For a small organization, the training was obviously a major undertaking, and a more comprehensive training evaluation might be more advisable.

QS 9000 AUDIT

Carol works for a small automotive supplier in Windsor, Ontario and is preparing for its QS 9000 audit in a few weeks. QS 9000 is a quality assurance program similar to ISO 9000. It requires documentation of a great many issues regarding how the company goes about its business.

Carol says that QS 9000 does not demand that the company conduct formal evaluations of its training. She continues, "We must train relevant employees in statistical process control (SPC), blueprint reading, and other skills. In an audit, an auditor can ask one of our employees questions related to SPC, and the employee better know the answer. If she or he does not, we better have a reason why. So evaluation is a good idea; we simply don't have the time or resources to do all the evaluation of training we would like."

To deal with the training, she says, "We send one of our employees out to training—

for example, SPC training. That person becomes our expert and trains others as required. Do we formally test them on SPC? No. We use reaction questionnaires to see how well they liked the training. We also put in place a performance review process that identifies areas of behavior that should emerge from the training. Supervisors are asked how often the trainee is observed performing SPC behaviors [or other trained skills]."

She goes on to say, "We do have specific certification requirements for operating forklifts, and for that we test people; it is a safety issue. I worked in a much larger organization before this, and there we had a much more comprehensive evaluation of training, but we also had a great many more resources. Here I think we are moving forward in our thinking about training and evaluation, and QS 9000 has been a driving force behind that push."

TRAINING AND EVALUATION AT SCEPTER MANUFACTURING

"ISO makes training mandatory," says Don Villers, plant manager of the 160-employee Scepter Manufacturing plant in Scarborough, Ontario. "We train everyone from the shop floor to the front office." The plant was ISO 9002 certified in 1994, and since then moved beyond the ISO training requirements.

In the company's rating system, supervisors are required to rate each of their employees on a scale from 1 to 10. An employee must reach 10 to be certified at that level and to be eligible for promotion. The rating system is

not seen as punitive, but developmental. It is used as a needs analysis to identify skill deficiencies, then as a learning measure, and finally as a transfer of training measure.

What about results? According to Villers, "Defective parts dropped from 5 percent to .1 percent. Scrap also dropped 50 percent." He attributes this success primarily to training. As a result of the success, the training budget is 10 times the $6,000 per year the company spent 3 years ago.

Source: Adapted from LeGault, M. 1997. In-house training that gets results. *Canadian Plastics*, February, pp. 14–18.

```
┌──────────────────────────────────────────────┐
│          THE TRAINING PROGRAM (FABRICS INC.)   │
├──────────────────────────────────────────────┤
```

Back to Fabrics Inc. Recall that we indicated that an evaluation using elaborate designs is nice, but seldom happens in reality. This case is just such a case.

The owner of Fabrics Inc. does not want us to assess any transfer of behaviors to the job. His argument is that his primary interest is in getting fewer complaints from employees and customers. He notes that in a small orga-

nization such as his, these changes (lowering of complaints) are proof enough that training was successful. We agree. So, the evaluation will consist of gathering weekly archival information on complaints from customers and subordinates as a baseline (gathering it for 2 months prior to the training) and tracking it for 6 months after training is complete.

SUMMARY

We began this chapter discussing the importance of a comprehensive evaluation. We end it suggesting that a comprehensive evaluation is not always necessary. With the understanding of validity and design issues, you now realize the difficulties that surround evaluation. It can be complex and in many cases costly. For this reason, we suggested throughout this chapter that evaluation is useful and important but not necessary at all levels all the time. Furthermore, good detective work can, in some cases, replace complex designs in assessing the validity of evaluation.

The decision as to what training should be evaluated and at what levels will be easier if the organization is proactive. By examining the strategic plan, you will be able to identify those areas of training that require evaluation and the extent to which you need to evaluate. Without such direction, the training department will need to identify its mission and goals as best it can and work from there to determine the training that needs to be evaluated. Even for a large organization, it is simply not practical to evaluate everything. Thus all organizations need to determine what training they need to evaluate and how they will do so.

KEY TERMS

- Affective questionnaire
- Control group
- Cost/benefit evaluation
- Cost-effectiveness evaluation
- Cost savings analysis
- Declarative knowledge
- Formative evaluation
- Internal referencing strategy (IRS)
- Job behavior outcomes
- Knowledge outcomes
- Learning outcomes
- Maturation
- On-the-job training
- Organizational results
- Outcome
- Procedural knowledge
- Process
- Random assignment
- Reaction outcomes
- Representative sampling
- Single-case designs
- Strategic knowledge
- Summative or outcome evaluation
- Utility analysis
- Utility questionnaire

CASE ANALYSES

CASE 1

You run Tricky Nicky's Carpet Cleaning Co., which cleans carpets for businesses. On average, one carpet cleaner can clean six offices per shift (work hours are 6:00 P.M. to 3:00 A.M.) Currently, 100 cleaners work for you, and they work 250 days per year. All carpets are inspected by a supervisor when the cleaner notifies him or her that the carpet is done. Because of Nicky's "Satisfaction Guarantee," when a carpet does not make the standard, it is redone immediately at no extra cost to the client. A recent analysis of the rework required found that, on average, one in every six carpets cleaned is not up to Nicky standards.

The profit averages $20 a cleaning. You pay your cleaners $15 per hour. When you reclean a carpet, you lose, on average, $20 in employee time. You still receive the same amount from the client, but, on average, your profit is gone.

Your training manager conducted a needs assessment regarding this issue at your request. He reported that half the employees are not reaching the standard one in nine times, and the other half are not meeting the standard two in nine times, for an average overall of one in six [(1/9 + 2/9)/2 = 1/6]. The needs assessment also indicated that the cause was a lack of KSAs in both cases.

The training manager proposes a training program that he estimates will reduce the recleaning by half, to 1 in 12. The training would take four hours and could handle 20 employees per session. ■

Costs associated with the training (assuming five training sessions and 250 working days in a year):

Developmental Costs

20 days of training manager's time for development at $40,000 per year	$ 3,200
Miscellaneous	800

Direct Costs

4 hours per session at $40,000 per year (trainer)	$ 400
Training facility and equipment	500
Materials	2,000
Refreshments	600
Employee salaries $20 per hour per employee (Nicky decides to do training on a Saturday and pay employees an extra $5 per hour as overtime)	8,000
Lost profit (none because training done on overtime)	

Indirect Costs

Evaluation of training	
10 days of training manager's time	$ 1,600
Material and equipment	600
Clerical support—20 hours at $10 per hour	200

CASE QUESTIONS

1. How much does the recleaning cost Nicky per year? Show all mathematical calculations.
2. If everyone is trained, how much will the training cost? How much if only the group with the most errors is trained? Show all mathematical calculations.

(continued)

(*continued*)

3. If everyone is trained, what is the cost savings for the first year? If only the group with the highest recleaning requirements is trained, what is the cost savings for the first year? Show all mathematical calculations.

4. What is your recommendation? Should both groups be trained or just the one with the most recleanings? Provide your rationale for your recommendation. Show any mathematical calculations used.

5. Let's back up and assume we're still at the needs analysis stage. Assume that employees had the KSAs needed to clean the offices effectively. What other factors might you look at as potential causes of the recleaning problem?

CASE 2

CASE QUESTIONS

1. In Chapter 5 you identified training that needed to be done in the MHC case and developed learning objectives for that training. Describe how you would go about evaluating that training.

2. Given the information in the case, indicate how you would evaluate whether the training you designed accomplished its objectives. Be sure to indicate the evaluation design(s) you would be using as well. Provide a rationale for both your measures and your design(s).

EXERCISES

1. Examine the reaction questionnaire your school uses. Is it designed to rate the course content or the instructors? Does it meet the requirements of a sound reaction questionnaire? Why or why not? Explain how you would improve it (if possible).

2. Break into small groups, each group containing at least one member who previously received some type of training in an organization. Interview that person on what the training was designed to teach, and how it was evaluated. Did the evaluation cover all the levels of outcomes? How did the trainee feel about the evaluation? Devise your own methods for evaluating each of the levels based on the person's description of the training.

3. Assume you are the manager of the training department of a large organization. Four employees are enrolled in a training course (assume it is this course). You are aware that for the course, reaction questionnaires and tests (to measure learning) are done at the school. Design a method for assessing the transfer of training to your department. What about a measure of organizational results?

QUESTIONS FOR REVIEW

1. What is the relationship among Kirkpatrick's four levels of evaluation? Would you argue for examining all four levels if your boss suggested you should look only at the last one (results) and that if it improved, you would know that training had an impact?

2. What is the difference between cost/benefit analysis and cost-effectiveness analysis? When would you use each and why?

3. What is the difference between cost-effectiveness analysis and utility analysis? When, if ever, would you use utility rather than cost effectiveness? Why?

4. Assume you were the training manager in the Westcan case (in Chapter 4). How would you suggest evaluating the training, assuming they were about to conduct it as suggested in the case? Be as specific as you can.

5. Of all the designs presented, which one would you consider to be most effective while also being practical enough to convince an organization to adopt it? If your design involved representative sampling, how would you accomplish it?

Appendix 8.1

This information is important to the understanding of effective evaluation.

EVALUATION: THE VALIDITY ISSUE

Once the decision to evaluate training is made, the evaluator must become familiar with a number of issues beyond the criterion issue discussed in Appendix 4.1. You want to be reasonably sure your findings on the effectiveness of training will be valid. After all, evaluation is both time-consuming and costly.

Let's say Sue is sent to a 1-week training seminar on the operation of Windows. According to the needs analysis, she clearly did not know much about how to operate a computer in a Windows environment. After training, she is tested and it is determined she learned a great deal. Training was effective. Perhaps—but a number of other factors could also result in her learning how to operate in a Windows environment. Her own interest in Windows might lead her to learn it on her own. The question is, how sure are you that the improvement was a function of the training you provided? In other words, does the evaluation exhibit internal validity? Once you are sure about the internal validity, how sure are you that the training will be effective for other groups who go through the same training; that is, does training show external validity? We will deal with internal and external validity separately. You should be aware that these "threats" are not specific to training evaluation but relate to evaluation in general. When we discuss each of the threats, therefore, we will indicate when it is not a serious threat in the training context.

Threats to Internal Validity

Internal validity refers to confidence that the results of the evaluation are in fact correct. Even when an improvement is demonstrated after training, the concern is that the change perhaps occurred for reasons other than training. To address this problem, you need to examine factors that might compromise your findings, which are called threats to internal validity.

History **History** refers to the events other than training that take place concurrently with the training program. The argument is that those events caused learning to occur. Consider the example of Sue's computer training. Sue is eager to learn about computers so she buys some books and works extra hard at home, as well as attending the training. At the end of training she demonstrates that she learned a great deal, but is this learning a function of training? It might just as well be that all her hard work at home caused her to learn so much.

On a half-day training seminar, is history likely to be a concern? Not really. What about a 1-day seminar or a 1-week seminar? The more that training is spread across time, the more likely history could be a factor in the learning that takes place.

Maturation **Maturation** refers to changes that occur because of the passage of time (e.g., growing older, hungrier, fatigued, bored). If Sue's 1-week training program was so intense that she became tired, when it came time to take the posttest, her performance would not reflect how much she learned. Making sure the testing is done when the trainees are fresh reduces this threat. Other maturation threats can usually be handled in a similar manner, by being sure that training and testing are not so intense as to create physical or mental fatigue.

Testing What is the influence of the pretest on learning? Suppose the pretest and posttest of KSAs were the same test. The questions on the pretest could sensitize trainees to pay particular attention to certain issues. Furthermore, the questions might generate interest, and the trainees might later discuss many of them and work out the answers before or during training. Thus learning demonstrated in the posttest may be a function not of the training but of the pretest. In Sue's case, the needs analysis, which served as the pretest for evaluation, got her thinking about all the material contained in the test. She then focused on these issues in training. This situation presents less of a validity problem if pretests are given in every case and if they are comprehensive enough to cover all the material taught. Comprehensive testing will also make it difficult for trainees to recall specific questions.

Instrumentation   The problem arising if the same test is used in pretest and posttest was already noted. If a different but equivalent test is used, however, the question becomes "Is it really equivalent?" Differences in the tests used could cause differences in the two scores. Also, if the rating requires judgments, the differences between pre- and posttest scores could be a function of different people doing the rating.

For Sue, the posttest was more difficult than the pretest, and even though she learned a great deal in the computer training, her posttest score was actually lower than the pretest, suggesting she did not learn anything. If the test items for both tests were chosen randomly from a large population of items, it would not be as much of a concern. For behavioral tests where raters make subjective decisions, this discrepancy may be more of a concern, but careful criteria development can help to deal with it.

Statistical Regression   The tendency is for those who score either very high or very low on a test to "regress to the middle" when taking the test again. This phenomenon, known as regression to the mean, occurs because no test is perfect and differences result as a function of measurement error. Those who are going to training will, by definition, score low for the KSAs to be covered in training and so will score low on their pretest. The tendency, therefore, will be for them to regress to the mean and improve their scores, irrespective of training. In the earlier example, Sue did not know much about computers. Imagine she got all the questions on the pretest wrong. The likelihood of that happening twice is very low, so on another test she is bound to do better.

This threat to internal validity can be controlled through various evaluation designs we will discuss later. In addition, using control groups and random assignment (when possible) goes a long way toward resolving these issues.

Initial Group Differences (Selection)   In some cases, in order to provide an effective evaluation, a comparison is made between the trainees and a similar group of employees who were not trained, called the control group. It is important that the control group be similar in every way to the training group. Otherwise the inherent differences between the groups may be the cause of differences after the training. Suppose that those selected for training are the up-and-coming stars of the department. After training, they may in fact perform much better than those not considered up and coming, but the problem is that they were better from the start and more motivated to improve. So if Sue is one of the highly motivated trainees, as are all her cohorts in training, they potentially would perform better even without training.

This problem does not arise if everyone is to be trained. The solution is simply to mix the two types so both the group to be trained and the control group contain both types.

Loss of Group Members (Mortality)   In this situation, those who did poorly on the pretest are demoralized because of their low score and soon drop out of training. The control group remains intact. As a result, the trained group does better in the posttest than the control group because the poorer scoring members left the trained group, artificially raising the average score. The opposite could occur if, for some reason, members of the control group dropped out.

This situation becomes more of a problem when the groups are made up of volunteers. In an organizational setting, those who go to training are unlikely to drop out. Also, all department members who agree to be in the control group are a captive audience, and it is unlikely they will refuse to take the posttest. Although some transfers and terminations do occur to affect the numbers of participants, they are usually not significant.

Diffusion of Training   When trainees interact with the control group in the workplace, they may share the knowledge or skill they are learning. For example, when Sue is back in the office, she shows a few of the other administrative assistants what she has learned. They are in the control group. When the posttest is given, they do as well as the trained group because they were exposed to much of what went on in training. In this case, training would be seen as ineffective, when in fact it was effective. This would be especially true if certain quotas of trainees were selected from each department. When such sharing of information reduces differences between the groups in this way, determining the effectiveness of the training could be difficult.

Compensating Treatments When the control group and training group come from different departments, administrators may be concerned that the control group is at an unfair disadvantage. Comments such as "How come they receive the new training?" or "We all are expected to perform the same but they get the help" would suggest that the control group feels slighted. To compensate for this inequity, the managers of the control groups' department might offer special assistance or make special arrangements to help their group. For example, let's look at trainees who are learning how to install telephones more efficiently. Their productivity begins to rise, but because the supervisors of the control group feel sorry for the control group, they help them to get their work done, thereby increasing their productivity. The evaluation would show no difference in productivity between the two groups after training is complete.

Compensatory Rivalry If the training is being given to one particular intact work group, the other intact work group may see this situation as a challenge and compete for higher productivity. Although the trained group is working smarter and improving its productivity, the control group works harder still and perhaps equals the productivity of the trainees. The result is that although the training is effective, it will not show up in the evaluation.

Demoralized Control Group The control group could believe that it was made the control group because it was not as good as the training group. Rather than rivalry, the response could be to give up and actually reduce productivity. As a result, a difference between the two groups would be identified, but it would be a function of the drop in productivity, not the training. Even if training were effective, the test results would be exaggerated.

These threats to validity indicate how important tracking the process is in the evaluation. Just as data are gathered about what is occurring in the training, it is also useful to gather data about what is going on with the control group.

External Validity

The evaluation must be internally valid before it can be externally valid. If evaluation indicated that training was successful, and threats to internal validity were minimal, you would believe that the training was successful for that particular group. The next question is "Will the training be effective for the rest of the employees slated to attend training?" **External validity** is the confidence that these findings will generalize to others who undergo the training. A number of factors threaten external validity.

Testing If the training is evaluated initially by means of pre- and posttests, and if future training does not use the pretest, it can be difficult to conclude that future training would be as effective. Those in the initial training perhaps focused on particular material because it was highlighted in the pretest. If the pretest is then not used, other trainees will not have the same cues. The solution is simple: Pretest everyone taking the training. Remember that pretest data can be gathered during the needs analysis.

Selection Suppose a particular program designed to teach communication skills is highly effective with middle-level managers, but when a program with the same design is given to shop-floor workers, it does not work. Why? It may be differences in motivation or in entering KSAs, but the important thing to remember is that you cannot be sure that a training program that was successful with one group of trainees will be successful with all groups. Once it is successful with middle managers, you can assume it will be successful with other, similar middle managers, but if you wanted to use it to train entry-level accountants, you could not say with confidence that it would be successful (that it had external validity) until you evaluated it.

One of the authors was hired to assist in providing team skills to a large number of employees in a large manufacturing plant. The first few sessions with managers went reasonably well; the managers seemed to be involved and learning a great deal. After about a month, training began for the blue-collar workers, using the identical processes, which included a fair amount of theory. It soon became evident that trainees were bored, confused, and uninterested. In a discussion about the problem, the project leader commented, "I'm not surprised—this program was designed for executives." In retrospect, it is surprising that lower-level managers received the training so well, given that it was designed for executives.

Reaction to Evaluation   In many situations, once the training is determined to be effective, the need for further evaluation is deemed unnecessary. Thus some of the trainees who went through the program were evaluated and some were not. The very nature of evaluation causes more attention to be given to those who are evaluated. Recall the Hawthorne Studies, which indicated the power of evaluation in an intervention. The Hawthorne Effect is explained by the following:[1]

- Taking the training was a novelty for the trainees.

- The trainees felt themselves to be special because of being singled out for training.

- The trainees received specific feedback on how they were doing.

- The trainees knew they were being observed, so they wanted to perform to the best of their ability.

- The enthusiasm of the instructor inspired the trainees to perform at a high level.

Whatever the mechanism, those who receive more attention may respond better as a function of that attention. As with the other threats to external validity, when you change the way groups are treated, you jeopardize the training's external validity.

Multiple Techniques   In clinical studies, a patient receives Dose A. It does not have an effect, so a month later she receives Dose B, which does not have an effect, so she receives Dose C and is cured. Did Dose C cure her? Perhaps, but it could also be that it was the combination of A, B, and C that resulted in the required effect. The use of multiple techniques could influence training when some component of the training is changed from one group to the next. For example, a group received one-on-one coaching, then video instruction. The members did poorly after receiving the coaching but excelled after receiving the video instruction, so video instruction became the method to train future employees. It was not successful, however, because it was the combination of coaching and video instruction that resulted in initial success.

What Does It All Mean?

It is useful to have an understanding of the preceding issues in order to recognize why it is difficult to ever suggest with certainty that training or any other intervention is the cause of any improvement. One cannot be absolutely certain about the internal or external validity when measuring things such as learning behavior and organizational results. Careful consideration of these issues, however, and use of well-thought-out designs for the evaluation can improve the likelihood that training, when shown to be effective, is in fact effective (internal validity) and will be effective in the future (external validity). This information is useful for assessing training and, equally important, helps assess evaluations of outside vendors.

EVALUATION DESIGN ISSUES

Here we go beyond the discussion conducted in the chapter and focus on issues specifically related to internal and external validity. For a more in-depth examination, a number of articles and texts address this subject.[2]

Basic Designs

Posttest Only   The posttest-only method occurs when training is provided (represented by $\times$) and then a posttest is given (represented by T_2). The design is represented as $\times T_2$.

The posttest-only design as it stands is problematic for assessing change. There could be a number of other competing causes for the change, as Table 8-1A suggests.

Pretest/Posttest   The other method used frequently by organizations is the pretest/posttest design. Using the same representations (and adding T_1 to represent the pretest), this design is expressed as $T_1 \times T_2$.

In this design, a number of threats to validity remain (see Table 8-1A). Although you can demonstrate that KSAs changed, you are not able to say that training is responsible for those changes. Therefore the prevailing wisdom is that a control group is necessary.

When a control group is not possible, and the pre/post design does in fact indicate change occurred, then other options are available to take the place of a control.[3] For example simply examining available information can help determine

TABLE 8-1A Sources of Invalidity

	Internal								External			
	History	Maturation	Testing	Instrumentation	Regression	Selection	Mortality	Interaction of Selection and Maturation	Testing	Selection	Relative to Evaluation	Multiple Techniques
Posttest Only (no control group)	−	−		−		−	−	−	−	−		
Pretest/Posttest (no control group)	−	−	−	−	?	+	+	−	−	−	?	
Posttest Only (with control group)	+	+	+	+	+	+	+	+	+	?	?	
Pretest/Posttest (with control group)	+	+	+	+	+	+	+	+	−	?	?	
Time Series Design	−	+	+	?	+	+	+	+	−	?	?	

Note: In the tables, a minus indicates a definite weakness, a plus indicates that the factor is controlled, a question mark indicates a possible source of concern, and a blank indicates that the factor is not relevant.

It is with extreme reluctance that these summary tables are presented because they are apt to be "too helpful" and to be depended upon in place of the more complex and qualified presentation in the text. No + or − indicator should be respected unless the reader comprehends why it is placed there. In particular, it is against the spirit of this presentation to create uncomprehended fears of, or confidence in, specific designs.

Source: Adapted from Campbell, D. T., and J. C. Stanley. 1963. *Experimental and Quasi-Experimental Designs for Research.* Chicago: Rand McNally.

whether extraneous occurrences influenced the improvement in learning.[4] History can be examined through interviews with the trainees. Maturation can usually be ruled out for adults, given that training is not generally long in duration. The point is that evaluation designs provide a mechanism for measuring the threats to validity, but simple investigation into the likelihood of these threats may be all that is needed. This method may be particularly relevant for the small business, where the size makes it easier to identify potential threats.

Internal Referencing Strategy Another way of dealing with the lack of a control group is internal referencing strategy (IRS), as indicated earlier in the text.

Many of the threats to internal validity do not exist with the IRS, because with no control group to react in an inappropriate manner, issues such as diffusion of training, compensatory treatment, compensatory rivalry, and others are not a concern. The only threats are history, maturation, testing, statistical regression, and instrumentation.

As previously noted, history can be investigated through examination of the time frame in which training occurred. Any events that potentially affected the trainees could be assessed as to their impact. Also, given that the relevant and nonrelevant items are similar in nature in the IRS, any historical event should affect both types of items in a similar manner. Maturation issues can be dealt with by ensuring that the training is designed to keep trainees interested and motivated, and to prevent them from becoming tired or fatigued.

The reactive effect of testing can be dealt with if parallel tests are used. Parallel tests cover the same content but do not use identical questions. This technique does lead to another potential problem (instrumentation), which can be addressed. If all trainees receive a comprehensive pretest, instrumentation is not an issue.

Instrumentation is a concern when two different tests are used. If a large pool of items are developed from which test items can be chosen at random, the result should be equivalent tests. Once again it is important to note that in any evaluation you can never be 100 percent sure that training caused the improvement. This design is not suggested to take the place of more stringent designs, when they are practical. It is appropriate, however, when the alternative is posttest only, or nothing. Again, some control is better than none at all.

More Complex Designs

As noted earlier, two factors need to be considered when developing a sound evaluation design: control groups and random assignment. Representative sampling is a more effective way of obtaining equivalent groups, although it must be pointed out that the assessments of the designs that use control groups (see Table 8-1A) assume random assignment.

Posttest Only with Control Group Posttesting only with a control group is represented by the following:

$$\text{Trainee Group (representative sampling)} \times T_2$$
$$\text{Control Group (representative sampling)} \quad T_2$$

As is noted in Table 8-1A, this design and the following one are equivalent in terms of dealing with internal validity, but remember that information in the table is based on random assignment.

The tendency is to downplay the effectiveness of this design because no pretest is given to assess equivalence of the groups before training. If you are able to create through representative sampling, an equivalent group, then most of the concerns regarding internal and external validity are addressed (See Table 8-1A).

Pretest/Posttest with Control Group The expression for pretest/posttest with a control group is:

$$\text{Trainee Group (representative sampling)} \, T_1 \times T_2$$
$$\text{Control Group (representative sampling)} \, T_1 \quad T_2$$

It is one of the more favorable designs for eliminating threats to internal validity. If random assignment was possible, all the threats to internal validity would be addressed (see Table 8-1A).

Threats to external validity related to using a control group are still a concern (compensatory treatments, rivalry, etc.). These issues might be managed by explaining to both groups the need for a control group and by treating the control group no differently except for the training. Reactive effects to testing can be dealt with by simply testing all those to follow, so that any cues that are provided will be provided to everyone. When a TNA is conducted, cueing will occur anyway. Careful test construction and administration will reduce concerns about trainees learning only answers to the test questions. Testing that causes trainees to focus on certain material will not be a problem as long as all receive the pretest. The reactive effect to being in the training is another concern that must be addressed. Treating the control group in a similar manner as the trainees (except for the training) will be a difficult task, and the Hawthorne Effect could influence the external validity of the training. Again, these threats do not mean the situation is hopeless, just that trainers and training directors must be diligent in their efforts to develop sound practices to alleviate these threats the best they can.

Time Series Design The time series design is represented by:

$$\text{Trainee Group } T_1\, T_2\, T_3\, T_4 \times T_5\, T_6\, T_7\, T_8$$

This design uses a series of measurements before and after training. In this way, the likelihood of internal validity threats such as testing or regression to the mean are small (see Table 8-1A). Also, when everyone attends training at the same time (a one-shot training program), this design can be used whether the number is large or small. It can still be argued that because no control group is used, history (internal validity) and many external validity concerns are not addressed. In applied settings, however, the goal is to be as sure as you can about the results, given organizational constraints. If enough measures are taken pre- and posttraining to deal with fluctuations in performance, the change after training is certainly suggestive of learning.

To make this design more powerful, consider adding a control group, expressed by:

$$\text{Trainee Group } T_1\, T_2\, T_3\, T_4 \times T_5\, T_6\, T_7\, T_8$$
$$\text{Control Group } T_1\, T_2\, T_3\, T_4 \quad T_5\, T_6\, T_7\, T_8$$

Here, you are able to deal with the concern regarding history. External validity issues remain a concern.

Multiple Baseline Design Multiple baseline design is represented by:

Trainee Group A	T_1	T_2	T_3	$\times$	T_4	T_5	T_6	T_7	T_8	T_9	$T_{10}\cdots$
Trainee Group B	T_1	T_2	T_3	T_4	T_5	$\times$	T_6	T_7	T_8	T_9	$T_{10}\cdots$
Trainee Group C	T_1	T_2	T_3	T_4	T_5	T_6	T_7	$\times$	T_8	T_9	$T_{10}\cdots$
Trainee Group D	T_1	T_2	T_3	T_4	T_5	T_6	T_7	T_8	T_9	$\times$	$T_{10}\cdots$

In this design, multiple measures are taken much as in time series, but each group receives the training at a different point in time. Each untrained group serves as a control for the trained groups. Issues related to external validity are dealt with, especially if Groups A through D represent all those to be trained. All will eventually be treated similarly, so concerns related to external validity are significantly reduced. Here the ability to say that changes measured by the test are due to the training is strong. If each group improves after its training, it is difficult to argue that something else caused the change.

Solomon 4 Group Once again, in this design caution must be given as we use representative sampling, and the value of the design is based on equivalence of the four groups. The Solomon 4 group is a thorough design that deals with all the concerns related to internal validity. It also deals with the reaction effect of the pretest. This design is represented as follows:

Group 1 (representative sampling)	T_1	$\times$	T_2
Group 2 (representative sampling)	T_3		T_4
Group 3 (representative sampling)		$\times$	T_5
Group 4 (representative sampling)			T_6

If you used this design, you would be able to confirm that pretesting did not have an effect on training success. On the basis of this information, you could suspend pretesting with the assurance that doing so would not affect the training success. As noted earlier, however, for the required complexity it simply makes sense to use the pretest consistently.

When this design is used, you can make a number of assertions based on the findings. First, if $T_2 > T_1$ and T_4, and if $T_5 > T_6$, and if $T_5 > T_3$, then the strength of your inference that training resulted in improvement is high. If T_6 is equal to T_1 and T_3, then history and maturation are not the cause of any improvement. If T_2 and T_5 are equal and both are higher than T_1, then the reactive effect of testing is not a concern.

What Design to Use

Determining the true impact of training requires an investigation into the validity of evaluation results. A number of methods are available, and the more complex the design, the more valid the results. However, other considerations arise when you are deciding on an evaluation design. Innovation can provide good substitutes when the best is not possible. Consider the multiple baseline design. It is a powerful design and certainly a possibility if a number of employees need to receive the training over time. However, what if multiple measures were not possible? The following design would address many of the same concerns, and although it is not as elaborate, it certainly deals with many of the validity issues. If pretest scores are all comparable, and posttest scores indicate an improvement, these results are a strong argument for showing training was responsible.

Trainee Group A	T_1	$\times$	T_2				
Trainee Group B		T_1	$\times$	T_2			
Trainee Group C			T_1	$\times$	T_2		
Trainee Group D				T_1	$\times$	T_2	

We already mentioned that most organizations do not evaluate all training at all levels. Furthermore, even when evaluating training, many organizations do not use pretest/posttest or control groups in a manner that would eliminate many of the threats to validity. Dixon indicated that of the companies she investigated in her article "New Routes to Evaluation," only one, Arthur Andersen, used designs that would deal with many of the validity issues.[5] Other companies, including IBM and Johnson Controls, follow such procedures only when asked by particular departments or higher-level management, or when they can defray some of the high cost of developing reliable and valid tests by marketing the final product to other organizations. The demand for certification in some skills (primarily because of ISO 9000 and other requirements) creates a need for these types of tests.

When you are evaluating training, if using control groups and or pretesting is not possible, remember other investigative methods can be used for assessing the likelihood that factors other than training account for any change in KSAs. By understanding the issues related to internal and external validity, you will be able to make good decisions regarding the design used in training evaluation.

Key Areas of Organizational Training

Learning Objectives

After reading this chapter, you should be able to:

■ Describe what organizations are doing in the following key areas of training and why this training is important:

- Orientation training
- Diversity training
- Sexual harassment training
- Team training

■ Use the training model to develop training in the key areas

■ Explain equity issues as they relate to training, specifically related to females in nontraditional jobs, the glass ceiling, and the disabled

■ Describe issues organizations need to consider related to basic skills training and safety training

---

Schrader-Bridgeport International (SBI) lost a civil suit that required them to pay more than $500,000 in damages. How did this whole situation happen? Ms. Conner and nine men (all graduates of a community college course) were hired at the same time for the position of "craftsman." Their job was to operate multi-spindle machines. The men were first sent to department 767 where special one-on-one, hands-on training took place for 6 months. This training taught them how to operate the machinery used at SBI, including how to properly load metal bars into the machines. Then they were transferred to

(continued)

(*continued*)

Department 710, where they began operating the machines. Ms. Conner was placed directly into Department 710, and did not receive the training.

On numerous occasions, George Schaefer, SBI's general supervisor in Department 710, stated explicitly that, in his view, women did not belong in the workplace at all. However, he admitted that Ms. Conner had "excellent mechanical ability," and estimated that of the 10 persons hired from the community college training program, Ms. Conner was "probably number three from the top."

When a machine malfunctioned, supervisor Bruce Boyd would explain and demonstrate to the male operators how to fix the machine, and permit the male machine operators to assist. If Ms. Conner's machine malfunctioned, however, Boyd simply fixed it without showing or explaining what he did. When she asked to participate in order to learn he "rolled his eyes" at her and refused. Ms. Conners then specifically asked Mr. Schaefer to see that she was provided with comparable training. He dismissed her request by responding that she had a high rate of absenteeism.

The machines the employees operated were idiosyncratic—each required its own particular techniques for it to perform well. New machine operators were typically assigned to a specific machine for a long period so they could learn how to keep that particular machine operating effectively. An inexperienced machine operator would advance to learning machine setup and unplanned tool-setting only after gaining basic operating skills on a single machine. As a result, the machine operator's efficiency and productivity were greater.

Mr. Schaefer, however, repeatedly moved Ms. Conner from one machine to another. These machine changes caused her to spend a much greater proportion of her time on machine setup and unplanned tool-setting rather than on production. She was always learning the idiosyncrasies of a new machine. For the period from October through April, Ms. Conner spent 139.3 hours on machine setup and unplanned tool-setting. The male operators each spent only 82.5, 48.3, 40.9, 15.5, 12.2, and 12.1 hours on these activities during the same time period.

Ms. Conner put up with a number of other things, such as ridicule, being forced to "mop up" the place, not receiving the same pay raise as the men, and so forth. She finally went to the personnel manager to complain. SBI's antiharassment policy required investigation of employee complaints "thoroughly and promptly to the fullest extent practicable." However, the investigation conducted by the personnel manager consisted of asking supervisors Schaefer and Boyd about her. It is not surprising that the findings indicated no problem.[1]

Yes, the preceding case really happened. No, it was not something from the 1950s or 1960s before we were more enlightened. It occurred in 1993. Was the company that "out of touch"? Perhaps, even though it did have an antiharassment policy. So what went wrong?

A number of possible reasons might explain why this company was unable to align the behavior of its employees with its policy. From an orientation perspective, neither managers, supervisors, or hourly employees went through a formal orientation to the workplace when hired. Orientations provide new employees with information about rules, policies, procedures, and the culture of the workplace.[2] A well-designed orientation program for supervisors might help them understand the importance of treating everyone on the basis of ability, not gender. An orientation for employees that introduced them to the procedures to follow if they wished to air a concern could help employees, such as Ms. Conner, deal with an issue early on before it gets out of hand.

Let's examine this issue from a diversity training focus. Diversity training for managers would expose managers to the differences people from various cultures bring to the organization and why these differences should be valued. Included in the discussion would be gender differences. Such a training topic would emphasize the value the organization put on these differences. Messages of this kind from upper management, if sincere, do affect how gender and ethnic differences are treated.

You can also view this problem from a sexual harassment training perspective. Some of the things Ms. Conner endured were clearly sexual harassment. Given that an antiharassment policy was in place, harassment training was perhaps conducted. If so, the training was not taken seriously. Furthermore, the policy on investigating harassment was clearly flawed. The HR manager only talked to the two supervisors, which would not meet the legal standards required when the case reached the courts.

From a team training perspective, you would probably uncover the negative attitude toward females during the needs analysis phase. You will see in the section on team training that attitudes among and toward team members are a vital factor in developing effective teams. Training can be designed to provide a forum for dealing with the issue.

In any event, no effective training took place at SBI in any of these areas, so the harassment continued. We return to the case at the end of the chapter, but for now let's examine each of these key training areas in terms of why they are important and what organizations are currently doing.

For the first topic, orientation training, we also take you through a hypothetical example to demonstrate how such a training program might be developed using our training model. You should be able to use this example to determine the issues that must be addressed in developing the other training programs.

Orientation Training

Orientation training introduces new employees to the organization, the job, and coworkers. It is often done on the employee's first day or soon thereafter. The orientation begins the socialization process for new employees, helping them to learn about the way the organization works and what it values. New employees eventually learn about these aspects whether an orientation program exists or not. So, why spend the time and money on an orientation program?

WHY IT IS IMPORTANT

From a learning theory perspective we know that new learning is based upon previous learning. New information is interpreted and understood in the context of what you already know. Thus, the best companies recognize that providing new employees with the information they need to understand the company and its expectations is a good investment. On the first day the new employee is anxious to impress, nervous about what this new job is all about, and excited about what is in store. It is the real first entree to the organization, so what happens to a new employee on that first day and the next few is critical. The first impression of the organization will be lasting, and it is important to orchestrate it in a manner that creates all the images and impressions that will enhance the effectiveness of the company and the employee.

Research shows that employees who attended orientation programs are more willing to adopt the organization's goals and values than those who do not.[3] Orientations also provide guidance to the new employee regarding management's expectations and informs the employee about job expectations. Effective orientations result in a number of positive outcomes for the

TABLE 9-1 Positive Outcomes Possible from an Effective Orientation

Reduce anxiety	Better understanding of expectations and formalized meeting of coworkers results in the new employee not feeling the higher level of anxiety associated with the first few days on the job.
Reduce role ambiguity	A structured opportunity to determine what is required on the job, and a comfortable feeling about approaching the supervisor and coworkers to ask questions about the job provides an opportunity to clear up any misunderstandings about job requirements.
Reduce turnover	Substantial evidence indicates that effective orientations reduce turnover.
Improved job performance	Better understanding of job requirements and the willingness to ask for assistance results in fewer errors, and the ability to get up to top production levels sooner, all of which translates to improved performance.
Higher level of commitment	Evidence suggests those who receive effective orientations are more committed, more involved in their job, and more likely to take on the values of the organization.
More effective/efficient organization	The organization with more employees getting to optimal performance faster, operating at a higher level of performance, showing a clearer understanding of their responsibilities, staying with the organization for a longer time, and being more committed to the values and objectives of the organization is definitely going to be more efficient, effective, and of value to its shareholders.

organization as depicted in Table 9-1. Higher commitment to the organization, increased job satisfaction, more job involvement, a clear role understanding, as well as increased tenure are all outcomes from an effective orientation.[4]

WHAT ORGANIZATIONS ARE DOING

The orientation is one of the most common types of training programs.[5] It is also one of the most neglected.[6] It is often done haphazardly with little thought to what should be included. In some organizations it lasts a few hours, in others it can be a few days. Large organizations often develop orientation packages, and forget about revising them until they are far out of date. Small organizations frequently develop them with little thought, if they do them at all.[7] The positive outcomes identified by research suggest that design and development of effective orientations is a good investment for most organizations.

Orientations do not require a long drawn-out process to provide positive outcomes. Training in Action 9-1 provides an example of what can be done in a day. A well-designed and implemented "1-day" orientation will be more effective than a poorly designed or outdated program that spans a year. Bison Transport, of Pine Falls, Manitoba, is a good example of how important orientation training can be. BT grew from about 35 employees in the early 1990s to more than 600 employees in 1999. To experience such growth and still be effective (twice chosen as one of the top 50 best-managed companies in Canada), it focuses on choosing only the best drivers. Bison relies on its 4-day orientation to assure a good match between company expectations and the new employee's expectations. The orientation is a method of continuing to screen new drivers to be sure of the "fit."[8]

For larger, more complex companies or higher-level jobs, it is useful to spread the orientation out over a longer time period. This approach minimizes the problem of information

---

EVEN A 1-DAY ORIENTATION CAN HAVE AN IMPACT

Texas Instrument's HR department put on a 2-hour orientation for its new assemblers. The new employees were told about the company, a bit about their job and the performance requirements that they would need to achieve, then they were introduced to their supervisor. The supervisor then gave the employees a short introduction to their job, and they were on their own.

Management at Texas Instruments noted a great deal of tardiness and turnover on the part of their assemblers. They conducted a TNA and discovered that new hires experienced a high level of anxiety when they started the job, and this anxiety increased because of the following reasons:

- New employees worried they would not be able to meet production requirements.

- Older employees would tell new employees they would never be able to reach performance requirements. This bit of hazing was considered a rite of passage.

- They were afraid to ask supervisors questions because they felt they would be seen as stupid.

Anxiety resulted in three important outcomes: low job satisfaction, tardiness, and high turnover.

Texas Instruments decided to see what could be done to affect these outcomes. They designed an additional 6 hours of orientation, which consisted of four specific points. New hires were told the following:

1. They were highly likely to succeed, based on statistics that indicated 99 per-

cent of new employees met expectations. They viewed the learning curves for production so they would understand that productivity would not be at the appropriate level at first. Throughout the 6 hours they were constantly told they all would succeed.

2. They needed to disregard the hazing (being told they would never make it). They were told to take it in good humor, but not to believe it.

3. They could take the initiative in talking with their supervisors. Supervisors were busy and would probably not come to each of them to see how they are doing. But supervisors are open to questions and new workers are expected to ask questions. No question was considered stupid.

4. They were told a bit about their supervisor—hobbies, personality, likes, and dislikes—to give the new employees a view of the supervisor as an approachable person.

The HR department wanted to be reasonably sure that any changes in turnover or tardiness could be attributed to the orientation. So, the next batch of new hires were separated into two groups: a control group (that received the typical 2-hour orientation) and the experimental group (that received the 2-hour along with the extra 6 hours of orientation).

The result: Better than expected. The experimental group showed 50 percent less tardiness and absenteeism, waste was 80 percent lower, and overall training time during the first year was reduced by 50 percent.

Source: Ivancevich, J. 1995. *Human Resource Management.* New York: Richard D. Irwin.

A LONG-TERM ORIENTATION AT CORNING

Prearrival	As soon as a decision is made to hire someone, the person receives orientation material and an orientation plan outlining what the orientation entails. Supervisor contacts new employee to assist in any way with settling in if a move was required.
First day	Breakfast with supervisor, processing at the HR department, attend a "Corning and You" seminar, and lunch with seminar leader. Get a tour of facilities, introduced to coworkers, and an opportunity to read through the "workbook for new employees."
First week	One-on-one interviews with supervisor, coworkers, and specialists. Learns the how-tos, where, and whys of the job. Must answer test questions in workbook provided earlier. Work with supervisor to develop an MBO plan.
Second week	Begin regular assignments.
Third and fourth week	Attend a community seminar and employee benefits seminar.
Second through fifth month	Assignments are intensified and include biweekly progress reviews with supervisor. Attend six 2-hour seminars which address issues like quality and productivity, performance management, employee relations and EEOC issues, and so forth. Answer workbook questions on each of the seminars, and review answers with supervisor.
Sixth month	Complete workbook questions. Participate in an MBO performance review with supervisor. Receive certificate of completion of Phase 1 of the orientation process.
Seventh through fifteenth month	Phase 2 of the orientation continues with more education about various aspects of the job, more reviews about salary and compensation.

Source: McGarrell, E. 1984. An orientation system that builds productivity. *Personnel Administrator* 29: 75–85.

---

overload. It also assures that opportunities for behaviors that management wants to encourage are practiced and feedback given. Corning developed such an orientation that continues over an entire year (see Training in Action 9-2).

So, given the importance of the orientation, how long should it be? Having read to this point in the book you know the answer is, "It all depends." The orientation is like any other training effort. So, lets go back to our model for developing training, and work our way through the TNA, design, development, implementation and evaluation phases.

TRAINING POINTS

The TNA

You might think a TNA is really not necessary for an orientation; after all, these are new employees and there are obvious things you need to convey to them. This is exactly what Meckelenberg County thought.[9] They provided new employees with a half-day orientation related to showing new employees how to operate some of the organizational systems (phone, e-mail), how to complete important forms, procedures to follow in an accident and so forth. Reaction questionnaires at the end of the orientation indicated the orientation was too long and boring. But Human Resources thought that such a response was to be expected. There were, after all, a number of mundane things that were necessary to learn even though they may be boring. So it was assumed that the orientation participants simply did not understand the importance of these things.

At one point, when the county was trying to change its image toward customers someone in HR suggested they also treat new hires as customers. To do this they would conduct a TNA and see what new hires wanted in the way of an orientation. The TNA included asking company executives, employees who had been through the present orientation, and new hires what they believed should be in an orientation. The resulting data indicated that the orientation would have to be even longer than a half day to provide all the information identified as necessary. After much analysis they put together a one-day orientation. Reaction questionnaires completed after the redesigned orientation indicated 94 percent of the respondents thought the length was just right, and it was interesting. Why the change? One reason was the TNA made it more relevant to their needs. So, orientations, like any training, will be more relevant and therefore more interesting and motivating for participants when their needs are met.

In addition to describing why orientation training is important and what organizations are doing in this area, we are trying to give the reader a feel for what it would be like to actually use the training model in developing orientation training. After reading the material that follows, including the hypothetical example, you should be able to see how interrelated the phases and steps are. You should also be able to appreciate that the model is not put into practice in linear form, that one step leads to the next. Rather, the practitioner will travel back and forth between the phases and steps within a phase.

Organizational, Operational, and Person Analysis   Recall from the training model, the TNA uses three inputs: organizational analysis, operational analysis, and person analysis. Previously we discussed these analyses separately. Here they are combined, because in practice, the analyses require moving back and forth among all three.

When a key performance indicator such as productivity, quality, tardiness, turnover, or employee satisfaction is below expectations, a TNA can be conducted to determine the causes. The output of the TNA is the identification of training needs and non-training needs. As we have said before, issues such as productivity, turnover, and so forth are likely to be caused by more than one thing. You will need to determine the causes of the deficiency to know what, if any, training will be useful.

Imagine, for example, that your company's product quality has not met expectations ever since the new quality standards were put into place last year and the VP of manufacturing has called you in to discuss a training solution (triggering event). A review of the strategic plan, adopted last year, reveals a high strategic importance placed on high quality products (organizational analysis). You then interview production employees (person analysis) and find they do not believe quality is very important. Because you use the training process model in this text, you know there may be aspects of the organizational structure and design that are causing or supporting the "quality-isn't-important" attitude. You engage in more organizational analysis and identify several factors that contribute toward the inappropriate attitude toward quality. You now realize that if training is to be a solution, you will have to provide an appropriate orientation to new hires, provide training to current employees that addresses the quality-isn't-important attitude and ensure that changes to the system are made (output: training and non-training needs).

Focusing now on the orientation program for new employees, you need to identify the specific KSAs new employees should have as they enter the job (operational and person analyses) as well as the organizational constraints that will be placed on the orientation (back to organizational analysis). For the orientation, you need to determine what non-technical information the new hires require before beginning their regular duties. A part of this will be what attitudes they need to hold about the quality of their work. At the operational level, the supervisor can provide this information. Keeping in mind the focus is on orientation training (not technical job training), you might cover such topics as early production expectations, policies and procedures that the department has in place, rules regarding absences, important dates and deadlines, how to use the phone and copy systems, and so forth. Supervisor interviews also allow you to determine what issues and requirements of the job might interfere with the goals identified by upper management.

At the Person Analysis level, you will want to ask recent hires what company knowledge and operational procedures they needed to know before they started their jobs. You also will need to explore the causes of the quality-isn't-important attitude in current employees. This information is likely to lead you back into the operational and organizational analysis. Asking those about to be hired what information they would like to know also provides information important to understanding the training needs. By the way, do not assume new hires know nothing about the firm. Many conduct a search for information prior to interviewing or even applying for a job. Similarly, different levels of experience working in quality systems may result in some new employees being very comfortable in such an environment, while others arrive disillusioned by their experience. Knowing where new hires stand on various issues such as work teams and quality, as well as their knowledge of the organization and their new job, will help in designing the orientation to be relevant and interesting.

HYPOTHETICAL EXAMPLE—TNA

Imagine then, you are the training manager for a midsized company of 800 employees. The company projected a loss of market share for this year for the second consecutive year. The VP of HR tells you that turnover among newly hired managers is much higher than the industry standard and increased significantly over the last few years. He suggests that an orientation program may be needed and wants you to investigate. Obviously, your first task is to conduct a TNA. Assume the following results from your TNA:

- The competitive strategy of your company is to maintain dominant market share through producing high-quality products, in large volume, within stringent cost parameters.

- The core values of the organization can be summed up in the phrase "quality products through teamwork."

- The entry and mid-level managers are relied upon to develop effective production teams to continuously improve "end product quality" while meeting cost and volume goals.

- The low morale of new management hires in the manufacturing area leads to high rates of turnover and poor attendance records, which results in a demoralizing effect on the production teams.

- Warranty claims increased slightly each month over the last two years.

- Many of those who stay with the company and rise to mid-level manufacturing managers show little interest in working with new hires (indicating not enough time, little incentive, and a survival-of-the-fittest mentality).

- Poor performance in new hires stems primarily from a failure to align the activities of their work unit to the strategic direction of the company (they sacrifice quality for quantity).

- From the mid-level managers you learn that managers are rewarded for quantity, not quality and that they feel a lot of pressure for productivity to remain high (this emphasis is confirmed by production team members).

(continued)

⟨ **HYPOTHETICAL EXAMPLE—TNA** ⟩

(*continued*)

- Exit interviews with managers who left the company after a relatively short tenure indicate they know little about the company when they start, rely on advice from the production team, and experience infrequent consultation with their boss (mid-level manager). A frequent response about company values was "everyone talks about quality, but the real pressure is on getting product out the door and keeping costs low." Policies and procedures were unclear, making it difficult to find out who is responsible for what.

TRAINING NEEDS

In discussing the results with the VP of HR, other members of top management, and high-performing mid-level manufacturing managers, you determine that most new hires lack the following KSAs when they start the new job:

- *Attitude:* Strong belief in the mission and core values

- *Knowledge:* Clear understanding of the market strategy and goals of the company

- *Knowledge:* A picture of how the company operates and how their job contributes to achievement of the strategy and goals

- *Knowledge:* Clear understanding of performance expectations over the course of the first year

- *Knowledge:* Important company policies and procedures and who is responsible for key operations

NONTRAINING NEEDS

You also identified some nontraining needs that must be addressed before training can be truly effective. One of these issues was the reward system that did not support the commitment to quality. If quality is in fact important you might suggest the following changes to the system so that it supports the quality core value:

- Provide managers with appraisals that give appropriate weighting to quality, quantity, and cost performance.

- Reward managers and workers only for reaching quality, quantity, *and* cost targets.

- Require operating units to produce and publicly display quality charts.

Unless the discrepancy between what we want managers to do and what the reward system encourages them to do is resolved, the orientation, no matter how well designed and implemented, will make little difference. Once any nontraining needs are identified and the process of appropriately addressing them begun, you can start the design phase of your training.

Design

The training model identifies the design inputs as the training needs from the TNA, the organizational constraints, and the training methods based on learning theory. For the hypothetical example we identified the training needs, including those already mentioned. Before we begin determining the training methods to use and the order of training, however, we need to consider the constraints.

Organizational Constraints   Constraints are placed on training by the organization, the environment, and the trainee population. They include factors such as how much time will be available to deliver the training, what mode of delivery is best suited to the trainees, the level of technology in the organization, and the facilities available. The TNA will at least partially identify the constraints. However, additional information will inevitably be required. Again, you will collect this information at the organizational, operational, and personal levels.

In our hypothetical situation, top management deemed the orientation to be important. You are authorized to develop an effective management orientation that is cost effective. Specific dates must be avoided for this training based on production schedules. However, you are able to work with the HR manager to assure that no new management hires are brought in during these periods. This arrangement gives you more freedom in terms of the timing, length, and quality of the orientation (remembering that you still must consider a return on investment). Based on your TNA and the preceding information you determine the orientation should take one full day and be periodically enhanced by meetings with the mid-level manager of the unit throughout the first 6 months.

Unfortunately for you, the problem of when to offer the training remains. Of the 800 employees in the company, 100 are management level. Based on turnover (one of the reasons the orientation program is being developed) of 15 percent, 15 new managers are being hired each year. But, they don't all come in at the same time and some replacements will be internal. Based on an average of 1–2 new managers per month, you can't justify the cost of getting a trainer up to speed in all of the areas and 12 days a year of the trainer's salary. You solve this problem by incorporating in-house subject matter experts (SME) into the training design. Each SME spends an hour or two with the new hire covering the SME's area of expertise. These people may require some train-the-trainer activities prior to the start of orientation to ensure they possess the KSAs necessary to be an effective trainer. This is an important factor to consider as you identify the SMEs who will participate in the orientation. Your design strategy so far provides multiple benefits:

- It addresses your cost-effectiveness issue; little additional cost is required in using the SMEs who are salaried and will "fit" the orientation module into their schedule.

- It provides experts in each of the areas covered by training rather than relying on the trainer to become an expert.

- It introduces the new hire to key people in the organization, helping to address one of the training needs.

Your organization has an adequate training facility but you will only be training one or two people a month and an office or small conference room will be better suited to your needs. Only limited technology is available to you for developing the training. You do not have the capability of producing high-quality in-house video or computer-aided instruction.

While reviewing your objectives, you note that initial learning of much of the material can be accomplished through reading or viewing a video. You know some useful materials already exist. These items can be duplicated for the training. Other material might require production by an outside vendor. You will keep this option in mind as you develop your training objectives, knowing you must do a cost-effectiveness analysis for outsourcing any of your training materials. All of these factors will influence what the orientation will look like.

Training Objectives Four categories of training objectives are developed: reaction, learning, transfer, and organizational outcomes. We will focus primarily on the learning objectives. Although your orientation program might have many objectives, we will focus on just a few as examples.

> ### HYPOTHETICAL EXAMPLE—OBJECTIVES

Continuing with your hypothetical trainer's job, you know that the new hires must develop a strong belief in the mission and values. Some prerequisite learning must occur. The new hire must first internalize the mission and values in order to be able to articulate them when asked. Second, the new hire must develop a positive attitude toward them. A learning objective for the prerequisite learning is:

- "Upon completion of the orientation, all trainees, upon request and with no assistance, will be able to state the mission statement and core values, with no errors."

Because the core values include teamwork, you need a learning objective related to the trainee's attitude toward teamwork. Recall that to affect attitudes, we do not train employees in attitudes per se, but rather provide information about teams that should result in a more positive attitude. You decide on the following:

- "By the end of orientation the trainee will be able to correctly list all the reasons why using a team approach to achieve continuous improvement of the production system is more effective than using individuals to accomplish the same task."

The third learning objective states:

- "Upon completion of the orientation, the trainee will be able to describe, to the satisfaction of a senior manager, how achievement of the mission and application of the core values will benefit society, the company, its employees, and customers."

New management employees also need to know the company's objectives and goals and how their job relates to their achievement. You state this learning objective as:

- "Upon completion of orientation, all trainees will be able to list the major goals and objectives of the company, without aids, and describe how their job relates to their achievement, in such a manner that anyone above them in the chain of command would approve of the statement."

Probably the new employees would not be expected to learn the many policies and procedures of the organization by heart. Rather, they should have a general idea of what those policies and procedures are and know where written descriptions of them could be located. A learning objective regarding a "procedure" in this case might read:

- "When asked to describe one of the company's policies or procedures, the trainee, using the company reference manual for policies and procedures, will be able to indicate the correct answer 100 percent of the time."

Transfer of training objectives would include the following:

- "Three months after the orientation the manager will be evaluated as 'strongly supportive of the mission and core values' by the immediate supervisor and production team members."
- "Three months after completion of the orientation program, all trainees will be rated by their teammates as highly supportive of team activities."
- "Within three months after orientation all manager trainees will develop goals and objectives for their unit that are aligned with those of the firm, as judged by their manager."

(continued)

```
        ╱ HYPOTHETICAL EXAMPLE—OBJECTIVES ╲
```

(continued)

- "On the first year performance evaluation, the trainee will be rated by the immediate supervisor as 'always' or 'nearly always' follows approved policy and procedure."

An organizational outcome objective is:

- "The average level of turnover for the first year of employment will be 20 percent less than the current average."

Based on these and other objectives, you are now ready to consider the methods of instruction that will most likely assure learning and transfer of the relevant knowledge and attitudes to the job. You note as you begin this process that the learning is focused on knowledge and attitudes. No skill development is included in your objectives.

Ensure Learning From learning theory we know that the lecture and lecture/discussion would be useful for conveying some of the declarative knowledge. However, this type of knowledge can also be provided ahead of time in written form, with the classtime used for practice, higher-level knowledge acquisition, attitude development, and explanation.

```
        ╱ HYPOTHETICAL EXAMPLE—DESIGN ╲
```

Based on the deficiencies identified in the TNA and the constraints placed on you, you developed objectives. From these training objectives, you make the following design decisions:

- The face-to-face portion of the orientation will be the new hire's first day of work.

- Most of the declarative knowledge related to mission, values, market strategy, company goals, company operations, policies, and procedures will be learned prior to arrival at orientation.

- Self-assessments for feedback purposes and formal pre-assessments of the informational learning can be done prior to and at the start of orientation.

- Orientation can be individually customized based on the input and pre-assessment data.

- The face-to-face time will focus primarily on procedural and strategic knowledge as well as the learning designed to affect attitudes. Some time will be devoted to addressing any deficiencies noted from the pre-assessment. Some time will used to assess learning objectives at the end of each module.

Pre-Orientation
You identified the following items that must occur prior to the new hire's arrival at orientation:

- Notify new hire that the first day of work will consist of an orientation and describe the program.

- Delivery of the pre-orientation instructions, training, and assessment materials to the new hire.

- New hire returns the formal pre-assessment materials and any input into objectives and agenda.

(continued)

(*continued*)

- Modify objectives and agenda based on input from new hire and pre-assessment data.
- Identify and reserve space that will be used.
- Reserve or acquire any equipment needed.

Start of Orientation

You developed the following goals and methods for the start of the orientation:

1. Create/maintain positive attitude toward orientation	• Introductions and welcome
2. Demonstrate the need for and value of the orientation	• Review the objectives (lecture/discussion) • Review day's agenda: Show what learning occurs when. Discuss usefulness in getting off to the right start. Ask if any additions or questions. (lecture/discussion)

During Orientation

Subject matter experts are identified and materials developed in the following areas:

- Company mission, goals, strategy, and core values: This presentation should be done by a high-level manager (perhaps the CEO). You decide to capture it on video and have a VP at the training session to answer questions.
- Company operations and how the new hire's job contributes to mission and strategy: The high-level manager covers company operations at the executive officer level. The director of manufacturing covers operations within the manufacturing area. The supervisor of the new hire covers operations within the department and in the new hire's unit.

- New hire's performance expectations for the first year: The supervisor presents this information.
- Company policy and procedures and people responsible for key operations: Trainer and the HR employment manager share responsibility for coverage of this material.

As you complete this list, you think of additional issues that need to be addressed in the development of the orientation, making these notes to yourself. Lunch and breaks need to be scheduled into the day. It would be nice if the entire training team could join the new hire for lunch. Each unit will be considered a module and will use a semi-formal lecture/discussion format. Each module will contain some structured content with the trainer determining how much additional coverage is needed based on the trainee's responses. Sufficient time must be provided at the end to allow for coverage of additional areas of interest to the trainee. Learning aids in the form of handouts will be provided in each module.

END OF ORIENTATION

After the last module and a break, the trainee tours the facility. During this time you meet with the other members of the training team to review your assessments of the trainee's learning and plan the feedback session. You note the following issues that must be a part of the feedback session:

- Identify the learning that took place and reinforce it. This assessment requires oral or written tests examining the learning expected (from learning objectives).
- Assess trainee's performance on the tests and identify areas where additional learning is needed. Reassure trainees that with so much to retain in one sitting, you want to reemphasize these areas.

> ◇ **HYPOTHETICAL EXAMPLE—DESIGN** ◇
>
> (*continued*)
>
> - Initiate a group discussion on how the additional learning can be accomplished. Get the new hire to commit to a plan.
> - Obtain public commitment from each member of the orientation team to be available to the new hire for assistance as needed.
>
> - Supervisor informs new hire of weekly meetings for first month to review knowledge of company and the job.
> - Thank the new hire for the time and energy given during the orientation and wish the new hire well on the new job.

Ensure Transfer   In the design phase you need to also consider transfer of the knowledge and attitudes toward the job. From the hypothetical example you can see the weekly meetings with the supervisor address this need in the short term. You will need to make sure the new hire documents the plan for additional learning and gives it to the supervisor. This documentation forms the agenda for the weekly meetings. At 3 months and 6 months, schedule half-day update sessions. You note that these will, by necessity, be custom developed a few weeks prior to the sessions based on the needs of the trainees. At these time intervals you will have more trainees who went through the orientation, so you can use small group meetings. You decide you will use your company intranet caucus to determine the types of information needed by the trainees and develop a system for prioritizing the lists.

The outputs from the design are the methods of instruction we determined are best for this situation (noted previously) and the evaluation objectives (to be discussed shortly).

Development

At this point you already identified what needs to be done to facilitate learning and transfer and the instructional methods for your training (inputs to the development phase). Now you need to produce the instructional material, manuals, and so forth, as well as identify the specific equipment and facilities required. In developing the material you need to carefully examine each objective and compare it to the material as it is being developed to maximize the likelihood that the objective can be met. Initial development involves formulating a plan of action for the orientation that anyone can follow.

> ◇ **HYPOTHETICAL EXAMPLE—DEVELOPMENT** ◇
>
> **PRE-ORIENTATION TRAINING PLAN**
>
> - Notify new hire that the first day of work will consist of an orientation and describe the program.
>   - Prior to making employment offer, each candidate is informed that should they be hired they will attend an orientation program their first day on the job.
>
> - Prepare notice of orientation date, purpose, objectives, and agenda. Indicate pre-orientation work is required and materials will be accessible on the company Web site once they receive a sign-on ID and password. Notice is included in employment package given to new hire on acceptance of the position.
>
> (*continued*)

(*continued*)

- Call new hire day after acceptance of employment offer. Welcome the new hire to the company and extend a reminder of the orientation and pre-orientation program. Ask if the new hire has any questions about the process. After answering any questions, provide a sign-on ID and password. Reiterate the date by which the formal pre-orientation assessment must be completed.
- Pre-orientation instructions, training, and assessment materials to the new hire.
  - Need to develop or acquire, and reproduce electronically, the following training materials:
    - Orientation objectives and agenda with explanation of how objectives were developed.
    - Mission statement with explanation of how achievement of the mission will benefit society, the customers, and company stakeholders, including employees.
    - Core values statement with explanation of why these values are held and how they benefit society, the customers, and company stakeholders, including employees.
    - General statement of the company's market strategy and goals. Because this information is proprietary, you will need to make sure the new hire signs and turns in the company confidentiality agreement prior to distribution of this material.
    - Organizational chart with description of key operations, titles, names, and pictures of key personnel.
    - Policies and procedures manual.
    - Two self-assessment questionnaires for each topic area.
    - Answer sheet to self-assessments.
    - Formal pre-assessment questionnaire on company Web site. New hire signs in and completes the questionnaire.

- Suggestions for orientation objectives and agenda.
- New hire returns the formal pre-assessment materials and input into objectives and agenda.
- Assessment scored and areas of strength and weakness noted. Feedback provided to new hire.
- Identify SMEs who will be training team for this new hire.
- Modify objectives and agenda based on input from new hire and pre-assessment data. New hire suggestions for additional objectives and agenda modification are considered by the team. If adopted, objectives are added and content and materials developed. Content for modules is also modified by results of assessment, emphasizing areas where learning does not meet objectives.
- Identify and reserve space that will be used.
- Reserve or acquire any equipment needed.
  - New hire must have compatible computer hardware and software to access pre-orientation materials. If not, must provide loan of company laptop.
  - No additional equipment will be required; all handouts in modules will be hard copies.

In developing the content of the materials you make a note that the following issues will have to be addressed:

- Provide information to create positive expectations for the orientation and the pre-orientation materials.
- Make the materials interesting and relevant to improve retention.
- Develop practice opportunities to allow for behavioral reproduction.
- Develop immediate feedback and reinforcement into materials to encourage learning.

(*continued*)

START OF ORIENTATION TRAINING PLAN

- Introductions (yourself and the other SMEs) and welcome.

- Review objectives of the orientation (describe how they were developed). The involvement of top management, unit managers, and other new hires will enhance credibility of the program.

- Review the agenda for the day, indicating the time frame and who will be the instructor for each portion of the orientation.

DURING ORIENTATION TRAINING PLAN

From learning theory we know that the lecture and lecture/discussion would be useful for conveying some of the declarative knowledge. However, some of this information will be provided ahead of time in written form, with the class time used for practice and explanation. For example, you might ask the trainee to articulate the mission statement (delivered ahead of time to the trainee as part of the orientation manual). If the trainee encounters difficulty with the material, use successive approximations to both teach and build confidence. Perhaps ask the trainee to open the training manual to the page and read the parts that are difficult to remember. During this process, you can ask the trainee to explain what the statement means. By discussing the meaning and underpinnings of the statement the trainee will more easily retain it in memory. Explain that each trainee will be meeting with a corporate officer who will be discussing in greater detail the mission, values, goals, and objectives. Your goal at this time is to simply prepare the trainee in a general way for that session.

You also include a discussion of the positive aspects of teamwork in the orientation to support the idea that the organization operates this way. You point out that the orientation itself is a form of teamwork, because multiple people must coordinate their activities to achieve the common goal of successfully orienting new employees to the organization. In fact, the entire team will be coming together for dinner with the new hire(s) to welcome them to the company and answer their questions at the end of the day. Although exercises to highlight the points related to teamwork would be ideal, with so few trainees, your options will be limited and more abstract than concrete. However, the interactions of the training team at dinner will go a long way in demonstrating how teams work in your company.

When your part of the orientation is completed, you introduce the new hire to the next SME (a peer manager), who will discuss how teams operate, the general procedures for handling routine office matters, and general office protocol. This session is followed by a meeting with the HR representative who will review policies and procedures related to compensation and benefits. This session is followed by a discussion with the high-level manager (preferable the CEO) about the mission, values, goals, and objectives. The trainee is then taken to lunch by the unit manager who explains first year job performance expectations. The manager also discusses how the new hire's job performance will affect the organization's goals and objectives. Providing an opportunity for the high-level and unit managers to answer questions considered important by the new employees assures these issues are addressed. These mini-sessions with individual SMEs continue until all your training components have been covered. The last SME returns the trainee to your office for evaluations and debriefing.

END OF ORIENTATION TRAINING PLAN

Prior to this phase, you met with the other SMEs to get their informal assessments of the degree to which the trainee met the training objectives. You begin the final phase of the program by asking the trainee to comment on the day's activities and which seemed the

⟨ **HYPOTHETICAL EXAMPLE—DEVELOPMENT** ⟩

(continued)

most valuable and why. You reassure the trainee that, because the 1 day of training covers a great deal, you will work together to develop some strategies for retaining the information. However, now you need to conduct a series of assessments to see whether the orientation training achieved its objectives.

Once the assessments are concluded, you make sure to provide the trainee with feedback. You identify the areas where the trainee did well and recognize any trainee accomplishments. Areas where the objectives are not fully met will be discussed further and additional practice provided where needed and when time allows. Reassure the trainee that carrying the great deal of information conveyed during

training back to the job without losing some of it will be difficult. Remind the trainee that orientation will conclude with dinner with the trainer and the supervisor to celebrate the beginning the new job. At dinner you work with the supervisor and new hire to develop strategies for transfer back to the job. At the end of dinner congratulate the employee again and reaffirm that refresher sessions will be conducted during the first year.

At this point we conclude our hypothetical example. Our intent with this example is to illustrate how the training process might play out. Obviously, it is difficult to illustrate the actual implementation of the training, so we will discuss the remaining phases of the orientation training process in more general terms.

Ensure Transfer   Recall that in the design phase you need to consider transfer of the knowledge and attitudes toward the job. Building in some refresher component is always a good idea. You cannot expect an employee on the first day or two of employment to remember everything. Built-in refreshers keep the focus and provide structured times when the new employee can ask questions. Consider Corning, where the orientation extends over a year, the focus is consistently on structured interactions with the supervisor and a performance (MBO) system. So, be sure to build in refresher sessions. Because the refresher sessions will include a number of trainees who previously attended the orientation, you can use small groups. In developing the content of these refresher sessions, use the new hires and their supervisors to determine training needs. For example, prior to the refresher session you can ask the trainees to each submit a list of what is going well and what is not going so well. You can either do the same with the supervisors, or after combining all items onto a single list, ask the supervisor to review and identify any additional items and prioritize the list. The final, prioritized lists can then be used for the development of the refresher agenda.

Implementation

All the outputs from the development are the inputs for the implementation. As mentioned earlier, it is difficult to illustrate implementation in words. Thus, we include a few reminders here from earlier portions of the book. Make sure to conduct a dry run to test out your plan. In addition to a few supervisors and a manager or two, the employees you ask to attend the dry run are best selected from among those recently hired and who show a positive attitude toward the organization and their work. After revisions, based on the dry run, you are ready to run your first orientation pilot. The pilot actually uses real new hires, but you gather data from them to make final refinements to the program. It would be helpful if all SMEs involved in the training could attend in entirety, both the dry run and the pilot. This gives them input into the modifications and a complete understanding of the orientation program.

Evaluation

Although this stage is presented after implementation, development of the evaluation measures takes place at the same time as development of training. Recall that the output from the design phase is both "identify alternative methods of instruction" and "evaluation objectives." So, evaluation measures are developed concurrently with the development of the training. The outputs here are both process and content measures. Again, we provide some reminders about what should be included in your evaluation plan.

Process measures focus on how closely the orientation training that was actually given matches the training that was developed. The types of measures you can use include the following:

- Interviews with new employees to ask what took place
- Sit-ins by orientation designers
- Logs by the trainer

Outcome measures deal with the four aspects of evaluation: reaction, learning, behavior, and results. They are based on the training objectives, so a review of those will clarify exactly what is necessary. As you can see, spending time developing good evaluation objectives makes development of the actual evaluation material much easier, because it clarifies exactly what must be assessed, and how.

A reaction questionnaire should be developed to assess how trainees feel about the orientation in terms of its content and process. You might want to use modified reaction questionnaire at the start of the refresher session, asking about the value of the orientation and what would make it better.

As indicated in the hypothetical example, learning should be measured through some assessment at the end of the orientation training. The assessment measures the learning objectives presented at the start of training, which will require some oral tests as well as some written tests.

Examination of the transfer of training objectives indicates that measures of behavior will be assessed through various methods. One will be performance appraisals conducted by the employee's supervisor (measuring support of company mission and core values, examining goals and objectives developed for their unit, and so forth). Another will be team members evaluating the manager's support of team activities. An organizational outcome will be to assess the level of manager turnover, as indicated by the objective developed at the beginning of the process.

Diversity Training

The makeup of the workplace continues to change. What was once predominantly white male is now a diverse group with a multitude of races and cultures, and increasing numbers of women. Fifty percent of the growth in the U.S. population each year for the next 50 years will be made up of Asians and Latinos. More than 60 percent of women are working or looking for work (compared to 40 percent in 1966).[10] The 65-and-older population in the United States will double by 2030.[11]

Much the same is occurring in Canada. Currently about 55 percent of immigration comes from Asia and the Pacific Rim with another 16 percent from Africa and the Middle East.[12] Almost 60 percent of women are in the workforce compared to only 35 percent in 1966,[13] and the 65-and-older population is higher than ever before, at about 13 percent. It is expected to top 21 percent in 20 years.[14]

This diversity within the workforce creates tension and conflicts in the workplace. One of the reasons is that supervisors (and people in general) tend to make decisions that favor those who are similar to themselves.[15] Thus, ratings of performance, promotion recommendations, and such are often biased in favor of those who are more similar to the person making the evaluation or recommendation. When employees perceive that decisions affecting their pay or status are biased by factors such as race or gender, they become upset. A recent study found that this similarity bias is directly related to a personal characteristic called "openness to dissimilarity."[16] People who are less open to differences between themselves and others are more likely to evaluate those who are different (in terms of ethnicity, gender, etc.) more harshly and those who are similar more favorably.

WHY IT IS IMPORTANT

Consider the case at the beginning of the chapter. Ms. Conner, who was identified by her boss, George Schaffer, as "one of the best new hires" was continually thwarted when she tried to get help in order to be more effective. Even though Mr. Schaffer acknowledged she was one of the best, he did nothing to assist her in being a productive employee. In fact, his attitude was that women did not belong in the workplace. Here is a motivated and talented worker who is being prevented from being as productive as she is capable. Is this practice good for the organization? Clearly not, and something needs to be done to ensure that all employees are nurtured to become highly effective employees.

Lack of acceptance by coworkers and management of those "different from themselves" leads to tension and biased treatment. Those "different" workers who are treated unfairly often quit; which, if the numbers are high, can be costly to the organization. The fact that the turnover of women in salaried jobs is double that of men, and the rate for blacks is two and a half times that of white males supports the notion that being different is too often a disadvantage for those employees.[17] The costs to the organization for this type of turnover include the following:

- Loss of a productive employee who could end up at a competitor
- Cost of recruiting a replacement
- Cost of retraining the replacement
- Loss of productivity during the preceding items

Furthermore, the resulting loss of reputation in the community entails its own costs (especially in metropolitan areas), such as the following:

- Minorities and women will stop applying for jobs, reducing the pool from which to hire.
- Minorities and women will stop being customers or boycott the company.
- Stock price may drop.[18]

Finally, costs are associated with having legal action taken by such employees. These costs go beyond the cost of the settlement if you are found guilty:

- Hiring legal staff to deal with the case
- Managers' time gathering the required information for a hearing
- Managers' time preparing to testify
- Managers' time testifying

Considering all of these costs as well as the millions it can cost in settlements, providing training to prevent such problems would seem the wise move. Consider, for example, if you end up losing in court, you will incur not only all the costs indicated, but also face the cost of training that is likely to be ordered by courts. Not all companies provide diversity training to their employees, however. A survey of more than 1,600 companies that employ 100 or more people found that 25 percent did not provide diversity training. Another 24 percent provided this training on an as-needed basis, and the other 51 percent provided diversity training on a regular basis.[19]

Diversity training focuses on understanding differences—race, age, ethnicity, gender—between individuals. Diversity in organizations is a fact of life. Diversity training can help everyone in the company understand how differences can be useful to an organization. With the changing demographics in North America, organizations need to be effective in attracting, promoting, and retaining a diverse workforce in order to be competitive.[20] Advantages to an effective diverse workforce are noted in Table 9-2. Effective organizations that recognize the issues revolving around employing a diverse workforce do something to capitalize on the advantages and at the same time deal appropriately with any negative aspects of diversity.

WHAT ORGANIZATIONS ARE DOING

Think about the ISB company in the opening case. Would providing a formal training program in diversity help to prevent the way Ms. Conner was treated? Would it put a company in a better position if it faces such charges in court? Consider the following:

- As part of a class action lawsuit settlement Smith Barney instituted a range of diversity training and paid about 1,850 women anywhere from $1,000 to $100,000.[21]
- Texaco Oil recently agreed to pay $176 million to settle what was called rampant discrimination among its top management.[22]

TABLE 9-2 Advantages of an Effective Diverse Workforce

Larger applicant pool	Maintaining an effective diverse workforce will contribute to a good reputation and more will want to join your organization. It will mean more people will apply for jobs, giving your organization a better likelihood of selecting better employees, which will translate into a more effective workforce.
Reduced costs	An effective diverse workforce will result in less turnover, which would translate into less rehiring due to quits.
	Also the tension created in organizations where they do not deal with diversity will not be present and the outcomes of such tension (lower productivity, absenteeism, fighting, refusing to cooperate on projects, etc.) will not be present.
	Those organizations with effective diverse workforces will not incur the costs associated with paying for legal representation and settling lawsuits for discrimination.
Access to more markets	The North American population is more diverse. The more your organization reflects this diversity the more likely a diverse customer base will be cultivated. Minorities and females will be attracted to an organization that employs a diverse workforce.
	As we become an international community with more international business, those organizations whose employees understand the culture of these international markets will do better.
Creative problem solving	The more diverse the group, the more diverse the ideas that are generated. Employees with different backgrounds are more likely to see issues from different perspectives, resulting in more creative ideas (other things being equal), which can result in better products and service.

Sources: Loudin, A. 2000. Diversity pays. *Warehousing Management*, April, pp. 30–33; Anonymous. 2000. Diversity: A new tool for retention. *HR Focus*, June, pp. 1–14; Hunsaker, P. 2001. *Training in Management Skills.* Upper Saddle River, NJ: Prentice Hall.

An early and serious investment by companies in diversity training may help avoid these types of costs and the resulting threat to their market position. However, just having a program is not enough. Many North American companies implement policy and training programs to deal with diversity issues, but these efforts often simply do not change anything.[23] Why? Like any intervention, training is only a part of it. GM certainly provided training on this subject. Yet in July of 2000 an employee walked into a GM plant wearing a mock KKK robe and hood. The company immediately held meetings to tell employees this behavior was not acceptable.[24] Was this action sufficient? GM articulates its employee guidelines in manuals, videos, and a hotline to deal with the diverse workplace and inappropriate behavior. Still, as one black man in the plant put it, "Sometimes it feels like this plant is run by white supremacists, but it is really worse for the women. They complain and are told to shut up, this is a man's job."[25]

Many of the above problems may result from lack of support from top management. Consider the survey of 785 human resource managers in which only 11 percent indicated that diversity training was initiated by their CEO, while another 50 percent indicated their CEO was only minimally involved in the implementation of training.[26] We indicated elsewhere the importance of upper management support in any successful intervention. This involvement is probably more important for diversity training. Without strong support from upper management many will see the training and policy as something the company requires from a legal standpoint, but not something that is really valued.

Which organizations realize successful programs? IBM is one example. They developed a diversity program that resulted in an increase in black executives (from 62 to 115) and female minority executives (from 17 to 54) in about 2 years.[27] Carrier Corp. formed diversity councils in all business units. They develop diversity business cases to assist in training and successfully increased the percentage of blacks in executive positions.[28] What the successful companies share in common is their understanding that training alone is not enough. Two key additional elements are required:[29]

1. Top management commitment/involvement
2. Tying diversity success to performance appraisals

Both these ideas are utilized in the new Texaco training initiative on diversity. In response to the court order[30] they trained 14,930 of their U.S. workforce (about 93%).[31] The training includes input from top management on the importance of diversity to their goal of excellence. They also tied managers' ability to promote diversity and equal opportunity within their departments to an incentive bonus plan.

So what does it take to see that the diversity training is effective and results in a positive climate for everyone? Table 9-3 provides information about what one successful company did.[32] With this information in mind, we examine key issues at each phase of the training model.

TRAINING POINTS

For the reasons stated in the preceding discussions, we recommend diversity training be provided to all employees. Once all current employees receive this training, it can be integrated into the company's orientation training.

We indicated in Chapter 4 that a TNA may not be necessary when you plan to train everyone. For diversity training, conducting at least a partial TNA may be beneficial for several reasons. In addition to developing the KSAs to support diversity, you must also align the organizational systems and policies to support the diversity goals. In organizations that are just implementing a diversity program you are likely to face resistance to the program. Using Lewin's force-field analysis, you can identify all the forces that are pushing for the status quo (e.g., resisting the diversity program). You will then intervene in ways to reduce those forces or create stronger opposing forces. One of the author's experience with a U.S. telephone company

TABLE 9-3 Agenda for Ensuring Diversity Remains an Important Part of the Organization

Develop a broad diversity refresher training session and implement throughout the plant.

Cover holidays that deal with diversity and publish throughout the plant.

Create a diversity council and maintain its image by sharing what it does throughout the plant.

Write articles about diversity in the plant newsletter.

Set up a booth on diversity at the company picnic.

Periodically invite nonmember managers to diversity council meetings.

Ask plant managers to share information monthly on what is going on in the way of diversity issues.

Establish a mentoring program to provide employees with a source for help.

Continue to address the guidelines supervisors need to be aware of when appraising and making training and development decisions.

Address any plant concerns regarding diversity in a timely manner and report back to person affected.

Monitor the impact of diversity efforts, praising the successes and investigating the failures.

back in the early 1980s serves as an example. Many men opposed the idea of women working in the telephone installation and repair units. This attitude resulted in harassment of the women who entered that job. The forces that created these attitudes in men were deep-seated and powerful. The change would need more than just providing KSAs. The phone company did provide training but also instituted a zero tolerance policy for harassment of women. A few did not heed the policy, and their employment was terminated. The message spread throughout the workforce that the company was serious about the policy and the incidence of harassment declined dramatically. Here a stronger force (job loss) was set up to counter the force of keeping the installation and repair job exclusively male. It was an important part of the intervention. Without a clear understanding of the nature and strength of the resistance, the success of the intervention is less certain. As an aside, we do not advocate a zero tolerance policy because each infraction should be investigated and treated on its merit; all behavior is not equal.

Some key aspects in the various phases of the training model deserve special attention for diversity training.

TNA Issues

1. Determine upper management's level of commitment to diversity. If top management is not committed, then the program is not likely to be successful. If the top management is committed, but significant segments of the rest of upper management is not, then training is indicated at this level. The American Institute for Managing Diversity suggests such training include a description of:[33]

   - Organizational culture and its impact on the change initiative
   - Steps involved in measuring how well you are managing diversity
   - Qualities of organizations that are beginning to manage diversity successfully
   - The responses of people to managing diversity
   - Three approaches to managing diversity: affirmative action, understanding differences, and managing diversity
   - The different motivations of people for implementing diversity

2. Identify the organizational goals/objectives related to diversity.
3. Obtain a good cross-section of attitudes and behaviors that reflect how the employees respond to diversity at their work site. Determine the strength of these attitudes/behaviors.
4. Determine the forces supporting diversity and those resisting.

Design and Development Issues

Prior to developing the training, pay special attention to the constraints you will face in trying to implement the training. Because you will likely be training everyone, the amount of time taken up by the training will be a constraint. You must balance the cost of the lost productivity against the value of the diversity training. It will involve making a careful match between the training objectives and the time needed to achieve those objectives. Related to this issue is the number of people you train at one time. The larger the number, the lower is the cost. However, the larger the number, the more limits you place on the types of training methods you can use. Thus, you need to examine the methods for achieving your objectives relative to the number of trainees that can be accommodated by the method. If training is to go beyond simply providing information, then the size of the training group will need to be controlled.

A number of factors help to ensure that the training is learned and transferred to the job. Diversity objectives need to be reflected in management performance appraisals. Effective interaction of employees in the department, and inclusiveness in training and promotional opportunities need to be a dimension of the performance appraisal, and part of managers' objectives. Those who are successful in meeting these goals need to be rewarded.

When developing the training, include the president or other high-level executive to introduce it and discuss the importance of diversity to the company. This presentation is best done in person, but if it is not possible, present it on videotape. When Wisconsin Power and Light developed its diversity training, it included a vice president or high-level manager opening each 1-day session with an explanation of the importance of a workforce that values diversity.[34] It is also a good idea if a senior manager is available near the end to answer any questions and reinforce management's commitment to diversity. Of course, the use of upper management in the training will be constrained by the availability and commitment of the upper management. To be effective, diversity training requires facilitated discussion among the trainees and between the trainees and the trainer. Building small group discussions into the training design allows trainees to encode the diversity concepts into their framework. Using cases from actual situations in the company for the small group discussions also increases the relevance of the training and improves the transfer of training to the workplace.

Evaluation

Management may be concerned about evaluating training because they might discover that training is not effective. The logic might sound something like: "It is better to provide the training, and if we get sued, we can point to the efforts of our training department as an indication of our commitment to diversity. But if it is evaluated and shown ineffective, we are worse off in a court of law."[35] As we noted earlier, however, this view looks at evaluation as a pass/fail system. The goal in evaluating diversity training is to provide input into the training process to create a continuous improvement system. Demonstrating continuous improvement of diversity training is a much more powerful statement to the court than simply saying "we provide training."

Sexual Harassment Training

Sexual harassment is one specific type of behavior that diversity training attempts to eliminate. It deserves special attention because of its legal definitions and extensive case law. Federal law banning sexual harassment was passed about 40 years ago in the United States. Relatively few complaints were filed, however, until after Anita Hill, a law clerk, filed a complaint against Supreme Court nominee Clarence Thomas a little more than a decade ago. Since then, the issue commanded more attention in both the United States and Canada. Sexual harassment complaints to the Equal Employment Opportunity Commission increased from 6,100 in the early

1990s to 15,342 in 1996.[36] Since 1996 the number leveled off and remained in the 15,000–16,000 range.[37] In Canada, 18 percent of the complaints filed with the Canadian Human Rights Commission in 2000 were related to sexual harassment.[38]

Sexual harassment is a form of sex discrimination under Title VII of the U.S. Civil Rights Act of 1964. It can take one of two forms: quid pro quo[39] and hostile environment.[40]

Quid pro quo harassment occurs when a supervisor makes an offer to the subordinate of some job perk (raise, promotion, easier jobs) in return for sexual favors. If a supervisor sexually harasses a subordinate, the company can be considered liable, even if no one else was aware of the harassment.[41] If an employee is harassed by someone other than a supervisor (such as a coworker or customer) the employer can still be liable if evidence shows that the employer was aware or should have been aware of it.

Hostile work environment (called poisoned work environment or gender discrimination in Canada) comes from the U.S. Supreme Court ruling in *Meritor Savings Bank v. Vinson*.[42] In this case, Vinson was abused verbally and sexually over a number of years by her boss, but was making good career progress. The court ruled that in this case the verbal and sexual abuse was "unwelcome" and sufficiently severe and pervasive to be abusive. This ruling broadened the definition to include verbal or physical conduct that creates an intimidating, hostile, or offensive work environment or interferes with an employee's job performance. Thus, if an employee is touched in some inappropriate and unwelcome manner, such as pinching or slapping the person on the buttocks, it is illegal. Even the use of foul language, telling sexually oriented jokes, or hanging sexually provocative pictures on the wall can be found to be sexual harassment. This notion of a "hostile work environment" is complex in terms of what is and is not considered sexual harassment. Sexual harassment training needs to define these concepts in ways that fit the specific workplace.

WHY IT IS IMPORTANT

More than 90 percent of *Fortune* 500 companies field sexual harassment complaints and more than one-third were sued for sexual harassment.[43] Just like the diversity issue, not paying attention to sexual harassment can be expensive. It cost Ford $7.5 million and Mitsubishi $34 million when they were sued for sexual harassment.[44] These figures do not include the costs associated with all the other related activities (as detailed in the diversity section). Furthermore, it is estimated that the damage to a company's reputation from a sexual harassment charge can decrease the firm's market value on the stock exchange by 5 to 30 percent.[45]

Just how many employees are sexually harassed? Some data suggest that sexual harassment is fairly common in the workplace. One survey in the United States reported 42 percent of the females and 15 percent of the males indicated being sexually harassed on the job.[46] In Canada, 48 percent indicated being sexually harassed in the previous year, with only 3 percent indicating the harassment was of the quid pro quo type.[47]

To win a harassment suit in which the supervisor sexually harassed someone, the organization must prove that the supervisor's harassment was against the company's harassment policy. Thus, maintaining such a policy is critical. Training supervisors in the use of these policies is accepted by the courts as compelling evidence of the company's concern regarding the issue.[48] In fact the court previously held that if you do not provide some kind of sexual harassment training to your employees, you will be liable.[49] So just for protection from lawsuits, training in the area of sexual harassment makes monetary sense.

Sexually harassed employees experience psychological distress and in some cases post traumatic stress disorder, both of which interfere with productivity.[50] A more direct impact on productivity is that these employees experience higher levels of absenteeism and turnover.[51] What is of real concern is the evidence that these outcomes manifest themselves in employees who, although they experience sexual harassment, do not define it as such and therefore do not report it.[52] This troubling tendency suggests that vigilance on the part of management is critical to stamp out such behaviors.

None of the preceding points addresses the ethical issues. Allowing an employee to be sexually harassed by others in the company is morally and ethically reprehensible. It is a part of a company's responsibility to the employees to protect their physical and psychological health while at the workplace.

WHAT ORGANIZATIONS ARE DOING

More than 80 percent of organizations offer some type of sexual harassment training.[53] For many companies it is effective. A survey of 663 human resource practitioners indicated that in 500 of the responding organizations, sexual harassment complaints declined after initiating training. Based on the information from these organizations, an effective strategy for dealing with sexual harassment was developed and is depicted in Table 9-4.[54] Training in Action 9-3 provides examples of what happens when an organization establishes the proper process for dealing with sexual harassment and provides appropriate training.[55]

On the other hand, many organizations are not doing a good job in this area. For that reason, we continue to hear of high settlements for such behavior. Going back to the SBI case, we note that a procedure was in place for dealing with harassment. This procedure was proper in that it did not expect the harassed employee to report the allegation to the supervisor (who was the offender) but instead to the supervisor's boss. The problem was that the boss apparently lacked training and failed to take the complaint seriously. In fact, many companies conduct minimal training and even less evaluation of the outcomes of the training.[56]

As noted earlier, sexual harassment of the quid pro quo type is most obvious, and its definition relatively clear. Defining sexual harassment when it relates to a hostile environment is difficult, and care in determining what is enforceable is important. Going too far in terms of punishment can be as costly as not going far enough. You may recall the "Seinfeld case," in which a manager at Miller Brewing Co. was fired for a discussion of a racy sitcom episode with a female employee.[57] Although the $26.6 million awarded the manager for wrongful dismissal was eventually overturned, the other costs associated with the original trial and the appeal were substantial.

The preceding examples show the importance of setting clear guidelines that are relevant to your organization. So, care needs to be taken in the development of the guidelines and the training. Those who develop and conduct the training must not bring their own values into the training. Rather, they must present the company's guidelines and their application. You do not want the training to create situations that are clearly not relevant and could quite likely lead to a backlash. For example, swearing on the shop floor is unlikely to be considered harassment nor is telling off-color jokes.[58] However, the same behavior at the management level might be. The preceding should not be interpreted as implying fixed and absolute guidelines. For example, the company may set a policy that is more stringent than the law requires. If policy bans the use of foul language or the use of derogatory names, appropriate consequences for violating the policy can be enforced. However, what is being enforced is company policy, not sexual harassment as defined by the courts.

TRAINING POINTS

As we indicated at the beginning of this section, sexual harassment is a component of an overall diversity program. Thus, the training points covered in that section also apply to this section. Some additional points relating to sexual harassment training bear reinforcing here.

Policy and Guidelines in Place

Before developing training, a sexual harassment policy and guidelines need to be in place. An acceptable policy contains the points suggested in Table 9-5.[59] Also, make sure a process is in place and a committee set up to deal with complaints. The policy and guidelines provide the basis

TABLE 9-4 Effective Strategies for Dealing with Sexual Harassment

Set an example at the top	Get their support for training, but also get their support in their behavior at the office.
Provide training	Everyone needs to know what is acceptable and what is not, which can only be provided in information sessions. Also examples and role plays are useful to make it clear what is not appropriate.
Check for understanding	Labor lawyers strongly recommend a written exam to determine (and demonstrate in the case of a suit) whether everyone understood the information provided. This indicates the importance of evaluating training at the learning level.
Refresher training	The executives in the study suggested refreshers once a year to keep everyone sensitized to the topic and current on the issues.
Investigate complaints quickly	Be sure an adequate complaint procedure is in place that does not involve a person's supervisor. Often it is the supervisor who is the problem. Also respond quickly to not only determine the merits of the case, but also to stop the behavior immediately if it exists.
Keep information confidential	Only those directly involved should know about the investigation. You do not want someone being intimidated because they filed a complaint. You may also want to remove the person from the workplace during the complaint (with pay) just to demonstrate you take all such complaints seriously.
Provide equal and effective punishment	Guidelines regarding sexual harassment should be clear and penalties for violation severe. Those who violate the guidelines need to be dealt with no matter who they are in the organization. It must be made clear that no one is free to take such liberties with any employee.

Source: Adapted from Moore, H., R. Gatlin-Watts, and R. Cangelosi. 1998. Eight steps to sexual harassment free workplace. *Training & Development*, April, pp. 12–13.

for much of the training. Part of the TNA would be an examination of the policy to identify the goals of training and the guidelines for the expected behaviors and the nature of the content that the training will embrace.

Training for Nonsupervisory Employees and Upper Management

Some organizations believe that sexual harassment training for nonsupervisors is unnecessary. All it will do is sensitize employees to the issue, and perhaps create more complaints.[60] This line of thinking is an error. The truth is, this type of training may surface complaints that can be addressed in the early stages. Studies show that training can reduce both the number of complaints and the costs of settling complaints. Everyone needs to know the policy, how it is implemented, what types of behavior are prohibited, and how to respond when an incident occurs.

Upper management may not believe training is necessary for them. This position is irresponsible if they really do understand the law. As we pointed out, if they don't go through training, it leaves the company vulnerable to lawsuits. In addition, upper management often is unaware of inappropriate behavior, as Training in Action 9-4 suggests. Interviews with those who interact with upper management will help determine whether a problem exists at that level. Even if no specific problem is uncovered, training is a good idea for everyone.

TRAINING IN ACTION 9-3

WHAT THE COURT SAYS IF YOU HAVE A PROCESS FOR DEALING WITH SEXUAL HARASSMENT

Ms. Brooks was a telephone dispatcher for the City of San Mateo, California. Steven was a coworker whom she alleged touched her in an inappropriate place. After she reported the incident, Steven was immediately placed on administrative leave, pending an investigation. He subsequently quit. Ms. Brooks was absent from work for 6 months recovering from the incident. Upon return to work she said a hostile environment was created by male employees who ostracized her and by her supervisor who mistreated her. She sued the city claiming a hostile work environment. She lost. The court indicated that her claim was related to a single incident that was dealt with quickly. Also, employers cannot force employees to socialize; therefore, it is not an adverse employer action. To the issue of mistreatment by the supervisor, as part of the program to help employees understand sexual harassment issues and what is not appropriate, group sessions were held at which she was asked to discuss the incident. This process was part of the city's effort to curb sexual harassment.

Leslie Kohler was hired as a project coordinator with Inter-Tel Technologies in California. Soon after being hired her supervisor began touching her inappropriately, making explicit remarks, calling her at home and leaving obscene messages. Citing intolerable working conditions, she resigned and filed a complaint with the Equal Employment Opportunity Commission indicating she was subject to a hostile environment. At the U.S. Court of Appeals, she lost the case. Inter-Tel had a comprehensive antiharassment policy in place. Kohler knew about the policy but chose not to report it to the human resource department or any other manager. The ruling was based on the notion that the first requirement in such instances it to use the company's process if they have one. She did not and her claim was therefore denied.

Customizing Training and Aligning Systems

To customize training to the environment of the company, you need to identify the types of problems that exist in the company. Use the committee set up to handle complaints to obtain initial information about problems and the effectiveness of the procedure for reporting problems. Remember, part of the TNA is used to identify roadblocks to transfer of training. Lack of an effective reporting procedure is one such roadblock. You can also meet with small, cross-sectional groups of employees. These groups should be homogeneous in terms of gender and level in the organization. Questions might include the following:

- What do you know about the issue of sexual harassment?
- Do you think anything you have ever done could be construed to be sexual harassment?
- Have you or anyone you know at this company ever been touched in a sexual manner?
- Have you heard about a supervisor indicating to a subordinate that sexual favors would help them get a raise, promotion, or any other perk?
- Do you know of anyone who might feel consistently uncomfortable in terms of the way coworkers or supervisors behave around them?

With these groups, it is good to conclude with a statement similar to the following: "If any, one wishes to tell me anything else about this important issue, you can contact me personally and

---

TABLE 9-5 What Experts Suggest Is Necessary to Include in a Sexual Harassment Policy

According to attorneys and experts a policy protects your organization if it:

—States the organization's strong opposition to sexual harassment.

—Explains what sexual harassment is with examples employees will find relevant to their jobs.

—Establishes a clear-cut procedure for reporting harassment that does not limit the reporting to a supervisor in their department or in human resources. A committee of employees that includes representatives from all levels of the organization is needed so employees can talk to a peer if that is what makes them comfortable. A "hotline" dedicated to such reporting can also be set up.

—Warns potential perpetrators that violations could be punished by discipline that could include dismissal, no matter what level in the organization they are.

—Pledges that investigations will be conducted promptly and no retaliation will be taken for reporting such issues.

Source: Ganzel, R. 1998. What sexual harassment training really prevents. *Training,* October, pp. 86–94.

TRAINING IN ACTION 9-4

SEXUAL HARASSMENT TRAINING IS NOT JUST FOR LOWER LEVELS IN THE ORGANIZATION

Katherine, the compensation manager was presenting a report on variable pay programs to the company executives. She suddenly felt a foot under the table touching her calf, and slowly moving up toward her thigh. She looked across the table to see Jay, the executive vice president of sales leaning back in his chair smirking. She stopped momentarily wondering what to do. As she proceeded with her presentation he made some minor counterpoints to her presentation as he continued moving his foot up her leg.

The options possible in such a situation are numerous, but many could be disastrous.

What did she do? She steadied herself carefully and reached down, grabbed his foot and yanked it up so everyone could see.

Her yank was so powerful that it nearly pulled Jay out of his chair. "OK, Kathy! Uncle, uncle! You win," he said, roaring with laughter. Katherine then completed the presentation, and after the meeting the employee relations manager came over to talk to her. "Look," he said, "you have to ignore those jerks. They are just testing you to see how tough you are. You've passed the test and from now on the rest is 'easy street.'"

Source: Moore, H., W. Gatlin-Watts, and J. Cangelosi, 1998. Eight steps to a sexual harassment free workplace. *Training and Development,* April, pp. 12–13.

---

we could meet to talk about it confidentially." It is a good idea to set up a schedule for times that employees could meet privately to discuss the issue.

Team Training

Teamwork is a pervasive part of organizational functioning in North America. A survey of *Fortune* 1000 organizations in the United States indicates about 70 percent of them use teams.[61] A survey of Canadian organizations indicates a similar percentage (76%) use teams.[62]

WHY IT IS IMPORTANT

Use of teams seems to make a difference in the effectiveness of an organization. A common characteristic of North America's 100 best organizations is the effective use of teams.[63] A great deal of evidence indicates that effective teams can significantly improve the effectiveness of an organization. For example:

- At General Electric in Lynchberg Virginia, team ideas saved the company more than $90 million since they began in 1987.[64]
- Westinghouse Furniture Systems increased their productivity 74 percent in 3 years.[65]
- FedEx cut service errors by 13 percent.[66]
- Campbell soup plant in Toronto reduced its costs to produce soup by $3.55 per case.[67]
- Volvo's Kalamar plant reduced defects by 90 percent.[68]
- Corning cellular ceramics decreased defect rates from 1,800 per million to 9 parts per million.[69]

In today's highly competitive environment, organizations are looking for ways to obtain an advantage. Effectively implementing the right kind of team concept can make the organization more responsive to customer needs, reduce manpower by requiring fewer levels of management, reduce waste, improve quality and productivity, and in other ways make the company more competitive.

Work teams are also a benefit to employees who are given the opportunity to be involved in more meaningful work.[70] More meaningful work leads to other positive organizational outcomes:

- Improved employee satisfaction and commitment
- Lower absenteeism and turnover
- Improved performance

So organizations see a reason to be moving toward this style of management in ever-increasing numbers.

WHAT ORGANIZATIONS ARE DOING

The use of teams began in earnest a few decades ago under names such as *quality of work life, quality circles, employee involvement,* and so forth.[71] They all centered around getting workers more involved in their work and helping in a manner beyond what was traditionally expected. These efforts were met with skepticism, particularly by unions, many of which believed it was simply a way for management to co-opt workers and reduce the workforce.[72] In some cases this assessment was probably true. In these early years many of these efforts failed.[73] One of the main reasons was the failure to address transfer of training and nontraining issues such as systems, procedures, and organizational design. After the initial training, refresher training, evaluation and feedback of team efforts, and the training of new members when they are brought on board are important components of a successful program.[74] From a nontraining perspective, maintaining support from the top, removing roadblocks, and creating systems and practices that support the team process (performance appraisals, compensation systems, and so forth) are critical to the success of the program.[75]

Today, there are a number of successful team efforts, and Training in Action 9-5 is but one of these.[76] The transition from a hierarchical system to a flatter more inclusive system is not easy, and training is one of the important ingredients for success. Coca-Cola's Baltimore syrup operation, for example, was a plant with high turnover, absenteeism, worn-out equipment, and an old-style management.[77] Mr. Bentley, the new plant manager, decided to change that. He promised to run the business competitively and provide the employees with the KSAs to do it now and in

---

TEAMWORK SAVES $1 BILLION AT CHRYSLER

Don Callahan and Brian Large were trying to determine why the warning light on the Dodge Intrepid was on when the system was working fine. What made this situation so different? Well, Don was an hourly assembly worker and Brian was a production engineer. If Dodge built the Intrepid like most American cars, the problem would not have been fixed, because the two workers would never meet. Brian would be too busy to contact anyone about the problem and Don would say it wasn't his problem. For this car, however, the manufacturing process depended on a team of workers, designers, and engineers collaborating on all stages of the car's development.

The result of the collaboration: the car reached production a full year less than the average production cycle for Chrysler. It also required 40 percent fewer engineers. The total cost for the car from its inception was just over $1 billion, less than half of the cost of two other well-known team efforts: the Ford Taurus at $3 billion and GM's Saturn at $3.5 billion.

Source: Hunsaker, P. 2001. *Training in Management Skills.* Upper Saddle River, NJ: Prentice Hall.

---

the future. Four years later it emerged as a highly successful plant with cost savings at $1 million. This transformation was accomplished primarily through the use of teams. To have effective teams you need training, however. Training was the second part of Mr. Bentley's promise and he came through on it.

The Coca-Cola training came in three categories: technical, interpersonal and team. For the technical training employees were encouraged to learn four different jobs to provide for flexibility in the organization. This increased knowledge also provided employees with a greater understanding of the operation of the plant, making them more valuable team members.

Interpersonal skills training was also provided, because of the belief that, before you can do anything effectively, you need to be able to interact effectively with others. All shop floor employees, supervisors, and managers were trained together. This way everyone was seen as regular human beings, not supervisor or worker. This approach helped employees work together as a team without necessarily seeing the other person as a boss or supervisor. The training included listening, handling conflict, and negotiation skills.

Team training included leadership, managing meetings, group dynamics, and problem solving. As members are provided these skills they are also provided with additional skills to explore future career or retirement options. Self-assessment, resume writing, and interview skills are all part of preparing employees for the future at Coke or anywhere else they decide to go. When people work for a company because they want to, rather than because they see no other options, it ensures that they stay because enjoy their work and want to be part of the Coke team. So, let's consider the steps you would take in the development of team training.

TRAINING POINTS

The team concept usually surfaces when key organizational outcomes are not achieved and one or more people in upper management suggest that implementing a team concept will "solve the problem." Of course an experienced and knowledgeable training manager will suggest that a TNA would be required to fully understand the cause of the problem.

TNA Issues

The first question to address in the TNA is: What organizational outcomes are not being achieved and to what degree are the work unit structure and job design responsible? A team concept is just one possible approach to achieving the desired outcomes. Once the cause of the deficit in outcomes is understood, the next question becomes "Will some type of team concept sufficiently improve the outcomes, and if so is it the best alternative?" Of the many types of team structure available, not all teams work equally well for achieving particular outcomes. Five of the major team types are listed here:[78]

1. Informal team (sense of togetherness and cooperation)
2. Traditional work units with a supervisor (more formal sense of togetherness and cooperation)
3. Problem-solving task forces, committees, or circles (teams outside of formal work unit)
4. Leadership teams, steering committees, and advisory boards (teams that integrate leadership from various areas of the company such as management and union leadership)
5. Self-directed work teams (teams that are their own work unit operating without a formal supervisor)

Space is not available here to describe each of these types in detail and identify the tasks and situations for which they are best suited. We recommend the book *Tools for Team Excellence,* by Gregory Huszczo, as a good source for this information. Once you identify the type of team(s) required, you can then identify the KSAs needed by team members for the team to be effective.

Even though the different types of teams require some training that is unique, many of the KSAs are common to all types. Seven factors are generally found to be components of all effective teams.[79]

1. Clear sense of direction
2. Members with the talents necessary to achieve the team's purpose
3. Clear and enticing responsibilities
4. Reasonable and efficient operating procedures
5. Constructive interpersonal relationships
6. Active reinforcement systems
7. Constructive external relationships

As you can see, some of these components carry direct implications for the KSAs required of team members. They also identify the types of nontraining needs that must be addressed if the teams are to be successful. The TNA should describe what each of these components consists of for the team(s). This description will then determine the KSAs and nontraining needs.

Design and Development Issues

Most training for teams requires KSA as well as "team-building" modules. The KSA portion addresses deficiencies in item 2 in the preceding list (talents necessary to achieve the team's purpose). Knowledge acquired here is primarily declarative and procedural. Examples of the types of training/learning possibilities include the following:

- Listening skills
- Techniques for seeking input from others
- Communicating positively in conflict situation
- Problem-solving techniques
- Consensus decision making
- Conducting an effective meeting

Trainees are typically provided with lecturettes to convey the necessary knowledge, and then they participate in exercises that develop the skills. In addition to providing the lecturettes and facilitating the exercises, the trainer assesses the KSA development of the team as a whole. After the trainer is confident the team shows sufficient development of KSAs trainees are moved into a team-building module. During the team-building module the trainer will be assessing the level of KSAs being applied and at the conclusion will work with the team to assess their performance. If additional work on the KSAs is necessary, the trainer will provide that training, otherwise the team will move on to the next set of KSAs or next team-building module. This process allows the trainer to ensure the appropriate level of learning occurs before moving to the next level. However, it also means that training must be done in small groups (teams), and this constraint will increase the cost of training.

The team-building portion allows the team members to use their newly developed KSAs to understand the constraints under which the team will operate and to build the team's processes, procedures, and relationships. However, this process encompasses strategic knowledge development as the team members learn how to work together to accomplish their objectives. For example, team members must work together to come to consensus on their goals and objectives. Even when objectives are provided by upper management, the team must all agree on what they are, what they mean to the team, and how they will be evaluated/measured. The team must also determine the constraints under which they must work. Thus, the team must determine their decision making authority, resources available, and so forth. The team must also come to understand which responsibilities are viewed as enticing by which team members and work together to make sure everyone is given work they find enticing. Together, they must develop the rules and procedures they will use in accomplishing their work. Working as an intact team builds a common understanding of the procedures, develops interpersonal relationships, builds trust among team members, and allows them active practice in skills such as listening, decision making, conflict management, and so on. By conducting training with intact teams, you are able to appropriately integrate the strategic knowledge development with the descriptive and procedural knowledge components. Because you are working with intact teams and the content of the training is directly tied to the job, transfer of learning is more likely.

If your company is changing from a traditional work flow to a team approach, the first type of training that is likely to be needed is informational (knowledge) and attitudinal. The first step is to reduce factors that may be creating resistance to the change. Here you would begin with a general orientation regarding the use of the teams. The orientation would provide everyone with the following:

- An understanding of why a team approach is being implemented
- The advantages for the company and the employee of the type of teams being implemented
- The difficulties involved in moving to a team approach and the support the company will provide employees in meeting these challenges
- A basic understanding of how teams operate as well as any company guidelines for team operations (e.g., decision making, reporting relationships, etc.)

It would not be necessary to include intact teams at the same orientation session. However, it is important that the same message is heard by everyone. Thus, a thorough pilot of the orientation is important. Any team training conducted after the general orientation to team training should be done with intact teams.

Evaluation

Even though the organization holds a vested interest in the effectiveness of the team concept, the team itself is at least equally vested in its outcomes. Thus, particularly for team training, the team should be involved in the design and assessment of the evaluation phase. First, the team approach is most often designed to be an ongoing aspect of how the company does its business, so continuous improvement of team training is critical to the success of the company. The implementation of teams is typically beset with difficulties in the beginning due to the departure from the traditional, more comfortable, work systems employees are used to. Therefore, it is important to examine each phase of the training process to identify what went well and what needs to be improved. Second, most team approaches are associated with a company's increased emphasis on quality and continuous improvement. Thus, from the TNA through implementation and evaluation, all phases must be carefully examined to provide a solid basis for understanding why desired outcomes were or were not achieved, and to identify what corrective action is necessary.

Process and Content Evaluation   Our approach to evaluation of team training is to involve the team in the design of a reaction questionnaire that will be used at the end of each training module. This use of a reaction questionnaire to measure process differs from our previous discussions in which the reaction questionnaire is used as an outcome measure. Even though it is also used here to assess outcomes (trainee reactions), the involvement of teams provides a unique opportunity to combine the two. Process evaluation is not only important for evaluating team training, it is a component of effective teams (it is part of the "reasonable and efficient operating procedures" component). Effective teams must periodically assess their process as well as their outcomes in order to make the appropriate process improvements that will lead to improving their outcomes. So team training must include a component on evaluation of process and outcomes. By designing the reaction questionnaire to look at both processes and outcomes you will be able to provide training while conducting a part of the evaluation.

As a trainer, you will need to spend some time discussing how to design a good reaction questionnaire. This process allows you to work with the team to design questions that measure the degree to which the team members feel that each learning objective was achieved. Each learning objective question is followed by questions about what seemed to be effective and what was less effective in that learning module. One advantage to this approach is that the team understands the meaning and intent of the questions (because they help design them), thus the validity of the results is increased. The real advantage, however, is the exercise is directly related to the team's need to develop evaluation procedures for their operation back on the job. Teams often encounter difficulty measuring the "soft" side of their operation (aspects such as interpersonal relationships, effective meetings, effective use of team's talent, etc.). The team's experience developing the reaction questionnaire is a good practice opportunity in preparation for developing an evaluation instrument for their "team process" back on the job.

After the trainees complete the reaction questionnaire, the trainer plays the role of a team leader and reviews the results with the team. The trainer may also identify outcomes that appear to be below standard, which the group did not identify. During this discussion the trainer asks for clarification and seeks consensus about the results. The trainer then outlines the training process for the module and asks the trainees to help identify ways to improve the process. Once this task is completed, the trainer asks the team to review the evaluation process they just went through to identify practices they feel would be useful to include in their operating procedures back on the job.

More formal content evaluation is not necessary if the trainer did a thorough job. The trainer observes the team members using the knowledge and skill during their exercises. These observations combined with continuous coaching throughout the day, and the use of the feedback from the reaction questionnaire makes formal testing redundant. However, a trainer who is less confident in his abilities in this area may use more formal measures.

Transfer of training should be built into the team's own evaluation process. The trainer should schedule a meeting with the team about 2 weeks after training to review how things are going. Additionally, a meeting should be scheduled approximately 6 months after training is concluded. Organizational results should be reviewed at least every 6 months to identify teams that may be experiencing difficulties.

Other Training Programs and Issues

The types of training provided and the way they are managed affect almost every aspect of organizational life. Training can assist an employee in doing a job more effectively: provide opportunities for promotion, transfers, increased pay, and employee well-being. It also prepares employees for dealing with emergencies and in some cases even saving lives. Let's examine a few of these types and the issues organizations need to consider.

TRAINING AND EQUITY

In the section on diversity training we deal with ways the organization can improve the ability of a diverse group of employees to work together effectively. **Training equity** means providing equal access to training to all its employees. Like hiring and promotion, training is a personnel decision that is subject to legal proscriptions and prescriptions. Even though we would hope the ethics of treating everyone equitably would predominate the world of business, unfortunately many lawsuits are filed each year because an individual or group feels treated inequitably. Of these suits a large number are based on an employee not being selected for a particular position. It may seem like a selection issue, but many times the organization's training practices played an important part in the outcome of the suit.

The majority of selection decisions within an organization involve current employees (transfers and promotions). Even if the promotion or transfer is based on who has the best set of KSAs for the new job, the company can be found guilty of unfair discrimination. This situation happens when one group of employees (e.g., minorities) are not provided with the same opportunities for training as another group (e.g., nonminorities).

Consider the female technician who worked for the Canadian Broadcasting Company (CBC).[80] She wanted to go on remote location assignments, but was refused because many took place at night and were not safe. When promotions came up at the CBC, she was not considered because one of the qualifications was a broad-based understanding of the types of assignments technicians go on. She never received the on-the-job training that going on remote assignments provided. The CBC's good intentions, protecting her, prevented her from developing important KSAs, which inhibited her advancement. Training is an important part in the development of employees, whether they want transfers, promotions, or simply to be better at what they do. It is the manager's responsibility to ensure that all employees are given opportunities to improve themselves and prepare for advancement.

In addition to the traditional performance review for the purpose of compensation and promotion decisions, many companies conduct a separate **developmental review**. This review provides the opportunity for the employee and supervisor to discuss career goals, areas of strength and weakness, and the opportunities for development that are open to the employee. This discussion benefits the organization, because it helps develop employees for higher-level positions in the company. It benefits the employee because it provides opportunities to grow and develop. In addition to traditional types of training programs, development plans may include off-site seminars, on-the-job training, being put on a task force, given a temporary assignment, and other ways the employee can develop the appropriate KSAs. The key is making sure all supervisors understand the importance of providing all employees with opportunities based on their current capabilities and developmental readiness, not on their gender, race, age, or other irrelevant criteria. Training in Action 9-6 provides an excellent example of an organization doing everything possible to provide opportunities for employees.

THE GLASS CEILING

The **glass ceiling** is a metaphor for an invisible barrier that prevents minorities and women from moving up the corporate ladder. It is an example of how training and development opportunities can limit the ability of employees to advance in the company. Let's examine the glass ceiling for

---

TRAINING IN ACTION 9-6

PROVIDING TRAINING FOR SUCCESS

Many women at Bell Telephone wanted to transfer from the operators job to the more interesting and lucrative jobs in installation and repair. When they applied, however, they failed to pass one of the tests required. Bell Telephone and the Communication Workers union got together to work out a way more women could be successful.

When women applied to the installation and repair department, they often were not accepted because they did not successfully pass the electronics test. It was an important criteria for acceptance, because much of the work involves understanding and working on the components of a telephone and its accessories. Women did poorly on the test because they usually did not take such courses in high school or follow it as a hobby as men seemed

to do. So management and the union worked out an agreement in which operators could apply for a limited number of special training slots created in installation and repair. Successful candidates were required to be able to climb a ladder, have a valid driver's license, and pass a color vision test. Those who were successful were chosen on the basis of their seniority as operators.

Once accepted into a training slot, the operators received 6 months of on-the-job training in installation and repair. Then they returned to their operator job until an opening became available and they applied like anyone else. The training they received prepared them for the test and resulted in many operators being selected into the position.

Source: Martin, D. 1993. Personal communication. Communication Workers of Canada, Toronto.

---

women. In the late 1980s, only about 2 percent of the corporate offices of the *Fortune* 500 were filled by women.[81] That proportion improved and passed 12 percent in 2000, but considering the number of females in the workforce, it still seems rather low.[82] Especially when considering Kraft Foods, one of the *Fortune* 500. It takes equity seriously, with more than 26 percent of its corporate positions filled by women.[83] What is the difference between Kraft and many others? One difference seems to be in the area of training. One of the main points, suggested by Mary Kay Haben, executive vice president of Kraft Foods, is their commitment to personal development and career advancement, both of which focus on training.

At Kraft, employees meet with their supervisor once a year (formally) to discuss performance, developmental progress, and career aspirations. They meet again (informally) 6 months later to review how things are going. At Kraft, they seldom hire from the outside for management positions, so opportunities for moving up are available. When they do lose a senior manager to the competition they are able to fill it within minutes.[84] To accomplish this level of preparedness, they developed an extensive human resource planning process with a heavy focus on preparing (training) employees for promotion. Part of this program takes place through an extensive mentoring program. They also formed a high-level committee that monitors how Kraft is doing regarding women and minorities at each level in the organization. When they identify a problem in any area, they go about solving it immediately. This example illustrates how a company can tie training to changes in the organizational environment to ensure equitable treatment to all employees.

DISABLED

Legislation in both the United States and Canada makes it unlawful, when hiring or training, to discriminate on the basis of a person's disability, whether physical or mental, if it does not prevent the person from doing the job. Basically, a job analysis describes the critical KSAs. Based on that information, you can assess whether the disability will negatively affect job performance. If not, then you must give that candidate the same opportunity to be hired, promoted, or trained as anyone else.

Consider Mary, who is hearing impaired but able to speak and read lips. She applies for the job of accounting clerk. The job analysis identifies all the critical tasks and KSAs, and she meets all of them. However, although not a critical task, the job requires using the phone from time to time. Can the employer refuse to hire her based on her inability to use a phone? Although each case needs to be examined on its merit, it would seem that such a refusal to hire her for the job would be illegal. The company faces, according to the law, a **duty to accommodate**. It would require the company to purchase a special phone used by the hearing impaired.

Duty to accommodate requires the employer to help the disabled do their job. Remember, these disabled employees possess the necessary KSAs to do the job, but require some help in certain areas. Accommodation may come in the form of special desks for wheelchairs, large computer monitors for visually impaired, removing an unimportant task from a job (that the disabled employee is not able to do), and so forth. Whether an employer needs to accommodate a disabled individual depends on whether it will result in **undue hardship** for the employer. Undue hardship is determined by a number of factors such as cost of the accommodation, financial resources of the organization, number of employees, and impact of the accommodations on the operation of the company.

Irrespective of the legislation, when considering the nearly 50 million disabled workers in the United States and 3.8 million in Canada,[85] it makes financial sense to include as many competent applicants in the selection pool as possible, disabled or not. After all, with more qualified applicants, the likelihood of selecting a strong candidate is higher. If the job analysis indicates that the job of operator requires answering phones and directing calls, someone who is legally blind can be considered. The main accommodation required in this situation is a phone in Braille. Training, however, may also require some changes in order to accommodate the special needs of someone who is blind. We return to that issue later.

So, let's go back to Mary, the hearing impaired accounting clerk. She moved up to the highest level in nonmanagement accounting. Six years later when she applies for the accounting manager position, she is turned down because she does not possess the requisite KSAs. Frank does demonstrate the required KSAs and gets the job, even though he worked there 3 fewer years. However, Frank got those skills through training courses offered by the company. Mary was never told about those training opportunities. If the skills Mary is lacking were available through training, and she was not told, the company failed to provide her with the same opportunities as others in the company. This failure puts the company in a vulnerable legal position. Perhaps more important, the organization potentially missed out on a competent supervisor and instead faces an extremely angry accounting clerk.

The Training Dimension   With the disabled, it is not only accommodation in the workplace, that needs to be considered but the implications for accommodation in training as well. Treating someone with special needs equitably in your training requires preparation. Proper furniture and accessibility to the training facility need to be considered. Training for the trainer if the person is going to be talking to some who are hearing impaired (through lip reading) or maybe the organization will provide other accommodations (such as a signer). The best way to deal with this issue is to meet with those who are disabled and ask them what they need.

Summing Up Training and Equity   Whether it involves not promoting a female to the job of technician, a minority or female to an executive position, or a hearing impaired person to supervisor, the issue is the same: The organization is losing out on potential. Career and personal development of everyone in the organization needs to be a top priority. Although this point seems intuitive, a recent survey of organizations noted that about one-third provided no mentoring or coaching for employees, and 16 percent did not provide personal or developmental planning.[86] How many of the remaining companies are just "going through the motions," rather than doing it properly, is also unknown. It is clear, however, that effort needs to go into helping all employees do their best if a company is going to compete. It makes good economic sense. To be sure it happens, organizations need to consider the following:

- Obtain support from the top that identifies the importance of the issue of equity for all employees.
- Write clear descriptions of job requirements and make them the focus of personnel decisions.
- Focus part of every manager's appraisal on the equitable treatment of employees.
- Assemble a steering committee that examines the issue and reports on progress each year.
- Establish a liaison and reporting procedure for dealing with issues of inequity.
- Provide extensive training to managers on issues related to equity at all levels.

What it comes down to is considering the implementation of an equity program as an intervention that will require training and changes in policies and procedures to assure that the forces pushing in the direction of equity for all are stronger than those pushing against.

BASIC SKILLS TRAINING

Literacy generally includes reading, writing, and basic arithmetic. The functionally illiterate are unable to use those skills even at the most basic level (reading instructions, balancing a checkbook, etc.). The problem may be getting worse as a result of the following factors:

- Lower standards in many high schools today
- More minorities and non-English-speaking immigrants entering the workforce
- An increase in skill requirements for most jobs

In the United States about 20 percent of the workforce is functionally illiterate. This figure translates into an estimated loss of $60 billion a year in productivity, through mistakes, accidents, and damage to equipment.[87] The problem is similar in Canada where about 22 percent of Canadian adults struggle with a severe literacy problem.[88] It translates into a productivity loss of about $4 billion (Canadian) per year.[89]

As far back as 1983, a presidential report, "A Nation at Risk," identified an inferior education system that would make it difficult for the United States to compete in an international marketplace.[90] Organizations find that, even when hiring high school graduates, they need to provide remedial skills training to get them ready for the job. A recent survey noted that of the new employees classified as requiring training in the basic skills, 67 percent did graduate from high school.[91] In addition to issues within the school system, immigration from non-English-speaking countries continues to increase. In the United States for example, 34 percent of immigrants in 1996 came from Asia.[92] At that same time, in Canada, only 21 percent of immigrants were from Europe and the United States.[93] With this immigration, new employees with English as a second language will be more prevalent, making reading and writing more problematic.

At the same time as skill level was dropping, most jobs began to require more skills. A machinist now needs computer skills to operate the computerized machinery, truck drivers need to understand logistics, inventory control, and flow analysis from the computer in their truck. Even parcel delivery requires data entry into a computer. Furthermore, many organizations are becoming ISO certified, requiring a new list of skills for the shop floor. Teamwork, which for years was the purview of management, is now also down on the shop floor, demanding that workers understand charts, know how to interact effectively with others, and so forth.

It is necessary then for organizations to upgrade their employees with these skills. Before they can, however, employees need to possess the basics. Just providing the basics can result in a positive financial impact. A survey of workplaces in Canada where literacy programs were installed revealed a drop in error rate in employees' work, improved morale, and a general improvement in health and safety.[94] Another positive outcome of such training is the improvement of employees' self-efficacy. Recall the importance of self-efficacy for training. Those with poor literacy skills will likely show a low self-efficacy. Providing employees with these skills will definitely lead to positive effects.

Developing **basic skills** (or literacy) **training** is similar to developing any other training program. The first step is a TNA. Here, more than in other TNAs, the need to ensure confidentiality is critical.[95] Workers who are illiterate generally take great pains to hide it out of embarrassment and shame. It may be advisable to use an outside vendor in this case to provide additional assurance that few in the organization would know. One company hired a consultant to provide outside assessment over a long period of time in order to encourage everyone who thought they might have a problem to go for assessment outside the workplace.

Outside vendors need not be the answer. Sea World did it themselves and was successful. They use company tutors. Trainees are given the option of a noncompany tutor, but most preferred someone from within the company. As with most things, no single way is always best.[96] The key is to keep the training relevant by using material that the employee uses every day. So for reading, use the memos received and typical instructions. This tie to actual work makes the success and value immediate. Some tips for improving employees self-efficacy in literacy training are shown in Table 9-6.

SAFETY TRAINING

Years ago, providing a safe work environment was considered a necessary cost because of legal requirements. That attitude is changing. Today, providing a safe work environment is an important part of the success of most organizations. Accidents and injuries cost industries billions of dollars each year, so any reduction translates to a positive result on the bottom line.[97] This change in focus may explain much of the reduction in the rate of illness and injury in the workplace over the past few years (see Figure 9-1).

For many organizations, a culture of safety is a requirement to be competitive in a global marketplace. In a survey of organizations considered to be on the cutting edge of safety training

---

TABLE 9-6 Tips for Improving Self-Efficacy of Those Requiring Literacy Training

Assure trainees that they are being asked to upgrade because of their importance to the company.

Do not call it "literacy training" or "basic skills training;" both can sound demeaning. Use a positive name that stresses job training.

Make participation rewarding, not punishing. Pay them for the time or conduct it on company time.

Always talk about "improving one's reading" rather than learning how to read.

Indicate the problem is widespread and that many similar employees successfully completed the training.

Provide early successes so trainee can see they are able to do it.

Use company-related examples to make sure it is not only meaningful and therefore easier to learn, but also useful right away.

Source: Tyler, K. 1996. Tips for structuring workplace literacy programs. *HR Magazine* 41:112–16.

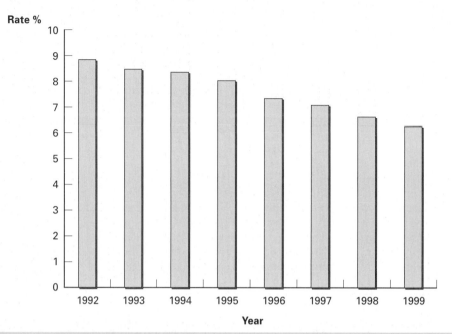

FIGURE 9-1 Percent of Full-Time Workers Reporting Occupational Injuries/Illness in Private Industry

Source: Bureau of Labor Statistics.

it was noted that they developed this "culture of safety" rather than a number of different training courses on safety.[98] In such an organization, **safety training** is not considered a cost, but an investment. This distinction may seem minor, but it changes the focus by looking at the benefits of safety training, rather than seeing it as forced compliance with OSHA or provincial health and safety legislation. So it is viewed as a cost savings. By evaluating training at the "results" level and identifying the cost savings in fewer accidents, less machine wear, lower compensation costs, and so forth provides continued support for this proactive approach to safety.

During years of consulting and training in organizations, we noted that most discussions with employees about safety training reveal how boring it is. From what you learned so far, you know this impression does not bode well for learning. Valerie Overheul, president of Summit Training Source, suggests a number of ways to make training interesting.[99] She indicates that in many years of training employees in various safety skills, the one comment consistent over the years is how interesting they are finding the training, which is not like previous safety training. Valerie's recipe for increasing trainee motivation in safety training it to "jazz it up." Get trainees' attention through the use of humor, familiar music, action clips, and dynamic graphics. Be sure the trainer is upbeat and interested in the topic. In a recent survey of the pulp and paper industry, where safety is a critical component of the job, one of the questions dealt with "obstacles to effective training." Fifty-two percent of the respondents indicated "boredom." The next closest response was scheduling, which only 22 percent indicated as an obstacle. These statistics reiterate a common theme in the text: motivate trainees by making training interesting.

Back to the SBI case. Recall that Ms. Conner requested that the personnel manager investigate her complaints, and he found no merit to her complaint. As a result, she filed a civil action against SBI based on the treatment she endured. The judgment was in her favor, awarding her more than $500,000 in damages.[100] Clearly much of this award is based on the hostile environment created by her managers and coworkers. The unequal training alone is not enough to result in such an award. However, consider the costs of simply going to court: time required for managers to get records together, preparations for trial, and the cost of legal representation. This potential expense alone is reason enough to motivate organizations to pay attention to such issues and provide appropriate training to see it does not happen.

SUMMARY

This chapter examined in depth four of the more prevalent training practices taking place in organizations today: orientation, diversity, sexual harassment, and team training. We discuss the importance of each and what is going on in organizations. With orientation training we provide an extensive hypothetical example of how to develop such training using the training model provided in the text. The development of the hypothetical orientation training is designed to show how to use the model in development of any type of training.

Additional issues and training programs were discussed more generally and briefly. Equity was discussed in relationship to employment and training opportunities. Employees are more often selected from within the organization than not. Even when promotions and transfers are based on the person's skills and potential, all employees regardless of their race, gender, or disability, must be provided access to training and development opportunities. The importance of equitable access in preventing costly litigation is understood, but it is more important in terms of fair treatment and obtaining the best employees in all positions.

Using a TNA as an assessment of basic literacy skills is useful in organizations today. The need for highly skilled, continually learning employees requires a solid foundation of basic reading, writing, and arithmetic skills. More and more companies are taking it upon themselves to provide these skills. However, those experiencing functional illiteracy are unlikely to admit it unless organizations take the time to develop and market training that addresses these skills.

Finally safety training is seen by many companies as a significant cost avoidance tool. In the past it was generally presented in an uninteresting manner, leading to poor learning and transfer to the job. If safety training is to achieve its cost avoidance potential, it needs to be designed to arouse the interest of the trainees.

KEY TERMS

- Basic skills training
- Content measures
- Developmental review
- Diversity training
- Duty to accommodate
- Glass ceiling

- Hostile work environment
- Literacy
- Orientation training
- Process measures
- Quid pro quo harassment
- Safety training

- Sexual harassment
- Team training
- Training equity
- Undue hardship

CASE ANALYSIS

Donna was born with no left arm below her elbow. She worked for the optical service department of a manufacturing company. The department provided digital scanning services to the organization, which meant scanning documents into a computer and indexing them. Donna's job was primarily indexing the documents, but she also prepared papers for scanning, maintained the copy machine, and occasionally ran the low-speed scanner. The company accommodated Donna by providing a special typing stand and other small things that made it possible for her to do the job, given her lack of a left arm. The company was generally happy with Donna's work and considered her an average or better performer.

Donna wanted to be trained on the high-speed scanner. She repeatedly requested the training but was refused. Use of the high-speed scanner was not a job requirement, and only 7 of the 21 employees in the department knew how to operate it.

The company's arguments for not training her on the equipment was that it was not a necessary part of her job, it did not affect on her pay or benefits, and would not influence her opportunities for advancement. Donna disagreed as far as the advancement was concerned. She believed she would be more marketable in the company if she possessed that particular skill. Besides, Donna pointed out that everyone else who expressed a desire to be trained was given that opportunity.

It was clear that the high-speed scanner was not a job requirement because only one-third of the department employees knew how to operate it. The supervisor admitted that he refused her training because he did not believe that Donna could operate the machine effectively because of her disability. More specifically, he commented, "It takes two hands to clear out the paper jams, and straighten documents that come out of the machine. The whole design of the machine is such that someone without a left hand could not operate it properly given the placement of the controls. Even if she could operate it somehow she would be too slow and would require assistance."

Of course Donna's response to being too slow and requiring assistance was that the company needs to accommodate her because of her disability. ■

Source: Based on Zachary, M. 2001. Training for the disabled. *Supervision*, November, pp. 23–26.

CASE QUESTIONS

1. Assume you are called in as an outside consultant to mediate this situation. What would you tell the supervisor and Donna separately? How would you recommend solving it? (Do not assume the law is on either side.) Support your recommendations with information from the diversity and disabled sections of this chapter and any additional information provided by the instructor.
2. Assume that the supervisor is correct in stating that Donna would require assistance with the machine given her disability, and that the decision to not train her is final. As her supervisor, what would you tell Donna? Explain your reasoning using concepts from the chapter.
3. Assume the supervisor gives in and Donna is trained, but the result is that she is slow and hurts productivity. What do you advise the supervisor to do?

EXERCISES

1. Over the next few days watch the instructor in the various classes you attend. Jot down notes about any differences you see in terms of how the instructor treats males, females, minorities, or the disabled. Share this information with the group and generate a list of

what differences exist and how you would deal with them. If you found no differences, indicate what specific things the instructor does to be sure everyone in the class is treated equitably.

2. Break into small groups. Each person thinks about a current job or one held in the past for which orientation training was provided.
   - If you never held a job that provided orientation training, just think of a job you held. Describe four things that a good orientation training would include to make breaking into the job easier. Post these activities on an easel under the heading "Wish they had done."
   - If you went through an orientation training, think about the orientation and list two things that were good about the experience and two things you thought were a waste of time or boring. Post these activities on an easel, with the positive under the heading "Glad they did" and the negative under the heading "Wish they wouldn't have."
   - After everyone contributes, discuss how the "Glad they did" and the "Wish they would have" tie into the training model in terms of what you need to do right. Do the same for the "Wish they wouldn't have" in terms of what to avoid.

3. Think about your role as a student in this class. Now think of a visually impaired, a paraplegic, and a hearing impaired person. What kind of accommodation to the training facilities (classroom) would need to be made for each to be successful? What about the trainer/teacher? What changes if any should he/she make to be sure the person is getting full value of the training/education?

4. Break into small groups to discuss the following situation. The vice president of human resources asked you, the director of training, to develop a sexual harassment training program for the company. During your needs analysis you discover that most of the executives do not believe they need this training and do not plan to attend. You identify a couple of instances in which an executive seems bordering on sexual harassment. You discuss your findings with the VP who then asks you to come back with a strategy for dealing with the resistance to training.

   Develop your response and be prepared to present it to the rest of the class.

5. Identify two organizations not used as examples in the chapter that are using orientations to good advantage. Describe your reasons for picking these two based on concepts presented in the orientation section.

QUESTIONS FOR REVIEW

1. What is an orientation designed to do? What are the characteristics of an effective orientation?
2. How are organizations dealing with diversity? Are they effective? Why or why not?
3. What are the important components of an effective sexual harassment strategy?
4. Why is team training necessary? What are the seven components of effective teams? What are some of the KSAs required of team members in effective teams?
5. How can training affect the selection of competent candidates for vacant positions? What would you recommend an organization do to ensure that everyone receives equitable opportunities for promotions?
6. Why is it important for organizations to focus on training of basic literacy skills in today's environment?
7. Why is safety training an important component of the training mix in so many companies? What is the biggest concern regarding safety training that was noted in the survey referenced in the chapter? Is it fixable, and if so how?

CHAPTER

Management Development

Learning Objectives

After reading this chapter, you should be able to:

- Identify and describe the roles and responsibilities of managers at different levels in the organization
- Describe the general competencies and characteristics of effective managers
- List the important organizational factors that determine which managerial characteristics are desirable at a given time and situation
- Explain how management training needs can be influenced by changes in organizational strategy
- Gather and feed back data as part of the management development person analysis
- Describe the unique developmental needs of technical managers
- Identify the various sources and types of training related to management development
- Identify the specific problems associated with training executives and some of the methods that can be used to deal with these problems
- Describe why development of executives is so critical to effective organizational functioning and the most effective way to deal with executive development

---

Linda Wachner Takes the Reins at Warnaco

In 1986 Linda Wachner took over as CEO of Warnaco, a manufacturer of women's lingerie, which was experiencing financial difficulty. Wachner's goal was to take the company public and ensure its profitability in a hostile, competitive market and fairly stagnant economy. She knew radical changes were needed to restore the company to

(continued)

442

(*continued*)

competitiveness. Since then, the company went public, the stock rose 75 percent above its initial offering, the debt was cut by 40 percent, sales increased by 30 percent, earnings before taxes increased by 140 percent, and operating cash flow almost doubled. Wachner pursued an unrelenting focus on the company's performance, which is closely tied to her personal financial situation since she owns 10 percent of the stock.

As the only female CEO of a *Fortune* 500 company at the time, her leadership was subject to careful scrutiny. Wachner continues to combine energy, drive, and enthusiasm with hard-core fiscal management. She maintains a focus on the customer and has high demands for her employees. Her employees view her as a tough boss, and often feel that she expects too much. Although her "do it now" philosophy focuses on responding to customer preferences in the short and long run, she also managed to reap considerable savings from cost cutting. For example, she reduced the corporate staff from 200 to 7. Some say that Wachner does not do a good job of managing people because of her single-minded focus on company profitability. She is unrelenting in getting to the point and requiring her colleagues to do the same.

"Have I yelled at meetings? No question. Do I think I've ever hurt anybody? I hope not. Look, I just want people to be good and I put enormous pressure on everyone to get this company moving in the right direction," she says. "I know I push very hard, but I don't push anybody harder than I push myself. Last year I travelled 200 days visiting stores, plants, and so on."

At the same time, she motivates her workers with her praise of their work. She visits the stitch room almost daily, picking up and examining the fabric, lace, and trim the stitchers are working on. "These are to die for," Wachner declares with a supremely satisfied smile as she holds up a garment. "Beautiful. Just beautiful." Maintaining the grueling schedule may be difficult for employees, but Wachner emphasizes creating an environment to which employees bring a high energy level and focus on a common goal. Her determination created a hard-as-nails image, but it's a style that gets the job done.

Why Focus on Management Development?

We already discussed in detail the training process and a great many training techniques. So why single out managers for special consideration? Don't the processes and techniques already presented apply to them? The answer is yes. However, several reasons prompt us to examine this part of the organizational community in more detail. Perhaps foremost is how important management development is in today's environment. Evidence indicates that those companies that align their management development with their strategic planning are generally more competitive.[1] So, we need to thoroughly understand such an important part of organizational competitiveness. Other related reasons include the following:

- Managers get a lot of training.
- Managers are accountable for success.
- Managers' jobs are complex.

MANAGERS GET A LOT OF TRAINING

One of the most frequent types of training provided by companies over the last several years is management development and executive leadership.[2] This is true across every industry from financial and banking institutions to manufacturing to communications to utilities. Management training is more important as the organization increases in size, but not dramatically. Eighty-eight percent of firms report management development programs, compared with 90 percent that provide executive leadership training.[3] For companies of all sizes approximately 37 percent of all training budgets go toward management and executive training. Thus, whether large or small, and regardless of industry, management training is seen as a vital part of improving organizational performance. A training professional needs to understand a part of the business that is in such demand.

MANAGERS ARE ACCOUNTABLE FOR SUCCESS

Managers carry a different and more complex burden for ensuring the success of the enterprise than nonmanagers. Think back to the opening case. How much responsibility does Ms. Wachner assume for the success of Warnaco relative to other employees? The business environment over the next decade is expected to place even more demands on management. Consider the following responsibilities of the manager of the new millennium:[4]

- Managers face a shrinking labor pool in terms of the skilled and educated. It is management's responsibility to grow and keep the talent necessary to be competitive.
- At the same time, more technologically sophisticated systems are being implemented, and management is responsible for ensuring that employees obtain the knowledge and skills required to perform their jobs.
- They must also deal with a more diverse workforce, and see that diversity is a strength, and not allow it to become a focus of divisiveness.
- Mergers, acquisitions, downsizing, and fast-paced changes must all be managed effectively.

In fact, it is management's responsibility to ensure that all systems and resources are appropriately integrated so the organization can achieve its objectives. No wonder companies place a high priority on developing the KSAs of their managers.

MANAGERS' JOBS ARE COMPLEX

Perhaps the most important reason to closely examine management development lies in the nature of managerial effectiveness. What makes a manager effective is more complex and difficult to ascertain than are most other targets of training and development. Thus it is more difficult to assess needs, to develop training content and methods and, most certainly, to evaluate the effects of training. Do you think Ms. Wachner is a good manager at Warnaco? What criteria are you using? Would everyone agree with those criteria?

A good training process first develops an understanding of the employees' training needs before designing the training program. For management development this is not easy. Typically, a manager's effectiveness is determined by how well his unit meets its objectives. However, determining his training needs from the performance of the unit is problematic. A complex alignment of many factors influences the unit's performance, and the manager can affect these factors in many ways. For example, Ms. Wachner's organization is successful. Would she be just as successful in a different company in a different industry? To understand a manager's development needs, you must first understand the context in which the manager and the unit operate. This context includes the strategic direction of the organization, the technology of the manager's unit, the human and financial resources available to the unit, and how the unit relates to the rest of the organization.

Information about the context in which the manager must operate is collected from an organizational analysis. The operational analysis identifies the managerial competencies required to create the appropriate match between the organization's strategy and the unit's structure, resources, and technology so the unit is able to achieve its objectives. To identify the manager's developmental needs, her attitudes, knowledge, skills, and behavioral styles are compared with the competencies required for the job. The job in this case is the management position in a particular unit. Determining all these factors is difficult enough, but it becomes even more difficult when you realize in how many ways a manager may go about achieving the unit's objectives. Just identifying a manager's developmental needs is a complex task filled with ambiguities. Identifying or developing a training program to meet those needs is just as difficult and ambiguous.

Our Approach to Management Development

It is only after the managerial process is understood that appropriate needs analysis can occur. This understanding is also required for the trainer to be able to select the instructional strategy that will best meet the manager's developmental needs. Although we identify some sources from which training programs can be acquired or developed, they are not the focus of this chapter. Literally thousands of programs are available, and new management development programs are developed frequently, as older ones fall out of favor and then many years later suddenly reemerge as a "favored" approach. Instead, the focus of this chapter is on increasing your ability to determine management development needs. Our philosophy is that the educated consumer makes wiser choices. Understanding the match required between managers and their organizational context provides two long-lasting benefits to the training professional:

1. An increased ability to determine a manager's development needs
2. An increased ability to assess accurately the appropriateness of a particular training program for meeting those needs

Thus we provide an integrated framework (a model) for assessing managerial behavior within the organizational context. Again, doing so takes a systems perspective in which we look at the manager within the unit and within the organization.

General Overview of the Managerial Job

A well-established principle of management holds that the effectiveness of particular manager styles, behaviors, and traits is contingent on other organizational variables.[5] That is, a successful managerial approach in one situation can be unsuccessful in another. How, then, can general statements be made about managerial duties and responsibilities across industries? Actually, no real contradiction arises here. The general activities carried out by managers seem to show more similarities than differences.[6] However, the frequency, the relative importance, and the manner in which these behaviors are performed differ greatly between organizations, even within the same industry. The first task is to understand the general makeup of the managerial job. With that understanding, we can turn our attention to some of the contextual factors that determine the frequency and style in which these activities are performed.

MANAGERIAL ROLES

Much of the research on managerial activity is integrated into general roles that are "customized" to fit into a particular management position in a particular organization.[7] Figure 10-1 illustrates the relationships among these roles, which form an integrated whole in which each role affects the others. One implication of this model is that managers must not only demonstrate the KSAs required to perform each role, but also the KSAs required for their integration. Although individual managers may give more or less importance to a particular role, eliminating or neglecting one role results in direct consequences on the performance of other roles, and hence on managerial effectiveness.

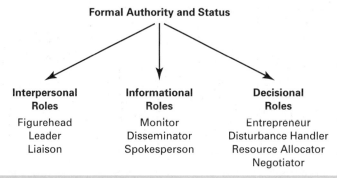

Formal Authority and Status

Interpersonal Roles	Informational Roles	Decisional Roles
Figurehead	Monitor	Entrepreneur
Leader	Disseminator	Disturbance Handler
Liaison	Spokesperson	Resource Allocator
		Negotiator

FIGURE 10-1 Mintzberg's Managerial Roles

Mintzberg defined a manager as anyone who is in charge of an organization or one of its subunits. The manager's roles derive directly or indirectly from the formal authority and status granted to the position. The nature of the activities required of each role is described in Table 10-1.

Some less systematic but more flavorful descriptions of day-to-day managerial work are listed here.[8]

- Engaging in brief, varied, and discontinuous activities
- Accommodating an unrelenting pace of activity
- Performing numerous regular duties, as well as handling the exceptions in their own as well as subordinates' routine
- Making decisions on the basis of judgment and intuition
- Providing subordinates with a clear understanding of their jobs and boundaries (yet jobs overlap and boundaries blur)
- Recognizing that routine and standardization are required to achieve efficiency but often must be sacrificed to create change; feeling comfortable doing either
- Needing controls and valid information, yet knowing that controls reduce information validity
- Regarding rules and standards as important constraints that must be observed, but acknowledging they are often inconsistent and making decisions about which must be ignored to meet others

From the descriptions of managerial activity above and those in Table 10-1, it is clear that managers operate in a dynamic internal environment where they must constantly act to meet the challenges of new circumstances. Managers of subunits must not only adapt to new circumstances themselves, but coordinate their actions with other subunits that are also adapting. Typically little time is available for careful planning and reflection. When careful planning occurs, it often won't reflect new circumstances that arose after the plan was developed.

Managers must be able to get their hands on the knowledge and skills necessary to meet these challenges as soon as they arise. This is not to say careful planning and reflective analysis are not important in organizations. Managers, however, often cannot take much time for this important activity. For that reason, many organizations maintain staff units whose job it is to provide the manager with recommendations based on careful planning and thoughtful reflection. A typical manager, however, must quickly diagnose a situation, develop an appropriate response, see that it is implemented, and move on to the next task. This process requires that the manager understand the organization, its strategies and capabilities, how his unit fits into the puzzle, and how his behavior will influence events. The next section addresses many of these issues.

TABLE 10-1 Description of Managerial Roles

Roles	*Activities*
Interpersonal	
Figurehead	Meeting the routine, obligatory, social and legal duties required of the head of a unit (examples: attendance at social functions, meeting with politicians, buyers, or suppliers)
Leader	Maintaining, developing, and motivating the human resources necessary to meet the needs of the unit
Liaison	Developing and maintaining a network of individuals outside the unit in order to acquire information and action of benefit to the unit
Informational	
Monitor	Searching for and acquiring information about the unit and its environment so that the manager becomes an information center for the unit and the organization; derives from liaison and leader roles
Disseminator	Distributing selected information to others within the unit or organization, some of which is transformed through integration with other information
Spokesperson	Distributing selected information to others outside the unit regarding plans, values, activities, and other elements of the unit and conveying the appropriate image of the unit
Decisional	
Entrepreneur	Proactively developing and adjusting the unit to take advantage of existing opportunities or meet anticipated threats in the environment; acting based on inferences and conclusions drawn from the evaluation and integration of information gathered in the monitor role
Disturbance Handler	Reacting to meet the immediate demands of the unit (examples: a wildcat strike, loss of a major customer)
Resource Allocator	Evaluating and choosing among proposals; integrating and authorizing activities and resource utilization
Negotiator	Bargaining to acquire the resources to meet the needs of the unit and organization

ORGANIZATIONAL FACTORS

Managerial context refers to the alignment of an organization's environment, strategy, structure, and technology as described in Chapter 2. These factors play a significant role in determining which managerial KSAs are necessary. Although many of the KSA requirements may be the same across organizations, different organizational contexts will require the KSAs to be used more or less frequently and in varying manners (or styles). The organizational analysis portion of a managerial needs analysis should carefully consider the factors discussed here and their relation to managerial requirements. You may wish to review Figure 2-2 (page 35) and the related material in Chapter 2 to refresh your understanding of organizational context.

INTEGRATING STRATEGY, STRUCTURE, AND TECHNOLOGY

Organizations seek to maximize the integration of strategy, technology, structure, and human resources through their design. Managers must monitor and manage these interactions within their unit to ensure their unit's activities are integrated with the strategic direction and technological base of the organization. This integration is depicted in Table 10-2.

TABLE 10-2 Strategy, Technology, and Structure Integration		
	Market Leader	*Cost Leader*
Technology	Nonroutine	Routine
Structure		
Design	Organic	Mechanistic
Decision Making	Decentralized	Centralized

As discussed in Chapter 2, the market leader organization will be subject to a more uncertain environment and thus require more nonroutine technologies. Rapid changes in technology create high levels of complexity in organizations that are driven by technology, which market leaders typically are. In these organizations, interactions among the factors that affect efficiency and effectiveness create ambiguity and uncertainty. As a result, less job specialization, more coordination, and more decentralized decision making are the strategy. On the other hand, recall from Chapter 2 that the cost leader strategy is more effective in environments with greater certainty. This type of strategy calls for more routinized technology, more centralized decision making, and reduced organizational complexity. These various strategies have direct implications for the skills, traits, and styles of managers within these different organizations.

Whereas a corporation or strategic business unit (SBU) faces an array of environmental forces, the individual subunit will face only a portion of those forces directly and must respond appropriately to these direct forces. Even though the subunits must support the organization's strategy, effective management practice for a subunit varies according to its own environment and its role in the overall strategy. However, on a general level, the environment of the subunits tends to reflect the organization's strategic environment.

General Characteristics of Managers

We indicated in Chapter 4 in the discussion of needs assessment that an employee's duties and responsibilities must be understood to determine the KSAs required to perform those tasks. Much of the management development literature, unfortunately, suggests that evidence of managerial effectiveness in one organization can be applied to other organizations. Whether this application is possible depends on the similarity of the organizational context. Remember our caution about copying other organizations without understanding the theory behind their practice. Nevertheless, this literature does identify many managerial characteristics that seem to be necessary for most managers.

The characteristics we discuss are, like managerial roles, general in nature and thought to be applicable across most organizations. Later, we provide a model you can use to integrate these general characteristics into various organizational contexts. As we review the empirical literature on managerial characteristics that are predictive of success, remember that the criteria used to determine "effectiveness" or "success" vary considerably across studies. Nevertheless, some aspect of effectiveness or success is associated with these characteristics. Certainly, the frequency with which they are reported in the literature gives support to their organizational utility in certain contexts.

MANAGEMENT STYLES

A wide variety of theories of management attempt to demonstrate the relationship between managerial behavior and the situation in which that behavior occurs.[9] Although we will not explore each of these theories, we do find a common thread running through the vast majority.

Managerial style seems to be related to two dimensions of leader behavior: employee-oriented and task-oriented.[10] Research on path-goal theory further differentiates these two styles. The **employee-oriented style** has two types: participative and supportive. The **task-oriented style** also has two types: directive or achievement oriented.[11]

Employee-oriented styles require higher levels of interpersonal skills (discussed in the next section). The **participative style** emphasizes involving subordinates in decision making, particularly in how they go about achieving their task. A **supportive style** is characterized by friendliness, empathy, and concern for meeting employees' needs.

Task-oriented styles require fewer human and more technical skills. In the **directive style**, subordinates are given instructions about what to do, how to do it, and when it should be done. The **achievement style** emphasizes goal setting and high-performance expectations for subordinates.

CATEGORIES OF MANAGEMENT CHARACTERISTICS

In addition to a manager's style, which represents her actual behavior, factors related to the manager's cognitive makeup also affect her effectiveness. The research we examined[12] can be organized into four major categories: conceptual knowledge/skill, technical knowledge/skill, interpersonal knowledge/skill, and personal traits. These categories are not independent of each other. Your personal traits influence your interpersonal skills, and both will affect how you carry out technical and conceptual activities. Most likely it is the integration of all four categories into a whole that determines the degree of a manager's success. Unfortunately, little research is available to tell us about how successful managers integrate these characteristics. Nonetheless, it is both convenient and useful to consider them separately for the time being.

Conceptual Knowledge and Skills

Conceptual knowledge and skills refer to the mental abilities required to analyze and diagnose complex situations and make appropriate decisions. They are essential and common to all (or nearly all) management positions. Listed here are some of the more frequently cited examples of the requirements in this category:

PLANNING AND DECISION MAKING

- Knowledge of decision-making alternatives and skill in their use
- Setting priorities
- Forecasting events
- Integrating organizational policies, procedures, and objectives
- Adapting to legal, social, and political environment

ORGANIZING

- Developing appropriate organizational structures
- Coordinating separate but interrelated activities
- Scheduling activities to reach time, efficiency, and quality goals
- Allocating resources to maximize return on investment

CONTROLLING

- Knowing how to apply various control systems
- Developing control systems
- Developing and supporting initiatives
- Developing policy, procedures, and objectives

Technical Knowledge and Skills

Technical knowledge and skills are necessary to carry out the operations of a particular functional area (e.g., marketing, engineering, human resources). For example, for a marketing manager advertising, direct sales, and consumer psychology are areas in which technical knowledge and skills are expected. Also included in this category are general technical knowledge and skills required for managing any organizational unit. The most frequently mentioned are financial analysis, budgeting, managerial accounting, and marketing goods and services.

Interpersonal Knowledge and Skills

Interpersonal knowledge and skills, often called "human" skills, refers to the ability to work with, understand, and motivate others, both individually and in groups. As Mintzberg's research indicates, managers spend most of their time interacting with others. It is primarily the manager's interpersonal skills and knowledge of human behavior that determines her success in influencing others and developing information networks. Examples of knowledge and skill elements in this category include the following:

- Understanding individual differences
- Motivating subordinates
- Developing subordinates
- Building a work team and providing team leadership
- Managing conflict constructively
- Adjusting behavior to fit situational demands (behavioral flexibility)
- Presenting a position in a compelling fashion (persuasion)
- Listening effectively
- Awareness of social cues
- Maintaining objectivity in social situations

Personal Traits

Personal traits are not knowledge and skills, but rather qualities of the manager as a person. In some ways you could think of them as attitudes, but they are considerably more complex. A personal trait is a relatively permanent predisposition to behave in a particular way. Early leadership studies consistently failed to identify personality traits that predict successful leaders[13] but research over the last 15 years found certain measurable characteristics that seem to be predictive of future success as a manager. You need to remember that personal traits may change markedly over the course of a manager's career. The traits discussed here were characteristic of early career stages and were associated with managers' success over the long term. However, the causal relationship is far from clear.

Earlier work by McClelland and his colleagues identified four need states that are predictive of effective and ineffective managers. We focus on three: need for achievement (nAch), need for power (nPow), and need for autonomy (nAut). Those high in nAch possess a strong desire to assume personal responsibility, wish to receive concrete feedback on task performance, and demonstrate a single-minded preoccupation with task accomplishment.[14] Those high in nAut show a strong desire to work independently. For situations in which they work alone, they prefer to control their own pace and procedure and not to be hampered with excessive rules.[15] These individuals tend to resist working in groups and indicate their need to be personally responsible for outcomes. Those high in nPow desire to lead, influence, and control the people and things around them.[16]

Recent research describes these need states in terms of two general characteristics: drive and leadership motivation.[17] **Drive** includes nAch as well as ambition, energy, and tenacity.[18] **Leadership motivation** relates primarily to nPow and distinguishes between a need for institutional power, which is directed toward organizational goals, and a need for personal power, which is focused on personal goals.[19] Institutional power needs are related to more successful managers and personal power to less successful managers and nonmanagers. The research also shows that those high in nPow (institutional), moderately high in nAch, and moderate to low in nAut are generally the most effective managers.[20] In addition, likeableness, resistance to stress, and career orientation are generally found to be predictive of future success.

We noted earlier that a common thread runs through the management style literature: the existence of two general styles of management. A second common thread is that leaders/managers must adapt their style to fit different situations. A manager's ability to be flexible or adaptable with respect to style of management is also highly predictive of success.[21] This **adaptability/flexibility** characteristic is found in the literature as both a personal trait and a skill, and it is clearly a necessary component for long-term success as a manager. However, it may be required more in certain kinds of organizations than in others.

INTEGRATING MANAGERIAL ROLES AND CHARACTERISTICS

When you examine the roles managers must perform and the characteristics needed by effective managers, you see that it becomes possible to match characteristics with roles. Table 10-3 depicts such an integration. For example, performing obligatory ceremonial duties (figurehead) will almost certainly require awareness of social cues, oral communication skills, and behavioral flexibility. The manager's personal traits, particularly likableness and resistance to stress, are likely to influence how they respond to those situations; conversely, it is not likely that a manager's technical or conceptual knowledge/skill will be much of a factor in this role. Using similar logic, we matched the other characteristics with roles.

Table 10-3 serves as a heuristic device in relating a manager's knowledge, skills, and traits to various aspects of managerial jobs. It is important to remember, however, that the precise nature of the roles and requisite managerial characteristics differ from organization to organization and even within the same organization. In particular, the evidence is reasonably conclusive that the importance of the various roles, and consequently the associated knowledge and skills, differs from level to level within the organization's hierarchy.

TABLE 10-3 Managerial Roles and Associated Management Characteristics

Managerial Role	Knowledge and Skills			Personal Traits
	Conceptual	*Technical*	*Interpersonal*	
Interpersonal				
Figurehead			yes	yes
Leader	yes		yes	yes
Liaison	yes		yes	yes
Informational				
Monitor	yes	yes		yes
Disseminator	yes	yes	yes	
Spokesperson	yes	yes	yes	
Decisional				
Entrepreneur	yes	yes	yes	yes
Disturbance Handler	yes	yes	yes	yes
Resource Allocator	yes	yes	yes	yes
Negotiator	yes		yes	yes

ROLES, KSAs, AND MANAGEMENT LEVEL

Lower-level managers primarily supervise and coordinate the work of nonmanagers. They are usually in daily contact with their subordinates and peers and are responsible for the day-to-day operations of their unit. They depend primarily on interpersonal and technical skills to get the job done.[22] Their roles are primarily leader, monitor, disseminator, disturbance handler, and negotiator. Usually other roles, requiring greater levels of conceptual skills, are made unnecessary because rules, policies, procedures, and upper management decisions take their place.

Middle managers coordinate the activities of lower-level managers. The manager in the middle (or sometimes "in the muddle," as they like to say) performs the role of liaison, spokesperson, resource allocator, and entrepreneur as well as most of the roles performed by the lower-level manager. Interpersonal skills remain important, but technical skills decrease in importance. Conceptual skills are somewhat more important.

Top managers coordinate the activities of the organization through their middle managers. Conceptual skills are of primary importance at this level, particularly the entrepreneurial role. Leader behavior is also important here to instill a sense of direction and motivate direct reports and employees in general. Informational, liaison, and figurehead roles are predominant, and the focus of the other roles changes from inside to outside the organization.

Organizations in general place higher priority on certain types of managerial KSAs at different levels in the organization, but the preceding discussion is not especially helpful in identifying the job requirements of managers in a specific organization. Each organization has its own context and the specific expectations of managers within that context. Thus even though it is generally helpful to know that supervisors typically are expected to rely on their technical more than their conceptual knowledge and skills, the relative importance will depend on the organizational context.

Integration: Strategies and Management Characteristics

Combining research on organizational environment, strategy, structure, and technology with the research on leadership provides some general prescriptions for effective managerial characteristics at each extreme of the strategy continuum. In the most general sense, effective managers possess technical, interpersonal, and conceptual skills.[23] The leadership research adds the concepts of personal traits and style. We examine these factors and assess the degree to which each is more or less relevant in market and cost leader organizations. Table 10-4 provides a summary of this discussion.

TECHNICAL COMPETENCE AND CONTEXT

Research indicates that technical competence is an important foundation for effective management.[24] Both market and cost leader strategies require managers with high levels of technical competence, but the technical sophistication required of market leaders is much greater because they operate on the leading edge of technology. Many technologies capable of significant flexibility in application are also required, making the environment more complex and less predictable. Thus in Table 10-4, market leader organizations are rated higher in the need for managers with technical skills.

TABLE 10-4 Strategy and Managerial Characteristics Integration

	Market Leader	*Cost Leader*
Skills		
Technical	More sophisticated and nonroutine	Less sophisticated and routine
Interpersonal	Higher	Lower
Conceptual	Higher	Lower
Traits		
Drive	High	High
Flexibility	Higher	Lower
Leader motive	High	High
Style		
Participative	Higher	Lower
Supportive	No difference	No difference
Achievement	Higher	Lower
Directive	Lower	Higher

INTERPERSONAL COMPETENCE AND CONTEXT

The market leader strategy uses a more organic, less formalized design, which requires the manager to interact more with higher-level managers, subordinates, and peers. These interactions are critical to coordinating activities within and between units. In cost leader organizations, the centralization of decision making and the formalization of rules, procedures, and policies decrease the importance of many of the interpersonal skills. These characterizations reflect a relative difference in the two types of organizations and should not be construed in an all-or-none fashion. Effectiveness in these "human skills" generally differentiates between successful and unsuccessful managers,[25] but logic suggests this is more likely in market leader organizations, where considerably more interaction is required (see Table 10-4).

CONCEPTUAL COMPETENCE AND CONTEXT

Again, because of the routine technology, mechanistic design, centralized decision making, and formalized coordination systems, the cost leader organization, by design, reduces the importance of managerial conceptual skills except at the higher levels of the organization. Market leader organizations, on the other hand, require managers with greater conceptual skills at all levels, because of their more complex organization and the need to reduce barriers to creativity. There is agreement that technical skills are more important at lower-level management positions, conceptual skills more important at higher levels, and human skills important at all levels. In other words, conceptual skills are more important at all levels in the market leader compared to the cost leader organization.

Studies generally support the notion that interpersonal and conceptual skills are more predictive of managerial success than are technical skills.[26] This conclusion, of course, makes sense if technical activities decrease in frequency as one moves from lower to higher management positions. The more effective managers are those who are able to handle the increasing demands of human and conceptual problems. In addition, individuals are typically hired or promoted to management positions on the basis of their technical competence at lower levels, so these skills are less likely to differentiate effective from ineffective performers. Particularly in technical units, new employees are rarely hired on the basis of interpersonal skills or ability to conceptualize complex organizational systems. When they are promoted to managerial positions, they are likely to need development in these areas.

PERSONAL TRAITS AND CONTEXT

For nearly all of the traits examined, no compelling evidence or logic suggests that managers high in these traits will be more or less effective in any particular organizational context. The only trait likely to be more useful in one organization than the other is flexibility. Because market leader organizations face more ambiguity and change than cost leaders, the manager with higher levels of adaptability would likely be more effective than one who was less flexible. This point is reflected in Table 10-4.

MANAGEMENT STYLE AND CONTEXT

Of the two employee-oriented styles, only the participative style is expected to show differences in effectiveness based on strategy. Logic suggests that participative styles are more effective in market leader organizations. Obviously, a decentralized structure promotes higher levels of participation in decision making. In the technical units of the market leader organization, this issue is especially important, because innovation and creativity are facilitated by multiple inputs and synergistic outcomes. In addition, because of the nonroutine nature of the technology, decisions relating to a particular area of that technology require the input of those most familiar with it.

We can expect the participative style to be less effective in the cost leader organization for several compelling reasons. Here the decisions are more centralized. The jobs are well defined by the routine technology, policies, procedures, and the structure. Few reasons or opportunities arise that would promote the participation of employees in decisions that would meaningfully affect their job. Remember, we are talking about an organization at the extreme end of the continuum. Even here, we are not saying no participation would take place, only that its value to the organization would be less.

We find no logic to support the notion that a supportive style is more or less effective in either organizational context. Although employees are likely to be somewhat different in organizations at opposite ends of the strategy continuum, there is no justification for postulating differences in need for friendliness, empathy, or concern from their managers. Our belief, supported by much of the research, is that this style is effective in nearly all organizations.

For the task-oriented styles, clear structural reasons suggest differences in the effectiveness of the achievement versus directive styles. For the market leader, the achievement style is more effective. This type of organization requires managers to reduce some of the ambiguity of their unit's task. The organization's task—to quickly identify and place in the market new products or significant modifications of old products—creates ambiguous expectations. Here the achievement-oriented manager clarifies goals, parameters, and performance expectations. In the cost leader organization, goals and expectations are well understood and standardized, leaving little need for the manager to exert effort in this area; in fact, subordinates are likely to see such behavior as redundant and negative.

Some amount of directive behavior will be useful in the market leader organization to the extent that it clarifies responsibilities and expectations. However, the detailed direction of who will do what, how, and when is contrary to the structural and technological systems of the market leader. For the cost leader, however, it is clearly important for the manager to monitor and ensure that the right people are doing the right things at the right time. In addition, the cost leader's design uses a centralized system in which operations are driven from the top. It is the manager's responsibility to ensure that changes in expectations are accurately conveyed to subordinates and that subordinates comply with the direction in a specific manner. We view the directive style as being more effective in the cost leader organization. Still, managers in such organizations must be discriminating in how it is applied. High or adequately performing employees in this organization may find additional direction from the manager irritating. Conversely, in the market leader organization employees may come to desire direction from their managers because of the absence of well-defined structure in their jobs. Nevertheless, the design of this organization favors the achievement style over the directive: providing employees with goals and objectives and giving them the autonomy to figure out the best way to achieve them (see Table 10-4).

The relationships described here between strategy and manager characteristics are generalizations, as are the relationships described between strategy, structure, and technology. Any given organization that adopts a market leader strategy will require some routine as well as nonroutine technologies. The point is that they will experience a greater preponderance of nonroutine technologies than if they followed a cost leader strategy. Likewise, the managerial characteristics related here to organizational strategy point to those characteristics that will be most effective with the particular structural and technology characteristics of that strategy. Perhaps the most appropriate use of Table 10-4 is at the organizational subunit level. If the subunit is structured in ways consistent with the strategy, the managerial characteristics associated with the strategy are likely to be more effective. Consideration could be given to using this table in developing a managerial needs assessment where the organizational context of the manager's unit can be measured.

Management Development Implications

The preceding model suggests that a key to effective management is knowing the context in which you are operating, knowing what is required of you in order to create the best match with the context, and having the KSAs to do what is required. Thus management development programs need to provide training programs that address these issues.

UNDERSTANDING CONTEXT

The most obvious implication of the context/management characteristics model is that effective managers must be able to adapt themselves and their unit to the needs of the organization, and to do so they need a clear understanding of the organization's strategy and their unit's part in that strategy. It is only with this understanding that managers can use their personal characteristics most effectively. Thus an important part of all management development programs should be the following:

- The clarification of the organization's situation
- Its strategy for coping with the situation
- How the various units fit into the strategy
- How the training program relates to these things

Organizations that develop their managers in this manner are able to obtain a competitive advantage.[27] Too often, however, management development programs try to provide managers with skills, knowledge, styles, and traits without an understanding of the context in which they are to be applied. In the worst case, the development is inappropriate for some units, and in the best case, in those units where the development is appropriate, the managers don't understand why it is appropriate.

SELF-AWARENESS AND DIAGNOSTIC SKILLS

Once managers understand what is needed from their unit and why, it is important that they understand how their own characteristics influence the activities within their unit and its relationships with other units. This understanding requires skills in self-awareness and diagnosis. To increase self-awareness, managers need to be able to access basic data required to diagnose cause-and-effect relationships between their behavior and others' actions.

Diagnostic skills are necessary to identify why gaps exist between what is expected of the unit and what actually occurs. Managers must be able to create the appropriate match between their behavior and:

- The structure/design of the unit
- The characteristics of the subordinates

Creating these matches requires the ability to diagnose the existence and cause of mismatches. Self-awareness and diagnostic skills are the basic requirements for managerial adaptability to changing conditions.

Of course an alternative is to place managers in situations that match their characteristics (a leader-match approach).[28] Although this approach may be effective in the short run, a guarantee that things will remain stable is simply not possible. It is preferable to try to develop these basic adaptability skills in all managers. However, for selecting new managers, particularly in technical areas, it would seem best to select those who most closely match the organizational context of the unit they will manage; they will likely be effective in the short term and their adaptability skills can be developed for the long term.

Once a manager understands the organizational context within which his unit operates and acquires the adaptability skills of self-awareness and diagnosis, he is ready for the appropriate development of knowledge, skills, and styles. For this, a managerial person analysis is required.

MANAGERIAL PERSON ANALYSIS

Identifying the required KSAs for a managerial job is difficult. Assume you already completed this identification and now you must determine whether the managers in unit A possess the required KSAs. How do you go about determining a manager's style, traits, and ability to interact with peers, subordinates, and superiors? One method gaining considerable popularity is the 360-degree feedback (360-DF) described in Chapter 4. This approach requires a sample of those with whom the manager interacts to fill out an anonymous questionnaire about the manager. The responses are then analyzed and graphed to provide feedback to the manager. The results show where general agreement lies among subordinates, peers, and superiors concerning how the manager "comes across." These data, combined with the data from the unit's operations and other measurement tools, can be used to identify areas of development for each manager. It can also be used during training to help the manager identify the cause-and-effect relationships between her behavior and others' reactions. The manager, of course, should be involved in identifying her areas of strength and weakness. If the manager is not involved, a scenario similar to the one described in Training in Action 10-1 is likely to occur.

This multiple-source feedback should be used only for development purposes, not for formal performance evaluations or for pay, promotion, or termination decisions.[29] If it is, the responses of those filling out the questionnaire are likely to change. Those respondents who are friends will inflate the manager's score, rivals (peers and some of the superiors) will lower their ratings somewhat, and the staff support person the manager complained about will cut him to the bone. However, the research shows that when assessment occurs for developmental pur-

---

TRAINING IN ACTION 10-1

FAST TRACK??

A major drug company chose one of its finance officers to attend a customized leadership program at the University of Pennsylvania's prestigious Wharton School, which cost the company more than $24,000 for the 5-week program. The finance officer went off to training assuming that he was being put on the fast track; after all, only a few executives were picked for this program every year. Instead, the company saw it as the last chance to improve the executive's interpersonal skills. After returning from the training, and two lateral moves later, he left the company. "Nobody was straight with me before I took the course," said the executive. "My bosses were looking for a changed man, but I wasn't any kinder or gentler. If anything, I suppose I was more aggressive, which to them, I guess, was more abrasive."

Source: Constructed from information reported in *The Wall Street Journal*, September 10, 1993, p. R-6.

---

poses, the validity of personal characteristics measurement is enhanced by the inclusion of supervisor, coworker, subordinate, and customer ratings.[30]

Though 360-DF often results in positive comments about the manager, it can also provide powerful, uncomfortable, and surprising information. In addition to the characteristics discussed in this chapter, 360-DF provides feedback about a number of other personal characteristics that typically do not show up in the research on management effectiveness. For example, one manager learned that he stood too close to people when talking to them and that little bits of saliva would fly out of his mouth when he spoke—not a good combination for a manager looking to advance his career. After feedback, he stood farther back and started speech therapy. Another manager, the head of Nestle's Perrier operation, found out that when he moved from head of sales and marketing to the CEO position, people changed their interpretation of his behavior. His temper and occasional "public whippings" of senior managers that was previously tolerated and seen as demonstrating forceful management became frightening after he became CEO with the authority to fire anyone, and managers stopped coming to him with problems and ideas.[31]

Because of the sensitive nature of the data, feedback must be carefully handled by the training professional to ensure that the manager sees it as "legitimate" and constructive. The most difficult comments to accept are those about interpersonal skills such as "untrustworthy," "poor listener," "uses poor judgment." These characteristics are seen as core competency skills and nearly every manager assumes she is strong in these areas. The Center for Creative Leadership estimates that only about one-third of all managers accurately predict how others view them. Another third hold inflated views of their talents. For these managers, the most surprises await, because subordinates almost always rate them the least effective.[32] For some hard-core control-oriented managers it sometimes takes massive doses of feedback before the message finally sinks in. Many will attempt to dismiss the results as inaccurate, inappropriate, or irrelevant. The training professional's job is to help the manager come to terms with and accept the results. When results are consistent (e.g., most people rate the manager in the same way), it is more difficult for the manager to explain them away. The most important part of the feedback agent's job is helping the manager understand that her intentions are not the same as other people's interpretation of her behavior. Once the manager makes this association, she can then begin to explore what she might do differently to achieve the desired results.

Sources of Knowledge/Skill Acquisition

The most obvious source of management training is the organization itself. However, most companies use a combination of internal and external sources to provide their managers with the appropriate mix of developmental opportunities. A survey of training managers[33] showed 93 percent of the companies providing both internal and external training to supervisors and middle managers, and 63 percent providing such training for executives. Only about 15 percent of the firms said they developed internal courses for executives, while more than 60 percent did so for middle managers and supervisors. These numbers tell us that few firms rely only on internal training resources, especially for upper-level managers and executives. Those involved in management development must be familiar with training and development opportunities outside their organization as well as being able to develop useful programs internally.

The following sections explore some of the more frequently discussed alternatives in the literature. This does not imply an endorsement of any particular source. Rather we present them to demonstrate the variety of sources that are available.

EXTERNALLY BASED TRAINING

Executive/management education programs at universities provide knowledge and skills of a general nature. These programs cover the range of management issues from traditional MBA programs to building strategically effective organizations. Other sources of management development activities are training companies, consultants, and professional associations. They supply a wide variety of training activities ranging from broad-based, general-application programs to those that are narrowly focused on limited areas of skill and knowledge. When the education is narrowly focused, dealing with specific topics such as project management, team building, financial analysis, or effective communication, the managers typically stay in residence at the training site for a few days to several weeks. When the focus is broader, dealing with general management domains (e.g., executive MBA programs), the manager likely attends training for a few hours to a few days periodically over periods of up to 24 months. Typically, the goal of broad-based programs is generic skill or content learning rather than job specific. Personal insight is generally not a goal; classroom-based methods tend to be used rather than games and simulations.[34] Personal insight and job-specific KSAs are more typically addressed in the narrow focus programs.

The principal advantages of externally based programs are as follows:

- They expose managers to the current thinking and theory in management.
- They remove organizational constraints in exploring new approaches.
- They allow interchange of ideas among managers from different organizational backgrounds.
- They cost less per person than internally developed programs.

Problems that may arise with externally based programs include the following:

- Inability to relate content to company-specific approaches
- Inconsistency of instructor effectiveness (some are excellent, others poor) and an inability of the contractor to choose the instructor (more typical with executive MBA programs than with residential programs)
- Inability to specify expected company outcomes as a result of the training
- Extended time away from the job
- Failure of the manager's company to provide on-the-job reinforcement of concepts and skills
- Inability to control the content of the training (the company can choose the course or program, but not the content)

Despite these concerns, most companies see externally based management programs as valuable tools. Enrollment in traditional MBA education is up, and enrollment in the growth of "for-profit" universities is up even more.[35] About 49 percent of companies utilize university-based residential or executive MBA programs, and most of these companies use some form of external short courses.[36] The primary reasons for utilizing these programs are credibility of the organization offering the program, the nature of the program topic areas, and managers' belief that it will meet their needs.

CORPORATE UNIVERSITIES

The growth of **corporate universities** is even higher than the growth of for-profit universities.[37] In an attempt to overcome some of the deficiencies of university-based education while maintaining many of its advantages, large corporations create their own internal "universities." Phillips Petroleum, General Electric, IBM, Motorola, McDonald's, and Xerox are just a few of the companies that developed their own university-type education. According to Jeanne Meister, president of Corporate University Exchange, about 1,600 corporate universities exist in the United States.[38] The reason organizations are exploring this approach is that after examining the characteristics of university-based versus external, nonuniversity-based formal educational programs for managers, they determined they could do better internally.[39] The primary reasons are as follows:

- The organization understands its own approach to management and can convey it better to its managers.
- Managers can obtain job-specific knowledge and skills.
- The company can ensure quality instruction.
- Because of the organization's size, the courses are cost effective.

Dr. Bill Lee explains why American Airlines developed its own university in Training in Action 10-2.

Public and private universities draw a wide range of managers to their management development programs. The diversity of backgrounds and interests requires that the concepts and methods taught must be general in nature so as to be applicable across most situations. Although students are usually encouraged to apply these concepts and methods to their own organization, faculty can do only a limited amount to facilitate transfer of this knowledge back to students' jobs.

The corporate university, on the other hand, can integrate the technical, conceptual, and interpersonal skills within the context of the organization's strategy, structure, and technology. The company can control and shape the curriculum to meet its own needs and values, provide the same content to everyone, and schedule instruction to be convenient for the organization and the trainee.

Some problems, however, exist with the corporate university approach. Matching the curriculum to the needs of the organization remains a difficult task. Pressures within the organization may discourage training in some areas or the use of certain methods while encouraging others. Although this situation reflects the political reality of the organization, it limits the organization's ability to develop new and more effective approaches. In addition, costs may actually be higher than for externally developed programs. Phillips, for example, found its costs to be about 50 percent more than for similar external training and education.[40]

This approach is possible only for large organizations. It is neither practical nor feasible for small to moderate-sized businesses to create their own university that includes faculty and attendance requirements. Smaller organizations must rely on public and private universities as well as other external training and development suppliers.

Regardless of whether training is provided internally or through external sources, the training department needs to match the content of the training with the context within which the

---

WHY AMERICAN AIRLINES DEVELOPED ITS OWN CORPORATE UNIVERSITY

American Airlines decided to develop a Corporate University (CU) because training was fragmented and many departments operated as cottage industries. Departments were hiring their own outside consultants, vendors, and so forth. Dr. Lee said, "We found that in many departments, the local management had contracts with the same off-the-shelf course providers and were all paying premium price." Other departments were hiring consultants to provide custom programs already developed by other departments. Before the CU was developed, this money came out of operations and no one was really tracking it.

"The CU is becoming a central clearinghouse for all material in the company, and is able to negotiate a better price with vendors and off-the-shelf providers as more and more departments come under the CU mantle," says Dr. Lee, "but there are still some groups that develop and provide their own training. We have reached out to them and offered to share what we have rather than trying to take them over. They have viewed that very positively and some groups have agreed to turn over their training to the CU because it is one less thing they have to manage. In many areas, such as publishing materials, we have saved thousands of dollars. In the area of government compliance we have saved literally millions by providing quality programs with consistent delivery."

Dr. Lee reports, "We are currently pursuing relationships with similar industries that are noncompetitive but have some of the same needs to reduce costs and maximize benefit."

Source: Personal communication with Dr. Bill Lee, Director of Measurement and Performance Analysis, American Airlines Corporate FlagShip University, Fort Worth Texas, September, 2002.

---

managers are to use it. Before adopting a management development program, the following questions are useful in assessing the match of a particular program to managers needs.

1. Do the program outcomes meet an identified need?
2. Will the learning that results from the training be supported on the job?
3. Will behavior resulting from the training conform to the organization's policies, procedures, and norms?
4. Will the individuals receive any personal benefit from the training?
5. What is the cost/benefit ratio of the approach compared with that of alternative approaches?

Another important point is the evaluation of such training. It is one thing to train managers and discover that the training is of little or no value. It is quite another to continue to do so, wasting training dollars and credibility year after year.

TYPES OF MANAGEMENT DEVELOPMENT PROGRAMS

A description of the full diversity of management development approaches and techniques is beyond the scope of this chapter. However, the following descriptions cover a variety of programs and techniques associated with the competencies of effective management described earlier. We are not necessarily advocating the use of any of them but are simply providing a glimpse possess the resources to acquire high-level instructors and develop the appropriate train-ing materials. These programs are also more easily tailored to fit the specific needs of the company.

Interpersonal and Management Style

e combined these approaches because it is difficult to separate management style from inter-rsonal skills. In fact, management styles are often addressed in training through emphasizing e or more interpersonal skills.

1. Interactive skills training: This approach uses simulations and feedback from observers to provide trainees with ways of interacting more effectively with others. It is an approach that makes managers more aware of how their behavior influences the way others per-ceive them and react to them.[49]

2. Leader match training: This program, based on Fiedler's contingency model of leadership, trains managers to diagnose their situation and themselves to determine the best fit.[50] Fiedler proposes that a manager's personal characteristics are relatively unchangeable, therefore the training provides ways of manipulating the situation to match the strengths of the manager. Thus, in this approach interpersonal skills are not modified, but rather managers are shown how to create the situation for which their particular style is most appropriate.

3. Grid management: The two most important managerial characteristics in this approach are the manager's concern for work outcomes and her concern for people (note the paral-lel here with "employee and task orientation"). The proposition here is that managers who have strong concerns in both of these areas are the best managers. Training focuses on developing the manager's ability to display these characteristics simultaneously. Even though the manager must respond to different situations with the appropriate behavior, it is the value orientation associated with both a strong concern for people and task that guides the manager's behavior.[51]

4. Workshops and seminars: Again, these are offered over a wide range of topics and by a wide range of providers. These programs typically focus on a particular skill area such as communication, managerial style, leadership, or team facilitation.

Developing Personal Traits

velopment of personal traits can be a part of many management development programs. A v programs that focus specifically on trait development are listed here.

1. Role motivation: The object of this program is to develop six motivational states in man-agers: favorable attitude toward authority; desire to compete; assertiveness; desire to exer-cise power; desire for distinctiveness; and a sense of responsibility. These motives help them deal with employee work deficiencies and meet organizational criteria for effective-ness (primarily in large organizations). It includes development of interpersonal skills but focuses primarily on self-examination and development of internal values.[52]

2. Need for achievement: This program of self-study, goal setting, and case analysis is designed to provide managers with an understanding of their need for achievement and develop-ment of that need so that it is focused on constructive behavior. This approach yielded the best results for small business owners, particularly at the early stages of their careers.[53]

3. Transactional analysis: This approach deals primarily with the orientation of the manager when interacting with subordinates. It suggests that unhealthy relationships within the work group arise from adult (manager) to child (subordinate) interactions rather than adult to adult. The training focuses on self-awareness and improving the manager's ability to develop adult-to-adult relationships with subordinates and superiors.[54]

of the diversity available. Those wishing to probe deeper into this
erences provided.

Knowledge/Skills Development: Conceptual

A variety of ways to develop conceptual skills in managers includ

1. Management/business games, simulations, and case studies (s
2. On-the-job training: Included in this are mentoring, coaching,
   understudy training, and junior boards. Mentoring and unde
   that the manager works closely with a senior manager to
   Understudy training occurs when the manager is assigned as
   senior manager; she learns by observing the senior manager
   of gradually increasing complexity and responsibility. Junio
   and on-the-job training techniques. A junior board of direc
   promising middle-level executives, who are given critical issu
   business and asked to provide senior management with recor
3. Decision making: Situations are diagnosed to determine t
   making a decision. For example, Vroom and Yetton provide a
   learns the relevant situational variables that determine whe
   made by the manager alone, delegated to a group of subordin
   in between.[42] Another approach to decision making is ratic
   uses simulations to develop managers' problem-solving ar
   unique feature of this approach is the use of actual situations
   identification, and elimination of potential problems. Unsolv
   problems are used for knowledge and skill development.[43] R
   conference method, where the focus is on group rather than
   and decision making.[44] Much of the foundation of current qu
   ity management training can be found in these approaches.[45]
4. Managerial roles: This approach, based on Mintzberg's model
   providing managers with an understanding of what they are
   observation and understanding of one's roles, effectiveness
   related approach, the incident technique, utilizes critical inci
   asking managers to identify the facts needed to address the in
   the skills especially needed to perform the monitoring and di

Knowledge/Skills Development: Technical

Technical training, especially professional skills training, is of
sources. About 60 percent of companies acquire this type of traini

1. Degree and certification programs: Degree programs in busir
   provide the technical foundation for most managers. In additi
   skills specific to a particular discipline are developed throug
   professional associations and through certificate training
   Society for Human Resource Management in the United State
   Professionals Association of Ontario, in Canada, provide tra
   human resource managers to take the certification exam. O
   (e.g., accounting, finance, engineering) provide similar types of
   ciations also provide opportunities for continual learning thro
2. Workshops and seminars: These are offered over a wide ra
   range of providers (e.g., universities, professional associatior
   panies). Larger companies, which prefer internally develope

The Special Needs of the Technical Manager

Technical managers usually go through academic training in their technical disciplines with little, if any, exposure to the study of organizational behavior and management processes. Organizations appear to rely on the premise that an individual with technical expertise can acquire organizational and managerial expertise on his own. Evidence shows that for technical managers, the management of unit morale, esteem, autonomy, and goal congruence were the primary predictors of subordinate turnover attitudes.[55] Training managers report that the content areas where training is most needed are managing people, strategic planning, decision making, and human resource management.[56] It is apparent, then, that a deeper understanding of the technical manager's developmental needs would be useful, along with a systematic approach to meeting those needs. Unfortunately, companies do not often seem inclined to determine the needs of their managers in general, much less their technical managers. For example, a survey of management training and education practices in the United States indicates that management needs assessments were conducted by only 27 percent of the companies.[57] The most frequent approach to management development was on-the-job training.

The literature indicates that technical experts' performance as managers is deficient in the following areas:[58]

1. Showing a willingness to reduce the focus on technical issues in favor of organizational and managerial issues
2. Understanding and using organizational priorities, requirements, and processes in decision making
3. Developing and maintaining interpersonal relationships with subordinates that generate their trust and confidence
4. Communicating with superiors, subordinates, and colleagues in an understandable, efficient, and positive manner
5. Managing conflict among subordinates constructively so their efforts are integrated to achieve the organization's goals

HISTORY AND EXPERIENCE

Technical professionals' skills, knowledge, and interests are generally related to things rather than people. Their education and training typically place them in solitary exercises and emphasize individual accomplishment. They are hired because of their expertise at manipulating and controlling things. They advance in the organization because of their good performance in the world of defined cause-and-effect relationships in their specialized field, and perhaps in their quantitative management of time, labor, and financial resources. Once the technical manager is moved into higher levels of management, he is expected to function in a multidisciplinary environment, attending to political, organizational, and business issues for which his history and education have not prepared him.

SKILLS

The effective technical professional, by definition, develops strong technical skills within her discipline. However, a great many technical employees received little education or background in the traditional management activities of planning, organizing, and controlling.[59] Just as important, the training and experience of the technical professional failed to develop the interpersonal (human) skills or the conceptual adaptability needed for managing people and organizations.[60]

TRAITS

Recall that those high in nPow (institutional rather than personal), moderately high in nAch, and moderate to low in nAut are the most effective managers. Unfortunately, technical professionals can generally be characterized as being high in nAch and nAut.[61] From the Kirkpatrick and

Locke perspective, we can say that their drive is perhaps too high because their focus on task accomplishment prevents them from being attentive to the effect of their behavior on others. Furthermore, their nPow, or leadership motivation, is typically based in the personal rather than the institutional domain. Their loyalties lie in their profession rather than their organization, and they see recognition from their peers as more valuable than recognition from their organization. Fortunately these need states appear to be changeable through training.[62]

LEADERSHIP STYLE

The technical professional, typically has no leadership training and is likely to mirror the styles used by his manager, or the personal style that has worked successfully up to the point of receiving the promotion. Unfortunately, these models are not the most appropriate if the promotion requires managing the work of others. The technical professional's past emphasizes a "best" methodology and a "right" answer. Ambiguities are eliminated and politics ignored. As a result of high loyalty to the profession, they remain heavily involved in the technology of the work they are managing and see themselves as the experts (that is why they were promoted, after all). As experts, they make all the important technical decisions, and when they delegate they provide specific instructions about the tasks to be performed. The directive leadership style fits comfortably with their past training (i.e., technical degrees, graduate studies), their past experience (e.g., running a lab), and their own self-image.[63] Many of the general requirements for successful managers are not typically inherent in technical professionals who are promoted into management positions. If these individuals happen to work in market leader organizations, they often possess even fewer of the required characteristics.

STRATEGIES FOR DEVELOPMENT OF TECHNICAL MANAGERS

Technical experts can learn to be effective and productive managers, provided both the organization and the experts themselves recognize the need to change and adapt to the realities of new requirements. Organizations must address the question of why it is essential that the technical experts be given managerial roles and what the expectations are for those roles. The organization can then develop a rationale for placing managerial components into the technical experts' job descriptions and assign jobs with an increasing degree of those managerial components. The model presented earlier for integrating organizational strategy, structure, technology, and managerial characteristics is at least a good starting point.

The technical expert needs to receive counseling to understand fully that the focus on technical issues will decrease. She also needs to recognize the potential risk of falling behind in technical expertise because of the shift to a managerial job.

The organization needs to establish a performance review program specifically oriented toward technical experts who are assigned increasing managerial responsibility. The objective is to assess continually his managerial training needs in order to enhance the potential for success as a manager. Finally, it is important in these instances to be sure that:

1. The technical expert learns appropriate behavior.
2. The technical expert transfers the behavior to the job.
3. The organizational structure facilitates this transfer.

If these results occur, the technical expert can indeed become the effective manager necessary in today's competitive environment.

Training for Executive-Level Management

One of the reasons cited earlier for providing a chapter on management training is that "managers are accountable for success," this is *especially* true at the senior level. Here the success of the whole company is at stake. Furthermore, the importance of aligning training needs to the overall strategy is absolutely critical at this level. Still, it is surprising how many companies still do not do it.[64] Consider the company that goes international. Then they discover that their executives do not possess the KSAs necessary for such a venture. Now what do they do? Such examples are numerous.[65] So, before any development takes place at this level a thorough examination of the strategic direction needs to be undertaken. Once the direction is set, the KSAs required to meet the strategic direction (operational analysis) can be determined. These KSAs are then compared to each of the executive's performance capabilities (person analysis) and developmental plans for each executive can be determined.

SKILLS, TRAITS, AND LEADERSHIP STYLE

An important duty for executives is to help formulate the strategic direction of the organization, plan for effective implementation of the plan, create mechanisms for assuring the strategic direction is followed, and track the progress of the change. These activities require strong conceptual skills in the entrepreneurial role and conceptual and interpersonal skills in the leader role.

President/CEO

The top executive must be effective in her role as entrepreneur (able to analyze the situation and choose the proper direction for the organization) and as leader (able to implement the plan through others). Although both of these roles are important, the more important one is leadership. The literature is full of examples of top executives coming in and revamping the organization; making it into what they view it should be; and more importantly, getting the employees to buy into that vision (see Training in Action 10-3).

TRAINING IN ACTION 10-3

LEADERSHIP'S IMPACT AT WALT DISNEY

When Judson Green arrived at Disney he decided a shift in focus was necessary. To remain a benchmark in creativity, customer service, and entertainment, he believed everyone needed to be active and involved in the process. He wanted to instill a passion in every employee to make the customer feel important.

He instituted what is called *Performance Excellence*. Judson believed that employees become passionately involved in the organization through effective leadership. To him a good leader is one who motivates, develops, and rewards subordinates. More importantly, it means his managers must view all employees from dishwashers to cleanup crews as creative, responsible employees.

So what does a manager do at Disney? He has open door board meetings, not executive board meetings. He spends 70 to 80 percent of his time in operating areas to see how things are going and to help out if necessary by working side by side with employees at peak periods.

The evidence shows that this change to a Performance Excellence model was successful. Business units that rate their managers as outstanding in listening, coaching, recognition, and empowerment also receive the highest ratings from customers. Also where a high level of manger involvement in the day-to-day activities occurs, employees indicate a high level of pride in their work.

Source: Taylor, C., and C. Wheatley-Lovoy. 1998. Leadership: Lessons from the Magic Kingdom. *Training,* July, pp. 22–25.

Even CEOs who come from within the organization need to examine the current environment and determine what changes in direction (if any) need to be taken. The important point is the employees need to feel confident in the CEO's ability and buy into the executive's decisions regarding the direction the organization is taking. To inspire this kind of loyalty requires sound leadership skills. Of course the importance of these skills will depend on the strategic direction being taken. The leadership skills for a CEO in a cost leader organization that is not making substantial changes in its strategic direction will not be as important as those for the CEO in a market leader that is beginning to move in a different direction. Take a look at Training in Action 10-3 again. Note that many of the leadership behaviors displayed and expected by Judson Green are trainable. As indicated earlier, personality traits certainly interact with interpersonal style, but anyone motivated to do so can learn these leadership behaviors.

Executives in General

One of the reasons for grooming your own higher-level managers to become executives is that they are already part of the organizational culture and possess many of the skills that are important to the type of organization they are in, whether market leader, cost leader, or somewhere in-between. This reasoning is especially applicable if management performance is based on a set of competencies. As long as promotion is based on sound appraisals, and development continues, managers should continue to be effective when they are promoted to the executive level. However, you still require a process for preparing them for the move.

STRATEGIES FOR DEVELOPMENT OF EXECUTIVES AND FUTURE EXECUTIVES (MANAGERS)

Note we are discussing two different levels of management here: development of executives and development of managers (preparing them for the executive level). Certain problems are specifically associated with training executives, such as the following:

- These people are at the top of the organization, which makes it difficult for them to ask for help or even be aware they need it.
- Who is capable of helping them, or at least has the credibility to be listened to by these executives?
- These busy individuals work long hours and don't have a lot of time for development.

Because of these issues, some strategies are better for executives and others are more likely to be used for developing managers (to be future executives).[66]

Coaching

Not long ago coaching was considered a corrective method for inadequate performance.[67] Not anymore. When Bob Peters was promoted to vice president of sales and marketing for American Science and Engineering, one of his perks was an executive coach.[68] A personal coach provides one way for the executive to deal with a busy schedule. It also, to some extent, deals with the credibility factor, given that these coaches are often experts from outside the organization. In a survey conducted by the International Coach Federation, more than 4,000 companies were using coaches for their executives.[69] For the CEO, a coach is the ideal training format. It can be done at the CEO's convenience, it is one-on-one, and it provides an opportunity for feedback from a professional. "It gets lonely at the top, and it's difficult to find someone to talk to about my concerns," says Mr. Venners, chairman of KFx a high-tech company in Denver.[70]

An advantage of this method is it can be done in short meetings, phone conversations, and Internet communications, when the executive has the time. It also focuses on specific areas identified as needing improvement. Again, the important first step is identifying the executive's specific developmental needs, which can be determined through 360-degree performance reviews.[71] An action plan is mutually determined by the coach and executive, followed by successive meetings and counseling by the coach.

For the manager, it is much more likely that any coaching would be done by her supervisor, although outside consultants are sometimes used for up-and-coming managers. Again the personalized approach helps the manager focus on specific needs and improvements.

Mentoring

The differences between coaching and mentoring are that mentoring generally is more of an ongoing relationship, and coaching is often for a shorter, more specific length of time. Also, meetings between a coach and the employee are generally more structured and regular than in mentoring.[72] Another difference is, for executives mentoring generally is done by someone inside the company and coaching is often done by an outside consultant.[73]

For the executive, "being a mentor" is an important developmental tool. The executive can learn a great deal from mentoring. By dealing with different mentees, the executive is given the opportunity to grow professionally by honing leadership skills and learning how to work with various personality types and backgrounds.[74] Executives sometimes also have mentors. In cases where the executive is new to the organization, a senior executive could be assigned as a mentor to help get the new executive settled into his new role.

For managers who are potential executive material, being mentored is a valuable method for preparing them to be future executives. This one-on-one interaction allows the mentor to determine what is required to improve the mentee's effectiveness. Once the mentor identifies an area/competency that requires work, the mentor can suggest relevant training. Also the mentor can provide opportunities to work on special projects that require use of the competency. A real advantage is realized through a mentoring program: it keeps your talent at home.[75] In a study conducted by the Center for Creative Leadership, 77 percent of companies indicated development of a mentoring program improved their retention rate.

Executive Development Programs/Executive MBAs

This type of training can take place at the organization's leadership center or at a university (public or corporate). It mixes classroom learning with real-life problem solving. In such environments the mix often includes both executives and middle managers. The training generally follows one of the following philosophies. Boot camp, as championed by Noel Tichy, or the less intense approach championed by Mintzberg.[76] The boot camp approach is designed to be stressful; which is generally what the executive's job is all about. Trainees are pushed to their limit, much like Navy SEAL or special forces training. Noel Tichy's point is that managers need to know how to operate in a stressful environment, so one is provided for them. Mintzberg does not agree. He says that "—these managers live boot camp everyday. The last thing in the world they need is more boot camp." Either way, both agree that the classroom is only a small part of the learning. Most programs offer some sort of action learning to accompany the classroom work. Action learning is where real company problems are given to trainees to work on. Take GE managers, for example. They are in a classroom in the morning, then given a real problem from GE to work on in a team for the day, and often into the wee hours of the morning. Sometimes these real-world projects provide a bonus for the company as described in Training in Action 10-4.

Action Learning

Although often a part of executive training programs, action learning can also stand alone. It is effective because it focuses on exactly what managers and executives need to do—come up with effective solutions to complex problems, implement, and evaluate them. It requires working in teams (to problem solve) and on their own (researching the issue and gathering relevant data),

---

TRAINING IN ACTION 10-4

U.S. POSTAL SERVICE GETS A BONUS

At the U.S. Postal Services' Advanced Leadership Program, one of the requirements is working on real Postal Service problems. At the end of week 3 of the training, a postal executive meets with each of the work teams that were formed at the beginning of training. The executive gives each of the teams a business problem. These problems are from ones submitted by executives from all across the country.

Over the course of the next 3 months the team works on the problem. When they return for the last week of the training, they present their solution to a panel of executives from the Postal Service. Generally, the solution is immaterial; it is the process that is important, and where the learning takes place. So where is the bonus?

Turns out that even though the important part of the exercise is the process of working out a solution, the solutions are often so innovative that they are implemented, and save the company money.

A team from California was given the problem of workplace violence. The team determined a common link to much of the violence was related to money problems. They recommended development of a 4-hour workshop on how to manage money. This recommendation was implemented in California and the workplace environment there improved.

Another group was challenged to increase retail income or reduce expenses in post offices. The result: Why not put advertisements on the rolls of receipt paper they used? In that way they could advertise their own products for free, hopefully increasing revenue. Or they could sell the advertisement space to others, decreasing their cost for receipt paper. Although neither of these options has been adopted yet, it is estimated that the use of external advertising to defray the expenses of receipt rolls would save about $13 million per year.

Source: Delahoussaye, M. 2002. Licking the leadership crisis. *Training*, January, pp. 24–29.

---

both of which are important for effective managers and executives. The difference between traditional meetings to solve problems and action learning is the focus on learning that takes place. To assure this learning happens, a facilitator is assigned to assist the team. The facilitator helps the team through debriefing after the meetings are over. Her focus would be on how members communicated with each other, how they provide feedback, how well they are following their plan of action. She also gets them to reflect how they are approaching the problem and how their basic assumptions might affect their view regarding the selection of a solution to the problem.[77] Specific training to help the team be more effective is determined by the group and "just-in-time" training is provided.[78]

The result: Not only do organizations get solutions to problems, but the team members develop skills necessary to be effective managers. And just as important, they learn how to continuously learn from the process.[79]

Job Rotation

For the executive, the job rotation takes on a different perspective. The executive is usually not simply going to another department. In some vertically integrated organizations (e.g., where the supplier is actually part of the same organization or a subsidiary), the job rotation might be to

---

TRAINING IN ACTION 10-6

THE DOWNSIDE OF AN EFFECTIVE SUCCESSION PLANNING PROCESS

GE is widely known for its ability to grow executive talent. This commitment to development of high-level talent was fortified by its recent CEO Jack Welch. His strong commitment to developing effective leaders is carried out through a comprehensive succession planning process. It is so effective that other companies, such as Polaris, emulate it. Each year top executives at GE meet to review the talent requirements and discuss plans for developing its managers. In looking for his replacement, Jack Welch, working with his board of directors, had some great talent to choose from.

When Jeff Immelt was chosen to succeed Jack Welch, Bob Nardelli was surprised and hurt. His record at GE was one of the best, and he simply did not understand why he did not get the job. As a result, he accepted a job as CEO of Home Depot. One of the other candidates in the running, Jim McNerney, also left to become CEO of 3M.

Source: Gale, S. 2001. Bringing good leaders to light. *Training,* June, pp. 38–42; Tyler, J. 2002. Succession planning: Charting a course for the future. *Trustee* 55:24–28.

---

cession plan prepares organizations to deal with sudden and even planned personnel changes with minimal disruption. So, with a succession plan, the assessment of the vice presidents (for the position of president) is an ongoing process of performance review. From the review, developmental activities to hone the executives skills would be worked out with the CEO (the vice president's boss). In such scenarios, the change from one CEO to another is often smooth and immediate. The downside must also be considered. When more than one candidate is working toward the promotion, those who are not moved up may be not only disappointed but also angry, as Training in Action 10-6 indicates.

So, as Training in Action 10-6 shows, in an effective succession planning process, where you are constantly grooming your best to become better, it is likely that when a promotion is made, those who do not get the promotion may leave. You lose good talent. However, because you are the one that grew the talent two important things happen. First, you get first choice of the talent you have grown, which should translate to the best person. Second, you get the person to fill the critical position immediately, which is a real advantage.

For Executives in General

With all the money spent on management training, it is surprising that so little is spent on leadership development. A recent survey indicated more than half the organizations either did not have executive development programs or only supplied them when needed.[83] Forty percent rate their approach to leadership development as low, or very low.[84] This statistic is problematic for a number of reasons:[85]

- The pool of available managers to fill executive positions continues to shrink.
- The cost of recruiting outside talent is increasing at a high rate.
- The average company expects 33 percent turnover of executives in the next 5 years.

This lack of preparing future executives is surprising given the importance of having effective executives. One reason for this problem is the continued downsizing taking place in U.S.

corporations.[86] When you are reducing employee numbers, little attention is spent on succession planning, and succession planning is the backbone of preparing relevant talent. Many of the middle managers let go in the job cuts were the potential future executives. This trend does not bode well for many organizations in North America, but those that are paying attention to the issue will be the winners in the long run.

All of *Training* magazine's "Top 50 training organizations" are constantly developing possible successors for their top positions through succession planning.[87] GE Lighting is one of those companies. In its succession planning process, executives meet twice a year to focus on the company's future needs, then determine the developmental needs of managers targeted for advancement.[88]

WHAT ABOUT SMALL BUSINESS?

Many of the ideas already mentioned for preparing managers to become executives are great for the organization that is large enough to devote the resources to take part in them. For smaller organizations, however, these options are simply too costly in most cases. So, what to do? Well, the senior manager/CEO or owner of the firm needs to take responsibility for the development of her managers. Some of the options include the following:[89]

- Articulate a vision and goals for the organization clearly and what these managers need to do to help you reach them.
- Help managers understand themselves and their shortcomings through feedback from the senior manager's own observations and the observations of others.
- Be sure the assignments provided to these managers are in line with their developmental needs.
- Provide managers with opportunities to learn the total organization through job rotation or different projects.
- Be a positive role model and coach.
- Let them shadow an executive for a week or so to fully understand what the responsibilities are for senior management.

Some real advantages are available to the small business leader when it comes to training future executives. Because the company is small, it is likely that doing all possible jobs and experiencing many of the issues that will arise is much more likely. Furthermore, under the guidance of the CEO, the manager surely will be learning what the CEO deems as important because the CEO is the one who designs and implements the development program. Morgan McCall, professor of management from the University of Southern California, says that leaders grow better under good tutelage than in a classroom.[90] The key is for the CEO to take the development of managers seriously and be that role model.

SUMMARY

All managers take on certain general roles, but the importance of these roles varies depending on the level of the manager and the type of strategy followed by the organization. Development of managers, therefore, needs to take these situations into account when determining what types of training to provide. The three main roles identified by Mintzberg are interpersonal, informational, and decisional. Within each of these roles are more specific roles: figurehead, leader, and liaison are within the interpersonal role; monitor, disseminator, and spokesperson within informational; and entrepreneurial, disturbance handler, resource allocator, and negotiator within the decisional role. For each of these specific roles, certain skills (conceptual, technical, and interpersonal) and traits are required. The key to effective management development is to determine the roles required for the position, and from these roles the relevant KSAs (operational analysis).

Then as in a traditional needs analysis you assess the current KSAs of the managers (person analysis). The 360-DF, when used properly, is an effective tool for determining the managers' current KSA levels.

A number of methods can be used to obtain the relevant training for managers, from externally based programs to corporate universities. Depending on the need—conceptual, technical, interpersonal, or even development of personal traits—all can be provided through various programs.

The technical manager faces special problems. When training is primarily technical, success is typically based on that expertise. So, when a technical professional is promoted and suddenly needs management skills to be effective, that person is often not prepared. Developmental plans to prepare the technical manager for moving into the management position will make the transition more successful. The manager needs to understand the importance of these skills and be provided with opportunities to develop them.

Development of executives is critical to organizational functioning but again, it is often ignored. Special attention needs to be focused here because executives are already at the top and likely feel competent or at least do not like to ask for help. It is difficult for someone who is a peer or lower to be credible enough to offer advice. Executives are also busy, often working long hours, making it difficult to find the time to receive any training. Executive coaching is one way to deal with these issues. Its use has grown at a tremendous rate over the last few years. Other methods are also available, and the key to smooth development is succession planning. An effective succession plan will allow all executives and high-level managers to be constantly appraised and provided with opportunities to develop using many of the methods mentioned, such as coaching, action learning, executive MBAs, and so forth.

KEY TERMS

- Achievement style
- Adaptability/flexibility
- Conceptual knowledge and skills
- Corporate universities
- Directive style
- Drive
- Employee-oriented styles

- Executive/management education
- Interpersonal knowledge and skills
- Leadership motivation
- Managerial context
- Managerial style
- Participative style

- Personal traits
- Supportive style
- Task-oriented styles
- Technical knowledge and skills
- Technical manager

CASE ANALYSIS

WILL TEAMS WORK?

An automobile parts manufacturer (APM) was attempting to institute employee problem-solving teams to improve quality. This action was strongly encouraged by its biggest customer, a major automobile manufacturer. The competition in the original equipment manufacturing (OEM) business is especially fierce. The major automobile manufacturers (Ford, GM, Chrysler, Toyota, Honda, etc.) now demand high-quality parts at extremely low costs, and they often play one supplier against the other in order to force the OEM industry to meet their standards.

(continued)

(continued)

A training needs analysis of middle- and first-level production managers was conducted. These managers were responsible for the operation of the parts production system, a system that is highly mechanized and somewhat automated. The labor force in this area is primarily high school graduates, but many have less education. The managers' responsibility prior to the change was to ensure that the hourly workers did their jobs in the proper manner and that the right amount and type of parts were produced to meet the production schedule.

The TNA showed low technical knowledge among these managers because they had been hired to monitor the hourly employees. They didn't really understand the machinery and equipment and had never operated it. Most of them use a confrontational style in dealing with their subordinates because they feel that if they took a gentler approach, the unionized workforce would take advantage of them. They were all selected on the basis of their high need to control their environment, high need to achieve, and willingness to work with others to get the job done. These traits still characterize this group of managers. ■

CASE QUESTIONS

1. What is the managerial context in which these managers will be operating? Do you think training designed to help managers understand the context they will be operating in will be helpful? Why or why not?
2. What types of competencies should be developed in the management training? Give your rationale.
3. What types of training should be used to provide the different competencies? How long will it take to provide this training? Give your rationale.
4. What are the alternatives to management development? Do you think one of these alternatives should be used? Why or why not?

EXERCISES

1. Bring a recent article (no more than a year old) that identifies KSAs that will be critical for managers in the immediate future. Be prepared to discuss the article and its management development implications in small groups or with the entire class.
2. Interview two managers with at least 2 years of management experience. One manager should come from a company whose strategy is toward the cost leader side, the other toward the market leader side. If possible they should both be in the same functional area. Determine what management development they received from their company. Determine how satisfied they are with the development they received so far. Bring this information back to class and be prepared to share it with others, and provide an analysis of how consistent these two experiences are with what the text proposes.
3. Research the Internet to see what the best companies do in management development. What are the similarities? Describe any major differences. Be prepared to discuss this information in class.
4. How does management education prepare a manager for her role? What are the ways in which management education occurs? Do some seem better to you than others? Why or why not? Can other forms of training substitute for management education? Why or why not?

5. Interview a manager with 5 or more years of experience. Record the manager's current position, previous positions, and education. Identify the manager's roles and responsibilities. Afterwards, answer the following:
   a. How do the roles and responsibilities compare to those described in the text?
   b. Identify the KSAs required to meet this manager's roles and responsibilities.
   c. How did the manager's previous experience and education prepare that manager for current roles and responsibilities?
6. Interview an HR person from a company and ask how its executives are developed. Find out how managers are prepared for executive positions. If the company uses a succession planning process, ask how it works and how often it is reviewed. If they do not, ask how they determine who to promote to executive positions when one becomes available. From the interview answer the following questions:
   a. How many different methods do they use for developing executives? For developing managers?
   b. If they do use a succession plan, how does it work? Do you think it prepares their managers for the higher-level management positions? If they do not, how do they fill higher-level positions?

Endnotes

CHAPTER 1

1. Bassi, L. J., and D. P. McMurrer. 1998. Training investment can mean financial performance. *Training & Development*, May, pp. 40–42.
2. McLagan, P. A. 1989. Models for HRD practice. *Training and Development Journal* 41(9):49–59.
3. Fattal, T. 1996. Quality is what ISO 9000 is all about. *Computing Canada* 22:30.
4. Dolack, P. 1996. ISO 9000 comes of age. *Chemical Marketing Reporter* 249:7–8.
5. Williamson, D. 1997. ISO rating the sign of the times. *Windsor Star*, July 16, p. F1.
6. Wisnia, S. 1997. Running to the rescue. *Industrial Distribution* 86:120–23.
7. Fleishman, E. 1972. On the relation between abilities, learning, and human performance. *American Psychologist* 27:1017–32.
8. Dunnette, M. 1976. Aptitudes, abilities, and skills. In *The Handbook of Industrial and Organizational Psychology*, edited by M. Dunnette. Chicago: Rand McNally.
9. Oskamp, S. 1991. *Attitudes and Opinions*, 2d ed. Upper Saddle River, NJ: Prentice Hall.
10. Kraiger, K., J. Ford, and E. Salas. 1993. Application of cognitive, skill-based and affective theories of learning outcomes to new methods of training evaluation. *Journal of Applied Psychology* 78(2):311–28.
11. Op. cit. Dunnette, 1976.
12. Op. cit. Oskamp, 1991.
13. Chuvala, J., J. Gilmere, and T. Gillette. 1992. The new kid on the training block. *Security Management*, August, pp. 65–72.
14. 2002 Industry report. Training budgets: How much do U.S. organizations spend on employee training?, *Training*, October 2002, pp. 24–73.
15. McMurrer, D., and M. VanBuren. 1999. The Japanese training scene. *Training and Development*, August, pp. 43–46.
16. Cascio, W., and J. Thacker. 1994. *Managing Human Resources*. Toronto: McGraw-Hill Ryerson.
17. ASTD. 1999. *State of the Training Industry*. Washington, DC: ASTD.
18. Le Gault, M. 1997. In-house training that gets results. *Canadian Plastics*, February, pp. 14–18.
19. Bennis, W. G. 1969. *Organization Development: Its Nature, Origins, and Prospects*. Reading, MA: Addison-Wesley; Beckhard, R. 1969. *Organizational Development: Strategies and Models*. Reading, MA: Addison-Wesley; Alderfer, C. P. 1977. Organizational development. *Annual Review of Psychology* 28:197–223; Beer, M., and E. Walton. 1990. Developing the competitive organization: Interventions and strategies. *American Psychologist* 45:154–61.
20. Griffin, R., and R. Ebert. 1996. *Business*, 4th ed. Upper Saddle River, NJ: Prentice Hall.
21. Deshpande, S., and D. Golhar. 1994. HRM practices in large and small firms: A comparative study. *Journal of Small Business Management*, April, pp. 49–56.
22. Banks, M., A. Bures, and D. Champion. 1987. Decision-making factors in small business. *Journal of Small Business Management*, January, pp. 19–26.

23. Szonyi, A., and B. Steinhoff. 1983. *Small Business Fundamentals*. Toronto: McGraw-Hill Ryerson.

24. Katz, D., and R. L. Khan. 1978. *The Social Psychology of Organizations*. New York: Wiley.

CHAPTER 2

1. Ozone House, Inc. 1999. *Strategic Plan*. Ann Arbor, MI.

2. Bower, J. 1982. Business policy in the 80s. *Academy of Management Review* 7:630–38; Chandler, A. 1962. *Strategy and Structure*. Cambridge: MIT Press; Jamison, D. 1981. The importance of an integrative approach to strategic management research. *Academy of Management Review* 6:601–8; Tichey, N., C. Fombrun, and M. Devanna. 1982. Strategic human resource management. *Sloan Management Review* 22:47–60.

3. Gutpa, A., and V. Govindarajan. 1984. Business unit strategy, managerial characteristics, and business unit effectiveness at strategy implementation. *Academy of Management Journal* 27:25–41; Jackson, S., R. Schuler, and J. C. Rivero. 1989. Organizational characteristics as predictors of personnel practices. *Personnel Psychology* 42:727–86.

4. Miles, R., and C. Snow. 1978. *Organizational Strategy, Structure and Process*. New York: McGraw-Hill.

5. Miller, D. 1987. The structural and environmental correlates of business strategy. *Strategic Management Journal*, January/February, pp. 55–76.

6. Op. cit. Miles and Snow, 1978.

7. Op. cit. Miller, 1987.

8. Porter, M. 1980. *Competitive Strategy: Techniques for Analyzing Industries and Competitors*. New York: Free Press.

9. Op. cit. Miles and Snow, 1978.

10. Op. cit. Chandler, 1962; Miles and Snow, 1978.

11. Duncan, B. 1972. Characteristics of organizational environments and perceived uncertainty. *Administrative Science Quarterly* 17(3).

12. Dowling, M., W. Boulton, and S. Elliot. 1994. Strategies for change in the service sector: The global telecommunications industry. *California Management Review*, 36(3):57–88.

13. Perrow, C. 1970. *Organizational Analysis: A Sociological View*. Belmont, CA: Wadsworth; Thompson, J. D. 1967. *Organization in Action*. New York: McGraw-Hill; Woodward, J. 1965. *Industrial Organization: Theory and Practice*. London: Oxford University.

14. Burns, T., and G. Stalker. 1961. *The Management of Innovation*. London: Tavistock.

15. David, F., J. Pearce, and W. Randolf. 1989. Linking technology and structure to enhance group performance. *Journal of Applied Psychology*, April, pp. 233–41.

16. Op. cit. Perrow, 1970.

17. Mintzberg, H. 1979. *The Structuring of Organizations*. Upper Saddle River, NJ: Prentice Hall, pp. 272–85; McDonough III, E., and R. Leifer. 1983. Using simultaneous structures to cope with uncertainty. *Academy of Management Journal*, December, pp. 727–35.

18. Mintzberg, H. 1987. Crafting strategy. *Harvard Business Review*, July/August.

19. Becker, B., and Huselid, M. 1999. Overview: Strategic human resource management in five leading firms. *Human Resource Management*, Winter, pp. 287–301.

20. Galvin, T. 2001. Birds of a feather. *Training*, March, pp. 58–67.

21. Gerhert, B., P. Wright, G. McMahn, and S. Snell. 2000. Measurement errors in research on human resources and firm performance: How much error is there and how does it influence effect size estimates. *Personnel Psychology* 53:803–34.

22. Hays, S. 1999. The ABC's of workplace literacy. *Workforce* 78:70–74; Stone, N. 1991. Does business have any business in education? *Harvard Business Review* 69(2):46–62.

23. Barron, K, and A. Marsh. 1998. The skills gap. *Forbes* 161:44–45.

24. Howard, A. 1986. College experiences and managerial performance. *Journal of Applied Psychology Monographs* 71(3):530–52; Porter, L. W., and L. E. McKibbin. 1988. *Management Education and Development: Drift or Thrust into the Twenty-First Century*. St. Louis: AACSB; Whetten, D. A.,

and K. S. Cameron. 1995. *Developing Managerial Skills*. New York: HarperCollins.

25. Op. cit. Porter and McKibbin, 1988.
26. AACSB (American Assembly of Collegiate Schools of Business). 1987. *Outcome Measurement Project, Phase III*. St. Louis: AACSB.
27. Calamai, P. 1999. The literacy gap. *Toronto Star*, August 28, pp. J1–J2.
28. Op. cit. Hays, 1999.
29. Tyler, K. 1996. Tips for restructuring workplace literacy. *HR Magazine* 41:112–16.
30. Becker, B. E., and M. A. Huselid (eds.). 1999. *Human Resource Management, Special Issue: Strategic Human Resource Management*. John Wiley & Sons, Winter.
31. Senge, P., C. Roberts, R. Ross, B. Smith, and A. Kliener. 1994. *The Fifth Discipline Fieldbook*. New York: Doubleday Currency; Nevis, E., A. DiBella, and J. Gould. 1995. Understanding organizations as learning systems. *Sloan Management Review* 36(2):73–85.
32. Garvin, D. 1993. Building a learning organization. *Harvard Business Review*, July/August; Senge, P. 1990. *The Fifth Discipline*. New York: Doubleday Currency; Shaw, R., and D. Perkins. 1991. Teaching organizations to learn. *Organizational Development Journal*, Winter, pp. 1–12.
33. McGill, M., and J. Slocum. 1993. Unlearning the organization. *Organizational Dynamics* 22:67–79.
34. DeVito, J. 1996. The learning organization. *The ASTD Training and Development Handbook*. 4th ed., pp. 77–103.
35. Marquardt, M., and A. Reynolds. 1994. *Global Learning Organization*. New York: Irwin.
36. Ackelsberg, R., and P. Arlow. 1985. Small businesses do plan and it pays off. *Long Range Planning* 18:61–66; Bracker, J., B. Keats, and J. Pearson. 1988. Planning and financial performance among small firms in a growth industry. *Strategic Management Journal* 9:591–603.
37. Sandberg, W., R. Robinson, and J. Pearce. 2001. Why small businesses need a strategic plan. *Business and Economic Review* 48:12–15.

38. Wheelen, T., and J. Hunger. 1995. *Strategic Management and Business Policy*. New York: Addison-Wesley.
39. Op. cit. Ackelsberg and Arlow, 1985; Buchele, 1967. *Business Policy in Growing Firms*. San Francisco: Chandler; Gilmore, F. 1971. Formulating strategy in smaller companies. *Harvard Business Review* 49:71–81.
40. Kargar, J., and R. Blumenthal. 1994. Successful implementation of strategic decisions in small community banks. *Journal of Small Business Management*, April, pp. 10–21.
41. Lang, J., R. Calantone, and D. Gudmundson. 1997. Small firm information seeking as a response to environmental threats and opportunities. *Journal of Small Business Management*, January, pp. 11–21.
42. Ibid.
43. O'Neal, H., and J. Duker. 1986. Survival and failure in small businesses. *Journal of Small Business Management*, January, pp. 30–37.
44. Op. cit. Kargar and Blumenthal, 1994.
45. Johnson, M. 1999. Anti-harassment training to shelter yourself from suits. *HR Magazine* 44:76–81; Ganzels, R. 1998. What sexual harassment training really prevents. *Training*, October, pp. 86–94.
46. Schuler, R., and S. Jackson. 1987. Linking competitive strategies with human resource management practices. *Academy of Management Executive* 1(3):207–19.
47. Carnevale, A., L. Gainer, and J. Villet. 1990. *Training in America*. San Francisco: Jossey-Bass; Tovar, R., A. Rossett, and N. Carter. 1989. Centralized training in a decentralized organization. *Training and Development Journal* 43:62–65.
48. Gerber, B. 1987. It's a whole new ball game at BC Tel. *Training* 24:75–81; and Lee, C. 1988. Where does training belong? *Training* 25:53–60.
49. Tichey, N. 1983. *Managing Strategic Change: Technical, Political and Cultural Dynamics*. New York: Wiley; Op. cit. Tichey, Fombrun, and Devanna, 1992.
50. Lewin, K. 1969. Quasi-stationary social equilibrium and the problem of permanent changes. In *The Planning of Change*, edited by W. Bennis, D. Benne, and R. Chin. New York: Holt, Rinehart, and Winston.

51. Rossett, A. 1996. Training and organizational development: Separated at birth? *Training*, April, pp. 53–59.

52. Golembiewski, R., C. Proehl, and D. Sink. 1982. Estimating the success of OD applications. *Training and Development Journal*, April, pp. 86–95; Nicholas, J. 1982. The comparative impact of organizational development interventions on hard criteria measures. *Academy of Management Review*, October, pp. 531–42.

53. Goodman, P., and J. Dean. 1983. Why productivity efforts fail. In *Organizational Development: Theory, Practice, and Research*, edited by W. French, C. Bell, and R. Zawacki. Plano, TX: Business Publications.

54. Op. cit. Rossett, 1996.

55. Ibid.

CHAPTER 3

1. Deming, W. E. 1986. *Out of the Crisis*. Massachusetts Institute of Technology.

2. Dobyns, L., and C. Crawford-Mason. 1991. *Quality or Else*. Boston: Houghton Mifflin.

3. Lawler, E. E., S. A. Mohrman, and G. E. Ledford. 1995. *Creating High Performance Organizations: Practices and Results of Employee Involvement and Total Quality Management in Fortune 1000 Companies*. San Francisco: Jossey-Bass.

4. Maslow, A. H. 1954. *Motivation and Personality*. New York: Harper & Row; Maslow, A. 1968. *Toward a Psychology of Being*, 2d ed. New York: Van Nostrand Reinhold.

5. Alderfer, C. 1969. An empirical test of a new theory of human needs. *Organizational Behavior and Human Performance* 4(2):142–75.

6. Ibid.; Schneider, C. P., and C. Alderfer. 1973. Three studies of measures of need satisfaction in organizations. *Administrative Science Quarterly*, December, pp. 489–505.

7. Thorndike, E. L. 1905. *The Elements of Psychology*. New York: Seiler; Thorndike, E. L. 1913. The psychology of learning. *Educational Psychology*, vol. 2. New York: Teachers College, Columbia University Press; Thorndike, E. L. 1932. *Purposive Behavior in Animals and Men*. New York: Appleton-Century-Crofts.

8. Skinner, B. F. 1953. *Science and Human Behavior*. New York: Macmillan; Skinner, B. F. 1968. *The Technology of Teaching*. New York: Appleton-Century-Crofts.

9. Ibid.

10. Grote, D. 1995. *Discipline Without Punishment*. New York: AMACOM.

11. Vroom, V. 1964. *Work and Motivation*. New York: Wiley.

12. Bandura, A. 1977a. Self-efficacy: Toward a unifying theory of behavioral change. *Psychological Review* 84:191–215.

13. Gecas, V. 1989. The social psychology of self-efficacy. In *Annual Review of Sociology*, edited by W. R. Scott and J. Blake. Palo Alto: Annual Reviews, Inc., 15:291–316; Gist, M. 1987. Self-efficacy: Implications for organizational behavior and human resource management. *Academy of Management Review*, July, pp. 472–85; and Manz, C. C., and H. P. Simms. 1981. Vicarious learning: The influence of modeling on organizational behavior. *Academy of Management Review* 6:105–13.

14. Ford, J., E. Smith, D. Weissbein, S. Gully, and E. Salas. 1998. Relationships of goal orientation, metacognitive activity, and practice strategies with learning outcomes and transfer. *Journal of Applied Psychology* 83:218–33; Locke, E. A., E. F. Lee, and P. Bobko. 1984. Effect of self-efficacy, goals, and task strategies of task performance. *Journal of Applied Psychology*, May, pp. 241–51.

15. Kozlowski, S., S. Gully, K. Brown, E. Salas, E. Smith, and E. Nason, 2001. Effects of training goals and goal orientation traits on multidimensional training outcomes and performance adaptability. *Organizational Behavior and Human Decision Processes* 85:1–31; Colquitt, J., J. Lepine, and R. Noe. 2000. Toward an integrative theory of training motivation: A meta-analytic path analysis of 20 years of research. *Journal of Applied Psychology* 85:678–707.

16. Ibid.; Op. cit. Ford et al., 1998.

17. Ibid.; Kraiger, K., J. Ford, and E. Salas. 1993. Application of cognitive, skill-based, and

affective theories of learning outcomes to new methods of training evaluation. *Journal of Applied Psychology* 78(2):311–28.

18. Schacter, D. 1996. *Searching for Memory: The Brain, the Mind and the Past*. New York: Basic Books; Squire, L., A. Shimamura, and P. Graf. 1985. Independence of recognition memory and priming effects: A neuropsychological analysis. *Journal of Experimental Psychology* 11:34–44; and Squire, L., and S. Zola-Morgan. 1991. The medial temporal lobe memory system. *Science* 253:1380–86.

19. Bruner, J. S. 1966. *Toward a Theory of Instruction*. New York: Norton.

20. Gagné, R. M. 1965. *The Conditions of Learning*. New York: Holt, Rinehart, and Winston.

21. Piaget, J. 1954. *The Construction of Reality in the Child*. New York: Basic Books.

22. Skinner, B. F. 1971. *Beyond Freedom and Dignity*. New York: Bantam/Vintage.

23. Knowles, M. F. 1984. Adult learning: Theory and practice. In *The Handbook of Human Resource Development*, edited by D. A. Nadler. New York: Wiley; Knowles, M. F. 1989. *The Making of an Adult Educator*. San Francisco: Jossey-Bass.

24. Latham, G. P., and L. M. Sarri. 1979. Application of social learning theory to training supervisors through behavioral modeling. *Journal of Applied Psychology* 64:239–46.

25. Gagné, R. M. 1962. Military training and principles of learning. *American Psychologist* 17:83–91; op. cit. Gagné, 1965; and Gagné, R. M. 1974. *Essentials of Learning for Instruction*. Hinsdale, IL: Dryden Press.

26. Pavlov, I. P. 1897. *Lectures on the Principle Digestive Glands*. St. Petersburg, Russia: Kushnereff; and Pavlov, I. P. 1912. Principle laws of the activity of the central nervous system as they find expression in conditioned reflexes. As reported by G. Murphy and J. Kovach in *Historical Introduction to Modern Psychology*. New York: Harcourt Brace Jovanovich.

27. Skinner, B. F. 1938. *The Behavior of Organisms*. New York: Appleton-Century-Crofts.

28. Kimble, G. A. 1967. *Foundations of Conditioning and Learning*. New York: Appleton.

29. Ausubel, D. P. 1963. *The Psychology of Meaningful Verbal Learning*. New York: Grune and Stratton; and Gagné, R. M., and W. Dick. 1983. Instructional psychology. *Annual Review of Psychology* 34:261–95.

30. Bandura, A. 1977b. *Social Learning Theory*. Upper Saddle River, NJ: Prentice Hall; op. cit. Bandura, 1977a; and Kraut, A. J. 1976. Behavior modeling symposium: Developing managerial skills via modeling techniques. *Personnel Psychology* 29:325–28.

31. Gagné, R. M., L. Briggs, and W. Wager. 1992. *Principles of Instructional Design*. Fort Worth: Harcourt Brace Jovanovich

32. Ibid.

33. Ibid, p. 190.

34. Based on an example from Gagné et al. 1992.

35. Baltes, P. B., and S. L. Willis. 1976. Toward psychological theories of aging. In *Handbook on the Psychology of Aging*, edited by J. E. Birren and K. W. Schaie. New York: Reinhold-VanNostrand.; Griffith, G., A. Tourgh, W. Barnard, and D. Brundage. 1980. *The Design of Self-Directed Learning*. Toronto: Ontario Institute for Studies in Education; Knowles, M. S. 1978. *The Adult Learner: A Neglected Species*. Houston: Gulf Publishing; and Pierce, J., D. Gardner, L. Cummings, and R. Dunham. 1989. Organization-based self-esteem: Construct definition, measurement, and validation. *Academy of Management Journal*, September, pp. 622–48.

36. Geddie, C., and B. Strickland. 1984. From plateaus to progress: A model for career development. *Training*, June, pp. 56–61; and Leibowitz, Z. B., C. Farren, and B. L. Kaye. 1986. *Designing Career Development Systems*. San Francisco: Jossey-Bass.

37. Blum, M., and J. Naylor. 1956. *Industrial Psychology*. New York: Harper Row.

38. Facteau, J., G. Dobbins, J. Russell, R. Ladd, and J. Kudisch. 1995. The influence of general perceptions of the training environment on pretraining motivation and perceived training transfer. *Journal of Management* 21:1–5; Tracey, J.,

S. Tannenbaum, and M. Kavanaugh. 1995. Applying trained skills on the job: The importance of the work environment 80:239–52.

39. Coch, L., and J. French. 1948. Overcoming resistance to change. *Human Relations* 1:512–32.
40. Op. cit. Facteau et al., 1995
41. Smith-Jentsch, K., E. Salas, and M. Brannick. 2001. To transfer or not to transfer? Investigating the combined effects of trainee characteristics, team leader support, and team climate. *Journal of Applied Psychology* 86:279–92.
42. Op. cit. Knowles, 1978; Knowles. 1984; and Tough, A. 1979. New conclusions on why and how adults learn. *Training*, January, pp. 8–10.
43. Op. cit. Knowles, 1984.
44. Westmeyer, P. 1988. *Effective Teaching in Adult and Higher Education*. Springfield, IL: Charles C. Thomas.
45. Belmont, J., and E. Butterfield. 1971. Learning strategies as determinants of memory deficiencies. *Cognitive Psychology* 2:411–20; and Brown, A., and A. Palicsar. 1982. Inducing strategic learning from texts by means of informed, self-control training. *Learning and Learning Disabilities*, April, pp. 1–17.
46. Borkowski, J. 1985. Sign of intelligence: Strategy generalization and metacognition. In *The Growth of Reflection*, edited by S. R. Yussen. New York: Academic Press; Kendall, C., J. Borkowski, and J. Cavanaugh. 1980. Metamemory and the transfer of an interrogative strategy by EMR children. *Intelligence* 4:255–70; and Walker, C. 1987. Relative importance of domain knowledge and overall aptitude on acquisition of domain related information. *Cognition and Instruction* 4:25–42.
47. Brookfield, S. 1987. *Developing Critical Thinkers*. San Francisco: Jossey-Bass; op. cit. Knowles, 1984; Marsick, V. 1987. *Learning in the Workplace: Theory and Practice*. London: Croom Helm.
48. Kanfer, R., and P. Ackerman. 1989. Motivation and cognitive abilities: An integrative aptitude/treatment interaction approach to skill acquisition. *Journal of Applied Psychology* 74:657–89.
49. Newstrom, J. W., and M. L. Lengnick-Hall. 1991. One size does not fit all. *Training and Development Journal* 45(6):43–48.
50. Adapted from Gordon, E., R. Morgan, and J. Ponticell. 1995. The individualized training alternative. *Training and Development*, September, pp. 52–60.

CHAPTER 4

1. Rummler, G. 1987. Determining needs. In *Training and Development Handbook*, edited by R. L. Craig. New York: McGraw-Hill.
2. Cascio, W. 1989. Using utility analysis to assess training outcomes. In *Training and Development in Organizations*, edited by I. L. Goldstein. San Francisco: Jossey-Bass; Cascio, W. 1991a. *Costing Human Resources: The Financial Impact of Behavior in Organizations*. Boston: PWS Kent.
3. Galagan, P.A. 1999. Training isn't the point. *Training and Development*, May, pp. 28–29.
4. Korth, S. 2001. Consolidating needs assessment and evaluation. *Performance Improvement* 40:38–43.
5. McGehee, W., and P. W. Thayer. 1961. *Training in Business and Industry*. New York: Wiley.
6. Op. cit. McGehee and Thayer, 1961.
7. Tannenbaum, S., and G. Yukl. 1992. Training and development in work organizations. *American Review of Psychology* 43:399–441.
8. Landy, F., and J. Vasey. 1991. Job analysis: The composition of SME samples. *Personnel Psychology* 44:27–50.
9. Dayal, I., and J. Thomas. 1968. Operation KPE: Developing a new organization. *Journal of Behavioral Science* 4:473–506.
10. McCormick, E. 1979. *Job Analysis*. New York: AMACOM.
11. Kraiger, K., J. Ford, and E. Salas. 1993. Application of cognitive, skill-based, and affective theories of learning outcomes to new methods of training evaluation. *Journal of Applied Psychology* 78:311–28.
12. Shoben, E. J. 1983. Applications of multi-dimensional scaling in cognitive psychology. *Applied Psychological Measurement* 7:473–90; Schvaneveltd, R. W., F. T. Durso,

and D. W. Dearholt. 1985. Pathfinder scaling with network structures. (*Memorandum in Computer and Cognitive Structures, MCCS-85-9*). Las Cruces, NM: State Univ. Computing Research Laboratory.

13. Ford, J. K., and K. Kraiger. 1995. The application of cognitive constructs and principles to the instructional systems model of training: Implications for needs assessment, design and transfer. In *International Review of Industrial and Organizational Psychology*, edited by C. L. Cooper and T. J. Robertson, 10:1–48; Goldsmith, T. E., and P. J. Johnson. 1990. A structural assessment of classroom learning. In *Pathfinder Associative Networks: Studies in Knowledge Organization*, edited by R. W. Schvaneveltd. Norwood, NJ: Ablex; Cooke N. M., and J. E. McDonald. 1987. The application of psychological scaling techniques to knowledge elicitation for knowledge based systems. *International Journal of Man-Machine Studies* 28:533–50; Champagne, A. B., L. E. Klopfer, A. T. Desena, and D. A. Squires. 1981. Structural representations of students' knowledge before and after science instruction. *Journal of Research in Science Technology* 18:97–111.

14. Parry, S. 1998 Just what is a competency? *Training*, pp. 59–64.

15. Miller, L. 1999. Editorial. *International Journal of Training and Development* 3:82–89.

16. Shippmann, J., et al. 2000. The practice of competency modeling. *Personnel Psychology* 53:703–40.

17. Rothwell, W., and Lindholm, J. 1999. Competency identification, modeling and assessment in the USA. *International Journal of Training and Development* 3:90–105. Op. cit. Shippmann, 2000.

18. Op. cit. Shippmann, 2000.

19. Ibid.

20. Op. cit. Rothwell, 1999; Mirabile, R. 1997. Everything you wanted to know about competency modeling. *Training and Development Journal*, August, pp. 73–77.

21. Dalton, M. 1997. Are competency models a waste? *Training and Development*, October, pp. 46–49.

22. Bernardin, H. J., and R. Beatty. 1984. *Performance Appraisal: Assessing Human Behavior at Work*. Boston: Kent.

23. Benedict, M. E., and E. L. Levine. 1988. Delay and distortion: Tacit influences on performance appraisal. *Journal of Applied Psychology* 73:507–14; Longenecker, C. O., H. P. Sims, and D. A. Gioia. 1987. Behind the mask: The politics of employee appraisal. *Academy of Management Executive* 1:183–93.

24. Payne, R., and D. Pugh. 1976. Organizational structure and climate. In *Handbook of Industrial and Organizational Psychology*, edited by M. Dunnette. Chicago: Rand McNally, pp. 1125–73.

25. Cascio, W. 1991b. *Applied Psychology in Personnel Management*. Upper Saddle River, NJ: Prentice Hall.

26. Herbert, G., and D. Doverspike. 1990. Performance appraisal in the training needs analysis process: A review and critique. *Public Personnel Management* 19:253–70.

27. Murphy, K. R., and J. N. Cleveland. 1991. *Performance Appraisal: An Organizational Perspective*. Boston: Allyn & Bacon.

28. Thorndike, E. L. 1920. A constant error in psychological ratings. *Journal of Applied Psychology* 4:25–29.

29. Bass, B. 1956. Reducing leniency in merit ratings. *Personnel Psychology* 9:359–69. Harris, M. M., and J. Schaubroek. 1988. A meta analysis of self–supervisor, self–peer, and peer–supervisor ratings. *Personnel Psychology* 41:43–62.

30. Farh, J., and G. Dobbins. 1989. Effects of self-esteem on leniency bias in self-reports of performance: A structural equation analysis. *Personnel Psychology* 42:835–50.

31. Williams, J., and P. Levy. 1992. The effects of perceived system knowledge on the agreement between self-ratings and supervisor ratings. *Personnel Psychology* 45:835–47.

32. McEnery, J., and J. McEnery. 1987. Self-ratings in management training: A neglected opportunity? *Journal of Occupational Psychology* 60:49–60.

33. Cheung, G. 1999. Multifaceted conceptions of self-other ratings disagreement. *Personnel Psychology* 52:1–35.

34. London, M., and R. Beatty. 1993. 360-degree feedback as a competitive advantage. *Human Resource Management* 32:353–72.

35. Brutus, S., M. London, and J. Martineau. 1999. The impact of 360 degree feedback on planning for career development. *Journal of Management Development* 18:676–93.

36. Pfau, B., I. Kay, K. Nowack, and J. Ghorpade. 2000. Does 360-degree feedback negatively affect company performance. *HR Magazine* 47:54–60.

37. Maurer, T., D. Mitchell, and F. Barbeite. 2002. Predictors of attitudes toward a 360-degree feedback system and involvement in post-feedback development activity. *Journal of Occupational and Organizational Psychology* 75:87–107.

38. Camp, R., P. Blanchard, and G. Huszczo. 1986. *Toward a More Organizationally Effective Training Strategy and Practice.* Upper Saddle River, NJ: Prentice Hall.

39. Seashore, S., E. Lawler, P. Mirvis, and C. Cammann. 1983. *Assessing Organizational Change.* New York: Wiley.

40. Cook, J., S. Hepworth, T. Wall, J. Toby, and P. Warr. 1981. *The Experience of Work: A Compendium and Review of 249 Measures and Their Use.* New York: Academic Press.

41. Robinson, J., R. Athanasiou, and K. Head. 1976. *Measuring of Occupational Attitudes and Occupational Characteristics.* Ann Arbor: Institute for Social Research.

42. Ford, J. K., and R. A. Noe. 1987. Self-assessed training needs: The effects of attitudes toward training, managerial level, and function. *Personnel Psychology* 40:39–53.

43. Fisher, C. 1979. Transmission of negative and positive feedback to subordinates: A laboratory investigation. *Journal of Psychology* 64:533–40.

44. Carrol, S., and C. Schneier. 1982. *Performance Appraisal and Review Systems.* Glenview, IL: Scott Foresman.

45. Michalak, D. F., and E. G. Yager. 1979. *Making the Training Process Work.* New York: Harper & Row.

46. Schneider, B., and A. Konz. 1989. Strategic job analysis. *Human Resource Management* 28:51–63.

47. Ibid.

48. Casner, J. 1989. *Successful Training Strategies.* San Francisco: Jossey-Bass.

49. Burns, T., and G. M. Stalker. 1961. *The Management of Innovation.* London: Tavistock.

50. Mintzberg, H. 1987. Crafting strategy. *Harvard Business Review,* July/August, pp. 66–75.

51. Keats, B., and J. Bracker. 1988. Toward a theory of small firm performance. *American Journal of Small Business* 4:35–43.

52. Banks, M., A. Bures, and D. Champion. 1987. Decision-making factors in small business: Training and development. *Journal of Small Business Management,* January, pp. 19–26.

53. Fairfield-Sonn, J. 1987. A strategic process model for small business training and development. *Journal of Small Business Management,* January, pp. 11–18.

54. Lee, W., and D. Owens. 2001. Rapid analysis model. *Performance Improvement Quarterly* 40:13–18; Rossett, A. 1998. *First Things Fast: A Handbook for Performance Analysis.* New York: Pfeiffer.

55. The list is partially based on Rossett, 1998.

56. Kuri, F. 1996. Basic skills training boosts productivity. *HR Magazine,* September, pp. 73–79.

Appendix

1. Thorndike, R. L. 1949. *Personnel Selection: Test and Measurement Technique.* New York: Wiley.

2. Blum, M. L., and J. C. Naylor. 1968. *Industrial Psychology: Its Theoretical and Social Foundation.* New York: Harper & Row.

3. Ibid.

4. Ibid.

5. Nunnally, J. 1978. *Psychometric Theory.* New York: McGraw-Hill.

6. Kraiger, K., J. Ford, and E. Salas. 1993. Application of cognitive, skill-based, and affective theories of learning outcomes to new methods of training evaluation. *Journal of Applied Psychology* 78:311–28.

7. Op. cit. Blum and Naylor, 1968.

CHAPTER 5

1. Galvin, T. 2001. Industry report. *Training,* October, pp. 40–75.

2. Ibid.

3. Marquardt, M., N. Nissley, R. Ozag, and T. Taylor. 2000. International briefing 6; Training and development in the United States. *International Journal of Training and Development* 4:138–49.

4. Mager, R. 1975. *Preparing Instructional Objectives*. Belmont, CA: Pitman Learning.

5. Langdon, D. 1999. Objectives? Get over them. *Training and Development,* February, pp. 54–58; Stoneall, L. 1992. The case for more flexible objectives. *Training and Development*, August, pp. 67–69.

6. Op. cit. Stoneall, 1992.

7. Op. cit. Langdon, 1999.

8. Colquitt, J., J. LePine, and R. Noe. 2000. Toward an integrative theory of training motivation: A meta-analytic path analysis of 20 years of research. *Journal of Applied Psychology* 85:678–707.

9. Lewis, J. 1981. Answers to twenty questions on behavioral objectives. *Educational Technology*, March, pp. 27–31.

10. Locke, E., K. Shaw, L. Saari, and G. Latham. 1981. Goal setting and task performance. *Psychological Bulletin* 90:125–52.

11. Latham, G. P., and G. A. Yukl. 1975. A review of research on the application of goal setting in organizations. *Academy of Management Journal* 18:824–45.

12. Op. cit. Lewis, 1981.

13. Filipczak, B. 1998. Old dogs, new tricks. *Training* 35:50–58.

14. Op. cit. Marquardt et al., 2000.

15. U.S. Bureau of the Census. 1998. *Statistical abstracts of the United States*. Washington, DC.

16. Ibid.

17. Cascio, W. 1995. *Managing Human Resources*. New York: McGraw-Hill Ryerson.

18. Anonymous. 1998. A stronger Canada. *Employment and Immigration Canada: 1998*. Ottawa, October 23.

19. Cronbach, L., and R. Snow. 1977. *Aptitude and Instructional Methods*. New York: Irvington.

20. Goldstein, I. 1980. Training in work organizations. *Annual Review of Psychology* 39: 229–72.

21. Ryman, D., and R. Biersner. 1975. Attitudes predictive of diving training success. *Personnel Psychology* 28:181–88.

22. Op. cit. Colquitt et al., 2000.

23. Camp, R., P. N. Blanchard, and G. Huszczo. 1986. *Toward a More Organizationally Effective Training Strategy and Practice*. Upper Saddle River, NJ: Prentice Hall.

24. Latham, G. P., and E. A. Locke. 1979. Goal setting: A motivational technique that works. *Organizational Dynamics* 8:68–80; Op. cit. Locke et al., 1981.

25. Ibid.

26. Reigeluth, C. 1999a. What is instructional design theory and how is it changing. In *Instructional Design Theories and Models: An Overview of Their Current Status,* vol. 2, edited by C. Reigeluth. Mahwah, NJ: Laurence Erlbaum Associates, pp. 5–29.

27. Op. cit. Latham and Locke, 1979; Op. cit. Locke et al., 1981.

28. Klatzky, R. 1975. *Human Memory: Structures and Processes*. San Francisco: Freeman.; Lindsay, P., and D. Norman. 1972. *Human Information Processing: An Introduction to Psychology*. New York: Academic Press.

29. Anderson, J. R., and G. H. Bower. 1972. Recognition and retrieval processes in free recall. *Psychological Review* 79:97–123; Bandura, A. 1977. *Social Learning Theory*. Upper Saddle River, NJ: Prentice Hall; Melton, A., and E. Martin. 1972. *Coding Process in Human Memory*. Washington, DC: Winston.

30. Anderson, J. R., and G. H. Bower. 1973. *Human Associative Memory*. Washington, DC: Winston.

31. Marquardt, M., and G. Kearsley. 1999. *Technology-Based Learning*. Boca Raton, FL: St. Lucie Press; Drucker, P. 1994. The age of social transition. *The Atlantic Monthly* 274:53–80.

32. Cascio, W., and J. Thacker. 1994. *Managing Human Resources*. Toronto: McGraw-Hill Ryerson.

33. Joinson, C. 1999. Teams at work. *HR Magazine*, May, pp. 30–36.

34. Schmitt, M. C., and T. J. Newby. 1986. Metacognition: Relevance to instructional design. *Journal of Instructional Development* 9:29–32.

35. Op. cit. Cascio, 1995.

60. Burke, L., and T. Baldwin. 1999. Workforce training transfer: A study of the effect of relapse prevention training and transfer climate. *Human Resource Management* 38:227–42.

61. Seyler, D., E. Holton, R. Bates, R. M. Burnett, and M. Carvalho. 1998. Factors affecting motivation to transfer. *International Journal of Training and Development* 2:2–16; Op. cit. Baldwin and Ford, 1988.

62. Orpen, C. 1999. The influence of the training environment on trainee motivation and perceived training quality. *International Journal of Training and Development* 3:34–43.

63. Noe, R. A., and S. L. Wilk. 1993. Investigation of the factors that influence employees' participation in developmental activities. *Journal of Applied Psychology* 78:291–302.

64. Hicks, W. D., and R. J. Klimoski. 1987. Entry into training programs and its effect on training outcomes: A field experiment. *Academy of Management Journal* 30:542–52.

65. Ibid.

66. Op. cit. Sayler et al., 1998.

67. Bergman, T. 1993. Job performance learning: A comprehensive approach to high-performance training design. *Employment Relations Today*, Winter, pp. 399–409.

68. Op. cit. Wexley and Baldwin, 1986.

69. Stark, C. 1986. Ensuring skills transfer: A sensitive approach. *Training and Development Journal*, March, pp. 50–51.

70. Ibid.

71. Op. cit. Orpen, 1999.

72. Tracey, B., S. Tannenbaum, and M. Kavanaugh. 1995. Applying trained skills on the job: The importance of the work environment. *Journal of Applied Psychology* 80:239–51.

73. Schneider, B. 1990. *Organizational Climate and Culture*. San Francisco: Jossey-Bass.

74. Op. cit. Orpen, 1999.

75. Op. cit. Burke and Baldwin, 1999.

76. Olsen, J. 1998. The evaluation and enhancement of training transfer. *International Journal of Training and Development* 2:61–75.

77. Schein, E. H. 1985. *Organizational Culture and Leadership*. San Francisco: Jossey-Bass.

78. Op. cit. Tracey, Tannenbaum, and Kavanaugh, 1995.

79. Op. cit. Cascio, 1995.

80. Thacker, J., and J. Cattaneo. 1992. Survey of personnel practices in Canadian organizations. Working paper series W92-04, ISSN 07146191.

81. Merrill, M. 1983. Component display theory. In *Instructional Design Theories and Models: An Overview of Their Current Status*, edited by C. Reigeluth. Hillsdale, NJ: Laurence Erlbaum Associates, pp. 279–334.

82. Romiszowski, A. 1999. The development of physical skills: Instruction in the psychomotor domain. In *Instructional Design Theories and Models: An Overview of Their Current Status*, vol. 2, edited by C. Reigeluth. Mahwah, NJ: Laurence Erlbaum Associates, pp. 457–81.

83. Reigeluth, C. 1999b. *Instructional Design Theories and Models: An Overview of Their Current Status*. Mahwah, NJ: Laurence Erlbaum Associates.

84. Reigeluth, C. 1999c. The elaboration theory: Guidance for scope and sequence decisions. In *Instructional Design Theories and Models: An Overview of Their Current Status*, vol. 2, edited by C. Reigeluth. Mahwah, NJ: Laurence Erlbaum Associates, pp. 425–53.

85. Gagné, R., L. Briggs, and W. Wager. 1988. *Principles of Instructional Design*. New York: Holt, Rinehart, and Winston.

86. Op. cit. Reigeluth (1999a).

87. Op. cit. Reigeluth (1999c).

88. Ibid.

89. English, R., and C. Reigeluth. 1996. Formative research on sequencing instruction with elaboration theory. *Education Technology Research and Development* 44:23–42.

90. Carson, H., and R. Curtis. 1991. Applying instructional design theory to bibliographic instruction: Macro theory. *Research Strategies* 9:164–79; Reigeluth, C. 1987. Lesson blueprints based on the elaboration theory of instruction. In *Instructional Theories in Action*, edited by C. Reigeluth. Hillsdale, NJ: Lawerence Erlbaum

36. Demster, F. 1990. The spacing effect: A case study in the failure to apply the results of psychological research. *American Psychologist* 43:627–34.

37. Dipboye, R. 1997. Organizational barriers to implementing a rational model of training. In *Training for a Rapidly Changing Workplace*, edited by M. Quinones and Ehrenstein. Washington, DC: American Psychological Assoication.

38. Donovan, J., and D. Radosevich. 1999. A meta-analytic review of the distribution of practice effect: Now you see it, now you don't. *Journal of Applied Psychology* 84:795–804.

39. Ibid.

40. Baldwin, T., and K. Ford. 1988. Transfer of training: A review and directions for future research. *Personnel Psychology* 41:63–105.

41. Adams, J. 1987. Historical review and appraisal of research on the learning, retention, and transfer of human motor skills. *Psychological Bulletin* 101:41–74.

42. Naylor, J., and G. Briggs. 1963. Effects of rehearsal of temporal and spatial aspects on the long-term retention of a procedural skill. *Journal of Applied Psychology* 47:120–26.

43. Blum, M., and J. Naylor. 1968. *Industrial Psychology, Its Theoretical and Social Foundations.* New York: Harper & Row.

44. McGhee, W., and P. W. Thayer. 1961. *Training in Business and Industry.* New York: Wiley.

45. Atwater, S. 1953. Proactive inhibition and associative facilitation as affected by the degree of prior learning. *Journal of Experimental Psychology* 46:400–4; Hagman, J. D., and A. M. Rose. 1983. Retention of military tasks: A review. *Human Factors* 25:199–214; Mandler, G. 1954. Transfer of training as a response to overlearning. *Journal of Experimental Psychology* 47:411–17.

46. Schendel, J. D., and J. D. Hagman. 1982. On sustaining procedural skills over a prolonged retention interval. *Journal of Applied Psychology* 67:605–10.

47. May, L., and W. Kahnweiler. 2000. The effect of a mastery practice design on learning and transfer in behavior modeling training. *Personnel Psychology* 53:353–73.

48. Kraiger, K., J. K. Ford, and E. S Application of cognitive, skille affective theories of learning o new methods of training evalua *of Applied Psychology* 78:311–2 R., and W. Schneider. 1977. Cor automatic information processi Perceptual learning, automatic and a general theory. *Psycholog* 84:127–90.

49. Thorndike, E. L., and R. S. Woo 1901. The influence of improven mental function upon the efficie functions. Functions involving a observation, and discrimination. *Psychological Review* 8:553–64.

50. Op. cit. Camp, Blanchard, and H 1986.

51. Locke, E., and G. Latham. 1990. *Theory of Goal Setting and Task Performance.* Upper Saddle Rive Prentice Hall.

52. Martocchio, J. J., and J. Dulebohn Performance feedback effects in The role of perceived controllabil *Personnel Psychology* 47:357–73.

53. Bandura, A. 1991. Social cognitive self-regulation. *Organizational Be and Human Decision* 50:248–87.

54. Marx, R. D. 1982. Relapse prevent managerial training: A model for r nance of behavior change. *Academ Management Review* 7:433–41.

55. Brownell, K. D., G. Marlatt, E. Lich and G. Wilson. 1986. Understandin preventing relapse. *American Psyc* 41:765–82.

56. Feldman, M. 1981. Successful posttr skill application. *Training and Deve Journal* 35:72–75; Op. cit. Wexley an Baldwin, 1986.

57. Op. cit. Wexley and Baldwin, 1986.

58. Marx, R. 1986. Improving managem development through relapse prevel strategies. *Journal of Management Development* 5:27–40.

59. Wexley, K., and T. Baldwin. 1986. Posttraining strategies for facilitating tive transfer: An empirical exploratio *Academy of Management Journal* 29:503–20.

Associates; English, R., and C. Reigeluth. 1996. Formative research on sequencing instruction with elaboration theory. *Education Technology Research and Development* 44:23–42.

91. Gagné, R., L. Briggs, and W. Wager. 1988. *Principles of Instructional Design*. New York: Holt, Rinehart, and Winston.

92. Ibid.

93. Hornsby, J., and D. Kuratko. 1990. Human resource management in small business: Critical issues for the 1990s. *Journal of Small Business Management*, July, pp. 9–19.

94. Deshpande, S., and D. Golhar. 1994. HRM practices in large and small manufacturing firms: A comparative study. *Journal of Small Business Management*, April, pp. 49–56.

95. Ahire, S., and D. Golhar. 1996. Quality management in large vs. small firms. *Journal of Small Business Management*, April, pp. 1–13.

96. McRae, C., A. Banks, A. Bures, and D. Champion. 1987. Decision-making factors in small business: Training and development. *Journal of Small Business Management*, January, pp. 19–25.

97. Op. cit. May and Kahnweiler, 2000.

CHAPTER 6

1. Broadwell, M. 1980. *The Lecture Method of Instruction*. Englewood Cliffs, NJ: Educational Technology Publications.

2. Brown, G. 1978. *Lecturing and Explaining*. London: Methuen and Co. Also see Bligh, D. 1974. *What's the Use of Lectures?* Middlesex, England: Penguin Education.

3. Op. cit. Broadwell, 1980.

4. Johnstone, A., and F. Percival. 1976. Attention breaks in lectures. *Education in Chemistry* 13:273–304; Lloyd, D. 1968. A concept of improvement of learning response in the taught lesson. *Visual Education*, Winter, pp. 23–25; Maddox, H., and E. Hook. 1975. Performance decrement in the lecture. *Educational Research* 28:17–30.

5. *Personnel Journal*. 1995. Interaction has its attraction. July, pp. 27–28.

6. Van Buren, M. 2001. *The 2001 ASTD State of the Industry Report*. February, pp. 19–20.

7. Gordon, S. E. 1994. *Systematic Training Program Design*. Upper Saddle River, NJ: Prentice Hall, p. 197.

8. Op. cit. Van Buren, 2001.

9. Steel-Johnson, D., and B. Hyde. 1997. Advanced technologies in training: Intelligent tutoring systems and virtual reality. In *Training for a Rapidly Changing Workplace*, edited by M. Quinones and A. Ehrenstein. Washington, DC: American Psychological Association.

10. Ibid.

11. Seidel, R., O. Park, and R. Perez. 1988. Expertise of ICAI: Development requirements. *Computers in Human Behavior* 4:235–56.

12. Ong, J., and S. Ramachandran. 2000. Intelligent tutoring systems: The what and the how. *ASTD Learning Circuits*. Available at www.learningcircuits.orgfeb2000/org.html.

13. Ibid.

14. Anonymous. 2001. Industry Report. *Training*. October, pp. 40–56.

15. Anonymous. 1999. Nugget introduces food safety training & certification through CD-ROM. *Restaurant Hospitality* 83:S6–7.

16. Grunberg, D. 1999. Multimedia Training. *Franchising World* 31:50.

17. Op. cit. Clark and Lyons, 1999.

18. Marquardt, M. 1999. *Technology-Based Learning*. Boca Raton, FL: CRC Press.

19. Op. cit. Steel-Johnson and Hyde, 1997.

20. Fister, S. 1999. Tech trends. *Training*, August, pp. 24–26.

21. Blumenthal, R., L. Meiskey, S. Dooley, and R. Sparks. 1996. Reducing developmental costs with intelligent tutoring system shells. Paper presented at the Workshop on Architechures and Methods for Designing Cost-Effective and Reusable ITSs. Montreal, June 26.

22. Ibid.

23. Op. cit. Marquardt, 1999.

24. Eurich, N. P. 1990. *The Learning Industry: Education for Adult Workers*, Lawrenceville, NJ: Princeton University Press.

25. Borthick, S. 2000. 10 gigabyte ethernet and the broadband revival. *Business Communication Review*, 30:28–35.

26. Op. cit. Fister, 1999.

27. Ibid.

28. Nash, N., J. Muczyk, and F. Vettori. 1971. The relative practical effectiveness of programmed instruction. *Personnel Psychology* 24:397–418; Burns, T. 1997. Multimedia and quality. *Quality Progress*, February, pp. 77–84; Stauffer, D. 1999. High-tech training a huge win in Marriott's high-touch culture. Available at www.traininguniversity.com; Fletcher, D. 1999. *Intelligent Tutoring Systems: Then and Now.* Workshop on Advanced Training Technologies and Learning Environments held at NASA, Langley Research Center, March, NASA/CP-1999-209339.

29. Op. cit. Fletcher, 1999.

30. Kearsley, G. 1984. *Training and Technology.* Reading, MA: Addison-Wesley.

31. Jensen, E. Personal communication, January 31, 2002.

32. Op. cit. Goldstein, 1993.

33. Ganger, R. E. 1990. Computer-based training works. *Personnel Journal* 69(9):85–91; Hannafin, M. J. 1984. Guidelines for using locus of instructional control in the design of computer assisted instruction. *Journal of Instructional Development* 7(3):6–10.

34. Gagné, R. 1977. *The Conditions of Learning.* New York: Holt, Rinehart, and Winston.

35. Op. cit. Goldstein, 1993.

36. Killian, D. 1976. *The Impact of Flight Simulators on U.S. Airlines.* Fort Worth, TX: American Airlines Flight Academy; Mecham, M. 1994. Cathay refines approach to simulator training. *Aviation Week and Space Technology*, January 17, pp. 35–37.

37. Op. cit. Killian, 1976; Parsons, H. M. 1972. *Man-Machine System Experiment.* Baltimore: Johns Hopkins Press.

38. Erwin, D. E. 1978. Psychological fidelity in simulated work environments. Proceedings of the American Psychological Association, Toronto, Canada.

39. Edwards, D., C. Hahn, and E. Fleishman. 1980. Evaluation of laboratory methods for the study of driver behavior: Relations between simulator and street performance. *Journal of Applied Psychology* 62:559–66.

40. Fink, C. D., and E. L. Shriver. 1978. Simulators for maintenance training: Some issues, problems and areas for future research. *AFHRL Technical Report*, Brooks Air Force Base, Texas, 78–127.

41. Barrett, G., T. Benko, and G. Riddle. 1981. Programmable simulator speeds operator training. *Bell Laboratories Record* 59(7):213–16.

42. Paffet, J. A. 1978. Ships' officers use simulators to learn vessel operation. *Minicomputer News* 4(8):11–13.

43. Slack, K. 1993. Training for the real thing. *Training and Development*, May, pp. 79–89.

44. Davis, L. 1973. Evolving alternative organizational designs: Their sociotechnical bases. *Human Relations* 30:261–71; Walton, R. 1975. From Hawthorne to Topeka and Kalmar. In *Man and Work in Society*, edited by E. Cass and F. Zimmer. New York: Van Nostrand Reinhold Co.

45. Barbian, J. 2001. Get Simulated. *Training*, February, pp. 67–70.

46. Dakin, S., and G. Wood. 1995. Learn TQM principles using jumbled proverbs. *Quality Progress*, October, pp. 92–95; Kaplan, R., M. Lombardo, and M. Mazique. 1985. A mirror for managers: Using simulation to develop management teams. *Journal of Applied Behavioral Science* 21:241–53; Goudy, R. 1981. Two years of management experience in two challenging weeks. *ABA Banking Journal* 73(6):74–77; Groth, J., and C. Phillips. 1978. What would you do if a crisis hit your firm? *Management World* 7(3):12–16; Zemke, R. 1982. Can games and simulations improve your training power? *Training* 19(2):24–31.

47. Op. cit. Barbian, 2001.

48. Argyris, C. 1980. Some limitations of the case method: Experiences in a management development program. *Academy of Management Review* 5:291–98.

49. Pigors, P., and F. Pigors. 1987. The case method. In *Training and Development Handbook: A Guide to Human Resource Development*, edited by R. Craig. New York: McGraw-Hill, pp. 414–29.

50. Huegli, J., and H. Tschirgi. 1980. Preparing the student for the initial job interview: Skills and methods. *American Business Communication Association Bulletin* 42(4):10–13; Op. cit. Goldstein, 1993;

Wexley, K., and G. Latham. 1991. *Developing and Training Human Resources in Organizations*, 2d ed. New York: HarperCollins, pp. 88–90; Sims, H., and C. Manz. 1982. Modeling influences on employee behavior. *Personnel Journal* 61(1):58–65.

51. Burke, M., and R. Day. 1986. A cumulative study of the effectiveness of managerial training. *Journal of Applied Psychology* 71:232–45; Decker, P., and B. Nathen. 1985. *Behavior Modeling Training: Principles and Applications*. New York: Praeger; Op. cit. Huegli and Tschirgi, 1980; Latham, G., and C. Frayne. 1989. Self-management training for increased job attendance: A follow-up and replication. *Journal of Applied Psychology* 74:411–16; Smith, P. 1976. Management modeling training to improve morale and customer satisfaction. *Personnel Psychology* 29:251–59.

52. Solem, A. R. 1960. Human relations training: A comparison of case studies. *Personnel Administration* 23:29–37; Fazio, R., and M. Zanna. 1981. Direct experience and attitude-behavior consistency. In *Advances in Experimental Social Psychology*, edited by L. Berkowitz. New York: Academic Press.

53. Gold, L. 1981. Job instruction: Four steps to success. *Training and Development Journal*, September, pp. 28–32.

54. Ibid.

55. *National Apprenticeship Training Program*. 1987. Washington, DC: Employment and Training Administration: Department of Labor.

56. Finnerty, M. 1996. Coaching for growth and development. In *The Training and Development Handbook*, edited by R. Craig. New York: McGraw-Hill.

57. Rothwell, W., and H. Kazanas. 1994. *Improving On-the-Job Training*. San Francisco, Jossey-Bass.

58. Gordon, E. E., R. Morgan, and J. Ponticell. 1995. The individualized training alternative. *Training and Development*, September, pp. 52–60.

59. Op. cit. Van Buren, 2001.

60. Ibid.

61. Honeycutt, E. Jr., T. McCarty, and V. Howe. 1993. Sales technology applications: Self-paced video enhanced training: A case study. *Journal of Personal Selling and Sales Management* 13(1):73–79.

62. Ibid.

63. Op. cit. Gagné, 1977.

64. Ibid.

CHAPTER 7

1. Broadwill, M., and C. Dietrich. 1996. How to get trainees into the action. *Training*, February, pp. 52–56.

2. Ibid.

3. Jolles, R. 1993. *How to Run Seminars and Workshops*. New York: Wiley.

4. Ibid.

5. Johnstone, A. H., and F. Percival. 1976. Attention breaks in lectures. *Education in Chemistry* 13:273–304; Lloyd, D. H. 1968. A concept of improvement of learning in the taught lesson. *Visual Education*, pp. 23–25; Maddox, H., and E. Hook. 1975. Performance decrement in the lecture. *Educational Research*, 28:17–30.

6. Palmer, A. 1981. Models of behavioral change. In *The 1981 Annual Handbook for Group Facilitators*, edited by J. E. Jones and J. W. Pfeiffer. San Diego: University Associates Press; Maddox and Hook, 1975.

7. Pfeiffer, J. W., and J. E. Jones. 1980. *The 1980 Annual Handbook for Group Facilitators*. San Diego: University Associates Press.

8. Ibid.

9. Baynton, D. 2001. Cyber learning fortunes. *Training* 38:22–23.

10. Ibid.

11. Swanson, S. 2000. Businesses share e-learning content. *Informationweek*, October, pp. 205–6.

12. Forlenza, D. 1995. Computer-based training. *Professional Safety*, May, pp. 27–29.

13. Anonymous. 1997. Release of the virtual reality training decision tool (news release). Available at www.rti.org/news/news.

14. Anonymous. 1993. Put SPIMM in your CBT. *Training*, February, pp. 12, 14.

15. Zenger, J., and C. Uehlein. 2001. Why blended will win. *Training and Development* 55:54–60.

16. Field, S. 2002. Personal communication, RTI International.

17. Lee, W. 2000. *Multimedia-Based Instructional Design: Computer-Based Training, Web-Based Training, Distance Broadcast Training*. SanFransisco, Jossey-Bass.

18. Anonymous. 2001. Training flexes small firms' competitive muscle. *Management Services* 45:6.

19. Faria, T. 1998. Business simulation games: Current usage levels—an update. *Simulation and Gaming* 29:295–308.

20. Faria, T. 2002. Personal communication.

21. Argyris, C. 1980. Some limitations to the case method: Experience in a management development program. *Academy of Management Review* 5:291–98.

22. Engel, H. 1973. *Handbook of Creative Learning Exercises*. Houston: Gulf.

23. Wohlking, W. 1976. Role playing. In *Training and Development Handbook*, edited by R. L. Craig. New York: McGraw-Hill.

24. Hequet, M. 1996. Video shakeout. *Training*, September, pp. 46–50.

25. Suzik, H. 1999. On-the-job training: Do it right. *Quality* 38:84–85.

26. *Apprentice Information*. 1995. Ontario Training and Adjustment Board. Toronto: Queens Printer.

27. Marquardt, M. 1999. *Action Learning in Action*. Palo Alto, CA: Davies-Black.

28. Orth, C. D., H. E. Wilkinson, and R. C. Benfari. 1987. The manager's role as coach and mentor. *Organizational Dynamics* 15(4):66–74.

29. Evered, R., and J. Selman. 1989. Coaching and the art of management. *Organizational Dynamics* 18(2):16–32.

30. Feldman, D. 2001. Career coaching: What HR professional and managers need to know. *Human Resource Planning* 24:26–35.

31. Kram, K. 1985. Improving the mentoring process. *Training and Development Journal*, April, pp. 40–43.

32. Phillips-Jones, L. 1983. Establishing a formalized mentoring program. *Training and Development Journal*, February, pp. 38–42.

33. Filipczak, B. 1996. Training on the cheap. *Training*, May, pp. 28–34.

34. Sneed, L. 1992. Making your video tell a story. *Training*, September, pp. 59–63.

35. Ibid.

36. Davis, I. K., and J. Hagman. 1976. What is right and wrong with your training room environment. *Training*, July, p. 28.

37. Chaddock, P. 1971. How do your trainers grow. *Training and Development Journal*, March, pp. 2–7.

38. Curry, T. 1977. Why not use your line managers as management trainers? *Training and Development Journal*, November, pp. 43–47.

39. Anonymous. 2001. Training flexes small firms competitive muscle. *Management Services* 45:6–7.

40. Blumfield, M. 1997. Learning to share. *Training*, April, pp. 38–42.

41. Anfuso, D. 1999. Trainers prove many heads are greater than one. *Workforce* 78:60–65.

42. Tyler, K. 2001. E-Learning: Not just for e-normous companies anymore. *HRMagazine* 46:82–88.

43. Leeds, L. 2002. Personal communication, Western Learning Systems.

44. Op. cit. Filipczak, 1996.

45. Ibid.

46. Abella, K. 1986. *Building Successful Training Programs*. Reading, MA: Addison-Wesley.

CHAPTER 8

1. Brandenberg, D., and E. Schultz. 1988. The status of evaluation of training: An update. Presentation at the National Society of Performance and Instruction Conference, April, Washington, DC.

2. McLaughlin, D. J. 1986. The turning point in human resource management. In *Strategic Human Resource Management*, edited by F. K. Folkes. Upper Saddle River, NJ: Prentice Hall.

3. Geber, B. 1995. Does your training make a difference? Prove it! *Training*, March, pp. 27–34.

4. Olsen, J. 1998. The evaluation and enhancement of training transfer. *International Journal of Training and Development* 2:61–75.

5. Goldwasser, D. 2001. Beyond ROI. *Training*, January, pp. 82–90; op. cit. Geber, 1995.

6. Purcell, A. 2000. 20/20 ROI. *Training and Development*, July, pp. 28–33.

7. Cattaneo, R., and A. Templer. 1990. Strategic contrasts: A comparative analysis of two examples of human resource management effectiveness. Proceedings of the Annual Conference of the Administrative Sciences Association of Canada, vol. 11, Whistler, B.C.: pp. 25–34.

8. McIntyre, D. 1994. Training and Development 1993: Policies, Practices and Expenditures. Toronto: The Conference Board of Canada.

9. Blanchard, N., J. Thacker, and S. Way. 2000. Training evaluation: Perspectives and evidence from Canada. *International Journal of Training and Development* 4:295–304.

10. Meals, D., and J. W. Rogers. 1986. Matching human resource management to strategy. In *Strategic Human Resource Management*, edited by F. K. Folkes. Upper Saddle River, NJ: Prentice Hall.

11. Spitzer, D. 1999. Embracing evaluation. *Training*, June, pp. 42–47.

12. Op. cit. Geber, 1995.

13. Ibid.

14. Geis, G. 1987. Formative evaluation: Developmental testing and expert review. *Performance and Instruction*, May, pp. 1–7.

15. Ibid.

16. Kirkpatrick, D. L. 1979. Techniques for evaluating training programs. *Training and Development Journal* 33(6):78–92.

17. Alliger, G., S. Tannenbaum, W. Bennett, H. Traver, and A. Shortland. 1997. A meta-analysis of the relationship among training outcomes. *Personnel Psychology* 50:341–58; Alliger, G., and E. Janak. 1989. Kirkpatrick's levels of training criteria: Thirty years later. *Personnel Psychology* 42:331–42.

18. Blanchard, P. N., and J. W. Thacker. 1998. Organizational Strategy and Management Development. Paper presented at the Global Business Trends Conference of the Academy of Business Administration, Acapulco, Mexico.

19. Korth, S. 2001. Consolidating needs assessment and evaluation. *Performance Improvement* 40:38–43.

20. Hamblin, A. C. 1974. *Evaluation and Control of Training*. New York: McGraw-Hill.

21. Saari, L., T. Johnson, S. McLaughlin, and D. Zimmerlie. 1988. A survey of management training and education practices in U.S. companies. *Personnel Psychology* 41:731–43; Yancey, G. B., and L. Kelly. 1990. The inappropriateness of using participants' reactions to evaluate effectiveness of training. *Psychological Reports* 66:937–38; Wexley, K., and G. Yukl. 1975. *Organizational Behavior and Industrial Psychology: Readings with Commentary*. New York: Oxford University Press.

22. Op. cit. Alliger et al., 1997.

23. Conroy, M., and M. Ross. 1984. Getting what you want by revising what you had. *Journal of Personality and Social Psychology* 47:738–48; Dixon, N. 1990. The relationship between training responses on participant reaction forms and post test scores. *Human Resource Development Quarterly* 1(2):129–37.

24. Op. cit. Alliger et al., 1997

25. Nunnally, J. C. 1978. *Psychometric Theory*. New York: McGraw-Hill.

26. Kropp, R., and E. Hankin. 1975. Paper-and-pencil tests for evaluating instruction. In *Evaluating Training Programs*, edited by D. Kirkpatrick. Madison, WI: American Society of Training and Development.

27. Glaser, R., and M. Chi. 1989. Overview. In *The Nature of Expertise*, edited by M. Chi, R. Glaser, and M. Farr. Hillsdale, NJ: Erlbaum.

28. Flanagan, D. L. 1990. Techniques for eliciting and representing knowledge structures and mental models. Unpublished manuscript. Naval Training Systems Center, Orlando, FL.

29. Kraiger, K., E. Salas, and J. Cannon-Bowers. 1995. Measuring knowledge organization as a method for assessing learning during training. *Human Factors* 37:804–16; Kraiger, K., J. K. Ford, and E. Salas. 1993. Application of cognitive, skill based, and affective theories of learning outcomes to new methods of training evaluation. *Journal of Applied Psychology* 28(2):311–28; Goldsmith, T. E., P. J. Johnson, and W. H. Acton. 1991. Assessing structural knowledge. *Journal of Educational Psychology* 83:88–96; Op. cit. Flanagan, 1990.

30. Means, B., and S. Gott. 1988. Cognitive task analysis as a basis for tutor development: Articulating abstract knowledge representations. In *Intelligent Tutoring Systems: Lessons Learned*, edited by J. Psotka, L. Massey, and S. Mutter. Hillsdale, NJ: Erlbaum.

31. Op. cit. Kraiger, Salas, and Cannon-Bowers, 1995; Gill, R., S. Gordon, J. B. Moore, and C. Arbera. 1988. The role of conceptual structure in problem solving. In *Proceedings of the Annual Meeting of the American Society of Engineering Education.* Washington, DC: American Society of Engineering Education; and op. cit. Means and Gott, 1988.

32. Ackerman, P. L., and L. G. Humphreys. 1990. Individual differences theory in industrial and organizational psychology. In *Handbook of Industrial and Organizational Psychology*, 2d ed. (pp. 223–82), edited by M. D. Dunnette and L. M. Hough. Palo Alto, CA: Consulting Psychologists Press; Lord, F. M. 1956. A study of speed factors in tests and academic grades. *Psychometrika* 21:31–50.

33. Gordon, M. E., and J. F. Isenberg. 1975. Validation of an experimental training criterion for machinists. *Journal of Industrial Teacher Education* 12:72–78.

34. Ostroff, C. 1991. Training effectiveness measures and scoring schemes: A comparison. *Personnel Psychology* 44:353–74.

35. Bernardin, H., and J. Carlyle. 1979. The effects of forced choice methodology on psychometric characteristics of resultant scales. Paper presented at the annual meeting of the Southern Society of Philosophy and Psychology; King, L., J. Hunter, and F. Schmidt. 1980. Halo in a multidimensional forced choice performance evaluation scale. *Journal of Applied Psychology* 65:507–16.

36. Stark, C. 1986. Ensuring skills transfer: A sensitive approach. *Training and Development Journal*, March, pp. 50–51.

37. Thacker, J. W., and M. Fields. 1992. Evaluation of steward training: Did it do what you wanted it to? Published in Proceedings of the 44th Annual Meeting of the Industrial Relations Research Association. New Orleans, January.

38. Thacker, J. W., M. Fields, and L. Barclay. 1990. Union commitment: An examination of antecedent and outcome factors. *Journal of Occupational Psychology* 63:17–20.

39. Clement, R. W. 1982. Testing the hierarchy theory of training evaluation: An expanded role for trainee reactions. *Public Personnel Management Journal* 11:176–84.

40. Op. cit. Dixon, 1990

41. Holton, E. 1996. The flawed four level evaluation model. *Human Resource Development Quarterly* 7:21; op. cit. Blanchard and Thacker, 1998.

42. Op. cit. Geber, 1995.

43. Cascio, W. 1991. *Applied Psychology in Personnel Management*, 4th ed. Upper Saddle River, NJ: Prentice Hall.

44. Op. cit. Geber, 1995.

45. Op. cit. Purcell, 2000.

46. Hassett, J. 1992. Simplifying ROI. *Training*, September, pp. 53–57.

47. Op. cit. Cascio, 1991.

48. Cascio, W. 1989. Using utility analysis to assess training outcomes. In *Training and Development in Organizations*, edited by I. Goldstein. San Francisco: Jossey-Bass.

49. Whyte, G., and G. Latham. 1997. The futility of utility analysis revisited: When even an expert fails. *Personnel Psychology* 50: 601–10; Latham, G., and G. Whyte. 1994. The futility of utility analysis. *Personnel Psychology* 47:31–46.

50. Dixon, N. 1996. New routes to evaluation. *Training and Development*, May, pp. 82–85.

51. Ibid.

52. Op. cit. Blanchard, Thacker, and Way, 2000.

53. Op. cit. Geber, 1995.

54. Sackett, P. R., and E. J. Mullen. 1993. Beyond formal experimental design: Toward an expanded view of the training evaluation process. *Personnel Psychology* 46:613–27.

55. Cook, T. D., D. T. Campbell, and L. Peracchio. 1990. Quasi-experimentation. In *Handbook of Industrial and Organizational Psychology*, 2d ed., edited by M. D. Dunnette and L. M. Hough, pp. 507–620. Palo Alto, CA: Consulting Psychologists Press; Cook, T. D., and D. T. Campbell. 1979.

Quasi-Experimentation: Design and Analysis Issues for Field Settings. Chicago: Rand McNally; Campbell, D. T., and J. C. Stanley. 1963. *Experimental and Quasi-experimental Designs for Research,* Chicago: Rand McNally.

56. Camp, R. P., P. N. Blanchard, and G. E. Huszczo. 1986. *Toward a More Organizationally Effective Training Strategy and Practice.* Upper Saddle River, NJ: Prentice Hall.

57. Wexley, K. N., and G. P. Latham. 1981. *Developing and Training Human Resources in Organizations.* Glenview, IL: Scott, Foresman.

58. Op. cit. Sackett and Mullen, 1993.

59. Ibid.

60. Ibid.

61. Haccoun, R., and T. Hamtiaux. 1994. Optimizing knowledge tests for inferring learning acquisition levels in single group training evaluation designs: The internal referencing strategy. *Personnel Psychology* 47:593–604.

62. Ibid.

63. Ibid.

64. Dixon, N. 1997. Personnel communication, July 9. Associate Professor, George Washington University, Department of Administrative Sciences.

65. White, L., D. Rosenthal, and C. Fleuridas. 1993. Accountable supervision through systematic data collection: Using single case designs. *Counselor Education and Supervision* 33:32–37.

66. QS 9000 Requirements. 1995.

67. LeGault, M. 1997. In-house training that gets results. *Canadian Plastics,* February, pp. 14–18.

Appendix

1. Goldstein, I. L. 1991. Training in work organizations. In *Handbook of Industrial and Organizational Psychology,* 2d ed., edited by M. D. Dunnette and L. M. Hough. Palo Alto, CA: Consulting Psychologists Press.

2. Cook, T. D., D. T. Campbell, and L. Peracchio. 1990. Quasi-experimentation. In *Handbook of Industrial and Organizational Psychology,* 2d ed., edited by M. D. Dunnette and L. M. Hough. Palo Alto, CA:

Consulting Psychologists Press; Cook, T. D., and D. T. Campbell. 1979. *Quasi-Experimentation: Design and Analysis Issues for Field Settings.* Chicago: Rand McNally; Campbell, D. T., and J. C. Stanley. 1963. *Experimental and Quasi-Experimental Designs for Research.* Chicago: Rand McNally.

3. Ibid.

4. Sackett, P. R., and E. J. Mullen. 1993. Beyond formal experimental design: Toward an expanded view of the training evaluation process. *Personnel Psychology* 46:613–27.

5. Dixon, N. 1996. New routes to evaluation. *Training and Development,* May, pp. 82–85.

CHAPTER 9

1. *Conner v. Schrader-Bridgeport International, Inc.* (2000). No. 98-2055 (4th Cir. 09/13/2000).

2. Fisher, C. 1986. Organizational socialization: An integrative review. *Research in Personnel and Human Resource Management* 4:104–45.

3. Klein, H., and N. Weaver. 2000. The effectiveness of an organizational-level orientation training program in the socialization of new hires. *Personnel Psychology* 53:47–66.

4. Allen, N., and J. Meyer. 1990. Organizational socialization tactics: A longitudinal analysis of links to newcomers' commitment and role orientation. *Academy of Management Journal* 33:847–58; Bauer, T., E. Morrison, and R. Callister. 1998. Organizational socialization: A review and directions for future research. *Research in Personnel and Human Resource Management* 16:149–214; Saks, A. 1996. The relationship between the amount of helpfulness of entry training and work outcomes. *Human Relations* 49:429–51.

5. Bassi, L., and M. Van Buren. 1998. The 1998 ASTD state of the industry report. *Training and Development* 52:21–43.

6. Tyler, K. 1998. Take new employee training off the back burner. *HR Magazine,* May, pp. 49–57.

7. Ibid.

8. Smyrlis, L. 1999. Trail Blazers: How Bison's executive team transformed a small

regional operation into Canada's best-managed fleet. *Motor Truck* 68:25–37.

9. McGiullicuddy, J. 1999. Making a first good impression. *Public Management* 81:15–18.

10. U.S. Department of Labor. 2000. The U.S. population is becoming larger and more diverse. Washington, DC.

11. Bolch, M. 2000. The changing face of the workforce. *Training*, December, pp. 73–78.

12. Anonymous. 1997. *A Stronger Canada*. Ottawa: Employment and Immigration Canada.

13. Stats Canada. 2001. Labour force and participation rates in Canada by age and sex. Ottawa.

14. Stats Canada. 2001. Population projections. CANSIM ll Table 052-0001.

15. Tsui, A. S., and C. A. O'Reilly. 1989. Beyond simple demographic effects: The importance of relational demography in superior-subordinate dyads. *Academy of Management Journal* 29:586–99; Wayne, S. J., and R. C. Linden. 1995. Effects of impression management on performance ratings: A longitudinal study. *Academy of Management Journal* 38:232–60.

16. Hartel, C. E., S. S. Douthitt, G. Hartel, and S. Y. Douthitt. 1999. Equally qualified but unequally perceived: Openness to perceived dissimilarity as a predictor of race and sex discrimination in performance judgments. *Human Resource Development Quarterly* 10(1):79–89.

17. Gilbert, J. 2000. An empirical examination of resources in a diverse environment. *Public Personnel Management*, pp. 175–84.

18. Wright, P., S. Ferris, Hiller, and M. Kroll. 1995. Competitiveness through management of diversity: Effects on stock price valuation. *Academy of Management Journal* 38:272–87.

19. Galvin, T. 2001. 2001 industry report. *Training*, October, pp. 40–75.

20. Naisbitt, J., and P. Aburdene. 2000. *Megatrends*. New York: Avon.

21. Smiley-Marquez, C. 2000. Updates on EEO/AA rulings. *Diversity Factors*, Spring, pp. 38–39.

22. Loudin, A. 2000. Diversity pays. *Warehousing Management* 7:30–33.

23. Gilbert, J., and J. Ivancevich. 2000. Valuing diversity: A tale of two organizations. *Academy of Management Executive* 14:93–105.

24. Lords, E. 2001. Sex, race charges hit GM in Pontiac. *Detroit Free Press*, August 23, pp. 1A, 11A.

25. Ibid.

26. Rynes, S., and B. Rosen. 1995. A field survey of factors affecting the adoption and percieved success of diversity training. *Personnel Psychology* 48:247–70.

27. Grossman, R. 2000. Is diversity working? *HR Magazine*, March, pp. 46–50.

28. Ibid.

29. Ibid.

30. *Roberts et al. v. Texaco Inc.* (1994). Civ. 2015.

31. Texaco. 1999. Second annual report of the equity and fairness task force for year ending June 30, 1999.

32. Gilbert, J., and J. Ivancevich. 2000. Valuing diversity: A tale of two organizations. *Academy of Management Executive* 14:93–105.

33. Loudin, A. 2000. Diversity pays. *Warehousing Management* 7:30–33.

34. Mueller, N. L. 1996. Wisconsin Power and Light's model diversity program. *Training & Development*, March, pp. 57–60.

35. Ibid.

36. Renolds, L. 1997. Sex harassment claims surge. *HR Focus* 74:8.

37. Anonymous. 2000. Sexual harassment charges EEOC & FPEAs combined. *The US Equal Opportunity Commission*. Available at www.eeoc.gov/stats/harass.html.

38. Annual Report. 2000. Canadian Human Rights Commission. Ottawa: Queens Printer.

39. *Pease v. Alford Photo Industries Inc.* (1987). 667 F. Supp. 1188, W.D. Tenn.

40. *Meritor Savings Bank v. Vinson*. (1986). 477 U.S. 57.

41. Anonymous. 1987. Court holds employer liable for harassment by supervisor. *Daily Labor Report*, June 1, pp. A1, D1-5.

42. *Meritor Savings Bank v. Vinson*. (1986). 477 U.S. 57.

43. Fisher, A. B. 1993. Sexual harassment: What to do. *Fortune*, August 23, pp. 84–88; Yang,

C. 1996. Getting justice no easy task. *Business Week*, May 13, p. 98.

44. Anonymous. 1999. Ford settles 7.5M case over sexual harassment. *Financial Times*, September 8, p. 27.

45. Foy, N. 2000. Sexual harassment can threaten your bottom line. *Strategic Finance* 82:56–60.

46. Flynn, K. 1991. Preventative medicine for sexual harassment. *Personnel* 68:17.

47. Anonymous. 2001. Study: Many employers unaware of subtle sexual harassment. *Halifax Daily News*, March 8, p. 12.

48. Johnson, M. 1999. Antiharassment training to shelter yourself from suits. *HR Magazine* 44:76–81.

49. Ganzel, R. 1998. What sexual harassment training really prevents. *Training*, October, pp. 86–94.

50. Magley, V., C. Hulin, L. Fitzgerald, and M. DeNardo. 1999 Outcomes of self-labeling sexual harassment. *Journal of Applied Psychology* 84:390–402.

51. Ibid.

52. Ibid.

53. Anonymous. 1999. Industry report. *Training*, October, p. 57.

54. Moore, H., R. Gatlin-Watts, and J. Cangelosi. 1998. Eight steps to a sexual harassment free workplace. *Training and Development*, April, pp. 12–13.

55. Greenwald, J. 2000. Court issues ruling on hostile work environment. *Business Insurance* 34:32–33; Anderson, T. 2001. Judicial decisions. *Security Management* 45:137–38.

56. Bingham, S., and L. Scherer. 2001. The unexpected effects of a sexual harassment educational program. *Journal of Applied Behavioral Science* 37:125–53.

57. Op. cit. Ganzel, 1998.

58. Ibid.

59. Op. cit. Ganzel, 1998.

60. Johnson, M. 1999. Use antiharassment training to shelter yourself from suits. *HR Magazine* 44:76–81.

61. Tata, J. 2000. Autonomous work teams: An examination of cultural and structural constraints. *Work Study* 49:187–93.

62. Way, S., and J. Thacker. 2000. Trends in human resource management. *HR Professional: Research Forum*, August/September.

63. Hunsaker, P. 2001. *Training in Management Skills.* Upper Saddle River, NJ: Prentice Hall.

64. Caproni, P. 2001. *The Practical Coach.* Upper Saddle River, NJ: Prentice Hall.

65. Whetten, D., and K. Cameron. 2002. *Developing Management Skills.* Upper Saddle River, NJ: Prentice Hall.

66. Ibid.

67. Cascio, W., and J. Thacker. 1994. *Managing Human Resources.* Toronto: McGraw Hill.

68. Op. cit. Whetten and Cameron, 2002.

69. Ibid.

70. Neuman, G., and J. Wright. 1999. Team effectiveness: Beyond skills and ability. *Journal of Applied Psychology* 84:376–89.

71. Cutcher-Gershenfeld, J., T. Kochan, and A. Verma. 1987. Recent developments in U.S. employee involvement initiatives: Erosion or diffusion. Paper presented at the Pacific Rim Labor Conference, Vancouver, Canada, June 25–26.

72. Wells, D. 1986. *Soft Sell.* Ottawa: Canadian Centre for Policy Alternatives.

73. Rankin, T. 1986. Integrating collective bargaining and collective bargaining. *Worklife Review* 5:3; op. cit. Cutcher-Gershenfeld et al., 1987; Greenberg, P., and E. Glaser. 1981. Viewpoints of labor leaders regarding quality of work life improvement programs. *International Review of Applied Psychology* 30:157–74.

74. Goodman, P., and J. Dean. 1983. In *Organizational Development: Theory Practice and Research*, edited by W. French, C. Bell, and R. Zawacki. Plano, TX: Business Publications Inc.

75. Anonymous. 1993. Why teams don't work. *Sales and Marketing Management*, April, p. 12.

76. Hunsaker, P. 2001. *Training in Management Skills.* Upper Saddle River, NJ: Prentice Hall.

77. Phillips, S. 1996. Team training puts fizz in Coke plant's future. *Personnel Journal* 75:87–94.

78. Huszczo, G. E. 1996. *Tools for Team Excellence.* Palo Alto: Davies-Black.

79. Ibid.

80. Anonymous. 1988. Pay for lost opportunities. *Canadian Human Rights Advocate* 4.

81. Haben, M. K. 2001. Shattering the glass ceiling. *Executive Speeches* 15:4–10.

82. Scott, M. 2001. For women the glass ceiling still persists. *Black Enterprise* 32:30.

83. Op. cit. Haben, 2001.

84. Ibid.

85. Nelton, S. 1998. Can-do attitudes and the disabled. *Nation's Business,* May, pp. 35–37; Facwett, G. 1996. Living with disability in Canada: An economic portrait. *Human Resources Canada.*

86. Salopek, J. 1998. Arrested development. *Training and Development* 52:65–66.

87. Hays, S. 1999. The ABCs of workplace literacy. *Workforce* 78:70–74.

88. Calamai, P. 1999. The literacy gap. *Toronto Star*, August 28, p. J1-2.

89. Tyler, K. 1996. Tips for structuring workplace literacy. *HR Magazine* 41:112–16.

90. Barron, K., and A. Marsh. 1998. The skills gap. *Forbes*, February 23, pp. 44–45.

91. Ibid.

92. U.S. Census Bureau. 1998. *Statistical Abstracts of the United States.* Washington, DC.

93. Anonymous. 1998. A Stronger Canada. *Employment and Immigration Canada: 1998.* Ottawa.

94. Anonymous. 1998. Workplace literacy training pays off. *OH & S Canada* 14:8.

95. Op. cit. Tyler, 1996.

96. Ibid.

97. Overheul, V. 2001. 20 years of safety. Occupational Health and Safety 70:70–74.

98. Ibid.

99. Overheul, V. 2001. A cure for boredom. *Occupational Health and Safety* 70:192–95.

100. Op. cit. *Conner v. Schrader-Bridgeport International, Inc.*

CHAPTER 10

1. Burack, E., W. Hochwarter, and N. Mathys. 1997. The new management development paradigm. *Human Resource Planning* 20:14–21.

2. Industry Report. 2002. *Training,* October; Industry Report. 2001. *Training*, October; Industry Report. 1996. *Training*; Industry Report. 1995. *Training.*

3. Op. cit. *Training*, 2002.

4. Cascio, W., and R. Zammuto. 1987. *Societal Trends and Staffing Policies.* Denver: University of Colorado Press; Offerman, L., and M. Gowing. 1990. Organizations of the future: Changes and challenges. *American Psychologist* 45:95–108; Patel, D. 2002. Managing talent. *HR Magazine*, March, pp. 112–13; Pater, R. 2002. Leadership skills for the 21st century. *Occupational Health and Safety*, March, pp. 6–15.

5. Howell, J., P. Dorfman, and S. Kerr. 1986. Moderating variables in leadership research. *Academy of Management Review* 11:88–102; Morden, T. 1997. Leadership as competence. *Management Decision* 35:519–26.

6. Campbell, J., M. Dunnette, E. Lawler III, and K. Weick, Jr. 1970. *Managerial Behavior, Performance, and Effectiveness.* New York: McGraw-Hill.

7. Mintzberg, H. 1975. The manager's job: Folklore and fact. *Harvard Business Review* 53(4):49–61.

8. Ibid; Sayles, L. 1979. *Leadership: What Effective Managers Really Do and How They Really Do It.* New York: McGraw-Hill.

9. Wexley, K., and G. Latham. 1991. *Developing and Training Human Resources in Organizations*, 2d ed. New York: HarperCollins.

10. Karmel, B. 1978. Leadership: A challenge to traditional research methods and assumptions. *Academy of Management Review*, July, pp. 477–79; Schein, E. 1980. *Organizational Psychology*, 3d ed. Upper Saddle River, NJ: Prentice Hall.

11. House, R. 1971. A path-goal theory of leadership. *Administrative Science Quarterly*, September, pp. 321–38; House, R., and T. Mitchell. 1974. Path-goal theory of leadership. *Journal of Contemporary Business*, Autumn, p. 83; Keller, R. 1989. A test of the path-goal theory of leadership with need for clarity as a moderator in research and development organizations. *Journal of Applied Psychology*, April, pp. 208–12; Mathieu, J. 1990. A test of subordinates' achievement and affiliation needs as moderators of a leader's path-goal relationships. *Basic and Applied Social Psychology*, June, pp. 179–89.

12. The primary and secondary research we examined that led us to the conclusions in this section are Andrews, J. 1967. The achievement motive and advancement in two types of organizations. *Journal of Personality and Social Psychology* 6:163–68; Bass, B. 1990. *Handbook of Leadership*. New York: Free Press; Bennis, W., and B. Nanus. 1985. *Leaders: The Strategies for Taking Charge*. New York: Harper & Row; Birch, D., and J. Veroff. 1966. *Motivation: A Study of Action*. Monterey, CA: Brooks/Cole; Bray, D. 1973. New data from the management progress study. *Assessment and Development* 1:3; Bray, D., R. Campbell, and D. Grant. 1974. *Formative Years in Business: A Long-Term AT&T Study of Managerial Lives*. New York: Wiley; Bray, D., and D. Grant. 1966. The assessment center in the measurement of potential for business management. *Psychological Monographs* 80:1–27; Brown, W., and N. Karagozoglu. 1993. Leading the way to faster new product development. *The Executive* 7:1; Byham, W. 1980. Starting an assessment center. *Personnel Administrator* 25(2):27–32; Gutpa, A. 1984. Contingency linkages between strategy and general manager characteristics: A conceptual examination. *Academy of Management Review* 9:399–412; Gutpa, A., and V. Govindarajan. 1984. Business unit strategy, managerial characteristics, and business unit effectiveness at strategy implementation. *Academy of Management Journal* 27:25–41; Howard, A., and D. Bray. 1988. *Managerial Lives in Transition: Advancing Age and Changing Times*. New York: Guilford Press; Katz, R. 1974. Skills of an effective administrator. *Harvard Business Review*, September–October; Kirkpatrick, S., and E. Locke. 1991. Leadership: Do traits matter? *The Executive* 5:2; Kouzes, J., and B. Posner. 1988. *The Leadership Challenge: How to Get Things Done in Organizations*. San Francisco: Jossey-Bass; Luthans, F., R. Hodgetts, and S. Rosenkrantz. 1988. *Real Managers*. Cambridge, MA: Ballinger Press; McCauley, C., M. Lombardo, and C. Usher. 1989. Diagnosing management development needs: An instrument based on how managers develop. *Journal of Management* 15:3; McClelland, D. 1961. *The Achieving Society*. New York: Van Nostrand; McClelland, D., and D. Burnham. 1976. Power is the great motivator. *Harvard Business Review* 54(2):100–10; McClelland, D., and R. Boyatzis. 1982. Leadership motive pattern and long-term success in management. *Journal of Applied Psychology* 67:737–43; Miner, J. 1978. Twenty years of research on role-motivation theory of managerial effectiveness. *Personnel Psychology* 31:739–60; Niehoff, M., and M. Romans. 1982. Needs assessment as step one toward enhancing productivity. *Personnel Administrator*, May, pp. 35–39; Porter, L., and L. McKibbin. 1988. *Future of Management Education and Development: Drift or Thrust into the 21st Century?* New York: McGraw-Hill; Smith, K., and J. Harrison. 1986. In search of excellent leaders. In *The Handbook of Strategy*, edited by W. Guth. New York: Warren, Gorham & Lamont; Starcevich, M., and J. Sykes. 1982. Internal advanced management programs for executive development: The experience of Phillips Petroleum. *Personnel Administrator*, June, pp. 27–33; Tornton, G., and W. Byham. 1982. *Assessment Centers and Managerial Performance*. New York: Academic Press; Zaleznik, A. 1970. Power and politics in organizational life. *Harvard Business Review* 48:47–60.

13. Bass, B. 1981. *Stogdill's Handbook of Leadership: A Survey of Theory and Research*, Revised and expanded. New York: Free Press.

14. McClelland, D. 1961. *The Achieving Society*. New York: Van Nostrand.

15. Birch, D., and J. Veroff. 1966. *Motivation: A Study of Action*. Monterey, CA: Brooks/Cole.

16. McClelland, D., and D. Burnham. 1976. Power is the great motivator. *Harvard Business Review* 54(2):100–10.

17. Kirkpatrick, S., and E. Locke. 1991. Leadership: Do traits matter? *The Executive* 5:2.

18. For ambition, see Howard, A., and D. Bray. 1988. *Managerial Lives in Transition: Advancing Age and Changing Times*. New

York: Guilford Press; for energy see Kouzes, J., and B. Posner. 1988. *The Leadership Challenge: How to Get Things Done in Organizations*. San Francisco: Jossey-Bass; for tenacity see Bass, B. 1990. *Handbook of Leadership*. New York: Free Press.

19. McClelland, D., and R. Boyatzis. 1982. Leadership motive pattern and long-term success in management. *Journal of Applied Psychology* 67:737–43; Miner, J. 1978. Twenty years of research on role-motivation theory of managerial effectiveness. *Personnel Psychology* 31:739–60.

20. Andrews, J. 1967. The achievement motive and advancement in two types of organizations. *Journal of Pesonality and Social Psychology* 6:163–68; Zaleznik, A. 1970. Power and politics in organizational life. *Harvard Business Review* 48:47–60.

21. McCauley, C., M. Lombardo, and C. Usher. 1989. Diagnosing management development needs: An instrument based on how managers develop. *Journal of Management* 15:3; Smith, K., and J. Harrison. 1986. In search of excellent leaders. In *The Handbook of Strategy*, edited by W. Guth. New York: Warren, Gorham & Lamont; Weiss, W. 1999. Leadership. *Supervision* 60:6–9.

22. Coleman, E., and M. Campbell. 1975. *Supervisors: A Corporate Resource*. New York: AMACOM.

23. Katz, R. 1974. Skills of an effective administrator. *Harvard Business Review*, September–October.

24. Bennis, W., and B. Nanus. 1985. *Leaders: The Strategies for Taking Charge*. New York: Harper and Row; Smith, K., and Harrison. 1986. In search of excellent leaders. In *The Handbook of Strategy*, edited by W. Guth. New York: Warren, Gorham and Lamont.

25. Brown, W., and N. Karagozoglu. 1993. Leading the way to faster new product development. *The Executive* 7:1; McCauley, C., M. Lombardo, and C. Usher. 1989. Diagnosing management development needs: An instrument based on how managers develop. *Journal of Management* 15:3; Kirkpatrick, S., and E. Locke. 1991.

Leadership: Do traits matter? *The Executive* 5:2.

26. Luthans, F., R. Hodgetts, and S. Rosenkrantz. 1988. *Real Managers*. Cambridge, MA: Ballinger Press; Op. cit. McCauley, Lombardo, and Usher, 1989; McClelland, D., and D. Burnham. 1976. Power is the great motivator. *Harvard Business Review* 54(2):100–10; Porter, L., and L. McKibbin. 1988. *Future of Management Education and Development: Drift or Thrust into the 21st Century?* New York: McGraw-Hill.

27. Op. cit. Bruack et al., 1997.

28. Fiedler, F., and M. Chemers. 1974. *Leadership and Effective Management*. New York: Scott Foresman; Fiedler, F., M. Chemers, and L. Mahar. 1976. *Improving Leadership Effectiveness: The Leader Match Concept*. New York: Wiley.

29. Frisch, M. 2001. Going around in circles with 360 tools: Have they grown too popular for their own good. *Human Resource Planning* 24:7–8.

30. Waldman, D., F. Yammarino, and B. Avolio. 1990. A multiple level investigation of personnel ratings. *Personnel Psychology* 43:811–35.

31. O'Reilly, B. 1994. 360 feedback can change your life. *Fortune*, October, p. 17.

32. Ibid.

33. State of the industry report. 1998. *Training and Development*, January, pp. 22–43.

34. Op. cit. Hall, 1986.

35. Schleede, J. 2002. The future of management education. *Mid American Journal of Business* 17:5–8.

36. Op. cit. *Training and Development*, 1998.

37. Op. cit. Schleede, 2002.

38. Ibid.

39. Eurich, N. 1985. *Corprorate Classroom: The Learning Process*. Princeton, NJ: Carnegie Foundation for the Advancement of Teaching; Starcevich, M., and J. Sykes. 1982. Internal advanced management programs for executive development: The experience of Phillips Petroleum. *Personnel Administrator*, June, pp. 27–33.

40. Camp, R., P. Blanchard., and G. Huszczo. 1986. *Toward a More Organizationally Effective Training Strategy and Practice*.

Upper Saddle River, NJ: Prentice Hall, pp. 285–86.

41. Op. cit. Mintzberg, 1975; Roberts, T. 1974. *Developing Effective Managers*. Stratford-upon-Avon: Edward Fox and Son.

42. Vroom, V., and A. Jago. 1988. *The New Leadership: Managing Participation in Organizations*. Upper Saddle River, NJ: Prentice Hall; Vroom, V., and P. Yetton. 1973. *Leadership and Decision Making*. Pittsburgh: University of Pittsburgh Press.

43. Kepner, C., and B. Tregoe. 1975. *The Rational Manager: A Systematic Approach to Problem Solving and Decision Making*. New York: McGraw-Hill.

44. Maier, N. 1963. *Problem-Solving Discussions and Conferences*. New York: McGraw-Hill; Maier, N. 1982. *Psychology in Industrial Organizations*, 5th ed. Boston: Houghton-Mifflin.

45. Scholtes, P. 1988. *The Team Handbook: How to Use Teams to Improve Quality*. Pittsburgh: Joiner & Associates.

46. Op. cit. Mintzberg, 1975.

47. Pigors, P., and F. Pigors. 1987. Case method. In *Training and Development Handbook: A Guide to Human Resource Development*, edited by R. Craig. New York: McGraw-Hill.

48. Op. cit. *Training and Development*, 1998.

49. Rackham, N., and T. Morgan. 1977. *Behavior Analysis in Training*. Maidenhead, England: McGraw-Hill.

50. Op. cit. Fiedler, Chemers, and Mahar, 1976.

51. Blake, R., and J. Mouton. 1985. *The Managerial Grid III: The Key to Leadership Excellence*. Houston: Gulf Publishing; Yukl, G. 1989. *Leadership in Organizations*. Upper Saddle River, NJ: Prentice Hall.

52. Minor, J., 1978. Twenty years of research on role motivation theory of managerial effectiveness. *Personnel Psychology* 31:739–60.

53. Op. cit. McClelland, 1961; McClelland and Burnham, 1976; Miron and McClelland, 1979.

54. Berne, E. 1964. *Games People Play*. New York: Grove Press; Harris, T. 1969. *I'm OK, You're OK*. New York: Harper & Row.

55. Shuman, J. 1989. Technical supervision and turnover among electrical engineers and technicians. *Group and Organizational Studies*, December.

56. Saari, L., T. Johnson, S. Mclaughlin, and D. Zimmerle. 1988. A survey of management practices in U.S. companies. *Personnel Psychology* 41:731–43.

57. Ibid.

58. Bettman, R. 1987. Technical managers mismanaged: Turnover or turnaround? *Personnel Journal* 66:64–70.

59. Badriu, A. 1987. Training the IE for a management role. *Industrial Engineering*, December, pp. 18–23; Eckerson, W. 1989. Techies need training for management roles. *Network World*, April, p. 10; Ford, B., and B. Kleiner. 1987. Managing engineers effectively. *Business*, October–December, pp. 49–52.

60. Op. cit. Badriu, 1987; Op. cit. Eckerson, 1989; Lennark, R. 1988. The cost engineer as manager. *Cost Engineering* 30:9.

61. Op. cit. Badriu, 1987; Rosenbaum, B. 1991. How to lead today's technical professional. *Training and Development Journal* 44:100–01.

62. Miron, D., and D. McClelland. 1979. The impact of achievement motivation training on small businesses. *California Management Review*, Summer, pp. 13–28.

63. Op. cit. Bettman, 1987; Op. cit. Ford and Kleiner, 1987.

64. Wellins, R., and W. Byham. 2001. The leadership gap. *Training*, March, pp. 98–106.

65. Ibid.

66. Thach, E. 1998. 14 ways to groom executives. *Training*, August, pp. 52–55; Zemke, R., and S. Zemke. 2001. Where do leaders come from. *Training*, August, pp. 44–48.

67. Tomlinson, A. 2002. The coaching explosion. *Canadian HR Reporter* 15:7.

68. Bolch, M. 2001. Proactive coaching. *Training*, May, pp. 58–66.

69. Ibid.

70. Ibid.

71. Caironi, P. 2002. Coaches coach, players play, and companies win. *TIP* 40:37–44.

72. Feldman, D. Career coaching: What HR professionals and managers need to know. *Human Resource Planning* 24:26–35.

73. Op. cit. Thach, 1998.

74. Op. cit. Thach, 1998.

75. Barbian, J. 2002. The road best traveled. *Training*, May, pp. 38–42.

76. Op. cit. Zemke and Zemke, 2001.

77. Op. cit. Zemke and Zemke, 2001.

78. Peters, J., and P. Smith. 1998. Action learning and the leadership development challenge. *Journal of Workplace Learning* 10:284–91.

79. Ibid.

80. Yelverton, J. 1997. Adaptive skills: Seven keys to developing top managers. *Vital Speeches of the Day* 63:725–27.

81. Tyler, L. 2002. Succession planning: Charting a course for the future. *Trustee* 55:24–28.

82. Ibid.

83. Galvin, T. 2001. Industry report. *Training*, October pp. 40–75.

84. Op. cit. Wellins and Byham, 2001.

85. Grossman, R. 1999. Heirs unapparent. *HR Magazine*, February.

86. Ibid.

87. Galvin, T. 2001. Birds of a feather. *Training*, March, pp. 58–68.

88. Ibid.

89. Tarley, M. 2002. Leadership development for small organizations. *Training and Development* 56:52–55; op. cit. Zemke and Zemke, 2001.

90. Op. cit. Zemke and Zemke, 2001.

Index